J. Alfred Minnick.

AMERICAN FOLKLORE AND LEGEND

READER'S DIGEST

AMERICAN FOLKLORE

The Reader's Digest Association, Inc.
Pleasantville, N.Y./Montreal

AND LEGEND

READER'S DIGEST GENERAL BOOKS

STAFF FOR AMERICAN FOLKLORE AND LEGEND

Editor • Jane Polley
Art Director • Vincent L. Perry
Associate Editor • David Rattray
Research Editor • Sharon Fass
Picture Researcher • Marion Bodine
Copy Editor • Zahava Feldman
Research Associates • Giza Braun, Laurel Gilbride
Assistant Artist • Barbara Jean Schneit

Contributing Writers • John Bowman, Zane Kotker, Wendy Murphy

SPECIAL CONSULTANT FOR AMERICAN FOLKLORE
Horace Beck, *Professor of American Literature,*
Middlebury College, Middlebury, Vermont

CONSULTANTS
Dan Fox, Music and Arrangements
Col. John R. Elting, *USA-Ret., U.S. Military*
Academy, Army and Frontier Lore

The credits and acknowledgments that appear on pages 424–432
are hereby made a part of this copyright page.

Library of Congress Catalog Card Number: 77-80638

ISBN: 0-89577-045-8

Printed in the United States of America

CONTENTS

INTRODUCTION

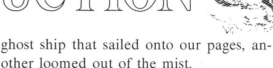

Scholars define folklore as the body of traditional customs, beliefs, tales, songs, and the like that are transmitted by word of mouth from one generation of a small society to the next. Such precision of definition, of course, is necessary to every academic discipline. In fact some folklorists deplore what one of them, Richard Dorson, has termed "fakelore"—that is, stories and characters popularly believed to be folklore, which are actually the product of a single writer or of the media. The editors have considered this academic definition of folklore and decided that they need not be confined by such exactitude. On the contrary, if characters such as Paul Bunyan and Snoopy, if stories about John Smith and Pocahontas and the jumping frog, have had such a strong hold on the American imagination, we reasoned, it would be wrong to exclude them from a book of lore meant to delight and inform the public.

That decision made, the editors set about the task of choosing from among the myriad stories, tales, legends, anecdotes, poems, and songs from every era the ones that were to appear on these pages. Some choices, such as "Paul Revere's Ride" and "The Big Bear of Arkansas," were clearcut—though the handling of material too long to fit our format was not always simple. More often the problem was the sheer volume of wonderful stuff. For every riproarin', rumsquattlin' Davy Crockett tale that we had room for, there were a dozen more as funny and exciting. For every

ghost ship that sailed onto our pages, another loomed out of the mist.

What we finally came to is a happy mix of dear and familiar tales with the sometimes shocking, sometimes unusual. Some of the stories here have not been read for a hundred years, except by a few scholars, and yet they constitute solid beams in the structure of American tradition that is even yet a-building.

The wisdom, imagination, and spirit of the common people that shine through all our lore inspired the feature essays on the customs, language, and superstitions of our country—as well as suggesting many others to be set aside for another time. Nor did we wish to forget that many of our finest literary works were inspired by what first belonged to the folk. Rousseau's philosophical romance with the "noble savage" germinated in tales about the American red men that reached the Continent; the historical Daniel Boone filtered through the fictions of several popular biographers and the folk to Cooper's pen and came out as Natty Bumppo, hero of the Leatherstocking Tales. Further examples abound.

The choices have been made and the result, we think, is a colorful, absorbing, and useful book. Fabulous creatures, fascinating stories, and delightful pictures pop out of every page. Browse through the book and linger where you will. As you do, we think you will discover a deeper dimension to the word "American."

The Editors

OUR POPULAR TRADITIONS

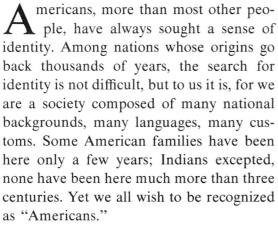

Americans, more than most other people, have always sought a sense of identity. Among nations whose origins go back thousands of years, the search for identity is not difficult, but to us it is, for we are a society composed of many national backgrounds, many languages, many customs. Some American families have been here only a few years; Indians excepted, none have been here much more than three centuries. Yet we all wish to be recognized as "Americans."

Tradition is a chief ingredient in any identification. In most countries tradition, based to a very large extent in folklore, history, and geography, has grown up over the centuries. Unfortunately, the U.S. is too young a country, and its inhabitants too diverse in character and too much on the move, for a folk tradition of the Old World type to have grown up. This book reflects that fact.

When I was asked to be a consultant to the present work, I suggested that the title be changed to "Popular American Traditions" because it deals in depth with just that. While it is true that there are items of folklore in this book, there is a great deal of material that is not folklore. Much of it was created by writers, such as Franklin, Longfellow, and Irving, who were deliberately attempting to build an American tradition.

Folklore, by definition, is the traditional knowledge of the folk. "Folk" are small groups of people living in isolation who pass along by word of mouth the information and opinions that enable them to live and thrive. This material has no known author or source. It is ancient and covers a plethora of topics from myths and legends, weather and planting lore, songs and games to medicine and language. Above all, it is oral and is known to a relatively small number.

Not only is folklore rather clearly defined by academic folklorists, but a clear-cut system of classification of terms and methods of study has been established. Myth, for example, refers to a certain kind of material with theological overtones. Folklorists talk of the Christian Myth much to the despair of the churchman who has been taught to believe "myth" is a polite way to say "colossal lie." On the other hand, legends are stories that tend to be based in historic fact, are narrowly located geographically, and are often an exaggeration of ethnic fears and aspirations. While folklorists make careful distinctions limiting superstitions, beliefs, and customs, the public is convinced that superstition is "anything not proved correct by scientific investigation and in which I do not personally believe."

Generally speaking, the academic folklorist is committed to an austere and rigorous method that requires that lore be set down in its entirety, including all textual mistakes and distractions. To this transcript the folklorist attaches as much personal data about the informant as possible. The material is studied, and the results are then

made available in a form interesting to other professionals.

The scholars also prefer that stories and lore be grouped into such categories as occupations, fractions of history and geography, and calamities. The editors of this book, however, have chosen to tell the story of America by following her historical development. Ignoring the classification system used by scholars, they have attempted to show the broad picture of a vast, restless, variegated land where people of every trade and background have mixed together to form a popular consensus of tradition that we call "American."

By the same token, the editors have chosen to take a broader view of what constitutes "folklore." A story by Washington Irving would not be considered folklore by folklorists even though it is based on an authentic folktale. Nor would Longfellow's "Paul Revere's Ride" or Bret Harte's "The Luck of Roaring Camp" qualify as folklore by academic criteria. Yet these very items are major ingredients in our popular lore. Americans derive a kind of shared experience by hearing that Washington cried for his troops on Christmas Day, that Barbara Frietchie risked her life for the American flag, or that General Jackson was so tough he was called Stonewall. It matters little that old George was crying because his false teeth hurt, that Frietchie never existed, or that when Jackson refused to attack, an irate officer exclaimed, "There stands Jackson just like a stone wall!"

American Folklore and Legend is really an anthology of popular lore—things Americans have been taught at home and in school, popular stories, poems, songs, and a considerable amount of folklore that has crept into the popular beliefs of modern Americans. Much of this material has been abbreviated, which is something the purist will condemn—yet, ironically, condensation often occurs in the transmission of lore among the folk. In fact deletion is the chronic, eventually fatal, disease of all folklore.

We hope the reader will be entertained by this book and his store of popular lore increased. *American Folklore and Legend* should help to develop that sense of identity so hard to find today. If the reader will stand back and assess the volume, he will have a better understanding of our national viewpoint and personality. Here are heroes different from those of other nations, a special kind of violence, humor, and sentiment that appeals to the majority of Americans. Where but in the United States does one lay so much stress on movement, low birth, self-education, upward mobility, cleverness, and large (if not colossal) heroes with a flair, not always intentional, for the comic?

This book is designed to entertain, while uncovering the foundation of our shared sense of national unity. If it succeeds in this, it will have accomplished its purpose.

Horace Beck

PART I

LAND of the PILGRIMS' PRIDE

New Lore in a New Land • The Inland Kingdom
In Search of Cibola • Pirate Treasure • The Spirit of '76

New Lore in a New Land

Christmastide 1620 saw work parties going ashore daily from the snow-swept *Mayflower* to build the first thatched huts of Plymouth. Many of the Pilgrims were deathly ill, but their hopes of founding a new society in the wilderness were as healthy as when they had embarked. Because that dream came true and gave birth to the American dream, Plymouth Rock has been rightly called "the cornerstone of a nation."

Unlike New Englanders, New Netherlanders were not given to grandiose visions of the future. Hudson Valley planters remembered Holland as a lost paradise. But the patroons flourished; and so did their trade with the Indians.

Others arrived from England and the Continent, where wars and economic woes were making life unbearable for many who were now eager to believe that the Earthly Paradise which folk tradition had long situated in the West might possibly lie just across the Atlantic Ocean in America. So they flocked in, settling Rhode Island, Pennsylvania, Maryland, Virginia, and Georgia. Most prominent of these colonies (and diametrically opposite in temper to New England) was Virginia, founded in 1607, 13 years before the coming of the *Mayflower;* its lore was Elizabethan in flavor, embodying all the aspects of rural Merry England that were anathema to the Puritans. However, the newcomers were all alike in that they tended to see the novel and wondrous things of the New World in terms of European folk stereotypes, making factual reports that seem to us today impossible (50-pound lobsters, pigeons so thick they darkened the sun), passing on rumors as eyewitness accounts, and interpreting evidence from the standpoint of the day (a dinosaur footprint was the track of the Devil, for example). But they were also well aware that their own deeds were opening an unprecedented era in human history. We begin with the saga of the Pilgrims because, more than any of the rest, they were the prophets of America's destiny.

This engraving illustrates the boastful settler Capt. John Smith's account of his last-minute rescue by the beautiful Indian princess Pocahontas—this is a favorite legend but probably isn't true.

Accused of witchcraft. Puritans thought Satan used traitors in their midst (as well as hostile Indians and demons) to force them to withdraw from "the spacious and mighty orchards of America."

WILDERNESS RIVALRY
The Courtship of Miles Standish

The oft-told tale of the courtship of John Alden and Priscilla Mullens is one of America's oldest and dearest. Doubtless the truths of the romance on which the adornments of legend have been hung are partly responsible for its durability. The young and handsome couple did woo and wed—and eventually produced 11 children—in the New World. Alden and Miles Standish really were friends, and a 19th-century Alden tradition describes the familiar triangle. But in history Standish did not play a part in the love affair. Of the story's retellings, the most popular is The Courtship of Miles Standish *by Henry Wadsworth Longfellow, who himself was descended from the Alden line. Herewith is an adaptation:*

Taunted for being a little man by an Indian enemy, Miles Standish "leaped on the boaster, and snatching his knife from its scabbard, plunged it into his heart."

In April 1621, 37-year-old Miles Standish, commander of Plymouth's small guard, had taken an extremely grateful and admiring John Alden into his home. Recently widowed and lonely, the captain requested of John, though he was "embarrassed and culling his phrases, 'Go to the damsel Priscilla, the loveliest maiden of Plymouth. Say that a blunt old captain, a man not of words but of actions, offers his hand and his heart. Not in these words. You, who are bred as a scholar, can say it in elegant language.'"

Standish had not guessed that John himself was desperately in love with Priscilla. "When he had spoken, John Alden, the fair-haired, taciturn stripling, all aghast at his words, surprised, embarrassed, bewildered, trying to mask his dismay by treating the subject with lightness," tried to persuade Standish to do it himself: "'Surely you cannot refuse what I ask in the name of our friendship!' Then made answer John Alden: 'The name of friendship is sacred; what you demand in that name, I have not the power to deny you!' So, friendship prevailed over love, and Alden went on his errand."

Though he was sent because he had read "of the pleadings and wooings of lovers," the handsome youth delivered his message bluntly. "Mute with amazement and sorrow, Priscilla the Puritan maiden looked into Alden's face, her eyes dilated with wonder, feeling his words like a blow, that stunned her and rendered

her speechless; till at length she exclaimed, interrupting the ominous silence: 'If the great captain of Plymouth is so very eager to wed me, why does he not come himself and take the trouble to woo me? If I am not worth the wooing, I surely am not worth the winning!'" Still the faithful Alden continued to speak on his friend's behalf. "But as he warmed and glowed, in his simple and eloquent language, quite forgetful of self, and full of the praise of his rival, archly the maiden smiled, and, with

"Alden listened and looked at Priscilla, thinking he never had seen her more fair, more divine in her beauty, he who but yesterday pleaded the cause of another."

eyes overrunning with laughter, said, in a tremulous voice, 'Why don't you speak for yourself, John?'"

The youth, filled with wild exultation, "rushed like a man insane, and wandered alone by the seaside," until he could bring himself to go home. "Then John Alden spake, and related the wondrous adventure, from beginning to end, minutely, just as it happened; how he had seen Priscilla, and how he had sped in his courtship, only smoothing a little, and softening down her refusal. But when he came at length to the words Priscilla had spoken, words so tender and cruel, 'Why don't you speak for yourself, John?' up leaped the captain of Plymouth, and stamped on the floor, till his armor clanged on the wall, where it hung, with the sound of a sinister omen. All his pent-up wrath burst forth in a sudden explosion, even as a handgrenade, that scatters the destruction around it. Wildly he shouted, and loud: 'John Alden! you have betrayed me! me, Miles Standish, your friend! have supplanted, defrauded, betrayed me!'"

Suddenly, in the midst of his ranting, the soldier was called away to fight hostile Indians, and John was left alone to brood about loyalty and love. Months passed, and still Standish was detained, bravely subduing native American foes. As for John, "oft when his labor was finished, with eager feet would the dreamer follow the pathway that ran through the woods to the house of Priscilla, led by illusions romantic and subtle deceptions of fancy, pleasure disguised as duty, and love in the semblance of friendship."

One afternoon, the young lover praised Priscilla extravagantly as she spun. Priscilla answered: "'Come, you must not be idle; if I am a pattern for housewives, show yourself equally worthy of being the model of husbands. Hold this skein on your hands, while I wind it, ready for knitting.' She standing, graceful, erect, and winding the thread from his fingers, sometimes chiding a little his clumsy manner of holding, sometimes touching his hands, as she disentangled expertly twist or knot in the yarn, unawares—for how could she help it?—sending electrical thrills through every nerve in his body.

"Lo! in the midst of this scene, a breathless messenger entered, bringing in hurry and heat the terrible news from the village. Yes; Miles Standish was dead; an Indian had brought them the tidings. Silent and statuelike stood Priscilla, her face looking backward still at the face of the speaker, her arms, uplifted in horror; but John Alden, upstarting, as if the barb of the arrow piercing the heart of his friend had struck his own, and had sundered once and forever the bonds that had kept him bound as a captive, wild with excess of sensation, the awful delight of his freedom, mingled with pain and regret, unconscious of what he was doing, clasped, almost with a groan, the motionless form of Priscilla, pressing her close to his heart, as forever his own, and exclaiming: 'Those whom the Lord hath united, let no man put them asunder!'"

On the bright wedding day friends were assembled together, when, "Lo! when the service was ended, a form appeared on the threshold, clad in armor of steel, a somber and sorrowful figure! Into the room it strode and the people beheld with amazement bodily there Miles Standish! Grasping the bridegroom's hand, he said with emotion, 'Forgive me!' Thereupon answered the bridegroom: 'Let all be forgotten between us—all save the dear old friendship.'"

FOLKWAYS

Courting in Cold New England

In the reality of 17th-century Plymouth, Priscilla Mullens would not have lived by herself; hence, when John Alden came courting, like the couple above, the lovers may have whispered endearments through a courting stick, a hollow wooden tube, designed to allow them some privacy in the presence of the girl's family. In a world of bitter winters and tiny houses with one fireplace as the main source of heat and light, other odd practices came into play, too, such as bundling. The custom was brought from Holland by the first Pilgrims, but Europeans gasped in hypocritical astonishment to hear of the austere Puritans encouraging a young couple to court in bed —albeit with most of their clothes on.

Promiscuous behavior by unbetrothed couples was treated very severely—in a few recorded cases offenders were hanged. Fortunately for engaged bundlers, modest allowances were made for the hot blood of youth. The many who became parents before the strictly construed ninemonth term were only punished with the lash, the stocks, or fines.

The Puritans were surprisingly modern in some ways. A maiden's family had to consent to a young man's courtship, but so did the girl. And if her father's objection to a suit was unreasonable, he could be haled into court by his would-be son-in-law and forced to relent.

Although Miles Standish's wish to marry within months of his first wife's death seems a mite hasty to us, he was slow getting to it by colonial standards. Wedded bliss was looked on as God's will; to be single was to be suspect. Widows and widowers often remarried within weeks of their bereavement. In Plymouth young bachelors were required to live in some established household. Perhaps partly for that reason, most boys married at a downy 19; their brides were about 16. A "thornback" (as any woman still unmarried at 30 was ungraciously known) was a real anomaly.

By about 1750, larger, better furnished houses enabled their occupants to sneer at "lower class" courtship customs, and clerics railed at them. Practices like bundling lingered on in rural areas, but for the most part they had served their purpose in the sparsely populated communities that nurtured them and were gone.

"WELCOME"
The Red Man's Greeting

From the moment Squanto uttered the legendary words "Welcome, Englishmen" to the Pilgrims who stepped ashore at Plymouth, the American Indians were a continued source of fascination—and sometimes fright—to the settlers. Whatever the case, their mutual encounters have created a rich store of folktales.

THE CRAFTY WOODSMAN

A New Hampshireman named Lovel was splitting logs when six Indians slipped from the woods and surrounded him. Knives and tomahawks in hand, they gestured that he was to go with them. Lovel agreed, asking only that they wait until he had finished chopping a big chestnut trunk.

Happy to avoid a struggle, the braves nodded. If the Indians would just lend a hand, Lovel suggested, the whole business would take less time. Again the Indians agreed. Driving a massive iron wedge into the split, Lovel asked the tribesmen to help pull the log apart. They did, and he swiftly knocked away the wedge, trapping their hands in the massive log. Then he killed all six with his ax and went on with his work as if nothing had happened.

MINISTER AND MAGICIAN

Rev. Richard Bourne was a Puritan missionary who worked among the Mashpee Indians of Cape Cod. His efforts were thwarted at first by an implacable shaman, determined to defend his people's ancient faith against the white man's religion. The conjurer muttered an angry tribal curse that magically mired the missionary's feet in quicksand. Immobilized but unruffled, Bourne challenged the magician to test his powers against Christian prayer. "Let us have a contest of wills," he said. "If I lose, I agree to serve you. If I win, you shall release me and trouble me no more." The witch doctor accepted the challenge. For 15 days and nights the dispute continued, each man in turn discoursing on the virtues of his own faith. Neither took time out to eat or drink or sleep.

The witch doctor eventually began to weaken; he started to sway, as his voice fell to a murmur. Bourne, on the other hand, remained fresh and alert, his great voice booming through the forest, for God had secretly sustained him. Every time he fell silent, a white dove fluttered down through the trees and placed a bright cranberry on his lips. At last, one berry fell to the ground. The conjurer saw it and realized what was happening, but his curses and spells had no effect on the dove.

Finally, the magician collapsed in a faint, breaking the spell that bound Bourne's feet. The missionary then hurried home to fetch a bowl of soup with which to revive his rival. When

FACT ? MYTH

The First Thanksgiving

To most Americans the first Thanksgiving is a "legendary" and real event, much as it is depicted in this modern painting: a decorous gathering of Pilgrims and their Indian friends meeting to offer thanks for God's bounty. Historically except for a brief grace, God was not mentioned. Instead, the Pilgrims hailed their first harvest in 1621 with a three-day banquet spiced with tests of skill and strength.

The settlers asked their Indian ally Chief Massasoit to dine with them and were momentarily staggered when he arrived accompanied by 90 uninvited ravenous warriors: no tribal women attended. The result was not a holiday for Plymouth's five women; they had to feed 145 diners.

The Pilgrims could not have been so elegantly dressed as they are in this romanticized view. The 10 months of hardship that killed half their original party must have taken their toll of their clothing too. The log cabin is also an anachronism. Pilgrim homes were fashioned of hewn planks and had wooden shutters, not leaded panes.

Revelers dined on venison and wild fowl, eel, shellfish, lobster, corn, dried fruit, and probably turkey—all washed down with homemade wine. Two traditional treats were absent: cranberry sauce and pumpkin pie. Except for knives, there were no utensils. One ate with one's fingers from wooden trenchers or scooped up food with crude clamshell spoons.

"The First Thanksgiving," by J. L. G. Ferris, is an imaginary version.

the grateful Indian had drunk the soup, he saw reflected in the bowl's silver bottom a vision of Judgment Day and the horrors that awaited unrepentant sinners. Terrified, he knelt before Bourne and from then on followed the Christian path.

Meanwhile, the berry that had fallen from the dove's beak took root and flourished. And that is how the cranberry came to Cape Cod.

THE CHEESE BRIGADE

New Hampshire pioneers John and Mary Corliss lived in the wilderness township of Alexandria. Their cabin was a point of special pride, for unlike most of their neighbors' homes, theirs had a cellar stairway with shelves for storage built above it. The Corliss dairy herd was richly productive, and the cellar shelves were lined with round cheeses.

One day John Corliss went off to town for supplies, leaving his young wife to guard home and herd against prowling Indians. All was peaceful for a time, the quiet of the clearing disturbed only by bird song and the chomping of grazing cattle.

Then Mary glimpsed a band of painted warriors waiting silently at the forest's edge. Alone and unarmed, she stood little chance of holding them off. Only her quick wits could save her. Crouching next to the cellar shelves, she called out, "Come on, boys," and hurled a cheese down the wooden stairs. Then she shouted, "Come, John," and followed with another cheese. She kept at it until the shelves were empty.

Mary peered out the window. The clearing was empty again. The Indians had mistaken the thumping of the cheeses for the footfalls of many defenders and had gone away rather than face the settlers' guns.

HEADWORK

One day Governor Joseph Dudley of the Massachusetts Bay Colony spied a young, half-naked Indian impassively watching while laborers sweated in the sun. Irritated by the Indian's apparent laziness, the governor asked him why he didn't get a

job and earn money with which to buy clothes to cover his nakedness. "Why don't *you* work, governor?" replied the Indian.

"I work headwork," answered Dudley, "and so have no need to work with my hands." Then, to demonstrate the rewards of labor to the Indian, he offered him a shilling to slaughter one of his calves for the

‘WORD LORE’

Necessary Additions

One day somewhere in southern New England a friendly Indian helped himself to a pipeful out of an English explorer's tobacco pouch. "How now, sirrah," said the explorer, "are you so saucy with my tobacco?" To his amazement, the red man repeated the sentence word for word. The incident was typical. English fishermen and traders had been coming for years, and Indians who had piloted and quartered them had learned to speak English. In turn, whites borrowed freely from native languages spoken along the Atlantic coast. Here is a sampling: *hominy*—prepared corn; *moccasin*—box, case, shoe; *opossum*—white animal; *papoose*—very small; *pemmican*—grease, fat; *pone*—baked (as in "corn pone"); *raccoon*—he scratches with his hands; *sachem* or *sagamore*—chief; *skunk*—small urinating animal; *squash*—green thing eaten raw; *squaw*—woman; *tomahawk*—ax; *wampum*—white strings; *wigwam*—dwelling.

table. The Indian killed the animal and returned. The governor objected that he had not dressed the calf. "No, no," said the Indian, "that was not in the bargain. I was to have a shilling for killing him. Am he no dead?"

Dudley had to agree that the calf was dead, and offered a second shilling to the Indian to finish the job. When he came again for his money, Dudley was moved to ask how the Indian had been able to outwit him.

"Headwork, governor," said the Indian, "headwork."

CHOCORUA'S CURSE

Chocorua, last grown survivor of his tribe, lived peacefully with his white neighbors in New Hampshire. He prized his handsome son above all things, for it was he who would carry on the ways of his fathers.

So friendly was Chocorua with the whites that when he went on a journey he entrusted his son's care to a settler named Cornelius Campbell. While Chocorua was away, the boy mistook a bottle of fox poison for a delicacy and drained it. When Chocorua returned home and found his son dead, he was maddened with grief. He refused to believe it had been an accident. When Campbell left his cabin for the fields several days later, Chocorua wreaked a terrible revenge: Mrs. Campbell and her children were brutally butchered.

Now it was Campbell's turn to call for vengeance. Rifles in hand, he and other grim settlers stalked the Indian for days until they finally cornered him atop the towering mountain since named after him. Throwing his rifle to his shoulder, Campbell ordered Chocorua to leap to his death. Chocorua stood his ground, his arms upraised, shrieking his final fury.

"A curse upon ye, white men," he thundered. "May the Great Spirit curse ye when he speaks in the clouds and his words are fire! Chocorua had a son, and ye killed him when the sky was bright! Lightning blast your crops! Wind and fire destroy your dwellings! The Evil Spirit breathe death upon your cattle! Your graves lie in the warpath of the Indian! Panthers howl and wolves fatten over your bones! Chocorua goes to the Great Spirit—his curse stays!"

With these words the Indian hurled himself onto the rocks below. Campbell and his companions returned to their cabins convinced the Indian threat was over, but Chocorua's curse outlived them all. Campbell went mad, became a hermit, and died within two years. For years after, valley crops are said to have failed, settlements were abandoned, and cattle that watered below Mount Chocorua wasted away.

MORTON'S MERRY MOUNT
A Peak of Revelry

In the mid-1620's a trading post near Plymouth started dealing with Indians in the dread French manner—exchanging guns and rum for beaver. At the site of present-day Maypole Park in Quincy, Massachusetts, life was a nonstop party. A Plymouth contemporary described it thus: "They invited Indian women for their consorts, dancing and frisking together like so many fairies, or Furies, rather." Their leader, a cavalier named Thomas Morton (or "mine host of Merry Mount," as he styled himself), hated Miles Standish, nicknaming him "Captain Shrimp." The outcome was dramatic. By the time Morton published this humorous account of it in his New English Canaan *(1637), the rise and fall of Merry Mount plantation had become a legend on both sides of the Atlantic.*

When the revels of Merry Mount were ended and the unregenerate Thomas Morton had been packed off to England, Governor Endecott caused the Maypole to be cut down, and upbraided the remaining ex-revelers for their profaneness.

FASHIONABLE REVELS

The inhabitants of Merry Mount did devise amongst themselves to have revels after the old English custom. They prepared to set up a Maypole and brewed a barrel of excellent beer and provided a case of bottles with other good cheer for all comers. And on May Day they brought the Maypole to the place appointed, with drums and other fitting instruments, and there erected it with the help of savages that came thither a-purpose to see the manner of our revels. A goodly pine tree, 80 foot long, was reared up, with a pair of buck's horns nailed on somewhat near unto the top, where it stood as a fair seamark for directions how to find out the way to mine host of Merry Mount.

To make their revels more fashionable, a merry song was sung with a chorus, every man bearing his part. They performed it in a dance, hand in hand about the Maypole, while one of the company sang and filled out good liquor like Ganymede:

"Drink and be merry, merry, merry, boys!
Let all your delight be in the Hymen's joys!
Lasses in beaver coats come away,
Ye shall be welcome to us night and day!"

This harmless mirth was much distasted of the precise Separatists [they were so called because they had *separated* from the Church of England]. From that time they sought occasion against my honest host of Merry Mount, and when his company were gone up into the inlands to trade with the savages for beaver, they set upon him at a place called Wessagusset, where by accident they had found him.

UNDER ARREST

Much rejoicing was made that they had gotten their capital enemy, and they sported themselves at my honest host, who meant them no hurt, and were so jocund that they feasted their bodies and fell to tippling.

Mine host feigned grief and could not be persuaded either to eat or drink, because he knew the contrary part would be so drowsy that he might have an opportunity to give them a slip. Six persons were set to watch him, but in the dead of night up gets mine host and got to the door, which, notwithstanding the lock, he got open and shut it after him with such violence that it affrighted some.

"Oh, he's gone! He's gone, what shall we do, he's gone!" The rest, half asleep, start up in amaze and like rams ran their heads one at another full butt in the dark.

Their grand leader, Captain Shrimp, took on most furiously and tore his clothes for anger, to see the empty nest, and their bird flown. The rest were eager to have torn their hair from their heads, but it was so short that it would give them no hold.

In the meantime, mine host got home to Merry Mount through the woods, finding his way by the help of the lightning—for it thundered, as he went, terribly. And there he prepared powder, three pounds dried, and four good guns, with bullets of several sizes, 300 or thereabouts.

Now Captain Shrimp takes eight persons and they embark against Merry Mount, where they beat a parlay and offered quarter—for they resolved to send mine host for England and bade him lay by his arms. At last, to save the effusion of so much worthy blood, mine host was content to yield. He had no sooner set open the door and issued out, but instantly Captain Shrimp and the rest laid hold of his arms, had him down, and fell upon him as if they would have eaten him—and so they made themselves masters of mine host of Merry Mount and disposed of what he had at his plantation.

THE INVISIBLE WORLD
Devilish Doings in New England

For the Puritans to doubt the existence of Satan and his "imps" would have been as blasphemous as doubting the existence of God himself, and they saw each event either as a divine providence or as evidence of the presence of the Devil and his minions. These excerpts from Cotton Mather's voluminous accounts of the struggle between good and evil in Massachusetts show just how real the Devil and the spirits of darkness seemed to the colonists—Mather got the details by conducting a survey, sponsored by Harvard College, of New England ministers. Given the witch-hunting temper of the times, it is not surprising that there flourished an abundant lore of witches, demons, and wonders from what Mather called "the invisible world."

BLACK MAN, BLACK MASS

That the Devil is come down to us with great wrath, we find, we feel, we now deplore. The things confessed by witches, and the things endured by others, laid together, amount unto this account of our affliction. The Devil, exhibiting himself ordinarily as a small black man, has decoyed a fearful knot of proud, froward, ignorant, envious, and malicious creatures to lift themselves in his horrid service by entering their names in a book by him tendered unto them. These witches have met in hellish *randezvouzes,* wherein the confessors do say they have had their diabolical sacraments, imitating the baptism and supper of our Lord. In these hellish meetings, these monsters have associated themselves to do no less a thing than to destroy the kingdom of Our Lord Jesus Christ in these parts of the world. First they each of them have their specters, or devils, commissioned by them and representing of them, to be the engines of their malice. By these wicked specters they seize poor people about the country, with various and bloody torments; and of these evidently preternatural torments, some have died.

INVITATION TO WITCHCRAFT

It is the general concession of all men that the invitation of witchcraft is the thing that has now introduced the Devil into the midst of us. The children of New England have secretly done many things that have been pleasing to the Devil. They say that in some towns it has been a usual thing for people to cure hurts with spells, or to use detestable conjurations with sieves, keys, peas, and nails, to learn the things for which they have an impious curiosity. 'Tis in the Devil's name that such things are done. By these courses 'tis that people play upon the hole of the asp, till that cruelly venemous asp has pulled many of them into the deep hole of witchcraft itself.

THE DEVIL DISTURBED

The New Englanders are a people of God now settled in those parts which were once the Devil's territories, and it may be supposed that the Devil was exceedingly disturbed when he perceived such a people here. The Devil thus irritated immediately tried all sorts of methods to overturn this poor plantation. But all those attempts of Hell have hitherto been abortive, wherefore the Devil is now making one attempt more upon us; an attempt more difficult, more surprising, more snarled with unintelligible circumstances than any we have encountered.

SUPERSTITIONS

The Demons of Newbury

In the year 1679 the house of William Morse of Newbury was "infested with demons after a most horrid manner," Mather writes. Bricks, sticks, and stones were thrown at the farmhouse by an invisible hand, and while the family sat at supper, ashes were heaped on their plates and on their heads. When Morse tried to write, his inkhorn was snatched away and his cap torn from his head. The demons pulled his hair, pinched and scratched him, stole his shoes, pricked him with awls and needles, and pelted him with clods of frozen cow manure. Mrs. Morse's milk pails were also befouled with dung, and she was imprisoned in the cellar when an invisible hand shut the trapdoor on her and pulled a table on top of it.

A little boy belonging to the family suffered most from one demon's molestations. He was flung about until it seemed his brains would be beaten out, hurled into the kitchen fire, "prick'd on the back" with a fork, an iron spindle, and knives. When possessed, he barked like a dog and then clucked. The specter snatched food from him and doused him with the contents of a chamber pot.

The child complained that a man called P---l had appeared to him and was the cause of it all. On one occasion the boy disappeared entirely, until at last he was found "creeping on one side, sadly dumb and lame." When he was able to express himself, he said that "P---l had carried him over the top of the house and hurled him against a cartwheel in the barn." And indeed, traces of barley from the barn floor were found clinging to his garments.

Before these torments came to an end, "the *invisible* hand which did all these things began to put on an astonishing *visibility*." Witnesses were able to discern a ghostly fist beating Morse and saw a vision of a black child. Later, they heard a drumming on the boards and a voice that sang, "Revenge! Revenge! Sweet is revenge!" Now they called upon God for help. "Whereupon there follow'd a mournful note, several times uttering these expressions: 'Alas! alas! we knock no more, we knock no more!' and there was an end of all."

THE WITCHES OF SALEM
"The Guilt of Innocent Blood"

Early in 1692 girls and young women of Salem village began to show signs of a frightening affliction. They fell into fits, uttered strange sounds, and screamed when they heard the Lord's Prayer. The diagnosis was not long in coming: they were bewitched. On March 1 began the series of hearings and trials that would lead to the arrest of at least 150 "witches" and the execution of 19 persons and two dogs. For many of the accounts of these trials and the testimony against the witches we look to Cotton Mather, whose Wonders of the Invisible World *stands as the contemporary report of the proceedings.*

THE GOSPEL WITCH

Martha Cory, whose husband, Giles, was later to be pressed to death beneath rocks for refusing to plead guilty or not guilty to yet another charge of witchcraft, was the first respectable member of the community to be accused by the afflicted girls. The Rev. Deodat Lawson of Boston describes her questioning by the testimony-gathering magistrates:

On Monday the 21st of March the magistrates of Salem were appointed to come to examination of Goodwife Cory. And at about 12 of the clock they went into the meetinghouse, which was thronged with spectators. And Goodwife Cory, being called to answer to what was alleged against her, desired to pray, which was much wondered at in the presence of so many hundred people. The magistrates told her they would not admit it; they came there not to hear her pray, but to examine her.

The worshipful Mr. Hathorne asked her why she afflicted those children? She said she did not afflict them. He asked her, who did, then? She said: "How should I know?"

The number of afflicted persons were about that time 10. These were most of them at Goodwife Cory's examination and did vehemently accuse her in the assembly of afflicting them by biting, pinching, strangling, etc. And that they in their fits see her likeness coming to them and bringing a book to them. She said she had no book. They affirmed that she had a yellow bird that used to suck between her fingers, and being asked about it, if she had any familiar spirit that attended her, she said she had no familiarity with any such thing: she was a Gospel woman. And the afflicted persons told her, Ah! she was a Gospel Witch.

It was observed several times that if she did but bite her underlip during the examination, the persons afflicted were bitten on their arms and wrists and produced the marks before the magistrates, ministers, and others. And being watched for that, if she did but pinch her fingers, or grasp one hand hard in another, they were pinched and produced the marks. After that, it was observed, that if she did but lean her breast against the seat in the meetinghouse (being the bar at which she stood), they were afflicted. After these postures were watched, if the said Cory did but stir her feet, they were afflicted in their feet and stamped fearfully.

The afflicted persons asked her why she did not go to the company of witches which were mustering before the meetinghouse. Did she not hear the beating of their drum? They

In this engraving after a painting by Howard Pyle, participants in a Salem witchcraft trial point accusing fingers at a bedeviled girl as stern judges look on.

 FOLKWAYS

accused her of having familiarity with the Devil during the examination, in the shape of a black man whispering in her ear. They affirmed that her yellow bird sucked between her fingers in the assembly.

She denied all that was charged upon her, and said, they could not prove her a witch. She was that afternoon committed to Salem prison, and after she was in custody she did not appear to them and afflict them any more.

DEVILED DOGS AND OXEN

Trim, tart-tongued Susanna Martin of Amesbury had a longstanding reputation as a witch. But only now, in the turmoil of the Salem accusations, did her victims come forward to recite wondrous tales of her witcheries to the assembled magistrates:

There was the tale of the Enchanted Oxen of Salisbury Beach. Fourteen head that John Allen had put out to fatten on the salt grass had one day been goaded by the Devil into swimming to Plum Island. When Allen traced them there and tried to round them up, the oxen ran from him "with a violence . . . wholly diabolic" and plunging into the water swam straight out to sea.

Faced with so ruinous a disaster, a good Puritan searches his conscience to see "what sin unrepented of" God is punishing him for. Allen may have started such a search, but he was interrupted by a memory ringing in his ears like a spiteful echo of the shrill voice of Susanna Martin. "Your oxen will never do you much service!"

It came back to him now. Just before he turned his oxen out to grass he had refused to hitch his oxcart to haul her some stones, and in those words had Susanna mocked him.

"Dost thou threaten me, thou old witch? I'll throw thee into the brook!" he had shouted, but Susanna had nimbly run across the bridge out of his way. Who but Susanna had sent the Devil into his cattle?

There was the tale of the Phantom Puppies. Susanna Martin owned these puppies. At first, they existed on the physical level; her bitch had

How To Tell a Witch

With the threat of infernal doings ever present, formulas for the detection of witches were collected and studiously discussed even by the best educated.

A typical list of "evidences" for detecting "a witch in league with the Devil" included:

1. A witch's mark, caused by the Devil touching or sucking the witch. "This mark is insensible, and being prick'd it will not bleed. Sometimes it's like a teat; sometimes but a bluish spot; sometimes a red one; and sometimes the flesh sunk: but the witches do sometimes cover them."

2. The witch's words, whether talking to her familiars, boasting of harm done, or threatening evil to come.

3. Deeds, "as when they have been seen with their spirits, or seen secretly feeding any of their imps. Or, when there can be found any of their pictures, their poppets [dolls], and other hellish compositions."

4. The witch's uncontrollable ecstasies, "with the delight whereof witches are so taken, that they will hardly conceal the same."

5. The confessions of fellow witches, bearing detailed witness against their colleagues "that they have seen them with their spirits, or that they have received spirits from them; or that they can tell, when they used witchery tricks to do harm, or that they told them what harm they had done; or that they can show the mark upon them; or that they have been together in their meetings.". . .

7. The witch's own confession. "It is no rare thing for witches to confess," the author concludes.

produced a likely litter, and John Kembal had contracted to buy one. But when he came to purchase it, Susanna would not let him have his choice and was wroth when he then refused to buy at all.

"I'll give you puppies enough!" she cried after him. And indeed she did. It began toward sundown with a little black cloud in the northwest. Kembal saw it when he came out of his woodlot with his ax over his shoulder, and at the same moment found himself in the grip of a power that made his feet unsteady. Though a broad, straight cartway lay before him, he began to weave from side to side, lurching into stumps, tripping

This woodcut showing Cotton Mather exorcising the Devil appeared in his book *Memorable Providences,* published in 1690.

and sometimes falling headlong, ax and all.

When finally he came out to the road near the meetinghouse, he found a puppy waiting for him. At least it was a Thing like a puppy: small, dark, and devilishly playful. It nipped at his heels, ran back and forth between his feet. Kembal took it for a real enough puppy until he swung his ax at it. Then the queer thing happened: the Thing leaped aside and vanished into the ground.

Kembal stared about him, rubbed his eyes, and stumbled on. Up the shadowy road waited another Thing, a large puppy, black as coal, and vicious. It sprang for his throat, his belly, and darting behind him made for his shoulders. Swinging his ax made no impression on it at all.

"In the name of Jesus Christ, avoid!" cried Kembal at last, and lo, the Thing was gone.

He was panting when he got to his kitchen but took care to say no word to his wife. It might scare her; besides, there is no knowing what a woman's inconsequence will suggest. It is common enough for maids to bring beer by the pailful to men working in field or woodlot; his wife might jump to the conclusion that he had refreshed himself too often.

His reticence made it the more remarkable that the story was all over town the next day. People grinned at him knowingly and asked for the puppies. How, he demanded, did they know? And he traced the gossip to Susanna Martin, who could have had only one way of knowing. She herself had sent her devils in the form of puppies to torment him.

THEN IT WAS OVER

On 22 September seven witches and one lone wizard were packed into a cart and hauled the long mile to Gallows Hill. The sheriff had not chosen the most convenient spot for his hangings, but he had chosen a conspicuous one, for the hangings were made a spectacle by intention. The Puritans never denied themselves this sort of show; it was considered a sound deterrent to immoral impulses, especially now when the Devil was so busy proselytizing the country. Besides, it was always interesting to watch. Those people who could not follow the spectacle at close range spied on it at a distance from their upper windows.

From Gallows Hill the witches in their turn could take one last look at the distant waters of the bay—gray today, for the sky was overcast and rain threatening—and at the brightness of the low rugged hills that rolled down to the shore, alight with goldenrod, rich with the smoky blue of the asters and the first turning of the leaves, for winter was coming, a winter for which they need cut and carry no wood.

At the steep ascent of the hill the cart stuck in the road. The accusers, riding close behind, plainly saw the Devil hold it back. At the gallows the wizard tried to address the people of Salem, protesting his innocence, but the waiting sheriff was smoking a pipe by his head and the smoke blowing into his face choked him off. The girls said that too was the Devil's work, though it seemed somewhat inconsistent of him.

Then it was over.

"What a sad thing," remarked Noyes, the sheriff, looking up at the oak tree with its heavy fruit, "to see eight firebrands of Hell, the Devil's familiars, hanging there."

INNOCENT BLOOD

Four years after the trials were over, 12 of the jurors who sat in judgment on the Salem witches acknowledged their own error in an extraordinary written statement that read in part:

"We confess that we ourselves were not capable to understand, nor able to withstand, the mysterious delusions of the Powers of Darkness and Prince of the Air. . . .

"Whereby we fear we have been instrumental with others, though ignorantly and unwittingly, to bring upon ourselves and this people of the Lord the guilt of innocent blood."

THE DEVIL'S NINE QUESTIONS

Freely

If you don't an-swer my ques-tions nine (Sing nine-ty-nine and nine-ty)
i'll take you off to hell a-live And you are the weav-er's bon-ny

What is whiter than the milk?
(Sing ninety-nine and ninety)
And what is softer than the silk?
Say you're the weaver's bonny.

Snow is whiter than the milk
(Sing ninety-nine and ninety)
And down is softer than the silk
And I'm the weaver's bonny.

What is louder than a horn?
(Sing ninety-nine and ninety)
And what is sharper than a thorn?
Sing, I am the weaver's bonny.

Thunder's louder than a horn
(Sing ninety-nine and ninety)
And death is sharper than a thorn
And I'm the weaver's bonny.

What is higher than a tree?
(Sing ninety-nine and ninety)
And what is deeper than the sea?
Say you are the weaver's bonny.

Heaven's higher than a tree
(Sing ninety-nine and ninety)
And hell is deeper than the sea
And I'm the weaver's bonny.

What is more innocent than a lamb?
(Sing ninety-nine and ninety)
And what is worse than womankind?
Say you're the weaver's bonny.

A babe's more innocent than a lamb
(Sing ninety-nine and ninety)
A she-devil's worse than womankind
And I'm the weaver's bonny.

Now you have answered my questions
(Sing ninety-nine and ninety)   [nine
You are God's child and not my own
And you're the weaver's bonny.

This riddle song goes back to the 1300's when riddles played an important role. Clever folks could outwit the Devil with a tough riddle or a quick answer. "Neck riddles" gave the condemned person a chance to escape the gibbet—we show a nodding acquaintance with that when we say, "I couldn't think of the answer to save my life."

New England Mourning

Strangely, funerals were the gayest communal occasions in the northern colonies. The Puritans severely limited their social activities. Perhaps for that reason, and because death was such a familiar event in early New England, celebrating it was a natural defense.

In 1683, after two of his four children had died, Edward Taylor could still write: "Christ would in glory have a Flower, Choice, Prime, and having Choice, chose this my branch forth brought./Lord take it. I thank thee thou takest ought of mine, it is my pledge in glory." In another poem, addressed to death, Taylor said: "Why camest thou then so slowly? Mend thy pace./Thy slowness me detains from Christ's bright face./Although thy terrors rise to the highest degree,/I am still where I was. A fig for thee!"

Death inspired other strange flights of fancy in the form of puns, anagrams, and verses. The 19th-century historian Alice Morse Earle lamented: "They seemed to reserve for these gloomy tributes their sole attempt at facetiousness." The pithiest were carved on headstones. Most were sweet: "Tears cannot restore her/ Therefore do I weep." Some of the quirkier were not: "Here lies as silent as clay Miss Arabella Young/Who on the 21st of May 1771 began to hold her tongue." "Here lies the body of Obadiah Wilkinson and his wife Ruth. Their warfare is accomplished." "He that was sweet to my repose/Now is become a stink under my nose."

Early Puritans shunned a funeral service as "papist," but they made up for it with a prolonged party at the home of the deceased. Neighbors often supplied and cooked the food, but the bereaved family was expected to pay for the mourning libations. Since the drinking sometimes started the night before the burial and went on long after it, that cost constituted a severe hardship for some families. Earle noted the relatively modest funeral expenses for a man, drowned in 1678. "By a pint of liquor for those who dived for him. .1s. By a quart of liquor for those who bro't him home. .2s. By two quarts of wine & 1 gallon of cyder to jury of inquest. .5s. By 8 gallons and 3 qts wine for funeral. £1 15s.

New England headstones often bore an extravagance of symbols. At upper left, backed by Father Time, skeletal Death, holding his fatal dart, snuffs out the candle of life. The sphere probably signifies the soul borne by birds—the Resurrection. Death has won the victor's laurel on the stone at the upper right. Angels and bats of Hell peer out from around the snake symbolizing eternity. The crowned soul effigies at the bottom are twined with hearts that represent the soul's love for God, and (bottom right) grapes meaning new life through the sacraments.

By barrel of cyder for funeral. .16s. 1 coffin. .12s. Windeing sheet. .18s."

The strong young men who carried the coffin to the grave, and their dignified elders who held the black or purple velvet pall over them and their burden, returned from the grave to find generous portions of gin and New England rum awaiting them. With such relaxants available, townspeople could converse freely and doubtless indulged in an unwonted laugh and did a little trading as they wished Godspeed to the departed one.

Gradually, funerals became more elaborate, and new expenses overshadowed catering costs. Gloves, originally believed to keep the spirit of the deceased from entering one's body, were presented to mourners. Samuel Sewall notes many such gifts in diary entries: "Went to the funeral of Mrs. Sprague, being invited by a good pair of gloves." At the funeral of Andrew Faneuil, a record-breaking 3,000 pairs were distributed. The quality of gloves

a mourner received depended on his status and relationship to the dead person. Social lions found themselves with more pairs than they could wear in a lifetime, such as a Reverend Eliot in Boston who received more than 2,900 sets. He and others supplemented income by selling the surplus.

Funeral fervor grew apace, and by the late 18th century long processions of people and horses draped in mourning paraphernalia followed the "corps" to its resting place. For their participation, friends were awarded gold funeral rings signifying a marriage of the body and soul. They were decorated with deathly symbols and bore such legends as "Prepared be/To follow me." One-fifth of Waitstill Winthrop's estate was spent on his funeral and its accouterments; in the face of such excesses a reaction set in against the spectacles. In 1741 Massachusetts enacted a law that little could be given away at a funeral (including rum), "upon the penalty of £50."

DUTCH TREAT
Holland on the Hudson

New Netherland survived only to 1664, but in their time the Dutch bought Manhattan for about $24, founded New Amsterdam (later New York), and built an overseas province that grew rich on its patroon-dominated tenant farms and fur trade. Their presence is still felt in place-names around New York and more widely in words such as boss, cookie, dumb, *and* snoop. *Much Dutch lore has vanished, except as retold—sometimes derisively—by Washington Irving. The storm ship story below is based on Irving; the others were recorded later.*

THE STORM SHIP

One day in the early years of the colony of New Amsterdam, a frightful storm descended on Manhattan Island. When it lifted, the watch at the fort at the southern tip of the island shouted that a ship was approaching from the Atlantic. Word passed quickly from mouth to mouth, for everyone had something to expect from a ship—loved ones, news from the homeland, supplies. The colonists assembled at the harbor and soon saw the sails coming over the horizon. They buzzed with excitement as the ship bore up the bay, but when she drew near and was hailed, no one on board replied. Sailing against wind and tide, the ship went on up the Hudson, leaving the good folk disappointed and mystified.

Week after week they waited in vain for the ship to return. Meanwhile, reports began to reach them of a strange ship spotted navigating up and down the river, especially when a storm was in the air. Some people claimed they could hear the captain shouting orders in Dutch. And as time passed, people along the river came to realize what they were seeing: It was the *Half Moon* of Henry Hudson, discoverer of the river in 1609—dead since 1611. Some said he was still seeking the Northwest Passage, others that he and his crew had returned merely to revel. But for many years people claimed to see the topsails of this ship glittering in the moonlight along the Hudson River, and when they did, troublesome times always followed.

STUYVESANT'S GHOST

This last and most picturesque Dutch governor died in 1672. His body was laid in a vault in the chapel he had

Peter Stuyvesant, last governor of New Amsterdam, in one of his notorious rages, is depicted by Asher Durand. Standing by is Anthony van Corlear, the trumpeter who rose ("like many a great man," wrote Washington Irving, "by sounding his own trumpet") to become Stuyvesant's assistant. Irving's caricatures of historical Dutchmen make them seem like folktale figures.

built in 1660, which has since been rebuilt into St. Mark's-in-the-Bouwerie. Almost immediately, family servants swore fearfully that they had seen the governor's ghost and heard tapping, as if by the famous wooden leg of the old warrior.

In 1774 his old manor house burned to the foundations, and at dead of night the angry wraith of the long-dead Stuyvesant was seen limping around. In the 1860's a church sexton visited the chapel late at night, only to flee in wild alarm; he had seen Stuyvesant, flame-eyed and timber-toed, advancing upon him. When impious commissioners began to cut Second Avenue through the graveyard itself, the bell began tolling. The sexton and others, roused by the angry song, hurried to the scene. The church was securely locked; as the searchers entered, the ringing ceased. Under the suddenly silent belfry hung a short length of rope, broken as if by a mighty jerk. The remainder of the cord was produced next day by the sexton, who insisted that he found it in Stuyvesant's vault.

A BAKER'S DOZEN

In the year 1655 on December's last day, a baker, Baas, was working late selling the New Year's cookies that had carried his fame far down the Hudson River. As trade grew less, he took an extra horn of rum and was about to shut up shop when an uncommonly ugly old woman thrust her way in, demanding a dozen of the special cookies bearing an effigy of Saint Nick.

When the baker handed her the fragrant bag, she said crossly: "One more cookie; I said a dozen." "You have a dozen," said Baas. "I counted them carefully—12 of my finest cookies." "One more cookie," said the old woman. "One more than 12 makes a dozen."

Baas grabbed her by the shoulder and pushed her to the door. "You may go to the Devil for another cookie!" he shouted. "You won't get it here." When he told the story to his wife, she suggested that on a holiday eve he should perhaps have given the extra cookie, but Baas reminded her that business was business.

In the days that followed, mysterious bad luck came to the little bakery in Beverwyck (Albany). Money and cookies seemed to be snatched up by invisible hands. Bread rose to the ceiling or fell flat as a pancake. A handsome brick oven collapsed. The stubborn Dutchman began to wonder whether supernatural powers were not at work. On New Year's Eve the memory of the old woman's appearance was so vivid that Baas exclaimed: "Holy Saint Nicholas, suppose that witch comes again! What shall I do?"

As the baker spoke these words, there appeared before him the benign saint, smiling with holiday kindness. "Well, Baas," said his saintship, "you were speaking to me so I thought I would drop in. This whole trouble can be resolved if you have the spirit which my holidays demand." The figure of the saint vanished; in its place stood the ugly old woman demanding a dozen cookies. Rapidly Baas counted 13 of them, presenting the bag to her with a bow and a "Happy New Year!"

"The spell is broken, Baas," said the witch. "Now swear to me on the likeness of Saint Nicholas that hereafter in Beverwyck and all the patroonship of Van Rensselaer 13 will make a baker's dozen." Baas took the oath and from that day to this when you say a baker's dozen, you mean 13. Before she left the shop the witch prophesied that someday 13 mighty states would unite to remind the world of her magic number.

FAIR TRADE

A Dutch trader went alone to buy beaver skins from Indians. He sat in their longhouse with 30 braves, wondering when they would stop chatting among themselves and get down to business. Finally, a chief leaned over and placed his hand on the Dutchman's heart. Feeling it beat quietly, the chief said: "He is not afraid. Now we can speak of skins. It is useless to deal with cowards."

Saint Nicholas

It was the Dutch who brought us Santa Claus, both the name and the concept of a magical gift-bearer. They, like the people in many European countries, had evolved their own myth from the stories about a real fourth-century bishop. Their dignified robed-and-mitered *Sinter Klaas* was loved for leaving goodies in children's shoes. Non-Puritan English settlers quickly added the kindly saint to their own elaborate Yuletide rejoicings—and Santa excited American children from then on. Saint Nick gradually changed his garb (though he always kept his Dutch pipe and fur trim) as his image moved back and forth between the people and the artists who pictured him for them. When Clement Moore wrote "The Night Before Christmas" in 1822, his jolly, plump, white-bearded elf became everyone's Santa Claus. Thence, artists drew him more or less based on Moore; but at that he was thin and threadbare compared to the robust man of our era. The quintessential Santa Claus of today is probably the one, portrayed for decades by Haddon Sundblom, who pauses to refresh.

RIP VAN WINKLE
Story With a Future

In relating the travails and triumph of Rip Van Winkle, Washington Irving created a minor literary masterpiece by adapting an old German legend about a goatherd. (He took pains, though, to make his delighted audience believe he had invented the tale.) Since its publication in 1820, the saga of Rip (condensed below) has gained in stature to become one of our most popular legends.

In a little village on the Hudson there lived a simple good-natured fellow of the name of Rip Van Winkle; he was a kind neighbor and an obedient, henpecked husband. The great error in Rip's composition was an insuperable aversion to all kinds of profitable labor. It could not be from a want of perseverance, for he would sit on a wet rock and fish all day without a murmur. He would carry a fowling piece for hours, trudging through woods and swamps.

If left to himself, he would have whistled life away in perfect contentment; but his wife kept continually dinning about his idleness. Times grew worse with Rip Van Winkle as years rolled on; a tart temper never mellows. He used to console himself by frequenting a kind of perpetual club of sages and other idle personages of the village, which held its sessions in a small inn.

From even this stronghold the unlucky Rip was at length routed by his termagant wife, who would suddenly break in on the tranquillity of the assemblage and call the members all to naught. Poor Rip was at last reduced almost to despair, and his only alternative was to take gun in hand and stroll away into the woods.

In a long ramble of a fine autumnal day, Rip had unconsciously scrambled to one of the highest parts of the Kaatskill Mountains. Panting and fatigued, he threw himself on a green knoll. He saw that it would be dark long before he could reach the village, and he heaved a heavy sigh when he thought of encountering the terrors of Dame Van Winkle.

As he was about to descend, he heard a voice from a distance hallooing, "Rip Van Winkle." He looked anxiously and perceived a strange figure slowly toiling up the rocks. He was surprised to see any human being in this lonely place, but supposing him to be in need of his assistance, he hastened down.

On nearer approach he was still more surprised at the singularity of the stranger's appearance. He was a short, square-built old fellow, with thick bushy hair and a grizzled beard. He bore on his shoulder a stout keg, and made signs for Rip to approach and assist him with the load. Though rather shy and distrustful, Rip complied, and they clambered up a narrow gully. Passing through a ravine, they came to a hollow, like a small amphitheater. On entering, new objects of wonder were to be seen. On a level spot in the center was a company of odd-looking personages playing at ninepins. They were dressed in a quaint, outlandish fashion. Their visages, too, were peculiar; one had a large beard, broad face, and small piggish eyes; the face of another seemed to consist entirely of a nose and was surmounted by a white sugarloaf hat.

What seemed particularly odd to Rip was that though these folks were evidently amusing themselves, yet they maintained the gravest faces. Nothing interrupted the stillness but the noise of the balls, which echoed along the mountains like rumbling peals of thunder. By degrees Rip's awe and apprehension subsided. He even ventured, when no eye was fixed upon him, to taste the beverage, which he found had much of the flavor of excellent Hollands. He was naturally a thirsty soul and was soon tempted to repeat the draft. He reiterated his visits so often that at length his senses were overpowered, his head gradually declined, and he fell into a deep sleep.

On waking, he found himself on the green knoll whence he had first seen the old man. He rubbed his eyes—it was a bright sunny morning. "Surely," thought Rip, "I have not slept here all night. Oh! That wicked flagon! What excuse shall I make to Dame Van Winkle?" As he rose to walk, he found himself stiff in the joints and wanting in his usual activity. "These mountain beds do not agree with me," thought Rip. With some difficulty he got down into the glen; he found the gully up which he and his companion had proceeded the previous evening, but to his astonishment a mountain stream was now foaming down it.

What was to be done? The morning was passing away, and Rip felt famished. He dreaded to meet his wife, but it would not do to starve. He shook his head and turned his steps homeward. As he approached the village he met a number of people, but none whom he knew; their dress too was different. They all stared at him with equal marks of surprise, and whenever they cast their eyes upon him invariably stroked their chins. The constant recurrence induced Rip, involuntarily, to do the same, when, to his astonishment, he found his beard was a foot long!

The very village was altered; it was larger, and familiar haunts had disappeared. It was with some difficulty he found his way to his own house, expecting every moment to hear the shrill voice of Dame Van Winkle, but he found the house gone to decay. He now hurried forth to his old resort, the village inn—but it too was gone. A large rickety hotel stood in its place. The appearance of Rip with his long, grizzled beard, his rusty fowling piece, his uncouth dress, and an army of women and children at his heels soon attracted the attention of the tavern politicians. An orator bustled up to him and inquired "on which side he voted." Rip stared at

For years this painting by John Quidor was believed to be Rip Van Winkle meeting the gnome; indeed, its "strange, uncouth, lackluster countenance" evokes the apprehension which made Rip's "heart turn within him and his knees smite together."

him in vacant stupidity. Another inquired "whether he was Federal or Democrat." "I am a poor quiet man, a native of the place, and a loyal subject of the king.!" Here a general shout burst from the bystanders. "A Tory! A spy! Away with him!"

The poor man humbly assured them that he meant no harm but merely came in search of some of his neighbors. "Well—who are they? Name them." Rip bethought himself a moment and inquired, "Where's Nicholas Vedder?" There was silence for a while, when an old man replied, "Why he is dead and gone these 18 years!" Rip's heart died away at the sad changes in his home and friends. At this critical moment a comely woman pressed through the throng to get a peep at the gray-bearded man. "Hush, Rip," cried she to her child. The name of the child, the air of the mother, and the tone of her voice awakened a train of recollections in his mind. "What is your name, my good woman?" asked he.

"Judith Gardiner." "And your father's name?" "Ah, poor man, Rip Van Winkle was his name, but it's 20 years since he went away from home and never has been heard of since." Rip had but one more question to ask, but he put it with a faltering voice: "Where is your mother?" "Oh, she died; she broke a blood vessel in a fit of passion at a New England peddler." There was a drop of comfort at least in this intelligence. The honest man could contain himself no longer. "I am your father!" cried he. "Young Rip once, Old Rip now."

All stood amazed. Rip's story was soon told, for the whole 20 years had been to him as one night. To make a long story short, Rip's daughter took him home to live with her; she had a snug home and a stout cheery farmer for a husband. Having arrived at the happy age when a man can be idle with impunity, he took his place once more at the bench at the inn door and was reverenced as one of the patriarchs of the village.

He used to tell his story to every stranger that arrived at the hotel, and it is the common wish of all henpecked husbands in the neighborhood that they might have a quieting draft out of Rip Van Winkle's flagon.

PEACEABLE KINGDOM
Vision of a Sylvan Paradise

Among the many English Protestants who sought refuge in America were the Society of Friends, better known as Quakers (because they were said to "quake" with religious fervor). There were Quakers all over, but most settled in their own colony of Pennsylvania, founded as a "Holy Experiment" by William Penn in 1681. Like many others before and after him, Penn saw America as a Garden of Eden and the Indians as descendants of the Ten Lost Tribes of Israel. Quakers gave voice to their own lore derived from their distinctive ways and worship.

TEN LOST TRIBES

In a tract written in 1683 William Penn explained his belief that the Indians' "language is lofty, yet narrow, but like the Hebrew, in signification full. For their original, I am ready to believe them of the Jewish race. I mean, of the stock of the Ten Tribes, and that for the following reasons. First, they were to go to a land not yet planted or known. In the next place, I find them of like countenance and their children of so lively a resemblance to the Jews of London. But this is not all. They agree in rites; they reckon by moons; they offer their first fruits; they have a kind of Feast of Tabernacles; and in other ways resemble the Jews in the Bible.

THE TRUTH MUST OUT

An elderly Quaker was mindful of the emphasis placed on cautiousness and veracity in speech. After brooding long, he arose to speak in meeting. "I have been greatly distressed over the new views being taught, and I have heard of an instance that shows how dangerous such views can be. A young man who had lost his faith went out sailing with a friend. A storm came up, and the youth who

"A Peaceable Kingdom," by Edward Hicks, a 19th-century Quaker preacher, is one of dozens of his depictions of an ideal image held by many colonists: America, the land where "the wolf will dwell with the lamb." In the background Hicks painted another legend: Penn signing a treaty with the Delaware Indians, an oft-depicted episode for which there is no conclusive evidence.

had lost his faith was drowned." The elder sat down, and the meeting was silent as everyone pondered this. But the elder was noticeably uneasy, and finally he arose a second time and said, "For the honor of truth, I think I should say that the other young man also drowned."

LEAD ON

A certain villager never attended either church or Friends' meeting, but he had to pass a meetingplace when he rode on horseback to the village square. As he approached the meetinghouse on a particular Sunday, he felt a strange attraction, but he resisted it. Suddenly, he threw the reins over the horse's head and said to himself: "If the horse turns into the meeting, I'll go. If it goes by, I'll go on." He was sure that the horse would proceed on the accustomed route, but the horse turned toward the meeting. So the man hitched his horse and slipped inside. A Quaker who was then speaking stopped, stood still for a moment, and then said, "It would have been well if thou hadst left it to thy horse years ago." The man was so moved by this that he became a leading Friend.

A HELPING KNEE

A Quaker woman tended to be moved to speak more than her share in meetings, but not always with much substance. As she was about to rise once again, her sister-in-law, sitting behind her, pressed her knee firmly against her dress. On the way home from meeting, the woman thus deterred remarked to her family, "I was about to speak, but the good Lord held me down."

CONFLICT OF INTERESTS

Two Quakers were engaged in what was, for all their restraint, an argument. Finally one said to the other: "William, thee knows I do not believe in calling anyone names. But if the mayor should come to me and say, 'Joshua, I want thee to bring me the greatest liar in this town,' I would come to thee and say, 'William, the mayor wants to see thee.'"

HOMELY AND EARTHY TALK
Pennsylvanians From Germany

William Penn's policy of religious toleration attracted oppressed Protestants from Switzerland and southwestern Germany to Pennsylvania. German-speaking Mennonites, Amish, Moravians, and others became known as Pennsylvania Dutch—in the 1600's "Dutch" meant "German" (Deutsch). They kept much of their Old World culture and many of the stories intact, including some about bumbling Till Eulenspiegel and the tale of the wild hunt, a version of the Flying Dutchman story. But most of their lore was rooted in more universal values of their life—farming, religion, conservatism, and the patriarchal family.

A RIDDLE SAVES A NECK

A young man about to be executed was brought before the king who, being in a kindly mood, promised the youth his freedom if he produced a riddle that no one at court could solve. The youth asked to be allowed to go home while he thought of one, and after putting on a different pair of shoes he returned with one: "In Inia I walk,/ In Inia I stand,/ In Inia I am happy and free./ Who can guess this riddle for me?"

The king and his court were baffled, and finally the youth was asked to explain. "I had a dog named Inia. On its death I flayed him, tanned the hide, and made this pair of shoes out of the leather." The king was so impressed that he freed the youth.

CRAFTY EULENSPIEGEL

Till Eulenspiegel was hired by a farmer to cut wood. The ax he used was so dull that when he struck the wood the ax rebounded. Said Till to the ax: "If you want to work so quickly, I'll work quickly, too." And he chopped away so hard that by noon he had a large pile of wood. The farmer, seeing this, said to his wife: "Look at all the wood he chopped with that dull ax. For this afternoon, I'll give him my sharp ax—imagine how much he'll cut!" After lunch, Eulenspiegel began to cut with the sharp ax. At the first stroke, the blade sank deep into the wood. Said Till to the ax, "Well, if you want to work slowly, I'll work that way, too." So he went easy all afternoon and cut only a little wood.

PENNY WISE, POUND FOOLISH

A frugal old farmwoman, determined to keep her costs to a minimum, reasoned that if she gave her horse a little less food day after day,

To the Pennsylvania Dutch the barn was the hub of life, and since about 1850 they have painted geometric designs on the spacious sides. The circles are called hex signs, suggesting they are to ward off witches, but they are probably just decorations.

she would eventually arrive at the point where the horse wouldn't need to eat anything. She thus proceeded, until finally she had him down to one grain. At the end of that day, the horse died. She told her neighbors, "If he had borne up just one day longer, I would have succeeded."

THE BEST OF THREE

A farmer was seeking a farmhand and came to see one likely youth. After discussing several matters, he casually asked, "How long can you plow with a stone in your shoe?" The youth answered, "All day." The farmer moved on, and while interviewing a second youth he asked the same question. This fellow replied, "Oh, half a day or so." The farmer continued on and came to a third youth. Again he asked the question, and this fellow replied: "Not a minute. If a stone gets into my shoe, I take it out right away." The farmer hired that young man on the spot.

CHRISTMAS EVE

There was a farmer who was very cruel to his horses. He had heard tell of mysterious happenings on Christmas Eve, when various spirits were abroad and even the animals were said to speak at midnight. He doubted all such tales, and when his friends persisted he decided one Christmas Eve to disprove them. So several hours before midnight he hid himself in the hay in the stable. Then, at midnight, he heard one horse say to another: "We have such a cruel master, and tonight we shall kick him to death." The farmer tried

to flee from the stable, but as he groped his way through the darkness, he stumbled and was kicked to death by the horses.

TWO COLONISTS MEET

A Yankee peddler, bound west with a team of horses and wares, stopped at a Pennsylvania Dutchman's inn. Because of the severe storm, he had to remain there several days. When he was able to move on he asked for the bill, and the Dutchman, figuring he'd never see the peddler again, charged him $10, almost double the regular rate. Then, pleased with his profit, the innkeeper offered a free mug of cider "for the road." The Yankee took a drink, and said, "Good—but it would make a fine wine if you converted it by a new secret process for which I have all of the necessary equipment." The Dutchman said he'd certainly like to hear more about how he could upgrade his brew, and eventually he

agreed to the Yankee peddler's terms. He gave the salesman $10 on the spot and promised to pay $50 more when the cider turned to wine. The Dutchman and the Yankee then went into the cellar, where the Yankee bored a hole into the barrel of cider. He told the Dutchman to put his thumb into it—"and wait until I get the special converter from my wagon." He left the Dutchman plugging the hole, went upstairs, finished his draft of cider, and drove off in his wagon.

TO EACH HIS WAY

Three Pennsylvania farmers—a Quaker, an Amishman, and a Hutterite—were given two cows each. The Quaker gave one of his cows to a less fortunate neighbor. The Hutterite turned his cows over to his communal group, which gave him some milk. The Amishman kept one cow and traded the other for a bull.

THE ETERNAL HUNTER

One summer when some early settlers were struggling to maintain a colony, there was a terrible drought. The crops failed, streams were waterless, and all the wildlife left the vicinity. The settlers were in dire circumstances, and as venison was their only source of meat, one of the old men decided to use his dogs to hunt and chase back the deer. Before taking off for the wilderness, he promised his people that he would hunt forever, even through the sky if necessary, to save the settlement

SUPERSTITIONS

Pagan Practices

The word "superstition" means, literally, "surviving belief," and superstitions are in fact survivals of old magico-religious techniques for influencing (to one's own advantage or to the detriment of others) the unseen forces that make things happen as they do. Although couched in ostensibly Christian language, the superstitious practices and beliefs of the Pennsylvania Germans, like those of other European colonists, harked back to the paganism of pre-Christian ancestors:

Put a scalded hand in hot water to ease the pain, and prevent blistering.

To win at cards, tie a bat's heart to your right arm with red silk string.

A girl can wash her freckles away with dew collected on May 1.

Put sugar in your armpit and then in your girl's drink; she won't resist you.

Smelling flowers that grow on a grave can destroy your sense of smell.

Say *Gesundheit!* ("Health!") when another person sneezes, to prevent that person from sneezing his soul out and to drive away evil spirits that may have come out of him with his breath.

The Amish

No group in America so deserves to be known as a living museum as the Amish. They cling to traditions and shun modern mores. Electricity and machines are not permitted on their farms. Married men must have beards and ride in closed, horse-drawn vehicles; single men and courting couples ride in open carriages. To this day a funeral may bring out scores of horse-drawn buggies.

The Amish take their name from Jacob Amman, a late-17th-century Swiss churchman who broke with the Mennonites over his strict interpretation of Biblical injunctions. The Amish

have since split into two main groups, and it is primarily the Old Order Amish who maintain the strict ways of their forebears. There are about 50,000 Old Order Amish in North America, most in southeastern Pennsylvania. Extremely close-knit, three-quarters of them bear less than 10 family names.

The Amish are justly proud of their generous dishes, such as scrapple, pickled beets, strudel, and shoofly pie (molasses and brown sugar).

The essence of Amish life is their absolute reliance on Biblical authority on all matters from ceremonial foot-washing to simple clothing. Outer garments are usually black, with hooks and eyes—buttons being signs of van-

ity. They avoid things that smack of the newfangled—radios, lightning rods, plumbing. A church building might become a source of pride, so they hold services in their own homes—and thus are also known as House Amish. Musical instruments, even part-singing, are banned. Suspicious of book learning, these farmers expect their children to leave school at 14.

Yet inconsistencies are present. The telephone is forbidden, but some use pay phones on the roadside. A good example of the kinds of incongruities with which the Amish are confronted in the 20th century is a new shopping plaza in Amish country, which has hitching posts in the parking lot.

from starvation. After he had been gone for a few days, the deer began to appear in the valley, but the old man never returned. Ever since then, on certain nights during the hunting season, people still hear the barking of a pack of hounds off in the sky. "The Eternal Hunter," they mutter.

THE BLUE GATE
A group of Amishmen were standing about after a worship service, when one said to another, "I've got a son that favors marrying soon." The second replied, "Well, I've got a daughter that wants marrying." While the other Amishmen listened,

it was agreed that the son would go courting "at the place with the blue gate." At the next worship service, the father of the marriageable daughter confronted the other man: "Why didn't your boy come courting?" The boy's father replied: "He did set out—but every man along the road with a daughter of marrying age had painted his gate blue."

THE WAY TO HEAVEN
A farmer in the Patch died, but as it was the very middle of the harvest season, his neighbors decided to send one of their boys to the funeral as their representative. The boy was

walking along the road to the Patch when a horse and buggy came up beside him. The driver invited the boy to ride with him, and as the boy settled down he asked the man, "Who are you?" "I'm a preacher," he said, "on my way to the Patch. Do you know where that is?" The boy replied that he was going there and would show the way, but after some moments a thought entered his head. "If you're a preacher," he said, "you must show people the right way to Heaven." "That's right, my son." "Then how is it," said the boy, "that you don't know where the Patch is when that ain't so far from here?"

PRODIGIOUS PORTENTS
Good (and Bad) News From Virginia

One of our oldest sayings about America is that its streets are paved with gold. Shakespeare's contemporaries said much the same of the new American commonwealth named "Virginia" in honor of their "Virgin Queen" Elizabeth I. (They pronounced the name "Vir-gin-yeh.") The cry of the hour was "Come, boys, Virginia longs till we share the rest of her maidenhead!" Talk was tall; there were rumors of easy-to-get gold, free land, and supernatural epidemics among the savages in Virginia, which a poet dubbed "Earth's only paradise."

Comets meant trouble. In 1607 Halley's comet appeared to the starving founders of Jamestown. The following winter was one of the coldest in recorded history.

GLITTERING GOLD

Gold is more plentiful there than copper is with us. Why, all their dripping pans and their chamber pots are pure gold. And for rubies and diamonds, they go forth on holidays and gather 'em by the seashore to hang on their children's coats.

EARTH'S ONLY PARADISE

The Atlantic crossing takes only six weeks. Even before landfall, one can smell a sweet smell—the Virginia coast. Grapes are so profuse, the vines tumble into the ocean and fill the treetops. The climate there is warmer than that of England, healthier too. Indeed, Virginia is as pleasant a land as ever the sun shined on, temperate and full of all sorts of excellent viands. Incredible quantities of game thrive there.

INVISIBLE BULLETS

There was no town where the savages practiced any villainy against us, but within a few days after our departure they began to die, a thing specially observed by us, as also by themselves. They were persuaded we might kill and slay when we would, without weapons, and not come near them. This marvelous accident in all the country wrought so strange opinions of us that they could not tell whether to think us gods or men. And the rather more that all the space of their sickness was no man of ours known to die, or much sick. They noted also that we had no women nor cared for any of theirs. Some therefore thought we were not born of women, and therefore not mortal, but that we were men of an old generation many years past, and risen again from immortality. Some would prophesy there were more of our generation yet to come, to kill theirs and take their places. Those that were to come after us they imagined to be in the air, yet invisible and without bodies, and that they did make the people die by shooting invisible bullets into them. To confirm this, their physicians would make the simple people believe that the strings of blood they sucked out of the sick bodies were the strings wherein the invisible bullets were tied and cast. Some thought we shot them ourselves from the place where we dwelt, and others said it was the special work of God for our sakes, as we had cause in some sort to think no less, our astrologers remembering especially the eclipse of the sun we saw the year before our voyage.

Elizabethans dreamed of America as a land of opportunity, where with luck anyone could become a lady or gentleman. Note the newcomers' sartorial extravagance.

THE LOST COLONY
Roanoke and Virginia Dare

One of the main objectives of England's first Virginia colonists in the New World was to collect sassafras, which in the late 16th century was being promoted as a great new remedy for all ills. The story of Roanoke and of the child born there has long been a part of our tradition, combining the elements of new life, hope, threatening red men, the mysterious disappearance of an entire settlement, and the subsequent reappearance of Virginia Dare in the form of a white doe. Certainly, the full story will never be known; here is the legend:

In the summer of 1587 more than 100 men, women, and children sailed from England to Roanoke Island, intending to colonize the place. They had been ashore less than a month when, on August 18, Governor John White's daughter Eleanor Dare was brought to childbed and delivered of a daughter. "Because this child was the first Christian child born in Virginia," the governor wrote, "she was named Virginia"; indeed, future Anglo-Saxon dominion seemed to be happily portended in that name—Virginia Dare. But that same summer hostile Indians grew so menacing that White felt obliged to return to England for reinforcements to save the colony from being massacred. On leaving, he made the settlers promise to mark in some conspicuous spot the name of their destination, should they move, and if need be, also to inscribe crosses as signals of distress.

Back home, White found England awaiting a Spanish invasion, for 1588 was the dramatic year Sir Francis Drake's small fleet was to defeat Philip II's "Invincible Armada." It took White more than two years to get back to Roanoke, and when he did, a shocking puzzle greeted him.

The arriving relief party sighted a column of smoke rising from Roanoke Island, which gave them hope that the colony might still be there. So—in spite of high winds, giant breakers, a strong riptide, and a sky full of thunder—they tried to land, but one of the boats capsized, drowning seven crewmen. At dusk the wind fell, and they tried again:

"We espied the light of a great fire through the woods. We rowed toward it, and when we were opposite the place we let fall our grappling anchor near the shore, sounded a trumpet call, and then played the tunes of many familiar English songs. We hailed the shore with friendly greetings but got no answer. At daybreak we landed, and when we approached the fire we found the grass and some rotten trees burning."

Nothing is known about the life of Virginia Dare beyond the age of nine days. Some have imagined that she grew up a robust young wench among fellow "lost colonists" who went native in the woods.

Footprints in the sand were the only sign of life. The base itself, completely rebuilt into a single fortress-like enclosure, was empty. One of the entrance posts was carved with the word "Croatan"—but without a cross or other mark of distress. This seemed to mean the missing colonists had moved across the bay to Croatan Island, whose inhabitants had treated previous expeditions with more friendliness than other tribes had. But at Croatan, White found no trace of either colonists or Indians. The wind blew harder, the ships' anchors began to drag, and the sailors' mood grew as foul and stormy as the weather. The searchers gave up and set sail for England. White believed his people dead.

However, they may have survived after all by "going native": 100 years later, gray-eyed Hatteras Indians told of grandparents who could "talk in a book" and of a ghost ship called *Sir Walter Raleigh's Ship* that appeared sometimes offshore—always "under sail, in a gallant posture . . ."

Concerning the fate of Virginia Dare, here is one old tale:

In the early 1600's Indians on Roanoke Island marveled at the sudden appearance of a milk-white doe. The mysterious creature was the most beautiful they had ever seen. Sometimes she stood alone, looking out to sea; sometimes she grazed in the melon patches round the deserted fort. She eluded every arrow, every snare and ruse. So the Indians organized a hunt, and the best archers came from far and wide. Among them was the young Wanchese who had been to England and returned with a silver arrow from the English queen, who had told him it would kill even the bearer of a charmed life. The hunt began, and the white doe bounded away over the sandhills as the hunters' arrows whizzed around her ears. At last she reached the beach. Wanchese appeared, facing her, took aim, and shot the silver arrow through her heart. At the moment she died, the white doe looked into her slayer's eyes and whispered, "Virginia Dare."

AN INDIAN PRINCESS
Pocahontas and John Smith

Indian prophets in Virginia had foretold that whites would invade three times, fail twice, and succeed on the third try. Events confirmed the prophecy. In 1570 Indians destroyed a Spanish mission on the Chesapeake Bay. A decade and a half later the Roanoke colony came to naught. Subsequently, to the tribal leader Powhatan and his counselors in 1607, Jamestown seemed the long-dreaded disaster. Chief among the enemy leaders was the redoubtable Capt. John Smith. But Powhatan's 11-year-old daughter, Pocahontas, became infatuated with the captain and (according to Smith) saved him from execution when he was captured. Their friendship led to a short-lived peace. Their legend arose from the boastful and probably apocryphal version of the events published by Smith 17 years later, in 1624. But we ought to begin with the account of the first summer:

POWHATAN'S CORONATION

The 10th of September 1608 we received presents and costly novelties for the coronation of Powhatan. (This strange coronation was done on direction from England.) Powhatan, being 30 miles off, was presently sent for. In the meantime, Pocahontas and her women entertained Captain Smith in this manner:

They made a fire before which, he sitting upon a mat, 30 young women came naked out of the woods, only covered behind and before with a few green leaves, their bodies all painted, some of one color, some of another, but all differing. Their leader had a fair pair of buck's horns on her head, an otterskin at her girdle and another at her arm, a quiver of arrows at her back, and a bow and arrows in her hand. The next had in her hand a sword, another a club, another a potstick, all horned alike, the rest every one with their several devices. Rushing from among the trees, they cast themselves in a ring about the fire, singing and dancing with most excellent ill-variety. Having spent near an hour in this masquerade, they departed. Then, having reaccommodated themselves, they solemnly invited Smith to their lodgings, where he was no sooner within the house than all these nymphs more tormented him than ever, with crowding, pressing, and hanging about him, most tediously crying: "Love you not me? Love you not me?" Once this salutation had ended, the feast was set.

The next day was appointed for Powhatan's coronation. The presents were brought him, his basin and ewer, bed and furniture set up, his scarlet cloak and apparel with much ado put on him, being persuaded they would not hurt him. But a foul trouble there was to make him kneel to receive his crown: he neither knowing the majesty nor meaning of a crown, nor bending of the knee, endured so many persuasions, examples, and instructions as tired them all. At last, by leaning hard on his shoulders, he a little stooped, and three (having the crown in their hands) put it on his head, when by the warning of a pistol the boats were prepared with such a volley of shot that the king started up in a horrible fear, till he saw all was well. Then, remembering himself, to congratulate their kindness, he gave them his old shoes and mantle.

BUILDING JAMESTOWN

Our drink was water, our lodgings castles in the air; but Captain Smith, by his own good example and good words, set some to mow, others to bind thatch, some to build houses, others to thatch them, himself always bearing the greatest task for his own share, so that in short time he provided most of us lodgings, neglecting any for himself. He conducted 30 of us downriver some five miles to learn to make clapboard, cut down trees, and lay in wood. Amongst us he had chosen two gallants, both proper gentlemen. Strange were these pleasures to their condition—yet lodging, eating and drinking, working or playing, they were but doing as Captain Smith himself did. All these things were carried on so pleasantly as within a week they became masters, making it their delight to hear the trees thunder as they fell. But the axes so oft blistered their tender fingers that many times every third blow had a loud oath to drown the echo. For remedy of which sin Captain Smith devised how to have every man's oaths numbered. And at night for every oath to have a can of water poured down his sleeve, with which every offender (including Captain Smith himself) was so washed that within one week's time a man should scarce hear an oath in a week.

SAVED BY POCAHONTAS

Now the winter approaching, Captain Smith went to search the country for trade and victual. Being got to the marshes at the river's head, he was beset with 200 savages. Two of them he slew, yet he was shot in the thigh a little and had many arrows that stuck in his clothes, but no great hurt. Being near dead with cold, he threw away his arms. Six or seven weeks those barbarians kept him prisoner; how they used and delivered him is as followeth:

Before a fire upon a seat like a bedstead, Powhatan (their emperor) sat covered with a great robe made of raccoon skins with the tails hanging by. (Powhatan is of personage a tall, well-proportioned man, with a sour look, his head somewhat gray, his beard so thin that it seemeth none at all.) On either side of him did sit a young wench of 16 or 18, and along on each side of the house two rows of men (and behind them as many women) all with their heads and shoulders painted red and many of their heads bedecked with the white down of birds. At Captain Smith's entrance before the king, all the people gave a great shout. Having feasted him after their best manner, a long consultation was held. The conclusion was, two great stones were brought before Powhatan. Then as many as could lay hands on Captain Smith dragged him to the stones and thereon laid his head, and being ready with their clubs to beat out his brains, Pocahontas, the king's dearest daughter (when no entreaty could prevail), got his head in her arms and laid her own upon his to save him from death. Whereat the emperor was contented he should live.

Two days after, Powhatan came unto him and told him now they were friends, and presently he should go to Jamestown to send him two great guns and a grindstone, for which he would give him the country of Capahowosick and forever esteem him as his son. So to Jamestown with 12 guides Powhatan sent him. The next morning betimes they came to the fort, where Smith showed Raw-

hunt, Powhatan's trusty servant, two demiculverins [long-barreled cannons] and a millstone to carry to Powhatan. They found them somewhat too heavy. But when they did see him discharge them, being loaded with stones, among the boughs of a great tree loaded with icicles, the ice and branches came so tumbling down that the poor savages ran away half dead with fear. But at last we regained some conference with them and sent to Powhatan and his women and children such presents as gave them in general full content.

THE STARVING TIME

Captain Smith's year as president being near expired, his powder bag fired accidentally, which tore the flesh from his body and thighs, 9 or 10 inches square, in a most pitiful manner. Seeing there was neither surgeon nor surgery to cure his hurt, he sent for the masters of the ships

that were to depart the next day and took order with them for his return for England.

Within six months after Captain Smith's departure, there remained not past 60 men, women, and children out of 500, and those were preserved for the most part by roots, herbs, nuts, berries, and a little fish. They that had starch in those extremities made no small use of it—yea, even the skins of our horses. So great was our famine that some did eat one another, stewed with roots and herbs. And one amongst the rest did kill his wife and powdered [salted] her, and had eaten part of her before it was known, for which he was executed, as he well deserved. Now whether she was better roasted, boiled, or carbonade'd [broiled], I know not—but of such a dish as powdered wife I know I had never before heard. This was that time which to this day we call the starving time.

Matoaks als Rebecka daughter to the mighty Prince Powhatan Emperour of Attanoughkomouck als Virginia converted and baptized in the Christian faith, and Wife to the wor:ᵗᵗ Mʳ Tho: Rolff.

The Indian princess Pocahontas made a sensation at the court of King James. "She was," said her old friend John Smith, "the very nonpareil of the kingdom." The king was much annoyed that John Rolfe, her planter husband, had as a commoner dared marry a royal person without obtaining prior permission from the Crown. The portrait at left, now at the National Portrait Gallery in Washington, D.C., was done from life when Pocahontas was 21. Above is one of many subsequent romantic visions of history's first "white Indian."

KIDNAPED
The First Blacks Arrive

"O, ancestors, do all that is in your power that our reigning princes and noble kinsmen shall never be sent away from here as slaves to America. We pray you, punish those who bought our kinsmen whom we shall never see again." These words have been heard even in recent times, in prayers to ancestral spirits in Dahomey, West Africa, where traditional memories of the biggest forced migration in history are still alive. Early black Americans' memories of that traumatic move were left unwritten for so long that individual family traditions concerning it faded away; but folk memory preserved it in stories like these:

THE BLACK SLAVE TRADER

There was once a black slave trader who was the terror of the Guinea Coast. In one year's time he could deliver more captives than all his competitors put together. His raiders struck far inland, bringing one coffle [slave caravan] after another to the coast. One day he received a parcel of Africans for delivery to a Yankee ship that was about to sail for America. He supervised the delivery in person. When the unfortunate prisoners had all been brought on board ship, the slave trader joined the captain in his cabin, to seal the transaction over a glass of rum. The rum was drugged. The next thing he knew, the slaver was lying shackled in the hold of the ship alongside his former

Africa's densely populated Gold Coast was for centuries styled the Slave Coast. The traffic enriched countless shippers, brokers, and others—one native king used to say, "Why should I not sell?"

captives. Like them, he was branded on the chest. Over him stood his friend the Yankee captain, laughing.

FLIGHT

According to an old story, Africans in ancient times could fly like birds. As late as slavery days, there were still some who retained the power of flight, though they looked like other men. One of these people once turned up on an out-of-the-way plantation in America. This is what happened. The plantation's cruel master had worked his slaves until they died of overwork in the burning sun. So, of a broker in the town, he bought a company of newly arrived native Africans to replace them. He put the newcomers at once to work in the cottonfield, where they worked from sunrise until dark, day after day. Among them was a young woman who had lately borne a child, her first, and she was still weak. Whenever the baby cried, she spoke to quiet it, in words the foreman could not understand, then gave it her breast and went back to chopping knotgrass.

But then one day, sick with the heat, she stumbled and fell. The driver struck her with his lash until she got up. She spoke to a man near her. He was the oldest there, tall and strong, with a forked beard, and the driver could not understand their talk. After another spell of work, she fell again. The driver whipped her to her feet, and again she addressed words to the old man. But he said, "Not yet." So she went back to work.

But when she fell down a third time, and the driver came running with his lash yet again, she turned to the old man, and this time he said, "Yes, daughter, go!" With that she leaped straight into the air and flew away, with her baby still astraddle her hip, sucking at her breast.

The driver hurried the others to make up for his loss. The sun was very hot indeed. Soon a man fell down. The driver lashed him. But the old man called out, in an unknown tongue, and when he had spoken, the man turned and laughed and leaped up into the air and was gone, flying over field and wood. Then another man fell, and the driver lashed him; but the old man spoke and stretched out his arms as he had done for the other two. Then the overseer cried to the driver, and the master cried to them both: "Get that old devil! Get him!" The overseer and the driver ran at the old man with lashes ready, and the master ran too, with a picket pulled out of the fence to beat the life out of the old man. But the old man laughed in their faces and then spoke some words loudly to all the Negroes in that field.

As he spoke, they all remembered what they had forgotten, and recalled the power which had once been theirs. Then all stood up together; the old man raised his hands, and they all leaped up into the air with a great shout and in a moment were gone over the field, over the fence, and over the top of the wood; and behind them flew the old man. The men went clapping their hands, the women went singing, and the children laughed and were not afraid. The master, the overseer, and the driver looked after them as they flew, beyond the wood, beyond the river, miles on miles, until they passed beyond the last rim of the world and disappeared in the sky like a handful of leaves. They were never seen by the master again.

They say, "Massa, you ain't gwine lick me," and with that they riz up in the air and fly 'way—right back to Africa."

TOBACCO

Queen Elizabeth once bet Sir Walter Raleigh he could not tell how much smoke there was in a pound of tobacco. Sir Walter took her up on it. His solution was ingenious: weigh the ashes from the pound after smoking it. The difference between the two weights, he asserted, must indubitably be the weight of the smoke. Convinced, or at least amused, the queen paid the wager, remarking that she had heard of many who turned their gold into smoke but that Raleigh was the first to turn smoke into gold. These were prophetic words. Within a generation scores of Virginia planters were turning smoke into gold. Tobacco had in fact become the mainstay of the new colony's economy, thanks to John Rolfe, husband of Pocahontas. In 1614, the same year he married the Indian princess, Rolfe had succeeded in developing a first crop of characteristically strong, sweet "Virginia" from the weak-flavored, bitter native leaf. So, at last, it was tobacco that put

Virginia on the map, years after Raleigh had been locked up in the Tower. (Sir Walter lived just long enough to witness this triumph and smoked at his own execution in 1618, thus anticipating the custom of the condemned man's last smoke.)

At that time, about a century after tobacco had first been exported from America, smoking was on the way to becoming a worldwide social habit. When Christopher Columbus' sailors first beheld the tobacco-smoking Carib Indians, they were amazed and fascinated. No such practice existed anywhere in the Old World. It had never occurred to medieval Europeans that one could pleasurably ingest certain kinds of smoke. Early explorers therefore likened native Americans to furnaces and chimneys. They encountered tobacco among the Indians everywhere, finding not only pipes, but cigars, perfumed cane cigarettes, chewing tobacco, and snuff. "Drinking smoke," Indians told them, keeps the

N. tabacum, *the mysterious plant Columbus found native West Indians smoking in big, trumpetlike cigars*

body warm and healthy. The whites needed no further encouragement. There had already been nicotine addicts among Columbus' crewmen— some confessed they smoked the weed constantly because they couldn't stop. Here is an early (1567) description of its effects on Europeans: "Sucking in as much smoke as they can, they say that their hunger and thirst are allayed, their strength is restored, and their spirits are refreshed; they are lulled by a joyous intoxication as the smoke fills the chambers of the brain with a sort of vaporous fragrance."

Medical men were soon prescribing tobacco as a wonder drug, and they continued to do so until well into the 1700's. (Tobacco was not finally dropped from the U.S. *Pharmacopoeia* until 1886.) In the early days, "tobacconists" (pro-tobacco people) were a majority of the medical profession, prescribing nicotine—applied in a poultice, to be taken in pill form, chewed and swallowed, smoked, sniffed, or drunk as a tea, according to the case—for all manner of aches and pains, swellings, snakebite, gunshot wounds, bad breath.

A minority disagreed. Tobacco was no panacea, they declared; if anything, it was a poison. King James himself wrote an anti-tobacco tract in which he told of the autopsy of a chain smoker whose body was found to contain a bushel of soot. Samuel de Champlain,

Sir Walter Raleigh was a tastemaker; he made smoking fashionable, but legend has it that the first time he lit up, his alarmed manservant acted to extinguish the fire.

the explorer, had a further unpleasantness to relate: "Its smoke dulleth the senses, and mounting up to the brains, hindereth the functions of Venus." Not only impotence, but sterility, brain damage, and blindness are blamed on tobacco in this contemporary quatrain:

Tobacco, that outlandish weed,
It spends the brain and spoils the seed:
It dulls the sprite, it dims the sight,
It robs a woman of her right.

There was doubtless more fancy than fact on both sides of the debate, which had grown as intense as it is today by the time Thomas Harriot, the astronomer and Virginia traveler who was Sir Walter Raleigh's fortuneteller, died of a possibly smoking-related cancer of the nose and mouth at his country residence in England in 1621. Like Raleigh, Harriot had become a heavy smoker; in fact, it was he who had taught Raleigh how to smoke in the first place, upon returning from Virginia in 1585. Yet no one at the time guessed that there might be some connection between Harriot's cancer and his 35-year smoking habit.

Meanwhile, traders succeeded in attracting increasing numbers of customers belonging to every race on earth, including the only New World people who had not previously used tobacco—the Eskimos. During the century after the introduction in the Orient of tobacco-smoking gear, opium, hashish, and marijuana pipes came into existence. Arabs were among the first to welcome tobacco as a new way to get high. In fact, the Arabic word *tabaq*, "euphoria-producing herb," is now thought to be the source of the word "tobacco." To this day it is the custom in some Arab countries to smoke marijuana blended with the strong, dark caporal tobacco leaf. Closer to home, the smoking of tobacco runs deep in the American grain. It is, in fact, the source of our oldest custom as a people. As a sign of hospitality and brotherhood, Indians shared peace pipes with the first European settlers. The custom of offering visitors a friendly smoke grew out of that and has been with us ever since.

The Sacred Smoke

The aborigines of America valued thousands of plants for their medicinal and supernatural properties, but from time out of mind they held tobacco in special reverence. Here is a myth linking the very origin of man with that of the leaf:

When the Great Spirit made the spirits of nature and the spirit ancestors of birds and animals, he conferred upon each a special power. Man he created last of all, but then found he had already given away every power, and there was nothing left to bestow upon this miserably weak, unendowed creature. So for man, the Great Spirit made a special plant: tobacco. At the first smell of it, the other spirits were filled with an insatiable craving for its fragrance. One by one, each petitioned to exchange his power for that of the new plant. The Great Spirit refused them all, saying that he too craved it, but that the gift was man's, and he was henceforth free to share the plant with other spirits or to withhold it from them as he chose. And so, ever since, humans have appeased the spirits and obtained their help by leaving offerings of the leaf buried in the ground, by casting it in the air or into lakes and rivers, and most important, by burning it in the ceremonial pipe bowl. (Some modern Indians liken the smoke from tobacco smoked in council to a telephone connecting the people with the spirit world.)

The peace pipe was thus a kind of censer at which alliances and contracts were made, friendships sworn, good traveling weather secured, and the like. The pipe had a stone bowl carved in any of a great variety of bird and animal shapes, and a cane stem decorated with feathers in almost every color save red. (Red feathers were reserved for war pipes.) When smoking these pipes (also called calumets) together, Indians commonly invoked the sun and sky, then blew smoke toward the four world quarters and the earth. In the Virginia of Powhatan's day, personal pipes often bore a design of concentric rectangles, symbolizing the cosmos. In some parts of America, smoking was for men only; in others, the teeth of men, women, and children were browned with tobacco juice.

The weed is even the source of our expression "Indian summer," which arose in Revolutionary times from the following native story:

In September and October the god of the north world quarter grows pleasantly drowsy as he watches the people feasting after harvest. Often the first frost rouses him just enough to enjoy a leisurely smoke before his annual hibernation. When this happens, there is a spell of smoky, mellow weather till the god dozes off contentedly and winter begins.

The Inland Kingdom

Decades before the founding of New France in 1605, French priests, trappers, and explorers began to chart North America's inland waterways in their quest for souls, skins, and a northwest passage to Cathay. Traveling by canoe and on foot, they established outposts as far from the Atlantic coast as the westernmost reaches of the Great Lakes and beyond, and learned the extent of the St. Lawrence, Ohio, and Mississippi rivers. They befriended the "savages," and many explorers and priests took the time to learn their languages and customs. There was one fateful exception: Samuel de Champlain sided with the Hurons in their ongoing war with the Iroquois. The ferocious members of the Six Nations never forgot or forgave the French for that.

Many explorers wrote accounts of their adventures, and few could resist embellishing. Some, like Father Hennepin, tried to claim credit for the deeds of their braver—or luckier—fellows. Others borrowed from imagination to fill in blanks in their information or repeated fanciful tales spun by fellow adventurers. At-home Europeans were fascinated, and in turn created their version of the New World, a paradise peopled with noble savages and fanciful beasts.

Many boys born in the Canadian settlements tried to slip into the forests to lead the lonely and adventurous life of a *coureur de bois* (woods runner) upon coming of age. Inevitably, the cultural lore of those French Canadians who succeeded was modified and reshaped by their Indian companions and wilderness milieu. Farmer settlers who came as part of the large-scale colonization, finally begun in the 1660's in part of Nova Scotia (Acadia), were not as affected by the wilds and clung to the French stories they had brought with them. But in 1755 the English expelled and scattered those Acadian farmers. Some of them were shipped to Louisiana, where their folklore expanded to include their exodus and acquired overtones from the lore of the Spanish and Negroes who were already at home there.

Louisianan voodoo rites (like that at left) were closed to whites until Mambo Marie Laveau made them into public spectacles in the 1830's.

The 19th-century artist E. W. Deming added his own touches to the story of Jean Nicolet who, thinking he had reached China, donned oriental robes before landing in Wisconsin.

THE STORYTELLERS
Explorers of New France

In 1564 Marc Lescarbot wrote of his fellow French explorers: "They write long but wholly undigested accounts." Their misrepresentations were not always innocent, either. The general tone of the reports was boastful; few writers could resist the impulse to exaggerate. The worst offender was Louis Hennepin, whose major conceit was that he—not La Salle—first discovered the mouth of the Mississippi. That self-serving lie appeared in a work that Hennepin revised and reissued after La Salle's death. The whoppers survive today as footnotes to history, but in their time they formed an important part of New World lore.

LESCARBOT'S LIGHTNING

Half a league from the French fort there fell a thunderbolt the like of which was never seen. It was at the end of August, at which time, although the meadows were all green and moist, in a moment this thunderbolt consumed more than 500 acres and by its fiery heat burned all the birds in the meadows. This lasted for three days, with continual fire and lightning. Much anxiety was caused thereby to our French, and not less to the Indians, who thinking that these thunders were cannon-shots fired at them by our men, sent orators to Captain Laudonniere to testify to him the desire of Chief Allicamani to maintain their alliance and to be employed in his service, and that therefore Allicamani considered passing strange the cannonade directed against his dwelling which had burned a wide stretch of verdant meadows, and consumed even what was under water, and came so near his house he expected it to be in a blaze. Laudonniere, concealing his contempt for the foolish notion of the man, joyously replied that he had ordered these cannonades on account of the rebellion made by Allicamani. He said that he had no desire to harm him but had contented himself with firing only halfway, to make manifest his power; he assured him, moreover, that as long as the chief remained willing to render him obedience, he would be his faithful defender against all his enemies.

The Indians were contented with this reply, and at the end of three days the thunder ceased, and the blaze utterly died out. But on the two following days the air suddenly became so excessively warm that the river almost boiled over, and so great a quantity of fish died of it that at the mouth of the river there were enough to load more than 50 wagons. From that there arose so great a stench that many severe contagious diseases broke out among the French, of which, however, by the favor of God, not a single one of them died.

FATHER HENNEPIN BOASTS

I had visited many parts of Europe, but not being satisfied with that, I was eager to see remoter countries and nations that had not yet been heard of; and in gratifying this natural itch I was led to this discovery of a vast and large country, where no European ever was before myself.

'Tis true indeed, I could not foresee the embarrassing difficulties and dangers I must of necessity encounter in this my painful voyage. But despite all the discouragements, I've perfected my design, the undertaking of which was enough to frighten any other but myself.

• • •

Betwixt the Lake Ontario and Erie there is a vast and prodigious cadence of water which falls down after an astonishing manner. The River Niagara is so rapid above this descent that it violently hurls down the wild beasts who endeavor to pass it to feed on the other side. They cannot withstand its current, which inevitably casts them down headlong above 600 feet. [In his first edition the author had described the spectacular 200-foot falls as 500 feet high.] The waters which fall from this vast height do foam and boil in the most hideous manner, making an outrageous noise; their dismal roaring may be heard from 15 leagues off.

• • •

I am resolved to give here an account of the course of the Mississippi

Explorer priests and traders engage in their favorite occupations in this highly imaginative 18th-century engraving. At the so-called Port of Mississippi, friars convert Indians while their countrymen corrupt them by trading whisky for pelts and other goods.

River; which I have hitherto concealed for the sake of M. La Salle, who would ascribe to himself alone the glory and the most secret part of this discovery. He was so fond of it, that he has exposed to visible danger several persons, that they might not publish what they had seen.

There is no man but remembers with pleasure the dangers he has escaped. I must confess that when I call to mind the perils that I was exposed to in the discovery of the Mississippi, my joy and satisfaction cannot be expressed. I was as good as sure that M. La Salle would slander me, and represent me to my superiors as a willful and obstinate man, if I presumed to go down the Mississippi, and therefore I was loath to undertake it. But on the other hand I was threatened by my two men if I opposed their resolution. So I thought it was reasonable to prefer my own preservation to the ambition of M. La Salle. So I agreed to follow my men, who seeing me in that good disposition, promised to be faithful.

The 25th we rowed the best part of the day and came to a point where the Mississippi divides itself into three channels. The water there began to taste brackish, but four leagues lower it was as salty as the sea. We rowed four leagues more

after that and we discovered the sea.

I undertook my whole voyage on the River Mississippi against M. La Salle's opinion. He has since made a voyage from the Illinois to the Gulf of Mexico in the year 1682, and two years after me.

BELLEFOREST'S MONTREAL

The royal citadel of Hochelaga stands on a mountain covered with plowed fields and gardens. The Christians called it Mount Royal, or Montreal. The entire compound is entirely surrounded by a wall two lances high. The interior of the wooden ramparts are lined with connecting platforms loaded with stones to cast down on besiegers and are accessible by ladders from within;

and it should not be imagined that this is at all strange or implausible, given that the finest and greatest towns of Muscovy are of no greater magnificence. Hochelaga is not the most populous city in the world; for it consists solely of a royal compound having but 50 palaces and mansions more or less, each being some 50 feet long and 15 wide, and all of wood.

Each house is built around a big courtyard, and in the interior of each are chambers, halls, etc.; and in the court they have their cooking fires, for they would never dare to have them inside, for fear of fire. These lodges are not so small but that they cannot accommodate two or three stories with attics on top of them, in which they store their corn.

The borders of areas claimed by England, France, and Spain in 1700 were fluid. Much of the territory was still unexplored, and there were constant claims and counterclaims as settlers moved or explorers entered regions new to them. This map shows a few of the most important white settlements at that time, most of which were clustered on the east coast. Indian peoples are indicated by general locality.

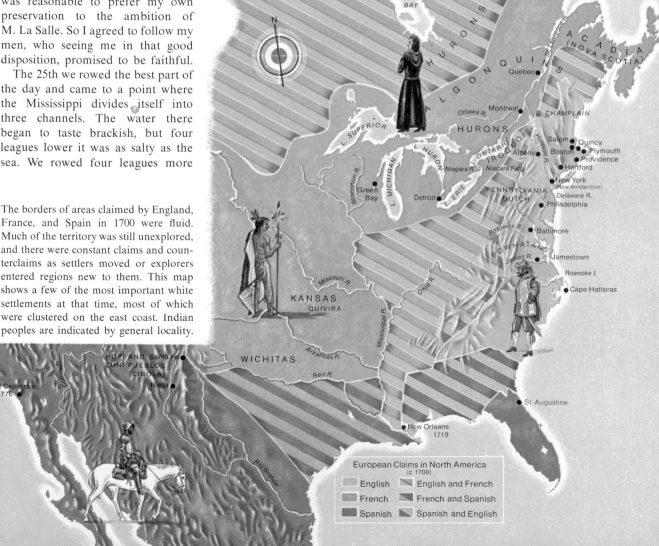

A BESTIARY
Beasts out of Mind

The flora and fauna of the New World were a delight and a puzzle to visitors. Writers eagerly repeated tales of strange beings, and artists illustrated their stories. It is safe to assume, however, that the explorers of North America were clever, so accounts like those below often exhibit a certain tongue-in-cheekiness.

Raretés des Indes, in which these animals appear, describes the beaverlike mammal as a "mountain rat big as a spaniel," and the others as a sea horse found near the St. Lawrence, a unicorn, and a tiger.

PLAYING POSSUM

The first marsupial ever seen by whites was the opossum. As described by one explorer, it "hath a head like a swine, and a tail like a rat, and is of the bigness of a cat; under her belly she hath a bag, wherein she lodgeth her young." Such a strange creature was bound to give rise to folklore. From the observation that mother opossums often sniff inside the pouch while giving birth, the notion arose that opossums copulate through the nose and then blow their young into the pouch.

THE GOUGOU MONSTER

A French boat sailed past an isle where dwells a frightful monster which the savages call Gougou. They say it is the shape of a woman but of exceedingly horrible aspect and of such size the savages declared that a ship's mast would not reach as high as the she-monster's girdle. Often she puts savages in her pocket when she succeeds in catching them, and then she devours them. Those who have escaped from the parlous toils of this wretched beast maintain that her pouch is so huge she could put a whole ship inside. The Christians sailed so close by the den of this dreadful monster that all hands plainly heard the hissing noises she made at their approach. We can only conclude the place must be the den of a devil appointed to torment them.

ARMOUCHIQUOIS

The savages were in terror of meeting their enemies the Armouchiquois, who are savages of an altogether monstrous shape: for their heads are very small and their bodies very stubby and their arms and hams as lean as any skeleton's, yet with legs long and strong and all of a size; and when they sit on their heels, their knees pass more than half a foot over their heads, which is passing strange. Yet they are of a powerful, strong temper and determined and therefore have the best lands around.

These strange creatures decorate *The Unknown New World,* published in 1673. The airborne beast at left, below, is identified as a "dreadful dragon with fiery eyes and a brown-blue back."

His companions are a two-tailed lizard and a cuttlefish. Two "baboons" (shown below, right), which were probably inspired by the uakari monkey, stroll among several strange serpents.

THE NOBLE SAVAGE

The New France of Champlain's day witnessed a bizarre theological debate between rival Jesuit and Franciscan missionaries on the issue of whether or not American Indians had souls to be saved. Were the savages fully human? Jesuits argued the affirmative. Indians might be a nature-folk, but they were still children of Adam and Eve. Arguing the negative, the opposing side held them to be descendants of a previously unknown subhuman species.

The Jesuits won the debate, referring to ancient legends situating humanity's birthplace on a remote isle of the Ocean Sea (America) on which our original ancestors were supposed to have dwelt in ideal simplicity and happiness—the Golden Age. Columbus himself had believed Indians were survivals of that era: "I am convinced that the Earthly Paradise actually exists . . . These are a handsome people, their eyes are beautiful, their speech sweet, gentle, and always with a smile. They go naked, without arms and without law. Many live in one house; it appeared things were common to all."

How had the savages come to possess so many admirable qualities? Unaware that the Indians' mental capacity was no lower than their own, Europeans assumed the virtues exhibited by savages—their simple communism, their belief in communal landholding, in group solidarity rather than individual competitiveness, and their lack of a concept of a distinction between animal and human personality—must come direct from nature. Reports of primitive lifeways in the wilds of America were eagerly received in oppressed, crowded Europe. Sick of civilization, people yearned, in the words of playwright John Dryden, to be "as free as Nature first made man, when wild in the woods the noble savage ran."

But primitivism, as the vogue of the fabled "noble savage" was called, was to find its greatest proponent in the philosopher-founder of Romanticism, Jean Jacques Rousseau. His doctrines of "innate goodness" and "natural liberty" were to be revolutionary slogans during the generation following 1776. The "noble savage" became a latter-day Spartan; in Rousseau's words: "I behold numbers of naked savages who despise European pleasures, braving hunger, fire, the sword, and death, to preserve nothing but their independence . . . What yoke, indeed, can be imposed on men who stand in need of nothing!"

"I am not of Rousseau's opinions," observed John Adams. "His notions of the purity of morals in savage nations are mere chimeras." The majority of Adams' countrymen shared this view —savages seemed anything but noble to them. However, 18th-century Americans still enjoyed yarns in which the red man's legendary virtues were highlighted. Here are two examples of that type of story:

BETTER BELIEVE IT
A bigoted Philadelphia lady went to the western frontier and set out to convert the savages. She started on the loyal chief Great Beaver's squaw but was rebuffed. So she sought out Great Beaver himself and exhorted him. He rejoined with a myth about a talking white bear. Unbelievable, the lady objected. No more so, Great Beaver observed, than the talking snake that spoke to Eve. "But *they* were inspired," she exclaimed confusedly. "So was the white bear," the chief replied. "But this is so excessively absurd," she cried, at which Great Beaver said, "I have not called your wonders absurd. I thought it more decent to believe."

COLLEGE NO GOOD
At a treaty meeting between some colonies and the Six Nations, Indians declined an offer from the English to take half a dozen of the brightest Indian lads and educate them in their college. The Indians replied that some of their youths had formerly been educated at that college but that it had been observed that long after they returned to their friends, they were still absolutely good for nothing—being acquainted neither with the true methods of killing deer nor catching beavers nor surprising an enemy. The commissioners' proposition they looked on, however, as a mark of good will meriting a grateful return. Therefore, if the English gentlemen agreed to send a dozen or two of their own children to Onondaga, the Great Council would take care of their education, bringing them up in what was really the best manner, and would make men of them.

Typical Huron weddings were quick and cool, wrote 17-year-old Baron de Lahontan: "They are altogether strangers to that blind fury which we call love."

VILLAGERS AND WOODSMEN
Cold Comforts and Icy Fears

By the early 1600's, there were a fair number of small French settlements in Canada. The colonists maintained peaceful relations with their Indian neighbors and joined them against their mutual bitter enemy, the Iroquois. Many even adopted native ways and wives, becoming coureurs de bois *who ranged the wilderness gathering valuable furs. So colorful did the coureurs' reputation become, so romanticized their genuinely arduous lives, that their legend tends to dominate the period, but there are stories about more prosaic people, too.*

THE LOUP-GAROU

There once lived in the village of Saint-Antoine in the district of Beauséjour a miller named Joachim Crête. Joachim was not a bad man, and though the villagers found his solitary bachelor ways rather odd, they tolerated him well enough. But they gossiped unmercifully about his hired man, Hubert Sauvageau, who was never seen in church. Repeatedly, when one of them would come to the mill to have his wheat or barley ground, he would draw the miller aside and complain that Joachim's helper was as religious as a dog.

Joachim was not impressed. Hubert's personal beliefs were no concern of his, the miller retorted. There was not a more diligent worker in all Beauséjour nor, he added privately, a better checkers partner. For when the day's chores were over and the night was hard upon them, Joachim and Hubert would take out their bottle of brandy, throw another log on the fire, and play checkers intensely, except when Hubert set off on one of his mysterious late night rambles.

On one such occasion Joachim was ruminating by the fire, doing nothing in particular, when he heard terrible shouting. He rushed out to find a young woman and her three children spilled out on the snow, their wagon overturned, and their horse rearing and snorting and all covered with sweat. When Joachim had calmed the little family down sufficiently to bring them into his house and seat them by the fire, he asked what had given them all such a fright.

"It is the *loup-garou*, the werewolf, which barred our path. Our poor mare was so frozen with fear that only when I beat her unmercifully did she finally take off and run, knocking the wolf aside before he could sink his teeth into her neck." Joachim, who was never one for tact, laughed at her foolishness. He had heard the story of the werewolf many times in recent weeks and dismissed it as just another bit of local superstition. But his guests could not be reassured, so he escorted them home.

For the first time in his life, Joachim was uneasy as he made the return journey alone later that night. He felt no better when, upon reaching the house, he found Hubert, looking even more unkempt than

The Montreal Fur Fair

Every spring after the waterways thawed sufficiently to permit passage by canoe, the *coureurs de bois* and their Indian suppliers headed for one of the French trading stations to sell their stock of furs. Though several small stations—more like military forts than mercantile centers—were established deep in the Canadian forests, it was to the brighter lights of Montreal in eastern Canada that most of the voyageurs went. Small wonder, for Montreal's fur fair offered both a ready market and a chance for indulging in a midsummer night's orgy of drinking, dancing, singing, storytelling, and general license.

Men coming from western Canada usually joined a flotilla of canoes at the French-held site of modern-day Green Bay, Wisconsin, on Lake Michigan and proceeded east en masse, until they reached their destination nearly 1,000 miles down the river. At the height of the fur trade, in 1693, the procession numbered more than 400 canoes, with some 200 coureurs de bois and 1,200 Indians. A chronicler of the day estimated the value of their cargo of furs at more than 800,000 livres, which suggests that they carried in excess of 200,000 skins.

As the huge party drew near to Montreal, discipline broke down progressively, for despite the orders of the king's agents, brandy was sold openly

Before bartering pelts with these French merchants in Montreal, two natives wisely inspect the trade goods offered.

at settlements along the route. By the time the Montreal stockades hove into view, many of the travelers had started celebrating and were ready for more.

The 10-day fair which followed traditionally began with formalities, with the berobed governor and bishop making speeches regarding French-Indian amity. After this, the local merchants were permitted to haggle for the furs. Beaver, used to make the highly fashionable beaver hats, brought the highest price, but mink, otter, marten, and other pelts were also welcomed and brought a decent price.

When the furs had all been sold, the carousing began in earnest. For the Frenchmen, it might have been a welcome—if debauched—reentry into the world they had left behind. For the Indians, whose traditional values were sorely tested by this brush with the modern world of commerce, it was at the very best a mixed blessing.

An engraving done c. 1700 depicts a French fisherman and trapper with quarries.

usual, in the deep sleep of one exhausted. After that the miller began to keep a closer watch on Hubert, but enjoying his company and needing another strong back to do the work, he tried to dismiss his uneasiness.

Autumn turned into winter and then Christmas Eve came. The miller and his helper cozied themselves for a night of holiday merrymaking, uncorking their best bottle of brandy before they sat down to their checkers. Neighbors passing on their way to midnight Mass stopped to invite Joachim along, but he only laughed. He even set the millstone to turning as if it were just another workday.

On the stroke of midnight, while the priest was intoning the first words of the Mass in the village, the mill stopped abruptly. The checkers players, both quite drunk by now, rose from the table and went out to the mill to set it going again. Nothing appeared to be broken, but they could not make the wheel turn. Stumbling about, swearing outrageously, they tried to find their way back to the warmth of the house. Hubert lost his footing and fell headlong down a flight of stone steps, and Joachim, by now barely sensible, decided to leave him there. Suddenly a huge dog, as big as a man and with eyes like torches, stood in his path. Joachim knew in an instant that he was looking at the muzzle of the loup-garou. "May God have mercy on me," he cried, going to his knees. He felt something sharp at his back and he reached around to find his sickle hanging on a nail on the wall. Grabbing the steel tool, he struck the wolf in the head. Then everything went black.

When Joachim awoke he found Hubert throwing water on him. He noticed that Hubert's ear was bleeding and he asked what happened. "You remember, two days ago I fell in the mill, and I struck my head on a bucket." But the miller knew otherwise. Shuddering with horror, he said, "It was you, Hubert, you are the werewolf!" and he fell back raving mad. Joachim never recovered his senses after that. Within a few years he died and his mill was swept away by the spring floods.

THE CHASSE-GALERIE
One New Year's Eve, four *coureurs de bois* in a cabin deep in the wilderness, remembering the fine parties, the fiddling, the dancing, and the girls they left behind, became unbearably homesick.

Trying to make the best of their misery, one of them, Philippe by name, leaped up. "Why are we sitting here when with the Devil's help we could be back in our village, arm in arm with a fine lusty wench!" So saying, he ran out the door, into the snow, and began to dig frantically at their great canoe buried in a drift. His companions, at once frightened at the thought of making a pact with the Devil and unwilling to be left behind, hurried to help.

Moments later the four men, their paddles in hand, took their places in the canoe. One by one they toasted the Devil and swore that in exchange

The miller Joachim Crête and his helper, Hubert, play a fierce round of checkers on Christmas Eve, ignoring the urgings of their neighbors to come to midnight Mass. The *loup-garou*, the devilish werewolf, will exact an extremely heavy price for their sins.

for a ride they would willingly surrender their souls if ever they should so much as utter the name of God or touch a cross before sunup. Then, with a great whoosh, the boat took flight and off they went, their canoe transformed into a magical flying canoe, the *chasse-galerie* that their fathers had told them of long ago.

The coureurs landed as planned just beyond the barn of one of their townsmen, where the cluster of wagons and the sounds of laughter gave witness to a grand party within. Soon they were dancing and shouting and warming themselves with great gulps of rum. Before they knew it, it was nearly dawn. They were very late leaving and had to paddle furiously.

Philippe, by now completely useless and very confused, stood in his place almost upsetting the boat. *"Mon Dieu,"* he exclaimed, forgetting his pact with the Devil, "my paddle is lost," and with that the canoe crashed to earth. When the men came to themselves they were in front of the cabin where they had begun; their canoe was a pile of splinters.

Philippe died not long after of mysterious causes, and the other three all came to bad ends. In their home village people wondered from time to time what had become of their adventurous young men; some swore that they had seen them briefly on New Year's Eve, but most people said that was impossible and laughed at so silly a story.

DANCE OF THE STARS

There once was a logger named Miette who would do anything on a dare. If he came to a mountain peak and had the choice of walking around it or going over it, more than likely he would scamper over the top, while his fellow woodsmen shook their heads. It was the same with treacherous rapids and ravines.

The bold logger was equally famous for his fiddle, and men would stop whatever they were doing just to hear him play. One autumn evening Miette appeared at a loggers' settlement and said he was going to celebrate that night because on the mor-

row he would marry a beautiful Indian girl. A big fire was lighted, great tankards of whisky were poured and poured again, and Miette began to play.

Every note was like a brilliant shaft of light piercing the darkness, and soon the loggers in their joy began to dance and leap about, first in the bunkhouse and then out into the winter night. Looking up, they saw that even the northern lights had begun to dance to the music. Some of the men were frightened and wanted Miette to stop, but the logger just played more magically than ever. He shouted to the sky, "Welcome, Marionettes"—for that is what he called the dancing lights—"come dance at my wedding."

The lights, as if obeying, began to soar higher than ever into the sky and to change colors. Miette, transported

Bound for Montreal and the annual fur fair

by his own music, played faster and faster. Soon the whole sky was alive and there was no blackness at all. Then, suddenly, as if a huge curtain had descended, everything went dark, the fire was extinguished, the music stopped. When Miette's com-

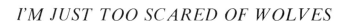

I'M JUST TOO SCARED OF WOLVES

I was a-coming from Vendée, (repeat)
Who should I meet with on my way . . .
– You make me laugh, you do:
Never will I leave home like you,
I'm just too scared of wolves.

Who should I meet with on my way, (r.)
Three cavaliers in brave array . . .
– You make me laugh, etc.

Three cavaliers in brave array, (r.)
Two of 'em mounted, one à pied . . .
– You make me laugh, etc.

He that did walk made bold to say, (r.)
Where shall we sleep tonight, I pray?
– You make me laugh, etc.

If you do with, with us you may, (r.)
Supper with you we'll share today . . .
– You make me laugh, etc.

And for you featherbeds we'll lay, (r.)
All three said YES without delay . . .
– You make me laugh, you do:
Never will I leave home like you,
I'm just too scared of wolves.

Rhythmic *chansons,* timed to the strokes of their paddles, were sung by *coureurs de bois* as they plied North America's lakes and rivers. In the late eighteenth and early nineteenth centuries canoeloads of *voyageurs,* transporting pelts for big fur companies, sometimes ran through 50 songs—of love, homesickness, adventure, and the bawdy life—in a day. A man with a large repertoire and good voice was considered such an asset that he often commanded higher wages than his fellows.

vent that took place each spring, a canoeload of Canadian Indian trappers (in gay beaver hats) paddle and sing their way downriver.

panions recovered from their surprise they looked about for the bridegroom, but the man was nowhere to be found. When his Indian bride came for him the next day he was still missing, and she went home disconsolate and in disgrace. Three days later a distraught and gaunt Miette returned, still holding his fiddle, the strings all broken, the bow worn through with playing. He would not say where he had been, and after gathering his few belongings, he set out for the mountains and was never seen again.

COURAGEOUS CADIEUX

Cadieux was one of the bravest of the brave coureurs de bois, and he was as trusted among the Algonquins as any sagamore [chief]. Once, when several families found themselves menaced by some Iroquois, they chose Cadieux to lead them out of their difficulty.

With one Algonquin companion, Cadieux set out through the woods, leaving a trail behind that they hoped would lead the Iroquois away from their main party. The ruse worked. The Iroquois chased Cadieux wherever he led them, getting close enough one day to capture and kill his companion. Then they gave up the hunt and returned to their own camp. The courageous trapper, cold, exhausted, and starving, could not light a fire for fear that the smoke would reveal his whereabouts.

Cadieux' friends, quite safe, returned to look for their hero. For days they searched and called but got

no reply, for the coureur could not summon the strength to answer. Finally, with all hope lost, he prepared his own grave, building a small shelter of pine boughs. He fashioned a cross, set it on the ground, and then lay down, placing his hands across his chest as in a peaceful sleep.

Several days later the Algonquins found the friend who had saved them, dead. Beside him, scratched on a sheet of birch bark, was a long poem that has since become one of the favorite ballads of French-Canadian voyageurs. It concludes:

Here I take leave of the world,
But I have faith in you, Savior of
    men!
Sainted Virgin, do not abandon me.
Let me die in your arms.

THE WENDIGO

Among the Indians a supernatural ogre called Wendigo was widely known and much feared. No one could describe this phantom of the forests, but his victims always submitted to him in the same terrifying way, answering his irresistible call when their time came.

Take the example of the Indian guide named Défago. One fall day while leading a party of Englishmen deep into moose country, Défago became very uneasy. He complained of smelling a strange, unearthly smell and kept looking over his shoulder. Though exhausted from a hard day's travel, he slept badly that night, and his companions heard him crying in his sleep. Suddenly, just before dawn,

the Indian jumped up shouting in a voice that seemed part terror, part delight, "My feet are burning! They are fiery wings and I must fly!" And as he disappeared into the woods, he continued shouting.

His companions, naturally terrified, waited until dawn to check out the Indian's disappearance. They found two pairs of tracks in the snow; one was of a moccasined pair of feet and a second belonged to some creature whose feet seemed as large as snowshoes. As they followed the trail, a curious change began to appear in the human's track—the footsteps began to assume the shape of the creature's until they were distinguishable only by their smaller size.

After following the trail most of the day without finding the missing guide but feeling more and more worried for their own safety, the Englishmen set out for civilization. Several days later as they were gathered around their campfire, a tattered, crazed-looking figure suddenly loomed in the flickering light. It was Défago, they were sure, but his face was barely recognizable, and his unshod feet were horribly scarred. The man no longer spoke intelligibly either, but from time to time he muttered one word they could recognize—"Wendigo." Despite their efforts to console and comfort him, the poor soul could not be brought out of his ravings, and he died soon after, whether of fright or by Wendigo's hand they never knew.

47

IROQUOIAN MYTH
"On the Other Side of the Sky"

The Iroquois were long the most powerful North American Indians. Commanding international consideration, their Six Nations League (which was comprised of the Mohawks, Oneidas, Onondagas, Cayugas, Senecas, and Tuscaroras) held sway over a vast region between the St. Lawrence and the Mississippi. This made for a high status among nations, and the universe of Iroquoian myth fully matched it in extent and depth. The stories were told only in winter, when people had less to do than in the busy summer months; also, it was said that in summer the snakes would come to listen, and when you stopped speaking, would strike.

THE LITTLE PEOPLE

Long ago there was a boy who went out daily to hunt small game. One day as he neared a ravine, voices from below reached his ears. Crawling to the edge, he saw at the bottom of the ravine two very small beings, human like himself, only much smaller. Both had tiny bows and arrows and were shooting at a black squirrel in a treetop almost in line with where the boy lay. Their arrows fell far short of the mark, but they kept trying, for (it seemed) they were anxious to get this black squirrel. Taking pity on them, the boy shot the animal, and it landed at their feet. They were much surprised, seeing the giant arrow that transfixed their kill. One of them looked up and saw the face of the boy hunter looking down at them. He scrambled down, and the three quickly made friends. One of the tiny beings explained to the boy that black squirrel was the most desired of all meat for the Little People—to them it was like buffalo meat to Indians. Then the other spoke up and asked the boy whether it was he who had shot the squirrel. Yes he had, the boy replied, adding that he would like to offer it to them as a gift. Accepting with alacrity, they invited their benefactor to come along to their house and (if he would be so kind) to assist with the squirrel, since it was much too plump and heavy for the two of them to carry unassisted. So off they went, the boy carrying the black squirrel in his hand and the two little hunters leading the way.

Their home was only a short way off. The boy was welcomed by his new friends' aged parents. The old man said: "We are what you people must henceforth call the Great Little People. We are divided into three tribes. My family are of the Hunters. We pursue the Great White Buffalo that travel under the ground and would cause great suffering to mankind if through negligence any were ever to escape through one of the entrances of the netherworld. The second tribe are known as Stone Throwers. They can uproot trees and hurl boulders. The third tribe are those of us who awaken plants, cause them to grow, make flowers blossom, and redden ripening fruit. We are also ordained to perform certain duties in behalf of your people. We have long awaited the proper season to make contact with you. Today this has come about, and from now on, our ceremony will be yours."

A feast of corn soup and squirrel meat then being in readiness, the mother struck a tiny drum three times, and all the Great Little People came trooping in. The boy sat next to the old man, and they partook of berry juice and tobacco. The boy was initiated in the mysterious Dark Dance, and all night long they drummed, danced, and sang. The same thing happened the next night and the next, till after several days the boy knew the entire ceremony by heart. Then they enjoined him to return to his people and instruct them in what he had learned, and they promised that at the first sound of his drum, they would come. And whenever he and his people heard the Little People's drum, they were to go to a ravine and cast in bundles of fingernail parings and tobacco.

And so his little friends led him to the cliff where he had first seen them. He found his way back to the village, but it was abandoned, the houses had been pulled down, and the site was overgrown. When at last the boy caught up with his people, he found them strangely aged. They greeted him as a man. Each day of his ab-

In mythical times cannibalistic Stone Giants preyed on the Iroquois, but the Creator trapped the ogres in mountain caves by means of an earthquake, grinding them to dust.

sence had been a human year. Three days later, they observed the ceremony, and from that day have never left off holding feasts for the Great Little People, whose good deeds in behalf of their human friends have never ceased.

THE SERPENT WOMAN

Long ago there were two young braves who were inseparable friends. They were the best hunters in the village. One of them, being especially handsome and kind, was quite popular with the girls. Several maidens wanted to marry him, but he refused all offers. His friend remonstrated with him and urged him to marry lest something happen that he should be sorry for. The handsome one promised he would choose after they had gone on a long hunt together. They went to their hunting ground and put up a wigwam. Each day they set out in opposite directions, and each night they returned. The one whom the girls liked the best always returned emptyhanded and sad, but his friend always got game.

The lucky one resolved to find out what was wrong. Next morning he trailed the handsome one and soon saw his friend running very fast toward a big lake. He shouted after him to stop but the other seemed not to hear, plunged straight in, and swam across. The lucky one ran around to the other side, but the handsome one got there first; they ran to a smaller lake, where they did the same, but this time the lucky hunter got to the other side first, so the swimmer turned back. The lucky hunter ran back past both lakes and hid in the bushes till his friend came ashore. Then he jumped out and caught him. But his handsome friend said: "If in the future you want to come see me, bring fresh tobacco and clean clay pipes, set them out on new-cut strips of bark on the shore, and then say to the lake, 'I want to see my friend.'" Having said this, he went back and married the big serpent in the lake.

That night, as the lucky hunter sat sadly by himself, there was a flash of

Imaginative pictures like this "Savage Chief and Savage Scalping His Enemy," by the diplomat and travel-book illustrator Grasset de Saint-Sauveur, served to reinforce stereotypes of the Iroquois Indians as a race of quaint childish and ferocious barbarians.

light, and a young boy stood in the doorway dressed in white and crowned with white feathers. "You seem to be in trouble," the stranger said, "but you are the only one who can help us. My chief sent me to invite you to our council." The hunter asked, "Where is the council?" The youth replied, "You came right past our wigwam, though you did not see it." So they went there, and the hunter saw eight chiefs, also

A Mohawk envoy (sketched by a French eyewitness) performs a ritual inviting neighbors to participate in sacred games.

crowned with feathers, sitting quietly on the ground, smoking a pipe. When the pipe came round to the principal chief, whose name was Thunderer, he rose and addressed the young man: "You have come to help us—your friend has married the big serpent in the lake, whom we must kill." Thunderer instructed the lucky hunter what to do, and said also: "We will come in the form of a cloud on the lake, not in the sky."

So the lucky hunter took the tobacco, the clean bark, and pipes provided by the thunder chiefs and summoned his friend. Soon there was a ripple on the surface of the lake, which then suddenly boiled up, and out of a fierce swirl of water came the handsome friend. He had a spot on his forehead and looked like a serpent and yet like a man. The lucky hunter said he was leaving for home and asked to see his friend's wife, saying, "I want to be able to tell your mother what she is like." "She may not want to come," said the serpent man, "but I will try." Lying flat on his belly, he put his mouth to the water and drank, then went down into the water, not swimming like a man but moving like a snake. Soon the water boiled up again and he returned, saying his wife would come. But she did not. The serpent man scanned the sky to see if it was clear. Seeing that it was, he went back into the water.

Presently a great sight was seen: The lake boiled again, not in one spot but all over, and waves crashed against the shore as if there had been a violent storm; yet there was not a breath of wind. The waves grew higher. The snake wife emerged, followed by the lucky hunter's friend-turned-snake husband. The serpent wife's glistening tresses streamed over her in the blinding summer sun, in which her body shone all silvery, but the silver seemed like scales. It seemed to the lucky hunter that the air they were breathing in that moment was unnaturally hot and still. He remembered Thunderer's words and at last, a great way off, descried—moving upon the water, not through the sky—a huge, black onrushing thing like a cloud. He asked his shiny-suited guests to join him in the woods, where the sun was not so hot. When they had sat down in the shade, he excused himself and, once out of their sight, ran as hard as his legs would carry him. The terrible cloud came at once over everything, and there was thunder and lightning where the serpent and her lover sat.

When all was quiet, the hunter went back, and there were a big and a little snake lying dead on the ground. The eight thunder chiefs were there, too, and they danced over their dead enemies. Then they cut up both serpents, making eight equal bundles of them. Each chief put one on his back. Then they all said to the hunter, "Ask us for what you want, at any time, and you shall have it." They went off in single file, seeming to step higher and higher, till they went up into the sky. Then there was a great thunderstorm. When he got home, he told the story to the mother of his friend. She was very sorry for the death of her son, whom she had loved, but adopted the lucky hunter in his place, and so the young man had two mothers.

THE REAL HIAWATHA
"He Eats Humans"

Everyone has heard of Henry Wadsworth Longfellow's narrative poem The Song of Hiawatha *(1855). Longfellow's title character should not, however, be confused with the real Hiawatha. The poem was based on the legend of the Ojibwa hero Manabozho, which Longfellow had read in H. R. Schoolcraft's pioneering work on American Indians. The real Hiawatha was the companion of the prophet Deganawidah, who was the founder of the Iroquois League.*

When Deganawidah set out to bring peace to his people, his first step was to cure them of cannibalism: "I shall visit first the house of Hiawatha of whom it is said, 'He eats humans.'" He went to Hiawatha's lodge, climbed to the roof, and lay flat on his chest next to the smoke hole. Hiawatha soon returned, carrying a dead body. He threw it down, cut it up, and boiled it in a kettle. Then he saw reflected in the water the face of Deganawidah looking down through the smoke hole, and he imagined it to be his own. He looked again, and once more saw the

Longfellow's young hero Hiawatha defies the sturgeon Nahma, King of Fishes, who is about to rise to the bait and gulp him down, canoe and all, in one oversize mouthful.

face. Thinking someone might be playing a trick, he looked up at the smoke hole, but there was nobody there. Presently he said: "So then it really is me—my personal beauty is most amazing. But perhaps my behavior is not so beautiful when I kill people and eat their flesh. Perhaps I should stop." He emptied the kettle in a stream; then Deganawidah appeared.

Hiawatha told him he was seeking a congenial friend and made him sit down by the fire. He gave him a full account of what had happened, at the end of which Deganawidah stood up and said: "Truly what has happened today is a very wonderful story. Now you have changed the very pattern of your life; now you are longing for righteousness and seeking someone to tell you what you ought to do, in order that peace may prevail in places where you have done injury among mankind." Deganawidah told him he too was seeking a friend, someone who was ready to work for the cause of Righteousness and Peace. Hiawatha agreed to join him.

Deganawidah bade him fetch water while he himself went hunting. He brought back a deer. It was on this, said Deganawidah, that the Creator intended men to live. They buried the remains of the human body and cooked and ate the deer. "What do you mean by Righteousness and Peace, and what will happen when these shall be realized?" Hiawatha asked. "By these," said Deganawidah, "I mean that this very day you have changed the disposition of your mind, and it shall come about that all mankind shall change their present disposition. That means that this reformation shall begin at once and that Righteousness and Peace shall increase continually." "What do you call this when it has taken place?" "It will be called the Completed House and also the Great Law." Hiawatha now understood and accepted Deganawidah's teaching. The next step was to prevent people from killing one another, and thus Deganawidah and Hiawatha began to organize the Iroquois League.

False Face Society

Iroquoian myth has it that a race of man-eating Stone Giants terrorized men long ago, until the Creator stamped them out in a cataclysm. A lone survivor escaped and periodically sent disease on the people. The

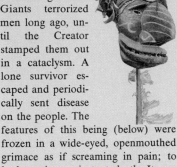

features of this being (below) were frozen in a wide-eyed, openmouthed grimace as if screaming in pain; to look on it was instant death. It was once the fate of a hunter, taking refuge from a hailstorm, to meet the creature in its cave. A voice boomed out in the dark: "Young warrior, beware! No human being has ever looked on me. I kill with one glance. You did not come to hunt me, so I will spare your life which is now mine. Henceforth you must obey my commands. Be wise and learn how disease is healed . . ."

The hunter fell asleep and dreamed he saw, issuing from the Stone Giant's head, a race of horrible beings, disease spirits in the shape of flying heads whose faces bore expressions of delirium and agony. He woke up at the foot of a basswood tree, and as he gazed at the crinkly patterns in its bark the tree slowly turned into a great mask and taught him its power: it could see behind the stars; it could create storms, summon sunshine, and remedy sickness and poisoning. The mask said: "My tree, the basswood, is

soft and porous; the sunlight can enter its darkness, the wind can whisper to its stillness, and it sees and hears. My wood is the life of Its Face: of all the forest there is none other." So the hunter carved the first False Face in the trunk of the living basswood, and the tree's life entered the mask. Then propitiating its spirit with an offering of tobacco, he gouged the mask out of its trunk. Years later, after many travels and strange adventures, the hunter returned home, founded the False Face Society, and instructed the first band in its ceremonies and ritual.

Ever since, False Face Society members have acted as healers and purifiers at certain feasts and have mobilized to drive away sickness. During an epidemic, False Faces guard each spring of water and march from lodge to lodge, taking from the inhabitants sweet corn mush and a strong decoction of sunflower seeds as they propitiate the Disease Spirit with clouds of tobacco smoke that are laden with their requests for deliverance.

Every New Year, they crawl on all fours into the longhouse among the assembled people, making very loud

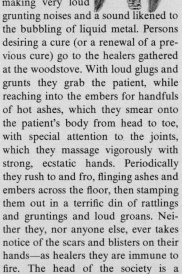

grunting noises and a sound likened to the bubbling of liquid metal. Persons desiring a cure (or a renewal of a previous cure) go to the healers gathered at the woodstove. With loud glugs and grunts they grab the patient, while reaching into the embers for handfuls of hot ashes, which they smear onto the patient's body from head to toe, with special attention to the joints, which they massage vigorously with strong, ecstatic hands. Periodically they rush to and fro, flinging ashes and embers across the floor, then stamping them out in a terrific din of rattlings and gruntings and loud groans. Neither they, nor anyone else, ever takes notice of the scars and blisters on their hands—as healers they are immune to fire. The head of the society is a woman; she has been given the title Keeper of the Masks.

LAUGHTER AND TEARS
A Gumbo of Cultures

The people along the bayous of southern Louisiana are known as Cajuns. This name, a corruption of "Acadians," identified them as descendants of the French dispersed in 1755 by the British from the eastern coastal region of Canada. In language and culture, Cajuns remained French, but old-fashioned and rustic, unlike the urban Creoles. Even a dip into their folklore confirms that Cajuns were like their favorite dish, gumbo: a stew of many ingredients. Tales like those about two rabbits, Bouqui and Lapin, are of probable Caribbean Negro origin. Foolish John is a European folk figure transplanted to the bayous, and Emmeline Labiche sounds suspiciously like Longfellow's Evangeline (whom Cajuns claim she inspired) and the heroines of many, many other tales of unhappy love.

FOOLISH JOHN

There once was a fellow living in the bayou country whom everyone called Foolish John. No one ever said he was malicious, just that he was slow-witted and literal-minded. Foolish John lived with his mother, and one cold, windy winter day she said to him, "Go milk the cow for me."

As his mother went back to her work, she heard a gunshot; Foolish John appeared emptyhanded in the kitchen. "Where is the milk?" asked his mother. "Why, Mother, I thought you told me to shoot the cow." (In French, the word *tirer* means both "to milk" and "to shoot.") "Ah, my foolish child," cried the exasperated mother, "you have killed our only cow! What shall we do? Well, now you must go skin her so we can at least sell the hide."

Foolish John strung the cow up on a tree and skinned her, leaving the head with its horns attached to the hide. Then he took the hide and set out for town. As Foolish John approached a large tree, he noticed its bare branches shaking and heard it groaning in the wind. "That poor tree must be cold," said Foolish John. "I'll cover it with the hide to keep it warm." He had just climbed the tree when seven robbers gathered at its base and began to divide their spoils, the chief doling money out of a sack.

"This is for me, that's for you," counted the chief as he went round the circle dividing the shares. Foolish John, watching from above, got so carried away by the situation that each time the chief counted, he plucked a hair from his cowhide and said, "And one for me!" One of the robbers heard him but unable to see anyone he exclaimed, "Listen, the Devil!" The chief ignored the comment and continued dividing up the enormous sum until all the money was apportioned—and Foolish John had picked his cowhide clean.

Just then he lost his grip on the limb and went crashing into the middle of the circle of thieves. The hide had come down with him, and since it was now hairless and the horns were still attached, the thieves saw a most extraordinary creature. Thinking it to be the Devil, they fled, leaving all their money behind them.

Foolish John gathered up all the money, which he placed back in the sack. Then the youth spread the hide over the cold tree, and returned home. As he entered the kitchen, his mother inquired, "Well, how much did you get for the hide?" "I collected a dollar for every hair on the hide," answered Foolish John as he set down the large sack of money. "My son, my son," exclaimed the woman, "sometimes I wonder if you are as foolish as people think!"

BOUQUI AND LAPIN

Bouqui and Lapin had agreed to farm together. Lapin proposed they split everything 50–50: Bouqui would take the parts that grew under the ground, while he, Lapin, would get the parts growing aboveground. Bouqui agreed, and since Lapin furnished the seeds, Bouqui even did all the plowing and planting.

When the crops were ready for harvesting, Bouqui discovered that they had grown only such things as corn, beans, cabbage, and melons. Lapin consoled him by offering him all the roots to feed his cow.

The next spring, Bouqui decided to be clever, and he demanded that this year he would have all the parts that grew aboveground. Lapin agreed, and once again provided the seed while Bouqui did all the plowing.

Autumn came, and Bouqui discovered that all they had grown were carrots, turnips, peanuts, and potatoes. And oh yes, there was one kind of thing growing aboveground—some inedible gourds. But Lapin consoled Bouqui by telling him he could make dippers out of all the gourds.

EMMELINE LABICHE

Several prominent Cajuns tell the tale as actual family history. Be that as it may, the story began long ago at the far end of the continent, in Nova Scotia, on Canada's shore. The French had made their first permanent New World settlement there in 1605, calling the area Acadia.

Among the French Acadians in the

This imaginative rendering of Evangeline and her lover sorrowing by a bayou manages to combine costumes appropriate to the period with a distinct 1930's aura.

52

mid-1700's was a young girl, Emmeline Labiche. Her mother had died when she was a child, but she was lovingly raised by her father. Attractive and sweet-tempered, Emmeline at 16 became engaged to her childhood sweetheart, Louis Arceneaux, a promising young man. Then, in 1755, the British—who had controlled the area since 1713—decided to punish the French Acadians for refusing to swear loyalty to Britain and to forsake Catholicism. British troops descended on the French communities and drove the inhabitants onto ships, to be dispersed among the various other British colonies to the south.

That event is recorded history. And the Cajuns say that this "great dispersal" took place just before Emmeline was to marry Louis. In any case, he and Emmeline were separated in the confusion at the ships, as were numerous other families and loved ones. Emmeline and her family were taken to Maryland. She by no means suffered there but she became a quiet, sad young lady. And although the Maryland colonists were not inhospitable to the Acadians, Emmeline's family continued to feel like strangers among their English-speaking neighbors.

So it was that, after several years, Emmeline's family moved on to Louisiana where they would be among fellow French. When their boat arrived in the bayou country, Emmeline did not even pretend to be happy, for she felt still farther removed from Louis. As she gazed about at her new home, she started. There, standing by an oak tree near the shore, was Louis Arceneaux. Emmeline rushed toward Louis, who looked at the young lady first in confusion, then in pleasure—and suddenly in pain. As Emmeline extended her arms toward her fiance, he turned away and spoke with a trembling voice. "Emmeline . . . I am unworthy of you . . . I thought I had lost you forever, and I have married another. You must forgive and forget me."

Some say Emmeline fainted at the foot of the oak, others that she merely turned pale and stared. All agree that Emmeline's mind was dazed with grief from that moment on. Melancholy and remote, she wandered and danced along the banks of the bayous as she picked moss and flowers. When she talked, it was of Acadia and her broken dreams.

Her health failed, and within a few months of arriving at this refuge for the Acadians, Emmeline died. Louisianans keep her memory alive and point out the oak where Emmeline Labiche found her beloved Louis.

In Louisiana the moron who tiptoed past the medicine cabinet so as not to wake the sleeping pills is Foolish John. Here, he is shown just before he falls from his perch and lucks into some money.

 SUPERSTITIONS

Bayou Wisdom

Along with their rich trove of tales, songs, games, festivals, and foods the Cajuns hedged their lives with countless superstitions. This common tendency of many an isolated, rural people was intensified by the very real threats of the Cajuns' swampy milieu—hunger, disease, and physical dangers. Not unexpectedly, either, Cajun superstitions were a compound of many cultures and influences. To their own Catholic European stock they added black African and American Indian elements. This mixture was then shaped to fit the peculiar conditions of the bayou world.

If you live too long in the swamps, you will become web-footed.

If an alligator crawls under your house, it is a portent of death.

Fishermen should beware of Letiche the monster, soul of an unbaptized infant who swims the bayous upsetting pirogues (dugout canoes).

Fish bite quicker on Good Friday than on any other day of the year.

Cook cabbage on New Year's Day to have good fortune all year.

When a snake bites you, race it to the water. If you beat it there and dip in the wound, it will die—not you.

Anyone bothered by asthma should wear a muskrat skin over the lungs.

Children should sleep on mattresses of moss from cypress trees to gain the strength of those trees.

Keep your house tightly sealed at night to keep out not only deadly germs but *loups-garous* (werewolves).

If you sleep in the moonlight, you will go crazy.

Reading the Bible backward keeps ghosts from entering the house. Reading it forward prevents those already inside from harming you.

If you are out on a picnic and it starts to rain, make a cross with two sticks and put salt on top of it. The rain will instantly stop.

Never eat both ends of a loaf of bread before you've eaten the middle, or you'll have trouble making ends meet in life.

Keep mirrors away from an infant lest the child become vain.

If you put your underwear on wrong side out, you must spit on it before changing it or have bad luck all day.

IN CREOLE CIRCLES
Cosmopolitan Romances

First settled by the Spanish, southern Louisiana was subsequently colonized by the French, who dominated it until 1803, when the United States bought the Louisiana Territory. New Orleans was the center of a society whose leading families, boasting of "pure" French or Spanish descent, were known as Creoles. Eventually they put a sophisticated gloss over traditional lore but they could not hide its roots. Creoles liked stories about old New Orleans houses, such as "The Devil's Mansion," but those were variations on age-old tales. Another common theme (given here in an adaptation from G. W. Cable) haunted many Americans: the terrible barriers and ambivalent feelings between the whites and blacks.

Madame John, a legendary New Orleanian, was forced to dance at a disreputable club so as to support her daughter.

'TITE POULETTE

In the olden days in New Orleans, one of the highlights of the social season was the quadroon ball. Quadroons were literally people with one-quarter Negro ancestry, but the term commonly included all light-skinned mulattoes. Although barred from full participation in white social life, those people were accepted in some situations, such as the quadroon ball (which allowed white Creole gentlemen to dance with quadroon girls). The dances, with their hint of the exotic and the forbidden, were exciting affairs. Yet all was open, elegant, and more or less respectable. Many mothers accompanied their daughters to make sure their reputations were not ruined by the more impetuous Creole men.

One of the frequenters of such balls was a distinguished Creole known as Monsieur John. One night his eye was caught by a young quadroon, the fair Zalli, whom all agreed was the loveliest of the girls. After several public encounters, Monsieur John became the "protector" of Zalli. Since the affair was in the open, Creoles considered it acceptable.

Zalli and Monsieur John had been together for many years when he fell mortally ill. He called for Zalli, and she came to his bedside carrying in her arms their baby girl. "Zalli," said Monsieur John, "you have been so faithful to me that I am going to leave this house to you and our little one." After she had inherited the house, she became known as Madame John, as was the Creole custom of the day. Her little girl, whom she called 'Tite Poulette, grew to be as fair and lovely as her mother. But because she was Madame John's daughter, Creole youths could not consider marrying her.

As she came of age, 'Tite herself occasionally dreamed of marrying a Creole gentleman. But she accepted her mother's teachings: "God made us just as we are—not more white, not more black." And as poor as she was, Madame John made certain that her daughter did nothing to compromise her reputation. When 'Tite Poulette was still a young lady, a Dutchman, Kristian Koppig, moved into the house across the street from Madame John's. Young Kristian was of a good family and had been sent to launch a new business in New Orleans. As a foreigner, he was most curious about the doings of his neighbors. As the days passed, he focused on Madame John's house, and particularly on 'Tite Poulette. Eventually he learned what few others knew: Zalli was forced to dance publicly at a disreputable club to earn enough money to enable her and her daughter to continue to live in Monsieur John's house.

One night, Kristian went to the dancehall and tried to persuade Madame John to give up her dancing. The manager was so furious that he ordered some hired hands to attack Kristian. They stabbed him, but Madame John took him to her home where she and 'Tite Poulette nursed him back to health. Inevitably, Kristian came to realize that he was in love with 'Tite Poulette. Yet he had learned the Creole code, so one night he tried subtly to ask Madame John if perhaps . . . the lovely, fair 'Tite Poulette . . . could she be the daughter . . . of someone else. Madame John briskly answered, "No," and ended the discussion.

The day Kristian was to move back home, he arranged to see 'Tite Poulette alone for the last time. Overwhelmed by passion, he defied the Creole rules and asked her to be his in honorable marriage. But 'Tite Poulette, who had grown to love him too, was resigned to her society's ways. Weeping, she could only say, "I cannot—it is against the law." At that, Madame John burst in. "It is not against any law," she cried. "Take her—she is white. Her real parents were Spaniards who died here of yellow fever. I was nursing them. Here are the sworn papers made out by Monsieur John."

Why had Zalli withheld the truth all those years? What was the truth? No matter, for 'Tite married Kristian in the full light of Creole society. And to this day there stands a house in New Orleans known as Madame John's Legacy, where 'Tite Poulette and Kristian saw love prevail.

THE DEVIL'S MANSION

The Devil himself once had a house in New Orleans. The immediate reason, or so it was said, was that he had taken up with a French Creole girl whom he established in a grand mansion. He was a very jealous lover, as she well knew, but as he was away most of the week on his other duties, the girl took a dashing Creole lover.

One night Satan returned unexpectedly, and aware of what was going on, he waited discreetly outside the house. When the youth emerged, the Devil accosted him and said: "You can hardly be expected to realize this, but I was that young lady's lover before you. No matter, I'm tired of her and I'd be only too happy if you'd take her far away. In fact, I'll even give you a million pounds to elope with her. I have only one condition: You must always be known as

Monsieur and Madame L."

The youth gladly agreed, and the next evening, as he and his loved one dined, he excitedly announced their good fortune. But the girl, instead of showing pleasure, began to shake with fright and fury. She realized what the youth did not: *L* stood for Lucifer! In a rage she rushed at her lover, whipped her napkin around his throat, and throttled him.

The Devil materialized, killed the girl, and carried both bodies to the roof where he devoured them completely except for their skins, which he gave to prowling cats. But he had forgotten in his jealous anger that he should not have exposed himself to the full moon. So he too was punished by death, except that his head was left alive. It was affixed to the gable of the roof by the sticky flesh of the mortals he had eaten.

As the years passed, the people of New Orleans would stare up at the living head of Lucifer glowering down at them from the gable of his

mansion. That was the least of this house's weirdness. In the dining room the drama was enacted over and over again. An elegant dining table and crystal chandeliers materialized; a young man and a girl sat down as though to eat; then the girl rose, her face contorted with anger, rushed at her companion, and strangled him with a napkin; finally, finding her hands drenched with blood, she frantically tried to wipe them clean. She never succeeded, however, and as she wept and wailed, the mirage faded from view.

Over the years, various families tried to make their home in the Devil's Mansion. But they could stand these ghastly manifestations only for a short time. Eventually the house was abandoned, and finally it had to be torn down. Only then were the shades of the girl and her Creole lover banished, and with them the living head of the Devil. But the people of New Orleans long remembered the mansion's story.

FOLKWAYS

Dueling

One custom of the lively Creole society that inspired a special lore was dueling. A duel to avenge some insult was an old European tradition. But what began as a genuine, if exaggerated, concern for personal honor became, in 18th- and 19th-century New Orleans, a grotesque parody.

Duels were often fought over trifling insults, real and imagined—a rude word, the wrong glance, a mere brush against another. The motivation for some was so absurd as to defy belief: One was fought to defend the honor of New Orleans coffee, another the Mississippi River. Anything that involved women evoked a challenge. Later, politicians and journalists participated in duels because they had offended others with their public statements.

An elaborate code governed the practice. Numerous books and pamphlets explained how to provoke or respond to challenges. A gentleman, of course, was expected to know how to

fence, and the fencing masters of New Orleans enjoyed the status of sports heroes in our age. Gradually, pistols—even shotguns and rifles—replaced the rapiers of earlier days.

Duels could be fought anywhere, but there were several favorite sites. One was the wooded area (pictured here) known as Dueling Oaks because the trees were a convenient pistol shot apart. Once blood was drawn, the duel ended, but sometimes one or both combatants were killed. If the two survived, etiquette required the par-

ticipants to reconcile. Aristocratic nonchalance was the ideal. One duelist is said to have appeared on a rainy day with an umbrella: He was prepared to die, but not to catch cold.

In the heyday of the deadly custom, there were sometimes several duels a day in New Orleans. In the 1800's efforts were made to outlaw dueling, but it survived late into the century, when it succumbed to new social values. All that remains today are the tales—and duelists' tombstones inscribed "Died on the field of honor."

VOODOO

While Louisiana was a colony of France, thousands of black slaves from Haiti streamed into New Orleans bringing with them a new religion, Voodoo. (In Fon and other languages of West Africa the word means "spirit" or "spirit medium.") Voodoo is a blend of several strong ingredients. Most important is the cult of Legba, youngest son of the Creator, a trickster deity controlling entrances and crossroads who "opens the way" for the gods during Voodoo rites (in other words, Legba helps put the congregation into the hypnotic trance without which there could be no ceremony). Next in importance is the cult of the Devil, who is pictured as "a light-complected man" in a white suit sitting on a horse, dragging a chain at the crossroads at midnight (an image possibly having some connection with slavery and the overseer). Finally, Voodoo mingles numerous elements of Roman Catholic ceremony with certain magical and religious practices of many of the various Caribbean Indian peoples.

In practice, Voodoo is based on two important components: first, its techniques for achieving hysteria and a trancelike state; and second, its ambivalence in attitude toward God and the Devil, both of whom are thought of as being simultaneously good and evil. Either may be invoked to do good as well as harm, and although once their help has been solicited it must be paid for, a clever man can avoid payment by tricking the Devil.

Voodoo rites are performed both at home and in public places. The ceremony may be held day or night, indoors or outdoors, in any place deemed suitable by the priests. Ritual equipment includes an altar, a snake, candles, and drums. The service is conducted by a man, the *hungan* (deity chief), and a woman, the *mambo* (priestess). The *voodoo* (divine spirit) is believed to be present in the snake. By handling the snake, priests receive messages from the spirit world in answer

The victim suffered a burst spleen if the spell cast with this Voodoo doll was successful.

to such questions as whether a candidate for initiation is acceptable or what tasks and tribute should be required of a given devotee. After this preliminary phase, the *loa* (guardian-angel spirits) begin to possess the priests and others, including those who have sponsored the service. As the loa takes hold of people, they stagger, fall, spring up again, shake spasmodically, and at last go into a hypnotic trance. Those who have experienced the trance speak of the loa *mounting* or *riding* the person being possessed. Other devotees begin to dance; many also drink. Soon all feel tuned in and start chanting, clap-

White-clad Voodoo devotees kneel by candlelight round the silk-cotton jumby (ghost) tree, singing and drumming to prepare for the descent of the loa *(possibly the animal shape on the hillside, upper left) that will possess them one by one.*

ping, and dancing to the drums. The hungan and mambo move through the swaying congregation, slapping some, spinning them around, spraying them in the face with liquor from their own mouths, guiding the devotees until together they achieve the desired experience of oneness with each other and the gods. Meanwhile some inhale flaming alcohol, while others roll in and out of fires, join in sexual union, climb trees, mimic and then sacrifice animals, drinking their blood and even tearing small ones apart and eating them raw.

Ceremonies conducted along these lines may be seen in Haiti today and were much the same in New Orleans in 1803, at the time of the Louisiana Purchase; they became even more spectacular during subsequent decades of the 19th century.

The most famous of all New Orleans mambos was Marie Laveau, who came to the forefront around 1830. Born a free mulatto, she was already a famous beauty when she set up as a fortuneteller and seller of charms, amulets, spells, and curses. It was not long before her rooms were thronged with persons of both races and every class. Two policemen were once sent to raid the premises; they went mad at the door, it is said, and barked like dogs. Four more were sent; they fought among themselves in front of the house, whacking one another on the head with their nightsticks. At last the entire station force mounted an assault, but all passed out cold upon reaching the front steps and slept soundly where they had dropped until Marie's lawyer arrived.

Marie started inviting paying visitors to Voodoo services at which she was the presiding mambo. Curiosity seekers flocked to Congo Square and nearby Lake Pontchartrain to watch. Each year, the story ran, on the night of June 24, she rose out of the lake with a big communion candle burning on her head and one in each hand, walked on the water to the shore, to preside over the Voodoo rites, and then went back the way she had come.

Marie was reputedly attended by a huge rattlesnake as long as she lived (her death occurred in 1881), but the day after she died the snake crawled off into the woods near Lake Pontchartrain and was never seen again.

Voodoo has also produced a very powerful kind of witchcraft-religion mixture called Obeah. Roots and potions are a great part of Obeah and other attendant witch cults, just as they are of Voodoo proper.

Historically, the lore of Cajuns and other southern whites has been deeply influenced by both Obeah and Voo-

Baron Samedi, or Three Spades, was one of the Guédé, Voodoo death spirits.

doo; and today, as West Indians migrate to the United States and Canada, the influence of Voodoo in North America generally, far from declining, is on the rise. (It is even reported that a Voodoo cult has appeared in Greenland.) As a result, there are thriving stores such as the Spanish *botánicas* (botany shops) in the Hispanic and black neighborhoods of every big city, where one can buy Dragon's Blood, High John the Conqueror, Compelling Powder, and all manner of other incenses, roots, elixirs, effigies, and spe-

cially anointed candles for practicing Voodoo, Shango (a Protestant-influenced equivalent of Voodoo originating in British-ruled parts of the Caribbean area), Obeah, Hoodoo, and the like. There are many terms for different types of practitioners: hoodoo men, conjure men and women, weed women, root doctors; others simply call themselves witches.

Here are some old Voodoo prescriptions. Lest you be tempted to put one of these into practice, bear in mind that only an experienced practitioner can expect to understand its inner meaning and obtain the desired results. And whatever the results, of course, one has to pay for them—or beat the Devil!

To make someone go mad: Sacrifice a snake and dry it in the oven slowly. Grind it up into a powder and put it on his doorstep; madness will follow. Snake Dust becomes a powerful type of War Powder when mixed with gunpowder or red pepper.

To detect poisoning: Tie a piece of silver money onto the patient's body; the silver will turn black if he is poisoned. If so, file some silver off the coin and give it to the patient in white rum or in milk from a red cow as an antidote to the poison.

To keep a worker from getting laid off: Write the boss's name three times on a slip of paper and the worker's name four times on top of it. Pour honey around a red candle, and also spice. Then light the candle.

To know whether a girl is chaste: Take a small piece of young radish, rub it in the palm of her hand, and she will reveal her secrets to you.

To make a man love you: Turn down the sweatband of his hat and pin two needles crossed inside where he won't find them, and he will love you.

To stop a troublemaker: Put cemetery dirt in a jar. Then put in the troublemaker's picture, face down on the dirt. Place an egg on top of it, to weigh it down. Burn some High John the Conqueror powder and force the smoke into the jar; then seal. The person will do no further harm.

In Search of Cibola

In 1539 the Franciscan monk Marcos de Niza journeyed north from Mexico in search of Cabeza de Vaca's fabulous enjeweled, gold-paved Seven Cities of Cibola. Perhaps deceived by a view of a distant Pueblo village inflamed by one of the Southwest's spectacular sunsets, Marcos de Niza returned to Mexico with the news that he had found Cibola and that its cities were indeed golden. Francisco Vásquez de Coronado's subsequent expedition proved De Niza wrong—but that did not prevent Coronado from ranging as far north as central Kansas in pursuit of a new chimera, "Quivira," where, it was said, even the crockery was made of precious metals, and golden bells chimed softly in the trees.

Concurrently, despite constant deprivation and danger, a group led by Hernando de Soto wandered the Southeast lured on by rumors of gold and discovered instead the bottom end of the Mississippi River, where De Soto died. The Spaniards' gold fever had various sources. In the case of Cibola, they doubtless misinterpreted the Aztecs' regard for the spiritual wealth of the Pueblos as awe of material riches; also, they may have credited tales of northern treasure because the natives' stories of gold in Mexico and Peru had proved true.

By the mid-17th century the conquistadors had given way to missionaries who in many places taught the Indians the art of sheep and cattle ranching. In the 18th century, after the founding of a mission, a small garrison of soldiers, followed by ranchers, was sometimes sent up from Mexico to guard the Spanish claim and enforce the conversion of the natives. Some of the Indians accepted Christianity, some melded old practices with new, and some (like the Pueblos) held fast to old beliefs while seeming to accept the Roman Catholicism of the "metal people," as the Pueblos aptly termed the Spaniards. Both peoples—Spanish and Pueblos—were proud, austere, and mystical. The coexistence and blending of their respective traditions over the past 400 years have resulted in a trove of lore that greatly enriches the American story.

"Gods dance there," conquistadors were told of the Pueblos and their dancing Supernaturals. Here, Talavai (Early Morning), Hemis (Chief Home Dancer), and a Mud Face "delightmaker" clown

Saint James was the patron saint of the conquistadors; his Spanish name was their battle cry: "Santiago!" Once, appearing on a horse in their midst, the saint turned the tide of battle in a fight against Comanches on the Rio Grande.

CORONADO AND THE TURK
Fictional History

The conquistadors' tireless treks through the South and West of America-the-Golden in hopes of riches beyond measure were spurred on by uncritical acceptance of tales told them by the Indians; the latter were quick to note that by confirming and embellishing such tales they could excite the Spaniards' hopes and keep them from settling down. The following 20th-century story, based on actual historical records of Coronado's Quivira expedition, is one illustration of how real events may beget a popular legend, and it preserves in the folk memory the hopes and tribulations of the early Spanish explorers.

One day, as Coronado's army was marching east, he came upon the encampment of advance-party leader Capt. Hernando de Alvarado, who had a prize—a strange Indian whom he called the Turk for his dark complexion. The Turk, said Alvarado, knew firsthand the paradise of legend and had shown the captain a finely wrought golden bracelet as proof of what he said.

At this, Coronado pricked up his ears. "Where do you come from, strange one?" he asked. "From the plains, far to the east, in the country of Quivira," replied the Turk, "where the river is six miles wide and the fish grow bigger than horses."

Coronado was eager to get on to the real subject. "But what of gold and silver? Are there precious metals in your land?" The Turk stalled: "On the great river are fine rowing boats with sails and teams of 40 oarsmen. And in these boats great lords recline in great splendor, amusing themselves with music and fine food." Coronado began to grow impatient, but the Turk continued unhurried: "Golden eagles surmount each prow, and golden bells jingle on the canopies so that a sweet tinkling accompanies each dipping of the oars."

To be sure the Turk was not confusing gold with a baser metal, Coronado showed him an object made of tin and asked, "Is this the gold that you are telling me about?" The Turk held the object to his nose to smell and replied confidently that it was not. "'Gold' we call *acochis,* and we also have fine silver plate and vessels

Ponce de León, in search of the elusive Fountain of Youth, discovered a land he called Florida. Ironically, though no such lifegiving waters were ever found, Ponce de León's Florida was to become a favorite retreat for the cold and the elderly.

in abundance." The Turk then began to digress on the matter of banquets and celebrations and festive occasions of which his people had many.

General Coronado was, by this time, quite convinced of the strange creature's truthfulness, but as final proof he asked to see the golden bracelet that Alvarado said the Turk wore. The Turk looked reprovingly at his captor. "My bracelet, lord, was taken from me at the pueblo where I was seized. Free me and on my life I will go back and retrieve it for you." Coronado ignored the request and motioned his men to take the Indian away. He wanted time to think.

A few days later the general summoned the Turk again. More questions brought more wondrous replies. How much gold was there, Coronado asked. "Some of the golden treasures had to be transported in enormous wagons," the Turk replied. But, he continued, "Quivira pales next to the richer lands of Harahey and Guaes, ruled over by a remarkable king named Tatarrax. And this king worships as no other Indians do, praying out of a book to a lady he calls the Queen of Heaven." Was the Turk to be trusted? Did he, as his cell guards claimed, hold conversations with the Devil? One of the guards had sworn under oath to Coronado that one day the Turk had revealed to him the exact number of Spaniards who had been killed in a recent battle with some Indians many miles from the encampment. And this without speaking to any mortal whatsoever! Coronado felt uneasy, but he could not dismiss information coming from such a man. He determined that the army should march come spring.

Finally, as the ice was breaking up in the mountain streams and the birds were taking flight on their spring migrations, Coronado and his army of 1,500 men and horses resumed their trek. Slowly they toiled across the plains, urged on by fabulous tales from the Turk. Although spring turned into summer and they still had not found Quivira, Coronado was not discouraged. In his mind the hardships encountered were

The caption for Theodore de Bry's engraving says: "System for collecting gold in the streams coming out of Apalachee." The Spaniards believed Apalachee to be a Floridian El Dorado until Cabeza de Vaca found it: "It was a place of unbearable squalor."

God's way of balancing accounts for the delights to come. But Coronado halted the main army and, taking 42 men, hurried forward. Nothing was heard of Coronado and his party for many weeks. Then, one day, they reappeared, tattered, exhausted, and emaciated—hardly the appearance of men bearing good news. Their comrades demanded to know what they had seen. "Nothing," came the barely audible reply, "only endless plains and sky. No gold, no gorgeous canoes, and as for King Tatarrax, he is a naked ancient whose entire wealth is the copper bangle he wears around his neck."

Gradually, a tale of suffering and disappointment unfolded. Coronado had put the Turk to death as a traitor and schemer, but the strange man had died still insisting that his words would be vindicated if the Spaniards would go but a little farther. Then Coronado's spirit seemed to lift. He stood up and clapped his hands, saying: "Enough. Winter is coming and there is no time for talk now. We will prepare ourselves to hold up here until spring and then we will speak further of gold. Somewhere beyond the sunrise I know for a certainty that a golden city lies."

WORD LORE

California an Island

Visiting the Lower California peninsula in 1535, the conquistador Hernán Cortés thought it an island and named it after the "island of California" described in *Deeds of Esplandián, Son of Amadis,* fifth book of a fantasy serial that was a bestseller then. Most literate Spaniards had read the adventures of the knight-errant and his son; hence, naming the new land California was as if astronomers upon discovering a planet were to name it Krypton, after Superman's home.

"California" in *Deeds of Esplandián* was an island inhabited by black Amazon pirates who joined an infidel expedition against Constantinople and its Christian champion Esplandián. The description:

"Not far from the shores of the Terrestrial Paradise, there was an island called California, peopled by black women, without a man among them, for they lived in the fashion of Amazons and raided many countries. And in the whole island there was no metal but gold. Their arms and armor were of gold, as were the harnesses of the griffins they rode and they fed them with the men they took prisoner and the boys they bore."

WORLD OF THE PUEBLOS
Hopi and Zuni "Death Talk"

Pueblos call storytelling "death talk." Believers in the annual death and rebirth of nature, they tell stories only in winter, when Earth lies shrouded in deathlike stillness, for at other seasons they are entirely occupied in scratching a subsistence out of the dry dirt and—being endowed with a metaphysical turn of mind—performing intricate ceremonials to obtain good crops. Also, tales are taboo in summer; they attract snakes and bring snow, it is said. But in winter, storytelling bees are all-night affairs in warm, dark rooms full of people seated on the floor with their backs to the walls, each in turn telling a tale. Most of the "death-talk" stories concern animals. Here are some typical examples:

TORTOISE VS. RABBIT

There was a tortoise who lived at First Mesa. Among his acquaintances was a rabbit. One day Rabbit challenged Tortoise to a race. "Very well," said Tortoise. "If you insist, let us run the race four days hence."

Unbeknown to Rabbit, Tortoise had a twin brother named Twin Tortoise, who lived at the far end of the agreed course. During the interval before the race, Tortoise visited him. Soon after the race began, Rabbit overtook Tortoise and came to a grove of cactus fruit, stopped there, ate his fill, and grew quite drowsy. "I'd better not fall asleep," he thought. "Not that I have any cause for worry." So Rabbit got up and scampered onward to the finish, where who should meet him but a sternly glaring tortoise, who said: "You were gorging yourself on cactus fruit when I passed you." Thereupon Twin Tortoise dispatched him. The pot was already simmering by the time his brother arrived.

COMING OF THE SNAKES

A youth named White Corn left home to find a wife. Provided only with a pouch of sacred cornmeal and four feathered prayer sticks, White Corn walked many days until he reached the sea, where the Sun Chief appeared and bade him tie his prayer sticks together and set them on the water; that being done, they became a raft with four gigantic feathers for a sail. Sun Chief told White Corn that a bride awaited him in the land across the waters, in the house of the great Snake Chief; but he must

"The Kachinas are coming!" Zuni children shout as the Shalako pageant begins each December, reenacting the Coming of the Supernaturals. Shown below is a giant Kachina (called a Shalako) dancing with one of the Koyemci, or Mudhead clowns.

The Supernaturals

According to Pueblo tradition, there was a famine many years ago when the people were rescued by a host of kindly visitants called Kachinas (Supernaturals), who brought food and water from their home far away in the mountains. Thereafter, the Kachinas returned every year for a time, staying from December 21 to mid-July, and imparted to the Pueblos the combination of irrigation agriculture and dry farming that has ever since insured their survival in a land of near-perpetual drought.

Then at length (again according to the myth), the Kachinas stopped coming in person. They arranged instead for members of a brotherhood of initiates, which was named the Kachina Society, to impersonate them in a yearly series of dances reenacting in esoteric pantomime the lore of the original visitations. Thenceforward, Pueblos believed that a Kachina Society member automatically became one of the 350 or more different Kachina personages by putting on a mask representing that particular Supernatural. The Kachinas are thus believed to be a real presence each time their impersonators appear, whether in the public dances in the village plazas or in the private rites held in each clan's kiva.

Kachinas are not mere patrons of agriculture, for along with sprouts, seedlings, and shoots, growing members of the community are also their charge, and the Kachina Society takes an active hand in educating the young by a system of edifying punishments and rewards. Santa-like Kachinas bring small replicas of themselves (called Kachina dolls) and other treats to reward good children, whereas disciplinarian Kachinas (called Whippers) make terrifying descents on bad children. They are attended by a group of sacred clowns (called Mudheads) who dance to the beat of a drum containing black butterfly wings, betokening sexual magic.

Kachina masks are made of cottonwood or of buckskin or canvas stretched over wooden frameworks, festooned with sprigs of new-cut spruce, feathers, leather thongs, cotton string, and horsehair, and each bears its supernatural owner's occult device patterned in colors bright and bold.

The Kachina pantheon was joined by a redoubtable ogre in 1539, when the discoverer of the Pueblos, a Hispanic Negro freebooter named Estebán, was executed (or in Pueblo terminology, "had the road closed against him") for molesting women and displaying other arrogant behavior at the village of Hawikuh. After a time, the deceased Moor reappeared in the guise of a new Supernatural, Black Kachina, whose impersonators have danced his role of Chákwaina (Monster) in the society's ceremonials ever since. Estebán's metamorphosis into Black Kachina is not the only sanguinary episode involving Kachinas. As in the traditions of many cults rooted in prehistory, hints of human sacrifice survive in Kachina lore. Here, for example, is a spooky cautionary tale told to eight-year-old boys during initiation into the Kachina Society:

One night long ago, when the Zuni village stood on the top of Corn Mountain, a young woman and her small boy watched the Kachinas dance. A few days later, when the children were out playing, a young man went by, and the boy said: "See that one? The other

night he was a Kachina maiden. Maybe the masked gods don't really come here after all." Thus he spoke, and the children heard him. When they went home, they told their elders: "Maybe the masked gods don't really come here after all." The elders demanded to know who had said that. The children told them, and the angered fathers talked of nothing else. They made new masks of dangerous monsters and, when the masks were ready, sallied forth to hunt down the child, whose mother had hidden him in the dust in the fourth inner room of her house. When the search party failed to find the boy, they sent word to the village of the Kachinas, and when the message arrived, the Kachinas arose. There came the four Exorcists, the White Bugaboo, and also the Mudhead clowns; all the Kachinas came. They made a house-to-house search, but when they reached the boy's house, his mother said, "He's not here." As soon as she said that, the Exorcist Kachinas jumped up on the roof. Two stood facing east; two stood facing west. Twice they rotated on their heels, and twice was heard this sound: Whoo-eesh! Whoo-eesh! And the earth shook twice. Again: Whoo-eesh! A cracking sound was heard. Once more: WHOO-EEESHHH! The walls of the house crashed to the ground—and there crouched the boy. They dragged him out and struck him. White Bugaboo stalked up and down, and the Mudheads screamed, "Quick, Grandpa! Knock his head off and let's get out of here." But White Bugaboo was so overwrought he ran round and round in circles in his rage, until at last—after a long time—he rushed up to the boy and seized him by the hair. Whack! He cut the boy's head off at the neck and flung it high in the air. It fell, but White Bugaboo kept flinging it up, again and again. Then the Mudheads kicked it all the way back to Kachina village, where they set it down on a nearby anthill.

Meanwhile, back at Corn Mountain, they buried the boy's headless body, thus enhancing the value of the Kachina Society. All this is secret. It happened long ago.

first seek out a rattlesnake named Big Rattler, who would guide him to the Snake Chief's mountain lair.

White Corn's voyage lasted 14 days. Upon touching dry land, the raft shrank back into a bundle of prayer sticks. White Corn walked inland until he reached a mountainside where a strange-looking old man appeared who had no nose or mouth and was carrying a stick with a crook at one end. Before White Corn had time to think, the old man hooked him with his stick and dragged him up the mountain at a furious rate. Then a storm broke. The old man was struck by lightning and sprawled on the ground but (because he was not really quite human) was unscathed. White Corn started to run, but his captor waved him back. Putting an obsidian knife in White Corn's hand, the old man ordered him in sign language:

"Make a slit from my forehead down to my chin, in a perfectly straight line the length of one prayer stick; then do the same across my face from ear to ear."

White Corn did as he was told. To his great wonder the old man's face peeled back, out popped a whole new face with a nose and mouth, and a young brave slipped out of the old man's skin. "You are no longer my prisoner," the brave said. The sky smelled of retreating thunder. Both young men broke out laughing and resumed the journey in high glee. After a while, they saw a river.

White Corn turned to his companion, but the latter had vanished. Pressing forward, he reached the river and sprinkled meal upon the water. Out of the tall grass beside him a tremendous snake appeared, its head held at eye level with his, its skin like a cascade of jewels. It told White Corn to tie his prayer sticks together and put them in the stream. As before, they became a raft. He got on, and was borne rapidly off.

Day became night, and the raft kept gaining speed. There were no clouds, no wind, no moon, and although moving much faster than a horse could run, the stream rushed

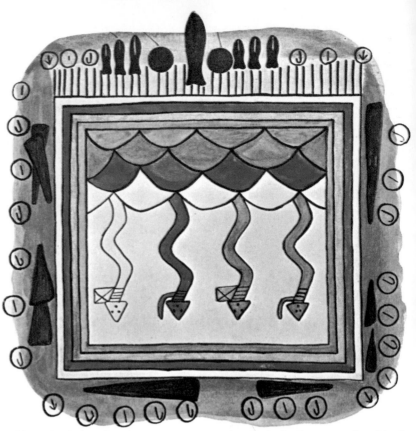

This sand painting of a rainstorm serves as an altar for Snake Dancers—rainmaking is a main function of the Snake Order. Snakes stand for lightning darting from clouds. Horns and squares mark males and females respectively. Colors symbolize the world quarters: yellow = N, red = S, white = E, green = W. The painting is first sprinkled with corn pollen, then obliterated when snakes are flung on it during ceremonies.

on in perfect silence, an immense pitch-dark loneliness in which all White Corn felt or heard was the night whistling in his ears. He continued in a state of wonderment until noon of the fourth day, when he perceived a sound as of an approaching rainstorm. This soon became an all-engulfing roar—a waterfall! The river seemed to be flowing into a rainbow. Then the raft was lifted by the waters and dropped on the bank at the foot of a mountain. Bruised and trembling, he climbed until, close to the summit, a certain rock attracted his attention. As he stood looking, a snake's head emerged from beneath. It was a large brown rattlesnake, and although there was nothing remarkable about its size or appearance, White Corn had a presentiment that this was the long-sought Big Rattler, who was to lead

him to the Snake Chief's cavern and his future bride. He sprinkled the earth with some cornmeal and placed his prayer sticks before the snake, which coiled round them and breathed on each separate feather. Then Big Rattler (for it was indeed he) spoke, instructing White Corn to proceed with certain ceremonies. White Corn now sprinkled the cornmeal in such a way as to describe a big circle on the ground, wherein he drew three intersecting lines, for the points whence came the different rains and winds. Then, without knowing how it happened, he found himself inside the hill, in a warm, bright cavern where he beheld a smiling throng of men and women in whose midst sat an old man of wrathful mien, the Snake Chief. Staring at White Corn, the Snake Chief rose and spoke: "The people have been watching in the east for one who shall smash open the barriers shutting them in from the vision of the sun and stars; but only through the ordeal of the Snake Order can the awaited one obtain for himself that liberation and in turn release others from the dark and lonely life."

White Corn was led down a narrow passageway to a chamber almost entirely inside the waterfall, where he threw his clothes aside and bathed. Emerging, he noticed for the first time that all the others had a peculiar skin, like a snake's, and that he himself was being enveloped in a similar covering. The Snake Chief then told him to choose a sweetheart, but he was unable to make a choice and asked the Snake Chief to select one for him. The old man then reached into a cloudy substance that hung beside him in midair and started pulling until a beautiful girl named Bright Eyes emerged and was given to White Corn for his wife. White Corn learned all the songs and ceremonials of the Snake Order during his subsequent sojourn in the cavern; and when he had at last received full initiation, the old Snake Chief led him and his bride through a secret tunnel to the earth's surface.

White Corn's village was in the middle of a drought when the couple arrived there, but Bright Eyes performed a ceremony, rain followed, and the crops grew. Then one night there was a storm. Soon afterward it was observed that Bright Eyes was pregnant, and the people rejoiced. They wished Bright Eyes to bear a son who would become their Rain Chief. When Bright Eyes reached term, White Corn took her away to a high mesa to the west of the village. After seven days they returned with her offspring—five snakes. The enraged people would have killed them all, but an old man came forward and said: "No, I will be their father. They shall come live with me."

That night, the people were startled by strange cries coming from the old man's house. Many ran to see, but thick smoke issued from the door and other openings through which outsiders might have looked in, nor did they ever find out what had happened. On the morning of the third day Bright Eyes took her snake children out into the valley, never to be seen again. The old man went with them but in the afternoon came back alone. As for White Corn, he stayed on and introduced the Snake Order among his people. Taking a new wife, he also founded the White Corn Clan and lived to see it become large and powerful before he died, when at last (as it is said by his people) he returned to the Sun whence he came.

Gripping hypnotized rattlesnakes between their teeth, Hopi Snake Dancers "summon the Cloud People" as they move to an incessant tattoo of drumbeats simulating a rainstorm. Significant colors are yellow = pumpkins, green = corn, and red = fruit.

THE SACRED AND PROFANE
Indian Influence, Spanish Tales

A royal edict proclaimed in Mexico in 1606 forbade further searches for gold in the north; the loss of men and money was too great. The Crown decided instead to gain riches by colonization. Missionaries and farmers moved into the area with horses, cattle, goats, and sheep and established hacienda ranching—grazing in miles of open range—which still exists in a modified way today. As these religious and dignified people learned the ways of the Indians and adjusted to the new environment, they developed a mission-centered lore illustrated by these tales. Though most stories are reverent, some, like Pedro's, tell of diabolical doings.

THE BLUE LADY

The Southwest abounds with legends of the Blue Lady, who some believe still roams the area causing blue flowers to bloom where she steps and bestowing love and riches on the unfortunate. Historians know her as María Coronel de Agreda (1602–65); here is a popular version of her story. In the city of Agreda, Spain, there lived a beautiful little girl, who was dainty, graceful, and spiritual and of noble parentage. The great issues and happenings of the day were discussed in her home, and tales of travels were recounted, to all of which little María listened with a sympathetic heart. The Indians, those strange people of the New World who knew not God, without any means of enlightenment, most excited her sympathy and fired her imagination, and she longed to bring light to their minds and salvation to their souls.

As she developed into womanhood, she determined to devote her time and means to doing all the good possible. To this end she founded a society that soon became famous throughout the country. The now learned and distinguished María Coronel de Agreda still retained her childlike heart and intense sympathy for the Indians. She spent hours on her knees in prayer, begging Providence to succor them, till at last it seemed to her that the way was opened to her to visit the New World. After a long and tedious voyage she found herself among certain tribes of Indians unheard of in Europe.

It being impossible for María Coronel to remain at length, she made frequent visits and obtained the Indians' promise that they would receive respectfully, as teachers, the white men in dark robes whom she would send to them to advance and raise their race and help them.

In the 1680's a missionary by the name of Damien Manzanet discovered in New Mexico some of the tribes referred to by María Coronel de Agreda decades earlier and founded a mission there. Manzanet and his companions were joyfully and kindly received and shown every consideration. The governor, or chief, of the Tejas Indians one day asked Manzanet for some blue baize in which to bury his grandmother when she died. Asked why he desired blue, the chief replied that it was because a beautiful woman who had come among them, and whom they reverenced, wore blue, and they wished to be like her on passing to Heaven.

The strange part of the story is that María herself had never been in New Mexico or in the New World at all, but during her state of intense longing and continued prayer, she must have dreamed about these tribes or visited them in ecstasy. So vivid, however, were her dreams—if dreams they were—and so often were they repeated that the Indians became as real to her as those among whom she had actually lived.

Stranger yet is the fact that the tribe actually seemed to believe that such a person had been there.

DIOS AND WAIDE

Pueblos never embraced Christianity wholeheartedly. A typical tale:

The Catholic god, Our Father Dios, and the Indian god, Our Father Waide, met to see who had more power and which of them could throw better. Our Father Waide said, "Well, Elder Brother, you throw to that spruce tree over there." Our Father Dios got his gun and hit the tree, and the bullet went through and even made a small hole. Then Our Father Waide shot with his thun-

Paintings of the Stations of the Cross were produced by California mission Indians in about 1779. Above, the Sixth Station: Veronica offers a cloth to wipe Christ's face.

derstick so that it thundered and lightninged, ripped the tree apart, and burned it up. "Well, Younger Brother," said Our Father Dios, "you have beaten me, but let's try another way. Let's see who will have the people." So Our Father Dios built a church. He rang the bells and the people flocked in, and the priest performed his ceremony at the altar. When the priest reached the middle of the Mass, Waide came with his drum. Standing a little way from the church, Waide began to drum, and all the people inside the church came out. "You have beaten me," said Our Father Dios, "but don't use the thunderstick except in war." Nor were the thundersticks ever again used otherwise. The people of Isleta, for example, once used them to recover a boy kidnaped by Navajo marauders. A violent storm broke over the abductors' village, so that the child was returned without a fight, but the Navajo enemies had partially mutilated the youth, and he died anyway.

THE MARGIL VINE
Within three days, a poor devout Indian boy was to attend his sixth Christmas program at the Valero mission (in Texas), and he had no gift worthy to offer the Holy Infant. That was the problem weighing on the boy's mind as he perched in a great poplar tree restlessly snapping off twigs. His reflections were inter-

An Indian artist who painted the Virgin Mary as a Pueblo unconsciously illustrated the cultural cross-fertilization that took place during the Spanish settlement.

rupted by Padre Antonio Margil, who observed the woebegone countenance of the boy. "Come down, my son," invited the old priest, "and tell me what is troubling you."

Shavano obediently scrambled down and stood staring at the brown earth, feeling ashamed that he had been found with tears in his eyes. Padre Antonio induced the boy to reveal the reason for his grief. He

enumerated his pitifully few possessions, from which he must choose a gift for the Christ Child. But Fray Margil placed his hand on Shavano's head and reassured him: "A gift is only a token that we give to show our love, my son."

But Shavano could not entirely understand the padre's reasoning. Had not gifts always been the proofs of love and good will among his people? He felt he must have something tangible to offer. The next day, Shavano wandered disconsolately to his poplar tree and leaned against its trunk. After a while his attention was drawn to a wisp of green, and he stooped to inspect it. It was a little vine, so tiny that it could have been trampled without being noticed. Shavano concluded that the plant would make a more suitable gift for the Christ Child than anything he possessed. He carefully dug it up.

He hurriedly got one of his mother's earthenware jars and planted the little vine in it. Rather shamefacedly, he carried the gift to the mission chapel and surreptitiously placed it out of view among the grander offerings about the manger. The boy lingered, fascinated by the assortment of beads, claws, and bright handmade articles, which represented incalculable wealth in his eyes. The objects that Shavano regarded with greatest admiration, though, were great antlers that must have belonged

FOLKWAYS

Cruel to Himself

Some 20 towns in modern Arizona and Mexico grew from missions established by the Jesuit priest Eusebio Kino (c. 1645–1711). An excellent administrator, founder of a thriving cattle business and farming system, and a fearless and tireless explorer, Kino nevertheless typified a certain kind of monastic more common to the Middle Ages. To see to the spiritual and physical needs of his vast Indian congregation Padre Kino spent much of his time on horseback, and then added endless rigors to that arduous life in order to achieve complete humility before God. His companion Padre

Luis Velardo wrote of him:

"His conversation was of the mellifluous names of Jesus and Mary, and of the heathen for whom he was ever offering prayers to God . . . When he publicly reprimanded a sinner, he was choleric. But if anyone showed him personal disrespect he controlled his temper to such an extent that he made it a habit to exalt whosoever maltreated him . . . And if it was to his face that they [insults] were said, he embraced the one who spoke them, saying, 'You are and ever will be my dear master!' even though he did not like him . . . After supper, when he saw us already in bed, he would enter the church, and even though I sat up

the whole night reading, I never heard him come out to get the sleep of which he was very sparing. One night I casually saw someone whipping him mercilessly [that is, as a means of penance]. He always took his food without salt, and with mixtures of herbs which made it more distasteful . . . He neither smoked nor took snuff . . . He was so austere he never took wine except to celebrate Mass, nor had any other bed than the sweat blankets of his horse for a mattress, and two Indian blankets . . . He never had more than two coarse shirts, because he gave everything else he had as alms to the Indians. He was merciful to others, but cruel to himself."

to some monarch of the forest, which were painted in stunningly brilliant colors. Shavano turned and crept away fearing that Christ might be displeased at the poverty of the little vine-weed.

Before daybreak the next morning the Christmas pageant was begun, starting with the appearance of the angels to the shepherds. Shavano was eager to witness the climaxing scene, but reluctant to appear as the donor of a worthless offering, he hung back as the crowd approached the church doors. As the shepherds reached the doors, those actors stopped and gazed fixedly within. Then to Shavano's ears there came the subdued cry: *"Milagro! Milagro!"* ["Miracle"].

Shavano wormed his way through the crowd. Perhaps, he thought, the Christ Child had bestowed some blessing upon the donor of the wonderfully painted antlers. Before the door he halted; then his whole being quivered with ecstasy, and tears of joy sprang into his eyes. His little vine had grown miraculously; it had twined itself about and over the crib of the Infant Jesus and had put forth a luxuriance of bright green leaves and brilliant scarlet berries so that it had become the most beautiful gift of all!

The Margil vine still grows in the San Antonio valley and is among the favorite Christmas decorations of the Mexicans of that region; they say that prior to the miraculous transformation of Shavano's gift, the plant was an insignificant weed.

PEDRO DE URDEMALAS

There were two brothers, Pedro and Juan, who lived with their bedridden mother and kept goats. One day when it was Pedro's turn to stay with the mother, he made a bowl of corn porridge with hot peppers (*chaquaqüe*) and gave it to her. When she could not eat it, he force-fed her till she choked to death. Then he dressed her nicely and propped her up against the door. He went out and when Juan came told him their mother was up and dressed, carding wool. Juan ran to see his mother and, by throwing the door open, knocked the old woman's body on the floor and thought he had killed her.

"You just killed my mother," Pedro said. "What do we do now?" Poor Juan started crying. "Don't cry, I know what to do," said Pedro, and he got a horse, and with Juan's help set the woman's body on the horse's back and then chased the horse into

their rich neighbor's wheatfield.

When the farmer saw that horse with its dead rider trampling down his wheat, he rushed out shouting, "Get off my land!" But the horse paid him no mind, so the farmer got a slingshot and shot the body off.

Then Pedro came running and screamed in his face, "That's my mother! You killed her!" When the farmer saw what he had done he begged Pedro's pardon, saying he hadn't done it on purpose but only to scare her. But Pedro kept on screaming until the farmer promised to pay for the funeral and, in addition, give the brothers 300 pesos.

Pedro de Urdemalas was so bad God ended up sending an angel of death after him. Pedro was sitting on a hill when the angel came, and he smeared some resin of turpentine on the spot where she would alight. So the angel got stuck, and when she went to carry Pedro away, she could not move. Then God sent a second angel, and the same thing happened. He sent another, this one under orders to beware. So the angel, instead of alighting, just grabbed Pedro by the scruff of the neck and bore him up to Heaven. God ordered Saint Peter to take him to Purgatory. They took him, but Pedro lashed the souls there with a whip. One escaped and told God what was happening. So God had Pedro transferred to Limbo. When Pedro got there, he heard the unbaptized babies crying, "Water! Water!" He heaved them into a nearby river, and they came up baptized and flew off to Heaven.

Seeing the trouble Pedro was causing in Limbo, God ordered that he be put in Hell. But on the way, Pedro put together a bunch of little crosses, which he carried in both fists, and when he got there the devils swarmed out to get away from the holy crosses. Then Pedro went and nailed the little crosses on the doors and windows of Hell, so the devils could neither enter nor escape. Finally, Satan himself got out by way of the chimney and went crying to the Lord. So God once more commanded wicked Pedro de Urdemalas to be brought into his

FACT ? MYTH

Exorcism by Pounding

Pueblo Indians thought of the recent dead as evil spirits and combined Roman Catholic rites with native ritual (derived from Spanish folk practice) to "chase the deceased from the village." In Isleta, New Mexico, it was also believed that the bodies of the dead might return from the grave, and so a drastic preventive measure—exorcism by pounding—formed part of the burial service. The dead person, dressed in a monklike habit and holding a crucifix, was lowered into the grave wrapped in a blanket and covered with a layer of soil. A male relative climbed into the grave with the "deadpounder," a 50-pound knot of cottonwood with fingergrips. He then pounded the soil, a local eyewitness related, "striking the corpse first over

the face, knocking the teeth out, then over all the body, to be sure that it is dead: otherwise, he (or she) may come to life and suffer in the dirt."

By way of further precaution, the positioning of the grave was such that the corpse, if it *did* come up, would rise facing the church and enter there.

But according to Isletans, the most irrepressible body in the place was that of a Roman Catholic priest. A 20th-century Isletan told the resurrecting padre's story thus:

"Long ago a priest was buried under the altar of the church. He comes out every seven years, and our padre sends word to the bishop. The dirt rises up, and up comes the coffin. He has gold teeth and no hair. Three times I know of this happening, and I have seen him with my own eyes. We don't know what he wants."

The religion-based lore of the Spanish settlers bespeaks their piety, but like most they also relished a good time. This detail of "Fandango," which was painted by Theodore Gentilz around 1848, depicts some early Californians in the midst of a wild frolic.

presence, and when Pedro got there Saint Peter met him at the gates of Heaven. Pedro said, "Open up and let me take a peek inside." Saint Peter opened the gates a crack, and Pedro jumped inside. God saw him and said, "Pedro, you will now turn into a stone." "A stone with eyes," Pedro interrupted.

So God turned him into a stone with eyes, and to this day Pedro de Urdemalas stands at the pearly gates and stares at all who enter there.

MIRACLE OF SAN FELIPE
Some Indians were enthusiastic converts, as this story relates:

The Indians of the northern pueblos were very much the enemies of the Spanish after the great rebellion against them in 1680. In a little while the *principales* of those pueblos held a *junta* in Cochiti and made it up to kill the padre and drive out the Spanish. The sacristan of Cochiti was a good Christian, and he ran to the padre: "I am your friend. They want to kill you but I will save you."

So the sacristan carried the padre across the river on his back, and then they took the *camino real* past Santo Domingo. The sacristan said: "This is the road; save yourself." It was already near day and the padre saw

that he must hide. There was a wooded island in the river and he went to hide there until night.

Now, by the grace of God, on that very day the Pueblos of San Felipe were making a great hunt, and the sentinel was on the mesa above the island to watch for game. When it grew more day, he saw something black moving among the cottonwoods and thought, "Already I see a bear." In truth it was the padre getting a drink. The sentinel made his signal and in very little the hunters found it was the padre from Cochiti. They were astonished, but he told them everything. Then at once the principales held council; they said, "We will save him and take him to our pueblo." Then they put him in their clothes and painted his face and hands. When they were coming to town they met many Cochitis asking for him. They said, "No, we have not met him," but then one of the Cochitis recognized him, and they demanded him with injurious words. There was a great fight, but they of San Felipe came safely inside with the padre. The next day, the Cochitis came with more of their own pueblo and of Santo Domingo, surrounding the town and wounding some. So the people of San Felipe retreated to the

top of the mesa. The others besieged them, and soon the water and food which they had carried up with them were all gone.

Then the padre pulled a little piece of paper out of his wallet. Upon this he made a writing with charcoal and told the sacristan to put it, writing upward, with stones on it. Then he made prayer for three days and nights and afterward sent the sacristan to bring the paper again. In truth there was also a writing on the other side. Who wrote it? *¿Quien sabe?* But we think the saints. When he had read the new writing, he broke a piece of topaz until it was sharp like a knife. And when the people had brought all their gourds, he made his arm bare and cut it with the stone knife and held it stretched out; and from the wound ran streams of water, the same as a clear river, and filled all the vessels. And all the people fell down and gave thanks to God.

A great while the enemy remained, but always when the water jars were empty the padre filled them again from his arm, till at last the Cochitis were tired and went away. Then the people went to the pueblo, taking the padre in great honor. No, we do not know his name. It is very long ago, and that has been lost.

THE MEZCLA MAN
Guardian of the Gold

Fortunately for delighted readers, Frank Dobie never kept a good yarn to himself. The story of the mezcla *man, which appears below in an adaptation, was first told to him by* vaquero *Elojio Juarez. Dobie said: "Thanks to an improved memory, I have doubled the length by putting in details that Juarez and I both forgot."*

There were no banks in the country then, so when the rich rancheros sold their wool and sheep, they brought the money home. It was gold, with some silver. Often they hid it in holes in the rock walls of their houses or buried it in the floors of dirt cemented with bull blood. Sometimes they put it outside.

Now one ranchero had more sheep and wool than any other. This rich old ranchero had more gold also than any other man, and he was very cunning. One time, after he had sold thousands of sheep and had conducted a caravan of carts loaded with wool to San Antonio, he brought home more gold than he had ever had before. But now, instead of hiding it in his house he carried it to the highest hill on his ranch. On its upper slopes black chaparral and catsclaw and other thorned brush grew so dense, a javelina [wild pig] could hardly squeeze through it. The top of the hill was flat, and in the middle of

the thicket was a small natural clearing. The trail to it was dim and thorny, for hardly anybody but wildcats ever traveled it.

The cunning old *rico* [rich one] knew it, though. It must have been right after a rain, for he found mud. There in the middle of the clearing, he made a great big man out of mezcla, which is a mixture of mud and straw or little sticks, the same as adobe. Big sticks supported the legs and neck and arms of the mezcla man. He was as big as a giant, and he was natural like a picture. He stood with his arms stretched to the east and west, and across his chest was this writing: "Dig out to the east and the west the way my hands are pointing and you will find the gold." Oh, but this mezcla man was strange, and his stomach was so big that anybody who looked at him would laugh.

After the cunning old rico had finished making the mezcla man, he kept his secret. He raised more sheep

and the shearers sheared more wool for him and he got more gold and hid it. They say that when he snored at night, his snores said, *"Más oro, más oro."* Then one night when he was snoring for "more gold, more gold," the bandits came as quietly as the owl flies and went into the snoring room. They grasped the rico. "Your gold," the chief of the bandits said. "There is none," the rico replied. "You had better say," the *bandido* said. "There is none," the rico repeated.

"Hang him," the chief of bandidos ordered. The others tied his hands behind him and took a hair rope, so that it would not cut his skin too much, and noosed him by the neck. Then they drew the other end of the rope over a beam and pulled him up until his feet were kicking nothing but air. When he went to breathing like a lassoed wild horse choking down, they lowered him.

"What is the name of the dance you are doing for us?" one of the bandits laughed. The rico said nothing. Again the leader asked and the rico refused to tell where the gold was. "All right," the leader cried, "hang him up again." Again he danced and again he strangled, but the dance was weaker, and the sound of the little air passing through the tight noose was shriller. The bandits let him down again. "For the last time," the bandit chief said, "I ask where is the gold." The rico was purple in the face and coughing, but he wheezed out, "There is none."

"May you go with God!" one bandit called. "And all you to the *infierno,*" the rico gasped back. "That's where you will snore now for more gold," another bandit taunted. After the rico's legs had made their last jerk, the taunter observed, "He loved his gold better than his life." "It was his pride that he loved," the bandit chief said, "even better than the Holy Virgin."

Then all went to searching. They looked everywhere there was to look inside the house and found not one piece of gold. When daylight came, they went to digging holes outside. One found the trail going up through

"There were robbers who came down from the north, and bandits who raided up from the other side of the Rio Grande. . . . One night they came as quietly as the owl flies."

the brush on the hill and followed it and came to the mezcla man. He came back yelling, "Now it is found!" What joy the bandits had! Quickly they dug under the hands of the mezcla man but found nothing. Now the bandits ran east and west the way the hands pointed, looking for likely places to dig. They were in a hurry, not only from eagerness for the gold but from knowledge that before long honest people would find out about the murder of the rico, a very important man, and begin trailing them down.

With all that traveling up and down the hill, from digging, to water and food, and back, the trail became as plain as the road to Laredo. On the afternoon of the second day the bandits heard horses galloping. They left the country.

When the ranchmen who were after the bandits came to the thicket and saw the strange mezcla man and read that writing on his breast, they forgot all about murder and justice. They thought only about finding the gold. Nobody was after them, so they could dig as deep and as far out as they wanted to. They would sight along the mezcla man's shoulders and along his arms and out his forefinger and out his middle finger, trying, trying to locate the right place on the ground to dig for gold. They even sighted out to a hill five miles away and dug a hole there. They cut paths through the brush east and west. But after they had dug and dug and found nothing, they became disgusted and quit.

Then the *pastores* [shepherds] began grazing their sheep up to the *Cerro del Rico* [Hill of the Rich One]. These pastores would leave their dogs to care for the sheep and go up the hill and dig all day long. They dug new holes and they dug the old holes deeper. But they did not find anything, and after a while they became disgusted and quit.

Only one old *pastor* did not quit. He was very astute, very wise. So he kept on coming to that high hill and digging. Every morning he would put his gourd of water down at the mez-

"Only one old *pastor* did not quit. He was more wise and had more knowledge than the other *pastores* . . . He could read in the stars . . . He was very wise, very astute."

cla man's feet, take his grubbing hoe and spade, and then for hours dig, dig, dig. One day after he had been working very hard and was thirsty and tired, the pastor regarded the writing for a long time. At last he said to the man of mud and sticks:

"Why, robbers came here and found you and read what you say and dug out to the east and west, and they did not find any gold. Then all the rich and important rancheros came. They had confidence in your word, and they dug out to the east and the west, and they did not find gold. Then after they quit, the pastores still believed you and they dug more holes. And I? Well, here I have been listening to you and digging my arms off for over a year, and I have never so much as found a copper *centavo*. Why you are just a billy goat of a liar!" He slapped him on his mouth.

The pastor was very indignant. "Shameless one," he said, "it is not

with your mouth that you deceive. Right now your lying to honest people will end." He seized his spade and hacked off the head of the mezcla man with his wide-open mouth. Then he chopped off the arms. And then, wow! he came with all his might down through the words on the mezcla man's breast and into his enormous stomach.

And when he did, gold coins, and some silver coins too, just poured out on the ground. They were so heavy that the pastor could not carry them all. You see, the cunning old ranchero had built the man to hold plenty, and then he fed him through his open mouth until he was full.

The pastor gave his master some of the money, and he kept the rest, and he never had to herd sheep any more. He went back on the other side of the river into his own country, and there he made a home and lived *muy contento* all the rest of his life.

The Saltwater Bandits

Pirating was among the hardest and most dangerous of the early colonial occupations. But it often paid extremely well. Many pirates began their careers as privateers—private licensees capturing enemy vessels in wartime. Later, unable or unwilling to fend for themselves as honest seamen in peacetime, they turned to pirating because it promised easy money and a freewheeling, glamorous way of life. The life was also filled with all the usual drudgery of a sailor's lot, and when a pirate failed to capture prizes for months on end, it could be lean pickings as well—for "no prey, no pay" was the rule. Nevertheless, pirates often enjoyed more freedom than they had ever known. The saltwater thieves of the Spanish Main frequently elected their own officers, including the captain, drank as much as they liked, and dressed exactly as they pleased. In many pirate companies there was no color bar, and the rule was share and share alike and one vote per head. Thus, the only truly "free" Negroes in the America of 1700 were aboard pirate ships, and it is hardly surprising that almost half the recorded piratical population at that time was black.

Like bandits of all eras, pirates treated their victims with varying degrees of gentleness or savagery. Some were themselves more or less innocent victims, having been shanghaied aboard ship and forced into pirating. Even that legendary archpirate William Kidd was in fact (as he himself protested) "the innocentest of them all" and the victim of a frameup. Pirates were themselves responsible for their fiendish folk image, fostering it in order to insure their frightened victims' cooperation. Ministers and politicians seized upon the negative image and inflated it. By 1800 the mythic buccaneer was a cherished figure in the American folk pantheon. To this day, pirates and hidden treasure live on in the lore of coastal localities from Maine to the West Indies, and many a mystery remains locked within the dozens of dead men's chests that lie buried yet.

"Up With the Jolly Roger!" Pirate captains knew it made merchant sailors' blood run cold to see the black flag with the skull and crossbones go up.

A pirate was "a sort of half horse, half alligator, with a streak of lightning in his composition." In this detail of a painting by F. J. Waugh, pirates board a ship wielding pistols and cutlasses.

CAPTAIN KIDD
Booty and the Beach

No man ever inspired so much pirate lore with so few piratical deeds as William Kidd. Born about 1645 in Scotland, he became a sea captain and by 1691 was a respected merchant in New York. Officially commissioned in 1695 to apprehend the pirate Thomas Tew, Kidd blundered into evidence that leading members of the English establishment were having dealings with their French opposite numbers although England was at war with France. Kidd was seized and, after a rigged trial in London in 1701, was found guilty of murder and piracy and hanged. Some of the highlights of his legend are related here.

KIDD'S DYING WORDS

This version of an anonymous English ballad that appeared on Kidd's execution day was very popular in America. For some reason, Kidd was called Robert in this ballad:

You captains brave and bold, hear our cries, hear our cries.
Tho' you seem uncontrol'd, don't for the sake of gold lose your souls.
My name was Robert Kidd when I sail'd, when I sail'd,   [sail'd.
My name was Robert Kidd when I
My name was Robert Kidd, God's laws I did forbid,
And so wickedly I did when I sail'd.
I curs'd my father dear when I sail'd, when I sail'd,
I curs'd my father dear when I sail'd.
I curs'd my father dear, and her that did me bear,   [sail'd.
And so wickedly did swear when I
I steer'd from sound to sound as I sail'd, as I sail'd,   [sail'd;
I steer'd from sound to sound, as I
I steer'd from sound to sound, and many ships I found,
And most of them I burn'd as I sail'd.
I'd 90 bars of gold as I sail'd, as I sail'd,
I'd 90 bars of gold as I sail'd.
I'd 90 bars of gold and dollars manifold,
With riches uncontrol'd, as I sail'd.
Then 14 ships I see as I sail'd, as I sail'd,
Then 14 ships I see as I sail'd.
Then 14 ships I see, and all brave men they be,   [sail'd.
And they were too hard for me, as I
Thus being o'ertaken at last, I must die, I must die,   [die.
Thus being o'ertaken at last, I must
Thus being o'ertaken at last, and into prison cast,
And sentence being past, I must die.
To Execution Dock, I must go, I must go,
To Execution Dock, I must go;
To Execution Dock, where many thousands flock,   [die.
But I must bear my shock, and must
Take warning now by me, for I must die, for I must die,   [die;
Take warning now by me, for I must
Take warning now by me, and shun bad company,   [must die.
Lest you come to Hell with me, for I

GARDINER'S ISLAND GOLD

Gardiner's Island, which takes its name from that of Lion Gardiner, the Englishman who acquired the island in 1639, is located in Long Island Sound, in the township of East

The spirit of pirate lore is caught by the famed illustrator Howard Pyle, who depicted Captain Kidd engaged in the activity at the heart of so many tales involving him: burying booty on a lonely beach.

The Astor Fortune

A classic sequel to the Captain Kidd legend is the story that the wealth of various families began with their discovery of Kidd's buried treasure. The tale is told of several American families along the northeast coast, such as the Gardiners, but the most persistent version involves the Astor fortune. It was first heard in the late 19th century and until recently was repeated—and believed. It goes like this:

John Jacob Astor was an obscure fur trader in the late 18th century when he employed a French-Canadian, Jacques Cartier, to buy furs from the Indians in Maine. In 1801 Cartier bought a few acres on Deer Island, in the mouth of the Penobscot River, from the owner, Cotton Mather Olmsted. Suddenly, Cartier's life changed. He retired from work and took to hunting, fishing, and drinking whisky.

Simultaneously, Astor's bank deposits leaped astronomically, and he received more than a million dollars from a London dealer in precious stones.

No one ever quite knew what to make of all this, until a descendant of Olmsted became suspicious. He was Frederick Law Olmsted, a distinguished landscape architect (and a designer of New York's Central Park). He explored Deer Island, and in a cave he found the imprint of a large chest. Eventually, he traced the chest through a junk dealer to the Astors—by that time one of the wealthiest families in America. Having proved that their fortune began with Kidd's treasure taken from Olmsted's island, he sued the Astors for millions.

These were the "facts." Actually, none of this ever took place. The whole tale was a hoax, begun in 1894 by Franklin Head, a friend of the Olmsteds, as a practical joke.

Hampton, New York. When, in June 1699, Captain Kidd put in at the island, the then "Lord of the Manor," John Gardiner, did not know that Kidd had been declared a pirate. Gardiner sold Kidd provisions and agreed to store some chests until the captain came back for them. In return, Kidd gave the Gardiners gifts. When Kidd was arrested soon thereafter, John Gardiner, realizing that Kidd's chests contained booty, turned them over to the authorities.

That much is part of the historical record. But many people knew that this was not the full story. The records did not tell how Kidd slashed Gardiner's hand with a cutlass as he landed. Or that among the gifts presented to the Gardiners was a cloth of gold, captured by Kidd from a ship off Madagascar and said to be part of the trousseau of the Great Mogul's daughter. To this day, Gardiner's descendants own remnants of that cloth of gold. Then there is the story that Kidd spent a night at the manor house on the island—some people even say he spent several nights there, and that during his stay Kidd lived high and handsome—that he forced Mrs. Gardiner to roast a

pig for him, that he dropped pearls in his wine, and that he tied Gardiner to a mulberry tree. The house later burned down, but after it was rebuilt, Kidd's ghost sometimes stalked about the rooms and corridors at night, tapping on walls.

Local people have long supposed that John Gardiner did not turn over all of Captain Kidd's booty. How else could the Gardiners have become so wealthy? Yet (the story goes) Kidd had in the end still managed to outsmart the Gardiners, for unknown to them he had buried another quan-

This woodcut illustrates the legend that Kidd—a minister's son—buried his Bible as a sign he had gone over to Satan.

tity of loot in a secret spot on the island. And—according to Edgar Allan Poe—anticipating that he might not be able to return to dig it up, Kidd "mapped" its hiding place with a cryptogram: the number 44106818. A popular (but untrue) legend has it that Poe visited Gardiner's Island and there deciphered the first seven numbers but failed to locate the trove. Poe was to recount all this in his story "The Gold Bug," which (itself based on genuine folklore) has become as much a part of America's popular tradition as of the nation's literature.

SCREECHAM'S ISLAND

Just off the coast of Cape Cod is a bleak islet where in Captain Kidd's day lived only two old women. They were the Screecham sisters, Sarah and Hannah. Sarah was a witch and lived alone in a little hut. Hannah dealt with pirates who prowled the Atlantic coast. Whenever they buried gold or other treasure on the islet, she provided a ghost to guard it.

One day Captain Kidd's ship appeared, and he came ashore with one sailor and some treasure chests. Hannah kissed the captain on the cheek and was presented with a shawl, a ring, and a locket containing a strand of Kidd's hair. The crewman then picked up the chests, and while Kidd waited on the shore, Hannah and the sailor made their way to a remote spot, where there was a deep, freshly dug pit. Hannah directed him to put the chests into the hole. As soon as he had done so, she shoved the man into the pit and helped her sister to bury the victim alive.

When she had finished, Hannah let forth a terrible screech like the scream of a gull in a storm. The wind carried it to Kidd, who shuddered with terror. But knowing that his treasure was safe, he rowed back to his ship. Since that day, no one has ever dared to look for the gold buried on Screecham's Island. For if anyone comes near, the ghost of the murdered sailor rises out of the pit, and Hannah Screecham shrieks across the sea, warning Captain Kidd.

BLACKBEARD
Scourge of the Spanish Main

Edward Teach, better known as Blackbeard, was a privateer under English letters of marque in Queen Anne's War. Teach turned pirate when peace came (1713), operating out of bases in the Bahamas and North Carolina, where Governor Charles Eden protected him in exchange for a share of the loot. Blackbeard was by nature a jovial exhibitionist with a taste for violence, wine, women, and song. After his death (1718), his skull was fashioned into a silver-sided punchbowl.

BLACKBEARD'S APPEARANCE

In real life Edward Teach was an abnormally big man, but the impression he made on people was so much larger than life that some considered him to be the Devil incarnate. Tall, well built, and phenomenally strong, the hirsute pirate had grown his beard when still a youth, and by the time he reached his prime it extended from his eyes down to his waist. He habitually wore it in pigtails tied with ribbons, some of which he fastened back behind his ears; and there was always a twinkle in his mad, bloodshot eyes. In time of action, Blackbeard wore a bandolier over his shoulders with three braces of pistols hanging in holsters and a fur cap with two slow-burning cannon fuses (made of hemp cord dipped in a solution of saltpeter and limewater) suspended from it on either side of his face, which had the effect of enveloping his head in a halo of black smoke. To add a finishing touch to this Satanic mien, Blackbeard had a favorite trick. He would mix gunpowder with his rum, set fire to it, and drink the flaming mixture down.

ABOARD SHIP

Blackbeard captured scores of ships in his day, and his treatment of unresisting prisoners was marked by a magnanimity that became as legendary as his beard. However, some captives balked at surrendering their money and valuables, and with them Blackbeard dealt summarily. For example, when one recalcitrant captive failed to give up a diamond ring voluntarily, the pirate chopped the piece of jewelry off, finger and all.

This engraving of "Capt. Teach, commonly call'd Black-Beard," was based on eyewitness details, exactly like a modern composite drawing of a criminal suspect.

Blackbeard expected absolute submission from his men and went to drastic lengths to enforce it. One night Israel Hands, Blackbeard's trusted confederate, was drinking with him in his cabin, when without provocation the pirate captain drew a pair of pistols and cocked them under the table. A second crew member who was present excused himself and stepped out on deck. Blackbeard blew out the candle, and the two men remained, locked in a silent war of nerves. Without a word, Blackbeard pulled both triggers. One pistol misfired. The other went off, and the ball from it struck Hands' knee, crippling him for life. Blackbeard offered this explanation: "If I did not now and then kill one of them, they would forget who I am."

Not long after this incident, crew members reported seeing a mysterious extra man on board ship. For several days the stranger was seen among them, sometimes below and sometimes on deck; yet no one could say who he was or where he came from—but the men all believed it was the Devil himself.

"Come," cried Blackbeard to his superstitious shipmates, "let us make a hell of our own and try how long we can bear it." Accordingly, he (with two or three others) went down into the hold and, closing up all the hatches, filled several pots full of brimstone and other combustible matter and set them on fire, then so continued until all the crew were almost suffocated and some of the men cried out for air. At length, Blackbeard opened up the hatches, not a little pleased that he had held out the longest.

BLACKBEARD'S LAST FIGHT

The forces of law and order (a small naval expedition consisting of two sloops commissioned by the Virginia government and led by Lieutenant Robert Maynard, Royal Navy) at last caught Blackbeard by surprise in one of his favorite coves, Ocracoke Inlet, 30 miles southwest of Cape Hatteras. As Maynard's sloop bore down on Blackbeard's vessel, they spoke to each other thus:

Blackbeard: "Damn you for villains, who are you? And from whence come you?"

Maynard: "You may see by our colors we are no pirates."

Blackbeard: "Send your boat on board so that I might have a look and see who you are."

Maynard: "I cannot spare my boat, but I will come aboard you as soon as I can with my sloop."

Blackbeard (taking up a bowl of liquor): "Damnation seize my soul if I give any quarter or take any from you."

Maynard: "I expect no quarter from you, nor shall I give any."

Thereupon Blackbeard gave a signal, and all eight of his cannons were touched off at once in a broadside, killing a score of Maynard's crew.

But the government force still outnumbered Blackbeard's people by more than two to one, so Maynard used a trick typical of the sea warfare of his day, sending all hands into concealment belowdecks. Although by this time only a short distance separated the two ships, gunsmoke concealed Maynard's stratagem from Blackbeard. The royal sloop continued to drift forward. When she was alongside, Blackbeard (seeing only dead bodies on her decks) shouted to his people: "They were all knocked on the head [killed] but three or four. Come on, blast you, board her and cut 'em to pieces!"

Yelling and shooting as they went, Blackbeard and 10 of his men scrambled aboard Maynard's sloop—only to be met by twice their number pouring up out of the hold. The pirates were shocked, just as Maynard had intended; but Blackbeard rallied his men, and a gory free-for-all ensued. Swinging his cutlass in a wild windmill attack, Blackbeard moved through the melee until he met with Maynard. Each shot at the other, but Blackbeard missed and was himself wounded by the ball from Maynard's gun. Then they fought with swords, and Blackbeard's cleaverlike cutlass snapped off Maynard's straight sword near its hilt. But as Blackbeard lifted his blade to strike the finishing blow, one of Maynard's comrades came up on him from behind and cut his throat. The cutlass swerved as it came down on Maynard and merely skinned his knuckles. The stricken pirate fought on, spouting oaths as blood spurted from his neck; Maynard and his people rushed him, and after five gunshot wounds and some 20 cuts Edward Teach, alias Blackbeard, fell dead.

Unwilling to run the risk that his vanquished enemy might somehow come back to life, Maynard had the pirate's head struck off and hung from the bowsprit, and at the same time caused the body to be chucked overboard. The instant Blackbeard's mutilated corpse hit the water, his head began to shout: "Come on, Edward!" And the headless body swam three times around the ship before sinking into the deep.

A HEADLESS SPECTER
Ever since Blackbeard's beheaded corpse sank and disappeared in the waters of Ocracoke Inlet, his ghost (which is also headless) has haunted Teach's Hole, a cove—on the Pam-

Blackbeard and Lieutenant Maynard are depicted in their famous fight to the finish in this painting by J. L. G. Ferris; a seaman approaches with uplifted sword to kill the pirate. It actually took 20 cuts and five gunshot wounds to kill him.

A galleon like the one shown under pirate attack in this painting by Howard Pyle was located recently by skin divers. Making their way inside, they discovered an intriguingly large, heavy box. When all other methods to open the chest had failed, the exasperated divers resorted to dynamite and blew the box apart. Out tumbled six hundred horseshoes.

ENCHANTED TREASURE

According to one of the dozens of Blackbeard treasure stories, some of the pirate's loot lies 15 fathoms deep at a place called Jake's Hole near the mouth of a creek on Maryland's Eastern Shore, where Blackbeard dropped it overboard in a big oaken chest. After his death, those who knew the exact spot went to Jake's Hole with ropes and grappling irons. But Blackbeard had left a spell on the treasure. It was easy enough to catch hold of the trove, but as soon as the treasure hunters hoisted it to the surface, their ropes burst into flames with an awful sulfur stink, and the chest sank back to the bottom of Jake's Hole. Many have tried it (the story continues) but the same thing happens every time, and they only lose their grappling irons for their pains. So the chest full of treasure is still there for anyone who can figure out how to get around the spell.

THIRTEEN WIVES

It was only natural that some of the many women he encountered should find a man like Blackbeard all the more charming for his devilries. Moreover, it happened that there was no pirate alive who was more chivalrous or respectful toward women. And so it was that over the years a total of 13 young women boarded Blackbeard's ship to stand up next to him before the first mate, who solemnly conducted a wedding ceremony and pronounced them man and wife. When the honeymoon was over, however, Blackbeard would sail away, and after a week or so of loud lamentations over the absent bride, he would forget all about her, and upon coming to the next port would set his heart on another girl.

The pirate did behave ungallantly on one occasion, and that was when he was rejected by Governor Eden's daughter, who was already engaged to another man. Blackbeard pursued her fiance, cut his rival's hand off, and threw him in the sea. Then he sent the severed hand in a jeweled casket to Miss Eden, who thereupon languished and died.

lico Sound side of Ocracoke Island—that was Blackbeard's favorite lookout spot in the area. Local fishermen report seeing the decapitated figure floating on the surface when the weather is propitious. It also swims round and round Teach's Hole in the dark of the moon. At such times it gleams with a phosphorescent glow and is plainly visible just below the surface of the water. People say the ghost is searching for its severed head, for Blackbeard is no more willing than the next man to meet the Devil without his head on

his shoulders. Also, how would his old shipmates recognize him if he were to arrive among them in Hell without his head? So the beheaded specter continues its search, sometimes coming ashore at night when there is a strong wind blowing inland. It is said that then one can hear the tramp of heavy boots and a voice roaring as if from a great distance, "Where is my head?" The specter carries a lantern. Thus, it has long been the custom in that locality to identify any unexplainable light appearing at night as "Teach's light."

GASPARILLA
King of the Pirates

Most of the revelers at the annual Gasparilla Carnival at Tampa, Florida, like to think of its eponymous hero as a well-dressed, courtly swashbuckler. José Gaspar's history is hopelessly mixed with lore; nevertheless, he can more accurately be described as a bloodthirsty, vicious rapist. An educated Spanish gentleman, he stole some royal jewels and consequently was outlawed; then he turned to piracy. He established himself on the coast of Florida where he kept a harem of beautiful captives and plundered the unwitting. Here is a version of his tale:

José Gaspar, falsely accused of robbery, captured a well-equipped navy bark. At his urging, his motley crew of escaped convicts voted to become pirates and sailed to the Caribbean. In the next few years Gasparilla, as he was now known, captured many prizes.

Male prisoners not needed as crew were knifed in the back and tossed over the rail. Many of the women and children who fell into Gasparilla's hands suffered the same fate. Some fared even worse. Those women whom Gasparilla allowed to live were divided among the officers and crew. On one occasion a Spanish maid spit in his face when he tried to remove the gold rings from her ears. He ordered her head to be bound to a mast by her long braids, after which he took his sword and sliced off both her ears in order to secure the trinkets without further insult to himself.

In time Gasparilla faced an important problem. He needed a land-based headquarters. Above all he felt a strong personal need for a place to relax among his books. Going back to *The Pirates' Who's Who*, we read: "He built a fort where he kept his female prisoners, all the male ones being killed. He kept his house on Gasparilla Island filled with young and beautiful women whom he captured from ships from every nation. These women's lives were usually short for he would soon tire of them and give them to his crew or behead them in a fit of temper, and each time a new face appealed to him, one of the less beautiful ones would in some way have to make room for the new."

On an inner island, Gasparilla built a village where the most vicious of his crew could carouse to their hearts' content and not disturb him with their yells and drunken fights. He also found it necessary to move the captives being held for ransom to a safer place—a deserted island to the south which was soon known as Cautiva (Spanish for "female captive"). In 1801 he captured a Spanish princess named Josefa, whom he was never able to conquer. He was said to have fallen violently in love with the young woman and to have tried every means to make her his willing mistress. He compelled the other women of his household to honor her every wish, and he showered her with jewels, fancy gowns, and even a private apartment. Gasparilla used amazing self-restraint in his courtship, but the girl called him hard names to his face. After a few months José Gaspar's patience reached the breaking point. He finally became insane over the girl's repeated rebuffs, and in a vile fit of temper neatly beheaded the princess with one mighty blow. Another version of this story adds: "For once, Gasparilla regretted his hasty action. He carried the body of the princess ashore and buried it in the island sand."

In 1821, thinking to take one last prize before quitting piracy forever, he bore down on an English merchantman, only to realize he had been tricked. False sides fell away to reveal rows of guns, and the American flag broke out at the peak of the Navy's *Enterprise*. Feeling his vessel going down, Gasparilla flung his sword aside with a fierce oath, twisted a length of anchor chain around his slim waist, shook his fist at the *Enterprise*, and threw himself into the Gulf of Mexico.

FACT ? MYTH

Walking the Plank

Did pirates really get rid of captives as shown in the 1887 Howard Pyle engraving at right? Probably not. According to ancient hearsay, the powdered and bewigged Stede Bonnet (a "gentleman pirate" who was briefly in partnership with Blackbeard) forced prisoners to walk the plank, but if so he was the only pirate who ever did. There were other ways to dispose of captives. For example, the buccaneer Thomas Cobham once tucked the entire crew of a small vessel inside her mainsail and then, as if drowning kittens, pitched the squirming parcel into the sea. But the classic technique for doing away with unwanted persons on board ship was simply to heave them overboard; and seafaring men—pirates and nonpirates alike—have been doing that since long before the prophet Jonah's day.

JEAN LAFITTE
Buccaneer of Barataria Bay

The Pirate of the Gulf, Jean Lafitte was called, even though he went to sea only once in his life, when he sailed from France to New Orleans in about 1809. Handsome and shrewd, with polished manners and the command of four languages, Lafitte amassed a fortune by smuggling slaves and merchandise past the local customs inspectors. Operating from his smugglers' roost on Barataria Bay, just off the Louisiana coast, and later from a fortified outpost on Galveston Island, Lafitte at one time controlled nearly the entire import traffic of the lower Mississippi valley. But his career as a high seas buccaneer is the stuff of legend.

During the years that Lafitte reigned over the smuggling trade of Louisiana, few dared to oppose him. One member of his crew, Grambo, once challenged his authority and called upon his comrades to overthrow Lafitte. The argument ended abruptly when Lafitte pulled out his pistol and killed Grambo. On another occasion, Lafitte hanged one of his men for daring to attack a ship against his orders.

By comparison, Gov. William C. Claiborne of Louisiana got off lightly when he tried to interrupt Lafitte's trade. When the governor offered $500 for his head, Lafitte offered $5,000 for the governor's head.

Enraged at this insult to his authority, the governor sent out an expedition to seize Lafitte's outpost on Barataria Bay and bring the pirate back to New Orleans for trial. Lafitte ambushed the approaching expeditionary force, which gave up without a fight. Whereupon, Lafitte displayed the nobility and generosity that were to make his name. Instead of executing the men who had come to take him prisoner, he loaded them with costly presents and allowed them to return to New Orleans.

SATAN OUTWITTED
According to an old French legend, Lafitte's fortified castle on Galveston Island—which he called Maison Rouge (Red House)—was built by the Devil himself in a single night. Lafitte had struck a bargain with Satan, offering in exchange for Maison Rouge the life and soul of

the first creature Lafitte cast his eyes on in the morning. Lafitte then arranged to have a dog thrown into his tent at daybreak, so that all the Devil got out of the deal was a dog.

LAFITTE'S DEATH
Lafitte apparently died in bed of a tropical fever in 1826. Yet the story persisted that he fell in a daredevil engagement with a British warship in the Gulf of Mexico.

Above the storm of battle, Lafitte's stern voice was heard, and his red arm, streaming with gore and grasping a shattered blade, was seen in the darkest of conflict. The blood now ran in torrents from the scuppers and dyed the waters with a crimson stain. At length, however, he fell. A ball had broken the bone of his right leg; a cutlass had penetrated his stomach. The British commander, also wound-

During the War of 1812, Lafitte (left) offered men and arms to Andrew Jackson and Governor Claiborne. This aid helped Jackson win the Battle of New Orleans.

ed, was laid senseless on the deck close by Lafitte, and the pirate, beholding his victim within his grasp, raised himself to slay the unconscious man. He threw his clotted locks aside, and drew his hand across his brow to clear his sight of blood and mist. But his brain was dizzy and his aim unsure, and the dagger descending only pierced the thigh of his powerless foe, and Lafitte fell back exhausted on the deck. Again reviving, he tried again to plunge the dagger in the heart of his foe, but as he held it over his breast, the effort to strike broke the slender thread of life, and Jean Lafitte was no more.

LAFITTE'S TREASURE
At one time or another, every inlet and island along the Gulf coast has been thought to be the hiding place of Lafitte's treasure. Lafitte himself helped spawn the tales, boasting that at Galveston alone he had buried enough money to build a solid-gold bridge across the Mississippi River. People living along the coast have been talking about the treasure for so long that it has become part of their daily conversation. For instance, if a Gulf coast man puts on weight, he's likely to be asked: "What you got there? Lafitte's treasure?"

LAFITTE'S RESTLESS GHOST
A tale commonly told about Lafitte's treasure is that the ghost of the smuggler continually wanders the earth searching for a worthy inheritor of his fortune: someone who will use the treasure for good rather than for evil or selfish purposes. Only when he finds such a person will Lafitte be absolved of his sins.

Most of these ghost legends seem to be based on a story told by a Confederate veteran about a night he had once spent in an old house near the town of La Porte, on the shore of Galveston Bay. It was a cold and blustery February day in the 1880's. Daylight was fading and he was dead tired. By the uncertain light of the moon he saw that he'd reached a stable; and beyond the stable, not many yards distant, he could barely make out the dark outline of a house.

Hitching his horse to a post inside the stable, he started toward the house with his saddle and blanket. He called out, but the only answer was the roar of the waves tearing at the bluff. Finding the great double doors of the house barred, he made his way in through a window. He struck a match and found himself in a room that gave promise of comfort. A stack of firewood lay beside the fireplace. Before long he had a fire going. Spreading his horse blanket close to the blaze and using the saddle for a pillow and the slicker for cover, he went to sleep.

"I do not know how long I slept," he said afterward, "when I became aware of a steady gaze fixed upon my face. The man was looking down on me, and no living creature ever stood so still. There was imperious command in the unblinking eyes, and yet I saw profound entreaty also.

"It was plain that the visitant had business with me. I arose, and together we left the room, passed its neighbor, and entered a third, a barren little apartment through whose cracks the wind came mercilessly. I think it was I who had opened the doors. My companion did not seem to move. He was merely present.

"'It is here,' he said, as I halted in the middle of the bare floor, 'that more gold lies buried than is good for any man. You have but to dig and it is yours. You can use it; I cannot. However, it must be applied only to purposes of highest beneficence. Not one penny may be evilly or selfishly spent. On this point, you must keep faith and beware of any failing. Do you accept?' I answered, 'Yes,' and the visitant was gone, and I was shivering with cold." Groping his way back to his fire, the traveler piled on more wood until he had a generous blaze. Then he dozed off, only to wake again in the presence of the visitant. "The still reproach of his fixed eyes was worse than wrath. 'I need your help more than you can know,' he said, 'and you would fail me. The treasure is mine to give. I paid for it with the substance of my

The numerous channels, bays, and estuaries of America's eastern and Gulf coasts made ideal havens from which Lafitte and other pirates could prey upon merchant ships. The respective domains of the three major rogue captains are illustrated on the map above.

soul. I want you to have it. With it you can balance somewhat the burden of guilt I carry for its sake.'

"Again we made the journey to the spot where the treasure was buried, and this time he showed it to me. There were yellow coins, jeweled watches, women's bracelets, diamond rings, and strings of pearls. It was just such a trove as I had dreamed of

In this detail of a painting attributed to John Wesley Jarvis, Jean Lafitte and his brother Pierre indulge in a little game of cards with pirate chief Dominique You.

when, as a boy, I had planned to dig for Lafitte's treasure, except that the quantity of it was greater. With the admonition 'Do not force me to come again,' my companion was gone. Once more I made my way back to the fire.

"This time I took up my saddle and blanket and went out to the company of my horse. The wind and the waves were wailing together, but I thought I saw a promise of light across the chilly bay, and never was the prospect of dawn more welcome. As I saddled up and rode off, the doleful boom of the muddy water at the foot of the bluff came to me like an echoed anguish."

Lafitte, it is said, still haunts the house at La Porte, steadily pursuing his object of finding a fit recipient for his dangerous gift. But he never succeeds, and his disappointment is terrible. Some folk believe that when there is a particularly dolorous moan in the wash of the waves, it is the despair of the thwarted pirate finding voice in the wail of the waters.

THE FAIR PIRATES
Mary Read and Anne Bonny

Anne Bonny and Mary Read each came to the New World to seek their fortunes; quirks in their natures and the work of fate made them pirates sailing out of New Providence Island in the Bahamas. Both were with Calico Jack Rackham when he was caught in 1720, but unlike Jack, they escaped the noose. A report of the two trials—men first, ladies second—omits many fanciful aspects included in Capt. Charles Johnson's account. His tale appears here in a condensed version.

THE FAIR PIRATES

Mary Read was born in England; her mother was married to a seafaring man who, going on a voyage soon after their marriage, left her with child. He was never to return. The mother soon proved with child again and to conceal her shame she went to the country and carried with her her young son. Soon after, her son died but Providence was pleased to give her a girl and this was Mary Read.

Her husband's mother was in some circumstances, and the wife meant to prevail upon her to provide for the child if she could pass it upon her for the son. She dressed her as a boy and her mother-in-law agreed to a crown a week for its maintainance. The grandmother died, the subsistence ceased and Mary Read, being 13 years of age, was put to work as a footboy, which employment she quit to board a man-of-war. She bore arms as a cadet in Flanders, behaving with a great deal of bravery; yet she could not get a commission, they being generally bought and sold. She took on in a regiment of horse, behaving so well in several engagements that she got the esteem of her officers but she fell in love with a comrade. She grew negligent in duty, for it seems Mars and Venus could not be served at the same time: her arms and accouterments were quite neglected. The troopers fancied her mad and even her comrade could not account for her until she let him discover her sex. He thought nothing of gratifying his passions, but found himself mistaken. She proved so reserved that he changed his purpose and courted her for a wife. When the campaign was over, they bought woman's apparel for her, were married, and set up an eating-house. But the husband died and the widow again assumed man's apparel, eventually shipping on board a vessel bound for the West Indies.

This ship was taken by English pirates and Mary was held until the crew took benefit of the king's proclamation and surrendered at New Providence. Being pardoned, they lived on shore until money grew short. When Capt. Woodes Rogers fitted out some privateers, Mary Read sailed with a crew that mutinied and returned to the piracy that she had often declared she abhorred. Yet men who had been forced to sail with them swore that in times of action no person was more resolute.

Her sex was not so much as suspected by any person on board till Anne Bonny, who was not so reserved in point of chastity, took a liking to her. To the disappointment of Anne Bonny, Mary Read let her know she was a woman also. This intimacy disturbed Captain Rackham, who was the gallant of Anne Bonny, and when he threatened to cut Mary Read's throat, Anne was forced to tell him the secret.

Captain Rackham kept the thing from all the ship's company; yet love found Mary Read out. So smitten with a captured craftsman that she could rest neither night nor day, Mary Read suffered her discovery by carelessly showing her breasts, which were very white. His passion was no less violent than hers. This young fellow had a quarrel with one of the pirates, and they appointed to go ashore and fight. Mary Read was anxious that the fellow might be too hard for her companion and quarreled with the pirate herself, appointing a time ashore two hours sooner. She fought him at sword and pistol and killed him.

When they were attacked and taken, none kept the deck except

Anne Bonny with pistol and Mary Read with cutlass donned male garb only to fight, witnesses at their trial reported.

They may have been practicing a trade older than piracy, though men who smuggled women aboard often risked death.

Mary Read and Anne Bonny and one more, upon which Mary Read called to those under deck to come up and fight like men; and finding they did not stir, fired her arms down the hold amongst them, killing one and wounding others. A witness at her trial deposed that to his question of what pleasures a man could have in such danger, Mary Read replied the threat of hanging was no great hardship, for were it not for that, every cowardly fellow cheating widows and orphans on land would turn pirate and so infest the seas that men of courage must starve. Being found quick with child, her execution was respited; soon after her trial she was seized with fever and died in prison.

Anne Bonny was born near Cork, in Ireland, her father an attorney at law. Anne was not one of his legitimate issue, but the daughter of a servant. Having a great affection for the girl, he turned what he had into ready money and with his maid and daughter embarked for Carolina. He became a plantation owner.

Anne Bonny's father expected a good match for her, but without his consent she married a young fellow not worth a groat and her father turned her out. The fellow shipped himself and wife for the Island of Providence, expecting employment. James Bonny was sober but Anne soon turned libertine and was courted by Jack Rackham. She proposed to her husband that Rackham give him money in return for which he should resign her; the governor threatened to have Anne Bonny whipped. Anne Bonny eloped to sea in man's clothes. After some time, she proved to be with child and was landed on the island of Cuba.

When any business was to be done, nobody was more courageous and particularly when they were taken. The day Rackham was executed, he was allowed to see her. She was sorry to see him there, she said, "but if he had fought like a man, he need not have been hanged like a dog." She was continued in prison until her lying-in; what is become of her we cannot tell, but she was not executed.

Mary Read fires at the cowards in the hold while Anne Bonny and friend face off men sent by Jamaica's governor to quell Jack Rackham—who has sneaked off in a longboat.

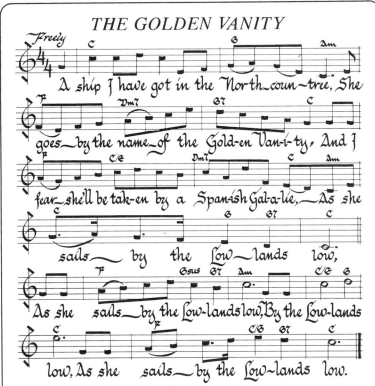

To the captain then upspake the little cabin boy.
He said, "What is my fee, if the galley I destroy,
The Spanish galalie, if no more it shall annoy,
    As you sail by the Lowlands low?"

"Of silver and of gold I will give to you a store,
And my pretty little daughter that dwelleth on the shore.
Of treasure and of fee as well, I'll give to thee galore,
    As we sail by the Lowlands low."

Then the cabin boy did swim all to the starboard side,
Saying, "Messmates, take me in, I am drifting with the tide!"
Then they laid him on the deck, and he closed his eyes and died,
    As they sailed by the Lowlands low.

"The Golden Vanity" tells of a cabin boy who sinks a Spanish pirate galley by boring holes in her side and is then cruelly requited for his brave (and improbable) feat. The song (about 300 years old) exists in several versions.

SATANIC SEA ROBBERS
Hellhounds of the Deep

Shakespeare once quoted a popular quip about "the sanctimonious pirate that went to sea with the Ten Commandments, but scraped one out of the table: Thou shalt not steal." Most real pirates went out of their way to disobey all the Commandments—some even enlisted Satan's help. Here are stories of the avowed Satanist Captain Lewis, ironically one of the nicest pirates on record; of Ned Lowe, a famous fiend who went in for mutilating New Englanders; and of the sons of Belial who turned the Palatine *into a horror ship and got away with it.*

A GENTLE SATANIST

Captain Lewis (or Louis—he may have been French) was a pirate from the time he was a little boy. Nothing is known about his origins, but he was fluent in English, French, Spanish, and Mosquil (a native Indian tongue), having spent his life from the age of four or five among sailors speaking those languages on board the ship of his guardian, the pirate Banister. When Lewis was no more than 10 years old, Banister's ship was captured by a British man-of-war. The pirates were all killed and thrown into the sea except for their captain and the child, for whom the captors reserved special treatment: Banister was hanged at the yardarm as the ship came in at Port Royal, Jamaica, while the young Lewis was dangled by his middle at the mizzen peak, badly frightened but unhurt.

The boy was released, and for several years he sailed with a merchantman out of Jamaica until, by this time a grown man, he was captured by the Spanish and taken to Havana. Before long, Lewis led six of his comrades in a successful escape, commandeering a Cuban fishing boat. Two of the fishermen crew joined Lewis and his men; now nine strong, they captured a turtling sloop and forced some of the hands to take on with them, discharging the others in the fishing boat.

Lewis continued with this small game, surprising and taking coasters and turtlers, until with forced men and volunteers he had made up a motley, polyglot company of 40 men. With them he made a series of daring captures, frequently swapping ships, until he had a fine, Bermuda-built brigantine of 10 guns.

He tacked the brigantine into the middle of a small fleet of merchantmen that were sailing in convoy because they had heard of his depredations and hoped to find safety in numbers. He captured several of these (while the others, rather than risk battle, sailed away) and took out of his prizes what he wanted, including 40 able-bodied Negro sailors and one white carpenter. The largest sloop, which was 90 tons, he kept for his own use and mounted her with 12 guns. His crew now numbered about 90 men, whites and blacks.

He cruised up to the Carolina

Brethren of the Coast

In 1700 American buccaneers had a name for themselves: Brethren of the Coast. The tougher and meaner a Brother was, the more his pirate Brethren admired him. But their lives were not all blood and thunder. Between cruises they gave themselves generous rest-and-recreation furloughs, becoming the West Indies' first vacationers. They camped out on the beaches, sunbathing, capturing parrots and teaching them to talk, eating pineapples and coconuts and green turtle soup (things unknown in England except to the very rich). They also barbecued sides of beef and whole lambs and pigs over Haitian-style cooking grills called *boucans*. (The word "buccaneer" comes from *boucan*, in fact.) The rest of their leisure time was devoted to drinking rum, fighting, and cavorting with the bawds of various ages, shapes, and hues—English, French, Spanish, mulatto, and half-Indian—who thronged the barrooms

coast, where he put in at an out-of-the-way creek and for a few days traded quietly with the locals, unloading his sugar and rum as well as a number of malcontents who took the opportunity to jump ship. He later sailed up the Virginia coast and on this cruise he seized and plundered several merchantmen.

At that time, most of his white crewmen were French. Hearing that the remaining Englishmen were plotting to maroon the French, and himself with them, Lewis had all the English put in a boat 10 leagues from shore, with only 10 pieces of beef among them. The unlucky plotters were never seen again.

Ranging as far north as the Grand Banks of Newfoundland, Lewis at length made for the Guinea coast of Africa, where he took many ships, English, Dutch, and Portuguese. Among these ships was one from Carolina, commanded by a Captain Smith. While Lewis was chasing the vessel, an incident occurred that made his men believe he had dealings with the Devil. His fore- and main-topmast being carried away,

Satan aided the gentle pirate Lewis, who threw a lock of his hair in the air and said: "Good Devil, take this till I come . . ."

Lewis ran up the shrouds to the maintop, tore out a handful of his hair, and threw it into the air with these words, which were heard by all: "Good Devil, take this till I come."

The ship immediately gained speed, moving faster than before the loss of her masts, and quickly ran down the Carolina ship. After Smith's surrender, Lewis treated him with great civility, giving him as much or more in value than he took from him, and, after swapping his own damaged ship for Smith's, released the latter, saying he would one day come to visit him in Carolina when he had got finished making money on the coast.

Lewis' unwillingness to use violence to solve problems caused his undoing in the end. Once again, his crew split into quarreling factions. A determined minority led by one Le Barre decided to secede and go off on their own, taking a large, newly captured sloop and such arms, goods, and provisions as they thought fit, while Lewis stood by and told them to take as much as they liked. But the runaway crewmen let their greed get out of hand and overburdened their sloop, encumbering her decks with goods and ammunition, making her topheavy. The wind began to blow

---

of such mariners' resorts as New Providence, the wide-open shantytown then standing on the site of present-day Nassau. Much of the money they spent while thus disporting themselves was Spanish—gold doubloons (worth about $12.50) and double doubloons, and silver pieces of eight—also known as Spanish dollars and worth roughly $1.00—so-called because they were often chopped into eight bits worth 12 cents apiece.

Once back on board ship, however, most pirates were all business and the typical pirate ship was as tight as any afloat, despite the democratic makeup of the company and the universally held belief of mariners that "rules were made for fools." In fact, written regulations (commonly called pirate articles) governed most buccaneering companies during the heyday of American piracy. Here is a rather elaborate set of rules that was drawn up by Captain Bartholomew Roberts for the benefit of his crew:

ARTICLES

I. To each a vote and an equal share of whatever fresh provisions or liquor seized.

II. To each a proper share of booty taken on board of prizes. If any defraud the company, marooning shall be his punishment.

III. No gambling.

IV. Lights out at 8 o'clock in the night. If any after that hour still remain inclined for drinking, they shall do it on the open deck.

V. Keep pistols, musket, and cutlass clean and fit for service.

VI. No boys or women. If a man be found seducing any of the latter, having carried her to sea disguised, he shall suffer death.

VII. Desertion of battle station to be punished by death or marooning.

VIII. No striking one another on board, but every man's quarrel to be ended on shore, at sword and pistol.

IX. No man to talk of breaking up our way of living till each has shared £1,000. If any man lose a limb or be crippled in the line of duty, he shall have $800 out of the public stock, and for lesser hurts proportionably.

X. The captain and the quartermaster each to receive two shares of a prize; the master, boatswain, and gunner, one share and a half; other officers, one and a quarter.

XI. Ship's musicians excused from seamen's duty on the Sabbath.

These articles were sworn to—sometimes on a Bible—by each new crewman. A frequent penalty for serious violations was marooning: leaving the offender on an island or unsettled coast far from regular shipping lanes, provided only with a gun and some ammunition and a bottle of water.

Few Brethren ever retired to enjoy the *dolce vita* many dreamed of for their old age. Death in combat or from wounds, starvation on a desert isle, drowning, poison, a knife in the ribs, the garrote, or the noose awaited the great majority instead.

hard, and they were obliged to find a sheltered cove, where they dropped anchor and prepared to ride out the weather. Lewis ran alongside with his guns loaded and primed and told them they were a parcel of rogues, and he would make them give back what they had taken. He ordered Le Barre to cut away his mast or be blown out of the water. Le Barre was forced to obey; then Lewis ordered the mutineers ashore. They begged the liberty of carrying their arms, goods, and provisions with them, but he allowed them only their small arms and cartridge boxes. Then he brought the sloop alongside, put everything back on board his own vessel, and sank the sloop. Attempting to play on Lewis' conciliatory nature, Le Barre and his men begged to be taken back on board and reinstated as crewmen. This Lewis denied; nevertheless, he held a farewell party for Le Barre and a few of his confederates, at which they exchanged many toasts and assurances of future friendship. This was too much for Lewis' black seamen, who sent him a deputation. Quietly drawing him aside, the Negroes informed Lewis that his guests had mounted a new plot. He replied that he could not withstand his fate, for the Devil had told him in his cabin that he would be murdered that night.

A few hours later, in the dead of night, the rest of the mutineers arrived in canoes and managed to get into Lewis' cabin, where they killed

him. His loyal crewmen beat off the mutineers after a fight that lasted more than an hour. Then they elected the quartermaster, John Cornelius, an Irishman, to succeed Lewis as captain. Nobody knows what became of them after that.

NASTY NED LOWE
Ned Lowe was a youth in Westminster at the time of Captain Kidd's trial and execution. He started his criminal career by stealing hats and

Captain Condent's men rode up and down the decks of a newly taken Spanish ship on the shoulders of captive priests.

wigs from the heads of bypassers in crowded London streets and was reputedly so successful at the trick that people took to tying their headgear on with ribbons, in order to prevent sudden removal.

When still a teenager, Ned went to Boston and for a time earned an honest living as a rigger, but at length he tired of that and sailed in a sloop to Honduras to steal logwood. Here he quarreled with his captain, tried to shoot him, and went off in an open boat with 12 other men. The very next day they seized a small vessel, in which they began their "war against all the world." Lowe's early days in Boston must have been disagreeable indeed, for he appears to have been a misanthrope with an especial hatred

for Puritans. Whenever he captured any of these unfortunates, he prepared tortures for them. He sliced off their ears and their noses, which he broiled before their eyes, and made them eat with salt and pepper.

Rather than go on the grand voyage to Africa and beyond, Lowe contented himself with acts of piracy from the West Indies to the Grand Banks of Newfoundland. Most of his activities, therefore, were confined either to fishermen or simple traders, and his booty was small. Still, because of his atrocities he was perhaps feared more than any other pirate.

Eventually, he overstepped himself by seizing a vessel from Block Island, Rhode Island, and maiming the crew before cutting them adrift in their lifeboat without oars, sail, or provisions. At that time Rhode Island—"that hotbed of Quakers and Baptists"—was considered immune to the attacks of pirates, for it was there that their contraband was traded and it was there that many pirates lived, and it was there that Kidd had come because he knew he would not be molested by the authorities.

Instead of vanishing, the fishing boat with her maimed crew was found, and a hue and cry went up. Lowe escaped, only to be subsequently marooned by his own men, but 26 of his crew were brought to Newport. They were tried, found guilty, hanged on Long Wharf, and buried on nearby Goat Island between high and low water.

Pirate chief Charles Gibbs carried a pretty Dutch captive on board his ship; unhappily, she was later poisoned by his crew.

Francis Spriggs taught his men to "sweat" captives, forcing them round and round the mast while thrusting knives at them.

According to a version of this story still current along the waterfront in the mid-20th century, the 26 condemned men were lodged in jail in double irons and under double locks, and the night before the execution there were still 26 prisoners, but when the guard came for them the next morning there were only 25. Neither the window nor the door had been forced, but there was a strong and unmistakable smell of sulfur and smoke throughout the jailhouse.

THE DOOMED PALATINE

The small *Palatine,* a Philadelphia-bound German immigrant ship carrying religious dissenters to the New World more than 200 years ago, reached the American coast and was driven off to sea again by a storm, in which the vessel lost her way. Meanwhile, as passengers and crew were running short on food and water, the captain died (some said he was murdered) and all shipboard discipline came to an end. The crew armed themselves and, taking possession of the remaining water and other provisions, demanded from the passengers huge sums for each bit of nourishment: 50 rix-dollars for a biscuit, 20 guilders for a cup of water, and so forth. Those who could not or would not comply were allowed to starve, and their bodies were thrown overboard. Having extorted all they could from the unhappy passengers, the crew took to the boats, leaving the stricken ship to the mercy of the winds and waves.

With no one left on board to navigate her, the vessel drifted on. Finally, on the last Saturday before New Year's, the *Palatine* fetched up on the southwest end of Block Island, and the natives rallied to the old cry "Ship ashore!"

Some say the survivors all came off the ship, except for one woman who had gone mad and refused to go ashore; she set fire to the ship and was burned to death. Others say the islanders who rallied to the ship were wreckers and killed all hands save for the crazy woman, whom they overlooked or were unable to catch.

The notorious Captain Spriggs took a Rhode Island vessel with a shipment of horses aboard. According to a survivor, Spriggs' men rode the horses at full gallop on the deck until the animals became infuriated and threw them, after which the pirates wreaked vengeance on their unfortunate captives for having neglected to provide riding gear.

While they were engaged in plundering the vessel, she floated off again with the rising tide, and the wreckers undertook to tow her to a neighboring cove, where they might dismantle her at their leisure. But a gale sprang up, and when by nightfall they saw that in spite of all their efforts the ship would be blown out to sea, they set her afire. None of the many men, women, and children who witnessed the scene were ever to forget the madwoman's screams as the *Palatine* burned to her waterline and sank.

Ever since that night, the vessel (seen as a bright glow offshore in fog) is said to rise and burn before great storms, and also on the Saturday between Christmas and New Year's, in commemoration of her loss.

Husband-and-wife piratical team Edward and Margaret Jordon are shown here attacking Captain Stairs of the *Three Sisters* after having massacred his crew. Stairs broke away and jumped overboard, to be picked up hours later by an American fishing schooner. Edward Jordon was later convicted and hanged; Margaret was acquitted.

The Spirit of '76

The mixture of restless colonists and new taxes and restrictive laws exploded—with results we all know. The American Revolution and the people famous for their parts in it form a solid basis for a U.S. national heritage. The rebellious colonists—by no means unified even among themselves, let alone in their resolve to break with the Crown—were impelled to invent a heroic, if recent, past. The Boston Massacre and the Boston Tea Party gave Revolutionary publicists an opportunity to do just that; and once the battle was joined, each minor victory had to be made into a triumph of bravery and military genius by the American press. The overall situation was bent into a myth perpetuated to this day—that of the untrained farmer militia staunchly struggling against a polished, battle-tempered British army. The British troops were in fact an ill-paid, untried lot, generally recruited from the dregs of English society, while many of the Continentals were highly motivated property owners (led by officers who as veterans of the French and Indian War were well-seasoned guerrillas). It is equally true that while the "Spirit of '76" did indeed exist, it existed only among a limited number of patriots.

The brand-new nation that emerged from the War of Independence had an even greater need for her own patriotic bywords; history held no precedent for her form of government, and culturally the United States was but a branch sawed from the tree of England. The new America stood in need of instant tradition, and starting with Benjamin Franklin, her native sons began to create it for her. People like Ethan Allen and Israel Putnam became genuine folk characters. But writers—from hack pamphleteers and balladmongers to the likes of Longfellow and Cooper—created many of the tales that we think of as an integral part of America's story.

As the nation came upon its Centennial, a new wave of Americanism swept over many writers; the literature of the time abounds in Revolutionary fictions. The end result has been a legacy of legend, fictionalized history, and romance as richly varied and fanciful as that of any nation on earth.

The eagle has long symbolized freedom, power, and vision; it was adopted in 1782 as national emblem of the United States (though Benjamin Franklin argued in favor of using the turkey).

"The Spirit of '76," by A. M. Willard, was inspired by the Centennial in 1876. The painting is a visual summation of the courage, hardihood, and patriotism that we traditionally associate with the winning of the War of Independence.

MYTHS TO MAKE MEN FIGHT

Radical Sam Adams and fellow propagandists had the difficult task of persuading some 2 million Colonials living in a rich land under relatively low taxes to risk their lives for complete independence. To help defame the British, Adams' had been characterizing their regiments, since their arrival in Boston in 1768, as depraved, claiming they beat boys and raped matrons and maidens.

One moonlit March night in 1770 a boy taunting a British sentry was joined by friends; as they flung chunks of ice the group grew into a mob of men armed with clubs who poked at the sentry and the eight redcoats with him. Shouting "Fire! You dare not fire!" the crowd, swollen to 400, pressed toward the frightened soldiers; then came the crack of shots ringing out. Three Americans were dead and two were dying.

This was the Boston Massacre described by Sam Adams as "MURDER . . . dogs licking human BLOOD in King Street." Now Adams had real blood to use, and he lost no time heralding the dead as martyrs. He got Paul Revere to engrave—from another's sketch—a deliberate misrepresentation of "The Bloody Massacre" for a broadside. Within three weeks the poster had been slipped under doors and pasted on posts across the city. That propagandistic version of the riot provoked by the mob had become the "truth" to many Colonials.

After the massacre Adams made sure that his cousin John Adams and Josiah Quincy defended the soldiers to assure a trial so fair (seven were acquitted) that no witnesses would be cross-examined and so tell the true story. It is possible that Sam Adams had even organized the scene, because he did have the power to raise a mob to create an incident. At any rate he did write inflammatory reports on disturbances, which he placed under various pseudonyms, in the seaboard's three dozen newspapers.

Revolutionary publicists made it clear that anyone not on "our" side would be hated by "the people." "Such Pilot will be marked for his Treason . . . and forever be recorded as the *damned traitorous Pilot* who brought up the *Tea Ship*," read a 1773 broadside. Not even nature would comfort the "wrong" side: birds that had nested for years under a Tory roof in Newport, Rhode Island, were reported in the spring of 1775 as moving to the dwelling of a Son of Liberty.

Britain's harsh retaliation after the Boston Tea Party—probably another Adams event—increased Adams' power in the Continental Congress in 1774. Partly as a result of his writing, the Massachusetts congress urged every county to arm and train a third of its men. Soon there were 15,000 men meeting three nights a week under veteran American officers of the French and Indian War. When the militia turned out at Lexington and Concord in the spring of 1775, it did so in highly mobile units of 50 and 60 men eager to try out their guns. And when 400 Americans fell on 100 British regulars holding a bridge during the battles of Lexington and Concord, they were attacking men serving a general who had not fought during 15 years of British peace. Yet from the pulpit and platform, in broadside and newspaper, these minutemen were referred to as "peaceable spectators" or "inhabitants collected at a bridge" or "peasants defeating veteran British soldiers." The result was that men ran to enlist in large numbers—something that was never to happen again in the course of the uncertain war.

Overlooking the shading in their own battle accounts, American publicists derided the British for false reporting. "WANTED" read an American advertisement in 1782. "A British commander . . . required to give security that he will not write home long epistles containing particular details of victories that never existed." By then, Adams' war of the pen had long given way to Washington's war on the field.

Paul Revere's misleading engraving stirred strong resentment against the British.

REVOLUTIONARY TEA

Rollicking tempo

There was an old la~dy lived o~ver the sea And she was an Is~land Queen~Her Daugh~ter lived off in a new~coun~trie With an o~cean of wat~er be~tween. The old la~dy's pock~ets were full~ of gold, But nev~er con~tent~ed was she, So she called on her daugh~ter to pay her a tax of three pence a pound on her tea, of three pence a pound on her tea.~

"Now, mother, dear mother," the daughter replied,
"I shan't do a thing you ax.
I'm willing to pay a fair price for the tea
But never the three penny tax."
"You shall!" quoth the mother and reddened with rage,
"For you're my own daughter, you see,
And sure, 'tis quite proper the daughter should pay
Her mother a tax on the tea,
Her mother a tax on the tea.

And so the old lady her servant called up
And packed off a budget of tea,
And eager for three pence a pound, she put in
Enough for a large familie.
She ordered her servants to bring home the tax,
Declaring her child should obey
Or, old as she was and almost woman grown,
She'd half whip her life away.
She'd half whip her life away.

The tea was conveyed to the daughter's door
All down by the oceanside
And the bouncing young lady poured out every pound
In the dark and boiling tide.
And then she called out to the Island Queen,
"0 mother, dear, mother," quoth she:
"Your tea you may have when 'tis steeped enough
But never a tax from me,
But never a tax from me."

Disguised in war paint and wrapped in "Indian" blankets (rather than sporting the feathers shown in the J.B. Beale painting at right), Sam Adams' men axed open 342 chests of taxed tea on the night of December 16, 1773, and dumped it "to steep," as the song says, in the harbor. "Revolutionary Tea," one of few songs surviving from that time, recounts the sauciness of an American daughter to her English mother. The mother soon boxed the daughter's ears, unwittingly turning more colonials into rebels.

PAUL REVERE'S RIDE
Rescue From Obscurity

Paul Revere rode out that "famous day" to spread the alarm that the British were coming and so did William Dawes. At Lexington they were joined by Samuel Prescott. As the trio raced toward Concord, Dawes and Revere were arrested briefly by a British patrol, but Prescott escaped to give warning to his countrymen. The next day the aroused minutemen won their first battle. The message, not the medium, had been important; but Henry Wadsworth Longfellow turned Revere's slight part in a "footnote to history" into one of our favorite legends.

Listen, my children, and you shall hear
Of the midnight ride of Paul Revere,
On the eighteenth of April, in '75;
Hardly a man is now alive
Who remembers that famous day and year. [march
He said to his friend, "If the British
By land or sea from the town tonight,
Hang a lantern aloft in the belfry arch [nal light—
Of the North Church tower as a sig-
One, if by land, and two, if by sea;
And I on the opposite shore will be,
Ready to ride and spread the alarm
Through every Middlesex village and farm, [arm."
For the country folk to be up and to
Then he said, "Good night!" and with muffled oar

Silently rowed to the Charlestown shore . . .
Meanwhile, his friend, through alley and street,
Wanders and watches with eager ears, [hears
Till in the silence around him he
The muster of men at the barrack door, [feet,
The sound of arms, and the tramp of
And the measured tread of the grenadiers,
Marching down to their boats on the shore.
Then he climbed the tower of the Old North Church, [tread,
By the wooden stairs, with stealthy
To the belfry chamber overhead, . . .
By the trembling ladder, steep and tall, [wall,
To the highest window in the

Where he paused to listen and look down
A moment on the roofs of the town,
And the moonlight flowing over all. . . .
A moment only he feels the spell
Of the place and the hour, and the secret dread
Of the lonely belfry and the dead;
For suddenly all his thoughts are bent
On a shadowy something far away,
Where the river widens to meet the bay—
A line of black that bends and floats
On the rising tide, like a bridge of boats.
Meanwhile, impatient to mount and ride, [stride
Booted and spurred, with a heavy
On the opposite shore walked Paul Revere.
Now he patted his horse's side,
Now gazed at the landscape far and near,
Then, impetuous, stamped the earth,
And turned and tightened his saddle girth; [search
But mostly he watched with eager
The belfry tower of the Old North Church, [hill,
As it rose above the graves on the
Lonely and spectral and somber and still. [height
And lo! as he looks, on the belfry's
A glimmer, and then a gleam of light! [he turns,
He springs to the saddle, the bridle
But lingers and gazes, till full on his sight
A second lamp in the belfry burns!
A hurry of hoofs in a village street,
A shape in the moonlight, a bulk in the dark,
And beneath, from the pebbles, in passing, a spark
Struck out by a steed flying fearless and fleet:
That was all! And yet, through the gloom and the light,
The fate of a nation was riding that night;
And the spark struck out by that steed, in his flight,
Kindled the land into flame with its heat. . . .
It was twelve by the village clock,

Grant Wood's "Midnight Ride of Paul Revere" was inspired by Longfellow's poem.

When he crossed the bridge into
    Medford town.
He heard the crowing of the cock,
And the barking of the farmer's dog,
And felt the damp of the river fog
That rises after the sun goes down.
It was one by the village clock,
When he galloped into Lexington.
He saw the gilded weathercock
Swim in the moonlight as he passed,
And the meetinghouse windows,
    blank and bare,
Gaze at him with a spectral glare,
As if they already stood aghast
At the bloody work they would look
    upon.
It was two by the village clock,
When he came to the bridge in Con-
    cord town. . . .
And one was safe and asleep in his
    bed   [fall,
Who at the bridge would be first to
Who that day would be lying
    dead,
Pierced by a British musket-ball.
You know the rest. In the books you
    have read,   [fled—
How the British Regulars fired and
How the farmers gave them ball
    for ball,   [yard wall,
From behind each fence and farm-
Chasing the redcoats down the
    lane,
Then crossing the fields to emerge
    again   [road,
Under the trees at the turn of the
And only pausing to fire and
    load.
So through the night rode Paul Re-
    vere;   [of alarm
And so through the night went his cry
To every Middlesex village and
    farm—
A cry of defiance and not of fear,
A voice in the darkness, a knock at
    the door,   [evermore!
And a word that shall echo for-
For, borne on the night wind of the
    Past,
Through all our history, to the last,
In the hour of darkness and peril and
    need,   [hear
The people will waken and listen to
The hurrying hoofbeats of that
    steed,
And the midnight message of Paul
    Revere.

ETHAN ALLEN
Green Mountain Boys

In 1770 Ethan Allen took command of the Green Mountain Boys, a raggle-taggle troop of Vermonters who had banded together to protect their land from encroaching New Yorkers. Their moment of glory—and Allen's beginnings as a legendary hero—came when they defeated the British at Fort Ticonderoga. Loud, crusty Allen was a hero to some and a traitor to others, but he captured the imagination, and most agreed with George Washington's assessment of him: "There is an original something in him that commands attention."

A DANGEROUS FOE

Strength, courage, and woodcraft made Ethan a dangerous foe. He was so brave that when a British guard spat on him while he was a prisoner, Ethan struck the man with his manacled hands and chased him back to his cabin. He was so tough that he bit the nails out of the handcuffs they had put on him. He was also a sensitive woodsman; when he gave three owl hoots, the Green Mountain Boys' signal, he was attacked by jealous male owls. Once he was hurrying through the woods to meet some friends and a huge panther leaped on his back. Ethan grabbed the beast, heaved it to the ground, and strangled it. When he arrived at the tavern he apologized for his lateness and appearance. "The goddam Yorkers," he explained, "have trained and set wild varmits against me!"

ETHAN THE GALLANT

Despite his gruff manner and rambunctious behavior, Ethan Allen was just as excessive in his kindliness when humble folk were in trouble. Once in his town in Vermont he chanced to be paying a social visit to the local dentist when a woman arrived suffering terribly from a tooth, which the dentist said he would have to pull. The woman took a look at the devilish gear the dentist was preparing to use and panicked. Ethan urged her gently to go ahead, but she resisted. At last Ethan said, "I shall show you, madam, that losing a tooth is nothing." He sat in the chair and instructed the dentist to extract a perfectly sound tooth. When it was

The homespun hero Ethan Allen leads his Green Mountain Boys in Robert Dowling's imaginative re-creation of the first defeat of a British post by the Colonials.

out, he turned to the lady and said, "There, you see, I didn't feel it." The woman thus encouraged had her tooth out—as Ethan stood by and suffered in silence.

ETHAN AND THE SNAKE

Along with his other attainments, Ethan Allen was reputed to be a drinker of heroic proportions. He

Allen was reported as saying that if he were reborn on earth he'd like to be a great white stallion, so as to roam and snort all over Vermont. After his death Vermonters saw such a stallion; above is a drawing of an old weather vane memorializing the tale.

had put away so much liquor over the years that there was speculation about what ran in his veins. Yet for all that, Ethan Allen never lost control of himself or events.

Once he was making a trip overland by foot with one of his Green Mountain Boys, Remember Baker. It was a hot day, and as the men had been up late the night before "celebrating," they decided to take a short nap in the woods. As they lay sleeping, Baker was suddenly roused by a noise. In his half sleep he gazed horrified: there on the chest of the sleeping Ethan Allen was a huge rattlesnake. It must have been five feet long. Before Baker could fully wake, the rattler bit Allen several times on the neck, arms, and hands.

Baker jumped up, grabbed his gun, and advanced on the snake. Just as he was about to knock the snake away, Baker was startled to see it glide to the ground. Its head was weaving from side to side, and its whole body was twisting in a way strange for any snake. Baker stood almost hypnotized when suddenly the rattler turned to look at him. The snake was cross-eyed! Then the snake gave a mighty "Buuurrrppp!" and passed out. "Drunk, by Jesus!" exclaimed Baker. When Allen awoke, all he complained about was "these eternal, damnable, blood-sucking mosquitoes" that had bitten him while he slept.

SHARE THE GLORY

One Sunday, disliking some remark by a Parson Dewey, Allen rose and started to stalk out. Dewey pointed at the bold Allen and shouted: "Sit down, thou blasphemer, and listen to the word of God!" Allen sat down but got his jocular revenge when Dewey was preaching a thanksgiving for the capture of Ticonderoga, giving rather more credit to God than Allen; he interrupted with mock pleading: "Parson Dewey, will you please mention to the Lord about my being there!"

ETHAN THE FREETHINKER

Although revered for his exploits with the Green Mountain Boys, Ethan Allen was also vilified in his day for his religious beliefs—or rather, his lack of religious beliefs. In his youth he had strayed from traditional Christianity and had become a deist, placing his faith in the powers of reason and science. Such a creed was suspect enough to his contemporaries, and he further scandalized them in his later years by writing a book, *Reason the Only Oracle of Man*. But when most of the first copies were destroyed in a mysterious fire at the printer's, everyone knew why: Jehovah had caused the fire as a sign of disapproval.

This book, plus Ethan's general reputation as a fighter, made him seem the Devil incarnate to some. So

it was that, when he lay dying, his wife anguished over her dilemma. She herself was a devout Christian, yet she knew how Ethan felt about such conventional pieties as deathbed rites. Finally, she decided to obey her own conscience, and she called in the local parson to comfort her husband in his final hours.

Now the minister was also well aware of Ethan Allen's opinions about religion and parsons, so he approached the deathbed most cautiously. Convinced that the old soldier was paralyzed and all but dead, the parson leaned over and said soothingly: "General Allen, the angels are waiting for you." At that, Ethan's eagle eyes sprang open and fired a glance like a musket shot. "Waiting, are they?" he rumbled like a cannon. "Waiting, are they? Well, God damn 'em, let 'em wait!" With that, Ethan Allen turned his face to the wall and died contentedly.

After his death his widow made another decision. Even though Ethan had denied the Christian idea of an afterlife, she made sure that a marble slab was placed over his grave. Years later, though, it was noticed that the stone had vanished. Again, the Vermonters knew why: Jehovah had crumbled it to pieces with a bolt of lightning—one final sign of displeasure with Ethan's rationalism.

But by 1850 that side of Ethan Allen's character was forgotten, or at least forgiven. The Vermont legislature voted funds to erect a monument to their state's founding father. When the people went to the graveyard and dug in the area where eyewitnesses confirmed he had been buried, none of his bones could be found. And after many searches for an explanation, the true story came out. It seems that years before, several medical students from Burlington had come and, as the owls hooted in protest from the nearby trees, dug up Ethan's body. They took it to their school and dissected it for their anatomical studies. So it was that Ethan Allen had the final word after all: he had always insisted that Science was to be the salvation of mankind.

THE SWAMP FOX
South Carolina's Robin Hood

Like Ethan Allen, Francis Marion of South Carolina has been compared to Robin Hood for emerging from the wilds to administer justice. In fact, stung by Marion's ability to pop in and out of the wildwood when least expected, his foe labeled him "Swamp Fox." According to one version of the story, Marion used the cry of the swamp fox as a signal—although no such animal exists in this country. He was a brilliant guerrilla and attracted followers in whom he inspired devout loyalty. That kind of man often becomes the focus of tales like these:

TUBER DINNER

Once when an exchange of prisoners had been agreed upon, a young British officer was sent to complete arrangements with Marion. He was conducted into camp blindfolded. When his eyes were unbandaged, a forest scene greeted his gaze. Groups of rudely costumed soldiers lay in the shadows of tall trees, and horses stood nearby ready to be mounted at a moment's notice. Before him stood Marion himself, short, slight, swarthy in complexion, with a quiet manner and a brilliant and searching eye. The young English officer was struck with astonishment. Were these the people who had filled the hearts of the Tories with terror? After business was over, the officer was asked to remain for dinner. He did so. Sweet potatoes smoking from the ashes were placed upon a piece of bark and set before the general and his guest.

"Doubtless this is an accidental meal," said the bewildered officer. "You live better in general?" "No," was the reply, "we often fare much worse." "Then at least I hope you draw a noble pay to compensate?" "Not a cent, sir," replied Marion.

When he finally returned to Georgetown, the officer reported that he had seen an American general and his officers, serving without pay and almost without clothes, living on roots and water—all for liberty. This officer resigned his commission for he felt that he could never again serve against such dedicated men.

MARION'S MEN SING

We follow where the Swamp Fox guides, [tree;
  We leave the swamp and cypress
Our spurs are in our coursers' sides,
  And ready for the strife are we.
The Tory camp is now in sight,
  And there he cowers within his den. [fight,
He hears our shout, he dreads the
He fears and flies from Marion's men.

BLACK MINGO BRIDGE

After weeks of futile pursuit the Tories gave up trying to catch the Swamp Fox, and he advanced southward. Information reached him that an enemy force was stationed on the Black Mingo River, and he determined to surprise and capture their camp. The only approach to it was over a plank bridge. Unfortunately, the galloping hooves of the horses as they crossed were heard through the stillness of the night, and an alarm gun warned the sleeping Tories of his approach. Marion then ordered a charge, and the patriots swept down on the enemy with irresistible fury. The Tories fled in confusion and their commander was killed. The surprise and the capture were complete. It is said that after this conflict Marion never crossed a bridge at night without first having his men spread blankets upon it to deaden the sound.

G. W. Mark's "Marion Feasting the British Officer" (detail below) well illustrates a famous tale, but Marion admirers would not believe that he'd put up with that cabin.

BRASH AND BOYISH DEEDS
Heroes of All Ages

Next to George Washington the most beloved soldier in Revolutionary America was Israel Putnam—a boy's hero, a "man of men." Like Cincinnatus of Roman legend, Old Put dropped his plow in midfield when he got the news of the battles of Lexington and Concord. A month later he was knee-deep in Chelsea Creek, brandishing a rifle at British swivel guns to show Goliath what could be done by the American David. The stories of his derring-do and that of many other brave Americans continued to be told long after the guns of battle had been silenced.

BOYISH HEROISM

On a fine May morning in 1780, as the family of Sheriff Firman, of Freehold County, New Jersey, was at breakfast, a breathless soldier burst into the room, stating that as he and another were conducting to the courthouse two men, taken up on suspicion at Colt's Neck, they had knocked down his comrade, seized his musket, and escaped. Firman, on hearing this account, mounted his horse and galloped to the courthouse to alarm the guard. The sheriff's son Tunis, a lad of about 17 and small for his age, seized a musket loaded only with small shot to kill blackbirds in the cornfields and, putting on a cartridge box, sent his little brother upstairs for the bayonet; then, forgetting to wait for it, he hurried off.

After running in a westerly direction for about a mile, he discovered the men sitting on a fence. Perceiving him, they ran into a swamp. As the morning was warm, he hastily pulled off his shoes and coat and darted in after them, keeping close to them for over a mile till they got out of the swamp and climbed into separate trees. As he came up, one of them discharged at him the musket taken from the guard. The ball whistled over his head. Feeling for his bayonet, he discovered that it was still with his little brother. He then pointed his gun at the man with the musket but deemed it imprudent to fire, reflecting that even if he killed him, his comrade could easily match such a stripling as himself. He compelled the man to throw down the musket by threatening him with instant death if he did not comply. Then, loading the fuse from his cartridge box, he forced his prisoners down from the trees and, armed with

In John Trumbull's flamboyant painting of the Battle of Bunker Hill (which actually took place on Breed's Hill), General Joseph Warren lies mortally wounded. The Bostonian had joined the battle as a volunteer and had chosen to fight in the ranks.

Down 100 stone steps the "old wolf" Putnam forced his horse as he escaped from Governor William Tryon whose 1,500 dragoons had almost reached him atop Horse Neck Hill in Connecticut. Putnam's 150 men had fired on Tryon and dashed to a swamp. As Putnam fled, a bullet passed through his hat; it is said Tryon sent him a new suit.

his two loaded muskets, drove them toward the courthouse, careful, however, to keep them far apart, to prevent conversation. Passing a spring, they requested permission to drink.

"No!" replied the courageous boy, understanding their design. "You can do without it as well as myself."

Soon after, his father, at the head of a party of soldiers, galloped past on the road within a short distance. Tunis hallooed but the clattering of their horses' hooves drowned his voice. At length he reached the village and put his prisoners in jail.

It was subsequently discovered that these men were brothers from near Philadelphia; that they had robbed and murdered a Mr. Boyd, a collector of taxes in Chester County, and, when taken, were on their way to join the British. As they had been apprehended on suspicion of merely being refugees, no definite charge could be brought against them. A few days later Sheriff Firman saw an advertisement in a Philadelphia paper, describing them, with the facts above mentioned and a reward of $20,000 (Continental money) offered for their apprehension. He, accompanied by his son, took them there, where they were tried and executed. On entering

Philadelphia, young Tunis was carried through the streets in triumph upon the shoulders of the military. In the latter part of the war this young man became very active and was the favorite of Gen. David Firman.

PUTNAM THE CAPTAIN

When a British major (during the French and Indian War) feeling himself insulted by Putnam sent him a challenge, Putnam requested an interview. The major came to Putnam's tent and found him sitting on a keg smoking a pipe: "I'm but a poor Yankee that never fired a pistol. If we fight with pistols, you have an advantage. Here are two powder kegs. I have bored a hole and inserted a match in each. If you will seat yourself, I will light the matches, and he who dares to sit the longest shall be called bravest." The matches were lighted. Putnam continued smoking. At length the major jumped up and, drawing out his match, cried: "Putnam, draw out your match. I yield."

"Don't be in such a hurry. They're nothing but kegs of onions!"

PUTNAM THE GENERAL

Shortly after the beginning of the war the Americans, guarded by a small

detachment of Putnam's men, were trying to move a herd of cattle toward Hog Island (now part of East Boston). They observed a red flag hoisted on the British schooner *Diana,* which was sailing with an armed sloop up Chelsea Creek nearby; she opened fire, providing cover for the British marines who advanced. Putnam ordered his men to dig in in the ditches alongside the creek, and when the British were a few rods from the Americans the order to fire was given and a surprisingly large number of English were killed.

Instructing his troops to get the cannons ready, Putnam went down to the shore close to the *Diana* and in his usual reckless fashion began to shout: "If you will surrender, you will be given the best of treatment." The British, exasperated by Putnam's nerve, fired two cannon shots. These were answered by cannon shots and reinforced by bullets from hundreds of rifles in the trenches. The British abandoned the *Diana,* and provincial soldiers set the schooner on fire. Then Putnam led his troops into the water up to their waists, and the Americans poured such fire into the sloop behind the *Diana* that almost everyone aboard was killed.

PRUSSIAN DISPATCH

Down south, when the governor of North Carolina put the cavalry of that state under Baron de Glaubeck's command, the baron found to his great astonishment that not a man among them had a sword. Therefore he ordered every man to supply himself with a substantial hickory club, one end of which he caused to be mounted with a piece of iron. Then, as an example, he threw aside his sword, armed himself with one of these bludgeons, and mounted his horse. Undaunted by their lack of proper arms, his whole unit rode toward Cornwallis' army, which had halted to take some refreshment. The baron seized this favorable opportunity, charged and routed two Hessian piquets, effectually bludgeoned three British regiments, and finally retreated with upward of 60 prisoners.

BENJAMIN FRANKLIN
Father of All Yankees

Benjamin Franklin is one of the first, and classic, cases of the American as a self-made man—in more than one sense. The poor, self-educated boy who by hard work rose to fame and fortune is true enough. Born in 1706 to a modest Boston merchant, he was so successful in his business ventures that by the age of 42 he could devote himself to public service and intellectual interests. Franklin was also a complex, sophisticated man, as comfortable with European aristocrats as with rustic colonials. Yet in much that he did he deliberately cultivated a folksy image, and thus he also made himself into the legendary Ben of popular lore.

POOR BOY

Although, in fact, Ben Franklin was an expert printer who rented a hotel room upon arrival in Philadelphia and found a job soon after, in his autobiography he preferred to dwell on the "poor boy" aspect of his life when he told of moving to the city. That story is adapted here:

I have been most particular in this description of my first entry into Philadelphia that you may compare such unlikely beginnings with the figure I have since made there. I was in my working dress, my best clothes to come round in a chest by sea. I was dusty from my journey. My pockets were stuffed with shirts and stockings. I was fatigued with traveling, rowing, and want of rest. I was very hungry, and my whole stock of cash consisted of a Dutch dollar and about a shilling of copper. I walked up the street gazing about, till near the market house I met a boy with bread. I inquired where he got it and went immediately to the baker's. I bade him give me three-penny worth of any sort. He gave me three great puffy rolls. I was surprised at the quantity but took it and, having no room in my pockets, walked off with a roll under each arm and eating the other. Thus I went up Market Street as far as Fourth Street, passing by the door of Mr. Read, my future wife's father, when she standing at the door saw me and thought I made, as I certainly did, a most awkward and ridiculous appearance.

HORSE SENSE

Travel was difficult in the American Colonies in Franklin's day, what with dirt roads, fractious horses, and exposure to the elements. And after hours of hard traveling, one often arrived at the only inn around to find it crowded. Once Franklin was passing through Rhode Island on a raw, rainy day. When he finally stopped at an inn, he discovered that numerous other travelers and locals had beat him there and were crowded around the fire. Wet and cold, Franklin quickly sized up the situation. In a loud voice he called to the boy on duty, "Boy, take my horse a quart of oysters." "A quart of oysters?" the boy exclaimed. "You heard me," pronounced Franklin as all eyes in the room turned on him. "A quart of oysters." Before the boy could do Franklin's bidding, there was a stampede out the door to see the phenomenal horse who ate oysters. But when the boy proffered the delicacies, as all the men stood by, the

No one has proved conclusively that Franklin flew a kite in a storm. He may have, but according to his own report he was 46 years old—not a patriarchal wizard surrounded by cherubs as depicted here in Benjamin West's famous portrait.

Poor Richard's Almanack

Franklin had been working in the printing and publishing field from the time he was 12. As owner of his own firm since 1730, he had printed others' almanacs and was well aware of their popularity. Along with the Bible, almanacs were among the few books found at every fireside. They featured helpful astronomical data—rising and setting of the sun, aspects of the moon, weather forecasts, and predictions based on astrology. Often they contained practical information on planting and harvesting, recipes, health aids, and a calendar of events such as fairs and court sessions. Some also contained odd facts, poems, even brief articles on scientific or other subjects.

That was standard almanac fare—dry and a bit dull—before Franklin brought out the first edition of *Poor Richard's Almanack* in 1732. It went through three printings in a month. His major innovation—and the fictional character that launched Franklin on his legendary career—was Richard Saunders, who spoke in the preface as the supposed author. Franklin molded him into "Poor Richard," a poor farmer, uneducated but full of horse sense, and pious but earthy. Because he and his wife, Bridget, were struggling to make a go of it, the average colonist could identify with them. Franklin astutely let Richard or Bridget write the preface to each edition. Beyond this, he had them refer to their domestic trials and triumphs, and this little drama gave a soap-operalike continuity to his almanacs. Since most writing in America till then had either religious or political themes, Franklin also deserves credit as an early American humorist. There was an element of comedy and even satire in much that Richard Saunders wrote—especially in his parodies of contemporary astrological predictions.

Franklin's gimmick of dispersing proverbs, maxims, and other sayings throughout the almanacs was not original. But Franklin exploited this tradition with a genius, for his sayings, coming as they seemed from Poor Richard, thus had a personal urgency. Franklin also ranged beyond the repertoire of proverbs familiar to his readers and took, as he himself admitted, "the gleanings of the sense of all ages and nations." He borrowed from other almanacs, ancient authors such as Aesop, as well as more modern writers, but he rewrote the material in a folksy style. "Fresh fish and newcome guests smell, by that they are three days old" became Poor Richard's "Fish and visitors stink in three days."

The best known of Poor Richard's sayings stressed the no-nonsense values of the ordinary colonist: hard work, thrift, moderation in tastes, prudence in all affairs. The most quoted (already ages old before Franklin adapted it) is "Early to bed and early to rise makes a man healthy, wealthy, and wise." Others include "Display is as false as it is costly" and "None preaches better than the ant, and she says nothing." Franklin occasionally also used the racy tone his age enjoyed: "Let thy maidservant be faithful, strong, and homely."

So it was that *Poor Richard's Almanack* became a bestseller in the colonies. It sold about 10,000 copies a year, approximately one for every 100 colonists. For the preface to the last edition, Franklin went through all his previous almanacs and skimmed off the many sayings about hard work, thrift, and ways to succeed. He strung these together as a speech given by "Father Abraham," an old man Richard Saunders heard at an auction. Then, following Poor Richard's advice on frugality, Franklin issued this preface as a separate volume, *The Way to Wealth,* one of the first American self-help books. That had an even greater success than the almanacs, going into several foreign translations and illustrated editions and was even issued as a children's book. Later attacked for its materialistic approach, it was deliberately one-sided in its aim —ironically, to help colonists save so they could pay their taxes to the British.

Franklin became so occupied with other affairs that he ceased publishing his almanac after 1758, but its influence continued. About 1796, a broadside called "Bowles's Moral Pictures" appeared with 24 woodcuts (some are shown here) illustrating such precepts as "Keep thy shop and thy shop will keep thee." Other almanacs and calendars trading on Franklin's name are being published to this day.

Kiteflying excepted, it is the almanac that is associated in most people's minds with Franklin today. And though by the time of the Revolution he was internationally known as a scientist, philosopher, statesman, and bon vivant, until his death most people identified Franklin with the pious, parsimonious, folksy Richard Saunders. When John Paul Jones named a ship outfitted for him by the French, he did not call it *The Franklin* or *The Washington*—but *Bonhomme Richard*.

horse refused to eat a single oyster. Some baffled, some bemused, they all trooped back into the inn. When they arrived in the main room, there was Benjamin Franklin sitting serenely in a chair close to the fire.

A WAY WITH THE LADIES
Along with his self-promoted image as the self-denying pennypincher, Franklin managed to create a second, if contradictory, image of himself as a ladies' man. True, he had an illegitimate son, but that was before his marriage and not uncommon in that age. It was during his years in Paris, as the colonies' representative to the French, that Franklin exploited his Casanova image to the fullest. Whether he really enjoyed the favors of all the ladies he was associated with can never be known. He was, after all, in his seventies, and most of the tales of his encounters come down to little more than flirtations. But he did realize the role that women played in high society in Paris—that their intelligence, wit, beauty, and other charms were often used to exert political influence. And so at times he had to be careful that his flirting did not make enemies for the colonies. Whenever he appeared in social gatherings, for instance, the ladies swarmed around him and exchanged kisses with him. Then each of the ladies would get him aside and ask if he did not care for her more than for any of the others. And Franklin would answer with words that combined his several reputations—ladies' man, honest Yankee, philosopher, diplomat, and scientist: "Yes, when you are closest to me—because of the force of attraction."

BEN THE MAGICIAN
If people were impressed with Franklin's diplomacy, they were fascinated with his electrical experiments; he was thought a sort of miracle-working wizard. Wherever he went, he was asked to demonstrate this incredible phenomenon, and he was not above playing such parlor tricks as animating tiny objects, firing pistols, burning materials, exploding gunpowder, or transmitting a charge through water. On at least one occasion he combined two of his interests—electricity and the ladies. He invited a young woman to sit on a special stool while he stood by with a concealed "wand" connected to a Leyden jar, a kind of battery. Then, as each young gentleman greeted her with a kiss, Franklin touched her with his wand. A light electric current rushed through her, and a spark from

One old folktale about Benjamin Franklin tells of his future wife falling in love with him at first sight. This picture is N. C. Wyeth's version of that magic moment.

her lips would drive the youth back, staggering and overwhelmed.

THE IMPERIAL GESTURE
En route to Paris in the autumn of 1776 as the delegate of the colonies, by then in open revolt, Franklin put up at a French inn. While registering, he was told that a fellow guest was Edward Gibbon, the English author of *The Decline and Fall of the Roman Empire*. Franklin sent his compliments to Gibbon's room and requested the pleasure of spending the evening in conversation. In response, Gibbon sent his card, stating that he could not have any conversation with a rebellious subject. So Franklin wrote a note to Gibbon, declaring that though principles compelled Gibbon to withhold his company, he, Franklin, still had great respect for the author. And if, as Gibbon wrote on the decline and fall of empires, the British Empire should come under his careful scrutiny, Franklin would be happy to furnish him with ample materials on the subject.

CHECKMATE!
During his many years in Paris Franklin became an avid chess player. He was apparently a fairly skillful player and his social drawing power made him a much-sought-after opponent whether at court parties or in cafes. And Franklin, well aware of the special thrill that the French got from playing against the noted American "revolutionary," had a favorite trick. He would wait until that point in a game when either his or his opponent's king was in check. Then he calmly reached down and took the king, pocketed it, and gravely continued the game. "Ah," his opponent would invariably say, though some said it more politely than others, "we do not take kings here." At which just as invariably Franklin replied, "We Americans do."

FATHER OF INVENTION
Franklin was responsible for several inventions and improvements of a practical nature—among them the lightning rod, a stove, bifocal spectacles. On one occasion he became convinced of the value of plaster of paris as a fertilizer. As a form of lime, it worked, but the conservative Pennsylvania farmers were reluctant to accept such a novelty. So Franklin chose a field close to the highway and wrote across it in plaster: THIS HAS BEEN PLASTERED. The locals were not especially amused but felt great glee as the letters vanished. Before long, however, the words reappeared—this time in a bright green that contrasted with the surrounding vegetation. The fertilizer had done its work, and Franklin had made his point.

INDEPENDENCE DAY
A Nation—and Myth—Are Born

A major tradition has it that America's independence was declared on July 4, 1776. In fact, the vote for independence was on July 2; its explanation, the Declaration, was accepted on July 4 and read publicly on July 8. As for the Liberty Bell, its role was the 1847 invention of George Lippard, whose stories about it (one is adapted below) did much to form our image of the Fourth.

THE FOURTH OF JULY

The mild clear light of a summer day was upon the roof and steeple of the old State House. It was toward the close of the day, when the trees shook their leaves in the rays of the setting sun. Not for its glorious beams alone does the scene arrest our attention but because the day marks an era in the history of Man. For all that day the Congress had been holding its secret session while the people awaited the result of its deliberations. Now from lip to lip a word thrills like electric fire—Independence!

Then, from that door with massive pillars come forth one by one the members of that solemn council. First a gentleman of mild appearance comes to the verge of the steps and stretches forth his hands. From lip to lip the murmur runs, "John Hancock, the President."

As he stretches forth his left hand, holding a parchment in his right, you see Franklin standing with uncovered brow. And over there, that form, tall and angular, the nether lip compressed, the nerves quivering with an emotion not the less deep because it is scarcely perceptible. It is Thomas Jefferson. Never king upon his throne, never conqueror on the battlefield, felt a deeper joy than thrilled Jefferson's bosom then!

Stouthearted John Adams stands between him and Franklin, his face beaming. An old soldier hobbles up to the foot of the steps and, with the marks of the Indian wars and Bunker Hill upon his face, gasps the words, "Well, President, is it all right?" Every ear in the throng hears his reply, spoken in calm, conversational tones. "It is. This day we have signed our Declaration of Independence! From this day there is no British dominion but the Republic of the United States of America."

Did you ever see a bolt of lightning stream in one red mass from the zenith and then scatter in a thousand rays? So these words rush into every heart and burst upon the crowd. The crowd is terribly still for a moment and then the murmur swells into a shout. At this moment, a little boy, whose golden hair tosses about his rosy cheeks, steals up the steps and clutches the President by the knee and whispers: "The old man in the steeple sent me down to ask you whether he should ring the bell."

Hancock presses his hands upon the head of the child and says: "You will live to see the day, my child, when the voice of that bell will have been heard by all the world! Tell the old man to ring!" Through the crowd, brave boy, and clap your tiny hands until the old man in yonder steeple hears you. Look! With his bronzed face and snow-white hair he bends from the steeple, he sees that child clap his hands. Then the old man bares his arm, and the bell on which is written, "Proclaim liberty throughout all the land unto all the inhabitants thereof," speaks to the People, and to a world that is in chains.

The tones of that bell go swinging over the city with a peal and a clang, saying to the kings on their thrones—and, of all the kings, to weak and wicked George of England—"Doom! Doom! Doom!" Then changing its peal it speaks to man: "Dawn! Dawn! Dawn!"

The Liberty Bell

This National Archives Building mural of the Founding Fathers (looking rather like classical heroes) is symbolic rather than factual. The signers of the Declaration were not able to gather at one time to ratify it; the signing took place over many months.

ICY MOMENTS
Courage and Long-sufferance

Two superhuman forces emerge from the folktales of the war against the English: winter and George Washington. The general's determination held steady against the ice at the Delaware Crossing in December 1776 and against the snow of Valley Forge a winter later. His resoluteness was matched by the "long-sufferance" he commended in his men—together they gave rise to legend. The following stories appeared 100 years after the war, so soldiers talk in 19th-century literary style.

John Frost's primitive of the Crossing (below) and Emmanuel Leutze's version (above) share a flag not designed until 1777.

Soldiers from Marblehead, Mass., former fishermen, rowed eight hours to ferry 2,400 men across the icy Delaware River from their retreat in Pennsylvania to battle Hessian mercenaries at Trenton, N.J. In the flagboat—Washington; on a raft—his white horse.

CROSSING THE DELAWARE

It was a dark and dreary night 99 years ago when in an ancient farmhouse an old man and his children gathered around their Christmas hearth. The old man, sitting in the full glow of the flame; his dame, a fine old matron; his children, a band of red-lipped maidens—some with slender forms just trembling on the verge of girlhood, others warming and flushing into the summer morn of womanhood! Had you, on that dark night while the December sky gloomed above and sleet swept over the hills, drawn near, you would confess that by that hearth burned a poetry like Heaven, that of Home!

Why does that old man's head droop down, his eyes fill, his hands tremble? He is thinking of the absent one, his manly brave boy, gone from the farmhouse for a year. But hark! A faint moan is heard over the wastes of snow from afar. The old man grasps a lantern and, with a young girl by his side, goes out softly over the frozen path. Something arrests the old man's eye, and they bend down, and they gaze upon that sight. It is a human footstep painted in the snow, painted in blood. "My child," whispers the old man, "now pray to Heaven for Washington! For by this footstep, stamped in blood, I judge that his army is passing near!"

Following those footsteps—one-two-three-four—the old man and the young girl reach a rock beetling over the river shore. There, the lantern flashes on the form of a half-naked man crouching in the snow. The old man looks upon that form clad in ragged uniform. It is his only son.

He called to him—and the young girl knelt and chafed her brother's hands. When she could not warm them, she gathered them to her young bosom and wept. Suddenly the brother raised his head and extended his hand. "Look there, Father!"

Bending over the rock, the old man looked. There, under the dark sky, a fleet of boats were tossing amid piles of floating ice. And that last boat just leaving the western shore of the Delaware, the old man saw that, too, and saw yon tall form, half muffled in a warrior's cloak, a warhorse by his side. "Father," gasped the brave boy tottering to his feet. "Give me my musket—help me on—for tonight—for tonight—" He fell and lay stiff and cold. On his lips hung faintly some words. "Tonight—Washington—the British—TRENTON!"

The old man did not know the meaning of that word until the next morning. Musketry to the south; booming along the Delaware the roar of battle. Then that old man with his wife and children gathered around the body of that dead boy, knew the meaning. George Washington had burst like a thunderbolt upon the British camp in TRENTON! The gleam of morning shone over yon cliff above the wintry river.

VALLEY FORGE

... The British took Philadelphia, and we took to the woods, into winter quarters at Valley Forge. We had dreamed of the winter in Philadelphia, of snug houses, warm clothing, full rations and sich, but General Howe had shut the door and we were turned out into the cold, the bare ground for our beds, the naked sky for a covering, and as for feathers for our beds, they came down presently, in the form of snowflakes.

Until our log huts were roofed in, we slept on the frozen ground, never taking our clothes off wet or dry, and they were often frozen so stiff that a man would rattle about in them as he walked, like a dried-up crab in his shell. Half a dozen of us would form a mess together, spread out straw, build a fire, and snuggle up close. One night the snow came swooping in whirlwinds. It stung like birdshot; the sentinels had to be relieved every 15 minutes so they would not freeze to death. When daylight came, some of the soldiers who slept in tents were under a foot of snow. These storms blocked the roads, and rations were cut down. For seven days the army was without a speck of meat. A thousand well-fed countrymen with old-fashioned flails could have thrashed the whole of us easy.

The soldiers sent up a committee to the officers. It was bread, or every man for himself. We knew perfectly well that the officers were hardly better off, yet pride kept them from complaining. We knew of their borrowing hats, coats, belts, yes, and even boots from each other, in order that they might appear decently before their commands on parade.

General Green promised to see what could be done by a personal appeal to the farmers of the Dutch country, who were mostly well off, snugger'n the bark of a tree; he was as good as his word. These little collections kept the army from disbanding.

Some folks imagine that while the soldiers were famishing, General Washington was living on the fat of the land, but that was not so. "Sir," his cook said one day, "we have nothing in the house to cook but the rations." "Well then, cook the rations," he replied.

Imagine a party of men with ragged clothes and no shoes huddled around a fire in a log hut; the snow about two feet deep on the ground, and the wind driving fierce and bitter through the chinks of the hovel. Many of the men had their feet frostbitten, and there were no remedies to be had. The sentinels suffered greatly as they paced before the huts. Washington often came over to see the poor fellows; I tell you, the men loved that man as if he had been their father, and would rather have died with him than lived in luxury with the redcoat general.

Josiah Jones was dying. He was lying on straw with nothing but rags to cover him. Josiah called out to us that he was dying and wanted us to pray for him. We loved him as a brother, but as for praying, we didn't exactly know how. To get clear of that duty, I ran for a drink of water to moisten his lips. While the rest were standing, not knowing what to do, someone heard the voice of George Washington in the next hut. Directly he came to our door, and the men told him the state of things. Now a commander in chief might have been justified in being angry that the regulations for the sick had been disobeyed, but he went up to Josiah and asked him how he was. Josiah told him he wanted someone to pray.

Washington knelt on the ground by him. We all knelt down too; we couldn't help it. He prayed to his Heavenly Father for mercy on the dying man's soul, to pardon his sins and take him to himself. Before the prayer was concluded, Josiah's spirit had fled. As a general, he was vigilant and skillful; but if he had been no more, we might have been crushed by the enemy. He had the love and confidence of the men on account of his character as a man.

On his white horse, Washington reviews troops at Valley Forge only 20 miles west of snug Philadelphia. The winter of 1777–78 was a mild one; nevertheless, 2,500 of Washington's 10,000 ill-supplied men died there and left a memory of blood on snow.

GEORGE WASHINGTON
Father to Us All

George Washington, with his modest yet commanding air and patrician looks, answered his countrymen's almost desperate need for a homebred hero. He also had enemies right up to the time of his death in 1799, who kept his image human. But the 19th-century writers—notably Jared Sparks and the self-serving Parson Mason Weems who wrote the cherry-tree episode and other stories as moral moneymakers—helped turn Washington into a rather dull, priggish cult object. By now, so much has been written about him that it is difficult to separate the man from the myth, but the stories that appear here are certainly pure invention.

WEEMS' CHERRY TREE

The following anecdote is too valuable to be lost, and too true to be doubted, for it was communicated to me by an excellent lady. "When George," said she, "was about six years old, he was made the wealthy master of a *hatchet!* of which, like most little boys, he was immoderately fond, and was constantly going about chopping. One day, in the garden, he unluckily tried the edge of his hatchet on the body of a beautiful young English cherry tree, which he barked terribly. The next morning, the old gentleman finding out what had befallen his tree, which was a great favorite, came into the house and with much warmth asked for the mischievous author. Nobody could tell him anything about it. Presently George and his hatchet made their appearance. *"George,"* said his father, *"do you know who killed that beautiful little cherry tree yonder in the garden?"* This was a *tough question,* and George staggered under it for a moment but quickly recovered himself, and looking at his father with the inexpressible charm of all-conquering truth, he bravely cried out: *"I can't tell a lie, Pa; you know I can't. I did cut it with my hatchet."* *"Run to my arms, you dearest boy,"* cried his father in transports, *"run to my arms. Glad am I, George, that you killed my tree, for you have paid me a thousandfold. Such an act of heroism in my son is worth more than a thousand trees, though blossomed with silver and their fruits of purest gold."*

JUDICIOUS GEORGE

Nothing was more common when the boys were in high dispute about a question of fact than for some little shaver among the mimic heroes to call out: *"Well, boys! George Washington was there; he knows all about it, and if he don't say it was so, then we will give it up."* *"Done,"* said the adverse party. Then away they would trot to hunt for George. Soon as his verdict was heard, the party favored would begin to crow, and then all hands would return to play again. . . . He was never guilty of so brutish a practice as that of fighting them himself, nor would he, when able to prevent it, allow them to fight.

"HERE!"

An Englishman in Philadelphia, speaking of the presidency of Washington, was expressing a wish to behold him. "There he goes!" replied the American, pointing to a tall, erect, dignified personage passing on the other side of the street.

"*That* George Washington!" he exclaimed. "Where is his guard?"

"Here!" exclaimed the American, striking his bosom with emphasis.

HERO WOMAN

Tory cutthroats are drinking and feasting in a farmhouse near Valley Forge, as they wait for 2 o'clock at night to kill Washington, whom they know will be passing then. Mary, the daughter of Jacob Manheim, one of the Tories, had been reared by her mother to revere this man Washington next to God. Yesterday afternoon, she went four miles, over roads

Grant Wood shows Parson Weems pointing to the famous scene that he created. The artist conveys the dehumanization that was wrought on George Washington by 19th-century orators, artists, and writers. Nathaniel Hawthorne was prompted to comment: "He had no nakedness but was born with his clothes on and his hair powdered."

Arnold Friberg illustrated Parson Weems' story about Washington praying in a lonely clearing near Valley Forge. A man who overheard him told his wife: "I am greatly deceived if God do not, through Washington, work out a great salvation for America."

of ice and snow, to tell Captain William the plot of the Tory refugees. She did not reach Valley Forge until Washington had left on one of his lonely journeys; so this night, at 12, a partisan captain will occupy the rocks above the neighboring pass, to "trap the trappers" of George Washington. Yes, that pale slender girl, remembering the words of her dying mother, had broken through her obedience to her father after a long and bitter struggle. How dark that struggle in a faithful daughter!

And now, as father and child are sitting there, hark! There is the sound of horses' hooves and the door opens—a tall stranger enters, advances to the fire, and in brief words solicits some refreshment and an hour's repose. Why does the Tory Manheim start aghast at the sight of that stranger's blue and gold uniform—then, mumbling something to his daughter about "getting food for the traveler," rush wildly into the next room? Ah—if we may believe the legends of that time, few men,

few warriors, who dared the terror of battle with a smile, could stand unabashed before the solemn presence of Washington. For it was Washington, exhausted with a long journey that had brought him thither earlier than the cutthroats expected, who was forced by a storm to take refuge.

In a few moments, behold the Soldier, with his cloak thrown off, sitting at that oaken table, partaking of the food spread out there by the hands of the girl, who now stands trembling at his shoulder. And look! Her hand is extended as if to grasp him by the arm—her lips move as if to warn him of his danger, but make no sound. One moment ago, *she heard the dice box rattle, as they were casting lots, who should stab George Washington in his sleep!* And now the words *"Beware, or this night you die!"* tremble half formed upon her lips when the father hushes her with a look.

"Show the gentleman to the chamber on the *left*, Mary. And look ye, girl—it's late—you'd better go into your own room and go to sleep."

While the Tory watches them, Washington enters the chamber on the left, Mary the chamber on the right. An hour passes. Before the fire are seven half-drunken men, with the father, Jacob Manheim, sitting in their midst, the murderer's knife in his hand. The lot had fallen upon him.

Even this half-drunken murderer is pale at the thought—how the knife trembles in his hand. The jeers of his comrades rouse him to the work. He enters the chamber on the left—he is gone a moment—silence!—there is a faint groan! He rushes down the stairs with the bloody knife.

"Look!" he shrieks, as he scatters the red drops over his comrades' faces, over the hearth. "It is his blood—the traitor Washington!" His comrades gather round him with yells of joy; already, in fancy, they count the gold which will be paid for this deed, when lo! that stair door opens, and there, without a wound, without even a stain of blood, calmly stands George Washington.

"What!" shrieks the Tory Man-

John McRae's engraving is supposed to show Washington arriving at the foot of Wall Street for his first inauguration. Despite the fact that the clothes are appropriate to the 1780's, the whole scene is pervaded with a rather exotic, Egyptian-barge quality.

heim, "can neither steel nor bullet harm you? Are you a living man? Is there no wound about your heart? No blood upon your uniform?" While Washington looks on in silent wonder, the door is flung open, the bold troopers from Valley Forge throng the room. Then a horrid thought crashes upon the brain of the Tory Manheim. He seizes the light—rushes upstairs, his blood curdles in his veins! Gathering courage, he enters. Toward that bed he struck at so blindly a moment ago! There, in the full light of the lamp, her young form but half covered, bathed in her own blood—lay his daughter, Mary!

In this pause of horror, listen to the mystery of this deed! After her father had gone downstairs, Mary silently stole from the chamber on the right. Then, though her existence was wound up in the act, she asked Washington in a tone of calm politeness to take the chamber on the opposite side. Mary entered the chamber when he left. Can you imagine the agony of that girl's soul as, lying on the bed intended for a death couch, she silently awaited the knife?

"Mary!" shrieked the guilty father—for robber and Tory as he was, he was still a father. Suddenly, she seemed to wake from that stupor. The strong hand of death was upon her. "Has *he* escaped?" she said, in that husky voice. "Yes!" shrieked the father. "Live, and tomorrow I will join the camp at Valley Forge."

Then that girl—that Hero Woman —dying as she was, not so much from the wound as from the deep agony which had broken the last chord of life, spread forth her arms, as though she beheld a form floating there above her bed, beckoning her away. She spread forth her arms as if to enclose that angel form. "Mother!" she whispered. "Mother, thank God! For with my life I have saved him—" That word, still quivering on the lips of the Hero Woman—that word choked by the death rattle—that word was—"Washington!"

NO WHITE MAN

Handsome Lake, an Iroquois prophet, told of a Christian-like heaven. But no white man ever got near there, with the exception of the Destroyer of Villages, as the Iroquois called George Washington. He lived in a fort with an enclosure around it, just outside the gate of heaven. Everyone who entered heaven saw him walking to and fro within it. His countenance indicated a great and good man. The Messengers told Handsome Lake: "The man you see is the only paleface who ever left the earth. He was kind to you when, on the settlement of the great difficulty between the Americans and the Great Crown, you were abandoned to the mercy of your enemies. The Crown told the great American that as for his allies, the Indians, he might kill them if he liked. The great American judged that this would be cruel and unjust. He believed they were made by the Great Spirit and were entitled to the enjoyment of life. He was kind to you, and extended his protection over you. For this reason, he has been allowed to leave the earth. But he is never permitted to go into the presence of the Great Spirit. Although alone, he is perfectly happy. All faithful Indians see him, recognize him, and pass by him in silence when they go to heaven. No word ever passes his lips."

FIRST IN WAR, FIRST IN PEACE, FIRST IN THE HEARTS OF HIS COUNTRYMEN

If Washington was a hero in life, upon his death he became a demigod. He was compared to Moses, Jesus, and the saints. He was portrayed in every noble guise, and nearly all American homes displayed his picture. Hundreds gained glory by claiming, "George Washington slept here." Countless stories and poems were written about him, and recounting his praises was a mandatory part of any public speech for more than 50 years after he died. In fact, orators had a major role in creating his legend. Here is a small sample of the flood of encomiums which washed away the real man:

Washington's fame will go on increasing until the brightest constellation in heaven is called by his name.

Like Moses, Washington led his countrymen through the dreary wilderness of the Revolution, and when the journey terminated he planted them upon the promised land of Freedom and Independence.

The old man's voice rang in deep solemn tones, while his eye burned as with the fire of prophecy: "The voice of God has spoken to me—'I will send a DELIVERER to this land, who shall save my people from physical bondage, even as my Son saved them from the bondage of spiritual death!'"

He is already become the saint of liberty, which has gathered new honors by being associated with his name.

Unbiased by mere emotions of the heart, he always regarded objects presented to his consideration with a steady eye and serene contemplation.

Washington was gigantic, but at the same time he was well proportioned and beautiful as in those fine specimens of Grecian architecture.

He is like the sun at meridian.

One artist chose to idealize the first president by dressing him as a Roman nobleman.

A Chinese painted Washington ascending to Heaven.

In an engraving after a C. W. Peale painting Washington is attired in armor, symbolizing knightly qualities.

This shield illustrates a 19th-century fable about the father of our country.

Noël Lemire's "Le Général Washington" (right) is suggestive of Napoleon in Egypt.

WITS AS WEAPONS
Women in the Revolution

Some stayed home and plowed. Some followed their men to the battlefield to cook and nurse, drawing half pay for themselves and quarter pay per child. Some filled the teacup to deceive the enemy. Some bound their breasts and put on pants to fight—it was not necessary to explain an unbearded face when there were so many soldiers of 14 and 15. The exploits of those who chose warfare, as well as of those who used wile, were romantically embroidered into popular legend.

MRS. MURRAY'S WILES

The British when they landed at Kip's Bay (in New York City in September 1776) made their way past the country seat of Robert Murray, a Quaker merchant of large wealth and known loyalty to the Crown. The merchant's wife and daughters, on the other hand, were ardent patriots and the day before had had Washington as their guest. When Howe and his staff (including Clinton and Cornwallis) and Governor Tryon reached this Quaker homestead near what is now Fifth Avenue and 37th Street, they were delighted to find Mrs. Murray and her lovely daughters at home and receiving guests.

"William, alight and refresh thyself at our house." "I thank you, Mrs. Murray, but I must first catch that rascally Yankee, Putnam." The general was not to be caught, however, if woman's wit could save him. "It is too late to catch him. Thee had better come in and dine."

The warmth of her welcome made him unmindful for hours of the task at hand and unaware that a battle was being waged several miles to the south. Finally, refreshed by good homemade cakes, heady homemade wine, and sprightly conversation, the officers rose, wiped their lips, and shook out the laces of their sleeves. But Dame Murray had another trick. The serving maid, to whom the officers had been paying superior attention, knew a song brought over from London—"Sally in Our Alley." Warmed with wine and flirtation, they settled down and listened through seven stanzas. When they emerged, the battle roar was dying down and clouds of black smoke were clearing from below. Then they learned that the British Army, for lack of staff direction, had let the Continentals slip through.

CROSS-EYED NANCY HART

In Elbert County, Georgia, there was a stream known as War-Woman's Creek—derived from the character of Nancy Hart, an uneducated and ignorant woman but a zealous lover of liberty and of the "liberty boys." She had a husband whom she denominated a "poor stick" because he did not take an active part in defending his country. This female patriot could

Her husband wounded, Molly Pitcher inspires the troops at Monmouth where 100 men died of the heat. "Sergeant Molly" got half pay for life from Congress. Rewarded for a similar deed, "Captain Molly" Corbin said: "Only *half* pay? No rum?"

boast no beauty; she was cross-eyed, awkward, and ungainly—but she had a woman's heart for her friends, and that of a tigress for the enemies of her beloved country.

One day a party of loyalists arrived at her cabin, entered unceremoniously, and ordered her to prepare them something to eat. "*That* you shall cook for us," said one, and raising his musket, shot down the turkey. She stormed and swore—for Nancy occasionally swore—but began cooking, assisted by her daughter, Sukey, a girl of 10, and sometimes by one of the party, with whom she exchanged rude jests, seeming in tolerably good humor. The Tories invited Nancy to partake of their liquor—an invitation which she accepted with jocose thanks.

Now the spring nearby was at the edge of a swamp, and a short distance within it was hidden a conch shell. Nancy sent Sukey for water, with directions to blow the conch for her father to "keep close" with his three neighbors. As the party had grown quite merry, the Tories stacked their arms before they sat down to feast. Water was called for and Sukey a second time dispatched to the spring to blow the conch. Meanwhile Nancy managed, by pushing out "chinking" between the cabin logs, to open a space through which she was able to pass outside two of the five guns. She was detected putting out the third, however, and the whole party sprang to their feet. Quick as thought, Nancy brought the piece to her shoulder. All were terror-struck, for Nancy's obliquity of sight caused each to imagine himself her destined victim. One made a movement and she shot him dead! Seizing another musket, she leveled it instantly. Sukey returned: "Daddy and them will soon be here." This information increased the alarm of the Tories, but each hesitated in the belief that Mrs. Hart had one eye on him. They proposed a general rush. She fired again and brought down another. Sukey had another musket in readiness, which her mother took and called the party to surrender "their d----- Tory

Cross-eyed Nancy Hart did not need to leave her Georgia cabin to enjoy a crack at local loyalists whom she wined, dined, shot at, and hanged; the 18th-century woman was expected to defend the home, which, as a married female, she did not legally own.

carcasses to a Whig woman." Her husband and neighbors came to shoot them down, but Mrs. Hart swore "shooting was too good for them." They were bound and taken out and hung. "A honey of a patriot—but the devil of a wife!"

SALLY SAINT CLAIR

About the beginning of the war, Sergeant Jasper of Marion's brigade had the good fortune to save the life of a beautiful dark-eyed Creole girl, Sally Saint Clair. Overcome with gratitude,

A patriot applies a broom to a redcoat who is trying to lower her country's flag.

she lavished upon him the depths of a passion nurtured by a southern sun. When he was called to join his country's defenders, the prospect of separation almost maddened her. She severed her long and jetty ringlets, provided herself with male attire, and set forth to follow her lover.

A smooth-faced, delicate stripling appeared among the rough and giant frames that composed the corps to which Jasper belonged. But none was more eager for battle or so indifferent to fatigue than the fair-faced boy. None suspected him to be a woman, not even Jasper. She fed her passion by gazing upon him in his slumber, hovering near when they stole through swamp and thicket, and being always ready to avert danger from his head. An eve before battle, by the flicker of watch fires burning low, reposed the warlike form of Jasper. The smooth-faced stripling bent down as if to listen to his dreams. Tears trace down the fair one's cheek and fall upon the brow of her lover. A mysterious voice has told her that tomorrow her life's destiny will be consummated.

On the morrow, foremost in battle is Jasper, and by his side fights the stripling. Suddenly a lance is leveled at the breast of Jasper, but swifter than the lance is Sally Saint Clair. There is a wild cry and at his feet sinks the maiden, the lifeblood gushing from the white bosom, which had been thrust as a shield before his breast. He heeds not now the din, but down by the dying boy he kneels. Then for the first time does he learn that the stripling is his love.

MOLLY AT MONMOUTH

It was hot on June 28, 1778; even at daybreak the air was still. Later in the day the temperature climbed to 100 degrees in the shade. Molly Hays, though a strong, sturdy woman, sometimes felt as if the Revolutionary War would never end. Even before the Declaration of Independence, she had gone with her husband into battle. Along with other wives, she did washing and cooking. She worked as a nurse during the fighting, and she also learned about cannons. John Hays, who had been a gunner before he joined the infantry, turned to his wife and said: "Get your things together. We're moving."

The Battle of Monmouth had begun. The burst of muskets never stopped. The air was cloudy with gunsmoke, and the heat smothered everyone. Molly Hays found a cool spring. Grabbing her pitcher, she scooped up water for the soldiers. One by one, soldiers dropped from gunshots or heat. She bent over a hurt soldier. "Chew on this cold rag." Pitcher after pitcher she carried, until the soldiers began calling her Molly Pitcher. She swabbed blood, cleaned out wounds, wrapped cloths around arms and legs. Running through musket fire, Molly Hays looked down at a young soldier. "Mam," he gasped, "get away. You will be shot." Gently she swung him on her strong shoulders and carried him out of the line of fire. She ran from stream to soldier, from soldier to stream. Then she spotted her husband loading a cannon. "John! Why aren't you with the infantry?" John Hays pointed to the ground; a soldier lay dead. "I am taking his place." Molly was filling her pitcher again when she saw her husband fall, badly wounded. She ran to him, when an officer spoke:

"Please move on, mam, we are going to move this gun away." "Give me that rammer staff!" She swabbed, loaded the cartridge and charged the cannon, ramming down the cartridge. "Aim! Fire!" Through the sweltering afternoon she swabbed, rammed, and fired. After the battle, General Washington asked her, "Madam, who are you?" "Mary Ludwig Hays, sir. They call me Molly." "You are now Sergeant Molly," he replied.

"ROBERT" SAMSON

As a youngster, Deborah Samson was taken from her poverty-ridden home and indentured to a kindly farmer. She was treated well and provided with food and clothing but not with an education. However, she borrowed books from children who passed the house to and from school, and persevered till she had learned to read. When she turned 18 the law released her from her indenture, and she began to attend the common school. Her improvement was rapid beyond example. Meantime, news of the carnage on the plains of Lexington and of the shooting at Bunker's Hill had reached every dwelling. Her youthful imagination was kindled by the brave deeds she was told of, and Deborah bitterly regretted she had not the privilege of shedding blood for her country. By keeping the district school for a summer term, she amassed $12, purchased a quantity of fustian, and slowly and laboriously made up a suit of men's clothing, each article being hidden in a stack of hay. Having completed her outfit, the lonely girl made her way to the American Army and enrolled, using her brother Robert's name. Accustomed to farm labor, she had acquired unusual vigor and strength.

"Robert" was a volunteer in several hazardous enterprises and once when wounded was carried to a hospital. Her leg burned with pain yet she could only think of one thing: that a doctor might find out she was a

The Revolution was fought under local banners: the 13-star flag that Betsy Ross shows to George Washington was not flown until 1783. The disputed legend of the Philadelphia seamstress' designing of the flag was first told by one of her grandchildren in 1870.

woman. She knew of a nearby cave where she could get the bullet out unseen and she managed to creep there from the hospital under cover of night. She cut her leg, deeper and deeper; at last, with a quick thrust, she pried the bullet out, and somewhat recovered, she limped back to take her place at her post; not for long, however. She was seized with a brain fever then raging among the soldiers, but she suffered most from dread that consciousness would desert her and the secret she guarded so carefully be revealed. Considered a hopeless case, she was carried to the hospital. "How is Robert?" "Poor Bob is gone." The doctor went to the bed, found her pulse still beating, and attempting to place his hand on the heart, perceived a tightly fastened bandage. Dr. Binney said not a word and had her taken to his house to give her better care. A young and lovely niece, an heiress, was touched by the pale and melancholy soldier and made known her attachment, offering to provide for the education of its object before their marriage. Deborah merely said they would meet again.

From the time of her removal into the doctor's family, she had anxiously watched his countenance and flattered herself that she was safe from detection. But he conferred with her commanding officer and "Robert" was ordered to carry a letter to George Washington; she could no longer deceive herself. Her heart sank as the chief bade her retire while he read the communication. She was summoned again and he said not a word but handed her a discharge, a tactful note of advice, and money sufficient to bear her home. Later she was granted land and a pension for her services.

POWDER FOR FORT HENRY

Her arms blackened with charcoal, Betty Zane lifted the ladle from the coals and poured the hot metal with a

The ladies of Edenton, North Carolina, look almost too busy to sign their resolution against drinking English tea or wearing English fabrics, which they were willing to do although it took a year to make a homespun suit.

steady hand. Too much or too little lead would make an imperfect ball. Lydia dipped the mold in water, removed it, and knocked it on the floor. A small, shiny bullet rolled out. She rubbed it with a greasy rag and dropped it in a jar. For nearly 40 hours the women had been at their post in Ohio, fighting Indians allied to the British. Silas Zane came running into the room: "The powder's gone! What can we do?" "Send someone to Eb's cabin fer powder. It's only about a hundred yards from here," answered Wetzel.

Three men stepped forward and volunteered. "They'd plug a man full of lead afore he'd get 10 foot from the gate," said Wetzel. "Send a boy, one as can run like a streak." "Harry Bennet might go," said Silas. "He is dead." The women covered their faces. "I will go." It was Betty's voice, and it rang clear and vibrant throughout the room. "I would rather die that way than remain here and wait for death."

"Silas, it ain't a bad plan. Betty can run like a deer. And bein' a woman they may let her get to the cabin without shootin'." "Betty, Heaven

bless you, you shall go," said Silas. "Run, but save your speed. Tell the colonel to empty a keg of powder in a tablecloth. Start back, run like you was racin' with me, and keep on comin' if you get hit."

The huge gate creaked, and as Betty ran out, taunting yells filled the air: "Squaw! Waugh!" The yells ran all along the riverfront, showing that hundreds of Indians had seen the slight figure running up the slope toward the cabin. She ran easily, and Colonel Jonathan Zane flung open the door. "We are out of powder. Empty a keg into a tablecloth. Quick!" He came out with a keg. With one blow of an ax he smashed in the top; in a twinkling a long black stream of the precious stuff was piling up in a hill. Then the corners of the cloth were caught up and twisted and the bag was thrown over Betty's shoulder. "Brave girl, so help me God, you are going to do it!"

Like an arrow Betty flashed out. Scarcely 10 of the 100 yards had been covered when angry yells warned Betty the keen-eyed savages knew they had been deceived by a girl. The leaden messengers of Death whistled past Betty, scattering pebbles in her path, striking up dust, and plowing furrows in the ground. A quarter of the distance covered! The yelling and screeching had become deafening, yet above it Betty heard Wetzel's stentorian yell. Half the distance covered! A hot, stinging pain shot through Betty's arm. The bullets sang over her head, hissed close to her ears, and cut the grass in front of her. Three-fourths of the distance covered! Betty saw the big gate swing. On! On! On! A blinding red mist obscured her sight; unheeding she rushed on. Another second and she stumbled, felt herself grasped by eager arms, heard the gate slam and the iron bar shoot into place. Silas Zane bounded up the stairs with a doubly precious burden in his arms, and a mighty cheer went up.

NAVAL UPS AND DOWNS
Games of Jones and Barney

Quick strikes at the enemy in Europe were the key to the Continental Navy's success. John Paul Jones, in a seemingly hopeless situation off the English coast, defiantly announced, "I have not yet begun to fight!" and proceeded to lead the crew of the Bonhomme Richard *to victory over the* Serapis. *Jones had a verve that inspired French women, American novelists, and Scottish taletellers. But verve could go awry, too, as the tale of Joshua Barney at Newport illustrates.*

JOSHUA BARNEY

Joshua Barney had a successful cruise, having taken $1.5 million worth of enemy shipping in 90 days, and sailed into Newport to refit. The people of that town were delighted. They lined the waterfront waving handkerchiefs and cheering. They even gave him a naval salute from the fort. Not to be outdone, and to show his appreciation, Barney ran out his guns and fired a broadside. Unfortunately, he had forgotten that the guns were shotted; the town was severely battered and one innocent bystander lost a foot.

On another occasion, Barney was bound for Bordeaux in a small privateer with a load of tobacco. On the way across, he captured a vessel loaded with a cargo of crowbars, some of which he took into his ship. Shortly after this, he was pursued by a large British privateer named the *Rosebud*. Barney tried to get clear, but the *Rosebud* was a better sailor and slowly gained on him until he was in reach of the *Rosebud*'s Long Toms. At this point, Captain Duncan and Captain Barney made a discovery. Barney's ship had no stern ports, so she could not return the Englishman's fire, and all the *Rosebud* had to do was to lie astern of Barney and pound the American to pieces.

During the night, Barney had a hole cut in his stern and a six-pounder mounted in his cabin. He also had a canvas dodger designed and fitted to cover this new gun port. Next morning the *Rosebud* again commenced firing from astern, and Barney allowed her to come very close. At the opportune moment he

Beneath Manhattan Bay, Ezra Lee cranked the propellers of David Bushnell's *Turtle* and moved out to Howe's *Eagle*. Lee was to drill into the *Eagle*'s copper-sheathed wooden bottom with an iron screw that floated a timed torpedo. But Lee drilled in vain at an iron plate. Dawn came; he set the bomb free but the ensuing explosion failed to "pulverize the British Navy," which shamed Bushnell.

dropped the canvas, ran out his gun, and delivered a charge into the bows of the unsuspecting Englishman. What made things even more shocking was that instead of loading his six-pounder with conventional ammunition, he had crammed it full of crowbars. The result was catastrophic. Forty men were killed, the rigging was shot away and the *Rosebud*'s mast so damaged she had to break off the battle to save herself, while Barney went on to Bordeaux to make money selling his tobacco.

JOHN PAUL JONES

Stories are still told in Scotland about Jones' less known harassment of the British in the old *Ranger* and his attempt to sack Edinburgh in the *Bonhomme Richard*.

It seems that word of Jones' activity had spread all along the coast, and when he appeared off the Firth of Forth the laird of the castle mistook him for a British man-o'-war. Either as an act of patriotism or as a device to ingratiate himself with the British, the laird sent his servant out in a small boat with a keg of powder and a letter requesting the captain to use said powder to destroy the Yankee pirate. Jones took the powder, wrote a thank-you note saying the powder would be used to good advantage, signed it, and sent the servant back with it to the laird.

While this was going on, word came to Edinburgh of Jones' intentions and position. The town was in dismay. There was neither sufficient ordnance nor troops in the area to repel the American force, and it seemed as if the town must fall. About the only thing that could save Edinburgh was a westerly gale, and that seemed unlikely. At any rate, word of the predicament reached the old bishop, and he decided to take stern measures. He ordered a chair and proceeded down to the shore. The tide was out, and the old man marched out onto the flats until his feet were wet. There he planted his chair and there he sat down. Raising his eyes and voice he prayed: "Lord, I have served you well over 40 years. Either send a gale to drive away the pirate who is coming to attack our town or I will sit here until I drown. Amen." The tide turned; the water rose to the old man's ankles. There sat the bishop grimly confronting the sea. The water reached his chest. Then the wind hauled west and blew a gale. The old man rose, retrieved his chair, and went ashore.

It is hard enough to beat up the Firth of Forth in a close-winded yacht in a heavy breeze. For Jones it was impossible. Every hour he was delayed was an hour in which relieving forces could draw closer. After a day and a night, John Paul Jones and his keg of powder squared away and departed in search of other game.

Mottoes of Revolution

In the 1760's the Thirteen Colonies' biggest grievance with the mother country was taxation. The British aimed to make every colonist a "bond slave," said Samuel Adams early in the decade. It fell to Boston attorney and radical publicist James Otis to coin (in 1761) the earliest and most effective of all Revolutionary slogans: "Taxation without representation is tyranny."

The Stamp Act of 1765 outraged Americans, and Patrick Henry gave voice to the people's anger in an inflammatory speech at the Virginia Convention that year: "Caesar had his Brutus; Charles I his Cromwell; and George III ["Treason!" shouted the Speaker] *may profit by their example.* If *this* be treason, make the most of it."

Almost 10 years later, Patrick Henry again climaxed a speech with fighting words: "I know not what course others may take; but as for me, give me liberty, or give me death!"

Just before the fighting began on Lexington Green on April 19, 1775, Capt. John Parker ordered his minutemen: "Stand your ground. Don't fire unless fired upon, but if they mean to have a war, let it begin here." A few moments later the roar of the guns marking the onset of the Revolutionary War was heard in Lexington; Samuel Adams is said to have exclaimed: "What a glorious morning is this!"

When Ethan Allen demanded the surrender of Ticonderoga, the British commander asked in whose name he spoke. The Vermonter supposedly replied: "In the name of the Great Jehovah and the Continental Congress."

At the Battle of Bunker Hill, Israel Putnam (or his comrade William Prescott) gave this celebrated military order: "Men, you are all marksmen—don't one of you fire until you see the white of their eyes."

Radical clergymen urged their flocks to support the Revolutionary cause. Preaching a farewell sermon in January 1776, the Virginian John Peter Gabriel Muhlenberg declared: "There is a time to pray and a time to fight. This is the time to fight." Then he threw off his minister's gown, revealing beneath it a militia officer's uniform.

When he finished writing his famous giant signature on the Declaration of Independence, the Bostonian John Hancock said: "There, I guess King George will be able to read that." On the same occasion Hancock also supposedly remarked: "We must be unanimous; there must be no pulling different ways; we must all hang to-

Patrick Henry folk portrait

gether." "Yes," Ben Franklin is said to have rejoined," we must indeed all hang together, or most assuredly we shall all hang separately."

Connecticut-born Nathan Hale accepted a spy mission in September 1776, but was arrested and hanged by the British at New York. His legendary last words: "I only regret that I have but one life to lose for my country."

Philadelphia radical Thomas Paine served in Washington's army in the dark days of December 1776 and

The Nathan Hale powder horn

wrote a tract, *The Crisis,* that was read aloud to inspire the troops on the eve of what was to be their victory in the Battle of Trenton: "These are the times that try men's souls. The summer soldier and the sunshine patriot will in this crisis shrink from the service of their country: but he that stands it *now* deserves the love and thanks of man and woman."

A favorite device, which appeared on various Revolutionary battle flags, was a coiled rattlesnake with the motto: "Don't Tread on Me."

The Scottish-born John Paul Jones was to make one of the most celebrated statements of American defiance in 1779 when his ship *Bonhomme Richard* was blown apart by cannon fire from the Royal Navy's *Serapis.* The British captain asked if the Americans were ready to strike their colors, and Jones replied: "Sir, I have not yet begun to fight!" (Two hours later, after a wild battle fought by moonlight, the *Serapis* surrendered and Jones transferred his surviving crew to the British warship, abandoning the *Richard.*)

"Soldier pastor" James Caldwell's New Jersey church was burned down by a Tory, and his wife was killed by a stray shot from a Hessian gun. Soon after the latter event, when Caldwell's comrades ran out of wadding to reload their muskets, he led them to a nearby church, where they ripped up a bunch of old Watts hymnals to serve as extempore wadding. Thereafter, when going into battle, Caldwell encouraged his fellows thus: "Put Watts into 'em, boys! Give 'em Watts!"

There was not only defiance but vast ambitiousness in the Spirit of '76. "An empire is rising in America," Sam Adams proclaimed, and his words were to be regularly repeated by other New England leaders, by advertisers in Philadelphia newspapers, and by southern planters. "The Almighty has made choice of the present generation," exulted William Henry Drayton of South Carolina, "to erect the American Empire. It bids fair to be the most glorious of any upon record."

YANKEE DOODLE DANDY

Sprightly tempo

Yan-kee Doo-dle went to Lon-don rid-ing on a po~ny, He stuck a feath-er
Fath'r and I went down to camp, A~long with Cap-tain Good-in'. And there we saw the

in his cap and called it mac-a~ro-ni.
men and boys as thick as has-ty pud-din'. { Yan-kee Doo-dle keep it up,

Yan-kee Doo-dle dan-dy; Mind the mu-sic and the step and with the girls be han-dy.

And there we saw a thousand men,
　As rich as 'Squire David;
And what they wasted every day,
　I wish it could be saved. (Chorus)

And there we saw a swamping gun,
　Large as a log of maple,
Upon a deuced little cart,
　A load for father's cattle. (Chorus)

And every time they shoot it off,
　It takes a horn of powder,
And makes a noise like father's gun,
　Only a nation louder. (Chorus)

And there was Captain Washington,
　And gentlefolks about him,
They say he's grown so tarnal proud,
　He will not ride without 'em.

He got him on his meeting clothes,
　Upon a slapping stallion,
He set the world along in rows,
　In hundreds and in millions

The flaming ribbons in his hat,
　They look'd so tearing fine ah,
I wanted pockily to get,
　To give to my Jemimah.

When the hated British regiments arrived in Boston in 1768, there were skyrockets and jollity as their band struck up "the Yankee Doodle Song" —a ditty that probably included insults about American cowardice during the French and Indian War. British fifers continued to taunt Bostonians with this tune and may even have played it outside their church doors during services. British drummers drummed it on the way to Lexington and Concord. After the Battle of Bunker Hill, the Americans took heart and snapped up the tune as their own. Eventually, they mortified the British by playing it triumphantly at the surrender proceedings after Saratoga and, some say, at Yorktown. By then the song had come to represent—and celebrate—brash, cocky America itself.

The tune, says folklorist Tristram Coffin, has links to Italian church music, Hungarian dance melodies, and various farm songs. Dutch reapers sang *"Yanker, dudel, doodle, down/ Diddle, dudel, lanther;/ Yanker, viver, voover, vown/ Botermilk and tanther"* to the tune. (Jan, the simpleton, will get milk and a tenth of the harvest.) According to Coffin, the Dutch brought this song to Nieuw Amster-

dam to sing against the English colonists who "affect a disgusting preeminence and take the lead in everything."

Coffin recollects the saying that a folksong's tune and its lyric are like Hollywood stars who meet, marry, and usually separate. The song's opening line stems from Oliver Cromwell's ride into Oxford after which the Cavaliers derided him with "Nanki" (whose meaning is obscure) "doodle came to

Macaroni hairdo provides base for Battle of Bunker Hill

town upon a Kentish pony." The feather called macaroni dates to a London fad of the 1760's and 1770's when the chic ate Italian macaroni every night, tied their hair in enormous topknots christened "macaronis," and wore tight clothes. Macaroni clubs formed, macaroni schools of music and art flourished: to be "in" was to be "macaroni." The admonition to "mind the music" remains from the melody's popularity as a dance tune.

Though no one knows who Captain Gooding was, most agree that a British army surgeon Richard Schuckburg wrote "Father and I," etc. One afternoon during the French and Indian War, Shuckburg watched the arrival of some Connecticut soldiers in Albany. He dashed off some rhymes about their bumpkinlike appearance, which brought laughter in the messhall. An undocumented coda says the regiment was led by Thomas Fitch whose wife Elizabeth—seeing the shabby state of the men bound for Albany—dashed into her chicken yard and plucked a few feathers for their hats. "Damn me," Schuckburg supposedly said, "they're macaronis!" The song grew, collecting myriad verses, and nearly became our national anthem.

The Legendary Backwoodsman

It had all started in the 1760's, despite the Crown's admonition not to go over the mountains. The land beyond the Appalachians was scouted by long hunters, so called for their protracted fur-hunting jaunts. Most famous them all was Daniel Boone, who led a party of pioneers through the Cumberland Gap into Kentucky. When the settlers spread out into the backwoods country west of the Appalachians, they developed a special strai of rugged individualism—brutal, brash, and boisterous. A new social type—the frontiersman—was born. As a legendary figure he was to be the prototype of all subsequent "western" heroes. More often than not, based o the exploits of real characters such as Boone and Davy Crockett, the frontiersman legend accurately reflects the fortitude and tribulations of the 300,000 who traveled up Boone's trail, the Wilderness Road, during the heroic perio

"A frontiersman speaking in a voice loud enough to be visible" (from a *Crockett Almanac*)

Daniel Boone and his party are shown viewing the unexplored plains of Kentucky from a vantage point overlooking the Red River, in this composition by T. Gilbert White.

of westward expansion. Others, passing through Ohio, camped down next to apple orchards planted by Swedenborgian missionary "Johnny Appleseed" Chapman (one of the rare white men to be well received by the Shawnees, whom he regaled with stories of visitations from spirits and angels). In a futile attempt to oppose the white invasion of their territory, the Indians of the Old Northwest formed a defensive confederation under the leadership of the Shawnee war chief Tecumseh (Shooting Star) and his prophet brother. They allied with the British in 1812, but the confederation collapsed when Tecumseh fell in a battle in 1813 won by the U.S. About a year later, frontier sharp-shooters under Andrew Jackson inflicted a crushing defeat on British regulars at the Battle of New Orleans. Overnight, the legendary frontier type was embodied in Jackson, a national hero destined to be the first "people's president."

In Revolutionary times, "horse-alligator" was a cliche for privateers like John Paul Jones. After 1800, the term described the ring-tailed roarer frontier type: "Men of the real half-horse, half-alligator breed grow no-where on the face of the universal earth but just about on the back-bone of North America."

DANIEL BOONE
Long Hunter of Kentucky

In 1767 the 33-year-old Daniel Boone made the first of his celebrated "long hunts" across the Appalachians into the Kentucky territory; he continued to explore that wilderness until he died. A chivalrous fellow in real life, Boone became a Robin Hood figure in legend, always arriving in the nick of time to save fellow pioneers from captivity or violent death, often by means of such time-honored folk stratagems as the knife-swallowing trick recounted here.

BOONE BRAGS

Once on a hunting expedition on the Green River as I rambled through the woods in pursuit of the sons of the soil, the Indians outwitted me. No sooner had I extinguished the fire of my camp and laid me down to rest than I felt myself seized by an indistinguishable number of hands, and I suffered myself to be removed from my camp to theirs without uttering a word of complaint. By so doing I proved to the Indians that I was as fearless of death as any of them.

When we reached the camp, great rejoicings were exhibited. I was assured by unequivocal gestures that the mortal enemy of the redskins would soon cease to live. The women fell a-searching about my hunting shirt for whatever they might think valuable and, fortunately for me, soon found my flask filled with Monongahela (that is, reader, strong whisky). The crew began to beat their bellies and sing, as they passed the bottle from mouth to mouth. As I observed that the squaws drank more freely than the warriors, the report of a gun was heard. The men took up their guns and left the squaws to guard me. In a minute they had my bottle up to their mouths again.

They tumbled down, rolled about, and began to snore; I rolled over and over toward the fire and burned my cords asunder. I rose on my feet, stretched my stiffened sinews, snatched up my rifle, and for once in my life spared the Indians, who were unprepared to defend themselves. Before leaving I was determined to mark the spot, and walking to a thrifty ash sapling, I notched it

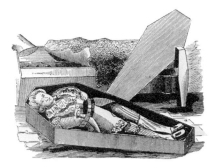

Legend has it that in later years Boone kept a coffin under his bed and, when the mood struck, he would try it on for fit.

three times with my tomahawk and ran off. Imitating Indian tracks so that my path would not be recognized, I soon was far out of danger.

Twenty years later, I was called as a witness in a lawsuit in Kentucky. It seems that a gentleman had used my tree markings as one of the locators in surveying some thousands of acres, and a corner of the land was described in the land deed as "at an ash marked by three distinct notches."

The tree had grown much, and the bark had covered the marks, losing the man proof of his property; somehow he heard the story of my escape and thought that I might remember the spot alluded to in the deed. He wrote to me offering to pay my expenses if I would come once again to Kentucky. I considered for a while and began to think that after all I could find the very spot, as well as the tree, if it was yet standing.

Off I went with the landowner to the Green River Bottoms. After some difficulties, I found at last the spot where I had crossed the river and, waiting for the moon to rise, made

for the course in which I thought the ash tree grew. On approaching the place, I felt as if the Indians were still there, so I camped till morning.

At the rising of the sun I mused some, staring at a particular ash tree. When I felt there was no doubt about it, I told my companion that his search was over. "Well, Colonel Boone," said he, "if you think so, I hope it may prove true, but we must have some witnesses"; and he trotted off to find some settlers whom he knew. When he returned, he was accompanied by three gentlemen. They looked upon me as if I had been George Washington himself, and walked to the ash tree as if in quest of a long-lost treasure. I took an ax from one of them and cut a few chips off the bark. Still no signs were to be seen. I cut again until I thought it was time to be cautious, and I scraped and worked away with my knife until I *did* come to where my tomahawk had left an impression in the wood. We now went regularly to work and scraped at the tree with care, until three hacks as plain as any three notches ever were could be seen.

BOONE KILLS A SHE-BEAR

Once when Boone was all alone in Indian territory, he found himself pursued by four Indians. After several unsuccessful attempts to shake them off his trail, he suddenly realized what he must do. Hastening on through the woods he found a large grapevine sufficiently strong to support his weight and, disengaging it from the roots, climbed it a few feet. When he had attained the necessary height, he gave himself so strong an impulse from the tree that he reached the ground some yards away and thus broke his trail.

Safe from the Indians, he soon met with a second adventure in which he encountered a foe scarcely less formidable. Hearing the approach of what he judged to be a large animal, he held his rifle ready and drew from its sheath a long and sharp knife. He determined to try the efficacy of his rifle first. As the animal came in sight, it proved to be a she-bear.

In this lurid lithograph published by Currier and Ives, Daniel Boone defends his family against an Indian's attack. The theme is as improbable as the costumes; in real life he coped with the "savages" by avoiding them or making friends.

As soon as the animal perceived him, it gave indications of an intention to make battle. Boone leveled his rifle and remained quiet, until his aim was sufficiently near to enable him to shoot with effect. In general, his aim was sure, but this time the wound inflicted only served to render the animal mad with rage and pain. It was impossible for him to reload and discharge his gun a second time before the she-bear would be upon him, and yet he did not relish the idea of grappling with it so closely.

His knife was the resource to which he instantly turned. He held it in his right hand in such a position that the bear could not reach his person without receiving its point. His rifle, held in his left hand, served as a kind of shield. Thus prepared, he awaited the onset of the formidable animal. When within a foot of him, it reared up to grasp him with its huge paws. In this position the she-bear pressed upon the knife until the

whole blade was buried in its body. Boone had pointed it directly to the heart of the animal. The she-bear fell harmless to the ground.

"The Abduction of Daniel Boone's Daughter," by Charles F. Wimar. Daniel's subsequent daring rescue of daughter Jemima from Chief Hanging Maw and his companions is a favorite Boone episode.

DANIEL MEETS HIS WIFE

Daniel was once, when a young man, out on a fire hunt with what might be called a boon companion. They had got into a heavily timbered piece of bottom skirted by a small stream, and the hunter's friend preceded him with the fire pan. All at once Boone gave the signal to stop, an indication that he had "shined the eyes" of a deer. Dismounting and tying his horse, he crept cautiously forward behind a covert of hazel and plum bushes, and sure enough, there were the two orbs turned full upon him.

Boone now raised his fatal rifle, but a mysterious something arrested his arm and caused his hand to tremble. Off sprang the game with a bound and the ardent young hunter in hot chase after it. On! On they go, when a fence appears, over which the nimble deer vaulted in a strangely human sort of way, while Boone, burdened with his rifle and hunting gear, clambered after as best he

Boone's Boys

Children have been following in Daniel Boone's trailblazing footsteps since 1905, when Daniel Carter Beard founded The Society of the Sons of Daniel Boone. The organization (divided into local forts) was dedicated to an appreciation of the outdoors and to the "old-fashioned virtues of American Knights in Buckskin." Each member started as a tenderfoot and worked to become a full-fledged scout. The two-fingered salute, used by Cub Scouts today, was originally the Indian sign for a wolf, scout of the wilderness. In 1910 the club was incorporated into the new Boy Scouts of America, which to this day continues to perpetuate the great Boone tradition.

could. Fighting his way through a score of snarling and scolding hounds, he knocked at the door of the house beyond the fence and was welcomed by farmer Bryan. The young hunter had scarce time to glance about inquiringly before a boy of 10 and a flushed and breathless girl of 16, with ruddy cheeks, flaxen hair, and soft blue eyes, rushed in.

"Oh, Father! Father!" cried out the boy. "Sis was down to the creek to set my lines and was chased by a panther or something. She's too skeared to tell." The panther and deer were now engaged in exchanging glances, and apparently the eyes of both had been effectually "shined," for, to make a long story short, that is how Rebecca Bryan became Rebecca Boone, the first white woman to go to Kentucky.

KNIFE-SWALLOWING TRICK

Boone and some of his followers were once eating in the woods when they were surprised by a large party of Indians. The Indians, hoping to lull the suspicions of the white men and thus seize a favorable opportunity for rushing upon them, sat down and also began eating. Boone affected a careless inattention but, in an undertone, quietly admonished the men to keep their hands upon their rifles. He then strutted toward the Indians unarmed and casually picking the meat from a bone. The Indian leader rose, just as casually, to meet him.

Boone saluted him and then requested to look at the knife with which the Indian was cutting his meat. The chief handed it to him without hesitation, and our pioneer, who possessed considerable expertness at sleight of hand, deliberately opened his mouth and affected to swallow the long knife, which, at the same instant, he threw adroitly into his sleeve. The Indians were astonished, and Boone, rubbing his stomach with satisfaction, pronounced the horrid mouthful *very good*.

Having enjoyed the surprise of the spectators for a few moments, he made another contortion, and drawing the knife, as they supposed, from his body, coolly returned it to the chief. He then sauntered back to his party. The Indians, dispatching their meal, marched off, desiring no further intercourse with a man who could swallow a scalping knife.

HERO'S DEATH

According to one legend, as Boone lived, so he died—with his gun in his hand. When he knew himself ready to breathe out his last, Colonel Boone rode to a deer lick and sat down within a blind raised to conceal himself from the game. While sitting thus, with his old trusty rifle resting on a log, his face to the breech of the gun, his rifle cocked, his finger on the trigger, one eye shut, the other looking along the barrel through the sight—in this position, without struggle or motion, he died so gently that when he was found the next day by his friends, although cold and stiff, he looked as if alive, with his gun in his hand, just in the act of firing. It is not altogether certain if a buck had come into the range of his gun, which had been the death of thousands, but the rifle might have intuitively obeyed its old employer's mind and discharged itself at a deer of its own accord.

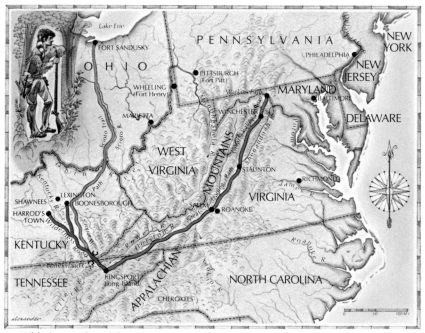

With the opening of the Wilderness Road, marked in red on this map, America's era of western expansion truly began. (Although the map shows important settlements in the Appalachian area c. 1780, modern state boundaries are indicated.) The 208-mile trail represented a prodigious three-week effort (March 10–April 1, 1775) by Boone and a team of North Carolinians who cleared a path through forest and over mountains for pioneers on foot. The new fort at one end of the trail was aptly named Boonesborough.

NATURE'S NOBLEMAN

"The Huron Flew Through the Air," by N. C. Wyeth (shown above), appeared as an illustration in Scribner's 1929 edition of James Fenimore Cooper's The Deerslayer.

When, in the 1770's, westward expansion began, a new breed of "noble savage" was born—the frontiersman. That hero's prototype was Daniel Boone, and the Boone-like pioneer has lived on in the American imagination to this day; but, as critic Arthur K. Moore has pointed out, this was a consequence not of folk tradition but of popular literature, most notably James Fenimore Cooper's hero Natty Bumppo who stars in the Leather-stocking Tales. Every latter-day "western" cliche is present in Cooper's hero. Natty was an expert woodsman, a sharpshooter, a protector of white women in the wilderness. As the noble savage had been, he was "a fair example of what a just-minded man might be, amid the solitary grandeur and ennobling influences of a sublime nature." While he was being tortured by Indians, "his notions of the duty of a white man stoutly made up his mind to endure everything in preference to disgracing his color."

In a word, "the man was of great simplicity of mind, but of sterling worth." For all his simplicity, Natty was a mass of contradictions. Despising civilization, he took to the wilderness—in order to tame it and thus enable an encroaching civilization to encroach faster; but in the role of Indian fighter, he scrupulously observed the rules of civilized warfare. Here is a typical episode, in which an implausibly chivalrous Natty appears under his sobriquet, Deerslayer:

"Deerslayer knew his adversary must be reloading, unless he had fled. The former proved to be the case, for the young man had no sooner placed himself behind a tree than he caught a glimpse of the arm of the Indian (whose body was concealed by an oak) in the very act of forcing the leathered bullet home. Nothing would have been easier than to spring forward and decide the affair by a close assault on his unprepared foe; but every feeling of Deerslayer revolted at such a step,

although his own life had just been attempted from a cover. 'No—that may be redskin warfare, but it's not a Christian's gifts. Let the miscreant charge, and then we'll take it out like men,' he muttered to himself.

"The savage's rifle was no sooner loaded than he glanced round and

Shy Natty turns away from an admirer.

advanced until he was fairly exposed. Then Deerslayer stepped from behind his own cover and hailed him, 'This-a-way, redskin, if you're looking for me—it rests on yourself whether it's peace or war atween us.'

"The savage was too well schooled to betray alarm, but dropping the butt of his rifle to the earth with an air of confidence, he made a gesture of lofty courtesy with the ease and self-possession of one accustomed to consider no man his superior. However, the volcano that raged within caused his eyes to glare and his nostrils to dilate like those of some wild beast. 'No, no,' Deerslayer continued, 'that will never do. I know it's war atween your people and mine, but that's no reason why human mortals should slay each other like savage critters that meet in the woods. Go your way and leave me to go mine. When we meet fairly in battle, the Lord will order the fate of each of us.' 'Good!' exclaimed the Indian."

DAVY CROCKETT
Ring-Tailed Roarer Turned Superman

Tennessee-born frontiersman Davy Crockett served as a scout under Andrew Jackson in the Creek Indian War, then went into politics, winning three terms as a U.S. congressman. Crockett's riproaring style delighted his plebeian constituents, and legend, much of it of Davy's own making, soon grew up around his deeds (for example, that he once killed 105 bears in eight months). After his death in the heroic defense of the Alamo in 1836, popular Crockett Almanacs *built up the legend of Davy as a backwoods superman. Some leading episodes:*

SURE CURE FOR TOOTHACHE
I was out with my rifle early in the spring on the banks of the Tennessee, making up my opinion about matters and things in general, when all of a sudden I heard a clap of thunder. I looked up, and again I heard it, but it was not thunder—for a whole swarm of swallows come bodily out of an old hollow sycamore, and it was the noise they made with the flapping of their wings. Now I thought to myself that them thar little varmints were doing some mischief in the tree and that it were my duty to see into it. For, you see, just then I felt hugeously grandiferous, for the neighbors had made me a justice of the peace. So I cut down a sapling with my knife and set it agin the tree and clumb up like a squirrel; for, you know, a sycamore has a smooth bark. As I were bending over the edge of the hollow to look down, the sapling broke under me, and trying to catch at something, I lost my balance and fell down into the tree, head foremost; and how to get out, I didn't know, for the hole was deep, and when I looked up I could see the stars out of the top.

Presently, I put my hand into something as soft as a featherbed and I heard an awful growling, so that I thought it was the last trump sounding to fall in for the Day of Judgment. But it was only an old b'ar I woke out of his winter nap, and I out Butcher [Davy's knife] to see which were the best man. But the critter was clean amazed and made a bolt to get out of the scrape, most cowardly. "Hollo, stranger!" says I. "We don't part company without having a fair shake for a fight." And so, saving your presence, I clenched hold both his posteriors. But finding the hair was like to give way, I got hold of his stump of a tail with my teeth, and then I had him fast enough. But still he kept on climbing up the hollow, and I begun to sorter like the idea; for, you know, he couldn't get up without pulling me up after him. So when he begun to get tired, I quickened his pace with an awful fundamental poke with my Butcher, jest by way of a gentle hint. Before long, we got to the top of the tree, and then I got to the ground quicker than he did, seeing he come down tail foremost. I got my shooting iron to be ready for him. But he seemed to got enough of my company and went off squealing as if something ailed his hinter parts, which I thought a kind of curious; for I've no opinion of a fellow that will take a kick, much less such usage as I give him. However, I let him go, for it would be unmanly to be unthankful for the service he done me; and for all I know, he's alive yet. And it was not the only thing I had to thank him for: I had a touch of toothache before, and the bite I got at his tail cured me entirely. I've never had it since, and I can recommend it to all people that has the toothache to chew two inches of a bear's tail. It's a certain cure. There are a wicked sight of virtue in bear's grease.

THE COONSKIN TRICK
While on an electioneering trip, Davy Crockett fell in with a group of thirsty constituents, and it became necessary for him to treat the company. They repaired to the local grog shop, which belonged to a skinflint Yankee. Davy's finances were rather low—he had but one coonskin about him. However, he pulled it out, slapped it on the counter, and called for its value in whisky, his supporters shouting, "Huzzah for Crockett!" The Yankee measured out the whisky

FOLKWAYS

To Nail a Coonskin

The hunter gets some dogs and starts out after dark. He releases the dogs and whistles them along in low, long tones. When the scent is struck, the dogs race through the underbrush, swamp briers, marshes, gulleys, and mudholes after the fleeing raccoon, baying as they go, and when they get close to the coon their baying becomes short and sharp. Once the coon is treed, the dogs alternate in a slow bay till the hunter arrives and sends a boy up the tree to shake him down. Once tumbled to the ground, the quarry fights lying flat on his back, using his teeth and claws with great precision and rapidity—on one occasion a hunter was moved to remark, "That

coon suttinly mus' larned his boxin' tricks sparrin' with lightnin'." The final flurry, punctuated by the barking and snarling of the dogs and the screeches of the doomed raccoon, often takes place in total darkness.

As shown in these *Crockett Almanac* woodcuts, backwoodsman Davy took equal delight in running an "Eelskin" (a Yankee) off his place at gunpoint and pulling a wildcat by the tail out of a tree.

and threw the skin into the loft. Davy, observing that the logs forming the loft were spaced wide apart, took out his ramrod and, when the merchant turned his back, twisted his coonskin out and pocketed it. When more whisky was wanted, the same skin was pulled out, slapped on the counter, and its value called for. This trick Davy played until they were all tired of drinking.

DAVY SPEECHIFIES

Friends, fellow citizens, brothers, and sisters! Jackson is a hero and Crockett is a horse! They accuse me of adultery; it's a lie—I never ran away with any man's wife that was not willing, in my life. They accuse me of gambling; it's a lie—for I always plank down the cash. They accuse me of being a drunkard; it's a damned eternal lie, for there's no whisky stilled that can make me drunk.

REMEDIA AMORIS

Thar ar a great many kinds of larning. I found it out when I went to Congress. Thar ar your mathematics, your geometries, your scientifics, and your axletricity. I knows nothing about the other ones, but the axletricity is a screamer. Thar war a feller in Washington that put the thunder and lightning into glass bottles, and when a feller had the rheumatiz' or the Saint Vitals' dance he would put the axletricity into his corpse jist like pouring whisky into a powder horn, and it cured him clean as a barked tree. So I seed how 'twas done and determined whenever anything ailed me to try it, only I didn't keer about the bottles, for I thort I could jist as well take the lightning in the raw state as it come from the clouds. I had been used to drink out of the Mississippi without a cup, and so I could take the lightning without the bottles and whirligigs that belongs to an axletricitifying machine. It fell out that some two years arter I had been to see this axletricity, I got a leetle in love with a pesky smart gal in our clearing, and I knowed it war not right, seeing I war a married man. So I combobbolated on the subject, and at last I resisted that I would explunctificate my passions by axletricity, so it must be done by bringing it right on the heart and driving the love out of it. So I went out into the forest one arternoon when thar war a pestiferous thundergust. I opened my mouth, so that the axletricity might run down and hit my heart, to cure it of love. I stood so for an hour, and then I seed a thunderbolt a-comin' and I dodged my mouth right under it, and plump it went into my throat. My eyes! It war as if seven buffaloes war kicking in my bowels. My heart spun round amongst my insides like a grindstone going by steam, but the lightning went clean through me and tore the trousers clean off as it come out. I had a sore gizzard for two weeks arterward, and my innards war so hot that I used to eat raw vittles for a month arterward, and it would be cooked before it got fairly down my throat. I have never felt love since.

SUNRISE IN MY POCKET

One January morning it was so cold that the forest trees were stiff and they couldn't shake, and the very daybreak froze fast as it was trying to dawn. The tinderbox in my cabin would no more catch fire than a sunk raft at the bottom of the sea. Well, seeing daylight were so far behind time, I thought creation were in a fair way for freezing fast. So, thinks I, I must strike a little fire from my fingers, light my pipe, and travel out a few leagues and see about it. Then I brought my knuckles together like two thunderclouds, but the sparks froze up afore I could begin to collect 'em. So out I walked, whistling "Fire in the Mountains" as I went along in three double-quick time. Well, after I had walked about 20 miles up the Peak O'Day and Daybreak Hill, I soon discovered what were the matter. The earth had actually friz fast on her axes and couldn't turn round; the sun had got jammed between two cakes of ice under the wheels, and thar he had been shining and working to get loose till he friz fast in his cold sweat. "Creation!" thought I. "This are the toughest sort of suspension, and it mustn't be endured. Something must be done, or human creation is done for." It were then so anteluvian [antediluvian] and premature cold that my upper and lower teeth and tongue were all collapsed together as tight as a friz oyster. But I took a fresh 20-pound bear off my back that I'd picked up on my road and beat the animal agin the ice till the hot ile [oil] began to walk out on him at all sides. I then took and held him over the earth's axes and squeezed him till I'd thawed 'em loose, poured about a ton of it over the sun's face, give the earth's cogwheel one kick backward till I got the sun loose, whistled "Push along, keep movin'!" and in about 15 seconds the earth gave a grunt and began moving. The sun walked up beautiful, saluting me with such a wind of gratitude that it made me sneeze. I lit my pipe by the blaze of his topknot, shouldered my bear, and walked home, introducing all the people along the way to the fresh daylight with a piece of sunrise in my pocket.

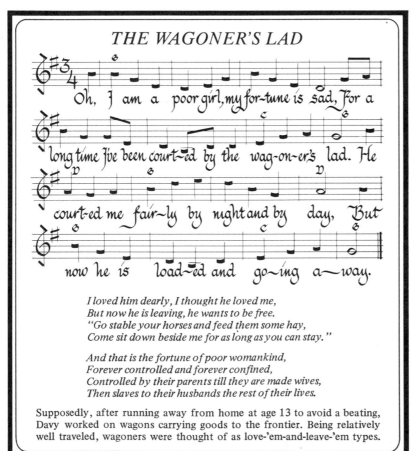

THE WAGONER'S LAD

Oh, I am a poor girl, my fortune is sad, For a long time I've been courted by the wagoner's lad. He courted me fairly by night and by day, But now he is loaded and going away.

I loved him dearly, I thought he loved me,
But now he is leaving, he wants to be free.
"Go stable your horses and feed them some hay,
Come sit down beside me for as long as you can stay."

And that is the fortune of poor womankind,
Forever controlled and forever confined,
Controlled by their parents till they are made wives,
Then slaves to their husbands the rest of their lives.

Supposedly, after running away from home at age 13 to avoid a beating, Davy worked on wagons carrying goods to the frontier. Being relatively well traveled, wagoners were thought of as love-'em-and-leave-'em types.

"Half-horse, half-alligator, a little touched with the snapping turtle," Davy was a comic-book hero before the funnies were invented—the four typical cartoons at right are from some *Crockett Almanacs*.

INFANT CROCKETT EATING HIS BREAKFAST

Arter awhile, I got old enough to eat knife and fork vittles. Bear's meat war my favorite, though I did take some wild fowl. It war thought best to wean me on whisky: so I had a bladder filled with whisky with a pipe in it, and I sucked at the pipe in the most soakoriferous manner. I would gnaw the meat off the bones before the rest had time to set down; and as for gravy, I used to drink it. That war one reason that I got to be so good a speechifier and war sent to Congress. As for mustard, I used to put the meat in one plate and the mustard in the tother, and arter I had done with my meat, I dove into the mustard for to give the meat a relish. Half a pint of it war only a taster. I always took a pint of whisky and mustard to give me an appetite for breakfast in the morning. Arter dinner, I always went round the table and licked out all the dishes and plates, which saved my mother the trouble of washing 'em. My mother liked it so well that arter I war grown up, she kept a tame bear to lick out the dishes, which saved a pesky deal of trouble, as well as the soap and dishwater.

OLD KAINTUCK

Shortly after I cum home from Kongress, the first time, Funk Winter attacked me about sumthing I had said in Washington. Funk was a great Polly Teashun in his own consate, and thort he could argufy like a lawyer. I skreemed one hour before I stopped—then I squeeled—then I hollered, and finally I began to nay like a hoss. Funk looked at his thumnale. I thort my biler would burst and called on the people to hold me. We both stood up at once, and Funk stood with his thumnale ready for a dive. I couldn't wait but I spit at him with all my mite. Then we closed in, and sumboddy got a pesky, all-gracious walloping. I've heard say it was Funk Winter.

DAVY'S UNCLE

The above portrait is a true likeness of one of Crockett's uncles. He is celebrated for the following peculiarities: he shaves himself with sheet lightning and eats pickled thunderbolts for his breakfast, and hailstone life pills when he's sick, picks teeth with a pitchfork, combs his hair with a rake, fans himself with a hurricane, wears a cast-iron shirt, and drinks nothing but kreosote and aquafortis.

AN APOLOGY

I'm often been thankful for my broughten-up. I war teeched perliteness when I war a boy; and when I did an imperlite action I war licked with a crocodile's tale, or a young saplin, till I greed to pollygize; but I should like to see that human that dared to tell Davy Crockett that he war in the wrong. Leaf Twig wonst ventured to do it, but he will never try it again. He sed I war wrong and de-manded a pollygee. I told him to have a ring formed so that everyone might hear the pollygee. So a ring was formed, and he stood to hear it. Sez I, what do you want me to say? Sez he, you must say that you are in the wrong. Then, sez I, it would be a mon-tracious lie. With that, he opened his mouth and cum at me. He got my head between his teeth and bit it ridiculous. I gave him a punch in the bowels, and he sneezed seven times. We both cum to the ground, but I rumsquattled him.

JOHNNY APPLESEED
A Native Genius

John Chapman was an eccentric who roamed the frontier establishing apple-tree nurseries and preaching Swedenborgianism, a very complex Christian theology. Little is known about him until, in 1797, at age 23, he appeared in northwestern Pennsylvania. During the next 48 years he moved between there and Indiana, preaching and planting. His legendary character took root in his lifetime—he even called himself John Appleseed—but first truly flowered in an 1871 Harper's *article. From then on, Johnny Appleseed's legend flourished in the American imagination, climaxing in the saint of nature still beloved today. Of the many tales about Johnny Appleseed, a few of the most typical are recounted below.*

THE APPLE MAN

Scarcely a community in America hasn't pointed to at least one apple tree it thinks descended from seeds introduced by Johnny Appleseed. Some people say he carried the seeds in leather bags on his shoulders, some say on horseback. But settlers from the Allegheny to the Wabash rivers, his main territory, reported seeing Johnny paddling up and down the rivers with two canoes lashed together carrying sacks of apple seeds. Whenever he came to a region being settled, Johnny would plant or distribute his seeds. His own plantings he let grow until the trees were big enough to be transplanted. He seldom charged money for seeds or trees, preferring to barter for food, clothes, or other necessities. Sometimes he took an IOU, but he usually either forgot or did not care to collect. And when his seed supply was exhausted, he went back to Pennsylvania, where he first began his mission, for a fresh supply at some cider mill. Why seeds instead of grafting, the usual way to propagate apple trees? Because Johnny believed cutting a tree was cruel.

CLOTHES UNMAKE THE MAN

Few hermits ever showed less regard for their personal appearance than did Johnny Appleseed. He started out wearing the basic homespun or buckskin of the settlers, but he turned to wearing the castoffs of others or anything he got as barter for his seeds. Eventually he settled for a coffee sack, merely cutting holes for his head and arms. On his head he first wore a tin pan, with which he also cooked, and then a cardboard cap he had made, with a large peak to protect his eyes from the sun. As for his feet, sometimes he wore homemade moccasins or sandals or castoff boots. But he refused to buy shoes and often went barefoot. Years and miles of walking shoeless had toughened his feet to the most extreme conditions. Once, though, traveling barefoot through mud and snow on a cold day, he encountered a neighbor who insisted it was sinful to go barefoot in such weather, and with this argument forced a pair of shoes on Johnny. A few days later, the neighbor came upon Johnny, his cold feet once again bare. The angry man asked Johnny to explain. Johnny said that he'd met a poor family moving westward, and as they had greater need, he gave them the shoes.

REVERENCE FOR LIFE

In Johnny Appleseed's day settlers could afford little sympathy for animals, but he showed an extraordinary concern for all living creatures. A grateful wolf he freed from a cruel trap followed him about for years like a dog. People said he talked aloud to the birds and animals as he tramped cross-country, and this attitude extended to the lowest forms of life. Once, while cutting grass, his scythe accidentally killed a snake. Johnny wept then and in years thereafter whenever he told of his deed.

One cool night when Johnny was preparing to sleep outdoors, he built a fire; he noticed that numbers of mosquitoes flew into the fire, attracted by the flame. Immediately, Johnny fetched water and quenched the blaze to spare other insects.

THE MEDICINE MAN

Johnny possessed almost supernatural powers of healing. The Indians considered him a great medicine man. When Johnny himself got cut, he seared the wound with a red-hot iron that no normal person could stand. And although not everyone knew this side of Johnny, along with apple seeds Johnny distributed many medicinal herbs and plants. Most of all, he spread the seeds of dog fennel, or mayweed, a plant he was convinced fought off malaria, then prevalent on the frontier. Later it was discovered that dog fennel has no effect on malaria. But it was too late. This foul-smelling weed took over everywhere, reminding one that even good old Johnny Appleseed could make a mistake and that for every good fruit there is a bad weed.

A VOICE IN THE WILDERNESS

Somewhere along the way, Johnny Appleseed became converted to the ideas of Emanuel Swedenborg, the 18th-century Swedish mystic, who denounced the vanities of this world. Johnny carried Swedenborg's works on all his travels and preached "news right fresh from Heaven" whenever he could corner a listener. But his own simple life was his best sermon. Once he stood on the edge of a group listening to an itinerant missionary. The preacher himself was smartly dressed from head to foot and employed elaborate rhetoric, but he constantly berated the assembly with the refrain "Where now is there a

The legendary Johnny Appleseed, barefoot, clothed in a coffee sack, and wearing his tin pan for a hat, is blowing a horn to warn settlers in the Ohio area of Indian threats during the War of 1812. He is garlanded by dog fennel and other symbols of his role as a demigod of nature.

man who, like the primitive Christians, is traveling to Heaven barefooted and clad in coarse raiment?" Finally, Johnny had enough of such hypocrisy. He went forward, put one bare foot on the stump serving as a pulpit, pointed to his coffee sack, and quietly said, "Here's your primitive Christian." The preacher left town.

FRONTIER PAUL REVERE

No one knew the trails and woods of the frontier so well as Johnny Appleseed. Even the Indians respected and almost venerated him, for they considered anyone with such strange habits as possessed by a God-given knowledge. At the outbreak of the War of 1812, many Indians eagerly joined the British in order to seek revenge for the injustices done their people by the settlers. There were numerous attacks by red men on the inhabitants of Johnny's region. And when Detroit fell to the British, the region was especially exposed to them. Because of his reputation, Johnny was allowed to move about as usual; yet, unknown to the Indians, he became a one-man warning system, alerting isolated settlements and families to imminent dangers. Once, when the people of Mansfield, Ohio, were under siege by natives, Johnny traveled 30 miles for aid, warning settlers along the route by blasting on an old powder horn.

At that time, a Frenchman, Bouvet, was living in the Missouri region. He had come there in flight from the French revolutionaries, and one night, alone in his cabin, he heard a noise at the door. When convinced that only one person stood outside, Bouvet opened the door. In walked a gaunt, peculiar-looking man who chanted: "I sow while others reap./ Be sure my warning keep./ Indians will come by break of day./ Indians hunting scalps, I say." With that, he walked off into the night. So warned, Bouvet was able to prepare the settlement, and when the Indians attacked at "break of day," the settlers repulsed them. Only later did Bouvet learn that the strange apparition was Johnny Appleseed.

THE WAR OF 1812
America at Sea

The War of 1812 was one of the more undefined, uninspired, and unnecessary wars in the history of the United States. It had several causes, but the most tangible was America's desire to stop the British from seizing her ships and seamen. Insufficiently organized to mount much in the way of either defensive or offensive actions, Americans were sure of only one thing: the British Navy, the most powerful in the world, had over 600 ships, and the young U.S. Navy had 12. So among the many surprises of the war was the series of American naval victories. Little wonder that much of the lore from this war has a nautical tang.

IN THE LONG RUN

We heard the other day a story related by an old sailor, Captain Jacob. It occurred during the last war. The captain, a native of Plymouth, was running onto the coast in a schooner loaded with flour. He had nearly reached his destination when he was overhauled by the enemy's frigates, who ordered him to heave a line aboard. There was no resisting. But the captain had a fair breeze aloft, and he was driving near a reef, and he knew the entrance well. Once inside, he was sure of making port.

Certain of this, he ordered one of

The best known legend of the War of 1812 is actually based in fact, although romanticized in this painting by Percy Moran. Francis Scott Key was detained on a British warship on a night when it bombarded Fort McHenry. When "by dawn's early light" he saw the flag, Key wrote his poem. It became an immediate hit when set to the tune of a popular English drinking song but did not become the official U.S. anthem until 1931.

his men forward with the line, and in a clear voice, perfectly audible on board the frigate, sang out: "Heave your line aboard!" Then he added, so as to be heard only by his men, "Heave it short." The Yankee sailor caught the hint and "hove" according to directions. The end of the line fell splashing in the water. Above the execrations of the English officer rose the roar of the indignant Yankee skipper. "Is that the way to heave a line, you lubberly son of a land crab? Heave the line shipshape, or I'll cut your liver out!"

Again the line fell short, and the English officer and Yankee skipper vied with each other in showering invectives on the blundering "landlubber." Meanwhile, the breeze was freshening and the schooner drawing nearer to the reef. Again and again the order to heave was given, with the same undertone addition, and with the same result. The Englishman began to smell a rat, and as the Yankee skipper and his men threw themselves flat on the deck, a shower of bullets came whizzing through the rigging. "Let them fire and be darned!" said the Yankee, and taking the tiller between his heels as he lay on the deck, he ran the schooner inside the reef. They were soon out of gunshot from the baffled frigate.

LADIES' AUXILIARY

One day about 1813, two British warships appeared off New London, Connecticut. The local militia manned the fort, but at the last moment discovered they had no cloth wadding for loading a cannon. Several men rushed off to find some flannel, but all the houses and shops were locked and the people had fled inland. Wandering around despairingly, they encountered a local resident, Mrs. Anna Bailey, and explained their plight. At once she reached inside her clothing and dropped her flannel petticoat. Coolly handing it to the soldiers, she asked them to "give it to the British at the cannon's mouth." The grateful men rushed back, and although the British ships withdrew before any shots were

"More Like a Nation . . ."

In June 1813 the fine old Revolutionary slogan "Don't give up the ship!" became once more the order of the day. It was revived by the mortally wounded Capt. James Lawrence, who supposedly repeated the words over and over before his death after his frigate, *Chesapeake,* had been shot to pieces. Three months later, on September 10, 1813, Commodore Oliver Hazard Perry sailed into the Battle of Lake Erie with the same slogan floated as a signal at his masthead. Victorious, he sent his famous dispatch: "We have met the enemy and they are ours." The romantic representation of the valorous Perry and some of his crew after the battle, at right, is by portrait painter John Wesley Jarvis.

That same year, Uncle Sam came into being as a counterpart of John Bull from someone's humorous interpretation of the letters *U.S.* on barrels of beef supplied to the U.S. Army by a New York meatpacker named "Uncle Sam" Wilson. "The people are more American; they feel more like a na-

tion," wrote one patriot at the close of hostilities. The new mood was well expressed by the naval hero Stephen Decatur in a victory toast when he exclaimed: "Our country, right or wrong!"

exchanged, Mrs. Bailey's petticoat inspired people all along the coast.

LONG BARNEY STRIKES

Still farther east, "down Machias way," lived Barney Beal of Jonesport. Barney was a huge man who liked to sit in a rocking chair. He never sought trouble, but when it came he managed to stop it. Once, in Portland, he threw two men through the side of a house when they crossed him, and he killed a dray horse by punching it between the eyes when it threatened to run over him.

Barney lived around the time of the American Revolution and the War of 1812. One day he was out with his seine net when a British man-o'-war sailed by and ordered him aboard, for they were looking for men to impress (the activity that political folklore tells us caused the War of 1812). Barney paid no attention and continued to fish, so a boat was manned with 12 men to go and get him and his crew. All hands were armed and Beal's companions be-

came nervous, but Barney waited until they were close enough. Then he stood up, threw the purse seine over the whole outfit—sailors, boat, oars, and guns—hauled in the strings, and bagged the lot. He then rowed ashore with the entire net load and marched the prisoners to jail.

OLD IRONSIDES

The *Constitution* was the most victorious participant of the war, but in 1830 the Navy decided she should be scrapped. Oliver Wendell Holmes expressed the indignation of many: Ay, tear her tattered ensign down!
Long has it waved on high . . .
Oh, better that her shattered hulk
Should sink beneath the wave . . .
Her thunders shook the mighty deep,
And there should be her grave;
Nail to the mast her holy flag,
Set every threadbare sail,
And give her to the god of storms,
The lightning and the gale!
The result was an instant legend that preserved the ship, which still rests in Boston harbor as a national shrine.

PRESIDENTIAL TIMBER
Old Hickory and Plucky Dolley

The War of 1812 produced victories at sea but disasters on land. The most humiliating episode was the hit-and-run attack on Washington, D.C., in 1814, when the British burned the president's house and most other government buildings. Perhaps to compensate for the shame of President Madison's flight, Americans converted his aristocratic wife, Dolley, into a popular heroine. The biggest gainer from the war was Andrew Jackson, an obscure Tennessee politician till he beat the British at New Orleans. That battle was fought after the war had ended, but it salved national pride and made Jackson's name a household word.

DOLLEY UNDER FIRE

Only hours before the British appeared in Washington, and with the sound of the cannon in the distance, Dolley Madison wrote a letter to her sister that was to make her legendary.

Tuesday, August 23, 1814
Dear Sister:

My husband left me yesterday morning to join General Winder. He inquired anxiously whether I had courage to remain in the president's house until his return; and on my assurance that I had no fear but for him and the success of our Army, he left me, beseeching me to take care of myself, and of the Cabinet papers, public and private.

I am accordingly ready; I have pressed as many Cabinet papers into trunks as will fill one carriage; our private property must be sacrificed.

Wednesday morning, 12 o'clock
Since sunrise, I have been turning my spyglass in every direction and watching with unwearied anxiety, hoping to discern the approach of my dear husband and his friends; but, alas, I can descry only groups of military wandering in all directions, as if there was a lack of arms or of spirit to fight for their own firesides!

3 o'clock Will you believe it, my sister? We have had a battle or skirmish near Bladensburg, and I am still here, within sound of the cannon! Mr. Madison comes not; may God protect him! Two messengers covered with dust come to bid me fly, but I wait for him. At this late hour a wagon has been procured; I have had it filled with the plate and most valuable portable articles. Our kind friend Mr. Carroll has come to hasten my departure and is in a very bad humor with me because I insist on waiting until the large picture of General Washington is secured, and it requires to be unscrewed from the wall. This process was found too tedious for those perilous moments. I have ordered the frame to be broken and the canvas taken out. It is done—and the precious portrait placed in the hands of two gentlemen from New York for safekeeping.

And now, dear sister, I must leave this house, or the retreating Army will make me a prisoner in it, filling up the road that I am directed to take. When shall I see or write you, or where shall I be tomorrow, I cannot tell!

Within a few hours, British troops entered the president's house to find a banquet prepared for the Madisons' expected supper guests.

SHARPSHOOTING

Andrew Jackson's political career depended greatly on his image as the buckskin frontiersman, or the new breed of American. That image, in turn, also depended greatly on the rough-and-ready militiamen he commanded at New Orleans. Many stories circulated about the sharpshooting skill of the Americans, until eventually legend had it that practically each dead Englishman had been picked off by a Leatherstocking. The climactic tale was about the British officer Colonel Rennie, killed in leading an attack. After the battle, some Americans began to argue over who had killed Colonel Rennie. One soldier spoke up: "If Rennie was shot just below the left eye, then I did it—for that's where I aimed." On inspection, it was found that Rennie had been shot just there.

Do not be startled, gentle reader at the picture before you. It is all true and every body ought to know it. Gen. Jackson having made an assault upon Samuel Jackson, in the streets of Nashville, & the latter not being disposed to stand still and be beaten, stooped down for a stone to defend himself. While in the act of doing so, Gen. Jackson drew the sword from his cane and run it through Samuel Jackson's body, the sword entering his back and coming out of his breast. For this offence an indictment was found against Gen. Jackson, by a grand jury, upon which he was subsequently arraigned and tried. But finding means to persuade the petit jury that he committed the act in self-defence, he was acquitted. Gentle reader, it is for you to say, whether this man, who carries a sword cane, and is willing to run it through the body of any one who may presume to stand in his way, is a fit person to be our President.

The more intensely an American president has been admired, the more vehemently his enemies have hated him. Andrew Jackson was no stranger to extreme actions: he had, in fact, killed a man in a duel. But this detail from an 1828 broadside (one of many efforts by Jackson's enemies to embarrass him) greatly exaggerates his wicked past.

GENERAL JACKSON AND THE INDIAN BABE IN FLORIDA.

Jackson's other image was that of an ideal great democrat, a diamond in the rough. This work employs a 19th-century art convention, placing Jackson in a heroic grouping. But the artist also shows the "Hero" surrounded by Indians and "plain folks."

THE COMMON TOUCH

Jackson had a not undeserved reputation as a roisterer and rakehell. As a young man, he was a law student in North Carolina, where he seems to have spent at least as much time with the girls and the horses as with his books. Years later, it came to the ears of an elderly woman that Andrew Jackson was being talked of for president. She remembered him as a law student—or rather, as a young man who was so disreputable that her husband would only share a drink with him in the stable. "What!" she exclaimed. "Jackson for the president? Well, if Andrew Jackson can be president, then I believe anybody can be!"

LOCAL BOY MAKES GOOD

Andrew Jackson, then 21 years old, rode into Jonesboro, Tennessee, in May 1788 and hung out his shingle; he practiced law there about two years. When, in 1815, a rumor reached Jonesboro that Andrew Jackson had killed the whole English army at New Orleans and had set sail to take possession of England itself, the townspeople were thrown into a frenzy of pride. One old grandpa threw his hat in the air and yelled: "Whoopee! Hurrah for Andy Jackson! Hell and thunder, I knowed he could whip anybody the day I seed him ride that hoss race at Greasy Cove!" "Andy Jackson, hell and thunder!" are the words still used there to express high feelings.

FRONTIER JUSTICE

Judge Jackson was holding court at a village in Tennessee. One day, a great hulking fellow, armed with pistol and bowie knife, took it upon himself to parade before the courthouse and curse the judge, jury, and all there assembled. "Sheriff," sang out Jackson, "arrest that man for contempt of court." Out went the sheriff but soon returned saying he found it impossible to take the offender. "Summon a posse, then," said Jackson. The posse didn't like the job any better than the sheriff, as the fellow threatened to shoot the first skunk that came within 10 feet of him.

Hearing of this, Jackson waxed wroth and cried out, "Mr. Sheriff, since you cannot obey orders, summon me too." "Well, judge, if you say so, I suppose I must summon you." Said Jackson, "I adjourn this court 10 minutes." Judge Jackson went out to where the ruffian was blaspheming and flourishing his weapons. Jackson walked calmly through the crowd with pistols in hand and confronted him. "Now," said Jackson, looking him straight in the eye, "surrender, you infernal villain, or I'll blow you straight through."

The man eyed the speaker for only a moment and then he put up his weapons and suffered himself to be led away. A few days later, when the man was asked why he had knuckled under to one person after refusing to allow himself to be taken by a whole company, he replied, "Why, when he came up, I looked him in the eye and I saw shoot—and there wasn't shoot in nary other eye in the crowd."

FIERCE SHAWNEES
Children of Heaven

In 1800 the Shawnees of Ohio, led by Tecumseh, formed the main obstacle to advancing "Big Knives," as Indians called white settlers. Tecumseh abolished the custom of burning and eating prisoners but was himself in the end reportedly flayed by Kentuckians and his skin used for razor strops (a report vehemently denied by his people, who claimed to have buried him in a secret grave). The Shawnees had a rich star lore and, curiously, a separate name for each star on the U.S. flag. The same stars, they believed, would descend from the heavens and advise Indians when the whites intended war. Here is another Shawnee star tale.

Waupee (White Hawk) lived in a remote part of the forest, where animals and birds were abundant. A tall, manly youth with flashing eyes, he was one of the most skillful and celebrated hunters of his tribe. There was no forest too gloomy for him to penetrate and no track he could not follow.

One day Waupee ranged farther afield than ever before, traveling through an open forest, which enabled him to see a great distance. At length he saw light breaking through the foliage, which made him sure he was on the borders of a prairie. It was a wide plain covered with grass and flowers. After walking some time without a path, he suddenly came to a ring worn in the sod, as if it had been made by footsteps following a circle. But what excited his surprise was that there was no path leading to or from the circle. Not the least trace of footsteps could be found in even a crushed leaf or a broken twig. So he thought he would lie in wait to see what this circle meant.

Presently, Waupee heard faint sounds of music in the air. He looked up and saw an object descending from the sky, which turned out to be a large basket filled with 12 beautiful sisters, the daughters of the Star Chief. The basket, Waupee believed, must have been lowered from a window in the heavens. As soon as the basket touched the ground, they leaped out and began to dance round the magic ring, striking a shining ball the same way Indians beat a drum. Waupee admired them all but was most taken with the youngest. Unable to restrain his admiration, he rushed out and tried to seize her. But the moment the sisters saw the form of a man, they leaped back into the basket and were rapidly drawn back up into the sky.

Regretting his bad luck and indiscretion, Waupee gazed after them and said to himself, "They are gone, and I shall never see them again." But the next day, he returned to the prairie and waited near the ring. In order to deceive the sisters, he assumed the shape of an opossum. He had not been waiting long when he saw the basket descend and heard the same music. The girls danced as before. Waupee crept slowly toward the ring, but the instant the sisters saw him they sprang into the basket. It rose only a short distance when one of the elder sisters spoke: "Maybe he came to show us how humans play our game." "Oh no!" said the youngest. "Let's get out of here!" And so, singing as they went, the sisters rose out of sight.

Waupee resumed his own shape and walked sorrowfully back to his lodge. That night seemed a very long one. He returned the next day, reflecting on the type of plan to follow in order be sure of success. On the way, he found an old stump, in which there were a number of mice. He decided such small creatures would not cause alarm and accordingly assumed the shape of one of them, having set up the stump next to the ring. The sisters descended and resumed their sport. "Look!" cried the youngest. "That stump wasn't there before!" With this, she started running toward the basket. But her sis-

FACT ? MYTH

The Noble Pioneer and the Ignoble Savage

Ohio and Kentucky meant "fine river" and "meadowland" respectively to their primeval inhabitants. They resisted furiously when the first waves of white settlers invaded their territory, which (although neither individual property rights were exercised nor even hard-and-fast boundaries between tribal lands observed) they believed to have been given them by God. The whites kept coming, and a new myth was generated, that of the brave pioneers who were forced to defend their right (also God-given!) to occupy the wilderness against hordes of bloodthirsty savages.

In line with the white "fact" of God-given right, Pennsylvania jurist Hugh Henry Brackenridge advocated Indian extermination: "These ringed, streaked, spotted, and speckled cattle have the shapes of men and maybe of the human species, but certainly in their present state they approach nearer the character of devils." The idea was eventually legitimized by right of conquest. The reality was forgotten but may still be recalled by the words of two who fought at the forefront on either side: "I've tried all kinds of game, boys, I've fit b'ar and painter [panther] and catamount, but thar ain't no game like Injuns, no sir, no game like Injuns." (Spoken by Adam Poe, an early pioneer)

On the other side, Chief Tecumseh stated the Indians' already-lost cause thus: "Will we let ourselves be destroyed in our turn, without making an effort worthy of our race? Shall we, without struggle, give up our homes, our lands, bequeathed to us by the Great Spirit? The graves of our dead and everything that is dear and sacred to us? I know you will say with me, Never! Never!"

"General Harrison and Tecumseh at Vincennes," by Stanley Arthurs. Future president Harrison wanted to purchase more Indian territory; the Shawnee chief made a derisive reply to him: "Sell a country! Why not sell the air, the great sea, as well as the earth?"

song was wafted by the wind, it caught her husband's ear, and he ran out to the prairie. But before he could reach the ring, Waupee saw his wife and child ascend. He watched till the basket became a small speck and at last vanished in the sky.

He bowed his head to the ground and was miserable. He mourned his wife's loss sorely, but the loss of his son was almost unbearable.

In the meantime, his wife reached her home in the stars and almost forgot that she had left a husband on the earth. She was reminded of this by the presence of her son, however, and as the little boy grew up he became anxious to meet his father.

One day the Star Chief said to his daughter: "Go, my child, and take your son down to his father, and ask him to come up here and live with us. But tell him to bring along a specimen of each kind of bird and animal he kills in the chase."

Accordingly, she took the boy and descended. Waupee, who was never far from the enchanted prairie, heard her voice as she came down from the sky. She told him her father's message, and he began hunting day and night, searching for every curious and beautiful bird or animal. He preserved only a tail, foot, or wing of each, to identify its kind. When he felt he had everything and was ready, Waupee and his wife and son went to the circle and were borne up.

Great joy was manifested on their arrival at the starry plains. The Star Chief invited all his people to a feast and, when they had assembled, proclaimed that each one might take of the earthly gifts whatever he liked best. Immediately, a strange confusion arose. Some chose a foot, some a wing, some a tail, and some a paw. Those who chose tails or paws were changed into animals and ran off. The others assumed the shapes of birds and flew away. Waupee chose a white hawk's feather. His wife and son followed his example, and all spread their wings and descended with the other birds to the earth, where many varieties of their kind are to be found to this day.

ters only smiled and, gathering round the stump, struck it playfully. Out ran the mice, Waupee among them. The sisters killed them all but one, which was pursued by the youngest sister. But just as she raised her stick to kill it too, the form of Waupee rose and clasped her in his arms. The other 11 girls sprang to their basket and were drawn up into the sky.

Waupee did all he could to please his bride and win her love. Wiping the tears from her eyes, he told of his hunting adventures and dwelt on the charms of life on earth as he gently led her toward his lodge.

Winter and summer passed quickly, and a baby boy was born to them. Waupee's wife still longed to return to her father, the Star Chief.

One day, she remembered a charm that would carry her home and so took occasion, while Waupee was out hunting, to construct a wicker basket, which she kept concealed. She then spent several days collecting such rarities from the earth as she thought would please her father, as well as the most dainty kinds of food.

When all was in readiness, she went out to the charmed ring, taking her little son with her. As soon as they got into the basket, she started singing, and the basket rose. As the

THE BELL WITCH
An Overseeing Haunt

The motivation of the John Bell family for moving to Tennessee differed from that of other settlers who were spiritual followers of Daniel Boone: the Bells were trying to escape mysteriously caused ruin. This version of their tribulations, given in condensed form, was collected by Arthur Hudson and Pete McCarter.

Back in the days before the Civil War, there lived somewhere in old North Carolina a well-fixed planter by the name of John Bell. Until he hired an overseer, Bell got along fine. The overseer was a Simon Legree sort of fellow; he tended to his business, however, though some say he had an eye open for Mary, the oldest daughter. And Mrs. Bell stood up for him, so he stayed on for a good while. Whenever he and Bell had a row—and their rows got bigger and bitterer—the overseer went out and blacksnaked three or four slaves. He was the worst kind of a bully, and a man of high temper. Mr. Bell had a tall temper too, and a stand-up fight was bound to come off. It did. Bell went away blowing smoke from his pistol barrel, and the overseer didn't go away at all. Bell pled self-defense, and the jury let him off.

That year and the next, the crops on the Bell place were an out-and-out failure. Bell had to sell his slaves one by one: finally, he went broke. He got what he could for his land and moved with his family to Tennessee. He bought himself a house and a patch of land near the home of old Andy Jackson, who had knocked off from being president.

Not long after the move, strange things began to happen in the Bell home. The children got into the habit of being tumbled out of bed and of waking up every morning with every stitch of the bedclothes snatched off and their hair all tangled. An old black woman told them it was the ha'nt, or witch, of the overseer Bell had killed. She was as superstitious as any other black, but she had spunk, and one day she allowed she would find out whether she was right by spending the night under the young-uns' bed. In the middle of the night Mr. and Mrs. Bell were fetched out of their bed by a squall like a pant'er's. When they lit a lamp and ran into the room, they found the old woman sprawled in the middle of the floor, dripping cold sweat like an ash-hopper, her face gray-blue as sugarcane peeling, and her eyes like saucers in a dishpan. "Fo' Gawd, hit's him! Hit peenched

me all over, stuck pins in me, snatched de keenks outen ma haiuh, an' whup me. Lawd Gawd, how hit whup me, whup me limber and whup me stiff, whup me jes' lack *him*."

The Bells were so scared they told some of the neighbors. Old Andy Jackson heard about it and decided to ride over. He didn't take any stock in ha'nts, and as he rode through the gate he spoke his mind out loud about tarnation fools that believed tales about them. He hadn't got the words out of his mouth before something whaled him over the head and skipped his hat 20 or 30 yards back down the road. Old Andy didn't say any more. He motioned his boy to hand him his hat, and he went away.

Mary would wake up in the middle of the night, screaming and crying that something cold and heavy had been sitting on her breast, sucking her breath and pressing the life out of her. One time she was getting ready to go to a play-party. Some of the young sprouts were waiting for her in the front room. While she was combing her long, black hair, it suddenly was full of cockleburs, and when she couldn't untangle it, she cried. "I put them in your hair," said the witch from the looking glass. "You've got no business going to the party. Stay here with me. I can say sweet things to you." Mary screamed, and the young fellows rushed into the room, and when she told them about the voice they shot at the glass with their pistols. But the glass didn't break. And the witch caught every bullet and pitched

it right back into their vest pockets and laughed. So they called it a draw and went out of there. And Mary stayed home.

Mary was now a beautiful woman. She had lots of beaux. But whenever one of them screwed himself up to the point of popping the question, he always found that the words stuck in his throat and his face and ears burned. They laid it on the witch and finally quit hitching their horses to the Bell fence. One night the witch spoke up from the andirons and told Mr. and Mrs. Bell he was in love with Mary. He said he wanted to marry her. Mr. Bell was shocked and surprised. He explained that he could never dream of letting a daughter of his marry a ghost. "Have you spoken to Mary?" he asked. "No, not spoken." "Well, how do you know she would have you?" "I don't. But I haven't got any reason to believe she wouldn't love me."

"What if you were to have children? Maybe half good human meat and bone, and the other half sight unseen. Do you think I want a passel of soapsuds young-uns floatin' round here and poppin' up into puffs of wind every time I p'inted to the stovewood pile or sprouts on a ditch bank? Not on your life. I reckon plain flesh and blood's good enough." "But, John Bell, I love Mary." "So do I, and that's why I'm not a-goin' to let you marry

her. Why, when she got old and hard-favored I reckon you'd quit her for some young hussy. You could do it easy enough. Mary'd have a hard time keepin' up with a stack of wind and a voice, and I'd have a hard time trackin' down and shootin' a low-down, no-count dust devil. When Mary marries, she marries a man that's solid and alive in body."

"But what kind of wedding would it be like?" Mrs. Bell put in. "Mary standing in front of the preacher saying, 'Do you take this woman?' to a vase of flowers." "About Mary, I'm going to talk to her right off." "Don't," said Mr. Bell. "Do you want to drive her crazy?" But the meeting was over, for there was no answer. And the fire had died down, and the andiron looked glum. The family noticed next day that Mary was drooping. For days she wandered about the house like somebody sleepwalking, and the color left her face. Finally there came a day when she didn't get up at all. In the evening a screech owl hollered in a cedar right by the gallery. That night her fever was high, and by midnight she was raving. The doctor came and said: "It's her mind and nerves. Medicine won't do her any good. Don't let her get lonesome. She's young, strong, and ought to come round in time."

But she never did. For a month she

lay there on the bed, looking at nothing and yet straining to see something. One night her ma was sitting there, holding Mary's hand and stroking the dark hair back from her forehead. Suddenly, Mary pushed her mother away and sat up and looked across the foot of the bed, as if somebody was standing there. "Mamma," she whispered, "I see him . . . at last. And I think . . . I'm going . . . to love him."

And she died with the only expression of happiness they had seen on her face in months. Some believe she was in love with the overseer from the first and didn't want to live because she knew she would never be happy with him until she too became a ghost. But she died just the same. And they say that on the day of the funeral, when the coffin was carried from the house to a wagon, a great black bird flew down from the sky. And around its neck was a bell that tolled in the mournfulest tone ever heard by the ear of man. And when the funeral procession began to move, the great bird floated just in front of it and circled round the grave during the burial, the bell tolling all the while. And when the mound was rounded up, the bird swung high up in the air and disappeared. But long after it was gone, the mourning notes of the bell floated back to those who stood and watched.

J. ENDEWELT

The *Western Engineer* (1819) was the first of a long line of Missouri River steamers. It was said they were so light in draft they could run on a heavy dew.

"Hello, stranger! If you don't take keer, your boat will run away with you!" Exchanging insults between raft and shore was a favorite sport on western rivers.

Riverboat Roarers

As homesteaders streamed into the vast, almost untenanted region between the Great Lakes and Louisiana, settlement tended to follow navigable rivers. The inland waterways provided not only cheap and easy passage to frontier zones but lines of communication linking western producers to markets in New Orleans and (after completion of the Erie Canal in 1825) New York. The rivers became crowded with "arks" (houseboats that often served as floating general stores, saloons, and raree shows) as well as rafts, barges, flatboats, keelboats, and—later—steamboats.

Boatmen had to have stamina and nerve as well as a fair measure of skill—navigation was a ticklish business.

Most early crews were impecunious backwoodsmen of the ringtail-roarer type who had signed on because the job promised fun, adventure, and freedom from responsibility in addition to money. It was not for nothing that they styled themselves horse-alligators and snapping turtles—many were indeed what we today would call animals. A contemporary wrote: "I have seen nothing in human form so profligate; their habits and education seem to comprehend every vice; their swearing is excessive and perfectly disgusting. Although earning good wages, they are in the most abject poverty." The reason for their poverty was of course that they squandered their wages ashore on wenching, drinking, and gambling. All this, together with the inevitable "Kentucky play" (fighting, especially dirty fighting), figures prominently in their lore, as do other more positive traits noted by Mark Twain: "[Rivermen] were in the main honest, trustworthy, faithful to promises and duty, and often picturesquely magnanimous." Worthy inheritors of the horse-alligator image associated with their piratical and backwoods predecessors, the western boatmen, along with their "illegal" brethren and sistren—river robbers, cardsharps, and ladies of easy virtue—provided an extravagantly colorful and wild phase in the development of America.

THE ERIE CANAL
Rowdy Life on the Big Ditch

The Erie Canal, America's first great engineering project, was completed in 1825 after eight years of grueling labor. Its 82 locks over a 363-mile course linked the Hudson River to Lake Erie, providing a water route from the Atlantic to the frontier, and greatly stimulated the nation's development. The canal also inspired a distinctive body of lore and legends. Popular fancy turned the Irish immigrants who built the Big Ditch into epic fighters and drinkers. And the "canawlers" who worked along it turned anything into legend, whether captain, cook, or mule.

CLASS WILL OUT

The Erie Canal was constructed mainly by Irish immigrants under local superintendents—often of English stock. One day, as Mr. Colt, superintendent of one of the links, was passing through a company of these laborers, he gave one of them a smart kick on his rear exposure for some real or supposed offense. The man instantly let go his barrow, and while with his left hand rubbing the seat of attack, with his right he very respectfully raised his hat, and rolling the quid in his mouth, with a peculiar knowing twinkle of the eye, said in the richest Irish brogue: "Faith and by Jesus, if yer honor kicks so hard while ye're a colt, what'll ye do when ye get to be a horse?"

WORK INCENTIVE

As work on the last locks of the Erie Canal progressed, the diggers lost no time. For the impatient residents of Buffalo, however, work moved too slowly. They watched and waited anxiously. Finally, a "Yankee" idea occurred to one of them. The next morning, when the Irish took their places in the ditch, they noticed barrels carefully placed at measured intervals along the route of the canal. They were not ordinary barrels, but whisky barrels. What was more, they were full. The game was soon out. As the Irish dug their way to a barrel, they drained it and moved on to the next and the next, until they reached the Little Buffalo Creek. Oldtimers had no trouble boasting that this was the fastest diggin' and drinkin' the canawl had ever seen.

SAINT PATRICK OF ERIE

Once the Erie Canal was in operation, snakes in and along the waterway became the bane of towpath life. A packet skipper named Joe seems to have been responsible for ridding the Erie towpath of them, helped by the indomitable descendants of Erin. Once, going through a school of water snakes, the canaler's boat lost an unlucky greenhorn overboard. According to the story, the fellow

This engraving of Lockport, New York (from Nathaniel Willis' *American Scenery,* 1840), captures life on the Big Ditch—rough, relaxed, rustic, and very picturesque. The rickety hotel (left) also reminds us that many of the "canawlers" led gypsylike lives.

hadn't washed since he left Ireland, and the snakes in the canal died of poisoning right then and there. This gave Joe an idea. Since most Irishmen carried a bowl filled with Irish field dirt, Joe took a handful of dirt from each of the Irish passengers aboard and scattered it liberally on the banks along the canal as he went. Since that day, there have been few snakes near the towpath.

THE ERIE'S PAUL BUNYAN

McCarthy, a canalboat mule driver, was supposed to have been the strongest man on the canal in the 1840's. One night, just after his team picked up the towrope for his six-hour trick, the line broke. McCarthy picked up the rope, put it over his shoulder, and hauled away for five hours, without anyone aboard knowing what was happening to the boat. Meanwhile the boat, a leaky tub filled with crushed stone, had her bottom ripped out on a sunken rock, and though she sank, McCarthy never stopped pulling. He hauled that barge along the channel for seven miles, its keel sinking deeper into the mud. The state legislature later voted him $500 for scooping the canal four feet deeper all along the way from Pittsford to Rochester.

THE GIANT SQUASH

One year a big drought hit the Erie, and the canal and its feeders were almost dry. A woman in Weedsport was arrested for filling her washtub from the Erie and thus stranding 15 canalboats. One fellow from Eagle Harbor made out all right, though. He had a squash vine that he had been nursing along by spitting on it every so often. When he finally stuck the roots into the canal to water them, the vine dragged out water like a big hose and left 10 miles of canal bottom bare. The plant swelled so fast, the farmer had to run to keep from getting squashed. The plants swelled like rubber balloons, and one section of the vine actually passed him by, going like a racer snake. He grabbed at a flowerbud, but by that time it had turned into a flower and

Sam Patch was a brash young millworker from Rhode Island who jumped to entertain crowds from towns that grew up or flourished because of the canal's existence. He died leaping 125 feet from Genesee Falls at Rochester, New York, in 1829. For many years after, Sam's feats inspired songs, plays, poems, and drawings.

then into a good-sized squash so fast it blew off his hand as a fistful of gunpowder would have done. He made a living for years selling sections of the vine's leaves—the veins made good drainage tile.

BRAWLING CANAWLERS

Cap'n Ed was a Civil War veteran who knew the canal intimately for half a century. The cap'n used to stop fights by stepping in and thrashing the combatants one at a time or, if they preferred, together. When he was about 75, he decided to follow a custom of hiring a fighter. On the first voyage out, it occurred to him that he hadn't tried his slugger to see whether he was up to canal standards; so he picked a fight and knocked out the professional.

But the classic tale at Buffalo is of the big battle between Charley and Jack. Jack bit off a piece of Charley's ear and spat it on the deck, whereupon there followed this curt dialogue: "There's your ear, Charley." "You bit it off, you cuss. Now eat it!"

The Erie Canal inspired songs from workers, travelers, and residents along the canal. Though some songs were derived from traditional airs and commercial "pops," others, like the "E-ri-e," are original folksongs from the canal period.

THE VOYAGEURS: EPIC LIVES

When the artist Mrs. F. A. Hopkins accompanied her fur-trading husband into the wilds of North America in the 1870's, she painted scenes that captured the strain of paddling through most of a 24-hour day, as well as the peaceful respite from labor (above) that the shelter of upturned canoes and the night's campfire provided.

The fur business in Canada was for a long time under the control of the French and later the Scots. The United States became involved in the fur trade in 1808, when John Jacob Astor founded the American Fur Company. But whoever was in command, the actual transport of the goods remained in the strong hands of the *voyageurs* who were hired by each outfit's chief trader, whose title was *le bourgeois*.

The voyageurs, most of them sons of French fathers and Indian mothers, ferried pelts along the rivers of America's West. Earlier, French boys born in the New World had shucked off civilization and vanished as *coureurs de bois* into the forests, where they took Indian wives and lived by trapping. During the 19th century their male descendants (along with Indian-Creoles of the South) turned, in the same lust for freedom, to the wild. But trapping was by then big business; the voyageurs, albeit free spirited, were hired hands and were treated, as John James Audubon was to observe, almost like slaves. They picked up pelts that trappers had bartered at scattered trading posts in Indian territory and eventually paddled, pulled, carried,

and sometimes—if the wind was right—sailed those furs back to such depots as Montreal and St. Louis. From those ports the pelts, especially beaver (then in worldwide demand for the manufacture of men's hats), were carried on larger craft to Europe.

Inured to the rigors of life in an often icy wilderness, the typical voyageur was only about five feet four or five inches tall, with a powerful torso and shoulders but surprisingly short, thin legs. Long-legged men could not endure the cramping confines of a canoe, where the added weight of a big man was more of a hindrance than a help. Those boys who reached adolescence short and bandy-legged could look forward to the brief but adventurous life of a voyageur. Working on three- to five-year contracts that required them to paddle as many as 20 hours a day in return for a yearly wage of $100 plus a few clothes, the voyageurs lived lives so strenuous that most of them died before the age of 40. Yet they took great pride in their strength and endurance. When voyageurs signed up with the American Fur Company, each promised to serve his particular bourgeois and "to do his

will, to seek his profit, avoid his damage, and refrain from trading on one's own account." They set out from the company's northern base at Mackinaw on the Straits of Mackinac between lakes Michigan and Huron, from its western base at St. Louis, or from smaller posts like that at Prairie du Chien on the Mississippi amid a flurry of "bon voyages." Though the bourgeois or his clerk traveled as overseer, once on the water the voyageurs informally took charge on the trips that sometimes covered 1,000 arduous miles.

Singing got the men working in unison and kept their strokes at 40 dips of the paddle per minute. This was a pace that, in calm water, could move a canoe 6 miles an hour or 100 miles a day. As great a motivator as song was, the natural pride and competitiveness of the men acted as an even greater impetus to keep at their grueling work. On occasion they paddled 24 hours nonstop in races among themselves, alternately singing and munching slices of pemmican.

At places along the route where rapids were too dangerous or where the river had to be abandoned for other reasons, the men vied with one another to carry the largest loads of supplies on the overland portage. "A rain during the day has rendered the path much worse than it otherwise would have been," recounts an observer. "Yet the men often take their keg of pork, 70 lbs., or two bags of flour, 160 lbs., or a keg, 230 lbs., and carry it half a mile before they rest. In a few instances, men have taken three bags—240 lbs." The men did not walk but ran at a dogtrot, sometimes through mud and water, over rocks and undergrowth, and slowed only to scale rock faces while the mosquitoes and flies buzzed about their faces. Broken limbs were not uncommon. Portaging was dangerous but much safer than the exhilarating sport of shooting the rapids: wooden crosses marked many places near riverbanks where voyageurs had met death in the white water. "When you are in the worst rapids," they would sing, "let the

Virgin Mary be your guide."

Up at 3 or 4 a.m., paddling a few hours before breakfast, often skipping lunch but never their numerous pipes, the voyageurs paddled and portaged until well past nightfall when, following supper, they would patch up the day's damage to the canoe with pine resin. Finally they settled for a last smoke as they sat by the campfire. Sipping a bit of rum, they told tales of the man-eating Wendigo, of the giant beaver, of the Folly of the Woods who stole men's minds, as well as of the more familiar "horses, dogs, canoes, women, and strong men who can fight a good battle."

On the wild Missouri River the voyageurs used heavy, hollowed-out pirogues; instead of portaging they removed to the riverbank and wrapped an end of a huge buffalo-hide rope around themselves so they could drag the boats along, inches at a time. Hundreds of miles up the Missouri they reached the mouth of the Platte River. Like the Equator is to deepwater sailors, that was considered a special line, separating the upper Missouri from the lower. Here boats stopped so the *hivernants* (winterers, or men who had spent a winter out in the wild) could initiate the greenhorns, or *mangeurs de lard,* whose nickname, "porkeaters," was a humorous reference to the typical tenderfoot's queasy dismay at being fed a daily ration of a quart of cornmeal hominy cooked in grease. The porkeaters' heads were shaved as part of their initiation, and they were taught many a superstitious saw during their first winter "outward bound."

Come spring, the men were on the lookout for omens; they hoped particularly to avoid seeing a bad-luck-sign crow. Pushing northward all kept their eyes peeled for fish, fresh meat, and honey trees. According to historian Grace Nute: "A beaver's tail was considered an especially dainty morsel, and the story is that the voyageurs ate it even during Lent. To determine how far they were sinning, the matter was referred to the Sorbonne, and, no doubt because the aquatic habits of the beaver so closely resemble those of fishes, the privilege of eating the tail in Lent was permitted."

The voyageurs stuck to the letter of their various agreements and expected like treatment, but they didn't always get it in the right spirit. "A story is told of M. Saint Jean, a trader on the upper Mississippi, who upon a certain occasion ordered one of his Frenchmen to accompany a party to the forest to chop up wood. The man refused. 'I was not hired,' he said, 'to chop wood.' 'Ah! For what then were you hired?' 'To steer a boat.' 'Very well; steer a boat, then, since you prefer it.' It was midwinter. The recusant was marched to the riverside and placed in the stern of the boat, which lay fastened in the ice. After serving a couple of hours at his legitimate employment, with the thermometer below zero, he was quite content to take his place with the chopping party, and never again thought it good policy to choose work for himself."

Many voyageurs left the company's headquarters in the fall to deliver the winter's supplies to outposts where they themselves would be forced to remain until spring. Then, boats loaded with pelts, each hivernant would sing his way back to Mackinaw, St. Louis, or some other entrepôt. The songs sounding through the woods alerted locals that canoes would soon be bursting into view as the voyageurs put on a last push of speed.

During the 1830's steamboats began to replace the paddlers, and within decades the free-spirited voyageurs had ceased to power along the rivers of *le pays sauvage* (Indian country) by muscle, song, and epic will.

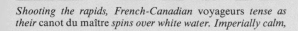

Shooting the rapids, French-Canadian voyageurs *tense as their* canot du maître *spins over white water. Imperially calm, the artist—wife of the Scottish secretary to the chief administrator of the Hudson's Bay Company—is seated amidships.*

JOLLY RAFTSMEN
Frontiersmen Afloat

When lumber, livestock, produce, and large numbers of people first moved along the central waterways into the Mississippi and downriver toward New Orleans, the bulk of the traffic was floated on rafts, which, after unloading at the point of destination, were themselves dismantled and sold for wood. Crewing the rafts was a scruffy assortment of "horse-alligator" backwoodsmen. Evicted squatters, ex-Indian fighters, and the like, Mississippi raftsmen were the earliest in a long line of hell-raising "Kentucky sailors." Here are a few highlights of their legend:

A RUDE AWAKENING

Every time the legendary riverman whipped his weight in wildcats, he talked up a storm about it afterward; and then (according to a contemporary observer) he became "not only loquacious but running over with the most extravagant superlatives in the broadhorn [Mississippi flatboat] dialect." Here is an example of the kind of broadhorn bragging one might have heard on the levee at Natchez, Mississippi, or many another river town dock around the year 1830:

According to legend, many pioneer families spent their lives on rafts like this one.

One day as I was sitting in the stern of my broadhorn, the old *Free & Easy,* on the Mississippi, taking a horn of midshipman's grog with a tin pot in each hand, first a draft of whisky and then one of river water, who should float down past me but Joe Snag. He was in a snooze as fast as a church with his mouth wide open—he had been ramsquaddled with whisky for a fortnight, and as it evaporated from his body it looked like the steam from a vent pipe. Knowing the feller would be darned hard to wake with all this steam on, as he floated past me I hit him a crack over his knob with my big steering oar.

He waked in a thundering rage. Says he, "Hallo, stranger, who axed you to crack my lice?" Says I, "Shut up your mouth or your teeth will get sunburnt."

Upon this, he crooked up his neck and neighed like a stallion. I clapped my arms and crowed like a cock. Says he, "If you are a game chicken, I'll pick all the pinfeathers off of you." (For some time back I had been so wolfy about the head and shoulders [in such a ferocious mood], I was obliged to keep covered up in a salt crib to keep from spoiling, for I had not had a fight for as much as 10 days.)

Says I, "Give us none of your chin music, but set your kickers on land and I'll give you a fierce licking." The fellow now jumped ashore, and he was so tall he could not tell when his feet were cold. Says he, "Take care how I light on you," and he gave a real sockdologer that made my very liver and lights turn to jelly. But he found me a real scrouger [crowder]. I brake three of his ribs, and he knocked out five of my teeth and one eye. He was the severest colt that ever I tried to break. I finally got a bite hold that he could not shake off. We were now parted by some boatmen, and we were so exhorsted that it was more than a month before either one of us could have a fight again.

A TALL TESTIMONIAL

According to popular tradition, the rivermen were much given to convivial banter of the Crockett variety. Here is a typical exchange between one raftsman and another who was passing him a bottle:

"Hey! Don't let that stuff drop like that on your boots! I spilt some on my new shore shoes last week and it ate the uppers clean down to the soles."

"Was them shoes tanned with oqueejum?" asked the other in a quietly interested way, as if he were seeking scientific knowledge.

"No, sir. That thar leather was tanned with the best hemlock bark, and the shoes cost me $3 back in Red Wing."

"Now, say, my friend," rejoined the other, "don't you know better than to buy leather tanned with hemlock? What you want is leather tanned with oqueejum, and then whisky can't eat it. You see, whisky and hemlock, they get together on social terms same's you and me, and then the whisky does its deadly work and swallows the leather.

"But whisky and oqueejum's enemies, and when they meet, the

whisky gets licked every time. That's why I keep my stomach lined with it. Oqueejum's made from the bamjam tree which grows in India to a height of more than 1,000 feet. Its wood is so hard, they have to cut it with a cold chisel. It stands to reason that it's stronger than hemlock. Try some on your stomach and then your liquor won't get to your head like this."

HAIR OF THE BUFFALO

The boatman's proverbial drink was "tanglefoot," otherwise known as forty-rod, a rotgut whisky reputed to kill at 40 rods distance and take the hair off a buffalo robe; but tradition tells of some Kentucky sailors whose cast-iron stomachs were equal to potations even stronger than the infamous forty-rod.

According to one story, a raft once put in at a river port and the already drunken crewmen became more than usually rumbustious, so the townspeople locked themselves in their cellars. Later the same night, one of the raftsmen was rummaging about an empty backyard and came upon what he thought was a still, from which the liquor was still dripping. He went back to the raft, fetched an empty bottle, and filled it with fluid that he described with joy as the finest corn whisky he had ever tasted. It turned out to be lye. The frugal pastor's wife had an upended barrel in the backyard, which she had filled with wood ashes preparatory to soapmaking. But the raftsman who had drunk it never turned a hair—or so they say who tell the story.

SEEKING JUSTICE

A tall, gaunt Hoosier, a flatboatman, walked in the door of a lawyer's house in a Louisiana river town. "Does a squire [lawyer] live here?" he asked. "They call me so," said the lawyer. "Well, squire," continued the intruder, "I have got a case for you, and I want justice, if it costs the best load of produce that ever come from In-di-an'." The man of the law asked what was the difficulty.

"It's this, squire: I'm bound for Orleans and put in here for coffee and other little fixins. A chap with a face whiskered up like a prairie dog says to me: 'Stranger, I see you've got cocks on board your boat. Bring one ashore, and I'll pit one against him that'll lick his legs off in less time than you could gaff him.' Well, squire, *I never take a dar* [take a challenge] lying down. Says I, 'Stranger, I'm thar at once.' And in 20 minutes the cocks were on the levee like perfect saints.

"We chucked them together, and then my bird—squire, now you mind, squire—my bird never struck a lick, not a single blow, but took to his heels and run, and by thunders, threw up his feed, actually vomited. The stakeholder gave up the money agin me, and now I want justice. As sure as fogs, my bird was physicked [dosed with a purgative] or he'd have stood up to his business like a wildcat." The lawyer heard the story with patience, but flatly refused to have anything to do with the matter.

"Perhaps," said the boatman, drawing out a fat wallet, "you think I can't pay. Here's the money; help yourself—give me justice, and draw on my purse like an ox team." To the flatboatman's astonishment, the lawyer still refused but gave his would-be client some free advice about going on board of his boat, shoving off for New Orleans, and abandoning the suit altogether.

The flatboatman was amazed and asked the lawyer if he was "a sure-enough squire." Receiving an affirmative reply, he sat down, put his hat aside, crossed his legs, and then, looking up to the ceiling with an expression of great patience, requested the squire to read to him the Louisiana laws on cockfighting. The lawyer said he did not know of a single statute in the state on that subject. The boatman started up as if he had been shot, saying: "No laws in the state on cockfighting? No, no, squire, you can't possum [fool] me—give us the law." The lawyer repeated what he had said, and the boatman demanded, "What's all them thar books about?"

"All about the law," said the lawyer. "Well then, squire, am I to understand that not one of them thar books contain a single law on cockfighting?" "You are." "And am I to understand that thar ain't no laws in Louisiana on cockfighting?" "You are." "And am I to understand that you call yourself a squire and that you don't know anything about cockfighting?" "You are." The boatman picked up his hat and started for the door, then turned round with a broad grin on his face to make this parting remark: "Any squire that don't know the laws of cockfighting, in my opinion, is distinctly an infernal old chuckleheaded fool!"

Mississippi rivermen as seen by a Romantic: William Baldwin's "The Merry Raftsmen"

MIKE FINK
King of the Keelboatmen

Most famous of all western boatmen was Mike Fink, a keelboatman who drank a gallon of whisky daily without staggering and wore a red feather in his hat proclaiming him king bully on the river. He left illegitimate children throughout the Mississippi Valley, and because his hair was red, any red-haired child seen playing on the riverbank was dubbed "Mike Fink's brat" by the other boatmen. According to one story, while engaged in his favorite sport of "shooting the cup" (off a friend's head), Mike aimed too low, killed the friend, and was himself shot dead by an avenger. Some of the many Mike Fink tales are related here:

All rivermen got "chawed up" now and then in a "free fight" (free-for-all).

OLD BANG-ALL

Like heroes of yore who bestowed names on their swords, Mike rejoiced in a .45-caliber Kentucky rifle he called Bang-All. It was "slicker'n a wildcat and quicker in action," he claimed, and handled like a "willow sapling in spring." The barrel length and the drop at the heel just suited his stumpy shoulders, while its hair-trigger action particularly pleased Mike's snapping-turtle disposition. Bang-All had been made to Mike's order—he himself had selected the tree that produced the beautiful full curly-maple stock, and he had sat on an old stump swapping tall tales while the gunsmith forged the crude iron bar into the long octagon barrel.

The gun's overall length was 58 inches; the stock was ornamented with 47 brass and silver inlays; on the cheekpiece was Mike's lucky six-point star inlaid in brass; and on both sides of the stock were etched figures of Indians in silver, of crescents, diamonds, dogs, deer, hearts, and, of course, the American Eagle.

MIKE'S BRAG

"I'm a Salt River roarer! I'm a ringtailed squealer! I'm a reg'lar screamer from the ol' Massassip'! I'm the very infant that refused his milk before its eyes were open, and called out for a bottle of old rye. I love the women an' I'm chockful o' fight! I'm half wild horse and half cockeyed alligator and the rest o' me is crooked snags an' redhot snappin' turkle. I can hit like fourth-proof lightnin' an' every lick I make in the woods lets in an acre o' sunshine. I can outrun, outjump, outshoot, outbrag, outdrink, an' outfight, rough-an'-tumble, no holts barred, ary man on both sides the river from Pittsburgh to New Orleans an' back agin to St. Louiee. Come on, you flatters, you bargers, you milk-white mechanics, an' see how tough I am to chaw! I ain't had a fight for two days an' I'm spilin' for plenty of exercise. Cock-a-doodle-do!"

FRESH PROVISIONS

Passing down the river one day, Mike observed a flock of sheep grazing on the shore, and being in want of fresh provisions but scorning to buy them, he hit upon the following expedient. He noticed that there was an eddy near to the shore, and, as it was about dusk, he landed his boat in the eddy and tied her fast. In his cargo there were some bladders of Scotch snuff. Mike opened one of these, and taking out a handful of the contents he went ashore, and catching five or six of the sheep, rubbed their faces very thoroughly with the snuff. He then sent one of his men in a great hurry to the sheepowner's house to tell him that he had better come down and see what was the matter with his sheep. Upon reaching the scene in answer to Mike's summons, the gentleman saw a portion of his flock very singularly affected: leaping, bleating, rubbing their noses against the

The wild men of the western river loved music—here keelboatmen stomp out a breakdown to the tune of "Jolly, jolly raftsman's the life for me," played by a fiddler.

ground and against each other, and performing all manner of undignified and unsheeplike antics. The gentleman was sorely puzzled and demanded of Mike if he knew what was the matter with the sheep.

"You don't know?" answered Mike very gravely. "I do not," replied the gentleman. "Did you ever hear of the black murrain?" asked Mike in a confidential whisper. "Yes," said the sheepowner in a terrified reply. "Well, that's it!" said Mike. "All the sheep upriver's got it dreadful. Dyin' like rotten dogs— hundreds a day." "You don't say so," answered the victim, "and is there no cure for it?" "Only *one* as I knows on," was the reply. "You see, the murrain's dreadful catchin', and ef you don't git them away as is got it, they'll kill the whole flock. Better shoot 'em right off; they've got to die anyway." "But no man could single out the infected sheep and shoot them from among the flock," said the gentleman. "My name's Mike Fink!" was the curt reply. And it was answer enough. The gentleman begged Mike to shoot the infected sheep and throw them into the river. This was exactly what Mike wanted, but he pretended to resist.

"It mought be a mistake," he said.

"They'll maybe git well. You'd better go an' ask some of the neighbors ef it was the murrain sure 'nough." The gentleman insisted, and Mike modestly resisted, until finally he was promised a couple of gallons of old peach brandy if he would comply. His scruples thus finally overcome, Mike shot the sheep, threw them into the eddy, and got the brandy. After dark, the men jumped into the water, hauled the sheep aboard, and by daylight had them neatly packed away aboard their boat and were gliding merrily down the stream.

AT ODDS WITH THE LAW

Mike was telling jokes one day in the "grocery" [tavern] in the tiny town of Westport, Indiana, opposite Louisville on the Ohio. All of the drinkers laughed heartily and uproariously at his yarns—all save one man, a little dried-up fellow, whose pensive face suggested that he was contemplating death and eternity. Mike at last walked over to him. "See here, mister," he said, "these yarns I been tellin' is funny, and you stand there as glum as a dead catfish on a sandbar. I tell snorters for folk to laugh at in a good-humored way, an' by God, I don't let no man make light of 'em." "Is that so?" the little man

asked negligently, and he sank back into his gloomy contemplations. Mike, at the bar, told another yarn, and the company dutifully howled. But the little man, sternly watched by Mike, looked positively tearful. Mike stamped across the floor. "Whoop!" yelled Mike. "Calamity's a-comin'! I'm a Salt River roarer, an' I'm chockful o' fight. I'm—"

But in the middle of his boast, Mike was surprised. For the wizened mourner suddenly leaped into the air, and as his body swooped downward his fist smacked Mike below the ear, and the keelboatman fell sprawling. "Is that so?" said the little man. Mike staggered to his feet, blood in his eye, roaring with anger. But as he came forward, his opponent doubled into a tangle of flaying feet and clawing fists, and Mike went into a whirl of flying arms and legs and emerged with a scratched face and a sinking in his stomach where a swift kick had landed. Angrier than ever, he flopped on the man again against a torrent of claws and leaping boots, and again he was able to do nothing. Four times more he tried in vain to seize or to strike his rival, and each time Mike looked more as if calamity and desolation had struck him. "Stranger," panted Mike at last, "I'm free to own I can't do nothin' with you. You're tougher to chaw nor [than] buckskin."

"Is that so?" dreamily asked the visitor. "Listen to me. I'm Ned Taylor, sheriff of this county; and if you and your crew don't get the hell out of here in 10 minutes I'll arrest the mess of ye!" "Five's enough," said Mike. "You're a snag, a riffle, and a sawyer all in one." In response to this compliment, the sheriff said, "Is that so?" and resumed his gloomy contemplation in the corner.

FINK MEETS CROCKETT

As the Mike Fink legend came to rival that of Davy Crockett, an encounter between the two was duly invented, appearing in the *Crockett Almanac* for 1839. The narrator of the yarn is Davy:

One night I fell in with him in the

According to one 19th-century writer, Mike Fink was "the William Tell of marksmen, the most daring of all wild-forest adventurers, and the prince of moose catchers."

woods, where him and his wife shook down a blanket for me in his wigwam. In the morning says Mike to me: "I've got the handsomest wife, and the fastest horse, and the sharpest shooting iron in all Kentuck, and if any man dare doubt it, I'll be in his hair quicker than Hell could scorch a feather." This put my dander up, and says I: "I've nothing to say agin your wife, Mike, for it can't be denied she's a shocking handsome woman, and Mrs. Crockett's in Tennessee, and I've got no horses. Mike, I don't exactly like to tell you you lie about what you say about your rifle, but I'm damned if you speak the truth, and I'll prove it. Do you see that ar cat sitting on the top rail of your potato patch, about 150 yards off? If he ever hears agin, I'll be shot if it shan't be without ears." So I blazed away, and I'll bet you a horse, the ball cut off both the old tomcat's ears close to his head and shaved the hair off clean across the skull, as slick as if I'd done it with a razor, and the critter never stirred nor knew he'd lost his ears till he tried to scratch 'em. "Talk about your rifle after that, Mike!" says I. "Do you see that ar sow away off furder than the end of the world," says Mike, "with a litter of pigs round her?" And he lets fly. The old sow give a grunt but never stirred in her tracks, and Mike falls to loading and firing for dear life, till he hadn't left one of them ar pigs enough tail to make a toothpick on. "Now," says he, "Colonel Crockett, I'll be pretticularly obleedged to you if you'll put them ar pig's tails on again," says he. "That's onpossible, Mike," says I, "but you've left one of 'em about an inch to steer by, and if it had a-ben my work, I wouldn't have done it so wasteful." So I lets fly, and cuts off the apology he'd left the poor cretur for decency. I wish I may drink the whole of Old Mississip, without a drop of the rale stuff in it, if you wouldn't have thort the tail had been drove in with a hammer. That made Mike kinder sorter wrothy, and he sends a ball after his wife as she was going to the spring and knocked half her coomb out of her head and calls out to her to

Flatboatman Jack Pierce knocked out Mike Fink by butting him but got his own skull stove in soon afterward by a ram.

stop for me to take a blizzard at what was left on it. The angeliferous critter stood still as a scarecrow in a cornfield, for she'd got used to Mike's tricks by long practice. "No, no, Mike," says I, "Davy Crockett's hand would be sure to shake if his iron war pointed within a hundred mile of a shemale, and I give up beat, Mike, and as we've had our eye-openers a-ready, we'll now take a phlegm-cutter, by way of an anti-fogmatic, and then we'll disperse."

WOMEN IN MIKE'S LIFE

Mike's relations with women were in keeping with the violent tenor of all his dealings. One story has it that he once tried—by way of a friendly practical joke—to throw a scare into Mrs. Davy Crockett by pouncing on her dressed in an alligator's skin. The undaunted Mrs. Crockett pulled out her "Arkansas toothpick" [bowie knife], ripped open the disguise at one swipe, and, finding Mike inside, went on to trounce him with her bare hands. Another—less edifying—tale has Mike curing his wife, Peg, of looking at other men by forcing her to lie down in a pile of leaves to which he set fire.

It was only fitting that the king of keelboatmen should be presented with a daughter who was cut of the same cloth as Mrs. Crockett. One of

the many stories describes Mike's sole acknowledged offspring thus:

If thar was a gal that desarved to be christened *one-o'-the-gals,* then that gal was Sal Fink, the Mississippi Screamer. She fought a duel once with a thunderbolt and come off without a singe, while at the first fire she split the thunderbolt all to flinders, and gave the pieces to Uncle Sam's artillerymen to touch off their cannon with. When a gal about six years old, she used to play seesaw on the Mississippi snags, and arter she war done she would snap 'em off an' so cleared a large district of the river. She used to ride down the river on an alligator's back, standen upright an' dancing "Yankee Doodle," and could leave all the steamers behind. But the greatest feat she ever did, positively outdid anything that ever was did. One day when she war out in the forest making a collection o' wildcat skins for her family's winter beddin', she war captered in the most all-sneakin' manner by about 50 Injuns an' carried by 'em to Roast Flesh Hollow, whar the blood-drinkin' wild varmints detarmined to skin her alive, sprinkle a leetle salt over her, an' devour her before her own eyes; so they took an' tied her to a tree, to keep till mornin' should bring the rest o' their ring-nosed sarpints to enjoy the fun.

Arter that, they lit a large fire, turned the bottom of their feet toward the blaze Injun fashion, and went to sleep to dream o' thar mornin's feast; well, arter the critters got into a somniferous snore, Sal got into an all lightnin' of a temper and burst all the ropes about her like an apron string! She then found a pile o' ropes, too, and tied all the Injuns' heels together all round the fire. Then fixin' a cord to the shins of every two couple, she, with a sud-denachous jerk, pulled the intire lot o' sleepin' redskins into that ar great fire, fast together, an' then sloped like a panther out of her pen, in the midst of the tallest yellin', howlin', scram-blin', and singin' that war ever seen or heerd on since the great burnin' o' buffalo prairie!

LOWLIFE
Robbers, Rowdies, and Rapscallions

Life on the Mississippi, Ohio, and other great waterways in the early 19th century could be idyllic, but there was a seamy side. Some river towns, like Natchez-Under-the-Hill, became nothing more than coarse dives for riverboatmen. Water traffic increased faster than society could organize or enforce the law. Travelers and goods were endangered all along the rivers and the shore routes by every kind of desperado. The most dreaded spot of all was Cave in Rock, Illinois, near the junction of the Ohio and Mississippi rivers; for decades it was the home of outlaws who preyed on river and overland traffic. The tales that spread about lowlife on the rivers were based in actuality, but the attraction-repulsion that attends villainy led to the kind of exaggeration which changes facts to legends.

COLONEL UNPLUG

The most famous of the river pirates on the Ohio in emigrant days was a certain Colonel Plug. His procedure was to go upstream from his riverside headquarters and pretend to be a traveler marooned on the riverbank. When kindhearted settlers took him aboard, he surreptitiously picked the caulking from the seams of their boat, nicely timing the operation so that the craft would sink in front of his establishment. Then his helpers rowed out to salvage the cargo and save the colonel—but not the emigrants. Plug met his end when he miscalculated the sinking time of a flatboat and drowned with his victims before his henchmen arrived.

THE FAMILY FORTUNE

One of the many outlaws based in Cave in Rock was James Ford. As a "front," he operated a ferry on the Ohio River where emigrants crossed from Kentucky to Illinois on the road west. Ford's gang robbed their victims along the roads leading up to and away from the ferry, and among his confederates was Billy Potts. Potts kept an inn near the ferry, and if the gang hadn't already gotten to a well-heeled client, Potts took his money—and often his life—during the course of the night.

Billy Potts had raised his son to take his place in the Ford gang. But young Potts, while holding up some travelers along the road, was recognized by local farmers who happened by. When Ford heard of this, he ordered young Potts to leave the area lest he bring the law down on himself, his family, and the whole Ford operation. So young Potts went off to distant parts and for several years made his own way. During this time he grew a beard, gained weight, and so changed that he felt confident no one at home would recognize him. That was confirmed when, approaching Ford's ferry, he was held up along the road by men he knew to be members of Ford's gang, and he had to produce considerable proof that he was young Potts before they agreed that they would let him go.

In the evening he arrived at his parents' inn, and as he anticipated, they did not recognize him. He had decided to conceal his identity until

The most notorious occupant of Cave in Rock was Samuel Meason, alias Wilson, who moved in about 1797. This 1938 illustration shows how Meason used liquor and women to lure riverboatmen; he not only took their cargoes—but their lives.

after he impressed his father with the money he had made on his own. That night, as they sat chatting, young Potts displayed a large roll of money and confided that he was glad to be in such a safe place. Still savoring the surprise to come, he asked for a drink of water. The old man led him out to the spring, and as the youth bent over to drink, his unknowing father stabbed him, took the money from his pocket, and buried the body.

The next morning, members of Ford's gang rode up to the inn to celebrate the return of their old friend. When they heard the father boasting of how he had dispatched a youthful guest, they were forced to tell him who the boy was. Both mother and father denied this, the father insisting that the fellow probably once knew his son and so fooled them. The mother said she could settle it, because her son had a distinctive birthmark on his back. They all went off to the grave and dug up the body. And as all looked on, the horrified, distraught father ripped the shirt away from the corpse and exposed the birthmark.

CLOSING THE CIRCLE

Many years ago, two brothers named Harpe appeared in Kentucky, spreading death and terror wherever they went. A savage thirst for blood, a deep-rooted malevolence against human nature, could alone be discovered in their actions. Finally, a Mr. Stegal, sole survivor of a family massacred by the Harpes, caught up with one of them and managed to sever his head from his body. This bloody trophy was placed in the fork of a tree, where it long remained a revolting object of horror. The spot is still called Harpe's Head. The other Harpe made his way to the neighborhood of Natchez where he joined a gang of robbers headed by Meason, whose villainies were so notorious that a reward was offered for his head. Harpe took an opportunity, when the rest of his companions were absent, to slay Meason, and putting his head in a bag, he carried it to Natchez and claimed the reward. The claim was admitted; the head of Meason was recognized; but so also was the face of Harpe, who was arrested, condemned, and executed.

ANNIE CHRISTMAS

A hoax is the tribute paid to the strength of a belief, and one of the great hoaxes of American folklore is Annie Christmas. She was concocted in the 1920's by two New Orleans journalists as a parody of the tales and traditions of the Mississippi. But it backfired, and their raunchy character is now often treated as a genuine folk figure.

Oldtimers say that the Negro longshoremen and all life on the riverfront are not what they used to be. In other days men were really men, yet the toughest of them all was a woman. Her name was Annie Christmas. She was six feet eight inches tall and weighed more than 250 pounds. She wore a neat mustache and had a voice as loud and deep as a foghorn on the river. The tough keelboatmen, terrors of the river in other days, stood in awe of her, and there wasn't a hulking giant of a stevedore who didn't jump when Annie snapped her black fingers. Most of the time Annie dressed like a man and worked as a man. Often she worked as a longshoreman. She would carry a barrel of flour under each arm and another balanced on

Tossing a victim's body off a cliff—a typical scene from the life of so-called Great Western Land Pirate, John Murrell

her head. Once she towed a keelboat from New Orleans to Natchez on a dead run and never got out of breath. Annie could outdrink any man in the South. She would put down a barrel of beer and chase it with 10 quarts of whisky, without stopping. Sometimes she got mad in a bar, beat up every man there, and wrecked the joint.

Then, every once in a while, Annie would get into a feminine mood. When this happened, she was 250 pounds of coal-black female, really seductive and enticing in a super sort of way. Of course, Annie was as magnificent amorously as she was a fighter and drinker and she always won first prize as a lover.

She would really dress up for these occasions, wearing red satin gowns and scarlet plumes in her woolly hair. She always wore a commemorative necklace containing beads for all the eyes, ears, and noses she had gouged from men, a bead for each one. The necklace was only 30 feet long, but then she only counted white men; there would not have been enough beads in New Orleans if she had counted Negroes.

Annie had 12 coal-black sons, each seven feet tall, all born at the same time. She had plenty of other babies, too, but these were her favorites. Whenever she got ready to have a baby, she drank a quart of whisky and lay down. Afterward she had another quart and went back to work.

Finally Annie met a man who could lick her and then she fell in love for the first time in her life. But the man didn't want her, so she bedecked herself in finery and her famous necklace and committed suicide.

Her funeral was appropriately elaborate. Her body was placed in a coal-black coffin and driven to the wharf in a coal-black hearse, drawn by six coal-black horses. Six on each side marched her coal-black sons, dressed in coal-black suits. At the riverfront the coffin was placed on a coal-black barge, and that coal-black night, with no moon shining, her dozen coal-black sons and the coal-black coffin floated out to sea on the barge and vanished forever.

SOMNAMBULISTIC PILOT
King of the River

The greatest trove of American riverboat writing is Mark Twain's classic Life on the Mississippi, *which mingles history and autobiography with folklore and fiction. According to Twain—a former steamboat pilot—the navigator-helmsman "knew better how to handle the boat than anybody" and so was "an absolute monarch who could do exactly as he pleased." In this selection from the book, Twain records a feat of piloting extraordinary even among those kings.*

A riverboat pilot steers his craft. Mark Twain asserted that the captain gave orders "in the pomp of a very brief authority while the vessel backed into the stream." After the boat had gained way she was "under the sole and unquestioned control of the pilot."

There used to be an excellent pilot on the river, a Mr. X., who was a somnambulist. Late one night, his boat was approaching Helena, Arkansas; the water was low and the crossing above the town in a very blind and tangled condition. As the night was particularly drizzly, sullen, and dark, Ealer [the other pilot] was considering whether he had not better have X. called to assist, when the door opened. Now, on very dark nights, light is a deadly enemy to piloting, so the pilothouse is kept pitch black. The undefinable shape that now entered had Mr. X.'s voice. This said: "Let me take her, George; I've seen this place since you have, and it is so crooked that I reckon I can run it myself easier than I could tell you how to do it."

"It is kind of you, and I swear *I* am willing. I haven't got another drop of perspiration left in me. I have been spinning around and around the wheel like a squirrel." So the black phantom assumed the wheel without saying anything, steadied the waltzing steamer with a turn or two, and then stood at ease, coaxing her a little to this side and then to that, as gently and as sweetly as if the time had been noonday. When Ealer, panting and breathless, observed this marvel of steering, he stared, and wondered, and finally said: "Well, I thought I knew how to steer a steamboat, but that was another mistake of mine."

X. said nothing but went serenely on with his work. He rang for the leads [sounding lines]; he rang to slow down the steam; he worked the boat carefully and neatly into invisible marks: as the leads shoaled more and more, he stopped the engines entirely, and the dead silence and suspense of "drifting" followed. When the shoalest water was struck, he cracked on the steam, carried her handsomely over, and then began to work her warily into the next system of shoal marks; the same patient, heedful use of leads and engines followed: then, under a tremendous head of steam, the boat went swinging over the reef and away into deep water and safety!

Ealer let his long-pent breath pour out in a great, relieving sigh: "That's the sweetest piece of piloting that was ever done on the Mississippi River!" There was no reply, and he added, "Just hold her five minutes longer, partner, and let me run down and get a cup of coffee." A minute later, Ealer was comforting himself with coffee. Just then, the night watchman happened in, and was about to happen out again when he noted Ealer and exclaimed, "Who is at the wheel, sir?" "X." "Dart for the pilothouse, quicker than lightning!" The next moment, both men were flying up the pilothouse companionway, three steps at a jump! Nobody there! The great steamer was whistling down the middle of the river at her own sweet will! The watchman shot out of the place again. Ealer seized the wheel, set an engine back with power, and held his breath while the boat reluctantly swung away from a sandbar.

By and by the watchman came back and said, "Didn't that lunatic tell you he was asleep?" "No." "Well, he was. I found him walking along on top. I put him to bed." "Well, I think I'll stay by next time he has one of those fits. But I hope he'll have them often. You just ought to have seen him take this boat through Helena crossing. *I* never saw anything so gaudy before. And if he can do such gold-leaf, kid-glove, diamond-breastpin piloting when he is sound asleep, what *couldn't* he do if he was dead!"

RIVERBOAT LIFE
Fun, Games, and Prayers

A steamboat captain seeking a pilot ignored two who assured him they'd never floundered in the Mississippi and hired a third because he'd "hit every snag and turned over in every eddy and been struck on every sandbar she's got." Knowing the river's treachery was essential to maneuvering the unstable paddle-wheelers with their airy oriental cabins fit for coquetry and cards. Thwarting or being thwarted by the river occupies many tales of the boats Twain called "finer than anything on shore" that plied the rivers in the 50 years before the Civil War.

CARRIED AWAY

On the levee before a Kentucky town, a gray-haired woman stood with a group of friends. She was wearing her Sunday-best hoopskirt and looked worried. Held tightly in her black-mitted hand was a steamboat ticket to New Orleans, where she was going to visit relatives. By her were several barrels of lard she was taking from her plantation to market in the Big Town Down the River. She looked with some trepidation at the white steamboat approaching. She had never set foot on one, and her friends had told her quite freely of the dangers of steamboat travel: snags, collision, fire, the perils of racing with its risk of bursting boilers. The boat circled in over the pale water.

"Captain," she said, "I want you to promise me, before we start, that you won't run this boat in any races."

"Madam, I never race; that is, hardly ever, and I promise you to do nothing dangerous."

"Thank you so much. I feel much safer. Are you sure my lard is all right? I'll go to my room."

Down the river steamed the boat, safely, sanely, and serenely, until one day a rival boat nosed alongside, and the firemen began to shake themselves, and the roustabouts started to yell excitedly.

"Goodness me! What does this mean? It is a race?" The Kentucky lady walked the cabin deck, twisting her fingers, watching the rival with bright eyes that made her face look younger. Suddenly she darted up the stairs to the hurricane deck. "Captain, you can take back your promise. I come from where they race horses, I do, and I won't be beat!"

A smile crossed the captain's tense face. "Madam," he cried, "we're doing the best we can."

"What! And you mean to say that boat is getting ahead?"

"Yes. She's putting oil on her wood—see the black smoke?—and we haven't any oil. We can't beat her on wood alone; can't get the boilers hot enough."

Just then, the stewardess ran up the stairs, a flatiron in each hand. "Cap'n, suh," she shouted, "if de engineeah want my ahns he can have 'em. Ah swo' las' time when dey got all rusty 'at ah neve' lend 'em again, but ah'll sand 'em 'nothah time befor' ah let dat pack o' stovewood an' scrap ahn beat me." "Thank you, Lucy," answered the captain, "but he won't need the irons. He's got a sledge hammer and two kegs of nails on the safety valve now."

The old Kentucky woman faced the captain and stamped her foot. "Captain, where is my lard?"

Engineer Jim Bludso of the *Prairie Belle* promised that if fire swept the boat he'd run her aground and hold her there till everyone got off safely, even if it cost him his life: "I'll hold her nozzle agin the bank till the last galoot's ashore." And the engineer died making good on that promise.

"Your lard? Why, it's perfectly safe. We haven't touched it."

"Safe! Bring up that lard this minute and put it on the wood, and get your old boilers hot!" The captain called an order, and up came the barrels to the forecastle. The fires leaped; faster turned the wheels. The boat quivered, strained, drew even—forged ahead. Up on the hurricane deck the old woman with glittering eyes stood by the roaring chimneys and laughed and wept and shook her fists at the rival boat, and waved her goodby.

SNAGGED

The captain stood on the deck of his boat which had struck a snag and was slowly sinking. He spoke: "Is there anyone among you who can pray?" A meek little man replied, "I can." "Good," said the captain. "You start praying while the rest of the passengers put on the life preservers. We happen to be one short."

WOODING UP

This story was told a bemused passenger aboard a steamer: We had been out a little more than five days, and we were in hopes of seeing the bluffs of Natchez on the next day. Our captain was easygoing and exceedingly fond of the card game brag. Our wood was getting low, and night was coming on. The pilot on duty above (the other pilot held three aces at the time, and was just calling out the captain, who "went it strong" on three kings) sent down word that the mate had reported the stock of wood was reduced to half a cord. The worthy captain excused himself to the pilot, whose watch was below, and the two passengers (anxious to learn the game) who made up the card party, and hurried to the deck, where he soon discovered by the landmarks that we were about half a mile from a woodyard, "right around yonder point. But," muttered the captain, "I don't much like to take wood of the yellow-faced old scoundrel who owns it. He always charges a quarter of a dollar more than anyone else. However, there is no other

A cool million was bet on the hot engines of the *Robert E. Lee* and the *Natchez* in an 1870 race from New Orleans to St. Louis that was telegraphed round the world. Legend says the *Lee* won because the *Natchez* crew hid her in a cove to give a longed-for victory to the name of Robert Lee. Actually, the *Lee* ran much farther ahead than shown above throughout the race because her captain had stripped her for speed and arranged for onriver fuel pickup. The *Natchez* tied up when she hit the Cairo shoals in a fog.

chance for a good ways along."

The boat was pushed to her utmost, and in a little less than an hour, when our fuel was about giving out, we made the point, and our cables were out and fastened to trees, alongside of a good-sized woodpile.

"Hollo, colonel! How d'ye sell your wood *this* time?"

A yellow-faced old gentleman, with strings over his shoulders holding up to his armpits a pair of copperas-colored linsey-woolsey pants—the legs of which reached a very little below the knee—rose from fastening our spring line: "Why, capting, we must charge you three and a quarter *this* time."

"The d---l! You charged me only three as I went down."

"Why, capting," drawled out the wood merchant, "wood's riz since you went down two weeks ago. Besides, when you're going *up* there's

no other woodyard for nine miles and—" "We'll take a few cords," the captain said and returned to his game of brag. In half an hour we felt the *Caravan* commence paddling again. Supper was over and I retired to my upper berth overlooking the quartet at the brag table.

"How does the wood burn?" inquired the captain of the mate, who was looking at the game. "It's cottonwood and most of it green," answered the mate. "Well, Thompson—three aces again, stranger. I'll take 10 and the small change, if you please. It's your deal . . . Thompson, I say, we'd better take three or four cords at the next woodyard; can't be more than six miles."

The paddles kept moving; at 11 o'clock it was reported that we were nearing the woodyard. "Head her in, then, and take in six cords, if it's good." The wooding completed, we

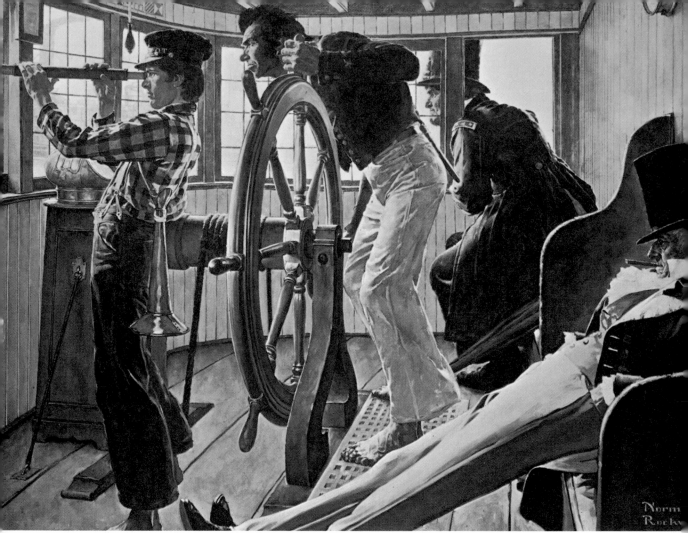

Despite former pilot Mark Twain's prejudiced dictum that a riverboat captain was little more than decoration, Norman Rockwell's painting of a pilothouse during a race properly depicts the skipper straining at the wheel while the pilot keeps a sharp eye out for snags. The bored-looking dude is probably a heavy bettor awaiting the race's outcome with admirable stoicism.

paddled again, the captain vexed that the price had been the same three and a quarter at that place.

From my upper berth (there were no staterooms then), I could observe the captain and the pilots (the latter personages took it by turns, steering and playing brag—when did they sleep?). One of them was invariably winning, while the two passengers went through the ceremony of dealing, cutting, and paying up their antes. At 2 o'clock, the captain asked the mate how we were getting on. "Oh, pretty glibly, sir! We are obliged to keep the middle of the river, and there is the shadow of a fog rising. This wood seems rather better than that we took in at old yellow face's, but we're nearly out again. I saw a light just ahead on the right. Shall we hail and see if they've wood?"

"Ring the bell and ask the price. Here's double kings."

The bell and the hail and a youthful voice on shore answered, "Three and a quarter!"

"Hollo!" ejaculated the captain, who had just lost the price of two cords to the pilot. "Are we never to get to a cheaper country? Deal, sir."

Day at length dawned and the brag party broke up; the passengers, in their first lesson, had lost $120. The captain winked at the pilot and said in an undertone, "Forty apiece for you and me and James" (the only name I knew for the other pilot).

I went out with the captain to enjoy a view of the bluffs. But there was nothing but fog and we were creeping near the shore for wood, the banks being invisible from the middle of the river.

The captain hailed, "Hollo! The woodyard!"

"Hollo, yourself!" answered a squeaking female voice.

"What's the price of wood?"

"I think you ought to know by this time, three and a qua-a-rter!" Then out crept the old man with the linsey-woolsey pants and the yellow countenance of the night before. "Since it's you, capting, I don't care if I do let you have it for three, as you're a good customer!" After a quick glance at the landmarks, the captain bolted; we had been wooding all night at the same woodyard!

SHOWBOAT'S COMIN'!

The frontier in the Middle West of about 1800 was often on the banks of a river. The goods, needed by the pioneers settled along the Ohio and Mississippi in towns of 200 or so, and in even smaller ones along the tributaries, reached them by water—and so did what little entertainment they got. Children and dogs were often the first to hear the sound of banjos or fiddles drifting downriver as whisky boats and quack-medicine barges passed. If they ran to the river, they might see acrobats or mimics on the flatboats tied at the wharf swinging into their acts.

In 1831 the theatrical Chapman family from England, who had played at Covent Garden, found itself unable to get work on the stages of New York. Following in the wake of a young troupe from New York State that had started a vogue for comedy staged on wharves, the Chapmans set out downriver. When their 100-foot barge topped by a crude barn had drifted to a settlement, the whole family would troop out with trumpets, stage a small parade announcing themselves, and tack or paste up handmade posters. At night, they played Shakespeare on the barge instead of the wharf and found the bard had just the right ring of culture and purity for settlers who usually brought the kids along and who feared corruption from the evil city or from sharpies of any kind. Versions of *The Taming of the Shrew,* "improved" by additions of song and dance, or tamperings with *Hamlet,* in which Ophelia got the star role, went off smartly. Though plenty of 50-cent tickets were paid for with bacon or blueberries, Chapman amassed enough money by 1836 to buy a steamboat. This meant the Chapmans could steam upriver and into the tributaries against the current.

The Chapmans did so well that soon they had all kinds of imitators, most of whom were amateurs, crooks, gamblers, and quacks who began to give showboating a bad name. The newly popular big circus boats escaped calumny, partly because the steamers that pulled the circus barges steered clear of the towns and drew up at the more populous cities. Built in 1851, Spauld-ing and Rogers' *Floating Circus Palace* carried clowns, acrobats, and 40 horses. It could seat 3,400 customers in varying degrees of luxury. One of its sideshows offered effigies of George Washington, Captain Kidd, and the Twelve Apostles in wax. Business was so good that city licenses shot up from $2.50 to $25. The *Palace* retaliated by keeping its gangplank a few inches aboveground, thus avoiding fees.

One of the magician-musicians aboard was August Byron French. He left when the Confederates seized the boat for a floating hospital, but he managed to revive the war-silenced river theater in the 1870's. He did it with a small barge (the first of several,

ever bigger *New Sensations*) and a wife a third his age, who played the blistering steam calliope with asbestos gloves. To quell ministers' fears, postwar showboaters offered Sunday afternoon programs of religious music on the calliope instead of the usual fare: *Oh Dem Golden Slippers* could be heard announcing arrival eight miles either side of the river. Shakespeare gave way to vaudeville—the grand march from *Aida* played on bicycle pumps—or to melodrama—*Bertha the Sewing Machine Girl* or *Ten Nights in a Barroom.* But in the 20th century the flickers and the Model T reached the Midwest, and the frontier was gone. Even though Ralph Waldo Emerson Gaches dressed his troupe in baseball uniforms to play the locals before presenting Broadway shows on his *Cotton Blossom,* showboating was doomed. By the time Edna Ferber's 1920's novel *Showboat* had become a musical and a movie, few showboats plied the rivers.

Horses cavort in Spaulding and Rogers' 1851 Floating Circus Palace *(below); the original* Cotton Blossom *(left) was built in 1903 as a floating theater.*

BLACKLORE
Working on the Levee

During the ante-bellum decades of steam on the Mississippi, the hands who loaded the boats and did heavy work on board were mainly Germans and Irishmen. After the Civil War, their place was taken by newly emancipated Negroes, who moved heavy loads including blue, seamed cotton bags over the gangplanks with a jerky, sidelong shuffle known as "coonjining" that helped maintain balance and pace—the word subsequently came also to mean the black roustabouts' work song, the coonjine. Living conditions aboard the steamboats were as poor for black crewman as they had been for their white predecessors. The men ate leftovers from the deck above and slept on gunnysacks. In spare minutes they gambled, sang, and swapped yarns. A few examples of their lore:

OUTWITTING THE MATE

When a certain steamboat left St. Louis, she carried a gang of Negro roustabouts to load and unload the freight. When the boat reached a landing, one of the hands of this gang could never be found. When the unloading of the freight was accomplished and the boat was again on its way, he would appear from somewhere. When asked by the mate where he had been, he said that he had been asleep. When the next landing was reached, the same man would be gone again. The mate searched everywhere for him but could not find his hiding place. This happened a number of times during the boat's journey. At last the mate, thoroughly mystified, called the malingerer before him. He promised him that if he would reveal his hiding place, he would not require any more work from him until the steamboat reached its destination. This being agreed upon, the mate asked the man, "Now will you please tell me where your hiding place was?"

"Why," answered the grinning black, "I'se been in your baid."

ROUSTABOUT HOLLER

Po' roustabout don't have no home,
Makes his livin' on his shoulder bone.
Wake up, sleepy, and tell your dream,
I want to make you 'quainted with two
 blue seams.
If yo' shoulder bone gets so' this time,
Git you a little sody an' turpentine.
I know my sweetie goin' open the do'

As soon as she hear the *Natchez* blow.
Did you hear Daniel in the lion den?
Lord, have mercy, hear me then.
Catch this here sack, boys, and leave
 it go,
Take her down the river further, 'cause
 they ain't no mo'.

NO MORE CARDS

I was traveling on a steamboat when Turtle, a fat roustabout who knew my interest in such mysteries, plaintively requested that I give him a spell to make him stop gambling. He was tired of losing his money; at the end of each trip, he went ashore without a penny to show for his labor. After some reflection I consented and, in the dark of the moon, taught him this

A steward (above) worked fewer hours on board than a roustabout, got more to eat.

verse: "Gambler's money is not for me. When I gamble, my money rolls out to the sea. Set my hand to shaking when I sit down by the cards." I informed the earnest Turtle that in the future, whenever he was about to play cards, he would see his right hand shaking like a leaf. In addition, I gave him a capsule filled with a white powder I had been employing as a preventative of malaria in the cypress swamps. Advising him to put the capsule inside the band of his hat, I announced that when the powder melted, the charm would be in effect.

I left the boat and, returning three months later, went below. The men were gathered in a tense circle, playing coon-can. Turtle sat watching with mournful eyes: "Captain, I played cards twice and the third time it come over me all of a sudden. And I can't play cards no more." Now he always urges me to remove the spell.

HER-GIRLS

Big Black was a Greenville black man a-rousting on the *Tennessee Belle*. But

Waiting on the levee, New Orleans, 1883; as roustabouts carried heavy loads on and off these boats, they sometimes chanted: "She took me to her parlor/And cooled me with her fan;/She whispered in her mother's ear,/'I love the steamboatman.'"

he got tired of the river and went on one of them ships that goes out of New Orleans to the sea. The weather kept getting hotter and hotter. And the mate seen him looking at the water and said, "Don't you go in swimming, Big Black." He didn't tell him why, though, and one day, when it was terrible hot, Big Black jumped in the ocean. And in a minute, a lot of them Her-Girls, that's half women, half fish, grabbed him and pulled him down to the bottom. They sit him up on a big rock, and then they all yelled at him: "Greenville man, do you like fish?"

Big Black was awful scared, and he didn't know what to answer. But he'd been getting too much catfish at Greenville, so he says mighty quiet: "If it's something to eat you wants to give me, if you'll please 'scuse me, I'd mighty like some pork chops or a nice chicken wing. I jest hates fish." And then all them Her-Girls clapped their hands. "If you'd a-said you liked fish,

we'd a-throwed you to the sharks," they told him. "You're the prettiest man we sure ever seen. We're going to make you our king." And they swum in with a big gold throne. He was their king for a mighty long time. Twice every year he used to go back to Greenville and give his mammy and pappy all the gold money they could carry and the finest pearls in the sea. But once he walked in the house, and there was a can of canned salmon laying on the table. He never come back to his house no more.

CHATTANOOGA'S GHOST

Piece o' Man constantly sees the ghost of his dead comrade Chattanooga. "That there Chattanooga was the smokingest rouster I ever seen," he will tell you. "Used to spend all his money gitting wonderful cigars. He kept 'em in the icebox to have 'em tasting right, he said. Every night after supper, he'd take one out and

smoke it and make big smoke rings come up in front of him. And when he had three of the rings going in a row, he'd take a match that was burning and throw it through 'em, all three of the rings at once. He seen it in a show, he said. One night he was wheeling coal off the fuel flat and fell in the river and was drowned. And I never expected to see Chattanooga no more. But sure enough, next night, the door of the icebox come open, and I seen him standing there, taking the cigars and feeling 'em to pick out the best one, like he always done. Then he set down and started blowing the smoke ring. He blowed the rings all right. But when he tried throwing the match, he couldn't get it through more than two. Every night he comes and tries to git the three. It makes him awful mad, and he sits there cussing and burning his fingers. But he can't git it through the three no-ways."

155

THE SPORTING LIFE
Gamblers and Suckers

In the early 1800's the South and the Mississippi Valley prospered so, that men had time and money for gambling. New Orleans supported stylish casinos, while the great steamboats encouraged impromptu games among passengers. Inevitably, this activity attracted professionals who used marked cards, sleight of hand, and such tricks. Often they worked as teams, gulling innocents into games, signaling the contents of "suckers'" hands. A few gamblers did live and dress in style, but most such tales arise from the universal fantasy of striking it rich. And when all else failed, the gamblers "reformed" and sold their memoirs as warnings.

THE GAMBLERS' GAMBLER

One of the most celebrated gamblers of the early Mississippi was a lame man named James Ashby, who exercised his talents in a field wherein there was little competition—he preyed almost entirely on his fellow card-sharpers. He usually worked with a part-

ner who was disguised as a gawky young backwoodsman, en route home after selling a drove of hogs. Ashby impersonated the young man's old pappy, who didn't have all his buttons and was forever playing snatches of tunes on his fiddle, especially after the young backwoodsman had been inveigled into a card game. Not for a long time did the gamblers

learn that the tunes were signals. Ashby was eventually exposed and dropped out of sight until the early 1840's, when he appeared in St. Louis and for several years operated the town's principal faro bank. During this period the lame gambler decorated himself with a great profusion of diamonds false and real, gold chains, rings, and bracelets; and when he went out he carried a gold-headed cane in each hand and a huge gold pencil, set with diamonds, in his mouth. He died in the early 1850's, and envious gamblers insisted that his death had been "greatly hastened by the enormous weight of jewelry with which he was accustomed to burden himself during his life."

THE CAPTAINS REMINISCE

"They was real sporty fellows, them gamblers," added ancient Captain Jake. "Dressed to kill, just like you see 'em now in the movies. And busting with tricks. One fellow used to always play in front of his stateroom, where a pal of his'd be sitting in the doorway pretending he was reading a paper. But he was really watching the transom; he'd tilted the glass so it showed all the cards of the men the gambler was playing with. Then, if the fellow watching scratched his ear, the gambler'd know the man he was playing against had a straight or a royal flush."

"Old days," commented Captain

Two styles of gambling that flourished along the Mississippi are seen in 19th-century illustrations: an impromptu riverboat card game (above); a casino table in New Orleans (right).

Jesse, "you'd make enough one trip pretty near to pay for your boat. And if things was bad, the gamblers came in real handy. Wasn't anything for a gambler to lend a captain $5,000. Then some night, when maybe the gambler'd got into bad trouble, like maybe some planter'd caught him with five aces, the captain'd land the boat out in the woods and let the gambler get away."

"My dad used to tell me a gambling story," added Captain Matt. "Swore it was true, but I don't trust no riverman. Even my own father. Two crooked gamblers tried to bribe the captain of a big boat to let 'em start a game. The captain kept on saying no, and the gamblers kept on raising the ante higher and higher. Finally, they offered him $10,000. This time, the captain got real mad. 'You fellows get off my boat right now,' he said. 'You're getting too close to my price.'"

THE TABLES TURNED
A clerk was sent from New Orleans to Pittsburgh to deliver $100,000 to a bank. A gang of sharpers found it out and determined to "pluck" him, for which purpose they took passage on the same boat. Before they had proceeded far, cards were introduced, and the clerk joined them in a game of brag. For the purpose of drawing him on, he was allowed to win a considerable sum, and then came the time for the big rush. The gamblers, believing they had all the clerk's money on the table, "saw" his last bet and went him $5,000 better. Endeavoring to persuade the gamblers to "show," but finding his efforts in vain, the clerk arose from the table, unlocked his trunk, and returned with the package of money. Throwing his package on the table, he exclaimed, "I see your $5,000 and go $95,000 better!" The gamblers left the table precipitately.

OCCUPATIONAL HAZARD
The famous gambler George Devol recalled in his memoirs: Another time, I was coming up on the steamer *Fairchild* with Captain Fawcett, of

Louisville. When we landed at Napoleon, there were about 25 of the "Arkansas Killers" came on board, and I just opened out and cleaned the party of money, watches, and all their valuables. Things went along smoothly for a while, until they commenced to drink pretty freely. Finally, one of them said: "Jake, Sam, Ike, get Bill and let us kill that d----d gambler who got our money." "All right," said the party, and they broke for their rooms to get their guns. I stepped out of the side door and got under the pilothouse, as it was my favorite hiding place. I could hear

This scene from an 1855 *Harper's* illustrates the roughhewn democracy that prevailed in steamboat bars and card games.

every word downstairs, and could whisper to the pilot. Well, they hunted the boat from stem to stern—even took lights and went into the hold—and finally gave up the chase, as one man said I had jumped overboard. I slipped the pilot $100 in gold, as I had both pockets filled with gold and watches, and told him at the first point that stood out a good ways to run her as close as he could and I would jump. He whispered, "Get ready," and I slipped out and walked back and stood on top of the wheelhouse until she came, as I thought, near enough to make the jump, and away I went; but it was farther than I expected, so I went down about 30 feet into the river and struck into the soft mud clear up to my waist. Some

parties who were standing on the stern saw me and gave the alarm and commenced firing at me, and the bullets went splattering all around me. The shooting brought the Negroes from the fields to the bank of the river. I hallooed to them to get a long pole and pull me out, for I was stuck in the mud. They did so, and I got up on the bank and waited for another boat.

WITH HIS BETS ON
One of the most exciting tales of the roulette tables of early New Orleans concerns a conservative old captain who, quite accidentally, almost broke the bank at a famous casino. His unvarying bet was 25 cents on each spin of the wheel, win or lose, and it was his wont to sit for hours at the table. On the fateful night in question, the captain placed his bet on the red and sat quietly, his hand cupping his chin, just as he did every night in port. Lucky on the first spin, the captain let his doubled bet ride on the red, which won a second time. Again breaking his rule of drawing down winnings, the old salt did not move a muscle, so that the bet was once more doubled as the red won once more.

Obviously transfixed by his great stroke of fortune, the captain allowed the winnings to ride again and again as the ball continued unfailingly to bounce into a red cup. By the 17th spin, his original quarter-dollar had grown to an enormous pile of $16,000 in banknotes. One of the excited onlookers reported later that at this juncture a husky voice called: "Haul in, old captain! You don't bet all that pile against this set of land pirates! Haul in!" It was the first mate of the captain's vessel, and he proceeded to scoop up the winnings in his cap. "Come, you have a full cargo. It's time to hoist sail," the solicitous mate coaxed, as he grabbed his arm.

At that moment, horrible to relate, the corpse of the captain toppled over upon him. The unfortunate captain had missed the most dramatic performance of his career, having passed on to his reward in the act of betting his first cents!

A contemporary cartoonist's view (right) of the greeting bestowed by Comanches on settlers arriving in Texas from the U.S.

"The Arkansas Traveler" by Currier and Ives (below) illustrates an Ozark tale about a "furriner" who broke the ice with an initially hostile squatter by playing a hoe-down tune in good style—he was then treated to conversation and venison and whisky and invited to "stay fur a week."

Arkansas to the Alamo

When, in the elections of 1835, his constituents failed to return him for a fourth term as U.S. congressman from Tennessee, Davy Crockett told them they could go to hell and he'd go to Texas. True to his word, he headed southwest across Arkansas. Arriving at Little Rock, he was given a hero's welcome. But when urged by his hosts to stay and hunt bear, Davy declined. He was bound for Texas "to join the patriots of that country in freeing it from the shackles of the Mexican government."

Arkansas was to remain a stronghold of bear hunters and pioneers of the old school. The Ozark woodlands represented a western limit of the Appalachian log-cabin culture—their folklore thus reflected the older background, but its emphasis on the land's poverty gave it a distinct Arkansas ring.

Those who pressed on to Texas were a new breed for whom "back east" meant any part of Texas east of the speaker, or any southern state. Like thousands of contemporaries coming out of Arkansas and East Texas, Davy Crockett found a treeless, waterless plain where his woodslore could not help him and the woodsman's guerrilla tactics were useless against mounted Comanche raiders. It was nevertheless a patriotic duty to proclaim that Texas had the best climate, prettiest women, and bravest men in the world.

Back east in Arkansas, however, Texas was said to be the destination of every rogue and reprobate that ever had to pick up stakes in the middle of the night. Thus, according to a humorous saying then current, a fugitive's forwarding address was GTT—"Gone To Texas." (It was said that the heroic Alamo commander, William Travis, was a GTT fugitive from Alabama, where he had killed a man for "annoying" his teenage bride.) Settlers in Texas talked as tall as their forebears had and—like them—preferred pungency to poetry. As armed newcomers kept pouring in, it was inevitable that they would clash with local Mexicans and Indians. When they did, a new era was born.

OZARK LORE
Hillbillies and Razorbacks

Settlers who moved into the Ozark Mountains and established the state of Arkansas (named after local Indians) found themselves isolated and poor, a situation which nurtured an exceptionally vigorous folk culture. Much of it partakes of broader American traditions, but Arkansans gave their ways a distinctive twang and twist. The Ozark hillbilly is the stock character in stories; the many forms of lore—legends, ballads, riddles, superstitions—are tuned to the local environment. Some of the best known bits, such as "The Arkansas Traveler" and "Change the Name of Arkansas?!" which appear here, are composed; whatever the source, Arkansas lore reflects a people who speak for themselves.

Betsy had to chop his feet out.

COLONEL WHETSTONE

Col. Pete Whetstone was created by an Arkansas lawyer, Charles Noland, in a series of humorous letters written over a span of some 20 years, starting in 1837. Noland caught the subtle differences—and similarities—between the provincial gentry and the more familiar hillbilly:

Well, I went to the play; I believe they call it a the-a-ter. It was mighty funny, I tell you. They were piled up as thick as pigs in cold weather, and such a hollering, "Down in front"— "Hats off"—"Music!" and all such noises. I didn't git the swing of the thing right off, for there sat four fellers on a platform, one going it on a little fife about as thick as a spike buck's-horn, one on a big thing sorter like a blowing horn, and then two fellers on fiddles. They didn't play "Old Zip Coon on a Rail," or sich like, but they were going it on the highfalutin order.

Well, presently a little bell jingled, and up went a green apron—and out came the queerest looking chap I ever see. Well, I tell you, he made us all laugh. When he got through, the crowd went it with a perfect looseness, *"On kore, on kore."* "On what?" says I. "That's French for him to do it again," said a nice-looking chap sitting by me. Then began the play—it was *Virginius,* and they call it tragedy. Tragedy or what, it ain't suited to that sort of a crowd—they want fun and laughing—no crying—and as to killing people, why, there is enough of that done in public without paying a dollar to see it.

HELL, NO!

The spelling and pronunciation of "Arkansas" have long been the subject of solemn dispute and humorous gibes. In the late 1800's there surfaced what was claimed to be the speech of a state legislator on this theme. Many versions have circulated, some extremely racy; the one given here satirizes both the rhetoric of the politician and the exaggerations of the backwoodsman.

Mr. Speaker: The man who would change the name of Arkansas is the original iron-jawed, brass-mounted, copper-bellied corpsemaker from the wilds of the Ozarks! Sired by a hurricane, damed by an earthquake, half brother to the cholera, nearly related to the smallpox on his mother's side, he is the man they call Sudden Death and General Desolation!

The man who would change the name of Arkansas would massacre isolated communities as a pastime. He would destroy nationalities as a serious business! He would use the boundless vastness of the Great American Desert for his private graveyard! He would attempt to ex-

I took her by the tail and tried to pump it out.

The drawings on these pages were created by Marion Hughes to illustrate *Three Years in Arkansaw* (1905). Their dry, witty line catches the spirit of Arkansas lore

tract sunshine from cucumbers! Hide the stars in a nail keg, hang the Arkansas River on a clothesline, unbuckle the bellyband of Time, and turn the sun and moon out to pasture; but you will never change the name of Arkansas! The world will again pause and wonder at the audacity of the lop-eared, lantern-jawed, halfbreed, half-born, whisky-soaked hyena who has proposed to change the name of Arkansas! He's just starting to climb the political banister and wants to knock the hayseed out of his hair, pull the splinters out of his feet, and push on and up to the governorship. But change the name of Arkansas! Hell, no!

She could hit a tomcat's eye.

THE BELLED BUZZARD

There was once a settlement along a river bottom in the Arkansas Ozarks. One bank of the river was bordered for miles by high unscalable bluffs crowned with scrub timber, the home and breeding place of thousands of buzzards. Hog raising was the main source of income of the community. One summer, hog cholera broke out among the porkers. The buzzards, feasting on the dead carcasses, carried the disease from one section of the country to another. There was an unwritten law that these birds should not be killed, but the farmers were aware that, unless some action was taken to check the spread of the disease, their hogs, together with their incomes, would be wiped out.

A meeting was called. It was decided to capture one of the birds and fasten a small sheep bell to it, in the hope that it would cause them to

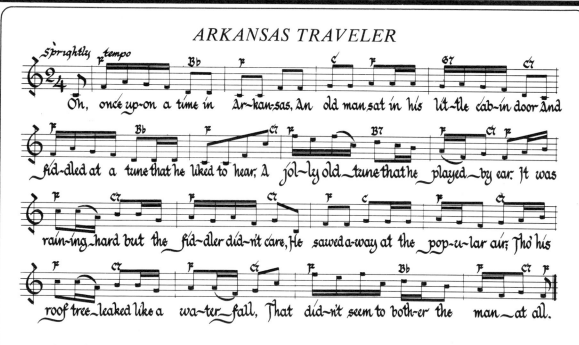

ARKANSAS TRAVELER

Oh, once up-on a time in Ar-kan-sas, An old man sat in his lit-tle cab-in door And fid-dled at a tune that he liked to hear, A jol-ly old tune that he played by ear. It was rain-ing hard but the fid-dler did-n't care, He sawed a-way at the pop-u-lar air; Tho' his roof tree leaked like a wa-ter-fall, That did-n't seem to both-er the man at all.

A traveler was riding by that day
And stopped to hear him practicing away.
The cabin was afloat and his feet were wet,
But still the old man didn't seem to fret.

So the stranger said, "Now the way it seems to me,
You'd better mend your roof," said he.
But the old man said as he played away,
"I couldn't mend it now, it's a rainy day."

The traveler replied, "That's all quite true,
But this, I think, is the thing for you to do,
Get busy on a day that is fair and bright,
Then patch the old roof till it's good and tight."

But the old man kept on a-playin' at his reel,
And tapped the ground with his leathery heel.
"Get along," said he, "for you give me a pain;
My cabin never leaks when it doesn't rain."

The tale recounted in the verses printed above is derived from the dialogue that began circulating in Arkansas in the 1840's. The tune is supposed to be the one begun by the squatter and finished by the traveler. First published in 1847, its authorship, like the dialogue's, is disputed, but it survives as a popular country song and fiddler's air.

They have one fault, they won't lay eggs.

leave. One of the birds was accordingly trapped and belled. His arrival among the others created a great commotion and in a few days the flock of buzzards disappeared, only the belled buzzard remaining. Finally, he, too, took flight.

At the end of the summer there was an epidemic of typhoid fever in the community. About that time the belled buzzard reappeared, the tinkle of his bell being plainly heard as he soared above the houses. He came and went time after time, and always following his reappearance some sort of calamity happened. Each return of the bird aroused apprehension and his presence became associated with misfortunes. People believed the repulsive fowl was possessed of an evil spirit. Many believe he still roams the skies, and to this day any report of the belled buzzard casts a spell of gloom over the community.

ARKANSAS TALL TALK
The tall tale thrives in Arkansas, and it frequently involves crops, animals, and the hardships of Ozark life:

The hoop snake of Arkansas has a poisonous stinger in its tail, and when it wants to go after somebody it tucks its tail in its mouth, forms itself into a hoop, and rolls after its victim like a wagon wheel. But if the snake gets caught in a tree or something, it's a goner, because it can't pull out frontwise. And the stinger's liable to poison the tree. Once an unsuspecting Arkansas woodcutter used a splinter from such a poisoned tree for a toothpick and he was dead before sundown.

Arkansas has a greater variety of hogs and less pork and lard than any state in the Union. The saw hog takes the premium for a freak of nature. They catch an old and poor sow, buckle a strap on her nose to keep her from biting their legs, then they turn her over on her back across a log, one man at each end a-hold of her legs for handles, one boy a-hold of her ears, and one a-hold of her tail. When they get started, you can hear the bark and splinters flying and the old sow squealing for three miles. The worst trouble with these saws is you can't file or set 'em. When they get pinching, you have to loose 'em.

It takes two men to plant corn in Arkansas; one pries the rocks apart with a crowbar; the other shoots the seed down the crack with a syringe.

According to Pogey Mahone, he had a potato grew so big it couldn't be dug nohow, so they built a new cabin over it and cut a trapdoor in the kitchen floor. Whenever the kids began hollerin' for victuals, Pogey just climbed down through the trap and shoveled up a big chunk of 'tater.

A man from the delta region of Arkansas reported: Here, the onliest time the sun ever shines is when it rains. Ma pores sprout watercress, ma houn' dawg has crawdads 'stid of fleas, and ma chickens air web-footed.

FACT  MYTH

Razorback Hogs

Among the leading characters in the Arkansas cast is the razorback hog. The name refers to the bristly, bony ridge of its back, so thin and sharp men claim they have shaved with it. This hog has other distinctive features: it is so spare it can only be shot sideways, so small it roosts like a chicken, and so swift and ferocious it attacks anything on legs—including men. In some tales the razorback seems half domesticated, but it is always assumed to be a unique species of wild hog.

In fact, any so-called wild hog in North America has been introduced here from the Old World. Although there may be a few pigs that have gone wild in Arkansas, zoologists do not recognize the razorback that stars in so many tales as a true species. Lack of official recognition does not daunt the University of Arkansas' football team, which uses the razorback as an emblem. Some years ago, a state official offered a reward for a razorback, dead or alive; he has not yet had a claimant. But all Arkansans know that razorback hogs roam the Ozarks, threatening anything that gets in their way.

Arkansas hog chasing a wolf

Ozark Practices

"God Almighty never put us here without a remedy for every ailment," said an Ozark resident many years ago. He was referring to herb remedies for physical ailments, but he might well have been expressing an Ozarker's general view of the world. To cope with potential danger from the unknown, Ozarkers drew on an extraordinarily rich store of superstitions.

Like superstitions throughout the world, those of the Ozarks operated on different levels. Many served a purely practical purpose: they worked because they incorporated a truth. "Keep cats away from an infant or they will suck the baby's breath away," warned the Ozarker. Although we no longer worry about a pet sucking away a child's breath we do recognize that a cat might sit on a baby for warmth

and suffocate it. Other saws enabled Ozarkers to deal with otherwise inexplicable phenomena. Thus a red birthmark was caused by the pregnant mother's craving for strawberries, a brown mark by her craving prunes. Although these marks were genetic accidents, folk beliefs about them had some possible benefit in cautioning pregnant women about their diet.

Marriage, of course, was the be-all and end-all for an Ozark woman, and since she moved in a small social circle, her future husband was probably already to be found among her male acquaintances. It made sense for a young girl to speculate as to the man destined to become her choice. Dreaming, peering into mirrors or wells, watching for the first man who passed under a horseshoe—these were some of the signs indicating a prospective husband. A girl might hang her handkerchief out to be dried of the dew by the sun on May 1, and then read the wrinkles for the initials of the man she would marry. Many of these practices

were related to ancient beliefs in fairies, who were considered to be sympathetic to such undertakings. But some superstitions allowed a girl to take an active role in getting a husband. "Give a man a drink with your cut fingernails in it and he'll marry you" was rooted in the age-old feeling that possession of a person followed possession of some part.

Once married, a woman's primary role was to bear and rear children. Great risks attended pregnancy in those days, but there was a strong belief that they could be circumvented by following various folk rules. "If a pregnant woman puts up fruit, it will spoil" meant that if she wanted what was inside her to come out unspoiled, she should not bottle up any image of its spirit. Any trying experience was to be avoided: shocks or frights; encountering unusual animals, unpleasant foods, or signs of violence. Modern medicine confirms that the fetus may be affected by foreign substances but does not subscribe to the Ozark belief that parents can determine the sex of their child by certain actions. "If a husband sits on his roof by a chimney for seven hours, his next child will be a boy" may be explained by ancient symbolism but not by modern science.

When a woman went into labor, it was suggested that a sharp ax under the bed would ensure easy delivery. "Be sure there is an empty hornet's nest hanging in the loft of a cabin where the woman is to give birth" went another folk saying. The symbolism of the former is obvious: a sharp blade cuts pain. The meaning of the latter is more obscure. But consider that hornets come out of a hole in a nest shaped like a womb—and may give pain; thus the woman's pain might be transferred to the nest. And in practical terms, since most homes

had a hornet's nest, it made sense to see that it was empty before a delivery. Another Ozark saying: "A woman doesn't suffer afterpains following the birth of her first baby"; the belief must have deterred many a girl from complaining lest it be thought she had given birth before in secret.

Since the first weeks of infant life in those days were extremely precarious, they were swaddled in superstitions. "Wash the palms of a newborn babe before the third day and you wash away luck in money matters" had to do with the hand grasping money, but behind it lay a widespread belief that a newborn barely possessed its soul before baptism. And as the child

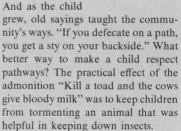

grew, old sayings taught the community's ways. "If you defecate on a path, you get a sty on your backside." What better way to make a child respect pathways? The practical effect of the admonition "Kill a toad and the cows give bloody milk" was to keep children from tormenting an animal that was helpful in keeping down insects.

And if the myriad warnings, signs, and significances could not ward off death, they could at least announce it—and help deal with it. A falling window sash, the howling of a dog at night, and many other occurrences symbolized the approaching end. "When a person dies, go out to tell the bees at the family beehive, which should also be draped in black lest the bees die or depart." That involved an old belief that bees were the souls of the departed. Finally, superstitions accompanied a person to the grave. "It's bad luck to halt a funeral procession." This allowed the soul of the deceased to proceed toward the afterlife swiftly and smoothly, as should all such launchings. It was also believed that quick burial prevented the spirit of the deceased from escaping from the body to haunt the community.

THE BIG BEAR OF ARKANSAS
Man Against the Elemental

One of the best known Arkansas "tales" was actually written by T. B. Thorpe, an American humorist who first published the story in 1841. The Big Bear, as a passenger on a Mississippi steamer, spins his yarn to a fascinated if captive audience. Interestingly, the tall-tale elements exaggerating the richness of the land are the opposite of those in the Ozark mountain lore. But the basics—the hunter who in certain ways becomes the hunted, his life somehow impoverished by bagging his beloved prey—have a universal appeal. Here is a condensation:

Big Bear walked into the cabin of a steamer, took a chair, put his feet on the stove, and looking back over his shoulder, passed the salute "Strangers, how are you?" Some of the company at this familiarity looked a little angry, and some astonished; but in a moment every face was wreathed in a smile. There was something about the intruder that won the heart on sight.

"Prehaps," said he, "gentlemen," running on without a person interrupting, "prehaps you have been to New Orleans often; I never made *the first visit* before, and I don't intend to make another in a crow's life. I am thrown away in that ar place, and useless, that ar a fact. Some of the gentlemen thar called me green. Well, prehaps I am, but I arn't so at home. They talked to me 'bout hunting, and laughed at my calling the principal game in Arkansas poker, and asked me if I lived in the woods, and didn't know what *game* was?

"At this, *I* rather think I laughed. 'Yes,' I roared, and says I, 'Strangers, if you'd asked me how we got our meat in Arkansas, I'd a told you at once, and given you a list of varmints that would make a caravan, beginning with the bear and ending off with the cat; that's meat though, not game. I'm from Arkansas: the Creation state, the finishing-up country.'"

"Whereabouts are these animals so abundant?" inquired a foreigner with increasing interest. "Why, stranger, the bears inhabit a neighborhood of my settlement, one of the prettiest places on old Mississipp—a perfect location, and no mistake. I once planted in those diggins a few potatoes and beets; they took a fine start, and after that, an ox team couldn't have kept them from growing. About that time I went off to old Kaintuck on business, and did not hear from them things in three months, when I accidentally stumbled on a fellow who had drapped in at my place with an idea of buying me out. 'How did you like things?' said I. 'Pretty well,' said he. 'The cabin is convenient, and the timberland is good; but that bottomland ain't worth the first red cent.' 'Why?' said I. 'Cause it's full of cedar stumps and Indian mounds, and can't be cleared.' 'Lord,' said I, 'them ar stumps is beets, and them ar mounds, tater hills.' As I had expected, the crop was overgrown and useless; the sile is too rich, and planting in Arkansas is dangerous.

"I had a good-sized sow killed in the same bottomland. The old thief stole an ear of corn and took it down to eat where she slept. Well, she left a grain or two on the ground and lay down on them; before morning the corn shot up, and the percussion killed her. I don't plant any more; nature intended Arkansas for a hunting ground, and I go according to nature."

Conscious that his association with so singular a personage would probably end before morning, a traveler asked him if he would not give a description of some particular bear hunt. The desire seemed to please him, and he squared himself round.

"On a fine fall day, long time ago, I was trailing about for bear, and what should I see but fresh [bear] marks on the sassafras trees, about eight inches above any in the forests that I knew of. Says I, 'Them marks is a hoax, or it indicates the d-----t bear that was ever grown.' In fact I couldn't believe it was real, and I went on. Again I saw the same marks, at the same height, and I knew the thing lived. That conviction came home to my soul like an earthquake.

"Well, stranger, the first fair chase I ever had with that big critter, I saw him no less than three distinct times at a distance: the dogs run him over 18 miles and broke down, my horse gave out, and I was as nearly used up as a man can be. Before this adventure, such things were unknown to me, who was allowed to be decidedly the best bear hunter around as possible; but, strange as it was, that bear got me used to it before I was done with him. He finally got so sassy, he used to help himself to a hog off my premises whenever he wanted one.

"Well, missing that bear so often took hold of my vitals, and I wasted away. The thing had been carried too far, and it reduced me in flesh faster than an ague. I would see that bear in everything I did; *he hunted me,* and that, too, like a devil, which I began to think he was. While in this shaky fix, I made preparations to give him a last brush and be done with it. Having completed everything, I started at sunrise, and to my great joy, I discovered from the way the dogs run that they were near him. Finding his trail was nothing, for that had become as plain as a turnpike road.

"On we went, and coming to an open country, what should I see but the bear very leisurely ascending a hill, and the dogs close at his heels, either a match for him this time in speed, or else he did not care to get out of their way—I don't know which. But wasn't he a beauty, though! I loved him like a brother. On he went, until he came to a tree, the limbs of which formed a crotch about six feet from the ground. Into this crotch he got and seated himself, the dogs yelling all around it; and there he sat eyeing them as quiet as a pond in low water.

"A greenhorn friend of mine, in

company, reached shooting distance before me and blazed away, hitting the critter in the center of his forehead. The bear shook his head as the ball struck it, and then walked down from that tree as gently as a lady would from a carriage.

"'Twas a beautiful sight to see him do that—he was in such a rage that he seemed to be as little afraid of the dogs as if they had been sucking pigs. I expected every moment to see him close in with the dogs and kill a dozen of them at least. In this thing I was mistaken; for the bear leaped over the ring formed by the dogs and, giving a fierce growl, was off—the pack, of course, in full cry after him. The run this time was short, for coming to the edge of a lake, the varmint jumped in. Finally, my best bear dog, Bowieknife, clenched with him, and they sunk into the lake together. Bowieknife came up alone, more dead than alive, and with the pack came ashore. 'Thank God!' said I, 'the old villain has got his deserts at last.' Determined to have the body, I cut a grapevine for a rope and dove down where I could see the bear in the water, fastened my rope to his leg, and fished him, with great difficulty, ashore. Stranger, may I be chawed to death by young alligators if the thing I looked at wasn't a she-bear and not the old critter after all.

"The way matters got mixed on that island was unaccountably curious, and thinking of it made me more than ever convinced that I was hunting the Devil himself. I went home that night and took to my bed—the thing was killing me. The thing got out 'mong my neighbors, and I was asked how come on that individ-u-al that never lost a bear? And if that same individ-u-al didn't wear telescopes when he turned a she-bear, of ordinary size, into an old he-one, a little larger than a horse?

"'Prehaps,' said I, 'friends'—getting wrathy—'prehaps you want to call somebody a liar?' 'Oh, no,' said they, 'we only heard of such things being rather common of late, but we don't believe one word of it; oh, no,' and then they would ride off and

"The dogs warn't slow in making a ring around him at a respectful distance, I tell you; even my best dog, Bowieknife himself, stood off. The way his eyes flashed! why the fire of them would have singed a cat's hair; in fact, that bear was in a wrath all over."

laugh like so many hyenas. It was too much, and I determined to catch that bear, go to Texas, or die—and I made my preparations accordin'.

"Well, stranger, on the morning previous to the great day of my hunting expedition, I went into the woods near my house, taking my gun and Bowieknife along, just from habit, and what should I see getting over my fence but the bear! Yes, the old varmint was within a hundred yards of me, and the way he walked over that fence—stranger, he loomed up like a black mist, he seemed so large, and he walked right toward me.

"I raised myself, took deliberate aim, and fired. Instantly the varmint wheeled, gave a yell, and walked *through* the fence, as easy as a falling tree would through a cobweb. I heard the old varmint groaning, like a thousand sinners, in a thicket nearby,

and by the time I reached him, he was a corpse. 'Twould astonish you to know how big he was; I made a bedspread of his skin, and the way it covered my mattress and left several feet on each side to tuck up would have delighted you. It was, in fact, a Creation bear, and if it had lived in Samson's time and had met him in a fair fight, he would have licked him in the twinkling of a dicebox.

"But, stranger, I never liked the way I hunted him and missed him. There is something curious about it that I never could understand—and I never was satisfied at his giving in so easy at last. Prehaps he had heard of my preparations to hunt him the next day, so he jist guv up to save his wind to grunt with in dying; but that ain't likely. My opinion is that that bear was an unhuntable bear and died when his time come."

JAMES BOWIE
Knight of the Long Knife

Born in Kentucky in 1796 and reared in Louisiana, James Bowie made his mark in the slave trade when still a young man, dealing with none other than the pirate Jean Lafitte, from whom he bought captive Africans at a dollar a pound for subsequent smuggling and resale. He then became a land speculator and searcher for lost treasure in Texas. Dying a hero's death at the Alamo with the famous knife, which bears his name, in hand, he was a terror to the last. Upon hearing Bowie's life story soon after the event, the hero-worshiping English author Thomas Carlyle exclaimed: "The man was nearly equal to Odin or Thor! The Texans ought to build him an altar." Here are highlights of the Bowie legend:

THE SANDBAR DUEL

The fame of James Bowie and his knife was established on September 19, 1827, by an event remembered in legend as the Sandbar Duel. This is how the story goes:

For years Bowie had made the Louisiana city of Alexandria, on Red River, his business headquarters. Once when pressed for money, he learned that Norris Wright, sheriff of the parish and director of the bank from which Bowie borrowed, had thwarted a loan of money to him. There was already bad blood between the two over politics. One day when they met on the street, Wright fired a pistol at Bowie, but the bullet

"Transactions" like the one depicted above were common on the early frontier.

was checked by a silver dollar in Bowie's vest pocket. Bowie's pistol snapped and he would have killed

Wright with his hands if men had not withheld him. The two parted, expecting to meet another day.

Bowie had told his brother, Rezin, of his pistol's snapping, whereupon Rezin gave him a knife: "Here, take old Bowie; she never misses fire."

The day Bowie and Wright met was not long afterward. The place was a sandbar noted as a dueling place on the west bank of the Mississippi across from Natchez. Bowie was one of four seconds, plus a surgeon, on the side of a principal in a duel. There were six men, likewise including a surgeon, on the other side. The duel turned into a general fight in which two men were killed and two badly wounded. Bowie had emptied his pistol and was down, shot in four places and cut in five. Norris Wright had emptied two dueling pistols. Without taking time to reload, he rushed against Bowie with a sword. Bowie, a ball in one hip, rose to standing position and stabbed the knife into his enemy, "twisting it to cut his heartstrings."

Bowie declared that he would wear that knife as long as he lived. So he did, and it served him well.

BOWIE TO THE RESCUE

One day in Natchez-Under-the-Hill, Bowie met the youthful son of an esteemed friend named Lattimore. The young man had just sold a large amount of cotton, and now "Bloody" Sturdivant, a notorious gambler and hard case, was cheating him of the money from the sale in a faro game.

"Young man," Bowie interposed, "you don't know me but your father does. Let me play your hand for awhile." The young man got up; Bowie sat down and before long exposed the cheater. He won back all the money young Lattimore had lost and gave it to him with the advice never to gamble again. Bloody Sturdivant, ignorant of who the rescuer was, challenged him to a duel, proposing that they lash their left hands together and fight with knives. Bowie accepted, and at the first stroke disabled his right arm and then magnanimously let the scoundrel go.

FACT ❓ MYTH

The "Arkansas Toothpick"

"They all carry knives, generally *Arkansas toothpicks*. When in expectation of a row, they begin picking their teeth with the point," reported Sir Richard Levinge, a British visitor in the early Southwest. "Arkansas toothpick" was actually a humorous term for the bowie knife, traditionally held to have been invented by James Bowie's brother, Rezin, in the early 1820's. Its design was more probably the work of many hands. The blade was 8–15 inches long, curved and double-edged near its point for slashing. Because of its superb balance, the knife could be thrown with accuracy. Popularized by sensational accounts of Jim Bowie's success with it in the Sandbar Duel, the knife became standard equipment for frontiersmen in the American West and was used as an all-purpose weapon and tool. It was the main eating implement not only in camps but in many a cabin. It served to skin and dress all kinds of game, mend saddles, and cut firewood. More than once it was also used to dig a grave on the lone prairie for a fallen comrade.

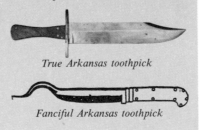

True Arkansas toothpick

Fanciful Arkansas toothpick

YANKEE NOTIONS
Peddlers and Pretenders

One of the stock confrontations in American lore is between the homespun settler and the slick stranger. The Yankee who occasionally appears in tales of the Southwest was one such stranger who had a complicated ancestry. In the 18th century the British saw all the colonists as humorous hicks—as in "Yankee Doodle." Americans quickly converted this image into "Jonathan Yankee," still a bumpkin but with impudent horse sense. By the 1830's, "Yankee" meant a New Englander with the sharp wits of a horse trader, shrewd and sometimes shady. Since the only easterners many Americans knew were peddlers selling everything from cloth to clocks, these strangers figured as the "Yankees" in their tales.

A YANKEE BESTED

Just before the frost come, one fall, a long-legged cream-faced Yankee peddler brot his plunder into the forest for to 'tice our gals out of their money. This peddler war most abominable onscrupulous in his dealings and knowed no more about handling a rifle than a goose knows about rib stockings; but he borrowed a rifle one afternoon and went out into the woods to kill some varmints. He didn't come back that night, so we raised the neighbors to go and hunt arter him.

We seed nothing of the peddler, so when it begun to grow dark we kindled a fire and sat down and took out the whisky. As the fire war made under the branches of a big tree, we looked up, and thar we seed a pair of long legs dangling down in the smoke. The peddler had seed a big snapping turtle come out of a pond that was close by and he thort it war a alligator. Arter we got home, the gals got hold of the story and the peddler cleared out pretty quick, for they used to shove a turtle in his face whenever he turned up wantin' to sell 'em anything.

JUST DESSERTS

I was jest a-goin' to tell you one of the cutest little dodges I ever hearn tell on. I guess there aren't many that's traveled much in the southern states but what's lit on a poor, tumbledown place called Camden, and if any of you ever had the misfortune to stop at a tavern, thinking to get dinner there, I guess you'll remember it. There was a stage full of passengers comin' this way, and one of 'em said that they were only five miles from Camden. "Pesky glad to hear it," said a Yankee-lookin' chap. "I'm as hungry as a dog."

"Sorry for you, then," says the man, "but you won't get three mouthfuls down afore up comes the stage. It's an old trick at that perticular house." "Trick or no trick," says the Yankee. "I intend to have a very hearty dinner for myself."

When they got to Camden, the dinner wasn't ready, and when it was, a man stood at the room door and taxed 'em four bits apiece when they went in. But they didn't get four bits apiece down their throats afore in comes the tavernkeeper and tells 'em the stage is ready and the driver wouldn't wait a minute for his grandmother. Away went the travelers, at least all of 'em but the Yankee. "You'll lose your seat, sir," said the tavernkeeper. "Don't keer a darn," said the Yankee. "I'll take a spoon to eat this here truck with." "Spoon, sir," says the man. "There was a dozen of 'em on the table; real silver, too." "Well," replied the Yankee, "you don't s'pose them chaps was a-goin' to pay 50 cents and carry nothin' away to show for it?" "Thunder and lightning!" roared the man. "See if I don't jest bring the whole of 'em to justice!"

Half an hour after, up came the same stage with the sheriff. In jumped the Yankee. "Hold on, stranger," sung out the tavernkeeper. "Now jest pint out the chaps that took them spoons, will ye?" "Well, mister," drawled the Yankee, "I guess if you'll only look in your coffeepot, I cal'late you'll find your spoons. I got my 50 cents' wuth that time."

"The Yankee Peddler," by John Ehninger, a 19th-century artist, is one of countless portrayals of this familiar frontier figure, who was suspect in real life, satirized in tales.

TAMING TEXAS
Rifles at the Ready

The first Arkansans to move to Texas in the second quarter of the 19th century found themselves among Indians who were determined to die before losing their ancestral lands. Newcomers, both men and women, learned to use their guns as calmly and efficiently as farm tools and taught their children how to sight before they even saw the ABC's. The lore that grew out of this state of tension betrays a sense of alertness to threat which was hardly eased by the rugged land.

BIG FOOT ARMOR

In the early foggy morning Big Foot Wallace looked out of his cabin door and saw that his horses were gone. The dogs had not whined or barked once during the night. Big Foot figured the Comanches had mesmerized them. Moccasin tracks around the corral were as thick as pig tracks around a corncrib. It was against Big Foot's religion to let Indians get away with his horses.

He walked down to the clearing in the brush where he had staked a gray mare named White Bean. She was still there. He threw his hull on her, crawled up into it, and took out on the trail. He was armed with Old Butch (his knife) and Sweet Lips (his rifle). He used to say, "Varmits don't like the kind of kisses Sweet Lips gives." The ground was moist, and he followed the trail of the stolen horses. He said he began to wonder just what he was going to do when he caught up with all those Comanches. Still, he kept on going, trailing as fast as White Bean could gallop. After a while, as he topped a hill, he saw smoke rising from a flat maybe a mile and a half ahead. He knew then the Indians had stopped and were cooking their favorite breakfast food, colt meat—one of his colts. The deed riled him and made him as hot as a bush red with ripe chilipiquines.

Before long he came into a heavily wooded swag in which grew many hickory trees. It was hickory-nut time. There wasn't much to them but the hard, thick shells, but they gave Big Foot an idea. He decided to armor himself with hickory nuts. Until the day he died, he liked roomy clothes as well as a roomy range. He tied the cuffs of his shirt about his strong wrists, and he tied the bottoms of his breeches legs at the ankles above his big feet. Then he began gathering the hickory nuts and stuffing them in until he was padded out bigger than Santa Claus.

Just before he got to the edge of the big prairie, he rolled off the horse—for he could not dismount in the usual way. He peeped through the brush fringe and saw smoke still rising and Indians lolling around.

He crawled through the tall grass until he was within maybe 100 yards of the Indians. There were 42. Then slowly, still keeping well hid in the grass, he squinted one eye and lined up the sights on Sweet Lips. She spoke, and a Comanche buck answered with his last yell. This time the Indians were wildly alert. They saw the gunsmoke, and now, all on foot, they took out for it lickety-brindle. Meantime, Sweet Lips in position, Big Foot raised up in all his majesty and all his stature and all his hickory nuts. He said those Indians halted "like they had been paralyzed." Those Comanches didn't seem to know whether they were facing some sort of supernatural giant or "just Old Big." They knew whose horses they had stolen. They seemed to debate for a minute or two. Then they must have decided. They came a-yelling and a-shooting. It was a mighty lucky thing for him, Big Foot said, that not a buck had a gun. But they were the most unerring marksmen with bow and arrow. Every time a bowstring twanged, an arrow hit a hickory nut, split it, and then fell to the ground. Big Foot said the arrows got stacked up in a three-inch pile in front of him. Well, when they finally ran out of arrows and saw that, though not an arrow had missed, the enormous target was still unharmed, they stampeded like a herd of longhorn steers.

"I stood there in my tracks," Big Foot said, "as still and solemn as a cigar Indian, until the devils were clean out of sight. Then I untied the strings around my wrists and ankles,

Having escaped Indians and Mexicans, starving settler John Duval had found shelter in an abandoned shack when he heard strange noises under the floor. He pried up a board, saw some pigs, pulled one out, clubbed it to death, and had a delicious dinner.

and the hickory nuts just rolled out. If there was a peck, there were two bushels, and you can kick me to death with grasshopper legs if a single, solitary hickory nut in the whole passel hadn't been split open."

THE VISION

One August day in 1833 Josiah Wilbarger set forth on a land-location expedition with a surveyor by the name of Christian and three young fellows who were hunting claims. They left the cabin of Reuben Hornsby, which was the last building of the white man, and struck out on horseback into the wilderness. They stopped to eat their lunch at noontime. Their horses were grazing—two of them saddled and the others hobbled—when 60 Indians tightened a circle about the little party.

A pandemonium of shrill yells, a cloud of arrows—that was the first notice that the white men had of their danger. Christian lay with a broken thighbone. One of the home seekers was dying with half a dozen feathered shafts in his body. His two companions leaped behind the nearest trees. Wilbarger dragged the surveyor to a little oak, propped him against the trunk, and placed a rifle in his hands. By the time he found cover, three arrows had lodged in his limbs. Heedless of the wounds, he lay behind a log, lining his sights, picking his targets. The Indians vanished from sight. They were better armed than most tribes at the time. Occasionally, a puff of smoke betrayed the hiding place of one who had a musket. The venomous buzz of arrows sounded on all sides. This kept up for perhaps an hour. Then one of the homesteaders managed to catch up the two saddled horses, and Wilbarger saw two men mounting. He shouted at them not to desert him; but they were off on the dead run.

So he found himself alone with the helpless surveyor and the dying man—and a ring of Indians closing in upon them. He did the best he could. He got his hands on Christian's rifle, and with the two guns he was able to shoot fast enough to hold

The White Steed of the Prairies, the White Mustang, and the Ghost Horse of the Plains were, in fact, several extraordinary white mustang stallions with like spirit. J. Frank Dobie tells of the Pacing White Stallion of Travis County, Texas, one of that breed. Like the others, he had a passion to live free: when caught and staked with grass and water within reach, he declined both and stood for 10 days until he lay down and died.

off the savages until a musket ball creased him in the neck and left him paralyzed. Then the Indians swarmed in. He saw them cut the throats of his two companions and scalp them. He beheld a warrior bending over him with an uplifted knife. Unable to move so much as an eyelash, he watched the blade descend. He felt the tug of fingers entwined in his hair. It seemed to him that he was blinded by a great flash of fire, and everything went from him in a roar.

Evening was well along when he recovered consciousness. The temporary paralysis had passed. The wound where his scalp had been torn away was throbbing terribly; the arrows burned his limbs like shafts of red-hot metal. He managed to crawl to a spring a mile away. He drank deeply and sank down in a swoon. The

hours passed. When the night was far along he awakened and crept toward the distant cabins of the settlers.

Meantime the two home seekers had fled to the cabin of Reuben Hornsby, where they gave it out that the Indians had killed all of their companions. An hour or two before the dawn, Hornsby's wife awakened him. "Wilbarger is alive. I know it," she cried. "I just saw him in a dream, covered with blood, standing by an oak tree, begging for help."

She told the vision to the posse of horsemen who came trooping to the cabin at sunrise, and that same morning they found Josiah Wilbarger standing by a tree just as the woman had described him. They brought him to his home, and so tough was the fiber of the man that he recovered within a few weeks.

COMANCHES
The Horse People

In 1836 Texas was inhabited by a volatile mixture of Mexicans, newly arrived U.S. whites—mainly southerners—together with their black slaves, and a beleaguered aboriginal population, the Comanches, nomadic buffalo hunters whose range extended from the Arkansas to the Rio Grande. In their perennial wars with the white man (which took place from about 1700 to 1875), they earned a reputation for courage and honor. Long noted as the finest horsemen of the plains, they gave this account of how they first acquired horses:

Frederic Remington's "In the Betting Ring—Comanches" depicts a popular game played with gambling bones to an accompaniment of singing and drumming. The object was to guess in which hand one's opponent held the marked bone. The articles wagered were piled up between the players, who sometimes staked all they owned on a single game.

MAGIC DOGS

In the old days the people walked wherever they had to go. They had to. They had dogs to pull or carry their loads, but no horses. Then one day a herd of strange animals came along. They were almost as big as buffalo, with long necks and tails, and humps on their backs. The humps were shiny and looked hard—as hard as stone. It was a very strange sight. Then a voice spoke from the hump of the leading animal. "Who are you?" it said in a man's voice. The animal suddenly split itself in two, and the hump got down off the creature's back and stood on the ground like a man. It was magic, all magic, because when the hump got down, the rest of the animal, with four legs on the ground, looked like a huge dog. The hump-man opened his mouth and pointed down his throat with his finger. The Comanches waited to see what would come out. Nothing did. Then the man rubbed his stomach with one hand and worked his jaws.

"I guess he wants food," said a woman. "What do you think he eats?" her husband asked. "Meat and bones, like a dog?" the woman wondered. But just then the lower part of the animal lowered its head to the ground and began to eat the grass. So the women sent their children out to gather grass, and they put a great pile of it in front of the creature. The lower part ate the grass, but the upper part still signed that it was hungry. "Bring him some meat and bones," the husband ordered, and the woman did. But the strange being wouldn't eat the raw meat and bones. He shook his head and pointed to the cooking fires. Two or three other animals split into upper and lower parts. "We are Spanish," they said to the Comanches. "Cook it, please."

When everyone had eaten, including the Comanches, the first stranger laid his face on the palm of his hand and closed his eyes, to show that he was sleepy. The Comanches gave them hides to lie on, and pretty soon the strangers were all asleep. "What shall we do?" asked one of the war chiefs. "We could kill them and take their magic dogs."

"No," said an old man. "Don't kill them. You wouldn't know what to do with a magic dog if you had one. Follow them. Then you will know."

The strangers stayed four days, and the one who seemed to be their leader even took his men down to the river, where they took off their shiny outer skins and went swimming. Under the outer skins they were white all over, as if they had been sick a long time. The sight of their hirsute bodies astonished the Comanches, because the Comanche people have almost no hair on their bodies and faces. But of course they were used to taking sweat baths and rubbing themselves all over with sage, and the old man said that was probably why they had so little hair, compared with these others.

Having bathed, the Spaniards put on some soft-looking clothes and got ashes from the cooking fires. They didn't even ask the women if they could have the ashes; they just took them. Then they rubbed the hard stuff until it was shinier then ever.

At the end of the four days, the Spaniards rode out of the Comanche camp toward the west. The war chief waited until noontime and then led his party after them. It was easy to follow their trail; they didn't try to wipe it out in any way. They traveled a long way, from waterhole to waterhole. The Comanches broke off yucca stalks and thrust them in the ground to stake the backtrail. All the time, the Comanches watched. They saw that at night the Spaniards took big pads off the dogs' backs, removed the guide ropes from their heads, and hobbled them so that they could not run away. When morning came, the Spaniards returned the big pads to the animals' backs, took off the rawhide bindings from their legs, and put the ropes back on their heads. They did these same things every day.

At first the war chief thought he could sneak into the camp at night and take a horse, but the Spaniards took turns guarding, so there was never a good chance to get at the horses. Finally, they came to a village of mud and stone. This village was square, not round like a camp circle. It made a solid wall around an open space. The Spaniards did not take their horses inside the wall but turned them out in a little grassy space. Then they went inside.

Late that night, the Comanche chief crept to the grassy spot. The horses were not frightened because they had gotten used to the Comanche smell by that time. The war chief had brought along a braided rawhide rope used to tie up bundles of firewood. He put the rope over a horse's head and led him away. Then another man did the same thing.

The Comanches followed their own backtrail until they had arrived among their own people. There they learned to ride the horses bareback. But because one horse was a stallion and the other a gelding, they did not mate. When they died, they were eaten. The Comanches knew they would have to get a female some way, but it was a long time before they did. Then they went north up the river to a place where another joined it, and found many Spaniards and horses. They came away that time with mares and stallions, and bred them. Then other Indians came and traded with the Comanches for their horses, and the Comanches became famous riders and raiders.

"The Buffalo Runner," by Frederic Remington. A major ceremonial hunt took place in summer, because buffalo symbolized long life and plenty. Replenishment was magically insured, the Comanches believed, by leaving the heart inside the skeleton.

FALL OF THE ALAMO
Not a Soul Surrendered

Just before dawn on March 6, 1836, some 2,400 troops led by Mexican dictator Santa Anna mounted a final attack on the 180-odd American defenders of a fortified mission compound called the Alamo (Spanish for "cottonwood"), outside San Antonio. Within 90 minutes the defenders, whose number included Davy Crockett and Jim Bowie, were all dead, but their heroic last stand was soon translated into a battlecry, "Remember the Alamo!" Thousands rallied to the cause of Texas independence, and the tables were turned. Some legends of the Alamo:

DEATH IN THE OPEN AIR

Ex-congressman David Crockett had arrived at the Alamo with a group of companions on the eve of the siege. Presenting himself to Travis, he said: "Here I am, colonel; assign me to some place and I and my Tennessee boys will defend it." Offered officer status, Crockett declined, saying he'd rather just be "a high private."

In the days that followed, Davy spent many hours on the walls, picking off Mexicans and shouting gibes at the besiegers, to whom it seemed that the tall man in buckskins with the coonskin cap must bear a charmed life. They called him Kwockey.

As the situation worsened and the men began to give way to despair, Crockett got out his fiddle and performed duets with a Texas Scot volunteer who was a bagpiper. A brave cacophony was produced that did all hands a world of good. But toward the end, Crockett had his own desperate moments. At one point he said: "I think we had better march out and die in the open air. I don't like to be hemmed up."

Soon after he spoke those words, Davy's wish for death in the open air came true. In the fierce hand-to-hand fighting that followed the Mexicans' final assault, he died shooting and defending the area in front of the Alamo chapel. "Won't you come into my bower?" he is said to have sung to the enemy soldiers as he greeted them with his rifle Betsy, four pistols, and a bowie knife. The big knife was still clutched in his hand when the Mexicans identified his body some time later. People were later to say that Crockett had been shot with a silver bullet because none other could kill him. It was also said that when Davy's body was brought along to where the bodies of the slain were heaped up for burning, a Mexican officer said, "So brave a man ought not to be burned like a dog." After a little hesitation, he added, "Never mind, throw him on." (In another version of this incident, the officer was Santa Anna himself and the body was Jim Bowie's.)

DEATH IN BED

For a short while after his arrival at the Alamo, James Bowie had been the men's elected commander, but was forced to resign when his tuberculosis suddenly worsened. When the end came, he lay near death in a cot in a remote room of the mission, but (according to a generally accepted tradition) at the sight of Mexican soldiers coming into the room, he rallied, shot two with pistols left with him by Crockett, and knifed several more before they finally blew his brains out. Thus Bowie kept his old vow to carry the knife bearing his name as long as he lived.

VICTORY OR DEATH

The commander of the Alamo was a young lawyer named William B. Travis, who with a group of friends had occupied the outpost about three months earlier in the belief that it would serve as a strongpoint to resist Santa Anna's planned advance into Texas. Travis was an ancient-history buff (his favorite author was Herodotus) and it seemed to him that the Texans' struggle against the Mexicans

A few days before Santa Anna's final assault, Texas commander William Travis drew a line in the sand, asking Alamo defenders who wished to stay in the fort and fight to the end to cross the line. All did, save for one man who went over the wall and escaped. The ailing James Bowie was carried across the line on a camp cot at his request.

Robert Onderdonk's "Fall of the Alamo" shows Crockett's legendary last stand—clubbing enemies with his rifle Betsy. Conflicting stories say he was captured and tortured to death or escaped, but most historians believe that Davy died fighting.

and their dictator had many points in common with the war of resistance waged by the Greeks against the Persian invaders. Specifically, Travis thought of himself and his Texans as vanguard fighters, as the Spartans had been in the Persian Wars, and aspired to do at the Alamo what the Spartans had failed to accomplish at Thermopylae—stop the invader. Travis thought the Alamo was the key to Texas and wrote, "I believe this place can be maintained." But even if it could not, Travis said, he would defend it to the death—an action which, like that of Leonidas and his 300 doomed Spartans, would at least serve to inspire his indecisive countrymen to fight.

Such was Travis' state of mind when, a couple of days before the besieged Alamo fell, it became apparent to the defenders that all was lost. Then (says a story first published a half century later) Travis took advantage of the lull before the fighting to address his men. He told them that death was inevitable and that he had detained them thus long in hope of reinforcements. When he had finished speaking, the silence of the grave reigned over all. Drawing his sword, Travis drew a line in front of his men and cried, "Those who wish to die like heroes and patriots come over to me." There was no hesitation. Every man, save one, crossed the line. Jim Bowie was too ill to leave the cot where he lay dying of consumption, but was not to be deterred. "Lads," he said, "I can't get over to you, but won't some of you be kind enough to lift my cot over?" In an instant it was done.

The man who did not cross the line was a Frenchman named Louis Rose, who had been a soldier in Napoleon's army in the retreat from Moscow. He had no more stomach for war horrors. Looking at Rose from his cot, Bowie said, "You seem not to be willing to die with us, Rose!" "No," said Rose, "I am not prepared to die and shall not do so if I can avoid it." Then Crockett also looked at him, saying, "You may as well conclude to die with us, old man, for escape is impossible." But legend has it that Crockett himself later helped Rose over the wall. The Frenchman is then said to have slipped through the Mexican lines and lived to tell the tale of his escape from the Alamo and of the line Travis drew.

Whatever the truth of that story, Texans reacted to the bad news exactly as Travis had foretold, and a proclamation was issued, opening with the words: "Thermopylae is no longer without a parallel!" Weeks later, Santa Anna's army was defeated in a bloody rout.

"I took ye fer an Injun," says one trapper to another in Frederic Remington's sketch of a once-over between two mountain men.

An apt if wry comment is made by the artist Charles M. Russell in the title of his work "Indians Discovering Lewis and Clark." Russell had a lifelong fascination for the 1804–06 trek.

Trailblazers and Trappers

Anxious to make sure France did not close the Mississippi, and therefore the Pacific, to the States, Thomas Jefferson managed to buy France's Louisiana Territory in 1803, which dramatically doubled the area of the nation. In 1804 Jefferson's exploration party led by Meriwether Lewis and William Clark was already canoeing up the Missouri.

The saga of far-western trailblazing, initiated by that early expedition, is marked by single names that have become part of the American legend, by single shadows against the sun-reflecting snow of the Rockies. It was Sacajawea alone who led Lewis and Clark over the rocky heights to open the secrets of the West, or so the legendmakers liked to whisper. After her came the solitary trapper-scouts, not unlike the 17th-century *coureurs de bois* who roamed the north woods, scrambling for pelts. One by one the mountain men faced harsh weather and cruel terrain and bands of Comanches, Blackfeet, Kiowas, and many others. Some took Indian wives, but most lived in self-imposed isolation. Alone they ran, hid, and crawled away from almost certain death, rehearsing privately their versions of The Great Escape to be told at the summer fur market—the Rendezvous—at the foot of the Rockies. An annual circus of shooting, gambling, gaming, carousing, and storytelling, the Rendezvous featured stories that were filled with a sense of superhuman exhilaration—for western tall tales were not unlike those told by the men who had crossed the Appalachians a generation earlier. They simply concerned men who were farther from home, who found themselves in a fabulously unfamiliar landscape, who were longer alone. By the last Rendezvous in 1840, trappers could draw maps of thousands of miles of Indian territory they had begun to think of as their own. But the wagons bringing settlers to Oregon were already preparing to roll, and the lone extravaganzas of the mountain men would soon be repeated only in their tales.

LEWIS, CLARK, AND SACAJAWEA
Legendary Reality

Meriwether Lewis and William Clark's exploration of the Northwest has mellowed into a legend that is based on the original, unembellished account of the journey, first published in 1904, exactly 100 years after the party set out. The story that most captivates modern imaginations is that of Sacajawea, the teenaged Indian wife of a French trader whom Lewis engaged as an interpreter. With her infant strapped on her back, she led the white men to her childhood home among the Shoshones, traversing country theretofore known to whites only by hearsay.

The mild Missouri, the bemused bear, and the leisurely gentleman of this 1813 drawing make unintentional spoof of Lewis' actual mad dash from a bear near the Great Falls.

Captain Lewis knew his company must winter east of the mountains and had a fort constructed. On Christmas morning the Stars and Stripes were hoisted above Fort Mandan near a Mandan village. All winter the men joined the Indians in the buffalo hunts, laying up pemmican [dried meat]. In February work was begun on the small boats for the ascent of the Missouri. By the end of March the river had cleared of ice, and six canoes and two pirogues were pushed out on the Missouri in the afternoon of April 7. A cheer arose from the traders and Indians on shore, and with flags flying, Lewis and Clark set sail for the unknown.

The current of the Missouri grew swifter, the banks steeper, and the use of the towline more frequent. On May 26 Captain Lewis had his first glimpse of the far-off, white "Shining Mountains" of which the Indians told—the Rockies, snowy and dazzling in the sun.

The Missouri had become too deep for poles, too swift for paddles, and the banks so precipitous that the men were often poised at dizzy heights above the river, dragging the towline round the edge of rock and crumbly cliff. Now the stream was so narrow it was hard to tell which was river and which tributary. Captain Lewis and four men went ahead to find the true course and heard the distant rushing of many waters. Above the prairie shimmered a gigantic plume of spray and Lewis and his men broke into a run across the open for seven miles to find cliffs 200 feet high. Spray tossed up a thousand shapes of wind-driven clouds. Lewis had found the Great Falls of the Missouri.

After sending back word to Clark, Lewis ascended a high hill when he suddenly encountered a herd of buffalo. It was near suppertime. Lewis fired. What was his amazement to see a huge bear pounce on the wounded quarry, and what was Bruin's amazement to see a thing as small as a man marching out to contest possession of that quarry? Man and bear reared, looked each other over. Bear had

been master in these regions from time immemorial. Lewis aimed his weapon to fire again when he recollected it was not loaded, and the bear was coming on too fast to recharge. Captain Lewis was a dignified man and he determined he would retreat at a walk. The rip of claws sounded from behind and Lewis glanced over his shoulder to see the bear at a gallop—and off they went in a sprinting match of 80 yards when the grunting of pursuer told pursued the bear was gaining. Turning short, Lewis plunged into the river and faced about with his spontoon [pike] at the bear's nose. A sudden turn is an old trick with Indian hunters; the bear floundered, reconsidered the sport of hunting this new animal, man, and whirled right about for the dead buffalo.

It took from the 15th to the 25th of June to portage the Great Falls. Cottonwood trees yielded wheels two feet in diameter, and the masts of the pirogues made axletrees. On these wagonettes the canoes were dragged. Grizzlies prowled the camp at night, wakening exhausted workers. Men fell asleep on their feet as they toiled, and spent half the night double-soling their torn moccasins, for the cactus had most of the men limping.

They entered the gates of the Rockies on the 19th of July; on the 25th the Three Forks of the Missouri were reached. Here Sacajawea recognized the ground and practically became the guide of the party, advising the southwest fork her tribe followed when crossing the mountains to the plains. It now became necessary to find Indians who would supply horses. Lewis with two men proceeded along what was plainly an Indian road, till the sources of the Missouri became so narrow one of the men put a foot on each side and thanked God he had lived to bestride it. The men came upon three squaws, who never moved but bowed their heads to the ground for the expected blow that would make them captives. Throwing down weapons, Lewis pulled up his sleeve to show he was white. The squaws led him toward camp. Pipes were smoked, presents distributed, and Lewis urged the warriors to come back up the trail to meet the advancing boats. To demonstrate good faith, Lewis rode on a horse behind an Indian, though the bareback riding over rough ground was jolting his bones apart. A spy arrived with news that one of the white hunters had killed a deer, and the company lashed to a gallop that nearly finished Lewis. Clark did not appear. If anything stopped Clark's advance, Lewis was lost. Though neither knew it, Lewis and Clark were only four miles apart.

Clark, Chaboneau, and Sacajawea were walking on the shore when the squaw began to dance with signs of extravagant joy. Looking ahead, Clark saw one of Lewis' men leading a company of warriors the squaw had recognized as her own people, from whom she had been wrested as a child. The Indians broke into songs of delight and Sacajawea, dashing through the crowd, threw her arms around an Indian woman, sobbing

Sacajawea elatedly wades along the shores of the Pacific in this painting by John Clymer. Long honored as guide of the Lewis and Clark exploration party, Sacajawea probably assured the expedition's success as much through simple womanliness—to hostile Indians hidden behind trees and rocks her presence meant this was no war party.

and laughing. Sacajawea and the woman had been playmates captured in the same war, but the woman had escaped, while Sacajawea became a slave and married Chaboneau.

Meanwhile, Captain Clark was being welcomed by Lewis and the chief, Cameahwait. Sacajawea was called to interpret. Cameahwait rose to speak and the poor squaw flung herself on him with cries of delight: she had recognized her brother.

The Indians discouraged the explorers about going on in boats. The stream was broken by rapids walled in with impassable precipices. Boats were abandoned and horses bought. Game grew so scarce that by October the company was reduced to a diet of dog flesh. Horses were left with the Flatheads and the explorers, once again in boats, glided down the Clearwater, to the Columbia. On November 8 they passed the last portage. When heavy fog lifted, there burst on the eager gaze of the voyageurs the shining expanse of the Pacific; shouts mingled with the roar of breakers.

The men fell ill in winter, their leather suits rotted from their backs; in March 1806 they left. Traders on the way up the Missouri from St. Louis brought the first news of the outer world, and the discoverers were not a little amused to learn they had been given up for dead. On September 20, settlers on the riverbank above St. Louis were surprised to see 30 ragged men passing down the river. Then someone remembered who these worn voyageurs were and cheers of welcome made the cliffs of the Missouri River ring.

FACT ? MYTH

Welsh Indians

One of the longest-standing legends about American Indians concerns a tribe descended from a band led by a 12th-century Welsh prince, Madoc, who was fleeing the enmity of his brother. The group supposedly landed in the Gulf of Mexico and made their way north. For at least two centuries explorers and wanderers told of one tribe after another speaking a tongue virtually interchangeable with Welsh. The story often included some Welsh object venerated by the tribe.

Eventually the legend centered on the Mandan Indians with whom Lewis and Clark's expedition spent its first winter (in North Dakota). Though the tribe nearly died out in the 19th century, their peculiarities, including features

Sah-ko-ka

such as gray eyes and beards, are well documented. George Catlin was so fascinated by them he lived with them for eight years and perpetuated the Welsh-origin belief. (He rendered the portraits shown here.) The Mandans themselves denied European origins. John Evans, who was specifically seeking the Welsh tribe, wrote in 1797 after a stay with the Mandans, "the Welsh Indians . . . from latitude 35 to 49 . . . have no existence." Yet writer Ellen Pugh speculates that Evans made that assertion because he was an alcoholic in the pay of Spain (which did not want to have any British claim substantiated).

Noted historian S. E. Morison dismisses the story as pure fable and the Bureau of Ethnology states: "There is not a provable trace of Welsh in any native American language."

Seehk-hee-da

TALES AS TALL AS THE LAND
The Mountain Men's Terrain

When trapper James Bridger told of Yellowstone's boiling rivers and geysers where "Hell bubbled up," people laughed at "Bridger's Lies." Easterners wondered if trappers were demented by the mountain air. Bridger or, some say, his listeners exaggerated his already fantastic reports; whichever the process, his tales began to parody themselves: a mountain described as glass next became invisible. Joseph Meek, a generation younger than Bridger, was formed in the same mold.

BRIDGER'S REPORT

Bridger gives a most romantic and enticing picture of the headwaters of the Yellowstone. A lake, 60 miles long, cold and pellucid, lies embosomed among high, precipitous mountains. On the west side is a sloping plain, several miles wide, with clumps of trees and groves of pine. The ground resounds with the tread of horses. Geysers spout up 70 feet high with a terrific, hissing noise at regular intervals. Waterfalls sparkle, leap, and thunder down

Jim Bridger's horse trotting neatly off a cliff onto petrified air illustrates a story as tall as any of the mountain men's tales.

precipices and collect in the pool below. The river issues from this lake, and for 15 miles roars through the perpendicular canyon at the outlet. Here are the "Great Springs," so hot that meat is readily cooked in them, and as they descend on the successive terraces afford delightful baths. On the other side is an acid spring, which gushes out in a river torrent; and below is a cave, which supplies "vermilion" for the savages.

THE GLASS MOUNTAIN

Coming one day in sight of a magnificent elk, Jim Bridger took careful aim at the unsuspecting animal and fired. To his great amazement, the elk not only was not wounded but seemed not even to have heard the report of the rifle. Bridger drew considerably nearer and gave the elk the benefit of his most deliberate aim, but with the same result as before. A third and a fourth effort met with a similar fate. Utterly exasperated, he seized his rifle by the barrel, resolved to use it as a club since it had failed as a firearm. He rushed madly toward the elk but suddenly crashed into an immovable vertical wall, which proved to be a mountain of perfectly transparent glass, on the farther side of which, still in peaceful security, the elk was quietly grazing. Stranger still, the mountain was not only of pure glass but was a perfect telescopic lens, and whereas the elk seemed but a few hundred yards off, it was in reality 25 miles away!

THE CRYSTAL MOUNTAIN

"Is there anything remarkable to be seen about here?" an inquisitive pilgrim asked him [Bridger] one day.

"W-al-l, there's a cur'ous mountain a few miles off, but the trouble is you can't see the blamed thing."

"That's curious," interrupted the pilgrim. "How large is it?"

"Wall, I should say it's nigh onto three miles in circumference at the base but its height is unknown. Didn't you ever hear of the Crystal Mountain?" "I never did."

"Wall, I'll tell you. It's a mountain of crystal rock, an' so clear that the most powerful fieldglasses can't see it, much less the naked eye. You'll wonder, p'r'aps, how a thing that can't be seen nohow was ever discovered. It came about this way. You see, a lot of bones and the carcasses of animals an' birds was found scattered all around the base. You see, they ran or flew against this invisible rock and jest killed themselves dead. You kin feel the rock an' that's all. You can't see it. It's a good many miles high, for everlastin' quantities of birds' bones are jest piled up all around the base of it."

THE OLD SCOUT'S ECHO

Opposite a certain camping ground where Bridger frequently stopped, there arose the bald, flat face of a mountain, but so distant that the echo from any sound that originated in camp did not return for the space of about six hours. Bridger converted this circumstance into an ideal alarm clock. Upon his retiring for the night he would call out lustily, "Time to get up!" and true to his calculation, the alarm would roll back at the precise hour next morning when it was necessary for the camp to bestir itself.

A LIKELY STORY

Somewhere along the shore an immense boiling spring discharges its overflow directly into the lake. The specific gravity of this water is less than that of the lake, owing probably to the expansive action of heat, and it floats in a stratum three or four feet thick upon the cold water underneath. When Bridger was in need of fish, it was to this place that he went. Through the hot upper stratum he

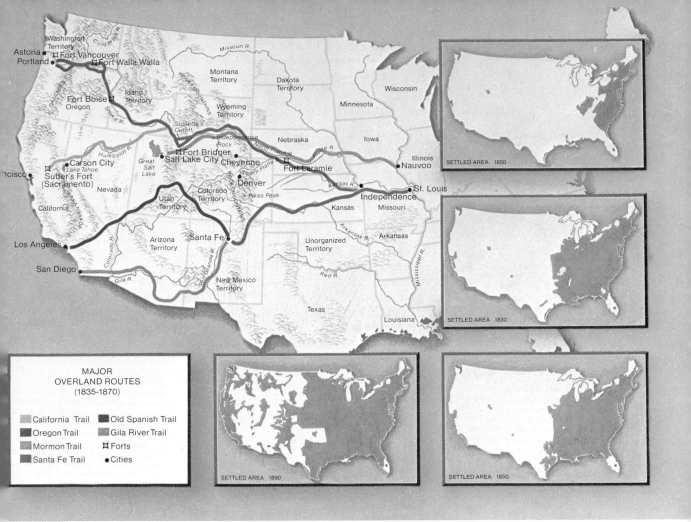

Go west and thrive: the American dream of land and liberty—and riches—lured wave after wave of young men and women westward. Because of English claims in the North and Spanish claims in the South, and plenty of land, there were still few Americans very far beyond the Mississippi in 1820. During the twenties and thirties the adventurous mountain men explored the Far West and discovered the trails over which pioneer wagons began to roll in the forties. In 1843 the first settlers' train reached Oregon country. In 1847 the first Mormons moved into Utah, and in 1849 the Gold Rush began. The seventies brought railroads and with them so many easterners that by 1890 a land once legendary and fabulous was mostly settled and deeded.

let fall his bait to the subjacent habitable zone, and having hooked his victim, cooked him *on the way out!*

THE PETRIFIED MOUNTAIN

According to his [Bridger's] account, there exists in the park country a mountain which was once cursed by a great medicine man of the Crow nation. Everything upon the mountain at the time of this dire event became instantly petrified and has remained so ever since. All forms of life are standing about in stone where they were suddenly caught by the petrifying influences, even as the inhabitants of ancient Pompeii were surprised by the ashes of Vesuvius. Sagebrush, grass, prairie fowl, antelope, elks, and bears may there be seen as perfect as in actual life. Even flowers are blooming in colors of crystal, and birds soar with wings spread in motionless flight, while the air floats with music and perfumes siliceous, and the sun and the moon shine with petrified light!

PETRIFIED EVERYTHING

What we did, finally, was come to a great wide canyon that appeared to cut me off from where I [Bridger] was going. At first I was worried, but then I got an idea, drove my pony to the edge of the canyon, and says, "Git up!" He turned around for a look at my face, naturally, to see if I was joking, the way I sometimes did with him, for we were old friends, you see. When he saw I wasn't, of course he stepped right ahead. He pranced right across the air in the canyon, the way I knowed he would. . . ."

"Wait a minute!" the tenderfoot said. "That's impossible!"

"Not there," Bridger told him. "You're educated and can see why, too, soon as I tell you. You see, *there, even the law of gravity is petrified.*"

"Have you any additional proof?" the tenderfoot asked. "Sure do. Some time later that pony got together three or four other ponies on the edge of Wildcat Bluff—to watch him. Then, with a smug smile on his face, he pranced out over the edge. I never saw a horse look as surprised as that pony did when he started to fall. We figured he was loco till Gabe told us why he done it. He was a good, logical pony. Only thing he didn't know, you see, was that in most places the law of gravity *isn't* petrified."

THE WILL TO ENDURE
Trial by Nature

Life in the wilderness took a heavy toll on the health and often the lives of the mountain men. Those hardy trappers, who roamed the Rockies in the 1820's and 1830's in search of beaver for the hats of eastern gentlemen, were exposed to hunger, thirst, heat, snow, and attack. Fact and fantasy are mingled in the stories of their heroic survivals and sudden deaths. And sometimes even the facts were so incredible that true stories were immediately elevated to the realm of legend.

MEEK'S MOUNT HOOD

The conversation chanced one day to run upon the changes that had taken place in the country since the earliest settlement by the Americans, and Joe Meek, who felt an honest pride in them, was expatiating at length, to the ill-concealed amusement of young officers, who probably saw nothing to admire in the rude improvements of the Oregon pioneers. "Mr. Meek," said one of them, "if you have been so long in the country and have witnessed such wonderful transformations, doubtless you may have observed equally great ones in nature; in the rivers and mountains, for instance?" Meek gave a lightning glance at the speaker, who had so mistaken his respondent.

"I reckon I have," said he slowly. Then waving his hand gracefully toward the majestic Mount Hood, towering thousands of feet above the summit of the Cascade Range and white with everlasting snows: "When *I* came to this country, Mount Hood was *a hole in the ground*!"

Old fancies in the New World's wilderness: artist Alfred Jacob Miller chose to dress the scout Jim Bridger in a suit of armor.

COLTER'S INDIAN RUN

Colter came to St. Louis in 1810, in a small canoe, from the headwaters of the Missouri, a distance of 3,000 miles, which he traversed in 30 days. I saw him on his arrival and received from him an account I shall relate. On the headwaters of the Missouri he trapped with a hunter named Potts; aware of the hostility of the Blackfeet, they set their traps at night and took them up early in the morning, remaining concealed during the day. One morning they heard a great noise and saw a party of Indians making their appearance on both sides of the creek. Colter and Potts, in the canoe, pushed off when an arrow was shot at Potts, and Potts leveled his rifle at an Indian and shot him dead—an act of madness, but if taken alive, Potts must have expected to be tortured to death. Potts was pierced with arrows. The Blackfeet now seized Colter, stripped him naked, and began to consult on the manner in which he should be put to death. They were inclined to set him up as a mark to shoot at, but the chief interfered and asked him if he could run fast. Colter knew that he now had to run for his life, with the dreadful odds of 500 or 600 armed men against him, and cunningly replied he was a bad runner. The chief led Colter 300 or 400 yards out on the prairie and released him, bidding him to save himself if he could. The horrid war whoop sounded in the ears of poor Colter, who ran with a speed at which he was himself surprised. He proceeded toward the Jefferson Fork, having to traverse a plain six miles in breadth, abounding with the prickly pear, on which he was every instant treading with naked feet. He ran halfway across the plain before he ventured to look over his shoulder. The Indians were scattered and he had gained ground. But one Indian, who carried a spear, was far ahead of the rest and not more than a hundred yards from Colter. A gleam of hope cheered Colter, but that confidence was nearly fatal to him, for he exerted himself to such a degree that the blood gushed from his nostrils and soon covered the fore part of his body. Arrived within a mile of the river, he heard the appalling sound of footsteps behind him and every instant expected to feel the spear. Determined to avoid the blow, he stopped, turned around, and spread out his arms. The Indian, surprised by the suddenness of the action and perhaps by the bloody appearance of Colter, attempted to stop but, exhausted with running, fell while endeavoring to throw his spear, which stuck in the ground and broke in his hand. Colter snatched up the pointed part, with which he pinned him to the earth, and continued his flight. The Indians, arriving at the place, stopped and set up a hideous yell. Colter succeeded in gaining the cottonwood trees on the borders of the [Jefferson] fork and plunged into the river. A little below there was an island, against which a raft of drift timber had lodged. He dived under and got his head above water among the trunks. The Indians arrived screeching and were frequently on the raft, seen through the chinks by Colter. In horrible suspense, he remained until nightfall when, hearing

"A Doubtful Guest," by Charles M. Russell, depicts two white men getting ready for trouble as an Indian approaches their camp. A mountain man's stock of pelts, traps, horses, and supplies made tempting quarry to red men—so did his white scalp.

no Indians, he swam silently down-river, landed, and traveled all night. He was completely naked, and the sun burned by day; the soles of his feet were filled with thorns of the prickly pear. He journeyed seven days to Lisa's Fort on the Bighorn, having subsisted solely on a root esteemed by the Indians, *Psoralea esculenta* [breadroot].

GLASS AND A GRIZZLY

Of the tales of survival in the western wilderness, few can match that told by mountain man Hugh Glass. Alone, unarmed, and crippled by a grizzly, Glass managed to crawl over more than 100 miles of hostile wilderness before reaching safety.

Glass' adventure began in the late summer of 1823, when he was headed for the Yellowstone River with a small party of trappers. Setting off alone one day in search of game, he was attacked by a grizzly. When his companions found him he seemed hopelessly mangled.

The men lingered for a few days, hoping Glass would either show signs of recovery or die; when no change took place they moved on. The leader of the party offered a reward to any person who would remain with the near corpse until he passed on. Two men, one of them supposedly young Jim Bridger, offered to do it.

Bridger and the other man, Fitzgerald, found time hanging heavy on their hands after their companions trekked away. They held a conference, decided that Glass was as good as dead, took what possessions he had—overlooking a razor—and hastened after the party. They reported Glass dead and buried.

But in a day or so Glass opened his eyes. In a blind, instinctive manner he rolled down to the spring of water beside which he lay, drank, and afterward crammed his stomach with chokecherries and buffalo berries that grew all around. Then he slept.

When he awoke the second time, however, his mind had cleared, and after cursing his companions, he settled down to decide what to do. Fort Kiowa in the Dakotas lay 100 miles away and looked like the best bet. So Hugh Glass, because of the way his back had been injured, crawled away—at an average rate of two miles from sunup to sundown.

There was, fortunately, plenty of water, and Glass drank a great deal to augment his diet of berries and such small lizards as he was able to capture. But his terrific exertion took toll of him, until at last starvation faced him unless he managed to secure more nourishing food. Strength drained from his arms and legs and he slumped forward wearily, on the point of total collapse.

A noise roused him—a buffalo calf pursued by three wolves. Glass sat up, wheezing with hope when the wolves closed in upon the calf. One of them hamstrung it and when the animal collapsed, they all darted in to dig fangs into the live body until it died. Then they settled to gorge.

Hugh Glass waited for the wolves to satisfy themselves. Then he crept forward. The wolves snarled, but their full bellies dulled their ferocity. They slunk off. "Anaaahhh!" Glass, no longer a man, screamed as he tore at the entrails of the dead calf. In time he paused, refreshed. And, hope rising now, he cut up what he could pack of the animal and crept away.

Eventually he saw Fort Kiowa and knew he had won. He crawled to the stockade; traders found him, took him in, marveled that this thing should be a man. Six weeks later, strong and well again, he set out for the upper reaches of the Missouri to find Bridger and Fitzgerald.

He presently rejoined his party, which months before had been convinced of his death. "Hugh Glass . . . it can't be! It's a ghost thing!" But Hugh Glass was no ghost. He was flesh and blood, and pretty tough flesh and blood at that. He continued in pursuit of Bridger and Fitzgerald, who had left the expedition. Months later he overtook Bridger but decided to go easy on him. "You're a young 'un, Jim. You're not even 18 yit. You didn't know what you was doin'. Tell you what—you fetch me back that rifle you robbed me of when you left me, an' we'll call this matter squar'!"

Glass' intentions concerning Fitzgerald were more elemental; he intended to cut off his ears and kill him by bits. But Fitzgerald joined the army and thus temporarily placed himself beyond Glass' vengeance. Before Glass could get to him, Glass found himself one day on the ice of the Missouri River, with Blackfoot Indians on both shores. The barren surface offered no protection, and the odds of life stood at 10,000 to 1 against Hugh Glass. This time he lost.

THE MASTER TRAPPER

William Sherley Williams, known as Old Bill, was a mythic figure even when he lived—and much of the myth was of his own making. Tall and gangly, with red hair and a red beard, he had been born in Kentucky and became, for a time, a circuit-riding Methodist preacher before deciding to give up the Bible for beaver.

Williams was, by his own admission, the best trapper in the mountains. He could likewise drink more liquor, spend more money quicker, swear harder and longer, and coin more queer and awful oaths than any pirate that ever blasphemed.

In keeping with his proud assessment of himself, Williams styled himself "William S. Williams, M.T.," which signified "Master Trapper," and he insisted that under all circumstances the title initials were to be attached to his name. In this regard he chanced at one time to fall into a mortal quarrel with a Blackfoot Indian, and upon achieving the advantage, he at once seized upon the red fellow's scalp lock.

"Bill Williams!" shouted the Indian, whose whole knowledge of English consisted of the capacity for pronouncing this singular old white man's name.

"William S. Williams, M.T., if you please," said the old man of the mountains, as he coolly darted the point of his knife around the Blackfoot's scalp lock and tore it off.

JEDEDIAH SMITH

As a pathfinder of the Far West, Jedediah Smith was without equal. While trapping and exploring beyond the Missouri, he opened three trails to California and the Pacific Northwest, and had enough adventures to satisfy 10 ordinary people.

Unlike most of his roughneck companions Smith neither swore nor smoked nor chewed tobacco, and he

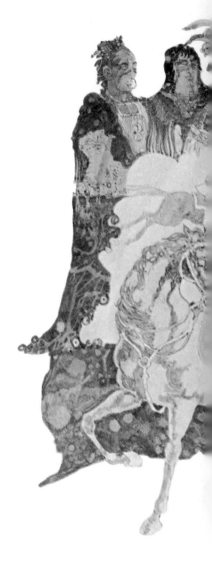

seldom drank. But no one ever accused him of being soft. During one trapping expedition he and a grizzly came face to face in a thicket. The bear took nearly his whole head in its mouth. When the beast finally let go, most of Smith's skull was laid bare and his right ear was hanging by a thread. Since none of his companions knew surgery, it was left to the injured man himself to direct the repairs. "One or two of you go for water," he said, "and if you have a needle and thread, git it out and sew up the wounds around my head."

Kit Carson was an unknown mountain man until chosen to guide John Frémont's expedition. Frémont's reports about Carson became the basis of his legend.

After all his other wounds were stitched up, Smith was told that the ear was beyond saving. "Oh, you must try to stitch it up some way or other," he insisted. He calmly gave directions on how to do it, and when the operation was over he mounted his horse and rode to camp.

KIT CARSON FIGHTS

Christopher "Kit" Carson may have been short and bandy-legged, with a soft voice and soft blue eyes. But legend made him into a giant of a man who stood well over six feet tall, who had the physique of a Hercules, and whose voice was like that of a roused lion. Who but such a strapping figure could have survived the combat with a mountain lion that Carson endured during one of his trapping expeditions in the Rockies?

As the story goes, Carson and a companion were working the streams that flow westward from the Rocky Mountains to the Great Salt Lake. Having left his partner back in camp preparing supper, Carson was walking along the bank of a stream checking his traps. He had a large rifle with him, as was his custom, and, seeing a turkey strutting along a few yards in advance, was preparing to shoot it when his attention was directed to a pair of fierce eyes gleaming out from behind the roots of a great tree, scarcely 20 feet away. A moment's inspection convinced Carson that he was in the presence of a powerful mountain lion.

To retreat, he knew, would have invited the attack he felt was about to be made, so raising his rifle he fired. But there was such a profusion of snakelike roots surrounding the lion's

183

♣WORD LORE♣

body that his shot resulted only in an exasperating wound as it struck the animal in the left shoulder. In the next instant the lion was upon him, roaring like its ancestral kith of the African jungles. Carson had no other weapon now save the large knife he carried, and with this he defended himself valiantly. But the sharp claws of the beast penetrated his flesh and cut like a two-edged sword. Carson's shirt was ripped off him, and while he slashed with his knife and time and again thrust it to the hilt into the lion's body, the infuriated animal still fought with such success that, weakened by the loss of so much blood, Carson was on the point of yielding.

But fortune at last favored him. The lion was also much exhausted. It fell under one of Carson's blows, and as it rolled onto its back with its dreadful fangs still fastened in the remnants of Kit's tattered shirt, a plunge of the knife into the animal's throat almost severed its head from its body and ended the battle at last—in Carson's favor.

But the victory was purchased at great expense, for the wounded trapper was so overcome by the lacerations of his flesh and sinews that he fainted and would undoubtedly have died had not his comrade-in-camp, alarmed at his long absence, begun to search for him. Discovering Carson's bleeding, unconscious body beside the dead lion, he carried Kit back to the camp, where his tender care renewed the life that had been so nearly extinguished.

DUEL IN THE DUST

Carson was as ready to stand up to a bully as he was to tangle with Indians or wild animals. One of his encounters was so famous that it became part of western folklore. It happened during the annual summer Rendezvous, where hundreds of mountain men and Indians had come to exchange their pelts for supplies from the East. Among the trappers who gathered at the Rendezvous was a big Frenchman named Shuman, who was particularly fond of bullying his companions. Riding about the camp with gun in hand, Shuman was having a fine time throwing insults at his fellow trappers. Special abuse was reserved for the Americans, whom he denounced as scullions and chicken-

Draped in furs, his packhorse burdened with peltries and supplies, a mountain man surveys his domain in this sketch.

livered scoundrels. This unprovoked language aroused Carson, who stepped forward toward the boasting Frenchman and said: "I am an American and no coward but you are a vaporing bully, and to show you how Americans can punish liars, I'll fight you here in any manner your infamous heart may desire."

Shuman boiled over with rage at this proposition. "If you want to be killed," he replied, "I have no objections to shooting you as I would a dog. Get on your horse and fight me, starting at 100 yards and riding toward each other, firing as we come together. Come on, you chicken-livered, pale-faced scullion!"

Kit returned no answer to this arrogant acceptance of his challenge but mounted his horse and prepared for the duel. The two rode apart, each divining the purpose of the other, until a proper distance was reached, then wheeled their horses and rushed toward each other. The entire camp stood by to witness the combat, the sympathies of the men being unanimously with Carson. Shuman was an excellent rifleman and had trained himself to fire from his running horse by shooting buffalo, and he therefore felt confident of putting a bullet through the head of his adversary. Kit carried a pistol but this was from choice, because he was an expert with that weapon.

The two determined men rushed toward each other like knights of medieval chivalry until within a few yards, when Shuman raised himself in his stirrups and, taking aim, fired. The bullet went so close to the mark that a lock of Kit's hair was seen to fall from above his ear. The smoke from the Frenchman's fire was still rolling away over his head when Carson presented his pistol almost as the heads of the two horses came together, and saluted his enemy. The ball struck Shuman in the hand and, passing upward in the arm, lodged near the elbow. Though not fatal, the wound was sufficient to humble the desperado and so change his disposition as to eliminate all braggadocio from his character.

ANIMALS THAT KNEW
As Much as Any Human Critter

When mountain men swapped stories, animal cunning and intelligence were a favorite topic. Jim Bridger used to tell how he was once surprised by a pack of wolves which he escaped by climbing a tree. The wolves waited at its base for about two hours, when finally all departed save one, and that one remained on guard. In about half an hour the pack returned with a beaver to chew down the tree. The rest of the story is now lost; but here are more tales in the same vein:

BEAVER BANTER

During a greenhorn's first winter west of the Platte, he was often subjected to a special kind of hazing by veteran companions sitting round the campfire at night. Typically, an oldtimer would tell the greenhorn a whopper with a straight face, and the greenhorn, though astonished, had to listen with a straight face, too, as well as a generally respectful demeanor. If he expressed amusement or disbelief, the group soon taught him to conceal his thoughts. Here is an example of the education of a novice trapper in backwoods manners:

"There was a beaver that lived with a trapper. In the daytime, when the trapper left the tent, the beaver would fall to work and make a dam across the floor of the tent, using the chest, skins, arms, and everything. That beaver was as near like a human bein' as any man present."

At this the greenhorn whistled, which seemed to give great dissatisfaction to all of the trappers present. One of them asked him: "Is that the way, youngster, you'se been educated in politeness of manners? If it is, I know a beaver who kin larn you somethin'. In the fust place, if a young beaver ever comes into the presence of the ole uns—especially if the ole un is a female beaver—the young un 'mediately fetches his right paw up to his forehead, jest 'hind the right eyebrow, an' makes a reverential bow of ceremony in salute. I'se seen that 'ar oftener than you've put one leg ahead of t'other yit, young un."

The trappers present all confirmed the truth of this statement by a sol-emn nod of assent to the query "Ain't that true, gentlemen?" Thereafter the greenhorn wisely refrained from his unceremonious whistling.

AN APPRECIATIVE BEAR

There was a Canadian by the name of Peno who trapped in the Powder River region. One day he shot and wounded a buffalo bull and the animal turned on him, gored his horse to death, and broke his leg. The trapper lost his gun and lay helpless on the bank of a little stream, now known as Peno Creek. Finally he regained enough strength to creep along down the creek bank in the direction of an Indian village. He lived several days on wild cherries. After crawling some distance, he fell exhausted to the ground and slept. Waking, he was horrified to find standing near him a large-sized silver-striped bear. Cold chills ran down his back, but he resolved that he must play dead. He closed his eyes and lay quiet.

After a while he looked to see if the bear had left, but no such luck. The monster was even closer. He then noticed that the animal held one of his paws in a position which indicated that he was asking for help. Realizing that the bear could do no more than kill him, Peno took out his knife and removed a sliver. With the pain thus eased, the animal lay down and slept. Peno crawled away. When the bear found him gone he trailed him. This continued several days. At last they reached a high point that overlooked the Indian village in a beautiful valley. The bear climbed on a huge rock and gazed earnestly in the direction of the village. He came back to the wounded man and looked at him in a manner almost human. Then he went quietly up the stream and disappeared, as much as to say: "I have done all I can for you."

Mountain man S. E. Hollister is shown in this contemporary lithograph fighting off an enraged mother grizzly bear whose cubs he had disturbed. Hollister lost a hand in the fight but managed nonetheless to fight on and kill the she-bear. He survived and mended.

A LIFE IN SKINS
Jim Beckwourth, Squawman

Trappers careful to befriend Indians could look forward to their hospitality in the mountains and on the plains; those who married into a tribe provided themselves with increased safety and improved terms of barter as well as with the pleasures of home. Some men settled into the Indian life with whole hearts, unlike devious Jim Beckwourth—son of a mulatto mother and white father—who lived with a number of Blackfoot, Snake, and Crow wives before returning to "civilization."

We spent the summer months at our leisure, trading with the Indians, hunting, sporting, and preparing for the fall harvest of beaver. We made acquaintance with several of the Blackfeet, who came to the post to trade. One of their chiefs invited Mr. Sublette to establish a branch post in their country, telling him that they had many people and horses and plenty of beaver. The Indian appearing sincere, Sublette proposed to establish a post among the Blackfeet if any of the men were willing to risk their scalps in attend-ing it. I offered to go, although I was well aware the tribe knew that I had contributed to the destruction of a number of their braves, but to the Indians, the greater the brave, the higher their respect for him, even though an enemy. So taking my boy Baptiste and one man with me, we packed up and started for Beaver River, which is a branch of the Missouri, and in the heart of the Blackfoot country.

On our arrival the Indians manifested great appearance of friendship and were highly pleased at having a trading post so conveniently at hand. I soon rose to be a great man among them, and the chief offered me his daughter for a wife. This alliance would guarantee my life as well as enlarge my trade; I accepted and, without superfluous ceremony, became son-in-law to As-as-to. To me the alliance was more *offensive* than defensive, but *thrift* was my object more than hymeneal enjoyments. Trade prospered greatly. I purchased beaver and horses at my own price.

After a few days I had difficulty in my family affairs. A party of Indians came into camp with three white men's scalps. The sight of them made my blood boil with rage but there was no help for it, so I determined to await with patience my day of revenge. In accordance with their custom a scalp dance was held, at which there was much additional rejoicing.

My *wife* came to me with the information that her people were rejoicing and that she wished to join the dancing and festivities.

I replied: "No, these scalps be-

longed to my people. My heart is crying for their death. You must not rejoice when my heart cries. You must not dance when I mourn."

She then went out, as I supposed, satisfied. My two white friends, having a great curiosity to witness the performance, were looking out upon the scene. I reproved them for wishing to witness the savage rejoicings over the fall of men who had probably belonged to our own company.

One of them answered: "Well, your wife is the best dancer of the whole party. She outdances them all." This was a sting which pierced my very heart. Taking my battle-ax and forcing myself into the ring, I watched my opportunity and struck my disobedient wife a heavy blow in the head with the side of my battle-ax, which dropped her as if a ball had pierced her heart.

I dragged her through the crowd and left her, then went back to my tent. This act was performed in such a bold manner, under the very noses of hundreds of them, that they were

Rendezvousing in summer at the base of the mountains or meeting in scattered camps during winter, trappers of various descents enjoyed a lively jug and an "Alouette" as in John Clymer's painting.

thunderstruck for a moment. Then the whole camp was in a blaze. "Kill him! Burn him!" was shouted throughout. Soon I heard the voice of my father-in-law crying above all: "Stop! Hold! Listen to your chief!" All was hushed.

"Warriors! I am the loser of a daughter, and her brothers have lost a sister; you have lost nothing. She was the wife of the trader; I gave her to him. When your wives disobey your commands, you kill them; that is your right. That thing disobeyed her husband. He told her not to dance; she disobeyed him; she had no ears. He killed her, and he did right. He did as you all would have done, and you shall neither kill nor harm him for it. I promised the white chief that, if he would send a trader to my people, I would protect him; this I must do and he shall not be hurt here. Warriors! Wait till you meet him in battle or, perhaps, in his own camp, then kill him; but here his life is sacred. What if we kill them all and take what they have? It will last but a few suns; we shall then want more. Whom do we get *sach-o-pach* [powder] from? We get it from the whites, and when we have expended what we have, we must do without or go to them for more. When we have no powder, can we fight our enemies with plenty? If we kill these three men, whom I have given the word of a chief to protect, the white chief will send us no more but his braves will revenge the death of their brothers. No, no. You shall not harm them here. They have eaten of our meat and drunk of our water; they have also smoked with us. When they have sold their goods, let them return to their homes in peace."

The chief then made a loud and long harangue, after which all became quiet. As-as-to next came to my camp: "My son, you have done right.

That woman I gave you had no sense; her ears were stopped up. But I have another daughter, who is younger than she. She is more beautiful; she has good sense and good ears. You may have her in the place of the bad one."

"Well," thought I, "this is getting married again before I have even had time to *mourn*." But I replied, "Very well, my father, I accept your kind offer." To refuse would be to offend.

My second wife was brought to me. I found her, as her father had represented, far more intelligent and far prettier than her sister, and I was really proud of the change. I now possessed one that many a warrior had performed deeds of bloody valor to obtain, for it is a high honor to wife the youngest daughter of a chief.

During the night, while I and my wife were quietly reposing, some person crawled into our couch, sobbing most bitterly. Angry at the intrusion, I asked who was there.

"Me," answered a voice, which, although well-nigh stifled with bitter sobs, I recognized as that of my other wife, whom everyone had supposed dead. After lying outside the lodge senseless for hours, she had recovered and groped her way to my bed.

"Go away," I said. "You have no business here. I have a new wife now, one who has sense."

"I will not go away," she replied. "My ears are open now. I was a fool not to hearken to my husband's words when his heart was crying, but now I have good sense and will always hearken."

It did really seem as if her heart was broken, and she kept her position until morning. I thought myself now well supplied with wives, having *two* more than I cared to have, but I deemed it hardly worthwhile to complain, as I should soon leave the camp, wives and all.

It is a universal adage, "When you are among Romans, do as the Romans do." I conformed to the customs of a pagan people. I was risking my life for gold that I might return one day with plenty, to share with one at home I tenderly loved.

FROM THE BLACKFEET
An Indian Odyssey

The Blackfeet, perhaps so called because they rubbed their moccasins with the ashes of their campfires, lived in the northwest corner of the Great Plains. These nomads had long hunted buffalo on foot, growing only a little tobacco as they moved their tepees to follow the hunt. Eventually they acquired both horses and guns and launched an offensive to hold their land, which made them much feared by trappers and other tribes. Blackfoot men who put tribe before self were revered, as was the magically born Blood-Clot Boy, off on an odyssey to do good.

BLOOD-CLOT BOY

Once there were an old man and woman whose three daughters married a young man who was supposed to hunt buffalo and feed them all, but he ordered his wives not to give meat to the old folks. Yet one stole meat for them.

The old man saw a clot of blood in the trail and said to himself, "Here at least is something from which we can make soup." He took the clot of blood home and requested his wife to make blood-soup. When the pot began to boil, the old woman heard a child crying. It seemed to be in the pot. She looked in and saw a boy baby, so she took the baby out and wrapped it up. That night the baby spoke to the old man, saying, "You take me up and hold me against each lodgepole." So the old man took up the baby and, beginning at the door, went around in the direction of the sun, and each time he touched a pole the baby became larger. When the last pole was reached, the baby had become a very fine young man. He said: "I am the Smoking Star. I came down to help you. When I have done this, I shall return."

When morning came, Blood-Clot took his father out to hunt. They killed a [buffalo] cow and Blood-Clot directed his father to eat. When the son-in-law saw this, he began to shoot arrows at the old man. Blood-Clot sprang up and shot the son-in-law. Then Blood-Clot Boy said, "Which one of your daughters helped you?" The old man told him it was the youngest. Then Blood-Clot went to the lodge, killed the two older women, brought up the body of the son-in-law, and burned them together. Then he requested the younger daughter to take care of her old parents. "Now," said Blood-Clot, "I will make a journey roundabout. Where are there any people? In what direction?" "Well," said the old man,

By 1911, when Remington Schuyler painted "The Disputed Trail," America's western Indian had become a permanently war-bonneted, stony-faced stereotype.

"up above there are some people."

So he started out. As he was going along in the mountains, some old women said: "Do not go there, for it is bad. Windsucker lives there. He will kill you." It pleased Blood-Clot Boy to know of such a thing, and he went to the mountains. A thunderstorm struck him and carried him to the mouth of a great fish. This was a suckerfish and the wind was its sucking. Blood-Clot Boy looked into his mouth and went in, and he saw a fearful sight. The ground was white as snow with the bones of those who had died. There were bodies with flesh on them; some were newly dead, and some still living. He spoke to a living person and asked, "What is that hanging down above us?" The person answered that it was Windsucker's heart. Then said Blood-Clot: "You who still draw a little breath, try to shake your heads [in time to the song], and those who are still able to move, get up and dance the Ghost Dance." Blood-Clot painted his face white, his eyes and mouth with black circles, and tied a knife on his head so that the point stuck up, and he began to dance. The others danced with him, and as he danced up and down, the point of the knife cut Windsucker's heart and killed him. Then Blood-Clot cut the heart down. Next he cut through between the ribs and let the people out. Then he asked: "Where are there other people? I want to visit all the people."

They said: "There is a camp to the west but you must not take the left-hand trail, because on that trail lives a woman, a handsome woman, who invites men to wrestle with her and then kills them." This was what Blood-Clot was looking for. This was his business in the world, to kill off all the bad things. After he had gone away, he saw a woman who called to him to come over. "No," said Blood-Clot, "I am in a hurry." However, the fourth time the woman asked, he said: "Yes, but you must wait a little while, for I am tired. I wish to rest. When I have rested, I will come over and wrestle with you." While resting, he saw knives sticking up from the ground almost hidden by straw. When he was rested, he went over. The woman asked him to stand in the place where he had seen the knives. "No, let us play a little, before we begin." So he began to play with the woman but quickly caught hold of her, threw her upon the knives, and cut her in two.

Then Blood-Clot went on. After a while he came to a camp where some old women told him that a little farther on he would come to a woman with a swing but on no account must he ride with her. After a time he came to a place where he saw a swing on the bank of a swift stream. There was a woman swinging on it. He watched her awhile and saw that she killed people by swinging them out and dropping them on the water. When he found this out, he came up to the woman. "You have a swing here. Let me see you swing," he said. "Well," said the woman, "Watch me." As the woman swung out, he cut the vine and dropped her in the water.

Again he went on and came to the place of a man-eater. Blood-Clot called to a little girl he saw nearby: "Child, I am going into that lodge to let that man-eater kill and eat me. Watch close, and when you can get hold of one of my bones, call the dogs and throw it down and cry out, 'Blood-Clot, the dogs are eating your bones!'" Then Blood-Clot entered the lodge and the man-eater seemed glad to see him, for Blood-Clot was a fat young man. The man-eater took a knife and cut Blood-Clot's throat and ate his body, limb by limb. Then the little girl said: "Pity me, man-eater. My mother is hungry and asks you for those bones." So the old man handed them to her and she threw the bones to the dogs, crying, "Blood-Clot, the dogs are eating you!" and when she said that, Blood-Clot arose from the pile of bones and slew the man-eater. "Now," said Blood-Clot, "I have rid the world of monsters. I shall go up into the sky as Smoking Star."

A rigid arm posture was part of the ritual performed by the Blackfeet after the first thunder of spring. Unwrapping the medicine pipestem, the priest prayed: "Listen, Sun! Listen, Thunder! Listen, Old Man! All Above Animals, All Above People, pity us! Let us not starve. Make the berries large and sweet." Then the Indians danced and smoked.

The Great Overland Adventure

Legend has it that when in 1848 Henry Clay was making his last homeward journey from Washington to Kentucky, he stopped and put his ear to the ground. When asked why, he replied, "I am listening to the tread of unnumbered thousands of feet that are to come this way westward." It did not take a prophet to hear those tramping feet. The dash for the Pacific coast had been underway since 1841, and every year had witnessed the departure of increasing tens of thousands setting out in wagon trains from the banks of the Missouri to carve out a share of the good life for themselves west of the Rockies.

Some 2,000 miles of prairie, desert, and rugged mountain lay between them and their goal, and the majority of pioneers had no experience and but scant knowledge of what awaited them along the way. The Great Plains were then commonly known as the Great American Desert and believed to be unfit for human habitation. It thus took considerable gumption to pack one's family and possessions

"Westward," by E. H. Blashfield, is a grandiose depiction of the opening of the plains. The allegorical figure with the book represents knowledge; her sister holds

into a wagon and head out, facing possible death by starvation, exposure, or Indian attack. Yet a blend of casual cheerfulness and bravado was the rule. Asked where they were heading, emigrants might reply, "Oh, going fishing."

The actual trip in most cases was not the grim death march it is often made out to have been. It was a grueling test of nerve and endurance, however, and many did fall by the wayside. Some of the latter, in accordance with their own or their families' wishes, were buried with their heads to the west—"pointin' the way they was goin'," as one old-timer was to put it. But most of the pioneers made it, sun-blackened and unkempt, only tougher from their ordeal.

Few fabulous Crockett-style heroes were to emerge from the overland journey. Instead, as noted by California Trail historian Julia Altrocchi, "it is more the trail itself that has become the hero. Oldtimers speak of 'the trail' with drawling respect. The human hero, if anything, is in the plural: 'them pioneers,' 'them covered-wagoners.'" Their story is thus more a saga than a collection of legends.

A New York editor wrote in 1845 that it was "our manifest destiny to overspread the continent." Most Americans agreed.

the Iowa State Seal while others scatter seed indicating coming civilization. The ladies at the rear holding models of a steam engine and an electric generator signify technology.

ON THE TRAIL
A Long Way From Home

A typical covered-wagon train was made up of 100 wagons, divided into four groups, each with its own captain. By the late 1840's the trails became so crowded that separate trains merged into one. "The trains passed our camp like the flow of a river," wrote one pioneer. The trek took about five months, ideally between May and October—leaving Missouri when the grass for livestock was green and crossing the Rockies before the first November snows. Some episodes follow:

WIND WAGONS
Contrary to the popular image of endless lines of identical prairie schooners, every imaginable kind of vehicle was used by the emigrants. In several instances wind wagons were tried. One party overtook such a vehicle about 10 miles west of Kansas City. It had four wheels, each about 20 feet in circumference, was about 9 feet across, and had a body like an omnibus. It was designed to carry 24 passengers. Rigged with a very large sail, schooner style, it plowed right along through the mud but was becalmed in a deep ravine where the wind failed to fill the sail. The captain of the 3,000-pound craft stated that when it was perfected he'd bet he could make it to the mountains in six days, but as far as is known he did not place his bet—and if he had he wouldn't have collected.

PARTING OF THE WAYS
The hardships of the westward trek were to put many a marriage and partnership to the test. Inevitably, some went on the rocks. For example, one man and his wife had such a violent quarrel that they cut their wagon in two, made a cart of each part, and divided their team equally, each taking a yoke of oxen. People remarked that there was no need for a judge, jury, lawyer, or fees to get a divorce out on the plains. Then there were the two men who had gone partners and prepared an outfit together at Independence but soon started squabbling over the traveling and camping arrangements. Their quarrels grew increasingly bitter and more frequent as the journey wore on. Finally, at Chimney Rock, one of the company suggested that they fight it out and be done with it. The mere suggestion was enough. Each drew his bowie knife and they closed in fierce combat. In a short time one fell and expired almost immediately. The other, fainting from loss of blood, was carried to the shade, where he died within an hour. At set of sun the combatants were laid next to each other in the same grave, nevermore to disagree.

NEVER STOP
Up and down the ever-moving columns of wagons, people, and animals the incidents of daily life went on as usual—there were courtships, marriages, births, and deaths in every train. One emigrant's record of a typical night noted a wedding in his own camp, while in another train a mile distant a young boy was buried by torchlight, and nearby in a third wagon camp the birth of a true pio-

An evening meal on the Great Plains. Provisions sometimes ran low in midjourney; when that happened, emigrants were lucky if they made it. Some of the fortunate could sing: "We lived on rotten buffalo hump and damned old iron-wedge bread . . ."

neer child was reported.

Less than a month after one party left civilization, a romance had developed to such a point that a church officer belonging to the caravan felt constrained to marry the couple on the Platte River, "without law or license," as he said, "for we were a long way from the United States." The fortitude of the women who walked the trail became legendary—one Mrs. Jeemes Taylor, who was already several months pregnant when she set out from her Illinois home, is an example. When it came time, she paused a few hours at trailside to give birth to a fine baby. Her husband inquired, "Do you feel able to go on, Sally?" "Oh yes, Jeemes, I feel pretty pert," she replied. "I reckon you'd better hitch up the steers." With this brief exchange, the proud husband hooked up and the onward march was resumed.

FLAYED ALIVE

Rawhide was a common commodity in the early West, and place-names along the emigrants' trail sprang from a variety of incidents involving it. At Rawhide Buttes, Wyoming, and a number of Rawhide creeks in Ne-

Many wagons halted once a week, so pioneers could observe the Sabbath—and make much-needed repairs. One man said: "Trains that laid by an' kept Sunday got to Californy first. You wouldn't believe it, but I've heard hundreds say the same thing."

braska, Wyoming, and California, the original incidents were forgotten and replaced by the legend that white men had been flayed there by Indians. Whether the story first arose from the conception of Indian tortures in general or from an actual occurrence in a specific place, from which the tale was carried in all directions by horrified pioneers, or whether it was derived from more than one incident along the trail cannot now be determined.

The first of these terrible "Rawhides" is on Elkhorn River, some 20 miles west of Omaha. The story is

FACT ? MYTH

Scarin' Off Injuns

Among certain Plains Indian peoples encountered by emigrants were individuals believed to harbor in a mysterious manner in their bodies some animal or object. On ceremonial occasions (and sometimes on the spur of the moment) such persons were wont to go into a trance, yank the object out of their mouths, and then (by a sleight of hand comparable to Daniel Boone's knife-eating trick) swallow it back down. Among the objects thus exhibited were buffalo and horse tails, birds' eggs and crow feathers, scalps, bullets, colored ribbons, and most commonly, parts of a bear's body, especially teeth or claws. During the Bear Song Dance of the Crows, for example, an ecstatic performer might spit up red paint and

then rush at terrified onlookers with bear teeth protruding from his mouth. All this related to the bear hunt and to associated forms of ritual medicine.

Not surprisingly, the memory of the spectacular bear cult performances of the red men—long familiar to trappers and mountain men—got mixed up in emigrant lore with an old favorite in which the white man frightens Indians by removing his wig, wooden leg, glass eye, or the like. A blend of fact and fancy, the covered-wagon version relates how an intrepid pioneer scared off a band of hostiles:

An emigrant named Harmanius van Vleck was crossing the plains in a small caravan. All the dangers of the deserts had been passed, and the company were camping in a grassy place under the first flanks of the Sierra.

Suddenly Van Vleck noticed a ring of Indian fires flashing signals from the hills. He decided that every one of his male companions should guard the campsite while he would try to handle the dangerous situation by himself. His technique was unusual. He rode up into the hills, toward the largest of the signal fires. When he was within a few rods of it, he straightened up in his saddle, assumed a ferocious expression, and galloped full speed up to the assembled Indians. When he was within the full glare of the campfire and all eyes were fixed upon him, he suddenly inserted his hand into his mouth, pulled out his upper set of false teeth, and flourished it in the faces of the terrified hostiles, who scattered in all directions into the dark, fleeing from this white wizard.

While mapping the Oregon Trail in 1843, John C. Frémont found emigrants navigating western rivers with arklike rafts loaded with their wagons, livestock, and families.

told that at one point a blacksmith, who had sworn he would kill the first Indian he laid his eyes upon, wantonly shot a Pawnee boy. The emigrants had had friendly dealings at Omaha with Chief Big Elk of the Pawnees. They could not allow the crime to go unpunished, and when pressed, they turned the murderer over to the Pawnees who, without qualms, tied him to a wagon wheel and skinned him alive.

There is another version of the legend at Schuyler, Nebraska. According to that story, an emigrant in one of the trains raped, then killed a squaw. The Indians surrounded the train and demanded the murderer on the threat of otherwise destroying the entire caravan. The offender was handed over and the Indians proceeded to flay him alive. They then turned him loose near the creek, into which he stumbled and died. The same story was told of a Rawhide Creek near Fort Laramie, Wyoming, and of yet another creek located in Woodside, California.

MASSACRE

Indian troubles gave rise to the greatest myth of the trail, that of the wagon train, its wagons drawn up in a circle, desperately fighting off a howling horde of Indians on horseback. The scene would be a pure fiction because such a defense was too formidable to the Indians—

except that something of the sort did indeed happen once, and that once was bad enough. The Massacre of Almo Creek, Utah, was the worst disaster in the history of the California Trail. It became the prototype of the Hollywood legend of the beleaguered wagon train.

The train involved consisted of 60 wagons with some 300 men, women, and children. The Indians suddenly appeared from ambush. The emigrants quickly and smartly formed the wagon circle, with the livestock inside. The Indians did not press the attack but kept the train under siege and prevented anyone from reaching water (there was a stream nearby). After a day and night without water the emigrants' situation grew critical. On the third day the animals grew so dangerously restive that they were released and were captured by the Indians. The emigrants dug wells but found no water. After darkness on the fourth day the guide and a young woman crawled through the sagebrush and escaped. Later, a man and two women, one of them with a small baby, also stole out of camp. The mother, crawling on hands and knees, carried the baby by holding its clothes between her teeth. They reached Raft River and hid in the bushes along its bank, eating rose hips and roots. The guide made for the nearest town—Brigham City, 100 miles east. An expedition was hastily

organized. The rescuers found the people who were hiding near Raft River. At the camp there were no survivers. The bodies lay scattered among the burned wagons.

A FALSE ALARM

Along with tales of Indian scares and massacres, people told stories about Indians who would come and beg for food. In one, a pioneer watches in dismay as a platter of fried eggs disappears down the gullet of one brave, while the others demand the same size serving. In another, an Indian eats a whole pot of half-cooked beans and is found dead the next day with his stomach distended. The theme of feeding the redskin blends with that of the Indian scare in a yarn that begins with a raiding party of Kansas and Osage tribesmen in red war paint swooping down on an emigrant wagon train. There was no time to form a defense; each wagon stood motionless, and guns were out and ready when about a hundred yards away from them the warriors came to a simultaneous halt.

The trail captain rode out to meet the marauders, shotgun in hand, and shouted, "What do you want?"

The leader of the raiding party caressed the scalp hanging from his belt and made ugly grimaces. A young brave acting as interpreter spoke to his leader at length. The leader replied with great passion, pointing first at the trail captain's wife and then at several other women nearby, who shuddered under his gaze. The interpreter translated his chief's words haltingly:

"We are—very proud—warriors—Osage, Kansas tribes. We hunting many days—White man scared off buffalo—Indians are hungry—Women—children—old people at Indian village very hungry. We want your women—"

The image of a wagon train drawn up in a circle under attack by mounted Indians has long been fixed in the popular imagination; actually the Indians weren't so foolish as to rush a group that was thus fortified and presumably well armed.

"Our women!" the trail captain shouted. He leveled his gun.

"—to give us food. We go away. Nobody hurt."

It was trickery, the trail captain thought. He pointed to the chief. "Nobody hurt! What about that scalp hanging there?"

The interpreter spoke to his leader, then said: "Chief found dead Sioux killed by snake. Took scalp. Had to come back from hunting trip with something!"

The trail captain started to laugh and couldn't stop. His whole body shook, his horse shook, and the whole wagon train swelled with one enormous laugh of relief. The Indians shifted from side to side and began to look embarrassed.

"We can't let our red brethren starve," the trail captain shouted. "Give them a bag of cornmeal, a side of smoked bacon, and a bag of flour from the main supply. We are getting away cheap at that."

The Indians were satisfied with the gift and rode away.

SWEET BETSY FROM PIKE

Oh, don't you remember Sweet Betsy from Pike, She crossed the high mountains with her lover, Ike, With one yoke of oxen, a big yellow dog, A tall Shanghai rooster and one spotted hog, Sayin', farewell Pike County, good-by for a while.

*One morning they climbed up a very high hill
And with great wonder looked on Placerville.
Ike shouted and said as he cast his eyes down,
"Sweet Betsy, my darlin', we've come to Hangtown."
Singing too-ral-i-al-ly too-ral-li-li-ay.*

Pioneers lightened the tedium of the trail by singing old songs and making up new ones. Most of the inventions were short-lived, but "Sweet Betsy," a sardonic relation of a Pike County, Illinois, couple's travails, is still a favorite.

GETTING THERE
On the Oregon Trail

Oregon's so lush that the milk of its buffalo cows squirts right out of the bags that hold it and when they're standing in a stream the current churns it into butter, or so such boosters as "Oregon" Smith put it to the stick-at-homes in Indiana. It was lush in promise, though hard to get to in reality. Early wagons that crossed the plains and the Rockies found they then had to navigate a 50-mile river channel with sides as high as 2,000 feet and a boiling downstream current that was almost matched by an upstream gale. Dark rumors reached home: beware.

COLUMBIA'S GORGE

Young Elizabeth Smith kept a diary of her trip to Oregon in 1844 with her husband Cornelius and their seven children. Their wagon train reached the Cascade Range in October, and when they arrived at The Dalles, the eastern entrance to the Columbia gorge, the train broke apart and it was each man for himself. Cattle had to be driven down the north bank to a point above the rapids, or Cascades, where they could be ferried across to the south bank. Meanwhile women, children, goods, and dismantled wagons rafted down the treacherous gorge. Storms of wind and rain were roaring through the gorge, and already the mountaintops on each side of the canyon were white with snow. *"It is rainy and cold,"* Elizabeth wrote calmly in her diary. *"The men are making rafts, the women cooking and washing, the children crying. Indians are trading potatoes for shirts."* The raft was finally finished, made of 40-foot pine logs lashed together. Three other adults joined the Smiths: gaunt, hollow-eyed Adam Polk and his wife, and an easygoing giant named Russell Welch. Polk had a suggestion: "It'll take three men to handle the raft. So how's this, Smith? You and me and your oldest boy take the raft through while Welch and your two younger boys drive the cows along the north bank. It ain't but 40 miles to the Cascades." "Good," Smith agreed.

On November 2 the raft shoved off. All the household goods and the dismantled wagons were lashed to it, and it was so unwieldy it required the combined efforts of all to fend away from the rocks. They made only a few miles the first day. *"It is impossible to sleep on the raft, so we clamber up among the rocks and build a fire to warm ourselves. All night the wind blows and the waves roll beneath."* The wind never stopped howling through the gorge. The rain changed to sleet. There was no turning back. Once in the gorge, they had to battle on. Each day they ventured out into the tossing current, inched downstream a few miles, then tied up again. Somewhere above the cliffs, in whitened timber, Welch and the two small boys were fighting the mounting drifts. Provisions on the raft ran out on the seventh day. Adam Polk stayed in bed, desperately ill. Mrs. Polk was gripped by fear of the ultimate tragedy to a woman on the trail: "My man's dying!" The younger children wailed with hunger in the night. One morning Smith decided to forage downriver on foot. He might meet some Indians or settlers. Mrs. Polk grew hysterical. "Don't let him go! He'll never get back. We'll be all alone in this terrible canyon." There was only the oldest boy to manage the raft. The women couldn't help, because there were four small children to watch each moment they were on the raft, and Mrs. Polk stayed with her husband; he was delirious now. They made less than a mile that day. *"The waves go over the raft and icicles hang from the wagon to the water. Adam Polk expired. We sat up all night while the waves were dashing below."* They remained tied to the bank that day and the next; on this stretch of the river they were facing the full sweep of the wind. The second night Cornelius Smith staggered in, exhausted from his struggle over rocks and ice-encrusted brush; he brought 50 pounds of beef. "Welch and the boys are down below. They had a tough time in the snow. They killed the red heifer. I grabbed this hunk and lit out, knowing you were starving. A feller's running a ferryboat down there, fetching cattle across to the south bank. But we got to wait our turn. And wait our turn hauling around the Cascades. It don't look good." "We'll make it," Elizabeth

Circled wagons beside the Sweetwater River on the Oregon Trail are seen from Independence Rock (where many emigrants scratched their names), in this painting by J. G. Bruff. Behind them lay the plains and ahead were the treacherous mountain passes.

"Then block the wheels, unyoke the steers; the prize is his who dares;/The cabins rise, the fields are sown, and Oregon is theirs!"

Pretty, but neither poet nor artists—not Currier, not Ives—convey the arduous physical exertion demanded of the pioneers.

said. The next morning they could make no headway against the wind.

The next day a lull came and they drifted to the point where Welch and the boys were waiting their turn to ferry the cattle. Cornelius was still weak: "I ain't sure I can handle that pole. The current's swift here." "We're the last ones at the ferry," Elizabeth pointed out. "Maybe we can persuade the ferryman to take us and the wagons down to the Cascades." "We already owe him for taking the cows across." "Then we'll owe him more. Think how much land we'll have in the valley!" The ferryman agreed. At the Cascades they assembled their wagons and prepared for the five-mile haul around the rapids, on a road that was all rocks and bottomless mud. After three days their turn came and the road was almost impassable.

Mrs. Polk had gone on with another family. Smith and Welch had gone with the cows, eager to arrange for a boat below the Cascades to take them to the valley. *We start this morning around the portage. It rains and snows. I carry my babe and lead another through snow and water to my knees.* In late afternoon the children collapsed. She had the boys unhitch and abandon the wagon. The oxen carried the little children into camp below the Cascades. Smith was alone there. He had built a windbreak and the family crept in, wet and chilled. "Where are the boats?" "Gone. There wasn't room for us. Welch has gone on with the cows. He'll be back with boats." When it turned colder Elizabeth with her own body protected her three youngest from the snow. When daylight came, Smith was too weak to move. Elizabeth sent

the boys back for the wagon; she built a fire. The third day passed, and the fourth. They had lived on beef alone for 10 days; now there were only bones. She caught occasional glimpses of the valley. On the fifth day Elizabeth wrote: *"I froze or chilled my feet so that I cannot wear a shoe, so must go barefooted. The whole care of everything falls upon my shoulder. I am not adequate to the task."* Welch came on the ninth day. They carried Smith down to the boats. The others made it alone: a little woman and very thin, carrying her baby and leading a two-year-old—the bigger boys bringing the others—walked through the snow. "Look at that!" Welch whispered. "Barefooted!" On November 27, 1844, Elizabeth Smith, her husband, and her seven children made it to the Willamette Valley.

PIONEER PARADISE
California Before the Gold Rush

In 1840 a tall-talking trapper named Joseph Robidoux returned to his post in Missouri from a stay in California. He told of an earthly paradise just beyond the Rockies, with vast tracts of fertile, unsettled land, eternal springtime, and air so pure a sick person was a curiosity. Land-hungry Missourians listened eagerly; within a year, a wagon train of them—the first American settlers to go overland to California—reached the San Joaquin Valley. Some samples of their lore below:

A BALMY CLIME

A story was told of a man who had lived in California until he had reached the age of 250 years. Such were the qualities of the climate that he was in the perfect enjoyment of his health and every faculty of mind and body which he had ever possessed. But he was tired of life. Having lived so long in a turbulent and unquiet world, he anxiously desired some new state of existence. Notwithstanding all his efforts to produce a result for which he daily prayed, health and vigor and life still clung to him—he could not shake them off. He sometimes contemplated suicide; but the priests admonished him.

A lay friend, however (his heir, probably), with whom he daily consulted on this subject, at last advised him to a course which, he thought, would produce the desired result. It was to make his will and other arrangements and then travel into a foreign country. This suggestion was pleasing to our venerable Californian patriarch in search of death, and he immediately adopted it. He visited an adjoining country and very soon took sick and died. In his will, however, he required his heir and executor, upon pain of disinheritance, to transport his remains to his own country and there entomb them. This requisition was faithfully complied with. His body was interred with great pomp and ceremony and prayers for the rest of his soul. He was happy in Heaven, it was supposed, and his heir was happy that he was there. But what a disappointment! Being brought back and interred in Californian soil with the health-breathing Californian zephyrs rustling over his grave, the energies of life were immediately restored to his inanimate corpse! Herculean strength was imparted to his frame, and bursting the prison of death, he appeared before his chapfallen heir reinvested with all the vigor and beauty of early manhood! He submitted to his fate and determined to live his appointed time.

BUFFALO STAMPEDE

A standard ingredient of the covered-wagon epic as told in later years by Californian veterans of this trail was the buffalo stampede. One old-timer remembered it this way:

"I was a boy travelin' with a wagon train. We were south of the Platte when we was forced to corral our wagons to keep our stock from bein' stampeded by buffalo. For five days an' nights 50 men kep' their guns hot killin' buffalo to keep 'em off the wagons. The sixth day the herd spread, givin' us time to yoke up an' cross the Platte, an' it's a damn good thing we did."

"Why?" asked a youthful listener.

"Well," said the oldtimer, "we no more than hit the high country north of the Platte, than lookin' back, here comes the main herd!"

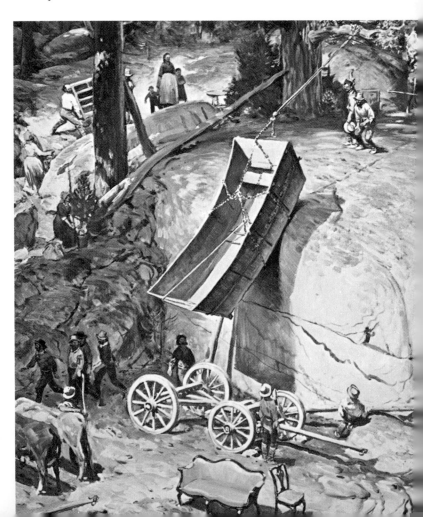

"Rough Going Over the Sierras," by Harold von Schmidt, depicts emigrants on the California Trail hoisting their dismantled rigs over Carson Pass with block and tackle.

BURIED BRANDY

One emigrant was carrying a large covered-wagon load of brandy to sell in California. The Indians had run off two of his oxen on the plains. The remaining two lay down in the sage and died. The traveler then dug a large pit near the trail, cached his dozens of jugs of brandy, mounded the pit over like a grave, made a headboard out of a wagon end, and printed on it with axle grease:

Here Lies
Mr. Bender Wild
of
Waterbury, Connecticut,
aged 66 years
Died July 1, 1850,
OF CHOLERA

"Of cholera" was written in large, terrifying letters. The trick worked to perfection because no one touched that grave. Meanwhile the emigrant hooked a ride with another traveler to California, concluded a fine deal for the brandy, returned the next spring with a new ox team to the "grave," dug up Mr. Bender Wild, proceeded with the wagon back to California, and made a handsome profit from his funereal ruse.

BRAINS DEFEAT BRAWN

Traveling in a party of eight wagons on the California Trail in the summer of 1845 was a Texan named Jim Kinney. He had a big wagon drawn by four yoke of oxen. His wife drove a light rig and a hired man was in charge of the big wagon. Kinney himself always rode a mule. He had long black hair, weighed about 225 pounds, possessed a violent temper, and was a good deal of a desperado. He would not obey train rules, but he was such a powerful man and apparently held life so lightly that no one wanted to cross him. As the train was creeping west across the desert, Kinney saw an Indian peeking out of the sagebrush and ordered his driver to stop. Since his wagon was in the lead, the whole train came to a standstill. Going to the wagon, he got out a pair of handcuffs and started back to the Indian. One of the members of the party, Jarvis Bonney,

The Old West witnessed a variety of novel approaches to the problem of desert transportation. Depicted here is a group of Mongolian camels imported to the Mohave.

asked him what he was up to.

"Where I come from we have slaves," Kinney said. "I am going to capture that Indian and take him with me as a slave." Bonney said, "The first thing you know, that Indian will escape and tell the other Indians, and they will kill all of us."

"I generally have my way," Kinney replied. "Any man that crosses me regrets it. I have already had to kill two or three men because they interfered with me. If you want any trouble, you know how to get it."

He waited a moment, and when Bonney said nothing more rode back to where the Indian was, jumped off his mule, and struck him over the head. The Indian put up a fight but was no match for the burly Texan. In a trice he had overpowered the red man, put the handcuffs on him, and dragged him back to the hack, tying him to it. Then Kinney told his wife to hand him his blacksnake whip. She obeyed at once, being as fearful of him as the men were. Kinney slashed the Indian across his naked shoulders with the murderous whip as a hint not to pull back. After a week or 10 days of beating him, Kinney untied the Indian and turned him over to his ox driver, telling him to break the Indian in as another ox team driver.

Kinney had a hound dog that was wonderfully smart. He had used him in Texas to trail runaway slaves. After

two or three weeks Kinney did not tie up the Indian any more at night, as he said if the Indian ran away the dog would pick up his trail and he could follow him and kill him to show the other Indians the superiority of the white man. He said he had killed plenty of Negroes and an Indian was no better than a Negro.

After the Indian had been with Kinney for over three weeks, one dark windy night he disappeared. In the morning, when Kinney got up, he found the Indian had taken a blanket as well as Kinney's favorite Kentucky rifle—a gun for which he had paid $100. He had also taken his powder horn, some lead, and three hams. Kinney was furious. Everyone in the train rejoiced that the Indian had escaped but they all appeared to sympathize with Kinney because they were afraid of being killed. Kinney saddled his mule, took his dog along, and started out to track the Indian. The wind had blown sand in ridges and hummocks, covering the Indian's trail. So after hunting for half a day in all directions and being unable to track him, Kinney returned to the wagon train and it started on.

There must have been great rejoicing when the young brave returned to his parents' lodge bringing the prize of a lifetime—a white man's gun. And the story of how he outwitted his captor must have been told many times around Indian campfires.

THE MORMON WAY
Earthy and Heavenly

Moving west to the "unwanted" Great Salt Lake area, the Mormons hoped to escape the hostility that their sect had sparked in the States. Heavenly light had shown the way to Joseph Smith in the 1820's but earthly rage at the sect's "holier than thou" attitude, as well as its prosperity and its practice of polygamy, had brought about Smith's murder. Nevertheless, Mormon folklore shines with the miraculous and smacks of jovial good humor over many aspects of Mormonism.

HEAVEN-SENT GULLS

In July 1847 when the ailing new leader Brigham Young rose from his cot to tell his persecuted followers, "This is the place," they stopped in the valley of the Great Salt Lake and planted a late crop. The hard winter gave way to spring when, as the Mormon's *Comprehensive History* says, the grain, which had sprouted early, had a rich color that promised a bounteous harvest. But before May had passed, an unexpected pest put in its appearance in the guise of millions of large black crickets that descended upon the new-made fields of grain. They devoured every blade of grain as they passed, cutting day and night with unabated appetites that left the fields bare and brown behind them. Ditches were plowed around the fields and an effort was made to drown or bury the crickets but all to no purpose—even greater numbers descended from the hills. Fire was tried, but with no result. Man's ingenuity was baffled. He might as well have tried to sweep back the rising tide of the ocean with a broom. Small wonder if the hearts of the colonists failed them. They were beaten by the ceaseless gnawing of this horde.

Then the miraculous happened, as men commonly view the miraculous. "When Sunday come we had a meeting," an eyewitness recounts. "Apostle Rich stood in an open wagon and preached out-of-doors . . . At that instant I heard the voice of fowls flying overhead that I was not acquainted with. I looked up and saw a flock of seven gulls. They came faster and in greater number until the heavens were darkened with them." Presently, continues the *Comprehensive History*, they lighted and began devouring the crickets. Others came —thousands of them—from over the lake. As they lit on the new wheatfields, they stretched upward, and then gracefully folded their wings and began devouring the devourers; to the cricket-vexed colonists they seemed like white-winged angels of deliverance. So it continued, day after day, until the plague was stayed and the crops were saved.

A NEPHITE VISIT

The word "Nephite" comes from the name of Nephi, son of a good man who, in Mormon tradition, sailed from Jerusalem to South America six centuries before Christ. After His resurrection, Christ preached to the man's descendants and transfigured three of them into everlasting life. These three old men go about helping Mormons in times of trouble.

It was on a hot summer day in 1874 at WaWa Springs—an oasis in the desert with nothing but sage and bunches of grass and hot sand—that Mrs. Edwin Squires saw the Nephite in the lumber shack where she lived with her husband and three small daughters. Mr. Squires and his hired men had gone on a roundup, leaving the family alone, miles from anyone. Her husband had told Mrs. Squires to have dinner ready.

It being about time for supper, she went to the spring for water and looked in every direction to see if the men were coming, but there was no one in sight. She took the water in and set it down and turned around, and there to her amazement was a man standing in the door. He asked if he would kindly give him a bit to eat, and although she was frightened she set out a humble but good meal. She told the man to eat and he did, as though he were famished. While eating, he said, "Sister, you are not well." "No, I have a pain under my shoulder." "That is your liver, but

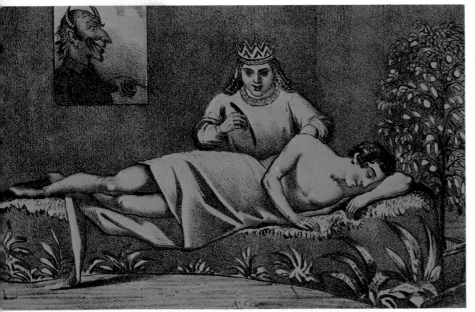

Hate literature ran strong against the Mormons in mid-19th century: here, in a picture from one of a series of tracts, a youth undergoes an "initiation" rite as the Devil looks on.

The temple at Nauvoo rises airily behind scenes of brutality as the Mormons, shorn of their murdered seer, are driven from their settlement in Illinois across the frozen Mississippi and toward Winter Quarters in Nebraska. Miracles occurred en route there.

you won't be bothered with that any more." Then he got up and started off, thanking her for her kindness and fine meal. "God bless you, sister. You will never want for anything."

As soon as she thought he had turned the corner of the house she went out to see in what direction he had gone, and there was no sight of him anywhere. This worried her more than ever. She went back in the house and, to her surprise, the table was just as she had set it. Yet she had seen him eat and drink the milk. But it was all there, and she then thought over how he was dressed so neat and his eyes were so bright and twinkled when he talked. He had a long white beard and his hair was gray. She was still worrying about it when her husband and the men returned and she

asked them if they had seen him, but they had not.

She could not get it off her mind for three months, and her mother came to make her a visit and she told her the story. The mother smiled and said: "Why, Lyda, have you forgot your Patriarchal Blessing? You were promised that one of the Three Nephites would dine at your table. That's who it was." Well, she had no more trouble with her liver, lived to an old age, and always had plenty.

PLURAL WIVES

Mormons have always had a saving sense of humor with regard to the complications of plural marriage. A favorite dialect story that makes the rounds in Utah yearly concerns the Danish saint who took three or four

of his wives boating in the park. They were drifting along close to shore where an English saint was strolling. The oars slipped off the boat and began to float away and the Britisher was the first to notice it. "I say, Brothe' Jensen," he called, "you' a-losing one of you' oars!" The Dane was indignant: "I'll haf you to know, brodder, dees is not 'hores; des is my lawfully vedded vifes vot I vas gif in de temple of de Lord."

Another story combines a comic appreciation of the human heart with the magic of a peculiar stone. One day Brother Samuel Parkinson lost a team of mules. He combed the whole country trying to find those mules but he found neither hide nor hair. So he went to a man who had a peepstone. There were a lot of stories around to the effect that people had found all kinds of things by looking in it. The man looked and he saw those mules lying down under a tree about four miles away. He then asked Sam if he wanted to look too; there were only a few people, he explained, that could see anything in the opaque stone but he always let them try.

So Sam takes a good look in the peepstone and there he sees his mules lying under the tree. He looks up and turns to his wife, who had accompanied him, and says, "Mama, is there anything you'd like to look in the peepstone and see about?" Well, Sam's wife says, "Yes! Look in and see if you kin find something about your other wives—if you are going to have any more." So Sam takes another look and there he sees two beautiful girls dressed exactly alike and standing arm-in-arm. He pulls his head away and blushes as red as a beet, so his wife grabs the stone and takes a look. "Do you see anything?" Sam ventured. "Yes! I kin see two beautiful girls a-standin' arm-in-arm." As they rode toward home, Sam asked, "Mama, if you ever see those two girls, will you let me marry them?" "Yes," she replied, "but you'll never see them."

Five years passed. Brother Parkinson and his wife moved to Idaho where he opened a gristmill with

Thomas Smart. Sam had become the first counselor to the bishop. Once as he was opening Sunday school, he looked down to the back of the meetinghouse and there he saw two girls enter—dressed alike and arm-in-arm as he had seen them in the peepstone. The curious thing is that they were Tom Smart's own daughters, girls Brother Parkinson had known for years but whom he had never associated with his peepstone vision for the reason that he had never before seen them dressed alike.

After meeting, Sam spoke to his wife: "Whom did Tom's girls make you think of today?" She confessed, "They looked exactly like the girls we saw in the peepstone." That is how Tom Smart's daughters became the wives of Samuel Parkinson.

J. GOLDEN KIMBALL

Thin and "75 inches tall," J. Golden Kimball preached the Mormon word for 60 years before "getting on over to the other side to find out how much of what I've been saying is true." Son of a Mormon, but fond of recalling his days as a cowboy, J. Golden had a homespun Lincoln-esque manner and a high, rasping voice still imitated within Mormonia. Most stories center around his infringement of church rules.

One Sunday evening J. Golden was all dressed up ready to go to church. He had on his finest suit, long black coat, and his silk shirt and his tall silk hat, and he was very handsome and well dressed. Just as he was about to leave for church, he discovered that the calf had not been fed, so he took the bucket of fresh, warm milk—the sudsy milk—and he went out to the corral in all his finery and fed the calf. And the calf came up and dived into the bucket very hungrily, and put its nose clear in under the foam, and got a mouthful, and then the calf raised his head and shook it, and shook milk foam all over the good brother. J. Golden said (shouting): "If I wasn't a member of the church, if I wasn't trying to for-swear swearing, if I wasn't a good brother in the priesthood, if I couldn't control my temper, I'd take your goddamn head and push it through the bottom of this bucket."

One day J. Golden was downtown at the rotisserie eating dinner with a fairly large group of friends, mostly lawyers, and he was seated at the end of the table, and the waiter came around to take his order first. As you know, being a good Mormon he was not supposed to drink tea or coffee, but he did like his coffee. Well, he ordered his dinner and the waiter wrote it down and then said, "What will you drink?" Brother Golden in a very weak voice said, "Water." And the fellow sitting next to him touched the waiter and said: "Oh, bring him coffee. He likes coffee." So the waiter wrote it down and went on around the table. Brother Golden didn't say anything until the waiter went away and then he said: "The Lord heard me say water."

A Danish convert to the Latter-Day Saints, Carl Christensen painted oft-told stories from Mormon history. Here, outside the jail at Carthage, Illinois, a beam of light deters a man with drawn bowie knife from beheading the slain prophet, Joseph Smith.

Paterfamilias

The most controversial doctrine of Mormonism was that of plural marriage, suspended in 1890 as a result of antipolygamy legislation. Under that doctrine, sisters might marry the same man, being sealed to him for time and eternity, or mothers and daughters could enjoy both wedding day and husband in common. Women shared the identities of their husbands; they did not have priesthood or status of their own. Perhaps more than anything else, plural marriage demonstrated woman's place in the patriarchal order that the Mormons tried—in imitation of Biblical mores—to restore to the Western World. The practice also made it possible for every woman who wished to to marry and bear children, in the belief that it was every woman's right to be a mother. And it reduced recourse to prostitution among men, for whom fatherhood was considered a duty and a sacrament. The more children a man had—the more heavenly souls for which he had provided bodies—the greater would be his glory in the afterlife.

In more mundane terms, polygamy meant that men were free to take younger wives when their own reached the transitional years: "After your grandma had raised 14 kids for him, one day he just brings home this young woman and introduces her to Mother as his plural wife. I thought she'd never get over it." She finally was able to do so, through prayer.

Even young women were exposed to being quickly, if only partially, supplanted by next year's bride. Only a year after marriage, a song laments, "When she gave her soft hand to my husband,/I knew that he thought me a toy/Beside this fair radiant glory,/This beautiful Christine LeRoy." Many young women were forced to become the plural wives of old men—business associates of their fathers, or men well up in the hierarchy of the church. "She'll expect more from you than just the laying on of hands," the plain-spoken preacher J. Golden Kimball warned an older man who asked him whether he should take himself a new young wife.

Such devices as the crystal-ball-like

A contemporary cartoon: two new beauties introduced to Brigham Young's already crowded bed get the business from older hands while he hides and babies bawl.

peepstone were sometimes used to persuade the girls that their futures lay with a balding elder. Mormon youths who fancied the same girl as an elder were on more than one occasion found beaten. Did the Mormons enjoy polygamy? There is more written on the good than the bad side of it, but informal testimonies are mixed. An old man smiles in affirmation; his wife presses her lips together and shakes her head no.

What about the children? There was a widespread belief that the children of polygamous families were smarter and stronger than others. Sometimes they lived with their father and their "aunts" and half brothers and sisters, sometimes in a house alone with a mother decreasingly visited by Pa; sometimes they were abandoned with Ma as in the bitterest of divorces. If their mothers ran off with gentiles—that is, with non-Mormons—the children would be sheltered and loved by the "aunts."

The men seemed, in jokes and tales, distant from the children; mistaken identity is the cue of many a laugh. "Brigham Young was walking down the street once and he met a boy about 14 years old. 'You're a fine looking young man,' he said, patting the boy on the shoulder. 'Whose boy are you?' 'Brigham Young's,' answered the lad." A less august polygamist was described as going into his yard at mealtimes and

shouting, "All you kids that belong te me, come an' git it; the rest uv yu hike along home."

Joseph Smith had married Emma and Eliza and Susan and Nancy and . . . It was he who had inserted the injunction to marry many virgins into his *Doctrine and Covenants*. Brigham Young made a public reacknowledgment of that doctrine in 1852, five years after the Mormons had reached Utah. Before a man could take a second or third wife, however, he had to get permission of the church president, who had to find him solvent and worthy. Then he asked his wives. But if they said no, he could go ahead against their wishes.

Congress ruled against polygamy in 1862, but the Mormons rebelled. Men required to shear themselves of extra wives went clandestinely from house to house. The situation became a battle of "cohabs" versus "deps" or cohabiters versus government deputies. The kids joined in, blowing trumpets at railroad stations if anyone resembling a dep debarked. Cohabs dressed as women to visit their wives. Wives and children had to pretend the children were illegitimate to keep their men from jail. Congress kept passing antipolygamy laws, and even tried to dissolve the Mormon Church as a corporation. Eventually the saints gave in and in 1890 the Mormons declared that polygamy was discontinued.

FROM A DIFFERENT WORLD
Lore of the Plains Indians

Contrary to popular legend, the Indians allowed wagon trains to pass without hindrance in most cases. They seem to have been interested in and amused by the sight of the long columns of people, animals, and wagons going by. And the emigrants could be cajoled or scared into giving gifts, which the Indians doubtless considered a kind of tribute. The ways of thinking of each side were as widely separated as if they had come from different planets. In view of this, it is remarkable that there was so little trouble. The Plains Indian tales that follow—told among the Cheyenne, the Arapaho, and others—strikingly illustrate the gap between Indian and white worlds. Many more have been preserved.

THE TREE HUSBAND

There was once a beautiful woman whose name was Rainbow Woman. A number of young men wanted to marry her. Every spring one or two tried to buy Rainbow Woman from her family. But she did not want to be married until a later time, when she could marry Young Eagle, a brave and handsome young man of whom she was very fond. But Young Eagle was killed in war. When Rainbow Woman heard this, she was so sorely grieved that she wanted to hang herself. She went to a river, looking for a place to die. As she came near a cottonwood tree, it suddenly called to her, "Come up quickly!" But instead she ran home and told her family she had been trying to hang herself and was so frightened by hearing a tree speak to her that she fled.

In the days that followed she continued to suffer from fits of terror, imagining that the tree would pursue her and take her as his wife. Finally she became pregnant, though without having married (except in her imagination, as she feared, the tree). One night a young tree grew out of her belly and took root, and she grew fast to it and became part of the tree. This is the reason that cottonwoods were much worshiped in former times. And after they heard this story, women no longer hanged themselves. Rainbow Woman had sung a lot when she was a girl, and for years afterward was still heard singing in the tree.

EATING BABIES

The trickster Nihansan was traveling down a stream when he saw something red in the water. He looked up and saw plums hanging on the tree above him. He ate and then filled his robe with them. Going on downriver, he came to a tent and saw a bear-woman go in. He threw a plum so that it dropped in through the top of the tent. When it fell inside, the bear-women and -children scrambled for it. Then he threw another and another. At last he went in and gave them the rest of the plums, saying, "I wonder that you never get plums when they grow so nearby." The bear-women wanted to get some more at once. He said: "Go up the river a little way; it's not far. Take all your children that are old enough to help pick. Leave the babies here and I will watch them." So they all went.

Then Nihansan cut the babies' heads off. He put the heads back into the cradles; the bodies he put into a kettle and cooked. When the bears returned, he said: "Have you never been to that hill? There were wolf cubs there." "In that little hill here?" they asked. "Yes. While you were gone I dug the cubs out and cooked

Painted by the artist Woody Crumbo of the Patawatomi tribe, "The Burning of the Cedar" depicts a phase of that tribe's peyote ritual. At left is the act's officiant.

204

Counting Coup

The Plains Indians had a military rating system known as counting coup. A coup was a "hit" inflicted on an enemy in any of a variety of ways. Some hits counted for more than others—their overall total determined a warrior's standing. Here is a typical case:

There was a Pawnee named Big Eagle who was feared by the Cheyennes. They agreed that whoever could count coup on him should be made war chief. After a fight on the Loup River, a Cheyenne warrior claimed to have counted coup on Big Eagle by thrusting a lance through his buttocks. He was accordingly made war chief. Years later, during a friendly visit between Pawnees and Cheyennes, the incident was mentioned. Big Eagle stood up and denied it. Throwing aside his robe, he called on the Cheyennes to examine him for the scars. None were found. The lying Cheyenne sank from the proud position of war chief to where he was an object of contempt to the meanest Indian in his tribe.

For some of the Plains Indians, counting coup included taking an enemy's horses at the risk of one's life. It was then customary to give the horses away.

---

them," he replied. The bears were pleased; they sat down and began to eat. One of the children said, "This tastes like my little sister."

"Hush!" said her mother, "Don't say that." Nihansan became uneasy. "It's too hot in here," he said, and took some plums and went off a little distance. There he sat down and ate. When finished, he shouted: "Ho! Ho! Bear-women, you have eaten your own children!"

The bears ran to the cradles and found the bear-children's heads. At once they pursued Nihansan. When they had nearly caught him, he came to a hole and threw himself in. The hole extended through the hill, and he came out on the other side while the bear-women were still standing at the entrance. He painted himself with white paint to look like a different person, took a willow stick, put feathers on it, and laid it across his arm. Then he went to the women. "What are you crying about?" They told him. "I'll go into the hole for you," he said and crawled in. Soon he cried out as if hurt and scratched his shoulders. He came out, saying: "Nihansan is too strong for me. Go into the hole yourselves; he's not very far in." They all went in, but soon came out again, saying, "We can't find him."

Nihansan entered once more, scratched himself bloody, and cried out: "He has long fingernails and scratches me. I can't get at him. But he's at the end of the hole and can't go any farther. If you go in, you can drag him out. He's only a little farther than you went last time."

They all went into the hole. Nihansan got brush and grass and made a fire at the entrance.

"That sounds like flint striking," said one of the she-bears. "The flint-birds are flying," answered Nihansan.

"That sounds like fire," said another. "The firebirds are flying about; they will soon be gone."

"That's just like smoke," called a third. "The smokebirds are passing. Go on, he's only a little farther, you'll catch him soon."

Then the heat followed the smoke into the hole. The bear-women began to shout. "Now the heatbirds are flying," said Nihansan.

When the bears were all dead, Nihansan put out the fire and dragged them out. "This is how to get food when you're hungry," he said. After that he went to sleep.

THE GHOST WRESTLER

A young man went alone on the warpath. As night was coming on he started a fire, by which he sat. Suddenly he heard someone singing loudly. He shouted to the singer, but the latter paid no attention to him. The young brave had a small quantity of *wasna* [grease mixed with pounded dried buffalo meat and wild cherries] and plenty of tobacco. So when the singer, who was a male ghost, came to him and asked him for food, the man replied, "I have noth-

ing." But the ghost said: "Not so. I know that you have some wasna."

Then the young man gave some of it to the ghost and filled the pipe for him. After the meal, when the ghost took the pipe and held it by the stem, the man saw that his hand had no flesh, being nothing but bones. The ghost's robe had dropped from his shoulders to his waist, and all his ribs were visible. Though the ghost did not open his lips as he smoked, the smoke was pouring out of him—through his ribs! When he finished smoking, the ghost said to the young man: "Ho! We must wrestle together. If you can throw me, you shall kill a foe without hindrance and steal some horses." The young man agreed, but before beginning, he gathered plenty of brush around the fire, on which he put an armful. Then the ghost rushed at him, grabbing his arm with his bony hands, which hurt but that didn't matter. The man tried to push the ghost away, but the latter's legs were very powerful.

However, the young man discovered that when the ghost was brought nearer the fire he became weak, and when he managed to pull his living opponent toward the darkness he grew very strong. As the fire got low, the strength of the ghost increased. The young man was becoming exhausted when day broke, and the struggle was intensified. As the two wrestlers drew near the fire the young man made a desperate effort and with his foot pushed a piece of burn-

While visiting the Blackfoot nation at the end of the Indian wars, Frederic Remington witnessed and sketched a horseback ceremony known as the Pony War Dance: 60 young men in warpaint and feathers galloped up and down, yelling and shooting off their guns—accompanied, as they believed, by ghosts of their kinsmen slain in battle.

ing wood suddenly into the middle of the fire; as it blazed up again the ghost collapsed, just as if he were coming to pieces. So the young man won and the ghost's prophecy was fulfilled. The man subsequently killed a foe and stole some horses. For that reason his people thereafter believed whatever ghosts told them.

DEER WOMAN

Long ago, when the Poncas still lived in Nebraska, young men sometimes saw the Deer Woman. Everyone in the village would be dancing and happy. Perhaps they were celebrating a victory, and the girls carried scalps on poles to show how brave their brothers were. The old men would build a big fire, and the young women would dance around it sidewise, in a ring. Sometimes they joined hands, linking the dancers, but the young men danced alone, leaping and prancing between the circling wall of women and the fire.

The woman came from nowhere, and nobody knew her. Suddenly she slipped into the ring between two girls, holding each of them by the hand. She was very beautiful. Her hair streamed like black water over her white buckskin dress. If the other dancers had glanced at the woman's feet, they would have seen that she had a deer's hooves, over which no moccasins would fit. But nobody ever looked anywhere but at her eyes. No matter how rude a person felt to stare so, he could not help gazing into those magic deep black eyes. Besides, everybody was busy dancing and being happy. They didn't think about looking down; all their thoughts and their looks were upward.

As the night lengthened, one young man would find a girl, and then a young girl would find a man. A couple at a time they slipped away from the dancing ring into the bushes, where they spent the night.

While she danced, the Deer Woman studied the young men and chose her partner, but only for the night. Whoever she chose was helpless. He could not go to any other woman, no matter how much he loved and wanted her. The Deer Woman held him with her magic eyes, and when the moon was lowest but the night not yet dark, she drew him away beside her.

In the morning someone found the young man. He lay dead on his back, his body stripped naked. Anyone who saw him knew how he had died, for when the Deer Woman had taken her pleasure from him she had beaten and trampled him to death with her knife-edge hooves.

All that was long ago, when the Poncas still lived in Nebraska. They lived in mat houses, cooked their meat in earthen pots, and carved their weapons from stone and wood. The Deer Woman came and went among them and they could do nothing to stop her.

To this day no one has ever caught the Deer Woman. She comes to the Ponca powwow every other year. Once the men were watching for her. They kept their eyes on the ground and would not look up at any woman's face. The men were not hypnotized by the Deer Woman's eyes, so this time they saw her feet. One sprang at her and almost caught her in his arms, but the Deer Woman jumped that seven-foot wall around the dance ring and was gone. Someday, say the Ponca men, they will catch up with the Deer Woman.

‛WORD LORE’

Sign Language

In the great treeless area of the plains, a score of nomadic Indian peoples, speaking as many languages, were in constant movement, following the buffalo on horseback.  War, trade, and ceremonies brought them together, and they overcame the language barrier by devising a system of hand gestures. The man at left, for example, signs "How many?" At right, Sioux chief Eagle Bull is signaling his name; the gesture means "bull." This sign language hardly fell short of the perfection (and speed) of a spoken language, and—as noted by a contemporary—it was the very poetry of motion.

SODBUSTERS
The Last Frontier

Not the western edge of America but the central plains once disdained by settlers bound for lush Oregon or California, the prairies were the last lands to be settled. Explorers Zebulon Pike and Stephen Long didn't help any, having mistakenly labeled the plains infertile—a Great American Desert. In 1862 the Homestead Act promised 160 acres to each and every man who could live on it. The plains were fertile all right. They were also too hot, too cold, too dry, too wet, and too quick to switch. Such is the subject matter of prairie lore; its style is the straight-faced lie.

Announcing the latest news, a frontier woman runs into the fields.

FEBOLD FEBOLDSON

From a bedrock of such stories rose the imaginary Febold Feboldson, the product of what would have been his own grandson's era had he been real. The Swedish sodbuster and natural scientist Febold represented the frontier use of ingenuity, and he did more than sell lumber for Wayne Carroll, the creative lumberman who invented him. He evoked for people of the plains their own forebears.

One day Febold looked at the sky, fiddled around with some of his instruments, and made a horrible discovery. "That's bad," he said. "Got to do something drastic." What he did was send a cable to London that read this way: "Send along a gross of your fanciest fog-cutters soon as possible, C.O.D. Febold Feboldson." Being a scientist, you see, Febold had figured out right away what a horrible time Nebraska was in for. He told Mrs.

Feboldson about the steps he'd taken that very evening while they were sitting trying to cool off a bit. "Cabled over to London today for a gross of fog-cutters," he said. Mrs. Feboldson's eyes stuck out so far they appeared to be on stems. "Fog-cutters?" she said, dazed-like. "Yes, fog-cutters, Mother," he said. "You see, they have the thickest fogs in London and they're inventive there, you know—a right smart race." "But I can't see as we need any fog-cutters. Look out the window, you'll notice there's no fog—nothing but land and sky, as far as you can look, with a hundred thousand heat waves."

"What's that dark gray thing no bigger than a man's hand?" says Febold. "Why!" Mrs. Feboldson said. "It's a cloud." Febold nodded. "How about that little toe of yours that warns you when we're to have rain?" "I'll swan it's a-twitching," she

told him. "We'll need those fog-cutters all right, Mother."

Along toward morning, there was the beginning of that horrible sound that people in Nebraska and parts of the neighboring territories kept nearly being driven crazy by for the next 40 days and 40 nights. The sound of steam—just one long burbling hiss. As soon as Febold came in from milking, Mrs. Feboldson asked what that horrible noise was. "It's working the way I figured," he said. "The rain's coming down like a dribbled ocean. But up there 10 miles or so, it's spattering down on the hot air that was piled up around here by the Great Heat. As soon as the rain hits the hot air, it turns to steam and makes that hissing noise. The steam will be the fog. Pretty soon the rain will hammer the fog down. Hope

John S. Curry's depiction of settlers dashing to stake a claim is supposedly an accurate depiction of the famous "Oklahoma Run" of 1889. Nevertheless, it is unlikely that one of tens of thousands who held claims that night arrived on a unicycle.

Smoke issuing from the soddy set in Karl Wimer's painting of the treeless but sunlit landscape of America's midwestern plains brings to mind the words of the plainsman's song: "I am looking rather seedy now while holding down my claim,/And my victuals are not always of the best./And the mice play shyly round me as I nestle down to sleep/In my little old sod shanty in the west."

those Englishmen hurry up with those fog-cutters."

Febold was right, as usual. There was a little fog at first, then more and more of it, until taking a walk alone was impossible. Two people would be needed so one could part the fog and hold it while the other walked through. Cattle didn't have to be watered, they could drink the fog. But the dirt farmers were scared speechless, because their crops were in a bad way. You see, some of the seeds had figured that the closest sunshine was in China, and had started growing downward.

The fog-cutters arrived, C.O.D. Febold started to slice the fog into big neat strips. "Can't leave them lying on the fields," he told Mrs. Feboldson, "or the seeds will keep growing downward. I know! I'll lay them out along the roads." Upshot was that he put those strips end to end all along the dirt roads of Nebraska. Some seeped down and some got so covered with dust nobody could see where Febold had buried the Great Fog. But every spring, when the sun begins to shine and the thaw comes, some of this old fog seeps up through the ground to the roads, turning them into the gooiest mess you ever saw.

FEBOLD'S CORNBALLS

It was strange weather even for Nebraska. For exactly a mile the sun shone, while the next mile was covered with rain clouds, and torrents fell from the sky. All Nebraska was striped like that—a mile of gray rain, then a mile of bright sunshine. It chanced that Febold's ranch was right where two stripes met. Down in the valley where the sun shone lay his field of corn. On the hill where it rained he had planted sugarcane. Well, the sun shone so hot on the cornfield that the corn started to pop. It popped right off the ears and lay all over the ground. The rain, drenching the hill, washed the juice from the sugarcane down the hill, a roaring flood of molasses. The force of that rush of molasses rolled the popcorn into huge balls no less than a hundred feet high. "Here's something worth eating!" cried Febold.

WIND, COLD, HEAT, CHANGE

I asked a seasoned farmer why Nebraska barns never have wind vanes. "No sense to it," he said. "When you want to see which way the wind is blowing, you just look out and see which way the barn is leaning."

"We had a corncrib," another farmer said, "filled with 500 bushels of ear corn. In the north side of the crib was a knothole. The wind blew one ear of corn at a time through the knothole, shelling the corn as the cob went through. When the wind went down we had a crib filled with shelled corn, and the cobs were piled up outside."

A fellow was once practicing his tuba when a Nebraska tornado screwed him 12 feet into the ground.

"I remember many cold winters. Many a time we had to get up on the roof to chop off the smoke clouds that had frozen on the chimney."

"It was so hot here in Nebraska that a lot of *stoves* burned up!"

"I was riding the range one Octo-

Burial was brief and simple, doubtless a match for the life of the child interred in William Ranney's painting "Prairie Burial."

Snow could cover everything. A woman stands on a snowbank as high as her soddy while her husband tries to dig out, in Harvey Dunn's "After the Blizzard." Inside, sheets hung over dirt walls from which snakes sometimes emerged. Under snow lay the "unshorn fields," as William Cullen Bryant called them, "boundless and beautiful,/For which the speech of England has no name."

ber day. The sun was bright and it was uncomfortably warm. Suddenly a blizzard broke and I started for the ranch as hard as the horse would go. For the full five miles it seemed as though we were riding neck and neck with the front edge of the storm. My face was warm from the sun and the summerlike day, while cold blasts from the blizzard were chasing up and down my spinal column. When we got to the ranch, the horse's neck and shoulders were covered with foam and lather while his rump was covered with snow and his tail was frozen so stiff that it came off."

DROUGHT AND CRITTERS

A farmer and his son met another ragged farmer on Main Street one day during a particularly bad drought. "Looks a bit like rain," the one opined hopefully. The other replied, "Well, it doesn't matter much one way or the other to me; I've *seen* rain. But," he went on, pointing to his teenage son, "the boy here . . ."

A man once stopped to visit a drought-stricken family in their soddy. He asked the farmer if crops were really as bad as they seemed. The farmer, chewing on an ear of roasted corn, answered, "For lunch we just et four acres of corn!"

Many oldtimers have told about rattlesnakes in their fury striking at hoe handles, which then swelled up to the size of telephone poles. "One such indiscriminate snake nearly caused a disaster when he struck at Custer Joe's horse one day and hit the wagon tongue instead. The tongue swelled up and broke the neck-yoke ring and Joe had to chop it off to save the wagon."

At the supper table Grandpa asked the kid: "Well, how did you get along with the sheep? Did you get them all in the shed?" "Oh I got along just fine," the kid replied. "But I had quite a time getting that one lamb in the shed." "Lamb? Why, there's not a lamb in the bunch." "Oh, yes, sir, there is, and I got it penned up with the rest." "This I got to see," remarked Grandpa. So they went out and into the shed. "There it is," said the kid pointing toward one corner in the shed. And darned if there wasn't one of them large Nebraska white-tailed jackrabbits crouched there.

One terrified homesteader awoke to see two huge figures standing in his doorway. He quickly recognized them to be mosquitoes. The one said, "Shall we eat him here or take him with us?" The other replied: "We better eat him here. If we take him

along, the big guys will take him away from us when we get home."

CIVILIZATION

"Neighbors were so far apart in pioneer Nebraska that everyone had to have his own tomcat."

"The late sleet storm made the grass on our sidewalks so slippery that one of our prominent jackrabbits fell and sprained one of his ankles so badly that he walks with a limp."

HARD TIMES

A poverty-stricken farmer entered a local, smalltown hardware store to buy three hammer handles at the price of $1. The next week he was back to purchase 8 more at the same price, and two weeks later 20 more. The hardware dealer, who had not sold more than 10 hammer handles in any one year since he had opened business, finally was compelled to ask the farmer what he was doing with the handles. He replied, "Selling 'em." "How much you getting for them?" "Fifty cents." "But that's less than what you're paying for them. You're losing 50 cents a hammer handle." The farmer shrugged with resignation, "That's a damn sight better than I was doing when I was dirt-farming."

UTOPIAN PIONEERS

"Butcher Boys on a Bender," by Olof Krans. Even drunk a colony's butchers maintain a calmly utopian mien, and only their oxen seem to be running wild.

Not every pioneer was a rugged individualist. Many were utopians who had embraced any of a dozen forms of communalism—or as they themselves put it, "living in community, being our brother's keeper." Shakers, Zoarites, Fourierists, Rappites, Icarians, members of such distinctive communities as Oneida, Amana, and Aurora, adhered to the tenets of self-devised social systems that ranged from complete communism to private ownership, from celibacy through monogamy to forms of group marriage. More than 100 of these communes dotted the map from coast to coast; by the eve of the Civil War, utopianism had involved at least 100,000 persons in the U.S.

The word *utopia* was first coined in 1516 by Sir Thomas More from Greek words meaning "nowhere." Where were U.S. utopians going? Like everyone else, they were going west. Believing themselves pioneers of the millennium, many thought the Great American Desert was as good a place as any to usher in the Kingdom of Heaven on earth. Typical utopian pioneers were the Christian communists who settled Bethel, Missouri, in 1844 when it was as wild and woolly a place as any west of the Mississippi. The Bethel colonists, many originally from Germany, were unlettered husband-

men, bakers, blacksmiths, cobblers, tailors, and tanners by trade. Their commune in Missouri had been flourishing for only about nine years when a group of younger Bethel colonists succumbed to the "Oregon fever" and set out, in 1855, for the Willamette Valley in Oregon Territory.

En route they were kindly received by the dreaded Pawnees who had killed so many other covered-wagon folk, perhaps because they met the red men's hostility by tenders of food, clothing, and sincere friendliness. Arriving in Oregon, they set up the Aurora community, which, with its orchards, sawmills, woolen and flour mills, distillery, school, and steepleless white church, came to be viewed as a model utopian settlement during the quarter century it lasted.

Most of the utopian communes failed soon after starting, because of a combination of defective planning, outside pressures, and intramural squabbling. Nonetheless they were trailblazers, especially as regards such resurgent issues as the back-to-the-land movement, the commune movement, pacifism, women's liberation, and vegetarianism.

The people of Oneida, for example, were famous in their day not only for their steel traps and silverware but for

their leader John Noyes' doctrine of "complex marriage," according to which carefully regulated spouse-swapping was practiced along with eugenics and birth control pioneered by the tall skinny visionary himself and fascinated ladies who fell under his spell. "There is no more reason why sexual intercourse should be restrained by law than why eating and drinking should be—and there is as little reason for shame in the one case as in the other," the 24-year-old Noyes wrote prior to his westward flight from Putney, Vermont, in 1847. One of the goals behind his advocacy of sexual communism was the liberation of woman from the "unequal contract"—child-bearing and -rearing, kitchen work, and the like. In line with the same objective, Noyes advocated no more than one hot meal a day, asserting that cold meals were healthier in any case.

Shakers approached women's lib from another direction, not allowing women's and men's duties to overlap. They were also the most radical of all regarding sex—they abolished it altogether. The government of the 20-odd Shaker communes, sprinkled over the map from Maine to Ohio and beyond, was dual, male and female, in all departments. Women had as much influence as men, and a woman held the first office in the overall organization for 25 years during its heyday. Shakers were particularly admired by Indians they came in contact with; Shawnee war chief Tecumseh marveled at their way of life no less than at their ecstatic "shaking" dance. Doubtless one of the reasons ordinary folk made fun of utopians was that their ideas seemed so outlandish. The Shakers' founder, for example, Anna Lee, was regarded by her followers as one who revealed God in female form, thus completing an incarnation that had begun with Jesus as the embodiment of God's masculine aspects. (Ironically, despite their celibacy and odd doctrines, the Shakers outlasted every primitive communistic sect other than the Hutterites and the Oneida folk; in fact, there were still Shakers living in the second half of the 20th century.)

Based on the doctrines of French reformer Charles Fourier, some 88 communes known as "phalanxes" made for the biggest single total of any U.S. utopian movement during the mid-19th century. Like many visionary leaders, Fourier was something of a fanatic. His dream of the "regeneration of the human body" to occur after 400 years of utopian living included a marvelously versatile tail, which he styled the "harmony arm," describing it thus: "It extends to the length of 144 vertebrae from the [regenerated human's] coccyx and is carried on the shoulder, rising to twice its owner's height, having at its extremity a tiny hand whose fingers are as strong as an eagle's claws, the index and pinky being lengthened and the middle fingers stubby, with an extremely elongated thumb and retractile talons like a lion's. When a man endowed with the harmony arm swims, it makes him swift as a fish. He streaks to the ocean floor where in a twinkling he sets out and fastens all manner of nets and traps for seafood. Back on dry land, the same man leaps by means of this marvelous limb into a lofty tree to pick

Utopian Charles Fourier declared man must continue to evolve and grow a tail.

fruit from its topmost branches. The harmony arm also serves as a rudder to steer balloons, and when playing musical instruments it doubles one's manual dexterity. When making a long-distance jump, the harmony arm shoots out in a spiral which at least triples one's normal momentum. It also cushions the shock of landing by

two-thirds. One spins it into a cone, which slows the body's fall by forming a parachute. If a mason is working atop a steeple, his harmony arm protects him from falling by wrapping itself round his body while at the same time leaving him the use of both hands as well as the harmony hand.

"The harmony arm is also a natural weapon, as redoubtable as it is industrious, placing an unarmed man on an equal footing with the most dangerous beast. (Its superiority if furnished with a sword may be readily imagined!) We might well ask why God did not favor our race with such a useful limb. The answer is simply that terrestrial humanity would destroy itself overnight if provided with this weapon. It may be objected that we will be exempt from such dangers when we pass into the state of Harmony. The observation is correct; it is nonetheless true that we were fated to live through several thousands of years of Discord during which God must needs refuse us the harmony arm. It will be ours only upon passing into the state of Compound Harmony, which is to begin after 16 generations of Simple Harmony—about 400 years hence."

The Shaker dance: "In their marching and dancing," wrote a witness, "they hold their hands before them and make a motion as of gathering something to themselves; this is called gathering a blessing . . . Their tunes are in quick time."

Gold! Gold! Gold!

Captioned "A Question of Title," this 1860 cartoon from *Harper's Magazine* accompanied an article on life at the gold sites where men lived in coyote holes and fought like so many beasts over their claims.

For the 100th anniversary of the California gold rush Harold von Schmidt painted this evocation of the droves of determined men who took pick and pack west. Many went overland, but easterners who could afford it, like these, went by ship.

In 1848, with the discovery of gold at Sutter's Mill, the legendary gold-strewn America once more seemed a reality. The epidemic of gold fever that had struck the Spanish and the Elizabethans raged anew, and would scarcely abate in 10 years time. "I looked on it for a moment," said a San Franciscan of a bag of newly panned gold, "and a frenzy seized my soul; unbidden my legs performed some entirely new movements of polka steps; piles of gold rose up before me; castles of marble; thousands of slaves bowed to my beck and call; myriads of fair virgins contended with each other for my love." He was off with pick and shovel as were sailors from their ships, farmers from their fields, servants from their yards, and clerks from their stores after hearing the news from California.

For most of the seekers it was a fool's rush to squalor and deprivation. Most of the thousands and thousands who made the five-month overland trek or spent six months rounding Cape Horn were lucky if they managed to pan $100 a month by dint of hard labor. They heard about the man who got $1,500 from one pan of gold, and they sang, "I'm going to Sacramento with my wash pan on my knee!" but they lived in tents or caves and had to pay 75 cents for 5-cent bread.

In 1849 California's population jumped from 26,000 to 115,000. Australians, Chinese, Irish, French, and Mexicans mixed in mutual distrust with the "Americans" in shoddy camps. Crime festered there and in the brawling burgeoning cities, especially in the fifties after most of the panable gold was gone. Legends of the gold rush sprang up almost as fast as the cities, many of them emphasizing the easy-come, easy-go nature of wealth: you find nuggets in your mule's stake hole in the morning and lose an ounce of gold dust by an ill-directed sneeze in the evening. The whopper-producing American imagination was momentarily stunned by the fact that there was gold in the dirt beneath one's feet. That was almost whopper enough, but not quite. Stories were told of tricksters, degenerates, and bandits, but mostly of lucky strikes, fabulous mines, the gold in them thar hills.

EUREKA!
Gold in them thar . . .

I'm rich! The color of gold, the shine of it, the sudden moment when a stone just turned revealed its speckled presence—the prospector lived for the future. He set his nose toward a new spot and moved along with a shout ringing in his ear: "I've found it, boys!" It was under the next hill, in the waters of the next river; hope never died, neither at the graveside, as the stories had it, nor in Heaven nor in Hell.

GOLD IN THEM THAR . . .

At Columbia a man pulled up a weed in his garden and found a $5,000 nugget tangled in its root.

Chickens were gatherers of nuggets and their gizzards were searched by cooks. At Diamond Springs one fowl was killed for a Sunday dinner whose gizzard panned out $12.80.

Even a lazy man could do well in diggings as rich as Columbia's. One of these firstcomers was too lazy to wash his drawers: he tied them to a limb that overhung a stream and let them dangle in the water. He figured the current would wash them. Next morning when he come to fish them out—lo and b'God—he found his drawers gold-plated.

On the Tuolumne a hunter shot a bear and the bear tumbled over the edge of a canyon, landing on a ledge. When the hunter climbed down, he found the ledge laced with gold.

A man who had been sitting on a rock moping in discouragement and homesickness arose and kicked the rock in anger. The rock rolled aside, disclosing a nugget of shining gold.

TO THE DEATH

In the winter of 1850, a mean wet season when men sickened with "lung fever" everywhere and the newly established graveyard on a little flat out of the camp claimed its tenants in increasing numbers, a funeral was in progress during a heavy rain. A parson down from Nevada City was indulging a particularly long-winded prayer while the wet dripped off bowed hats of the handful clustered around the newly made grave. One of the mourners thought he saw something glimmer in the fresh mound of dirt. He stirred the dully shining point with his boot. A nugget! And snuggling right 'longside that nugget another—a whopper! The mourner sneaked away. One by one his fellows followed . . . "And now, O Lord, dust to dust and ashes to ashes; and the speerit of our beloved brother—" The parson happened to look up. He saw all the mourners pacing off 15-foot claims. "Hey, boys, you gotta give me a show when I finish!"

A WHIZZER, OR TRICK

It was in the spring of 1850 when word of the incredible richness of Downie's Flat swept downstream and sent a crowd of wild-eyed boomers hurrying thither. Original discoverers were digging a pound of gold a day, to the man, out of the rock there with the point of a butcher knife! So the rumor exploded.

When the first of the rush lowered themselves hand over hand down the precipitous wall of the gorge to Downie's camp, they were not cordially received by the dozen original discoverers who'd spent a hard winter there. Pike Sellers had an inspiration one day when he saw one of the boomers, pack on back, crawling precariously downtrail. Pike scrambled up out of the streambed and commenced furiously prying at the bark slabs on a jack pine. Just as the stranger came up, Pike pushed two fingers behind a shag of bark and withdrew a fat gold nugget. "MY Gawd! I hearn ye was diggin' the yaller stuff outa cracks in the rocks, but I didn't know she grew on trees." "Gits lodged thar when the tree's pushin' up through th' soil." Pike found a couple more nuggets.

The boomer whipped out his bowie and started on a nearby pine. "Hold on thar!" from Sellers. "Yo're on my claim." Where could he stake himself to a tree? Sellers abandoned work to stride through the forest to a jack pine of smaller growth. "She's richest nigh th' top. Ye can climb this one." The newcomer dropped his pack and, bowie in teeth, commenced to shin up. "Higher up's better," bawled Pike. "Nothin' but flake gold low down." Sellers sifted back to the streambed and later reaped fame as the father of a whizzer.

ULTIMATE STAKES

Two prospectors died and contrary to expectation found themselves in Heaven. A third was admitted by Saint Peter with hesitation. "I have let you in," said Saint Peter. "You've always worked hard for your grub-stakers, and you've worshiped God under the stars and played fair and haven't told any lies that would do anyone any real harm. But I must admit, I let a couple of prospectors in a while back and they've been tearing up the golden streets." "Well," said the newcomer, "I'll fix that."

A day or so later the two prospectors appeared at the gate and asked to be released. Saint Peter warned them that once out they couldn't come back but cheerfully let them go. All was peace in Heaven. Saint Peter came upon the third prospector. "You did very well," he said. "How did you arrange it?" The prospector grinned. "I just let it drop that there was a rich new strike in Hell," he said. But a few days later the prospector approached Saint Peter. "I'd like to get out," he said. "I been thinkin' about that new strike in Hell, an' I believe I'd like to get down there ahead of the rush an' stake me a few good claims."

The moment of Finding It is caught by an artist in this composite depicting the forty-niners. After the trek, after the labor with pick and pan, a lucky few would hoist golden nuggets, having struck it rich.

AT CAMP
Impolite Society

The backbreaking labor of placer mining was glamorized as male. Male meant the tough, raucous, hard-drinking, gambling, practical-joking, unwashed life Tom Sawyer might have looked for. Indeed, it was at the camps that Samuel Clemens met miners who would appear in his stories, as they do in his first hit: "The Celebrated Jumping Frog of Calaveras County." Clemens probably based that story on oral tradition, though earlier versions—such as the one below—were printed in newspapers. Bret Harte funneled camp machismo into his famous short story "The Luck of Roaring Camp," which is presented here in a condensation.

A TOAD STORY

A long, stupid-looking fellow frequented a gambling saloon and was in the habit of promenading up and down but never speaking. At night he spread out his blankets on an empty monte table and lived like a gambler, except that he talked to no one nor gambled a cent. He became, at length, an acknowledged character, slunk in and out, and the boys tittered as they saw him pass. One day he came in with an important air and said, "I have got a toad that'll leap farther than any toad you can scare up." They soon surrounded him, and roared and laughed. "Yes," says he, "I'll bet money on it. Barkeeper, give me a cigarbox to hold my toad in." The fun was great, and the oddity was the talk of all hands. A gambler, in the evening, happened to come across a big frog, fetched him to the gaming house, and offered to jump him against the Yankee's toad. "Well," says Yank, "I'll bet liquors on it." A chalk line was made and the toad put down. They struck the boards behind the toad and he leaped six feet, then the frog leaped seven. Yank paid the liquors, but next morning he says aloud: "My toad waren't beat. No man's toad can leap with my toad. I have two ounces and two double eagles, and all of them I bet on my toad." The boys bet with him again, and his toad leaped six feet, but the frog leaped only two feet. "The best two out of three," said the gamblers. "Very well," says Yank. But still the frog could not go over two feet. Yank pocketed the bets. "My frog is darn heavy this morning," says the gambler. "I reckoned it would be, stranger," says the Yankee, "for I rolled a pound of shot into him last night."

THE LUCK

There was a commotion in Roaring Camp. It could not have been a fight, for in 1850 that was not novel enough to have called together the entire settlement. The whole camp was collected before a cabin on the edge of the clearing. Conversation was slow, but the name of a woman was frequently repeated: "Cherokee Sal."

Perhaps the less said of her the better. She was a coarse and, it is feared, very sinful woman. She was the only woman in Roaring Camp and was lying in sore extremity when she most needed the ministration of her own sex. A few were, I think, touched by her sufferings. Sandy Tipton thought it was "rough on Sal" and, in the contemplation of her condition, for a moment rose superior to the fact that he had an ace and two bowers in his sleeve.

Deaths were by no means uncom-

In "The Music Man," by Robert Abbett, prospectors, passing the time with a banjo concert, wend their way from the dig to town.

The frog that was not stalled by a shot-filled belly leaps toward the bar, in this illustration from Harper Brothers' 1903 edition of Mark Twain's famous frog story.

mon in Roaring Camp, but a birth was a new thing. "You go in there, Stumpy," said a prominent citizen known as Kentuck. "Go in there, and see what you kin do." Perhaps there was a fitness in the selection. Stumpy, in other climes, had been the putative head of two families; in fact, it was owing to some legal informality in these proceedings that Roaring Camp—a city of refuge—was indebted to his company. The crowd approved the choice and the door closed on the extempore surgeon and midwife; Roaring Camp sat down outside, smoked its pipe, and awaited the issue.

The assemblage numbered about 100 men. Physically, they exhibited no indication of their past lives and characters. The greatest scamp had a Raphael face, with a profusion of blond hair; Oakhurst, a gambler, had the melancholy air and intellectual abstraction of a Hamlet; the coolest and most courageous man was scarcely over five feet in height, with a soft voice and an embarrassed, timid manner. The strongest man had but three fingers to his right hand; the best shot had but one eye. By degrees the natural levity of Roaring Camp returned. Bets were offered: 3 to 5 that "Sal would get through with it," even that the child would survive; there were side bets as

to the sex and complexion of the coming stranger.

Above the swaying and moaning of the pines, the swift rush of the river, and the crackling of the fire rose a sharp querulous cry, a cry unlike anything heard before in the camp. The camp rose to its feet as one man! In consideration of the situation of the mother, only a few revolvers were discharged; for Cherokee Sal was sinking fast. Within an hour she had climbed, as it were, that rugged road that led to the stars, and so passed out of Roaring Camp, its sin and shame, forever.

"Can he live now?" The answer was doubtful. The only other being of Cherokee Sal's sex and maternal condition in the settlement was an ass. The experiment was tried: it was less problematical than the ancient treatment of Romulus and Remus, and apparently as successful.

When these details were completed, which exhausted another hour, the door was opened, and the anxious crowd of men who had already formed themselves into a queue entered in single file. Beside the low bunk, or shelf, on which the figure of the mother was starkly outlined by the blankets, stood a pine table. On this a candlebox was placed, and within it, swathed in staring red flannel, lay the last arrival

at Roaring Camp. Beside the candle-box was placed a hat. Its use was soon indicated. "Gentlemen," said Stumpy, with a singular mixture of authority and *ex officio* complacency, "gentlemen will please pass in at the front door, round the table, and out the back door. Them as wishes to contribute anything toward the orphan will find a hat handy." The first man entered with his hat on; he uncovered, however, as he looked about him, and so unconsciously set an example to the next. In such communities good and bad actions are catching. As the procession filed in, comments were audible—criticisms addressed perhaps rather to Stumpy in the character of showman: "Is that him?" "Mighty small specimen." "Ain't bigger nor a derringer." The contributions were as characteristic: a silver tobacco box; a doubloon; a navy revolver, silver mounted; a gold specimen; a very beautifully embroidered lady's handkerchief (from Oakhurst the gambler); a diamond breastpin; a diamond ring (suggested by the pin, with the remark from the giver that he "saw that pin and went two diamonds better"); a Bible (contributor not detected); a silver teaspoon (the initials, I regret to say, were not the giver's); a Bank of England note for £5 and about $200 in loose gold and silver coin.

THE DYING CALIFORNIAN

Lay up near-er, broth-er, near-er, For my limbs are growing cold And thy pres-ence seem-eth dear-er When thy arms a-round me fold.

I am going, surely going,
But my faith in God is strong.
I am willing, brother, knowing
That He doeth nothing wrong.

Tell my father when you greet him
That in death I prayed for him,
Prayed that I one day might meet him
In a world that's free from sin.

Tell my mother, God assist her
Now that she is growing old,   *[her*
That her child would fain have kissed
When his lips grew pale and cold.

'Twas for them I crossed the ocean.
What my hopes were I'll not tell.
But I've gained an orphan's portion,
Yet He doeth all things well.

Originally a stage song, this sentimental recital of the fate of countless forty-niners who went to California by sea was eventually taken over by the folk.

"The Luck" grabs Kentuck's finger as miners file past Stumpy's setup for the new baby, in this detail of an illustration for Bret Harte's classic, and sentimental, morality tale.

During these proceedings Stumpy maintained a silence as impassive as the dead woman on his left, a gravity as inscrutable as that of the newly-born on his right. Only one incident occurred to break the monotony of the curious procession. As Kentuck bent over the candlebox half curiously, the child turned and, in a spasm of pain, caught at his groping finger and held it fast for a moment. Kentuck looked foolish and embarrassed. "The d----d little cuss!" he said, as he extricated his finger with perhaps more tenderness and care than he might have been deemed capable of showing. He held that finger a little apart from its fellows as he went out, and examined it curiously. The examination provoked the same original remark in regard to the child. "He rastled with my finger," he remarked to Tipton, holding up the member, "the d----d little cuss!" It was 4 o'clock before the camp sought repose. A light burned in the cabin where the watchers sat, for Stumpy did not go to bed that night. Nor did Kentuck.

The next day Cherokee Sal had such rude sepulture as Roaring Camp afforded. After her body had been committed to the hillside, there was a formal meeting of the camp to dis-cuss what should be done with her infant. A resolution to adopt it was unanimous and enthusiastic. But an animated discussion in regard to the manner and feasibility of providing for its wants at once sprung up. Tipton proposed that they should send the child to Red Dog, where female attention could be procured. The suggestion met with fierce opposition. The introduction of a female nurse in the camp also met with objection. No decent woman could be prevailed upon to accept Roaring Camp as her home, and the speaker urged that "they didn't want any more of the other kind." This unkind allusion to the defunct mother, harsh as it may seem, was the first spasm of propriety—the first symptom of the camp's regeneration. Stumpy averred stoutly that he and Jinny—the mammal before alluded to—could manage to rear the child. Stumpy was retained.

Strange to say, the child thrived. In that rare atmosphere of the Sierra foothills—that air pungent with balsamic odor, that ethereal cordial at once bracing and exhilarating—he may have found food and nourishment, or a subtle chemistry that transmuted ass's milk to lime and phosphorus. Stumpy inclined to the belief that it was the latter and good nursing. "Me and that ass," he would say, "has been father and mother to him! Don't you," he would add, apostrophizing the helpless bundle before him, "never go back on us."

By the time he was a month old, the necessity of giving him a name became apparent. Gamblers and adventurers are generally superstitious and Oakhurst one day declared that the baby had brought "the luck" to Roaring Camp. It was certain that of late they had been successful. "Luck" was the name agreed upon, with the prefix of Tommy for greater convenience. "It's better," said the philosophical Oakhurst, "to take a fresh deal all round. Call him Luck, and start him fair." No allusion was made to the mother, and the father was unknown. Stumpy stepped before the crowd: "I proclaim you Thomas Luck, according to the laws of the United States and the state of California, so help me God." It was the first time that the name of the Deity had been uttered otherwise than profanely in the camp.

And so the work of regeneration began in Roaring Camp. The cabin assigned to "The Luck" was kept scrupulously clean and whitewashed. Then it was boarded, clothed, and papered. The rosewood cradle—packed 80 miles by mule—had, in Stumpy's way of putting it, "sorter killed the rest of the furniture." So the rehabilitation of the cabin became a necessity. Again Stumpy imposed a kind of quarantine upon those who aspired to the honor and privilege of holding The Luck. It was a cruel mortification to Kentuck—who had begun to regard all garments as a second cuticle, which, like a snake's, only sloughed off through decay—to be debarred. He thereafter appeared regularly every afternoon in a clean shirt. The shouting and yelling which had gained the camp its infelicitous title were not permitted within hearing distance of Stumpy's.

The Luck was usually carried to the gulch from whence the golden store of Roaring Camp was taken. There, on a blanket spread over pine boughs, he would lie while the men

This print, entitled "A Pleasant Surprise," appeared in the March 19, 1853, *Ballou's Pictorial.* Miners returning to their tent find a bear there warming its paws.

were working. There was a rude attempt to decorate this bower with flowers, and generally someone would bring him a cluster of wild honeysuckles, azaleas, or the painted blossoms of *las Mariposas.* The men had awakened to the fact that there were beauty and significance in these trifles, which they had so long trodden carelessly beneath their feet. "I crept up the bank just now," said Kentuck one day in a state of excitement, "and dern my skin if he wasn't a-talking to a jaybird. There they was, just as free and social as anything you please, a-jawin' at each other." Such was the golden summer of Roaring Camp. They were "flush times," and The Luck was with them.

It was proposed to build a hotel in the following spring and to invite one or two decent families to reside there for the sake of The Luck, who might profit by female companionship. A few held out but meekly yielded in hope that something might turn up to prevent it. And it did.

One night the North Fork suddenly leaped over its banks and swept up the valley of Roaring Camp. In the confusion of rushing water, crushing trees, and crackling timber, the cabin of Stumpy, which was the nearest to the riverbank, was gone. When morning broke, they found the body of its unlucky owner; but the pride, the hope, the joy, The Luck, of Roaring Camp had disappeared. A shout from the bank: it was a relief boat from down the river. They had picked up, they said, a man and an infant two miles below. It needed but a glance to show them

Kentuck lying there, cruelly crushed and bruised, but still holding The Luck in his arms. As they bent over the pair, they saw that the child was cold and pulseless. "He is dead," said one. Kentuck opened his eyes. "Dead?" he repeated. "Yes, my man, and you are dying too." A smile lit the eye of the expiring Kentuck. "Dying!" he repeated. "He's taking me with him. Tell the boys I've got The Luck with me now"; and the strong man, clinging to the frail babe as a drowning man is said to cling to straw, drifted away into the shadowy river that flows forever to the unknown sea.

FOLKWAYS

Camp Women

Miners would run from afar to view and celebrate a live, legitimate woman on their site, though there was rarely such an occasion; very few women appeared in the temporary mining camps. In one camp the remnant of an unknown woman's hat was stuck on a stake draped with a blanket to resemble a female; for two days reveling miners danced around the apparition. Most miners had to be satisfied with such fantasies, though in fact a few prostitutes did work the camps.

If women's favors and their civilizing qualities were missed by the prospectors, so was their domestic labor. "Six days shalt thou dig or pick all that the body can stand under," ran the fourth of the popular "Miners' Ten Commandments" printed up in 1853 by a disappointed Englishman who had found little gold, "but the other day is Sunday, yet thou washest all thy dirty shirts, darnest all thy stockings, tap thy boots, mend thy clothing, chop thy whole week's firewood, make up and make thy bread, and boil thy pork and beans, that thou wait not when thou returnest from thy claim weary." And the 10th commandment directed: "Thou shalt not forget absent maidens nor neglect thy first love."

JOAQUIN MURRIETA:
Terror of the Mother Lode

The Joaquín Murrieta legend grew out of actual conditions in gold country. Hostility toward Mexicans was especially fierce on the Mother Lode, where would-be landowners were eager to expel those earlier settlers. As gold became scarcer, criminal gangs developed, so some dug and washed the mineral that others would steal. There were several different Joaquins, but much of the hero-outlaw legend attached itself to Murrieta. Such Robin Hood-like ideals exist in the folk mind, awaiting a historical person to clothe them with life. He is handsome, loved by the ladies, pushed into crime by evil society, and dies young. He is loyal to friends, partial to the poor, and impeccably cool at all times.

ROSITA

The glances that followed Rosita in Saw Mill Flat—the mining town to which the 18-year-old Sonora native had brought his bride—were for the most part the tributes of clean-minded men to beauty abloom with health. Rosita walked serenely, unmindful either of admiration of the better sort or the burning glances of drunken satyrs. She was chaste as a lily. For her there was only one man in the world, her husband.

Joaquín and Rosita sat in the front room of the adobe under the old pine on the hill. The afternoon was waning. Cool shadows filled the valley. Saw Mill Flat was quiet, awaiting the night's revelry. The walls of the room were neatly whitewashed; the floor was of clean, hard earth. On a little bracket stood a painted plaster image of the Holy Virgin. On a table lay Joaquín's bowie knife. Rosita sat in a corner idly plucking the strings of a guitar. Suddenly five American miners marched in, bent on trouble. "You've got to pull out o' these here diggin's," blurted out the leader.

"Who are you?" Joaquín arose.

"We're good American citizens—that's who we are and who you ain't. This here's a white man's camp and no greasers wanted."

"There are plenty of Mexicans in Saw Mill Flat."

"They're thick as flies, crowdin' in here; they've took up some of the best claims on the creek. But we're goin' to pack 'em up and clear 'em out. California belongs to the U.S. of America. The Mexican War done settled that. These here greasers pannin' out our gold are robbin' us American miners of what American soldiers fit and bled fer."

"There's no law barring Mexicans from mining."

"Git balky and you shore air liable to go out in a pine box." His heavy fist crashed into Joaquín's face. Joaquín fell to his knees but was up in a flash and sprang for his bowie knife. "Look out, boys. Don't let him git that knife." The five men leaped upon Joaquín and drove him fighting desperately back and forth across the room. Rosita snatched the bowie, but with Joaquín in the center of the furiously swirling battle, she could not reach him. The gentle girl turned tigress. If Joaquín could not have the knife, she would use it. Springing at the leader, she aimed a thrust at his heart. The giant seized her wrist and, twisting the knife from her hand, pinioned her in his arms against the wall. "You little wildcat," he snarled.

Joaquín went down time after time until, battered and mangled, he lay insensible, a pool of blood spreading slowly about him. Rosita, pale with horror, watched her husband grow limp and apparently lifeless. Now that the hurly-burly was over, the ruffians looked her over.

"Take a look at that figger," said one. "I bet she could love a feller to death," added another. "Tried to kill me, eh?" purred the scoundrel who still held her. "Naughty baby."

"Holy Virgin protect me!" The relentless blackguard dragged the screaming girl into the back room. The others crowded in with him.

Then the cabin was silent. The five miners had disappeared. "Rosita? Where's Rosita?" Joaquín staggered into the back room. There lay his wife, as white and still as if she were dead, her clothes torn. "I am cold," she murmured. "It is growing dark." Folding her to his breast, Joaquín could feel the beating of her heart. It grew fainter—and ceased.

Months later some prospectors in a wild ravine stumbled upon five skeletons lying about the ashes of an old campfire. Through each of the five skulls was a neat, round hole made by a bullet.

JOAQUIN'S REVENGE

Joaquín moved to Murphy's Diggings and tried to make an honest living running a monte table. But his brother Jesus was accused of stealing a mule. The two Mexicans confronted a druken mob led by a Bill Lang. "You sold me that mule and took my money for it," Joaquín's brother protested. "You're a liar," Lang bawled. "Git a rope, fellers." The noose was made tight around the neck of Jesus and the loose end of the rope thrown over a limb of the oak. Stripped to the waist, Joaquín was bound to the trunk of the same tree. "All ready? Let her rip." Jesus shot into the air. For a few moments his body twisted with contortions. Wave-like spasms of shivering swept over him. Gradually the writhings ceased and his limp form dangled motionless. With eyes uplifted to the ghastly spectacle, Joaquín watched.

Sleeves rolled up, a rope in his hand, Lang stepped into position for the flogging. The crowd roared approval. "Bear down, old hoss. Blister him good." A strong man was Bill Lang, cruel, merciless. Whirling the rope, he brought it down across Joaquín's back. Another full-armed swing. "I'll beat you black and blue, you mangy horse thief." Three, four, five. "Fetched the blood that time." Nine, ten, eleven. "I'll cut you into mincemeat." He worked himself into a frenzy. Thirty-seven, thirty-eight. He paused. "Here's the last one. I'll make it a jim-dandy." The rope ripped with slashing force across the mangled and blood-smeared flesh. Joaquín took his punishment with grim, set face, no sign of suffering.

The crowd went back into town and lined up at a bar. "Did you notice that greaser's eyes while Bill was lacin' him? He kept them eyes rovin' round the crowd from one to t'other of us like he was fixin' us in his mind." Murphy's Diggings gossiped

over the lynching for weeks. Then a dead man was found in the chaparral, one of the 20 who had flogged Joaquín. The body was covered with stab wounds, the ears sliced off, and about the neck a deep red scar made by the noose of a rawhide lariat. Evidently the man had been lassoed, dragged into a thicket, and tortured.

In the next few weeks the bodies of four other men were found. All had been members of the lynching party. About each throat was the mark of a lariat. One by one Bill

Lang's stranglers stole away from Murphy's Diggings and scattered to the four winds. But eventually Joaquín had slain 18 of them; one had been shot by another man and one hanged by law. Joaquín Murrieta was no longer just another Mexican. His name had become a synonym for terror.

SUTHERLAND'S SON
Jack Sutherland, a well-to-do cattleman, lived on a ranch on Dry Creek and when he went to Stockton on business left his son, Billy, in charge. Billy sold a bunch of steers for several thousand and counted it on the kitchen table, piling it in glittering stacks of gold and silver. Suddenly Murrieta and a half dozen of his outlaws stalked into the house; Billy's heart sank.

"Aren't you afraid to be here with that money?" asked Joaquín.

"There ain't much danger," answered Billy, putting on a front.

"What if Joaquín Murrieta paid you a visit?"

"He wouldn't rob me."

"He wouldn't, eh?"

"My dad did him a favor once. Murrieta never harms his friends."

"What's your name?"

"Billy Sutherland."

"You Jack Sutherland's son?"

"That's what I am."

"All right, Billy," said Joaquín. His eyes lingered on the shining heaps of money. "Give your dad my best. And if any of the sheriff's men pass this way, forget we've been here."

ROBIN HOOD
Murrieta with several of his men arrived one night at a ferry on the Tuolomne River. Thumping on the door of a cabin with the butts of their

Murrieta's dedicated gaze illuminates this early painting. The legendary outlaw once vowed he would "revenge my wrongs and take the law into my own hands. The Americans who have injured me I will kill, and those who have not, I will rob because they are Americans. My trail shall be red with blood; those who seek me will die."

pistols, they aroused the ferryman. "We want to get across," said Joaquín. "But first we would like all the money you have."

"We've got no time to lose," snapped Three Fingered Jack drawing his bowie. "Shell out quick or I'll work on you." The ferryman handed over a purse containing a hundred dollars, which he had concealed under his pillow. "You'll have to dig up more than this," snarled Three Fingered Jack. "That's all I've got." "All?" asked Joaquín. "Every cent in the world. I'm very poor. I make a bare living out of my ferry." "Take back your purse then," said Murrieta. "There are plenty of rich fellows to rob. I don't need your money."

REWARD

A reward of $5,000 was offered for Murrieta dead or alive. A crowd gathered one Sunday morning around the flagpole in the public square in Stockton on which a placard announcing the reward had been posted. The crowd stared as a handsome young Mexican, superbly mounted, came riding into the square, a feather in his hat, his serape tossed back over one shoulder revealing a glimpse of gold-braided jacket and scarlet sash: a gallant figure sitting his horse jauntily and glancing about him with cool unconcern. The placard caught his eye. He reined to a stop at the flagpole and, bending from his saddle, gazed intently at it: "$5,000—REWARD—$5000 Offered by the Citizens of Stockton to Anyone Who Delivers to the Proper Authorities JOAQUIN MURRIETA Dead or Alive."

Dismounting, the Mexican stepped closer and read the placard again. Suddenly, as if a happy idea had occurred to him, he drew a pencil from his pocket and scribbled something at the bottom. Then swinging into the saddle, he rode off leisurely across the square. The onlookers crowded around to read this message inscribed in a bold, free hand: "I will add $10,000—Joaquín."

JOAQUIN'S DEATH

Surrounded by California Rangers at his campsite, Joaquín leaped on his horse and, chased by three of them, fled for his life with bullets whispering death around him. One Ranger shot at his horse, and the animal floundered. One by one the Rangers fired and each of their bullets found its mark. Murrieta pitched to the earth with a heavy thud. His horse, in its last throes, gave a few violent lunges beyond him and fell dead. Getting to his feet with a painful effort, Murrieta ran unsteadily in a desperate effort to escape. But nothing could save him. Ranger Henderson drew a steady bead. His six-shooter spouted fire. The bullet passed through the outlaw's body. Wounded to the death, Murrieta turned with quiet acceptance of fate and, facing his enemies, raised his right hand. "It is enough," he said in a clear voice. The job is finished. I am dead." An ashen pallor overspread his bronze face. He dropped to his knees and sank on his side. It was as if, after his violent life, death had gathered him gently in its arms.

JOAQUIN'S GHOST

For years, according to his own story, Henderson was haunted by Murrieta's ghost: I was riding at dusk one day from Los Angeles to my ranch when a headless horseman wrapped in a black serape suddenly appeared at my side. Who are you? I demanded. I am Joaquín, replied the phantom, and I want my head. Joaquín, I said, I do not know what became of your head . . . Many times after that the phantom appeared to me as I rode along some lonely road, and at night I would awake to hear a voice calling me in the darkness. I am Joaquín, it said, and I want my head. Give me back my head.

That women swooned in his embrace, that he could be slain only by a silver bullet, that the superbly mustached pickled head—which was widely displayed by the California Rangers for a dollar a peek—was not really his, that he had escaped the Rangers and set up a ranch in Mexico, were but a few of the flourishes attached to Joaquín's legend.

CITIES OF GOLD
And the Root of Evil

First there were the tents along a river, next frame shanties announced that a town was born, then the thousands of gold seekers came, and brawling cities grew: Stockton, Sacramento, San Francisco. Initially all male, mining towns naturally attracted loose women but gradually became fit for "ladies." In the cities, gambling palaces and fancy houses vied with miners' rough bars for patronage.

HAPPY FEET

Across the street from the Mississippi House was a mudhole and this mudhole was at the back door of a saloon. In the 1850's a bartender there practiced an original bit of larceny that had an original flair to it.

It was the custom for miners to pay for their drinks out of a poke of gold dust. A pinch of dust for a drink—and the bartender did the pinching—so men with big thumbs were in demand for the job. This bartender not only had a big thumb but a careless habit of letting some of the dust spill onto the bar. Not enough to excite any of the miners, however. Always neat, he brushed the dust off the bar onto the floor—on his side. Every hour or so he would slip out the back door and coat his boot soles with the sticky mud from the hole. He would then tread over every inch of the floor behind the bar. Each night he would go home to his cabin, stepping carefully in order not to dislodge any of the mud, and would wash the dirt from his boots into a pan. It is said that he washed out as much as $30 on weekdays and $100 on Sundays and holidays.

BLOOD WILL TELL

It was one day in the rainy winter of 1854 and 1855 and too wet to work, so me and the boys begun to wander in at the Long Tom in Columbia, California. By noon all the tables was full and the gambling got more exciting as the day wore on. Gambling fever's catching and it'll spread through a crowd like any other fever. At some of the tables they was betting on the turn of a card, and they was one crowd having a spitting tournament at the stove. But the greatest bet in betting history was laid that night by young Ad Pence.

"Boys," says Ad, pounding on the bar, "luck's been agin me so far, but I've got 500 here that says I've a louse

Many residents and visitors in early San Francisco found its streets no better than the average hog wallow during floodtide or when it rained, which meant most of the time. Neither boots nor mules prevented one from getting mired either, a fact of life that satirical artists eagerly lampooned. The lithograph here is titled "The Winter of 1849" and pokes fun at pedestrian problems.

Tea, coffee, and chocolate were offered at this gambling house, and doubtless much more. Whatever the appeal—ladies of leisure, money to be won, or inebriation—the Portsmouth Square saloon depicted by Friedrich Gerstaecker in 1859 looks very popular.

jumping because it was so hot. The boys was cheering and yelling and standing on chairs to see.

Well, neck and neck it was at the start, but Ad's louse pulled ahead a bit and he was the first to reach the rise of the rim. Then come the hard pull for the edge. He started up the rise, but when he got about halfway up he lost his footing and slid down. So he back up and took another run for it, but again he slid back. He was a game one, that louse. He tried again and again. No, sir, it was on that last hard pull up the rim that the blood of Saint Patrick began to tell, for Larry, he started up slow and careful and he kep on a-pulling and a-scrambling and up and up he went and *over* the edge to victory. A hero he was! "Three cheers for Larry and the blood of Saint Patrick!" The boys roared out three cheers.

"Stranger," Ad said, "it was a fair race and the best louse won. But I've one request. Just let me borrow Larry till tomorrow." "What for?" says the stranger. "Why, man," says Ad, "I want to improve my breed!"

COLUMBIA'S BIG LOU

We had our full share of gold here in Columbia, so, naturally, we had our share of fancy women, too. Big Lou had her fancy house on State Street, and it was a *real* fancy house with big gilt mirrors and red plush chairs and all the fixings. But she was a great drinker, Big Lou was, and she used to go on terrible sprees. Now that wouldn't of been so bad if she'd stayed in her own house to do it, but she'd go out and rampage all over the town and be so loud and noisy she'd make a big disturbance. Well, one day she was off on a big bender and having a regular whoop-up. She was standing out in front of the Columbo Saloon, on the boardwalk, when Mrs. Dealey come along. This Mrs. Dealey was the schoolteacher then, and a saint if ever they was a live one. And when she saw Big Lou there, taking up so much of the walk, she lifted up her skirt and stepped out into the street. That made Big Lou mad.

"Who'd a thought it?" she says

that can beat, in a fair race, any louse that ever cut his teeth on any miner's hide." He'd caught a good lively one and held him up for all the boys to see. "I'd say this louse is the champeen, for I've been chasing him around my carcass for a week and I've only just caught up with him. Five hundred backs him against all comers." At that, all the games stopped short and everybody crowded up to the bar, but none of the boys would admit that he kept this kind of stock. Then a stranger, a big Irishman with a red beard, come elbowing his way through and up to the bar.

"Will ye let me have a look at that louse?" he says. So Ad held it out. "A dainty crayther indade," says the stranger, "but I think no racer. His belly's too low and his legs too short. Now wait a bit and I'll have something to show ye." So the stranger put his hand inside his shirt and scrabbled around in there for a minute, and when he pulled it out, between his thumb and finger he held a struggling louse.

"Me boy," he said. "Your 500 is as good as gone. Yours, he's but a mongrel. *This* is the greatest racing louse in the world, and he has the most distinguished pedigree. Just before me old grandfather died, back in Ireland, he said: 'Granson, I'm a pore man. But there's wan threasure I have, Katie, the finest little seam squirrel in all of Ireland and a direct descendant of one that fed on Saint Patrick. She'll bring ye luck.' Now, me boy, this louse ye see here is Larry, Katie's great-great-great-grandson, and the blood of Saint Patrick himself runs in his veins, so I'll lay 1,000 to that 500 ye bet on yer mongrel!"

So Ad and the stranger placed their stakes, and side betting begun in the crowd. "There can be no race without a racetrack," says the stranger, and he calls to the bartender. "Bring us a plate. Now boys, the middle's the start, the edge is the goal, and the first little pants rabbit over the rim is the winner."

The bartender brought the plate, and the stranger felt of it. "No louse would ever set a good pace on this cold plate. Let's hate it up a bit." So they heated the plate piping hot and set it where all could see. One, two, three, go! Each man dropped his louse in the middle of the plate, and they were off, a-scrambling and a-

224

"The angel walks on two legs, just like Lou," and then she let loose with some fancy cussing. Well, of course this embarrassed Mrs. Dealey, and the story spread around, and everybody agreed that this was a general insult to the good women of the town and that something ought to be done.

Now it happened that Number Two Engine Company was having a meeting that night, and when this subject of Big Lou come up, Bob Mullan says: "We can't let this go on. When this rip gets to insulting our good women, she's going too far."

"Well, you're the marshal, Bob," somebody says. "Why don't you lock her up?" "Sir," says he, "I run a respectable jail. I won't have it turned into a fancy house! And besides, we don't want to lock her up and keep her here. What we want is to get rid of her. She's a disgrace to the fair name of Columbia," he says. "I make a motion that this company turn out with the engine and wash Big Lou out of town!"

Well, they put it to a vote and it passed unanimous. So the meeting adjourned right then and there and the boys hauled that big Number Two Engine down Main Street and set it on the cistern on State Street. They put on an extra-long hose so as they could get in the house. Then the fellows on the brakes was pumping as hard as they could go, and the hosemen, first they turned the stream on the outside of the house and broke the windows and tore up the shades. Big Lou, she come reeling out, letting the G.d's and the s.o.b.'s fly in all directions, but the boys, they just turned the hose on her to cool her off and washed her out into the street. Then they run the hose inside, and the stream would hit the fine mirrors, and bing! they'd bust. They hosed off the plush chairs and sofas and rugs and almost washed the whole house away. And every time Big Lou would start to cuss, they'd souse her again. So that was the end of Big Lou and her fancy house in Columbia. Yes sir, old Number Two Engine Company washed her right out of town.

WIDEMOUTHED MAYHEM

When a thousand ground sluicers were washing an old river channel down to rich bedrock at Galena Hill, life ran high. Saloons and gambling halls never closed. The hurdy-gurdy gals came and went, dispensing their favors at a dollar a dance. And there was Madam Sharp's fandango house.

Now Madam Sharp was hardly a lady. But she ran a good house: no fights or loud swearing—or practically next to none. Things went smoothly at the Maison Sharp until one Blazer Bill hit the diggin's. A fightin', swearin', cantankerous son of a gun was this Blazer Bill; got himself run out of Brandy City for slitting a gal's silk stocking for the nugget she had under her garter. Starts right in makin' his mark in Galena Hill. Got away with it until one night he runs foul of Madam

John Stobart's painting of Vallejo Street Wharf in 1863 gives no hint of the brawling town San Francisco really was at that time.

The engraving reproduced above appeared in *Old Block's Sketch Book, or Tales of California Life,* which was published in 1856. Two forty-niners, hardly spilling a drop of their high spirits, are hard at the task of shopping while on horseback—much to the dismay of the proprietor of the store, his pets, and some more genteel customers.

Sharp, which she's a bad old catamount to tie into once she goes on the warpath. One word leads to another until finally the two of 'em lace into a scuffle, and Blazer so far forgets his gentlemanly instincts and early trainin' as to bite the lady. Next day she has him arrested for what-you-call-it—mayhem.

Looks like Blazer's in for a stiff term in county jail until he gets old Judge May to defend him. "I'll get you a change of venom to Downieville," the judge says. "You can't get a fair trial, what with the prejudice raised agin' you." Which he does. And trial day you couldn't wedge a thin half-dollar between folks jamming that courtroom.

Madam Sharp takes the stand to tell judge and jury about her bein' bit by Blazer, and she don't miss nothin' in describing the attack. "Now, Madam Sharp," says Judge May, "kindly show judge and jury where you was bit." The old girl backs and fills and pulls a blush, but the judge he clears the court after a lot of trouble. Then madam shows where she was bit—a double row of purple toothmarks plain as a signpost. Then Judge May puts Blazer on the stand. "This is the man you claim to have bit you?" "Yessiree!" "Blazer," says Judge May, "turn an' face the jury." Blazer does. "Blazer, open your mouth wide." He does. Blazer didn't show a tooth on his whole upper jaw! A' course the jury had to acquit him. And when Blazer got back to Galena Hill, Judge May give him back his upper teeth.

❦WORD LORE❧

It All Panned Out

In some parts of the United States at the height of the gold rush it seemed as if all the young men had departed for California. It wasn't long before most returned, disappointed. Having enriched their vocabulary, if nothing else, they carried prospectors' jargon to virtually every locality in the land. Examples: *claim*—piece of land taken for mining (hence *stake a claim*—assert title to something—and *jump a claim*—usurp title to something); *grubstake*—help provided to launch someone on a project (California merchants *staked* needy prospectors to *grub*—food and supplies—in return for a share in their discoveries); *bonanza,* a rich vein of gold or silver (American Spanish for "good luck"); *pay dirt*—ore-laden earth. Many other terms originated in the digs or were popularized there: *prospecting, striking it rich, panning out,* as well as such now-commonplace words as *gulch, canyon,* and *saloon* (in the sense of

"barroom"). Having few other ways to amuse themselves, the miners were heavy drinkers—a pinch of gold dust paid for a half tumbler of one's favorite tanglefoot—and to them we owe the finely expressive synonym for "delirium tremens," *the jimjams.* (The word is a humorous deformation of the Latin medical term.)

Arriving miners were wont to name a new settlement after some memorable event, wisecrack, or circumstance. One such place's unpromising original name of Dry Diggings changed to Hangtown following the hanging there of three men who, according to a contemporary, "had exhausted the patience of the miners." Finally, as the digs and diggers' tempers improved, the settlement went on the map with the respectable name of Placerville.

The western vogue for funny place-names went back to the era when the Allegheny frontier was still the West. But, notes H. L. Mencken in his monumental *American Language:* "It was after the plains and the Rockies were crossed that the pioneers really spit on their hands and showed what they could do. Many of their inventions have become part of the romantic traditions of the Pacific Coast . . . Humbug Flat, Jackass Gulch, Gouge Eye, Red Dog, Lousy Level, Gomorrah, and Shirt Tail were very real . . . In the years since then many of these names have been changed to more elegant ones, and others have vanished with the ghost towns they adorned, but not a few still linger on."

LEGENDARY MINES
Found and Lost

Walz the Dutchman and Pegleg Smith both drank a lot and then talked of fabulous hidden mines. Walz stole his mine from three Mexicans, and men who tried to follow him to it were killed. Some think Walz was simply bragging about the slayings, but he did confess on his deathbed that he had in fact murdered those who tried to learn his secret. That mine has never been found again. Pegleg could not relocate his rich mine after his initial discovery, but that did not stop him from selling treasure maps at $5 a throw to the tenderfeet in San Diego's bars.

PEGLEG'S LOST GOLD

In 1837 a trapper named John G. Smith (known as Pegleg because of an accident that had left him with one leg) started from Yuma for Los Angeles. Being pressed for time, he attempted a shortcut but lost his way. To regain his bearings, Smith climbed a hill. While reconnoitering, he noticed some lumps of black, burned-looking ore thickly sprinkled with yellow particles of varying size, which literally covered the hill. Attracted by the curious appearance of the rock, Smith gathered up a few samples and carried them with him to Los Angeles, where an expert pronounced the yellow particles pure gold. Pegleg organized an expedition to relocate the hill, but at an early stage of the trip all of the party's animals were run off by the Indians. Smith died before he could outfit another expedition. Subsequently many prospectors started out from Yuma and Los Angeles in a vain search for Pegleg, as Smith's discovery had come to be called. The skeletons of some of those unlucky searchers continue to be found to this day.

However, the location of the lost gold was known to at least one native of the region. In the 1860's a Mexican employee of a ranch on the edge of the desert, being refused an advance by his boss, said, "All right, I know where there's plenty of gold." He disappeared into the desert, to return at the end of three days with a few thousand dollars worth of burned black gold of the Pegleg, and reveled to his heart's content. Thereafter, whenever his funds ran low, he would leave the ranch and soon return, his pockets filled with nuggets. The Mexican's secret died with him a few years later. A while after that, the Pegleg seems to have been found and lost a third time when a miner who was cutting across country accidentally climbed the same hill as Smith and noticed he was standing on a mass of broken quartz and free gold. Filling his saddlebags with the precious stuff, the miner took careful note of the surroundings and continued on to Los Angeles, where he fell sick and died, leaving a small fortune in Pegleg gold to the doctor who attended him. But the whereabouts of the marvelous hill remains a riddle to this day.

LOST DUTCHMAN MINE

Jacob Walz acquired the nicknames of Dutchman and Old Snow Beard. His beard was the freakish, gleaming white that is ghostly and frightening, and his fierce eyes gleamed above it. Walz was a German—not a Hol-

Eight feet tall, walking aimlessly, with a lantern dangling in his chest cavity, this skeleton appeared at night to prospectors who were camping near Borego, Arizona.

lander—taciturn and cranky, and little children were by no means the only ones who feared him. One day in the 1870's Walz made a short cut across the Superstition Mountains when an Indian's arrow nicked him. He ducked and ran. When nightfall came he did a lot of plain and fancy crawling. He was suffering from thirst and hunger. By noon, Walz came upon the camp of three Mexicans. "Water!" he pleaded with them, and they hastened to supply him. "What are you camped here for?" Old Snow Beard demanded. "*Por el oro, señor.* The gold. We get heem. The mine, eet ees ours." They took Walz to their digs and Old Jake's eyes nearly popped. Walz edged from his hosts and spoke. "Ain't that some men a-coming yonder?" All three turned away. Walz lifted his rifle and fired. He dragged all three corpses about 150 yards into a crevasse and piled rocks on them.

Walz collected all the golden nug-

SUPERSTITIONS

"Cousin Jack" Lore

The first waves of California gold hunters were mostly greenhorns when it came to mining, but soon after 1850, Cornishmen (known as Cousin Jacks) who brought with them centuries of experience in hard-rock mining began flocking in from Michigan, the East Coast, and the old country itself. Their ability to "smell" ore became proverbial; and it was they who discovered the original Mother Lode, biggest vein of gold ever found, in California's Sierra Nevada.

Cornish mining lore included a wealth of superstition. One belief Cornishmen shared with the "farmers"—as they called placer miners—was that the appearance of unwanted persons at diggings jinxed the ore and caused it to pinch out. (Obviously, a placer miner who was cleaning the gold out of his sluice boxes did not relish being surprised by somebody coming up on him; such a person might bring bad luck in any number of different ways.) The "Cousin Jacks" had many another taboo. For example, never kill a rat in a mine. For this offense, a greenhorn was sure to get his ears pinned back. The reason was that the rats' superior hearing and intuition made them valuable indicators of impending cave-ins. "When the rats move out, so does the miner." Another taboo: if your candle goes out, you go out, too. This made sense because a candle won't burn in bad air; so if you see your candle flickering out, you may be on the point of asphyxiation and not know it.

Yet another: no whistling in the mine during the night shift (because

sharp sounds were thought to set up vibrations that could cause a cave-in). The most unlucky time of night was from midnight to 2 a.m. (because, said the oldtimers, the ground moves more at that time than at any other, the earth being asleep and snoring).

The Cornishmen also believed in "Tommy Knockers," mine-dwelling gnomes that were so called because of their habit of knocking or tapping on the walls of mine shafts just before a cave-in. It was widely held that the first man to hear Tommy Knockers tapping in the case of a disaster would be the first to die, either that time or the next. Apart from this sinister office, the Tommy Knockers were a beneficent if occasionally mischievous lot—they sometimes even assisted in finding ore. In appearance they were like little old men, the size of two-year-olds, with big, ugly heads; they dressed in leather jackets, peaked hats, and water-soaked boots. Clay images of the Tommy Knockers were placed by Cornish miners at the entrances to tunnels until within recent memory.

gets he could, came to Phoenix, and got drunk. "I got a private graveyard in th' mountain and enough gold to pave this street!" Bartenders' eyes bulged at the nuggets he showed. The old man was followed when he next set out for the mountain. Quick shots broke the still of evening: some cowboys found the remains of two well-known Phoenix men not far from where Walz had been camping.

A man named Phipps backtrailed the Dutchman one week and came onto his mine. He hastened to his home camp and went down into an abandoned mine shaft to get a pick. Nobody ever knew just what happened, but something caused the shaft to cave in, and Phipps was killed in the disaster.

Another man, named Deering, found Walz' mine. He got drunk and soon a fellow tippler had had enough of him and drove a dagger through Deering's heart. Oldtimers say Deering was the seventh direct victim of the Superstition Mountains gold spell.

Walz wrote back to Germany and asked his own nephew Julius to come and help. And come he did! Uncle and nephew took out a burro load of the ore and headed for Phoenix. All the way Julius was garrulous, full of plans for spending the money. At Phoenix, Julius became a spendthrift and did a lot of boasting. Encamped near the present town of Tempe, the old Dutchman snatched up his rifle and put a bullet through his own nephew's brain.

Walz then moved to Phoenix and shortly thereafter contracted pneumonia. The dying Walz tried to tell his friend Dick Holmes the location of his mine but died after he had confessed to the murders and had revealed only: "The key is a stripped paloverde tree with one limb left on, a pointing arm. It points away from Weaver's Needle. About halfway from between it and Weaver's Needle, and 200 yards to the east, is the richest mine I ever heard of." Holmes spent 28 years trying to find the property. His sons still have hopes. None of them has ever located the paloverde with the pointing arm.

GOING HOME
Mostly Busted

Contrary to Samuel Butler's counsel that pondering large zoo animals was an antidote to despair, discouraged miners felt beaten by what they came to call "the elephant." After years of backbreaking work for themselves or mining companies, many who had left home with high hopes returned with broken spirits. "I have seen the elephant," they said. "I'm going home." It was all too large, too unbeatable. Some, including many foreigners, stayed on to make California an international state. Others went back to the kitchens of their waiting wives.

"DADDY'S HOME!"

Jeff Clarke had been gone from Oregon over a year. One September evening near sundown his children were playing by the creek, out of sight of the cabin. Elvie's mother was setting the table when Elvie hurried in, excited and breathless. "Maw—you'd better get the rifle down! There's a tramp coming across the swale!" "Maybe it's an Indian!" said her mother, alarmed. "I'd better call the children in!" "No," Elvie said, looking around the cabin, "he's no Indian—he's got whiskers! But he's awful ragged. Come look."

Her mother came to the corner.

"Your eyes are better than mine. What's he doing? It looks like he's crawling." Elvie laughed. "He just fell in the creek. There, he's up again. Look at him stagger along! I'll bet he's drunk." "No, he's just weak, poor man. See how he walks, with his head hanging . . . Elvie!" her mother gasped, then her voice rose strongly: "*Jeff!* Oh, Jeff, honey—wait, *wait!* I'll help you . . ."

Yes, it was Jeff Clarke, home from the goldfields. When he had recovered from malaria in Sacramento and had returned to his claim, he found his helpers had stripped the ground of its last grain of gold. Jeff had exchanged the last of his nuggets for boat passage to Portland. He was still apathetic as he sprawled on the kitchen chair. "I'm just naturally a failure. I had my hands on it—I was *rich*—but it got away from me. And you and the kids are practically starving here!"

"There's more gold right here, Jeff, than they'll ever find in California. Right here in the valley." "Yeah?" Jeff said, rousing, "Where'd they find it? On Gales Creek? How much is it running to the pan?"

"No, listen. We bought eight heifers while you were gone. We've got four cows milking. We've got three good workhorses." "Well, I'll be—" Jeff peered up at his wife. "Where'd you get all this livestock? Who do you owe?" "I paid for them." "With what?" "With California gold." "But doggone it—where did you get gold?" "From the wheat we sold. Elvie and I put up 20 acres of wheat. We harvested 800 bushels. We saved some for flour and seed and sold the rest for $2.50 a bushel! They paid for it with gold that just came up from California."

"That's right—flour's four bits a pound up on the gold creeks!"

"Do you know how much seed I saved out? Enough for 80 acres. There's 80 acres in the big meadow, all ready to break. Don't you *see?*"

All of a sudden it was as though a bad dream was over. "Joe! Betty! Come and get washed for supper. *Hurry! Daddy's home!*"

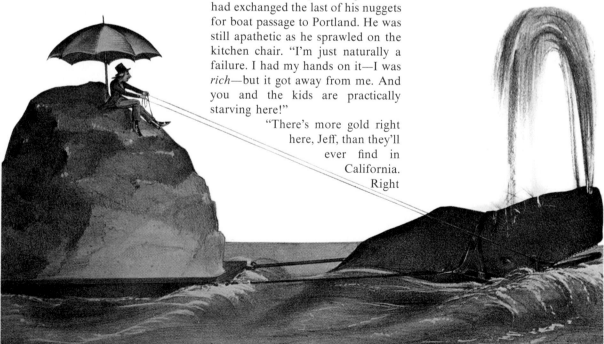

Going home in 1849, when the gold rush was young, meant to lithographer Nathaniel Currier simply lassoing a sperm whale and letting him pull you and your hill of solid gold around Cape Horn and from there to the admiring cities of the East.

Blow the Man Down

American interest in speed at sea was much intensified by the discovery of gold in California, and the result was the superb clipper of the 1850's. In two years the voyage to San Francisco from New York via Cape Horn was cut from half a year to 90 days. After discharging cargoes and passengers in San Francisco the clippers raced for the Orient; during the decade, their great speed and immense carrying capacity enabled them to capture the cream of the China trade. Until the Civil War changed priorities, more and more young men sought berths in the clippers and for some the rewards were great. Captains not yet 40 retired in elegance to their new-built mansions on Main Street.

From the outset America had been a maritime nation. The settlers all arrived by boat, and fishing, shipbuilding, and ocean transport were among her first significant sources of income. The merchant marine grew with the country because shipping long remained cheaper and faster than the developing roads and rails. As the maritime industry grew and flourished, a considerable body of folklore naturally developed around it. Many of the stories told here have an American ring, but the majority stem from the Old World and, moreover, are as ancient as the ark. Beliefs and superstitions, legends and customs, were picked up in one far corner of the world and disseminated in another. The lore was perpetuated because sailors believed it offered a means to survive at sea and it gave voice to their fears and desires. The sea is vast, hostile, and treacherous. Only those steeped in sealore, physically fit, and indescribably tough survived to become salts. To the seafarer the adventure, the wonder, and the hope of great reward made up for all the hardships and risk. The land was not for sailors. As the fabled tar Stormalong once said of farming: "Nothin' but green grass an' trees an' hills an' hot work. Nary a breeze or a smell of the sea. Never a storm to make a man pull out all the best that's in him." The sea makes captives of her children.

America's Phillips Whaling Fleet, which was famous for its filth, makes its way through crowded waters in this oil on a panel attributed to painter W. H. Luscomb.

All was not a breeze in sailing days; here a Marblehead sailor hangs onto a line for dear life under the bow of the brig *America*. A fellow seaman, still hatted, looks cheerful enough in the bright but ominous sea: the gouache is by Michel Felice Cornè.

BIGGEST OF THEM ALL
Whalers' Tales

"There she blows!" Whaleboats were lowered and rowed quietly to where the Leviathan had been spotted. When it surfaced, the harpooner went to work. Once hit, the thrashing whale would sound and pull fathoms of shrieking, smoking line out of the boat and sometimes swim off dragging the whalers behind him. When he tired, the whale was lanced and if his wound proved mortal he spouted blood. "He spouts tar!" they shouted. Later, seamen gathered in the forecastle and recounted other adventures. Herman Melville turned whaling into tragic allegory but the whalers treated their life-or-death work with whimsey or factuality.

INSIDE THE WHALE

After years of slaughtering the great bulls, Yarmouth's Ichabod Paddock had at last met his match in a giant battle-scarred "crook-jawed sparm bull," a monster who would make 200 barrels of oil if he'd make a thimble. Time and again Captain Paddock had let fly at old Crook-Jaw from the small boat, but never once had he made fast. Come at him anywhere, stem, stern, or amidships, and your iron would glance off like a dull ax on green pine. One windy day Ichabod raised Crook-Jaw lolling in the choppy waters of Handkerchief Shoal, sound asleep and snoring like a sated sinner. Heaving to about a mile to leeward, he pulled off his long-leggers and plunged overboard. Straight up to the whale he swam and waited. Half an hour he waited, treading water, and at last he got what he was waiting for. Crook-Jaw opened his great mouth and yawned. Wider until the huge jaws stood apart so that a cart upon wheels might have gone into it. Then, arching like a porpoise, in dove Ichabod.

It was parlous close for air inside the whale, but once down below, the captain thought he saw a light and started aft. Sure enough, on squeezing through, he came into a snug lamplit cabin where two people were sitting at cards. One was a betaking young wench with hair the color of Eastham corn and a hitherly glance in the five-fathom green of her eyes. The other was the Divil. As Ichabod entered, the Divil slammed his cards on the table, and sparks singed their edges. Getting to his feet, he vanished in a huff. "I'm very sorry, ma'am," Ichabod said. "I didn't come purposing to break up the game." The girl laughed. "The game was over anyway."

"Your friend was mortal put out," Ichabod remarked. "Could a body inquire what the stakes might be?" "Captain Paddock, *you* were the stakes!" And she raised the brows above her green, green eyes and added softly, "You might oblige me, sir, by bearing witness that I won."

So it happened that Ichabod was given up for lost by his crew; but at dawn they saw the waters of Handkerchief Shoal set a-dance by the

In this 1877 oil study for a panorama, "All in a Day's Work," by C. S. Raleigh, a whaleboat is neatly split by the flip of a fluke.

arms of a returning figure, and Ichabod climbed wearily aboard. Now, it had become evident to the captain that the green-eyed woman of Crook-Jaw had not spent all her life inside the whale's body; either that, or Ichabod himself had not been the first to venture through those gaping jaws. His queasy conscience being eased on certain essentials, the next evening he again plunged overboard and was seen no more by his crew until morning.

This happened continuously until the vessel had to make in for a new fitout. Ichabod was losing both his reputation as a whaler and a certain instinctive trust in which he had been held at home. The next time he came ashore, his good wife, a handsome creature not yet 30, made him a gift—a shiny new whaling iron. He was somewhat less pleased, when he went to sea again, to hear her insist that his father-in-law go with him. A few days later old Crook-Jaw spied the captain's vessel and, having come to regard Ichabod as a friend and guest entitled to a certain amount of civility, stood by. Ichabod on the deck beside his father-in-law watched him. When the old man began to exclaim at the size of the creature and to beg Ichabod to lower for him, he could not properly refuse. Over they went in the small boat, and with a mighty heave the whalemaster sent his new iron whistling through the air. He was confident the whale would understand and there would be no harm done, but to his astonishment, he made fast! The beast churned and thrashed the water and finally died. When they cut him up, all that Ichabod Paddock found inside, where his cozy cabin had been, was a strand of seaweed which had bleached to the color of Eastham corn and two round sunstones of pure emerald green.

As for the explanation of the killing of Crook-Jaw, I have not heard whether Ichabod's wife ever confessed. But the shiny "iron" she had given him was made of pure silver—the only metal that could pierce the heart of a witch.

Historically, whaling began on the beaches, moved to the open sea, spread to the South Pacific, and finally reached the cold poles. George Halm's watercolor illustrates a story about a whale that was suspended 250 feet above sea level in an iceberg showcase.

NANTUCKET SLEIGH RIDE

A harpooned whale will usually "sound" at once, going down deep and remaining under for the better part of an hour. On rising he will often "run," that is, swim away at high speed, dragging the boat after him by the whale line: this is known as a "Nantucket sleigh ride."

One old whaleman given to drawing the long bow once entertained an interested group of summer people with a story the truth of which we do not vouch for: "We was fast to an old bull whale, an' the minute he broke water he started off to looard lickety-split. Sufferin' cats! How that whale did travel! We fleeted aft's fur's we could git, but even then the water poured over the gunnel for'ard and kep' us all bailing's hard's we could to keep her afloat. All of a sudden I happened to look aft, an' there was an empty whaleboat follerin' in our wake astern. For a minute or so she follered us close; then we gained on

her an' gradually she fell off. The next wave struck her, an' she went to smithereens, an' that was the last of her."

"But where'd the other boat come from?" "Wal, 'twas a mystery to us till we got aboard ship and h'isted our boat up on the davits. Then we see her plankin' was as clean as the day she come out o' the shop. You see, that thar whale went so fast he pulled our boat clean out o' the paint, an' what we seen was jest the shell o' paint follerin' after us!"

THE RECKONING

The story was told of a tremendous whale captured and killed in the Indian Ocean. The throat of this whale was so extremely large that a swallowed whaleship was lodged there; the crew of the successful ship boarded her, walking the deck in fear and trembling as they realized what their own fate might have been. As they prowled about the deck of the

Gulp!

There are many stories about people swallowed by whales—and toothed whales, which ingest whole squid, could bolt down a human being. With the miraculous exception of Jonah, however, there is no evidence that one of these great creatures has ever done so. British seaman James Bartley was found in 1891 inside the belly of a sperm whale—unconscious but alive and whole—facts verified by a noted French science editor. But some 50 years later an American expert explained why a man could not survive in a whale and labeled the story "unadulterated bunk." The June 1947 edition of *Natural History Magazine* printed the report of Dr. Egerton Y. Davis, Jr., who in the 1890's did an autopsy of a sailor found dead inside a whale's carcass. The man's chest had been crushed but his body had not been dismembered by the beast's jaws. A letter writer revealed, however, that "Egerton Y. Davis" was the pseudonym used by the famous doctor Sir William Osler, a noted prankster. (The 1890's were the heyday of hoaxing by British aristocrats.) Although a prominent oceanographer has perpetuated the Davis story, it seems to have been a journalistic hoax.

swallowed ship, they heard voices coming from the cabin. Warily they peered down the companionway; there they saw the captain and mate, arguing about the reckoning.

WRECK OF THE ESSEX

In 1821 Owen Chase, mate of Nantucket's *Essex,* published an account of what happened one day in the Pacific when he was forced back to his ship because a whale had stove a hole in his whaleboat. Two other boats were still out when, to the amazement of those on the *Essex,* a whale appeared and attacked the ship. Aspects of this incident were retold in Herman Melville's *Moby-Dick.* As Chase put it:

A very large spermaceti whale, about 85 feet in length, broke water off our weather bow. He spouted two or three times and then disappeared. In less than two or three seconds he came up again, about the length of the ship off, and made directly for us, at the rate of about three knots. The ship was then going with about the same velocity. He came down upon us with full speed and struck the ship with his head; he gave us such an appalling and tremendous jar as nearly threw us all on our faces. The ship brought up as suddenly and violently as if she had struck a rock, and trembled for a few seconds like a leaf. We looked at each other with perfect amazement, deprived almost of the power of speech. He passed under the ship, grazing her keel as he went along, came up alongside of her to leeward, and lay on the top of the water (apparently stunned with the violence of the blow) for the space of a minute; he then suddenly started off to leeward. Recovering, in some measure, I concluded he had stove a hole in the ship and that it would be necessary to set the pumps going. Accordingly they were rigged but had not been in operation more than one minute before I perceived the head of the ship to be gradually settling down in the water. I ordered the signal to be set for the other whaleboats, which scarcely had I dispatched before I again discovered the whale, apparently in convulsions, on the top of the water, about 100 rods to leeward. He was enveloped in the foam of the sea that his continual and violent thrashing about in the water had created around him, and I could distinctly see him smite his jaws together as if distracted with rage and fury. He remained a short time in this situation and then started off with great velocity, across the bows of the ship, to windward. The ship settled down in the water and I gave her up as lost. I turned to the boats with an intention of clearing them away.

I was aroused by the cry of a man at the hatchway, "Here he is—he is making for us again." I turned around and saw him about 100 rods directly ahead of us, coming down with twice his ordinary speed and, to me at that moment it appeared, with tenfold fury and vengeance in his aspect. The surf flew in all directions about him; his head was about half out of water, and in that way he came upon and again struck the ship. I bawled out to the helmsman, "Hard up!" but she had not fallen off more than a point before we took the second shock. I should judge the speed of the ship to have been at this time about three knots and that of the whale about six. He struck her to windward, directly under the cathead [strongest part of the ship], and completely stove in her bows. He passed under the ship again, went off to leeward, and we saw no more of him. We were more than a thousand miles from the nearest land, and with nothing but a light open boat. I or-

"John Tabor's Ride" took place atop a speeding whale: Tabor uses a stuck harpoon for helm in J. Ross Browne's work from his 1846 *Etchings of a Whaling Cruise.*

Hidden Meanings

Few hidden meanings lurk in the seacraft of scrimshaw, but tattooing, the carving of figureheads, and the tying of knots are fraught with symbolism. Tattooing originally developed among primitive peoples as a way of providing themselves with magical protection. The signs they used had special, mostly forgotten meanings—American sailors believed, for example, that a pig tattooed on one foot and a rooster on the other would prevent drowning, because those animals despised the water. Actually the symbols stem from days when the rooster's power to dispel the demons of night by his crowing had made him sacred to Persephone, queen of the underworld. The pig, too, was sacred to Persephone and even

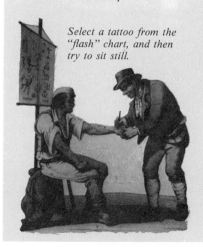

Select a tattoo from the "flash" chart, and then try to sit still.

The lady is Hope, from a ship of the same name; the man, unknown.

more so to her mother, Demeter, the great earth goddess. Those deities, it was believed, would come to the aid of a drowning man.

HARD LUCK tattooed on the knuckles of the hands would bring good luck to one; a lover's knot kept the sweetheart true; a cross on the right arm ensured shore burial to the dead sailor cast on Catholic shores; a dripping dagger on the left arm meant bravery. Done with a pin or needle and ink, tattooing tested the young sailor who showed himself a man by bearing up stoically under this initiation rite: later he could flex his biceps and make the naked woman there writhe seductively. At one time U.S. sailors had to get dresses tattooed on such dancers on reenlistment.

Knowing knots was a sailor's business. He knotted the rope closing his own bag of possessions with a thief's knot that resembled the ordinary reef knot. The looter would retie with a reef knot and so alert the owner. A hangman's knot with 13 turns jinxed a ship, so there existed a taboo against tying one while underway.

In ancient Egypt and India, eyes were painted on either side of a craft's prow to allow the boat, anthropomorphized, to be on the lookout for danger in fogbanks or darkness. Later, vessels bore identification that suggested the name of the ship, or its owner, or the city from which it came: the Athenians, for instance, carried statues of Athena on their ships and by appropriate rites could induce the goddess' protective presence aboard. The terrifying Norse boats were designed with dragons' heads at their bows, tails at their sterns, and oars to resemble moving legs in order to scare off enemies and sea creatures. Centuries later American ships signaled their identity by carrying such figureheads as Indians or an Abraham Lincoln.

---

dered the men to cease pumping and everyone to provide for himself; seizing a hatchet at the same time, I cut away the lashings of the spare boat and cried out to those near me to take her as she came down. The steward had in the meantime gone down into the cabin twice and saved two quadrants, two practical navigators, and the captain's trunk and mine; all of which were hastily thrown into the boat as she lay on deck. The ship had filled with water and was going down on her beamends. We shoved our boat into the water, all hands jumping in her at the same time, and were scarcely two boat's lengths distant from her when she fell over to windward and settled down. From the time we were first attacked by the whale, to our leaving in the boat, more than 10 minutes could not have elapsed! We lay in our boat, about two ship's lengths off from the wreck, in perfect silence, calmly contemplating her situation, and absorbed in our own melancholy reflections when the other harpoon boats were discovered rowing up to us. The sudden and mysterious disappearance of the ship was first discovered by the boatsteerer in the captain's boat, and with a horror-struck countenance and voice he suddenly exclaimed: "Oh, my God! Where is the ship?"

(It may be noted that of the twenty in the crew, eight survived. The three whaleboats got to an island whence three crew members who chose to stay were later rescued. The others set off again. One boat was lost but the others sailed a total of 3,700 miles to safety—one of the greatest feats at sea. Two men were given a sea burial but the next seven to die were eaten, among them a cabin boy who had drawn the lot of sacrifice.)

GHOST SHIPS
And Spectral Sailors

After the schooner Haskell *accidentally cut the* Johnston *in half off George's Bank during the 1870's, the* Johnston's *26 drowned sailors appeared aboard the* Haskell *as dripping shades who fished over her rail with shadowy gear whenever the unfortunate schooner anchored there. When word got around, no one would sign on the* Haskell *and she rotted at a Gloucester pier. That the dead return to aid or harm the living is one of the oldest beliefs of man, and it surfaces in sinister marine versions. Ghost ships are an elaboration of the same fearful tradition.*

SALEM'S SPECTER SHIP

We were Salem men aboard the *Neptune* ending a 16 months' voyage on the shortest day of the year, in time for Christmas. Salem's a town that holds people wherever they roam— we remain Salem men until death. Legend has it that no matter where its body dies, the spirit returns.

Captain Low had taken two of us boys on the voyage. There I was, not yet 15, returning from a voyage that had doubled both capes, I who had yet to see Boston, 16 miles from Salem. I had some 80 silver dollars due me, silk for a dress for my mother, a pipe for my father, a Chinese doll for my sister, and genuine Calcutta bandannas for all my relatives. Our practical education was in the hands of an elderly sailmaker, "Sails." We learned to knot, reeve, and splice, to hand, reef, and steer.

We learned the sealore, the legends, and the salty speech. Sails' favorite topic was the ghost ships. He had seen them all, the *Flying Dutchman,* the *Carmilhan,* the *Palatine,* the *Breeze,* and *Jessie.* Many were the watches we spent on the cold wintry deck while doubling the Cape of Good Hope looking for the Dutchman. "Do not speak to him," Sails said. "If he asks your position, shrug your shoulders; if he asks for water, point to the sea. His last appeal will be for you to take letters for his beloved wife. Do not take them, for your ship will never reach port."

Now returning to Salem, we had but one regret, we had seen no ghostly ships. The Old Man always boasted of his ship, so responsive she could be brought to port by a couple of boys, and now I was at the helm and Jack was on lookout. Darkness

had already fallen. Old Sails was standing near the wheel. The pilot, Mr. Cates, was giving his orders in his quiet voice. We would make a running moor, take in our canvas, and warp into our berth. The men were laughing and telling each other what they'd be having for supper.

Then Jack screamed: "Astern! Look astern! Ship ho!" Thoughtlessly I turned and looked aft. A great ship, under full sail, four times the size of the *Neptune,* was bearing down upon us. I threw the helm over hard to port, believing I could throw the brig over enough to ease a dead-on crash. The wheel was roughly taken from my hands and I was crowded off the grating. The wheel spun back to its old position, and a calm voice was saying, "Steady, lad, steady." The crash I had been expecting did not come.

Lifting my head I saw the giant vessel veer slightly and come along our starboard side, crowding us, but with no splintering of wood against wood, no rush of water—and she was making 15 knots to our 8—no creaking and straining of ropes and canvas, only a grim and glowing silence. Every sail was set, every rope taut or coiled and flemished on her deck, yet with not a sailor in sight. The strange ship seemed to fade away as though she had entered a dense fog. Old Sails was sucking his breath, eyes bugging out of his gaunt features, his knees shaking. Mr. Cates was pressing a silver flask on the old man and saying in his quiet voice: "It's the Ghost Ship. A proper Salem man has died somewhere and the ship is bringing his spirit home to Salem, home for Christmas."

THE LUCY JACKSON

The *Lucy Jackson* was such a splendid craft that it was hard for the Gloucester people to understand why she changed owners so often. Somebody would buy her, fit her for a run to the Banks, then suddenly sell her for less than she had cost him. When the *Lucy* had been sold four times in as many weeks, the men of Gloucester demanded the reason.

Common in both the folklore and real-life experience of the sea is the person adrift in the lifeboat, a situation eerily depicted in Albert P. Ryder's painting "Constance."

The *Lucy,* it was learned, had a ghost. The various owners tried to sell before damaging rumors had gone too far. There was no question but that several people had seen a white figure that moved about the deck and entered the cabin to lose itself among the smells and shadows of the hold. This was no invention of nervous persons, for it had been seen by unsuperstitious fishermen.

The last purchaser was Jake Davenport. "What do I care for ghosts?" he asked. "They say the *Lucy* lost some men on the Banks—if it's any comfort to the poor devils to keep their berths, I guess we can let them stay." Brave words. Davenport knew, as well as anybody, he would have a hard time shipping a crew. He went down to the wharf and "botched around" till night fell and the harbor was deserted. A fog came in, dulling the few lamps to be seen ashore, so he lighted a lantern and continued his explorations. She was a lonesome tub, he had to admit. He also decided the mice, rats, and roaches emphasized the loneliness more than usual. He found the forecastle, smelling of stale pipe smoke and moldy boots, in a dreadful state and he began to pile up old boxes, tin pans, and torn oilskins, intending to pitch them overboard.

Suddenly he was interrupted by a groan. Standing motionless, Jake listened intently, and then began to relax, for he heard merely the schooner rubbing against the timbers of the wharf. Possibly the wind was coming up. He would just gather the rubbish and come around in the morning to finish clearing up, before his lantern went out.

At that moment he heard the groan again! Jake felt a sudden chill, and for a moment his legs refused to move. Giving way to panic wouldn't help. The groan came again, this time from below deck. Climbing down the narrow, greasy companion hatchway, Jake held the lantern above his head and looked around. It was deserted. There was a faint roll in the water, with the noise of choppy gurgles from under the wharf, nothing else.

Tied to the old tales of Cain, of compact with the Devil, and of the sailor cursed to endless wandering, the Flying Dutchman's saga is worldwide. His ship glows; its figurehead is a skeleton; its sailors all are specters: the illustration here is by Howard Pyle.

Going aft, he found that he had left his peajacket in the cabin. Putting it on, he started to leave. Hardly had he passed the hatch when an awful groan was heard, and something in white came slowly up the ladder.

Jake's scalp started to slide back. His eyes began to pop, while his mouth pulled open in a grin of abject terror. In a frenzy he clutched a swordfish lance. The specter was on deck, groaning and reaching toward him. Taking careful aim, Jake flung the spear. The ghost fell to the deck with a shriek. This seemed human and substantial, and therefore comforting. Jake put his lantern close to the mystery. It wore boots—No. 10's.

It was bleeding, for the spear had grazed its neck. It was also swearing. Jake tugged at the white wrappings.

"Abe Dimmock, you old fool! This is pretty business for a grown man. And you the skipper of this very boat once. Well, I've got my flask of Medford rum. Take a pull, and I'll tie up your neck." Later the former captain confessed he had been playing ghost to bring a bad name to the schooner, so that her cost would be brought down to $3,000, the amount he had. He recovered, sailed aboard the *Lucy Jackson* as mate, and was drowned off the Cape years later. Since becoming a real ghost, he has not been seen on board at all.

SHIPWRECK!
Disaster at Sea

Shipwreck is the most terrifying event at sea. When such a disaster occurs, it inevitably makes cowards of some and heroes of others like Rasmus Midgett who rode his horse seven times into the ebbing tide near Hatteras Island, North Carolina, to rescue survivors of the Priscilla; *when the horse tired, he swam back and forth himself for the last three. Pathos abounds in disaster stories, where starvation and freezing are as threatening as the all-feared death by drowning.*

THE WRECK OF THE ASIA

Longfellow's "Wreck of the Hesperus" is reminiscent of the story of the wreck of the *Asia*. During a February storm in 1898, the Nantucket Shoals caught the *Asia* and she heeled over. Capt. George Dakin was frantic with fear that his wife and 11-year-old daughter, Lena, who were aboard, would be lost. But he did his utmost to maintain discipline. Suddenly his little daughter came rushing on deck in her nightclothes. "Oh, Daddy, what will we do?" "Everything will be all right. Don't worry, Lena," he said. Chief Mate Cook called the captain aside. During the voyage from Manila he had been a friend to the girl: "No matter what happens, I'll look out for Lena," he told the father. Captain Dakin knew what was ahead. He was not going to be able to aid his family

when the time came, as he would obey the traditions of the sea and be the last to leave the ship. He looked at Mr. Cook. Cook waved his hand and the captain was reassured.

Without warning, the sea burst over the side. Captain Dakin forced the others out the hatchway onto the deck. When his turn came, he was tumbled by a giant wave into the cabin and drowned. The ship began to break up. As Lena clung to Mr. Cook, she began to cry. "Oh, please throw me overboard! So I can go to Jesus. For I know Jesus will take me!" The mizzenmast plunged into the surf. Next the starboard quarter went, carrying away Cook still holding Lena. Later the bodies of Cook and Lena were discovered frozen to death, tied to fragments of the starboard quarter. The chief officer was found clinging to the body of the

blue-eyed girl he had sworn to protect from the sea. Cook had kept his word—for although the girl had frozen, she had not drowned.

FIRE!

All that is left of the ancient ceremony of christening a ship is the breaking of a wine bottle and the naming, but to sailors these are of great importance. Accidents on this occasion give the ship a bad name, and the use of anything but alcohol is sure to bring ill luck. Such was the case of the *Great Republic,* biggest clippership of its time, launched at Boston in 1853 in the presence of a huge crowd. It had long been East and South Boston's boast that they had more grogshops than public waterpumps. Just before the launch, the water mains bringing in the new Cochituate water were completed, and it became the aim of temperance advocates to see that water got an even break with whisky. The shipbuilder was pressed to permit his great vessel to be baptized in water from this new source. He consented, and his brother, who was to command the new ship on her maiden voyage, broke a bottle of water over her bow, naming her *Great Republic.* So violently did the ship resent this treatment that she literally leaped from the ways, and it was only through the use of two heavy anchors and a powerful tugboat that she was kept from venting her wrath on the Chelsea Bridge. After receiving her spars at the Navy Yard, the *Great Republic* was towed to New York. By midnight on the eve of sailing, she was almost loaded at her Front Street pier. The two brothers sat aboard her, drinking to a successful voyage, when the cry of "Fire!" rang out—somehow the ship's tightly furled main topgallant sail had caught fire. Flames ran along her cordage to the main royal and skysails. The top of the 130-foot mast could not be reached with water from a hand en-

Calamity reigns in the hostile sea of C. J. Vernet's oil "Seascape: The Storm."

"They're Saved! They're Saved!" And just in time, in this scene by Currier and Ives.

gine. The brothers offered $1,000 to any man who would go aloft and cut off the fire and the mainmast, but no one took them up on it. No one at the time went so far as to charge that the disaster was due to the water baptism, but there can be little doubt that many sailors would have preferred other berths to sailing in a vessel that had been humiliated in such a manner.

IN THE RIGGING

During the blizzard of January 7, 1866, some 20 vessels and 100 sailors were lost between Cape Elizabeth and New York. On Martha's Vine-

yard the roaring of the blizzard was so strong that Cape Poge's lighthouse keeper, George Marchant, could not hear 20 feet away. During the first part of the storm, Marchant worried about a schooner which was close to Hawes Shoal. Late Monday a partial clearing developed and Marchant sighted the shape of an ice-covered schooner. A breaker hit the schooner and went nearly 60 feet into the air. The storm shut in again and the wreck faded from sight. Marchant sent a message to Edgartown. As he expected, the lifesavers believed it would be some time before they could venture out.

When the schooner *Christina* had hit the shoal Sunday, the surf drenched the six men aboard. Mate Tallman knew that all would freeze to death if help did not come soon. "Let's dress heavily," he suggested. The men treated his remarks with contempt, as three out of five sailors drowned at sea and the average sailor didn't learn to swim. At least they didn't need to weigh themselves down. The schooner settled into the shoal, her bottom torn open, but her hull was strong. The men watched as the water rose higher and higher. Tallman proceeded to dress himself in layers of clothing and crawled into his bunk. Monday the crew agreed they should climb into the rigging. Most were soon in the shrouds, looking down at the thundering surf. Captain Leach stayed such a long time getting his valuables that he was wet up to his armpits when he climbed. Leach died within an hour. Two of the crew froze to death before nightfall: one dropped off into the sea; the other froze to the rigging.

During the settling of the schooner, Tallman's feet had become wet and he lost his mittens when he went aloft, but sighting the church spires of his village, he was determined to stay alive. Every so often he would beat his hands against the rigging to

FOLKWAYS

Frognostication

Sailors can read weather signs in the action of wind and water, fish and birds, and from sounds and lights. This ability to predict the weather has always been vital to safe sailing. When today's sophisticated measuring machinery konks out, sailors still rely on the old lore. As the cartoon from the 1878 *World Almanac* suggests, the old ways are very reliable. There is the barometric bottle and its accouterments—but all you really need is the frog. A frog croaks before rain.

Much lore was based on observed responses to a change in barometric pressure: if a teakettle boils quickly, the weather will change. Lore also

arose from observations combined with common sense. A red moon means wind; a pale one, rain. A ring around the moon means a storm due as many days later as there are stars within the ring. On the North Atlantic coast, when the stars appear far off and dim there will be foul weather. If they seem near, it will be cold. Phosphorescence in the water on a summer night indicates a blow. Swallows flying low over water mean rain, and gulls go inland before a gale. Dew on a spider-web means good weather. If spiders run an extra line around their webs, you can be sure of bad weather, as you can when you hear the "singing of the sea" or the sound of stones being drawn to sea in the retreating waves.

regain circulation. The surviving members of the crew were the cook and the cabin boy, and they began to freeze on Tuesday. Early in the afternoon the cook died, leaving Tallman and the cabin boy. They talked about their chances for life and had practically agreed to join hands and leap into the sea, but Tallman changed his mind. Less than an hour later the boy froze to death.

At daybreak Wednesday, Tallman's thirst was so overwhelming he climbed down to the icy ratlines above the sea and broke off chunks of ice to eat. When he climbed back into the rigging he became sick, for the saltwater ice acted as an emetic.

At the lighthouse the keeper had been observing the wreck with his spyglass. When Tallman started down the rigging, Marchant sent his second message to Edgartown. The rescue team would leave before dawn on Thursday. On the wreck Tallman watched Wednesday's darkness gather and, believing he might fall off his perch into the sea, climbed just under the futtock shrouds, through which he forced his arms. All that long night he hung suspended, his feet twisted into the rigging below. When the first glow of dawn was seen, Tallman offered a prayer to God for still being alive. Then he saw the whaleboat approaching. Almost blind from the frozen salt covering his face, he tried to shout and discovered his jaws were frozen together. Rescuers started up the icy ratlines. They reached the body of Leach, which had jackknifed in the rigging. Next came the body of the cabin boy. Ten feet higher they saw Tallman, now groaning as hard as he could in his efforts to be noticed. Finally the two men climbed to him and made sure he was alive.

"Lower away," came the order, and the near-frozen mate was let down into the lifeboat. Stimulants were poured down his throat. Two days later the local physician was forced to amputate the ends of his fingers, and later both feet. For the remainder of his life the only way he could walk was on crutches.

OLD STORMALONG
Super Sailor

Old Stormalong, a super sailor who stood fathoms, rather than feet, tall, was invented by the men who sailed out of the New England ports. The seagoing giant was undaunted by the worst blow and unintimidated by the largest whale. In fact, it was said he could throw a harpoon 25 fathoms and haul the beasts directly aboard ship, eliminating the need for whaleboats. Other samples of his talents:

Of the oldtime Yankee deep-water sailormen, Alfred Bull-top Stormalong, A.B.S., soon became the popular hero. He was familiarly known as Old Stormie and every old salt knew him or had heard of him. The *A.B.S.* placed after his name stands for "able-bodied seaman." He was a master mariner and after years became the skipper of a big square-rigger. Hundreds of tall yarns of his prowess have been spun on the decks of old wooden sailing ships. No literary shark could gather them all.

Old Stormalong was a great eater. When he settled down to a repast he kept the sea cooks busy scurrying about with his viands. He ate his whale soup from a Cape Cod boat. Whale and shark steaks rare were his favorite meats. He liked ostrich eggs for breakfast, either boiled or poached. But these were not always obtainable. Because of his great fondness for them quite a trade in ostrich fruit was early built up between New England and the Dark Continent. His favorite beverages were whale oil or whale milk cut with Maine hard cider. This was conveyed to him through a firehose. It took a big vat of this liquid nourishment to wash down his food. After his repasts he would walk the deck, picking his teeth with a marlinespike.

Once, when the whaling fleet was on the whaling grounds in the North Atlantic, Old Stormie sighted a whole school of whales. The skipper gave the order to hoist the mudhook and take after them. They pulled and hauled with all their might but could not budge it. A wily old giant devilfish bent on mischief had taken hold of it. With some of his arms he had

hold of the cable and with the others he was holding to the rocks and seaweed on the bottom. Stormie leaped over the side of the ship with his big knife in his teeth. What he did to that devilfish it would take a month of Sundays to tell. Stormie succeeded in freeing the anchor. In a spirit of revenge he tied the arms of that devilfish in sailor's knots. Some of them the monster was never able to undo.

The biggest ship he ever sailed on was the *Albatross,* a huge four-master out of Boston, even though Boston Harbor was not big enough for her. When she arrived at a port, her cargo had to be transferred to ordinary ships to land it. This vessel was so large that all of the officers and some of the crew were mounted on horses. No sailor, however sharp his eyesight, could see from one end to the other. There was a whole hour's difference in time between her bow and her stern. The rigging was so immense that no man could take in her sails at a single glance. It took five men, each looking as far as he could, to see the top of a mast. Her masts penetrated the clouds. The tops were hinged. Thus they could be bent down to let the sun and the moon go by. Her sails were so immense that all of the sailmakers in Boston were taken into the Sahara Desert, where there was plenty of room, to sew them. Young men who were sent

Old Stormie was the tall tale gone to sea, the personification of the sailor's desire to conquer unconquerable nature and rule the ocean. The Great Captain appears at right with nineteenth-century ships and some creatures as fantastic as he.

241

aloft to furl or unfurl them generally came down as graybeards. The skipper had to order all hands aloft a week before a storm. At that some of them got to the yards too late.

The *Albatross* carried a crew of 1,000 sailors. None of these Jack Tars ever saw even a quarter of their shipmates. When all hands were ordered forward, it took some of the unmounted ones a whole week to get there. Some of the seamen got lost because they failed to take their compasses along.

It took 34 men to turn the ship's steering wheel. Old Stormie was the only man who could do it alone. Turning it easily with one hand, he helped himself to a bite of Navy Twist with the other. With him at the wheel she could ride out any storm that ever blew. She was so big that she had to keep to the ocean. Some of the deep bays in America's coastline are merely dents she made in turning around. Once she managed to navigate through the English Channel. The skipper had her sides well soaped for that. She got into those British waters by mistake, and she had to see the adventure through. The Dover cliffs scraped off all the soap on her starboard side. This, they say, explains their pure white color.

Stormie visited many foreign countries during his voyages. Once, in Italy, he leaned for just a few minutes against the tower of Pisa, and it has been away out of plumb ever since. In Australia he cast away his clothing and bought new gear at a slopshop. The fleas all got away. They call them kangaroos down there now.

When Old Stormie "passed in his checks" he was mourned by American sailormen on every sea in every port. It took 10 acres of silk sailcloth to make his shroud. His burial at sea was most impressive. The funeral procession of ghost ships was led by the famous *Flying Dutchman*. Legions of sea horses followed in their wake. Thus passed from human sight Alfred Bulltop Stormalong, A.B.S., legendary hero of the oldtime Yankee deepwater sailormen.

ANOTHER HAND

Many songs that today evoke a nostalgia for days under sail were actually the necessary accompaniment to the sailor's backbreaking work. "A chantey," said one old salt, "is another hand on the rope." Chanteys helped the men establish rhythm and precise timing as they pulled together to haul ropes, hoist sails, and weigh anchor.

The use of songs to increase efficiency goes back to ancient times; the height of sea chanteying, however, was reached during the mid-19th century when whaling, merchant, and fishing vessels crossed the seas to ports all over the world. Three types of chantey were sung, depending on the work to be performed: the short-haul was the simplest, used for hauling jobs that took only a few quick but vigorous pulls; the halyard or long-haul chantey accompanied longer jobs, such as hoisting the yards (rods that support sails); the capstan or windlass chantey was still more elaborate, sung at slower tempo and suited to the sustained effort of "breaking out" a heavy anchor from the bottom.

Another type of sea song was the "fo'c'sle" song, sung strictly for enter-

THE STATELY SOUTHERNER

'Tis of a state-ly south-er-ner who flew the Stars and Stripes, The whist-ling wind from west nor'west blew through our pitch-pine spars, We had our lar-board tacks on board as we hung up-on a gale, And Greb-le Is-land light shone bright from the old head of Kin-sale.

What looms upon our starboard bow, what nags upon the breeze?
'Tis then our good ship hauled her wind abreast the old Saltees.
For by her ponderous press of sail and by her stunted spars
We saw that our morning visitor was a British man-o'-war.

What did our daring foeman do? A shot ahead he passed,
Clewed up his flowing courses, laid his topsails to the mast.
Those British tars gave three huzzas from the deck of their black corvette,
But we answered back with a scornful laugh as our starry flag we set.

Out spake our noble captain then, not a cloud was on his brow:
"Stand by, my gallant heroes all, the enemy's on us now.
We carry aloft the Stars and Stripes against old England's boast.
Paul Jones, the terror of the sea, will fly them on her coast!"

ainment. Sometimes accompanied by an accordion, the men sang ballads of ships, lost loves, storms, shipwrecks, battles, and sudden death. "The State-y Southerner" is a forecastle ballad escribing one of John Paul Jones' aids during the Revolution. It became o popular that even the "limeys" ved and sang it.

The lyrics of "The Drunken Sail-r," a halyard chantey, mirror the self-nposed belief that all sailors went on debauched binge when they hit port ter months—or years—aboard. (At ght, three drunken sailors disrupt ctivities on a New York wharf.) The ort-haul chantey "Boney Was a War-or" celebrates Napoleon's exploits.

THE DRUNKEN SAILOR

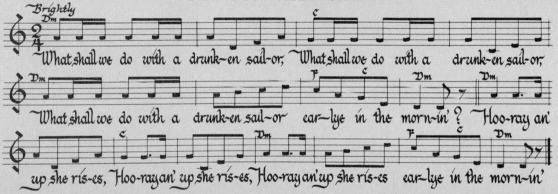

What shall we do with a drunk-en sail-or, What shall we do with a drunk-en sail-or,
What shall we do with a drunk-en sail-or ear-lye in the morn-in'? Hoo-ray an'
up she ris-es, Hoo-ray an' up she ris-es, Hoo-ray an' up she ris-es ear-lye in the morn-in'

Put him in the longboat till he's sober,
Put him in the longboat till he's sober,
Put him in the longboat till he's sober,
Earlye in the mornin'.

Pull out the plug and wet him all over,
Pull out the plug and wet him all over,
Pull out the plug and wet him all over,
Earlye in the mornin'.

Sailors pass time in the forecastle gossiping, yarning, fighting, and singing.

BONEY WAS A WARRIOR

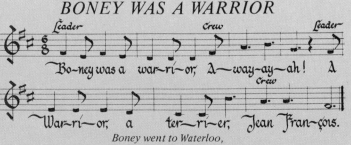

Bo-ney was a war-ri-or, A—way-ay-ah! A
War-ri-or, a ter-ri-er, Jean Fran-çois.

Boney went to Waterloo,
Away-ay-ah!
There he got his overthrow,
Jean François.

MERFOLK AND SEA SERPENTS
Enchantresses and Creepy Creatures

Merfolk, tritons, sirens, and sea serpents have inhabited people's imaginations the world over from time immemorial—Dagon, one of the chief gods of the Phoenicians, was a merman; the horned serpent of the Aztecs, the Loch Ness monster, and the creatures that rise out of the deep to make the earth a living nightmare in today's chillers are all of a piece. Along the same lines, 19th-century America could boast not only such literary creations as the white whale of Melville's Moby-Dick *but a rich folklore of marine prodigies. Here are a few good examples:*

TALLEST OF THEM ALL

A retired whaling captain in Sag Harbor, Long Island, had the tallest sea serpent story of them all for his grandchildren. If pressed, he would allow that he hadn't been an eyewitness himself, though "it was easier to tell that way"—but maintained that it had all really happened to some of his crewmen:

On that voyage we'd set sail on a Friday [an unlucky day for a whaling voyage to start] and as a result of this bad move were having a very poor catch. Then we lost our bearings in a storm below the Cape and drifted for days. After a while we realized we were in the waters of the Antarctic. One day we fetched up at an island. We tried to put ashore, but the thing moved—it was a sea serpent. We

rested quietly, hoping he wouldn't harm us. But the sea serpent put his tail in his mouth and went to sleep, enclosing us in a lagoon. We were really in a fix. How would we ever escape? Finally we got an idea. He was so big that if you cut a canal through his back, he'd never even feel it—it would be just like a pin scratch. So we started cutting the blubber away, and this animal's blubber was such as we had never seen before. So we tried it in the trypots and discovered that it was the finest oil that you could ever find. It was even better than the best whale oil we had ever prepared. Our catch was bad, and we thought the monster wouldn't miss a few ton of his hide. We loaded the ship with blubber and oil. What we couldn't boil down we

"Old Father Neptune and his Wife" were spotted and sketched in November 1852 by a whimsical passenger on board a San Francisco-bound clipper as she crossed the Equator 25 days from New York.

stored, because we wanted to get out of that place as quick as we could and take as much of the oil and blubber as possible. But just as we had pulled out of the canal we had cut, the serpent woke up and started chasing us. His breath was so strong that we put up full sail and could keep a good distance ahead of him. We had a cannon aboard ship and used all our ammunition on him, but the cannonballs bounced off his hide like marbles. Finally we took a keg of nails and fired them into his mouth. They went in his throat, and he at last gave up the chase.

After the reported appearance of the Gloucester sea serpent in 1817, the beast surfaced down the coast in Boston Harbor and upset a fishing vessel. A Frenchman engraved this version of the event after it was described to him by an American eyewitness.

KELPIES

From Scotland we get another fabulous creature of the Celtic imagination, the kelpie, who appears on dry land as a beautifully harnessed horse and specializes in enticing children and travelers to ride him in order to drown them. To women and girls it may also appear as a handsome youth with seaweed in his hair, or water dripping from his clothes. At certain spots along America's east coast the story lives on to this day; Marylanders say the kelpie is a red horse that comes out of the sea and seems friendly. If you mount him he will take you down under the sea, where you can live—but it is impossible to return to land. A boy saw a kelpie and, not knowing what it was, stroked its muzzle. Instantly he was glued to the beast and found himself being carried headlong toward the sea. Quick as a flash, he drew his knife and slashed off his hand. He was none too quick, for the waterhorse plunged into the sea, leaving him on the very edge.

SIRENS

One form Mediterranean mermaids often took was that of a siren, one of the sweet-voiced swimming and flying denizens of the deep who enticed sailors to their death by drowning. Appropriately, when sirens crossed to the New World they headed for Southern California, if the tale told by the first U.S. settlers of the region is to be believed. According to the forty-niners, local Mexicans considered Santa Barbara Island in the Pacific, 40 miles offshore from Los Angeles, to be a headquarters of sirens because of the yells and screams and strange songs fishermen heard as they sailed past it. When that happened, the story goes, Mexican crewmen regularly crossed themselves and begged their captains to give the rock a wide berth. But the Anglo newcomers soon found out what was causing the weird noises: Santa Barbara Island's sole inhabitants turned out to be cats, the meowing, caterwauling offspring of a tabby shipwrecked in a bygone age. What

American primitive artist Mary Ann Willson depicted this "Marimaid" in about 1820 as a decently clad lady with the hind quarters of a sea serpent wrapped in a crazy quilt. The prim mermaiden holds a lance and a snake instead of the traditional mirror and comb.

sounded (when heard out on the water) like the siren's song was in fact the noise of cats quarreling over their supper—dead fish and seagull eggs —of which there was never quite enough to go around.

MERFOLK

The idea of a race of near humans inhabiting the sea is age-old and widespread. Although American Indians believed in a kind of merfolk, the sailors' mermaids and mermen came to us direct from the mother country and are most deeply rooted in the folk traditions of its Celtic peoples—Irish, Scots, Cornish, and Welsh. Human from the waist up and fish beneath, merfolk all yearn for a soul but can get one only by marrying a mortal; to this end they sometimes entice human beings to live with them beneath the sea. Moreover, the mermaids' song (like that of the sirens, with whom they are often equated) may send a man to sleep or

drive him mad. Their "note" (as Shakespeare called it) is also a portent of impending storms, for merfolk enjoy storms and are sad in calm weather. In fact, when becalmed, they sometimes board ships at night and weight them down, sinking them. Mermen are often considered to be the spirits of drowned sailors. Both male and female merfolk take terrible vengeance when wronged.

SEA SERPENT OF 1817

A huge sea serpent was reportedly seen by many persons in and around Gloucester Harbor in August 1817. It was later sighted in Long Island Sound, while at the same time back in Gloucester, where many people believed it had come ashore by night to lay eggs, a three-foot blacksnake was killed in the belief that it was a hatchling sea serpent—much to the delight of skeptics. A debate not unlike that which in recent times has centered on the existence of the Loch

Ness monster was to continue for several years thereafter, and a number of affidavits from purported eye-witnesses were collected by members of New England's Linnaean Society in Boston. A typical example:

"I, MATTHEW GAFFNEY, of Gloucester, in the County of Essex, Ship Carpenter, depose and say: That on the 14th day of August, A.D. 1817, between the hours of four and five o'clock in the afternoon, I saw a strange marine animal, resembling a serpent in the harbor in said Gloucester. I was in a boat, and was within 30 feet of him. His head appeared full as large as a four-gallon keg, his body as large as a barrel, and his length that I saw I should judge 40 feet at least. The top of his head was of a dark color, and the underpart of his head appeared nearly white, as did also several feet of his belly that I saw. I supposed and do believe that the whole of his belly was nearly white. I fired at him when he was the nearest to me. I had a good gun and took good aim. I aimed at his head and think I must have hit him. He turned towards us immediately after I had fired, and I thought he was coming at us; but he sunk down and went directly under our boat and made his appearance at about 100 yards from where he sunk. He did not turn down like a fish but appeared to settle directly down, like a rock. My gun carries a ball of 18 to the pound, and I suppose there is no person in town more accustomed to shooting than I am. I have seen the animal at several other times but never had so good a view of him as on this day. His motion was vertical, like a caterpillar."

The Linnaean Society official in charge of the sea serpent investigation later questioned Gaffney:

Q. How fast did it move?
A. I should say he moved at the rate of a mile in two or at most three minutes.
Q. Does he turn quick and short, and if so, what is the form of path that he makes in turning?
A. He turns quick and short, and the first part of the curve that he makes in turning is in the form of a staple [i.e., the sea serpent made U-turns], but his head seems to approach rapidly towards his body, his head and tail moving in opposite directions, and when his head and tail come parallel they appear almost to touch each other.
Q. Did he appear more shy after you had fired at him?
A. He did not, but continued playing as before.

The witness was then sworn on a Bible as to the truth of his statements. A short while later a bigger and better sea serpent was reported in Provincetown, on Cape Cod. The Gloucester serpent's head had looked to Matthew Gaffney like a 4-gallon keg; the Provincetown monster's head was like a 200-gallon cask, rose 30 feet in the air, with six red and green eyes and four rows of teeth. First observed by the town crier, who lay hidden in a plumberry bush, the creature rose out of Herring Cove, slithered across the dunes, mowing down underbrush and scrub pines in its path (which afterward had a burned, sulfurous look as if seared by a hot iron or a passing dragon), until it reached Pasture Pond and dived in headfirst like a duck. As the tip of its tail went under, the water began to recede from the shore. The waterline sank lower and lower, until a deep hole appeared in the pond's center. Sounding leads were lowered 300 fathoms down the hole, but no bottom was found.

BELOW THE BELT

The mermaid's reputation as an enchantress and cause of fatal allurements made her a natural subject for some mildly bawdy humor centered on the bottom half of her anatomy. For example, Capt. John Smith of Jamestown fame once sighted a mermaid in the West Indies. What he could see of her from the deck he examined closely—she was swimming about with extraordinary grace, he noted. He was very critical and found her finely shaped nose too short, and her well-formed ears too long—yet all in all, he thought, she was a very attractive woman. Just as he was about to lose his heart, the lady turned over, revealing an unbroken expanse of fish scales below the waist. His heart remained intact.

Merfolk often appeared as characters in the funny books of our great-grandparents' day. Here a shipwrecked sailor laughs in his merman rescuer's face: "'You,' says I, 'are the livin' image o' Teddy Mulcahey, what were fust mate o' the *Smokin' Sarah* an' were drowned. Are you him?' 'No, I are not him,' says he to me. 'My name are Benjamin B. Seagrave an' I never were a sailor, 'cause I are by birth and perfession a merman.'"

Seacurity

With nothing between himself and eternity but thin, wooden planks, the seaman lived in an uncertain world that he tried to shore up with myriad superstitions, customs, and beliefs. Some American sea superstitions stem from Christian Britain, but others involve some of man's oldest beliefs.

A ship had to be properly launched. That meant that no ship should be commissioned on a Friday, for that was the day of Christ's crucifixion. Today a proper launching involves a woman breaking a bottle of champagne on the new ship's prow. Until the 19th century the rite was performed by a minister or priest, a tradition that reaches far back into the pre-Christian era. The wine is a symbolic substitute for the blood of humans sacrificed to appease the gods of the elements and sea, who, happy with this initial smearing, would spare the lives of the craft's sailors. Vikings rolled new ships to the sea over bound slaves, whose crushed bodies provided an ample offering. The Greeks and Romans used wine to symbolize the blood of slain animals, which had replaced human sacrifices in some places. Occasionally, teetotaling Americans have christened ships with poor, thin stuff—water. According to legend, "Old Ironsides" balked twice at such treatment and did not budge until madeira was produced.

After the launching, clergy were taboo on board. They were the Devil's natural enemy and he would attack a clergy-bearing ship with winds—which all belonged to him. Whistling mocked the Devil and he responded to the insult with his infernal winds: so whistling was good when a ship was becalmed but deadly and forbidden in a blow. Women were unwelcome on board, and so were cats because of their connection with witches.

Anyone dressed in death's black might be a Jonah. A Jonah, as in the case of the unwilling prophet God called to distant travel, would only attract devilish forces and bring destruction, so once identified he had to be cast into the sea to calm the resulting storm. After he drowned he sank (unlike the original Jonah) into the ever-open locker, or coffin, of Davy

This dramatic painting by Howard Pyle illustrated a story in Harper's Monthly. *The belief that rats' departure from a ship means that it is sinking is accurate; living in the bowels of a ship the vermin are the first to be flooded out.*

Jones. All sailors buried at sea landed there. The name Jones was a corruption of Jonas or Jonah, and Davy comes from the word Deva, an abbreviation of "Devil."

During the first month on board, most sailors worked without pay. They'd gotten it on shore and spent it. When the second month loomed near, they gathered up old bedding and such and molded it into the shape of a horse. Then they pushed the horse into the sea. A 19th-century sailor would explain he was burying the "dead

horse" he felt he had been laboring for. But behind all that probably lay the ancient rite of sacrificing a horse to Neptune, god of both the sea and horses. Coins are set under masts or tossed into the sea for Neptune, too. So is the first fish caught, even today.

Sailors have long refused to kill certain birds that follow a ship, because they are believed to be the souls of dead seamen. On the other hand, a ship's crew rushed to kill trailing sharks because their presence meant a sick comrade would die.

THE SAILORS' UNDERWORLD
Villains and Victims

Sailors have a well-earned reputation for traveling in fast company, though historically they have more often been victims than villains. Ports of call were traditionally their undoing and San Francisco, where most of the tales recounted here originate, was among the most perilous. The ports offered temptations to match the wildest imaginings at sea—fast women, cheap liquor, and weeks of leave in which to spend their accumulated wages. Hordes of clever "crimps," or shanghaiers, saw to it that many of these travelers were back at sea sooner than they wished. As for marine crime, smuggling, with its aura of glamour, has enjoyed a certain measure of public approval, as some of the stories suggest.

The *Ark,* Asa Smith's bawdy houseboat in New Bedford Harbor; built on an old hulk, she was the scene of much shanghaiing until a mob smashed her up and sank her. A second "ark" of no better character replaced that one and before long met with a similar fate.

THE CRIMPS' TRADE

It was commonplace in ports like San Francisco, Port Townsend, Portland, and Seattle for whole crews to go off with "crimps," men engaged, often illegally, in the procurement of sailors. Masters dared not prevent these louts from boarding their ships because they knew they would be compelled to go to them for crew when the time came to leave again. The crimps were powerful, and they were a recognized institution.

As soon as the anchor of an arriving vessel was down, the crimps' runners would come over the side bringing bad whisky and worse promises. Within half an hour the ship, which had come in with a fine band of clean-living men, was transformed into a bedlam, and the sailors, their minds besotted with drink, were going off with the runners in boats to the shore, shouting and cursing and looking forward to a job with unlimited dollars. Anything did as a promised source of riches, even picking oranges or serving in a steam schooner on the coast. The very same night, if there were a homeward-bounder stuck for crew, those men might well find themselves, still stupid with drink, shipped away for a Cape Horn voyage. The boarding master would pocket their advance wages—and charge the ship whatever he could get for providing her with a crew, usually $100 a head.

Time and again the same man would submit to this kind of treatment. Why? The answer was in part that no one else welcomed him, and coming in after a long voyage, he was not his normal self. The smell of the land that first day put the lonely sailor off balance. He became a little lightheaded, perhaps, and the runners came quickly and took advantage of his vulnerability.

SHANGHAI KELLY

Most infamous of the crimps on the Barbary Coast [San Francisco's harbor district] was a slovenly, thickset Irishman, an irritable, red-whiskered fellow known as Shanghai Kelly. Though he would stop at nothing to get a crew, he preferred to handle real sailors, and by supplying them with "free" women, liquor, and accommodations, he attracted many who waited their turn to be shipped out. When there was a scarcity of hands, he often resorted to novel techniques to make up the deficiency.

On one such occasion, three ships lay in San Francisco Bay, all of them ready to sail as soon as crew could be provided; one was the notorious "hell wagon" *Reefer* of New York, and not a sailor could be found. The crimp's lieutenants spread the word along the Barbary Coast that it was Kelly's birthday and that all his friends were invited to join him for an excursion. There would be free food, drinks, and entertainment. Kelly had chartered the old paddle-wheeler *Goliath.*

When 90 men were aboard, word was given to cast off. As the craft churned out into the bay, the riffraff fell to eating and drinking. The *Goliath* cruised slowly until the doped liquor began taking effect on the guests. She then ranged alongside the waiting ships, and the picnickers were passed up, to be revived by mates when they were offshore and outward bound.

MISS PIGGOTT'S TRAP

Miss Piggott was a ferocious old woman who operated a saloon and boardinghouse on Frisco's Davis Street during the 1860's and 1870's. No one ever knew her first name; she insisted on being addressed, with proper respect, as Miss Piggott. Her only rival of importance as a female crimp was Mother Bronson, whose establishment was in Steuart Street. Both these ladies were their own bouncers and chief bartenders, but neither enforced her edicts with a bludgeon or a slungshot, as did some other notorious ladies elsewhere along the Barbary Coast. Miss Piggott remained faithful to the bung starter, a sort of wooden mallet used to knock out plugs in barrels, and in the use of this implement as a weapon she developed amazing skill. On the other hand Mother Bronson, who was nearly six feet tall and broad in proportion, scorned to use any other than Mother Nature's weapons. She possessed a fine and strong set of teeth, which she delighted to sink into the anatomy of an obstreperous customer; her enormous feet were encased in No. 12 brogans, and her fist was as hard as a rock and resembled in size a small ham. With the toe of her boot she once hoisted a Chinese from the floor of her saloon to the top of the bar, and she often boasted that she could fell an ox with one blow of her fist.

Sometimes Miss Piggott lacked enough sailors to round out an order, whereupon Nikko, her runner and right-hand man, prowled through the Barbary Coast until he found a likely-looking prospect and enticed him into the Davis Street saloon. There he was nudged along the bar until he stood upon a trapdoor built into the floor. Then Nikko called loudly for drinks, which were served by Miss Piggott in person. The runner received beer, while for the stranger Miss Piggott prepared a concoction much used in shanghaiing circles and called a Miss Piggott Special. It was composed of equal parts of whisky, brandy, and gin, with a goodly lacing of laudanum or opium.

While the victim was shivering under the terrific impact of this beverage, Miss Piggott leaned across the bar and tapped him on the head with a bung starter, while Nikko made matters certain with a blow from a slungshot. As the prospect began to crumple to the floor, Miss Piggott operated a lever behind the bar and dumped him into the basement,

A sailor is being shanghaied via a trapdoor from Penny's notorious San Francisco bar. Sometimes, sailors claimed, a corpse was thus shipped, under the pretense of its being a live body in a stupor.

where he fell upon a mattress that Miss Piggott had thoughtfully provided, realizing that the man might receive an injury that would lessen his value. When the object of all these attentions awoke, he was usually in a ship bound for foreign climes, with no very clear idea as to how he got there. All of Miss Piggott's regular customers knew the exact location of the trapdoor and kept away from it, for it was an unwritten law of the establishment that any man who stood upon the fatal spot was fair game. The spectacle of Miss Piggott drugging and then slugging a stranger and dropping him into the basement excited no particular attention. The bystanders might comment judiciously upon the force and accuracy with which the old lady

"Smugglers' Cove," by Albert P. Ryder; like the pirates of yore, smugglers made heavy use of caves and coves for concealment.

delivered the knockout blow, but that was about all. What happened to him was his own affair.

CHLOROFORM KATE
Catherine Johnson got her nickname from her habit of sniffing—or even swigging—chloroform as a sort of chaser for the raw whisky she swilled. Kate was the widow of Shanghai Johnson, who specialized in kidnaping whalers on the Barbary Coast. She had been a barmaid when he was flourishing and she took over the business after his demise. Although Kate would drink and carouse with her customers, and though she mothered some of the regulars like a hen with a brood, she was likely to answer fresh seamen with a crack on the head.

One day a Royal Navy seaman lurched into her barroom, three sheets to the wind, and tried to embrace Kate. While Harry the Ape, one of the regulars, used his fists on the sailor, Kate belabored him with a belaying pin. The Royal Navy sank by the stern but was soon followed to the floor by Kate. The exertion plus the chloroform-spiked beer she had been tanking up on all day were too much for her heart. The drunken, tearful customers tenderly picked her up and placed her on a table where they splashed water in her face

(probably the first time *that* liquid was used in Kate's place). These attempts to arouse her were without effect. She was dead.

The regulars decided to give Chloroform Kate a decent burial at sea, but their booze-fogged brains could not come up with any ideas as to how to get her out to the Golden Gate. God knew, they had neither the money nor the pull to secure a boat to transport the body out to sea. Suddenly Harry the Ape shouted: "I have it! We'll take her aboard the barge at Howard Street Wharf!" A chorus of approving cries and back-slaps greeted this suggestion and, after having one for the road, the men bundled the corpse into a tarp and staggered their way under the burden to Howard Street. Sam, as chief mourner, followed Harry and the other pallbearers, carrying an old litho of the clipper *Glory of the Seas* that graced the wall of Kate's bar. They scooped out a shallow grave in the mass of refuse in the scow, and Red Sam gallantly placed the picture with the body. They then sprinkled some brown and wilted gladioli over the tarpaulin and covered her up. When San Francisco's heavily laden garbage scow was towed out the Golden Gate next day, Chloroform Kate made her last voyage and was consigned to the deep.

MEN OF STRAW
Though ships' captains naturally preferred to hire on strong, able-bodied men, when forced to resort to crimps for their crew they took what they could get. Accustomed to seeing whole boatloads of men sodden with drink or drugs, and consequently quite limp and lifeless when delivered, captains could on occasion be tricked into "buying" a dead man or two. The presence of a corpse was seldom discovered until the ship was at sea, and then the captain usually thought the poor fellow dead of alcohol rather than foul play. The body was heaved overboard, with word of the murder never reaching the police on shore.

Another way in which the crimp fleeced the shipmasters was to include a dummy among the sailors whom he delivered. A suit of clothes was stuffed with straw and properly weighted, while that part of the dummy which represented the head was swathed in mufflers or other heavy cloths. For a few hours after his arrival on board he generally looked better than some of his hungover flesh-and-blood companions.

GLAZIER SAILOR
A land shark, lacking men to make up a crew, met a German glazier on Long Wharf with a pack of glass on

his back and said to him, "Hi, my good fellow, I want you to put some glass in the stern of that ship." So off they went. As the German sat in the stern of the boat, much pleased with the prospect of a good job, the shark gave him a cigar. The glazier sat and puffed away as he used to do in his Faderland, but before they reached the ship he tumbled over in the bottom of the boat—the cigar was impregnated with opium. The shark threw the German's pack of glass into the bay and, running alongside, hailed: "On deck there, lower away and haul up this man!" A rope was lashed around him and he was hauled up. The shark ran to the captain's office, saying: "Captain, I've got you a first-rate sailor here. He's a little boozy today, but he'll be all right tomorrow."

The poor German woke up at sea with a longer job than he had engaged for, and the worst of the business was he not only had to work for nothing but be cuffed through the whole voyage for having the presumption to impose himself on the ship as an able seaman when he knew nothing about the job.

SMUGGLERS' WILES

Part of the charm of a smuggler's life was the continual battle of wits he waged with the law. Success in getting the goods to their destination was just a little sweeter when it was accompanied by some great chase.

Way back in 1772, for example, a small sloop belonging to a Rhode Island trader named John Brown came into the bay and was promptly intercepted by the British cutter *Gaspee*. Since the vessel had a cargo of contraband aboard (goods which the British had forbidden the colonies to receive), Brown's skipper crowded on sail. Drive as hard as he would, he could not shake the Crown's vessel, and he was rapidly running out of room. Fortunately he knew the bay, and he set his course for Namquit Shoal, just barely easing his shallow draft over it. The *Gaspee*, in hot pursuit, fetched up and ran aground until the next tide while the smuggler sailed on to Providence, seven miles away, to spread the news of the *Gaspee*'s predicament. As a result John Brown outfitted a whaleboat and mounted an attack that night before the cutter could be floated. After the *Gaspee*'s officers and men had been captured and taken ashore, the smugglers set the cutter afire just to let the king know what they thought of his regulations.

During the rumrunning days of Prohibition, an almost identical stunt was pulled on the Old Bull, a rock awash farther down the bay. A Coast Guard cutter pursued a rumrunner named the *Black Duck*. When the *Black Duck* came to the rock, she turned out her stern light—which she had neglected to do during the first part of the chase—dodged around the rock, and relit the light. The Coast Guard, as one might expect, kept straight ahead. Only their bottom stayed on the horns of the Old Bull. The rest of the ship and her crew went down in deep water several boat lengths beyond, and the *Black Duck* proceeded leisurely "up-river" to unload.

One of the most humiliating tricks pulled by a group of smugglers on the opposition was that of a little sloop named, appropriately, the *Artful Dodger*. She was to pick up a load of liquor and tobacco at Martinique and land it on a nearby English island. All went well until they landed, when it was discovered that a revenue officer was hiding under a propped-up rowboat on the beach waiting to catch them redhanded and receive a large reward. As soon as the captain got word of the officer's presence, he and another man rowed ashore. They sneaked up on the rowboat, kicked the supports from under her, and sat on her keel, with the revenue officer neatly pinned inside. As the cargo came ashore, they regaled him with a running account. "Two hundred cigars, one keg of brandy . . ." When the cargo was all ashore and on its way, they lashed the boat to the beach with their lines fastened to pegs and went about their business, leaving the officer to find his way out.

Below is a smugglers' cave on the Atlantic coast. The population of one such lawless stretch was so hard a lot that people there went to church armed with shotguns.

CAPTAINS COURAGEOUS
And Otherwise

Whether he was timid or overweening, lamb or lion, the sea captain had absolute power over his men. He could order up a hanging, lashing, or keelhauling—in which the bound sailor was dragged against barnacles under the ship—for insubordination, but seldom did. Most captains, like most men, were neither heroic nor despicable but something in between. As a captain's character and judgment determined a sailor's share of the profits and, more important, his safe return, the Old Man was closely scrutinized by his crew. If nothing else could be done about any peculiarities noted, they could be added to the forecastle banter.

RESOURCEFUL

A stuttering foremast hand, seeing a shipmate fall overboard, rushed aft to tell the captain, but so excited was he he could only mouth helplessly, "B-b-b-b-!" "Sing it, man," roared the captain (for 'tis well known that stutterers can always sing). Whereupon the sailor chanted:
"Overboard goes Barnabas
Half a mile astern of us."

OVERWEENING

Years and years ago there was a great rivalry between the fishermen of Gloucester and those of Lunenberg. Every year they had a race called the Fisherman's Race, and great honor in Canada and in the United States went to the winner. At that time the greatest fish killer in all New England was a man named Ford. Now Captain Ford had made a lot of money on the Grand Banks and he took all that money to build himself a vessel. He said that vessel was going to be the largest and the fastest fishing vessel ever built and he was going to win the Fisherman's Race with her. He went to work building, and he got engaged to a girl named Mary and decided he would name the vessel the *Mary B. Ford*. She was the biggest fishing vessel ever, and when he went to paint her, instead of painting her gray or black like all the other schooners, he painted her white. She was so big and clumsy she got stuck when launched, but they pushed her in, towed her around, and rigged her out, and the *Mary B. Ford* with a fine crew of Gloucester seamen set out

This intransigent gunner emulates everyman's captain in an 1854 Currier print; he refuses to abandon his gun even though arctic waves are washing aboard his ship.

for a shakedown voyage to the Grand Banks. She sailed past Thatcher's Island and disappeared into a fog bank and that was the last that was seen of her.

Years passed, the schooners began to disappear from the Grand Banks, and steam trawlers took their place. One calm summer night there was a French trawler dragging on the banks with a wire drag and suddenly the drag stuck. The captain was reluctant to cast off the drag and lose his fish, so—hoping to make the drag break loose—he put on more steam and more steam and suddenly the trawler began to move ahead again. It was a full moon, no sea, a little mist—you could see about a quarter of a mile,

the moon was a ghostly thing through the mist. Then the water astern rippled and broke and a great bowsprit came out, and then the forward end of a vessel, and then the foremast, with the sails still hanging on the spars and stays, seaweed there and barnacles growing on the mast and booms. This great vessel rose slowly higher and higher against the moon. The French captain turned his light on her and there it was: her name in gold letters in the one space not covered with barnacles and seaweed, absolutely clean—the *Mary B. Ford*. She rose up out of the water, came level with the top of the net, toppled over the other side, and disappeared quietly and slowly down into the sea again. And that is how men finally knew what had become of Captain Ford, his vessel, and all his men.

GREEDY

Long ago there was a poor man and his wife. It was almost Easter and there was no ham. The husband went into the forest to think how he might get a ham. There he met a little man who asked for food, which the man gave him. In gratitude, the little man told his benefactor that if he went to Hell and offered the Devil some bacon, the Devil might give him a quern that would grind anything asked. All one needed to do was say, "Grind such and such," and the mill would grind out the object until the command "Grind no more such and such." The poor man returned home, took up bacon, and set off for Hell. He found the quern in a corner and bargained with the Devil successfully for it. Before he reached home the man said, "Grind ham." The mill began to whir and one grand ham after another popped out. He said the magic words, the mill stopped, and he went home. The man and his wife prospered mightily. One day a sea captain came to the house and saw the mill in operation. He asked the farmer how to start it and that night the captain stole the mill and put to sea. At the fishing bank they caught a large number of fish, and being in need of salt to preserve the catch, the

Sailor Talk

English as spoken by mariners is an occupational dialect of our language dating back to Viking times. Though in its present form Nautical English has continued pretty much unchanged since 1750 and is common to American, British, and other English-speaking seamen, it was enriched during the era of clipper ships and whaling by an influx of Yankee words and expressions. Some examples: *beachcomber*—a sailor, especially a whaleman, who jumps ship to live as a loafer on a Pacific island; *to breach*—for whales to leap out of the water: whether they actually do jump clear up in the air is a much disputed question, but when one breaches even two-thirds of his length, it looks almost as if he were flying; *caboose*—a ship's kitchen. The word later came ashore to designate the tail car of a railroad train—like other railroading terms such as *all aboard, berth, steward, crew, shipping,* and so forth; *cracklin's*—dry leavings of whale blubber after the oil is extracted. Whalemen occasionally ate cracklin's as a snack while trying out, or rendering, the blubber: they taste like fishy toast. On such occasions fish, chickens, and popcorn were likewise sometimes cooked in the boiling whale oil; *dead whale or a stove boat*—the whalemen's slogan, equivalent to "Do or die"; *it don't amount to Hannah Cook*—is of small size or value. The phrase is supposed to derive from "a hand and a cook"—crew of a small coasting vessel; *doughboy*—a small round doughnut served to sailors on shipboard with hash. (Earlier, it had been a dumpling originating among buccaneers on the Spanish Main.) During the Civil War the word transferred to a brass button shaped like the sailors' dumpling, worn by Union infantrymen, and from that use it finally came to mean a foot soldier in the U.S. Army; *Fiddler's Green*—where good sailors go when they die. A 19th-century dictionary of Americanisms defines it as "a sailors' elysium in which wine, women, and song figure prominently"; *gam*—a social meeting at sea or a conversation between persons in two boats. *To gam* also means to gossip; *hurrah's nest*—a big mess. When,

Nantucket sleigh ride. A finback whale might do 60 m.p.h.—fast enough to make a whaleboat shed her paint.

for example, a heavy sea swept the deck of a ship, pitching everything about in grand confusion, the resulting tangle of ropes and displaced gear might be called a hurrah's nest—"everything on top and nothing at hand." Pronounced hooraw; *lay*—a share of returns from a whaling voyage, given in lieu of wages. If, for instance, a crewman was "on the two-hundredth lay," he was entitled to the proceeds from one barrel out of every 200 taken on board; *sky-scraper*—a triangular skysail also known as a moonraker, which adventurous skippers set above the royals (highest sails normally carried on a square-rigged ship) when in calm latitudes. The word came ashore in the 1880's to designate tall U.S. buildings; *tell it to the marines*—meaning "I don't believe it." The expression was originally "That will do for the marines, but the sailors won't believe it." The marines in question were soldiers serving on board British warships—to sailors they personified all that was lubberly, ignorant, and clumsy.

As noted by seafaring folklorist Horace Beck, mariners tend to expand their occupational language to fit requirements other than at sea: "The sailor ashore *swabs* the floor of his house. When it rains he tells his wife to *close the hatch!* His clothes *slat* on the line, and he persists in saying *port* and *starboard.* Someone moving fast is *carrying sail.* Should a sailor go on a trip, he *takes a cruise* and *ties up* for the night . . . Eventually the old salt, his *voyage complete, slips his cable* and departs for *Fiddler's Green.*"

These American cod fishermen on the Grand Banks are engaged in dressing down their catch, the process of splitting and salting the fish. The modern expression "dressing down," meaning a tongue lashing, probably comes from this term.

skipper ordered the mill to grind salt. The mill began to whir and it wasn't long before he had plenty of salt. The problem was how to stop it. The mill filled the cabin and then the companionway and finally the hold with salt until the vessel foundered, taking the crew with her. To this day the mill lies on the bottom grinding salt. If you don't believe this story, taste the seawater.

INDECISIVE

Seamen and mates talked long about their captains—usually paying special attention to their faults. "Indecision is bad," said Dashy Noyes. "Cap'n Tripp had indecision—had it in his vitals. A good master, a thorough seaman, a perfect gentleman, but bewildered by nature, sort o' boneless. When he gave an order it was either too soon, or too late, or the thing never needed to be done. His special anxiety was carryin' sail.":

We was bound on the regulation China passage, sailed in midwinter, on the tail of a nor'wester. The wind was dead aft and howlin' and the weather fine, but what did Cap'n Tripp do but keep her down to lower topsails? There we was joggin' off at 6 or 7 knots when we might ha' been makin' 12. The second day I couldn't stand it any longer.

"Don't you want to set them upper topsails, cap'n?" I asks. He looks all around the horizon. "No-o, I guess we'll let her run along easy," he says in his way. "You don't gain much in the end by carryin' sail."

"Well, sir, if you call this carryin' sail—" "I don't know," he says, looking aloft again. "I suppose she might stand the main upper topsail." "Stand!" I cries. "She'd stand three royals!" 'Twas disrespectful but this joggin' along had strained my nerve. "Three royals, Mr. Noyes?" asks Cap'n Tripp. "You young fellers are so extravagant. We'll try her with the main upper topsail and see how she behaves." I'd called the men and sent a couple of 'em aloft to loose the sail when I see the Old Man wave his hand. "I guess we won't set it, after all, Mr. Noyes," says he. "Not set the

upper topsail, sir?" I asks. "No, not just now. I'll feel safer to let her run as she is."

Cap'n Tripp seemed too young a man to be in his dotage. I knew he wasn't drunk. Most o' the day the Old Man shambled back and forth on the quarterdeck; and, knowin' him as I do now, I can understand that this weighty problem was worryin' him distracted. Had he ought to set that topsail? . . . Would she stand it? . . . O' course she would! . . . Still, it was blowin' pretty stiff . . . Better keep it furled . . . And yet, maybe, 'twould be well to set it. Indecision, you understand—

Saint Elmo's Fire was a luminous flame that often settled on a mast or in the rigging before a disastrous storm. Two together were dubbed Castor and Pollux.

he warn't a timid man. Once on a given tack, he hated to go about. Neither was he incompetent; he knew too cussed well what ought to be done. But he couldn't quite make up his mind to do it, leastwise not till afterward; and when he'd said the word, he'd wish he hadn't and try to take it back. I figured life must ha' been distressin' hard for the Old Man Tripp. A man who'd rather go hungry than pick out a breakfast from the bill o' fare ain't what you might call well fitted for a world o' pull and haul. And o' course luck went against him right along.

We pegged along to the China Sea and managed to arrive at Hong Kong in 140 days. More and more as I sailed with him, I come to like the

Old Man. He tickled me. He meant right in his heart. 'Twas the fault o' the world that he didn't make more showin'. The man warn't selfish enough. He'd always given in to someone else, and the habit had knocked the tar out o' him. I had got to enjoy him thoroughly on the passage out, so I didn't care what sort o' time we made.

Ships lay around us the first evenin' in Hong Kong. All along the slope o' the hill the lights was twinklin' and the air smelled strong o' land. "Seems good to be at anchor, sir, don't it?" I says. "Mr. Noyes," says he, "I thank God every time I arrive in port."

The ship *Paul Revere* lay in Hong Kong and Dan Sands was mate o' her, a chum o' mine from home. I told Dan all about the Old Man. "Some day when you sight a ship on the line," I says, "hove to under a goose-winged topsail, that's us. Or you might see us on the coast in a howlin' northeaster, with royals set." "The *Paul Revere* is a clipper, my boy," he'd answer. "We'll beat you by about 30 or 40 days." It made me mad. I'd seen enough o' the *Vigilant* to know that with proper handlin' she could *sail*. When Dan waved his hand to me from the *Paul Revere,* as we was goin' out by Green Island side by side, I vowed I'd find some way to make a decent passage home. We parted company with the *Paul Revere* on the second day out, and the weather seemed made to order for Cap'n Tripp—a fair wind most o' the time, not too light and not too strong. It did him a world o' good. The vessel sailed herself; we rounded the Cape o' Good Hope and took the trades across the South Atlantic. Seventy days we'd been from Hong Kong to the line, no slouch of a run. I began to polish up the *Vigilant* for port, plannin' what I'd say to Dan when he come straggalin' in. The third day it breezed on heavy. The Old Man paced the quarter deck, skittish. He'd cast his eye aloft, then look to windward, then walk aft and examine the wake. I knew the symptoms; my heart dropped into my boots. A

great ship came swingin' along our wake and I clapped the glasses on her: *Paul Revere.* The Old man had gone down below to sleep. Hardly stoppin' to think, I locked the companionway on the outside and took the key. "Come to the door a minute, sir," I cried. "What is it, Mr. Noyes?" he says, rattlin' the knob. "You're a prisoner, cap'n. You'll be comfortable, and your meals'll be sent in regular. The *Paul Revere* just passed us and I'm goin' on deck and make sail." "Well, I wouldn't set everything, Mr. Noyes," he says deliberate, on the other side o' the door.

Then I drove her. I found a set o' stunsails below that I rigged out on bamboo poles lashed to the yardarms. I covered her with staysails. She looked like a backyard with the washin' out. On the fifth day we crawled up on the *Paul Revere* and was sailin' side by side. Pretty soon they set signals. "Is captain sick?" I suppose they'd been watchin' with their glasses. I took the signal book and found: "Captain desires me to inform you . . . In bad health."

Side by side we sailed, day after day. The Old Man himself seemed happy as a clam at high water. Now and then I'd peek at him through the skylight; usually I'd find him readin'

in the big armchair, without a care in the world. We passed Barnegat one day about noon and it was nip and tuck to the lightship. I hung the balloon jib over the bow and the *Paul Revere* dropped into our wake. The moment that the anchor fetched bottom, my courage ebbed. "We're anchored off quarantine, sir," I says after I unlocked the cabin door. "And we beat the *Paul Revere.*" "Did we?" says he. "Well, now, I'm glad to hear it." "I want to apologize for

what I've done." I hitched from one foot to the other. "The doctor is comin' aboard, and I told the pilot you was sick abed; and now I don't know what to do." He got up kind o' slow and smiled. "Well," says he, "I guess I'd better get to bed."

DEVOTED

Captain Eleazer was skipper of one of the trimmest schooners in the "Injies trade." His vessel, the *Bulldog,* was "built to split a drop of water into a half moon while she heeled," and he had let the town know he was proud of her. He married a girl named Abigail Bangs, and townsfolk began asking if he planned to change the name of the vessel to the *Abigail.* His reply was "No, I don't see fitten for to change the vessel's name. But if Abigail keeps on steady being a good girl like she is, I've been thinking I might have her rechristened Bulldog."

A two-clipper race on the 100-day run home from China was a frequent if rarely viewed occurrence in the later 1800's. Montague Dawson painted *Ariel* and *Taeping* in a neck-and-neck contest.

When Cotton Was King

A Mississippi planter was once asked by a visitor if he knew where a night's lodging could be had. "Why, at any house in the state, sir," was the reply. This stereotype of the ever-hospitable southern planter-gentleman dates back to well before the Civil War, as do the other leading figures of southern folklore, the banjo-strumming Negro and the poor white, whose lives, like the planter's, were focused on a single means of livelihood: cotton. For cotton (and its agent, the cotton trader) was indeed king in Dixie.

The great majority of the hands who planted its green seeds and harvested its cream-colored wool from the Atlantic tidewater to the river bottoms of East Texas were black. These "cotton Negroes," who in many places lived side by side with the poor whites, brewed up for themselves a heady blend of inherited and acquired tradition. Where they embraced the whites' Protestant faith, for example, church services were transformed into "shouts" and hymns took on an unmistakably African sound. Music had a way of getting into every occasion of Negro life, or so it seemed to whites, who came to imagine that blacks had somehow naturally "got rhythm." Less conspicuously, the slaves also combined their ancestral heritage of signs, dream and ghost lore, taboos, and charms with a hoard of superstitions and ghost stories borrowed from the whites. The history of their ordeal in America they transmitted in many ways. It came through in animal tales of the Uncle Remus type, some of which were actually parables of the struggle between races; in jokes about a clever slave who always outwitted his master; in escape fantasies involving magic; and, more often than not, in the recital of unvarnished facts.

The era of the cotton boom was one of false prosperity and increasing recklessness—more and more debt-ridden planters gambled their crops, their slaves, and even their plantations to regain solvency, while to win freedom more and more slaves gambled their lives. Not surprisingly, the folklore that arose from such a volatile mixture of people and circumstances was hot and spicy.

Harriet Beecher Stowe's *Uncle Tom's Cabin* presents the irrepressible slave child Topsy as an opposite number to sweet little Miss Eva.

John Whettan Ehninger's "Old Kentucky Home" illustrates a favorite cliche in the traditions of th slaveholding class: blacks' devotio to their owners' offspring.

MORE AND MORE
Making Good the Cotton Brag

Cotton planters' profits depended on the volume of the fall-winter picking season. By the combined efforts of men, women, and children, slaves averaged 100 pounds a day but were driven hard to produce more; they were also offered bonuses— tobacco, molasses, calico, liquor, etc. Likewise, picking contests were held, and whites made bets among themselves as to the outcome—a planter's boast of having harvested the greatest poundage with a given number of slaves was called his cotton brag. Here are stories told by cotton-bragging folk rich and poor:

THE COTTON GIN

The invention by Eli Whitney in 1793 of the cotton gin meant a huge increase in productivity for planters. The following account of how the invention came into being was handed down in one family's tradition and corresponds quite closely to the actual events as recorded at the time: Eli Whitney invented the cotton gin while a guest at Mulberry Grove near Savannah, Georgia, home of an old friend and college mate of Whitney's named Phineas Miller. By various repairs and tinkerings about the premises, Mr. Whitney upheld the reputation of Yankee ingenuity and inspired the family with such confidence in his skill that on one occasion when Mrs. Miller's watch was out of order she gave it to him. Not long thereafter a gentleman called to exhibit a sample of cotton wool and incidentally remarked while displaying the sample, "There is a fortune in store for someone who will invent a machine for separating the lint from the seed." Mrs. Miller turned to Whitney and said, "You're the man, Mr. Whitney, for since you suceeded so well with my watch I am sure you have ingenuity enough to make such a machine." After this conversation Mr. Whitney confined himself closely to his room for several weeks. At the end of this time he invited the family to inspect his model for a cotton gin. It was constructed with wire teeth on a revolving cylinder. However, there was no contrivance for throwing off the lint after it was separated from the seed, and it wrapped around the cylinder, thereby greatly obstructing the oper-

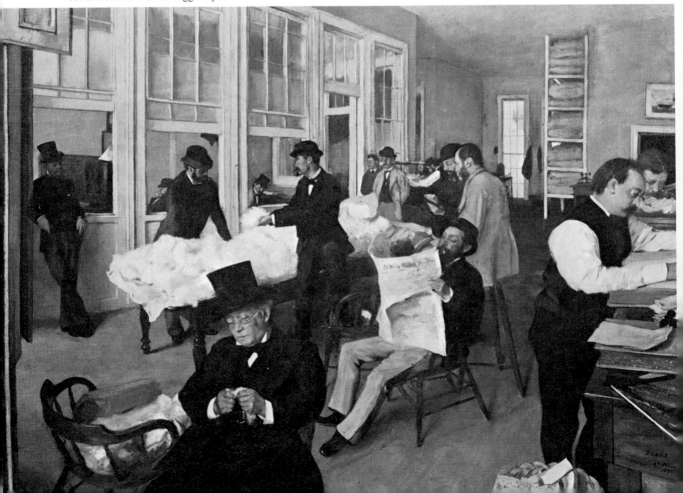

Because of the South's dependence on a single-crop economy, cotton brokers were its biggest tycoons. The New Orleans Cotton Exchange (shown here as depicted by Edgar Degas) witnessed an annual turnover unrivaled save in New York and Liverpool.

ation. Mrs. Miller, seeing this difficulty, seized a common clothesbrush, applied it to the teeth, and caught the lint. Whitney delightedly exclaimed: "Madam, you have solved the problem. With this suggestion my model is complete!"

G.P.C.

Not all of the cotton was produced by slave labor on big plantations. Some of it came from small farms worked by poor whites with no slaves or but a few. From that world came the following cotton joke about a rascally young church member who suddenly claimed to have had a miraculous vision and demanded on the strength of it to be ordained as a minister:

The church was in an uproar. The congregation was badly divided on the question of granting a young brother, whose reputation for piety was none too good, a license to preach the Gospel.

A few of the older conservative members were a little doubtful about the young man's sudden call to the ministry and wanted to put him off until they could be a little surer about the reality of the call. Many of the younger brethren were very enthusiastic about the wonderful conversion and vocation of the applicant. They thought a real miracle had happened and were anxious to see him licensed and put to work in the Lord's vineyard. They recounted with great seriousness how the Lord had appeared to the young man in a vision and had shown him the three letters "G.P.C." flaming in the sky and how a still, small voice had said, "Follow these." There could be no doubt about the interpretation. "G.P.C." meant "Go Preach Christ." And the young man should be sent on his way.

But the old deacon was on his feet, replying: "Brethren, I do not deny the vision. I am sure that the Lord has spoken to this young man. But knowing this young man as I do, and appreciating to some degree the great wisdom of the Lord, I am sure that you all misinterpret what this vision meant. 'G.P.C.' in this case can only mean: 'Go Pick Cotton!'"

SUPERSTITIONS

Cotton Magic

King Cotton enjoyed a different kind of prestige in the eyes of the slaves who worked the plantations. To them, cotton was a source of signs, "conjure," and folk medicine, based in part on the belief that cotton contained spirits of the dead. When the cotton was still green, spirits haunted the plants, it was said, but when the crop ripened the spirits emerged to haunt people and animals, continuing even after the fields were gleaned. For example, a story was told that one cold December night after a heavy snowstorm some horses were in a cottonfield when the ghosts of long-dead Indians came and mounted them. Next morning not a horse was alive; they had all been run to death. This tale may reflect real-life observation, because cotton contains a poison from which animals occasionally die like the horses in the story, gasping, a bloody froth at the mouth, as if run to death. (The poison, a yellow pigment called gossypol, is present especially in the seed and sometimes occurs in toxic quantities in processed cottonseed used in livestock feeds.) The same poison in smaller doses was used as a medicine.

Cotton was chewed as a toothache remedy, and a preparation from it was locally applied for chronic headaches—a use honored to this day in India, cotton's Old World homeland, whence the plant was introduced to Africa in antiquity, long before most European whites had ever seen or heard of it. Likewise, and again precisely as in India today, Negro slaves used a decoction of powdered cotton-root bark as a stimulant and to induce miscarriage. Perhaps by association with those powers, cotton was at once credited with aphrodisiac virtues and blamed for conjugal unhappiness. Sometimes a young couple would keep a boll to symbolize their marriage. If the boll turned white, the marriage would be successful; if it changed to a creamy color (meaning that the gossypol content was high), the couple would soon separate. To insure that they would never lack money a couple had to sleep on a cotton mattress on their wedding night.

Bolls were a source of much other prognostication concerning sex and

Cotton was constantly on a plantation slave's mind. Above, one of dozens of William Walker's depictions of field life

marriage. If an unmarried girl found a twin boll, one of her suitors was on his way to claim her; if a newlywed couple found it, twins could be expected within the year. It was taboo to use a cotton tablecloth on one's wedding day—crippled offspring would result, it was believed. It was also said that good luck was bound to come to anyone who made love during daylight hours in a cottonfield at harvest time. This belief relates to the universal idea that sex in the fields promoted good crop growth and general welfare; and anyone performing the feat was likely to be young, vigorous, and bold—a better-than-average candidate for good luck. Associated with this was the notion that the plant possessed powers of attraction—not only people but fish could be lured with it. So when going fishing, black fishermen were wont to carry 20 dried cottonseeds and to place them at the water's edge to insure a bite. In slavery days it was dangerous to find a boll with no cotton inside— some of one's kin would be sold before night unless one dropped everything and counted slowly to 10. It was also widely believed that anyone who dreamed of a cottonfield would shortly be compelled to pick cotton. By the outbreak of the Civil War, several million Negroes in the U.S. South were obliged to do just that.

259

UNCLE REMUS
An Old Head Informs

An African love of humanizing animals is reflected in slave tales told in America, tales overheard by a white boy named Joel Chandler Harris on a plantation and later gathered by him as a reporter. Harris eventually took over an "Uncle Si" column in Atlanta's Constitution *and began to turn out his collected "Uncle Remus" stories, eventually filling 10 books. Though Harris presented Remus as content with slavery, the tales he tells themselves belie this—overtly, as in "The Deluge," and covertly, through the powerless yet ever-victorious brother rabbit.*

THE TAR-BABY STORY

"Didn't the fox *never* catch the rabbit, Uncle Remus?" asked the little boy the next evening. "He come mighty nigh it, honey, sho's you born—Brer Fox did. One day Brer Fox went ter wuk en got 'im some tar, en mix it wid some turkentime, en fix up a contrapshun w'at he call a Tar-Baby, en he tuck dish yer Tar-Baby en he sot 'er in de big road, en den he lay off in de bushes fer to see what de news wuz gwine ter be. En he didn't hatter wait long, needer, kaze bimeby here come Brer Rabbit pacin' down de road—lippity-clippity, clippity-lippity—dez ez sassy ez a jaybird. Brer Fox, he lay low. Brer Rabbit come prancin' long twel he spey de Tar-Baby, en den he fotch

up on his behime legs like he wuz 'stonished. De Tar-Baby, she sot dar, she did, en Brer Fox, he lay low.

"'Mawnin'!' sez Brer Rabbit, sezee—'nice wedder dis mawnin',' sezee. Tar-Baby ain't sayin' nothin', en Brer Fox, he lay low. 'How duz yo' sym'tums seem ter segashuate?' sez Brer Rabbit, sezee. Brer Fox, he wink his eye slow en lay low, en de Tar-Baby, she ain't sayin' nothin'. 'How you come on, den? Is you deaf?' sez Brer Rabbit, sezee. 'If you is, I kin holler louder.' Tar-Baby stay still, en Brer Fox, he lay low.

"'You er stuck up, dat's w'at you is,' says Brer Rabbit, sezee, 'en I'm gwine ter kyore you, dat's w'at I'm a-gwine ter do,' sezee. Brer Fox, he sorter chuckle in his stummick, he did. 'I'm gwine ter larn you how ter talk ter 'spectubble folks ef hit's de las' ack. Ef you don't take off dat hat en tell me howdy I'm gwine ter bus' you wide open,' sezee. Tar-Baby stay still, en Brer Fox, he lay low. Brer Rabbit keep on axin' im, en de Tar-Baby, she keep on sayin' nothin', twel present'y Brer Rabbit draw back wid his fis', he did, en blip he tuck 'er side er de head. Right dar's whar he broke his merlasses jug. His fis' stuck, en he can't pull loose. De tar hilt 'im. But Tar-Baby, she stay still, en Brer Fox, he lay low. 'Ef you don't lemme loose, I'll knock you agin,' sez Brer Rabbit, sezee, en wid dat he fotch 'er a swipe wid de udder han', en dat stuck. Tar-Baby, she ain't sayin' nothin', en Brer Fox, he lay low. 'Tu'n me loose 'fo' I kick de natchul stuffin' outen you,' sez Brer Rabbit, sezee, but de Tar-Baby, she ain't sayin' nothin'. She des hilt on, en den Brer Rabbit lose de use er his feet in de same way. Brer Fox, he lay low. Den Brer Rabbit squall out dat ef de Tar-Baby don't tu'n 'im loose he butt 'er cranksided. En den he butted, en his head got stuck. Den Brer Fox, he sa'ntered fort', lookin' des ez innercent ez a mockin'bird.

In this charming Winter depiction, Uncle Remus speaks afresh to his traditional audience—a small white boy. Children could see themselves in the canny rabbit.

"'Howdy, Brer Rabbit,' sez Brer Fox, sezee. 'You look sorter stuck up dis mawnin',' sezee, en den he rolled on de groun' en laughed en laughed twel he couldn't laugh no mo'."

Here Uncle Remus paused and drew a two-pound yam out of the ashes. "Did the fox eat the rabbit?" asked the little boy to whom the story had been told. "Dat's all de fur de tale goes," replied the old man. "He mought, en den again he moughtent. Some say Jedge B'ar come along en loosed 'im—some say no. I hear Miss Sally callin'. You better run 'long."

TOO SHARP FOR MR. FOX

"Uncle Remus," said the little boy one evening when he had found the old man with little or nothing to do, "did the fox kill and eat the rabbit when he caught him with the Tar-Baby?" "Law, honey, ain't I tell you 'bout dat?" replied the old man,

Brer Rabbit caught in a trap set by Brer Fox, who had suspected him of "grabblin'" in his goober patch—by beloved illustrator A. B. Frost.

chuckling slyly. "I 'clar ter gracious I ought er tole you dat, but old man Nod wuz ridin' on my eyeleds twel a leetle mo'n I'd a dis'member'd my own name, an den on to dat here come yo' mammy hollerin' atter you. 'Fo' you begins fer ter wipe yo' eyes 'bout Brer Rabbit, you wait en see whar'bouts Brer Rabbit gwine ter fetch up at.

"W'en Brer Fox fin' Brer Rabbit mixt up wid de Tar-Baby, he feel mighty good, en he roll on de groun' en laff. Bimeby he up en say, sezee, 'Well, I speck I got you dis time, Brer Rabbit,' sezee. 'You been runnin' roun' here sassin' atter me a mighty long time, but I speck you done come ter de een' er de row. En den you er allers sommers whar you got no bizness,' sez Brer Fox, sezee. 'Who ax you fer ter come en strike up a 'quaintance wid dish yer Tar-Baby? En who stuck you up dar whar you iz? Nobody in de roun' worl'. You des tuck en jam yo'se'f on dat Tar-Baby widout waitin' fer enny invite,' sez Brer Fox, sezee, 'en dar you is, en dar you'll stay twel I fixes up a bresh pile and fires her up, kaze I'm gwine ter bobbycue you dis day, sho.'

"Den Brer Rabbit talk mighty 'umble. 'I don't keer w'at you do wid me, Brer Fox,' sezee, 'so you don't

The rabbit has the upper hand, temporarily, and is thoroughly enjoying the luscious contents of the dinner pail of Brer Fox, whose tail is nailed to the roof in the Milo Winter illustration, above left. In the other Winter painting an innovative young rabbit is admonished by Big Money, the witch: "Ef you git any mo' sense, son, you'll be de ruination ev de whole settlement."

This famous story is known around the world: in the illustrations above, Brer Fox admires his handiwork once again; and Brer Rabbit, once again enraged by the Tar-Baby's silence, gets himself thoroughly gummed up, much to Brer Fox's great delight.

fling me in dat brier patch. Roas' me, Brer Fox,' sezee, 'but don't fling me in dat brier patch,' sezee. 'Hit's so much trouble fer ter kindle a fire,' sez Brer Fox, 'dat I speck I'll hatter hang you,' sezee. 'Hang me des ez high as you please, Brer Fox,' sezee, 'but fer de Lord's sake don't fling me in dat brier patch,' sezee.

"'I ain't got no string,' sez Brer Fox, sezee, 'en now I speck I'll hatter drown you,' sezee. 'Drown me des ez deep ez you please, Brer Fox,' sez Brer Rabbit, sezee, 'but don't fling me in dat brier patch,' sezee.

"'Dey ain't no water nigh,' sez Brer Fox, sezee, 'en now I speck I'll hatter skin you,' sezee. 'Skin me, Brer Fox,' sez Brer Rabbit, sezee, 'snatch out my eyeballs, t'ar out my years by de roots, en cut off my legs,' sezee, 'but do please, Brer Fox, don't fling me in dat brier patch,' sezee. Co'se Brer Fox wanter hurt Brer Rabbit bad ez he kin, so he cotch 'im by de behime legs en slung 'im right in de middle er de brier patch. Dar wuz a consider-abul flutter whar Brer Rabbit struck de bushes, en Brer Fox sorter hang 'roun' fer ter see w'at wuz gwine ter happen. Bimeby he hear somebody call 'im, en way up de hill he see Brer Rabbit settin' crosslegged on a chinkapin log koamin' de pitch out'n his ha'r wid a chip. Den Brer Fox

know dat he bin swop off mighty bad. Brer Rabbit wuz bleed'n fer ter fling back some er his sass, en he holler out: 'Bred en bawn in a brier patch, Brer Fox—bred en bawn in a brier patch!' en wid dat he skip out lively ez a cricket in de embers."

THE DELUGE

One time, way back yander 'fo' enny un us wuz borned, de animils en de creeturs sorter 'lecshuneer roun' 'mong deyselves, twel at las' dey 'greed fer ter have a 'sembly fer ter sorter straighten out matters en hear de complaints. En w'en de day come dey wuz on han'. De Lion, he wuz dar, kaze he wuz de king, en he hat-ter be dar. De Rhynossyhoss, he wuz dar, en de Elephent, he wuz dar, en de Cammils, en de Cows, en plum down ter de Crawfishes, dey wuz dar. Dey wuz all dar. En w'en de Lion shuck his mane, en tuck his seat in de big cheer, den de seshun begun.

Dey spoke speeches, en hollered, en cusst, en flung der langwidge 'roun'. Howsumever, dey 'ranged der 'fairs en splained der bizness. Bimeby, w'ile dey wuz 'sputin', de Elephent trompled on one er de Crawfishes. Co'se w'en dat creetur put his foot down, w'atsumever's under dar wuz squshed, en dey wa'nt nuff er dat Crawfish lef' fer ter tell

dat he'd bin dar. Dis make de udder Crawfishes mighty mad, en dey sorter swarmed tergedder en draw'd up a kinder peramble wid some warfo's in it, en read her out in de 'sembly. But, bless grashus! sech a racket wuz a-gwine on dat nobody ain't hear it, 'ceppin maybe de Mud Turkle en de Spring Lizzud, en dere enfloons wuz pow'ful lackin'.

Bimeby, w'iles de Nunicorn wuz 'sputin' wid de Lion, en w'ile de Hyener wuz a-laughin' ter hisse'f, de Elephent squshed anudder one er de Crawfishes, w'at dey wuz lef' un um, swarmed tergedder en draw'd up anudder peramble; but dey might ez well sung "Ole Dan Tucker" ter a harrycane. De udder creeturs wuz too busy wid der fussin' fer ter 'spon' onto de Crawfishes. So dar dey wuz, de Crawfishes, en dey kep' on gittin madder en madder en skeerder en skeerder, twel bimeby dey gun de wink ter de Mud Turkle en de Spring Lizzud, en dey bo'd little holes in de groun' en went down outer sight.

Dey bo'd inter de groun' en kep' on bo'in twel dey onloost de foun-tains er de earf; en de waters squirt out, en riz higher en higher twel de hills wuz kivvered, en de creeturs wuz all drownded; en all bekaze dey let on 'mong deyselves dat dey wuz bigger dan de Crawfishes.

SO THAT'S WHY
Stories That Explain

The long-term edification of children and their short-term amusement have often combined to spur impromptu manufacture of "how come" tales. Here a woman's patient voice rises out of a cautionary turtle tale. Her voice takes on an edge—irony, self-hatred—when she tries to explain how the blacks got the short end.

THE TURTLE

De turkle ain't han'some lak de yothah critters; he ain't got no haiah lak mos' ov 'em, an' he ain't got but mighty little hide, an' some o' his fambly kin go inside an' shet de front do' an' de back do' an' you can't see neither dey haids ner dey tails. But dey wa'n't allus dat-a-way. Dey use' to be a good-lookin' fambly, an' hit all come about along o' de 'speriunce an' troubles dat de turkles got into in de early days a-playin' wid fiah.

In dem times de turkles had sof' skin an' haiah all ovah 'em des lak de yothah crittahs. An' dey was mighty fon' o' wheat an' dey use' ter go on picnics to de wheatfiel's an' pull down de wheat an' eat it. But one day de turkle fambly got into a wheatfiel' dat mek 'em trouble al de res' o' dey lives. Dey was all in dere a-eatin' de wheat, but dey done lef' two o' de children by de picnic fiah, an' dey done tole 'em to keep de dawgs away from de kitchin things an' to *be sho' an' not play in de fiah.* Well, suh, putty soon dem children forgit all about not playin' in de fiah, an' dey begin to make red ribbons wid de chunks, an' de fus' thing yo' know de fiah cotch de wheat an' de win' blowed it.

Well, suh, dem 'ar turkles nevah was much of a fambly fur runnin', but dey natchelly lit out o' dar when dey seed de fiah a-comin' to'ds 'em. But 'twan't no use; de fiah cotch up wid 'em, an' dey hides was so buhnt an' swunk up dat dey was all out o' shape an' dere eyes was all blood-shot. An' mo'n dat, de fiah was so hot an' hurted 'em so dat dey all crope to de creek an' got into de watah to suage de pain. An' when dey done dat, de bubbles come to de top an' de watah jes' sizzled an' mek dey hides hahd lak a piece o' hot iron when de blacksmith put it in de watah. An' eva sense dat time de turkles has all stayed in de watah or mighty close to it whar dey can drop in an' git out'n de way if any trouble comes along. An' to dis day wheneva Mr. Turkle jumps in de watah de bubbles come to de top.

An' dat's what meks me tell ye, honey, if ye want to grow up han'sum, don't nebber play wid fiah.

HARD WORK? TWO REASONS

God made up a great big bundle and let it down in de middle of de road. It laid dere for thousands of years; then Ole Missus said to Ole Massa: "Go pick up dat box. Ah want to see what's in it." Ole Massa look at de box and it look so heavy dat he says to de slave, "Go fetch me dat big ole box out dere in de road." De black been stumblin' over de box a long

Yanked by a sartorially splendid Devil through a hole in the wall, the snake loses his legs forever and abandons all hope of regaining the good will o' 'spectable folk.

Froggy went a-tippling and that's how he learned his blissful call "jug-o-rum!" Both John Branner pictures date from 1921.

time so he tell his wife, "'Oman, go git dat box." So de black 'oman, she runned to git de box. She says, "Ah always lak to open up a big box 'cause there's nearly always something good in great big boxes." So she grabbed a-hold of de box and opened it up and it was full of hard work. Dat's de reason de sister in black works harder than anybody.

Aw, no, dat ain't de reason blacks is working so hard. God let down two bundles 'bout five miles down de road. So de white man and de black man raced to see who would git there first. Well, de black outrun de white and grabbed de biggest bundle. He was so skeered de white man would git it away from him he fell on top of de bundle and hollered back, "Oh, Ah got here first and dis biggest bundle is mine." De white man says, "All right, Ah'll take yo' leavings," and picked up de li'l teeninchy bundle layin' in de road. When de black man opened up his bundle he found a pick and shovel and a hoe and a plow and chop ax and then de white man opened up his bundle and found a writin' pen and ink. So ever since then de black been out in de hot sun, usin' his tools, and de white man been sittin' up figgerin' ought's a ought, figger's a figger; all for de white man, none for de nigger.

HAVE YOU GOT RELIGION?
Certainly, Lord!

When captive blacks came to America, their new owners often prohibited the practice of their traditional tribal African religions; the result was that many of them embraced Christianity. "Praise houses" became the major focal point of what social life Negroes had—a church in which visions, ecstasies, and "speaking in tongues" regularly accompanied the making of a joyful noise unto the Lord. The following selections—the first a typical sermon and the second a convert's testimonial—show how it felt to "walk all over God's Heaven" in the exuberance of an all-night "shout" led by a preacher who was really a poet-singer.

BEHOLD THE RIB

The oldtime Negro preacher followed traditional African call-and-response song patterns, starting slowly and softly and rising to a climax punctuated with the congregation's amens:

"I take my text from Genesis 2:21. Behold de rib! Now, my beloved, behold means to look and see. Look at dis woman God done made. But first thing, ah hah, Ah wants you to gaze upon God's previous works! Almighty and arisen God, hah!

Peace-giving and prayer-hearing God, high-riding and strong-armed God, walking acrost his globe creation, hah! Wid de blue elements for a helmet and wall of fire round his feet, He wakes de sun every morning from his fiery bed wid de breath of his smile and commands de moon wid his eyes, and oh, wid de eye of Faith I can see Him! Even de lion had a mate, so God shook his head and a thousand million diamonds flew out from his glittering crown and studded de evening sky and made the stars.

So God put Adam into a deep sleep and took out a bone, ah hah, and it is said that it was a rib! Behold de rib! A bone out of a man's side. He put the man to sleep and made wo-man, and men and women been sleeping together ever since. Behold de rib! Brothers, if God had taken dat bone out of man's head, He would have meant for woman to rule, hah! If He had taken a bone out of his foot, He would have meant for us to dominize and rule. He could have made her out of backbone, and then she would have been behind us. But no, God Almighty, He took de bone out of his side, so dat places de woman beside us, hah! God knowed his own mind. Behold de rib! I can *see* Him seize de mighty ax of his proving power and smite the stubborn-standing space and laid it wide open with a mighty gash—making a place to hold de world. I can see Him—molding de world out of thought and power and whirling it out on its eternal track, ah hah, my strong-armed God! He set de blood-red eye of de sun in de sky and told it, 'Wait, wait! Wait there till

This outdoor "shout" was among the exotic sights sought out by the Russian painter Pavel Petrovich Svinin, who visited the United States during the mid-19th century. Revival religion gave the oppressed blacks an opportunity to let off some steam.

"A Pastoral Visit," by Richard Norris Brooke. Black ministers enjoyed high prestige among their followers, and the best of them tended to be sympathetic listeners as well as fiery preachers.

Shiloh come!' I can *see* Him mold de mighty mountains and melting de skies into seas. Oh, behold, and look and see, hah! We see in de beginning He made de beasts every one after its kind. De birds that fly de trackless air, de fishes dat swim de mighty deep—male and fee-male, hah! Then He took of de dust of de earth and made man in his own image. And man was alone. Let us all go marchin' up to de gates of Glory. Tramp, tramp, tramp! Oh, behold de rib! And let's all sct down in Glory together right round his glorified throne and praise his name forever."

GREEN PASTURES

An old lady born in slavery on a cotton plantation recalled late in life the visionary experiences that led to her conversion:

The first time I heard the voice, I was in the cotton patch. A voice said, "Behold, I move you by the still waters." The voice was like muttering thunder. I did not join the church, and a little later I had my soul fixed up. I saw myself standing on a pretty white rock with nothing around it. I was afraid I was going to fall into the deep pit. It seemed that there was nothing to pity me. I was a little image and my body was standing beside me. While I stood there, a little man came before me and said, "Don't you know that you will be devoured in here?" With this he took me in his arms and journeyed on a narrow white path that seemed no wider than a spider web. I saw three devils, one very large, one smaller, etc. They threw three large balls at me and I cried and said, "Lord, if those balls should hit me they would tear me to pieces." We journeyed on and saw two lions lying by the side of the path. They were cream-colored. They did not move as we passed. We journeyed on and came to a beautiful green pasture with beautiful green grass. Every spring seemed even. There was a beautiful willow tree and every limb seemed even. My guide put me down and said, "I leave you in the hands of the mother." She arose, a very tall woman who was wearing a long white robe and she dressed me the same way, and when she was through she said, "Everything just fits." I then began to shout and praise God with the rest of the angels. We must see, feel, and hear something, for our God talks to his children. I joined the church after nearly 10 years of experience and I rejoice ever in the love of God. The love of God is beyond understanding. It makes you love everybody.

STEAL AWAY

Steal a—way, Steal a—way, Steal a—way to Je—sus,
Steal a—way, steal a—way home, I ain't got long to stay here.
My Lord— calls me, He calls me by the thun-der, The
trum-pet sounds with-in-a my soul, I ain't got long to stay here.

Green trees bending, poor sinner stands a-trembling,
The trumpet sounds within-a my soul,
I ain't got long to stay here.

My Lord calls me, he calls me by the lightning,
The trumpet sounds within-a my soul,
I ain't got long to stay here.

"Steal away to Jesus" had a double meaning: "Escape to freedom!" Negro spirituals are full of references to the oppressed Jews of Bible times, with whom slaves came to identify. The music blends white and African elements.

GHOSTS AND GRAVEYARDS
Shudders and Belly Laughs

A pastime much enjoyed by field Negroes was the storytelling sessions that were held secretly in the quarters of different plantations on long winter nights—favorite themes were "ghosties," witches, Jack-o'-lantern, the evil eye, etc. Despite owners' efforts to prevent the gatherings, slaves hiked from one place to another in order to attend. Some stories were downright terrifying; folks were even known to refuse to leave the fireside before morning, they were so frightened. In other tales a blend of the shudder and the belly laugh predominates:

JACK-O'-LANTERN

Jack-o'-lantern, or Jack for short, was a goblin haunting swamps and luring folk with his lantern into bogs and pools where they drowned. The ancestry of Jack's story, like that of many of its narrators, was mixed—English, Scotch-Irish, and African. On the European side the swamp-haunting Jack-o'-lantern was another name for will-o'-the-wisp, fox fire, or ignis fatuus [foolish fire], a kind of glow emitted by decaying timber. Often seen in marshy places at night, this light seemed to recede, then vanish, and then reappear. The Irish tradition that Jack-o'-lantern was the wandering soul of one who had been refused admittance to both Heaven and Hell was taken over by southern blacks. Others said he was the spirit of someone they knew, recently deceased. He was described as a hairy creature, with goggle eyes and huge mouth, that bounded along like a human-size grasshopper. Yet, they said, if you met Jack, despite his fearsome and repulsive appearance you would be filled with an irresistible impulse to follow him and his lantern. You might be immune to his power, though, if you wore your coat or pockets inside out or carried a new knife that had never cut wood. According to one old root doctor, Jack was originally a man who sold himself to the Devil at the crossroads one night at midnight. For seven years all power was given to him to do as he pleased, but at the end of that period his soul belonged to the Devil. When old Satan called for him, Jack was ready. He had tacked a piece of old shoe sole up above the door and asked the Devil to get it for him. When the Devil stood on a chair and reached for it, Jack took a hammer and nailed the Devil's hand fast, slipping the chair out from under him. Upon a promise of his freedom, Jack then released old Satan. Finally Jack died. He went up to Heaven, but those in charge would not let him in. He went down to Hell, but the Devil threw a chunk of fire at him and told him he was too smart for Hell. Jack, deprived of a home, was forced to pick up the chunk of fire and to spend all his time wandering about the earth luring people into swamps and mudholes at night.

SEEING GHOSTS

Sea Island, Georgia, Negroes held that a special fluid if put on the eyes would make one "double-sighted," or able to see ghosts. In the view of ordinary folk it was an unlucky power. As one aged Gullah exclaimed upon recalling a youthful sightseeing trip to the invisible world: "Spirits sure worrisome!" His story:

When I been a young boy my

A boy seeking a peek at the invisible world took a "coat" from his dog's eye

granny tell me exactly what for do if you want to experience ghosts. She say you must take a coat out of a dog eye and place 'em in you eye. I try that plan one night just for deviltry. You know how boy-kind is—always want to try some new prank. Well, as I say, I try the plan out. I got a old dog name Lion. I sneak up to Lion when he been sleep by the fire and stick my finger in he eye. The dog let out a yell and jump through the window. Goodby dog. After he gone, I stick the same finger that been in Lion eye in my own eye, and I put on my cap and leave the house. Well, sir, I scarcely gone two task [a task is roughly 100 feet—a local land measure] 'fore I see something dance 'fore my eye like a swarm of big bird. I know they ain't bird, though, 'cause they got long leg and long arm sekker [same as] people but they fly round just like buzzard. They start for whoof and whiff. Then I really get scare. I shut my eye tight and run. That night I reckon I knock 'gainst every tree in Big Wood, but I ain't care. Got to get 'way from them ghost 'fore they take my mind away. After that, I ain't never take coat out dog eye and put 'em in my eye. I done satisfy myself about ghost, bubber. You liable for see ghost anyhow in you travelin'. Ain't no use to seek 'em out.

PLAT-EYE

Plat-eye was the name of a kind of evil spirit with fiery eyes that attacked wayfarers in the woods, swamps, and other solitary places. A black great-grandmother, questioned about plat-eye, told of a youthful encounter thus:

One time—I have my bloom on me [I was young] and was clamming in them days—and the tide been very late in the evening. It was dusky dark when I hit the Parsonage Lane, and when I been come to the footlog [a single-log bridge] I turn my eye up and there was a cat—black cat with he eye like balls of fire and he back all arched up and he tail twitchin' and a-switchin', and he hair stand on end. He move front of me 'cross that

"An Oldtime Midnight Slave Funeral," by W. L. Sheppard. On some plantations it was the Negroes' custom to bury their dead at midnight, or as close to it as was possible.

cypress log; and he been big, large as my little yearling ox. And I say: "I ain't for fear nuttin'. Ain't no ghost! Ain' no plat-eye! Ain' no nuttin'!"

And that plat-eye ain't give me back my word [didn't reply]. He move forward, and he tail swish same like big moccasin tail when he lash the rushes. My short-handled clam rake been in my hand, and I sing, "God will take care of me,/ Walkin' through many of dangers."

And then the mind come to me, "The Lord helps them what helps theyself." When I raise up my rake, and I come right 'cross that critter's head. If that had been real cat, I'd ha' pin him to that log. But that critter ain't feel my lick. And I'se wrastle like Jacob with the angel. I been strong and have my bloom on me, but it ain't 'vail nothin'. No, man! Mr. Plat-Eye just as pert and frisky as 'fore he been hit. And I 'buse him and I cuss him and say, "You devil! Clear my path!" And if that critter didn't paw the air and just rise up that big bamboo vine, and me for hit him every jump! My mind come to

me, "Child of God, travel the woods path!" And I turn back and make haste, and I hit that path. Just as I was giving God the praise for deliver me, there that cat! This time he big as my middle-size ox, and he eye been blaze! And I lam [fled] and I lam, and just as I make my last lam, that critter rise up 'fore my eyes, and this time he been big as my cousin Andrew full-grown ox. And he vanish in that old box pine as you quit the deep woods. Yas'm. I ain't believe in plat-eye till then, but I minds my step since them days. And when I travels the deep woods where the moss wave low, and Mr. Cooter live, and Mr. Moccasin crawl, and the firefly flicker, my pocket for load [is loaded]. Yas'm. I'se ready for 'em. Gunpowder and sulfur. They is say plat-eye can't stand them smells mixed. Uncle Murphy he witch doctor and he been tell me how for fend 'em off. That man full of knowledge, he must have God mind in him. So I totes my powder and sulfur, and I carries stick in my hand and puts my trust in God.

MARDI GRAS

Mardi Gras, the famed celebration that takes place on the Tuesday just before Lent in New Orleans and a number of other southern American cities, has origins that can be traced all the way back to prehistoric rites of spring. Anthropologists have identified annual celebrations of the end of winter and the birth of the new year in almost every society in the world. By the time of Roman hegemony, elements of the modern festivities, such as the wearing of masks (believed to protect one from the supernatural) had become fixed in the ritual. With the spread of Christianity the festival was incorporated into the holy calendar as *carne vale*—literally, "farewell to meat," or possibly, "farewell to fleshly delights"—in reference to the solemn 40 days of penitence that follow. Mardi Gras (properly speaking, only the last day of carnival) translates as "fat Tuesday," descriptive of the great feasting that marks the finale. Typically, the old French Mardi Gras was marked by street parades, carousing, the wearing of elaborate costumes and masks, and the "worship" of a master of revels, a lord of misrule.

All of these elements have descended intact to French-influenced parts of the southern United States, where Mardi Gras is marked with more good-natured gusto than any other event of the year. Just when Mardi Gras was first celebrated in the New World remains in dispute. The name, at least, entered our vocabulary in 1699 when Pierre le Moyne, sieur d'Iberville, and his party of Mississippi Delta explorers honored fat Tuesday by naming their camping place on that day Bayou Mardi Gras. In the years of French settlement that followed, colonists marked the day with casually organized parties and dances. The Spanish, who took over the region in 1769, continued the custom, though they tried to prohibit masking in order to cut down crime and wild behavior. With the Louisiana Purchase in 1803 and the establishment of American rule in the Delta area, still more strictures were placed on Mardi Gras, and in 1806, when it was rumored that the adventurer Aaron Burr was scheming an attack on New Orleans, the authorities banned the celebrations altogether for fear that the Burr forces would slip into town unnoticed because of the general excitement.

For 21 years fat Tuesday was little more than the day before Ash Wednesday, but in 1827 a group of young Creoles, recently returned to New Orleans from their studies in Paris, revived the revelries. At first they were satisfied to merely form chains of celebrants and run through the streets shouting and cavorting. But in 1838 some unnamed hero had the idea of organizing the day into what turned out to be the first cousin of the Mardi Gras festival as it exists today.

The New Orleans *Commercial Bulletin* excitedly reported: "The European custom of celebrating the last day of the carnival by a procession of masqued figures . . . was introduced here yesterday . . . The principal streets were traversed by a masquerade company." Even more enthusiastic was the story in the *Daily Picayune:* "A large number of Creole gentlemen of the first respectability went to no little expense with their preparations. In the procession were several carriages superbly ornamented—bands of music, horses richly caparisoned—personations of knights, cavaliers, heroes, demigods, chanticleers, punchinellos, etc., all mounted. Many of them were dressed in female attire and acted the lady with no small degree of grace."

The following year, by all accounts, the display was even greater and, times being good, so were the balls and parties that preceded it. For those not actually engaged in the parading, there was a kind of spectator involvement in throwing flour on the marchers—a

curious custom which grew each year until it was said the white stuff was so liberally dispensed that it looked as though a blizzard had struck the city. This innocent form of fun came to an end a few years later when rowdies took to substituting bricks, dust, and quicklime for the flour, and the authorities once again attempted to impose some rules of conduct.

The first of the great "krewes," or secret carnival organizations, made its debut in 1857. Calling itself the Mistick Krewe of Comus (Comus being the ancient Greek god of revelry), the group produced a well-organized parade, complete with splendid costumes, all devoted to the theme "The Demon Actors in Milton's *Paradise Lost*." For five glorious years they were the main attraction of Mardi Gras. In 1862 the Civil War banished all thoughts of merrymaking. But only temporarily—after the war the Comus Krewe was back again, soon to be joined by numbers of other krewes, whose memberships became highly sought social prizes and whose plan-

ning activities sometimes occupied the better part of each year. Carnival time began to stretch backward as the parties multiplied, until it overlapped Twelfth Night in early January. But fat Tuesday was and remains the climactic day of the year in Creole America.

"When Rex and his train enter the queer old streets," wrote a mid-19th-century onlooker, "the balconies are crowded with spectators." Rex, or King, was the title of the presiding masker in the festival, and the Parade of the King and His Minions was—and still is—a highlight of the Mardi Gras.

MAGPIES AND MAGNOLIAS
Skeletons in the Closet

"In many families every child had his individual slave," wrote a 19th-century visitor. "Great gentlemen almost openly kept their concubines; great ladies half dozed through the long summer afternoons on their shaded piazzas, mollified by the slow fanning of their black attendants and by the laving of their feet in water periodically fetched anew from the springhouse." Such was the white South as others saw her and as she at times saw herself. To round out that picture, a couple of eerie planter-family legends current in the pre-Civil War era appear below:

THE GILDED MIRROR

A wealthy Alabama planter's daughter married a young New Yorker she had met through his sister who was a classmate at finishing school in New York City. The bride's father presented the young couple with a substantial plantation, and they began their married life happily. The New Yorker's health, however, was not equal to the rigors of Alabama life, and he was soon bedridden and under a doctor's care. The physician was a gallant young southerner who proved so sympathetic and engaging that before long he and the wife became lovers, and every afternoon old Joshua, the lady's favorite slave since childhood, hitched up a team and drove his mistress to a secluded trysting place out in the woods.

One day while the lovers were thus absent, a lone visitor walked his horse up to the big house, gave over his reins to a slave, and went to the master's room. Soon loud voices were heard, and the visitor strode out of the house and rode off quickly.

The next morning, the invalid came downstairs from his sickroom and had Joshua brought to the whipping post next to the house. He sat in a big cushioned chair while a black overseer methodically lashed the skin from old Joshua's bare back. During the overseer's pauses to rest, the slave was asked what his mistress did each day, at which he swore there was nothing to tell. Finally the master, believing that no man could endure such torture without breaking down and telling all he knew, had Joshua taken away and cared for.

The exertion of going back upstairs proved too much for the master, however, and he had gone only a few steps when he suffered a heart attack. The young doctor was summoned. He ordered the big four-poster bed brought down and set up in the reception room just to the left of the front door, saying it would be dan-

Folklore and fiction of the white antebellum South dwell on aristocratic romance in a setting of mansions and moss.

Mistress of Peckatone

There were few haunted places in John Smith's Jamestown or in the surrounding forests of tidewater Virginia during the Old Dominion's second and third generations. But with the rise of a slavery-based tobacco gentry, many a fine house came to reecho the vicissitudes of former occupants. Typical was Peckatone, where stood one of the earliest great houses on the Potomac. In addition to lofty brick walls, sweeping facade, porches of marble, and spacious, well-lit rooms, it boasted extensive wine cellars from which earthenware bottles stamped "Peckatone" are still being found today. But gradually, after festive beginnings, the house fell silent and empty.

The mansion's fourth proprietor, Martha Turberville (nee Corbin), an only child who had spent much of her childhood at Peckatone, inherited the house when she was a young woman and occupied it thereafter with her husband, George Turberville. Turberville became known as a tyrant over his slaves, distinguishing himself by such actions as leaving a black coachman chained to the box of his coach while dining abroad with friends. "The fellow is inclined to run away," said George Turberville. With or without her husband's influence, Martha began to indulge her own sadistic urges. She used the wine cellars as a dungeon in which she incarcerated fractious overseers and acquired a taste for whipping her slaves. Some, it is said, she even whipped to death. Meantime, leading a double life, Martha became favorite aunt to a generation of tidewater belles, throwing gay parties with lots of dancing. At the same time, she took to sallying forth in her coach on mysterious nocturnal errands, armed with pistols and other guns, and carrying an ax—to remove all obstructions, she said. One night she went out in a storm and was caught in a sudden twister. She, her coach, coachman, and horses were all carried away, lifted into the heart of the whirlwind, never again to be seen. Afterward, from time to time there were reports of blood-curdling shrieks and groans and of lights moving from room to room in the darkened house, which stood empty for years. A century later, in 1888, it burned; and at last the ground it had occupied was claimed by the Potomac.

gerous to move the patient even as far as his room. This solicitude caused the doctor to be found out; as he said farewell to his beloved in the secrecy of the front hallway, the great gilded mirror above the marble mantel betrayed their guilty embrace to the sick man's eyes.

The New Yorker said nothing but thought of his friend who had warned him and been rudely dismissed for his pains. He sent for the friend, asking forgiveness. The narrative so distressed the reconciled friend that it gave him a headache, so the invalid suggested that he join him in taking a dose of a sedative powder the doctor had prescribed. A few moments after swallowing the medicine, both men were dead.

As was to be expected, suspicion of murder fell upon the doctor, but he suggested that the victims of his medicine had been drinking and had taken too many of the powders. He pointed out that none of those left on the bedside table contained a lethal dose. There was no tangible proof that the doctor's deductions were false.

Free now to do as they pleased, the lovers waited a few months for the whisperings of foul play to die down. They waited in vain; so at length the two sold their property, got married, and went to France where they lived happily, as far as anyone knows, for many years.

THE GHOST BRIDE

Fenwick Hall on Johns Island near the mouth of the Stono River was the setting for one of South Carolina's most tragic romances. The Fenwick family business was the raising of racehorses and life at the Hall was prideful and gay, for the best young bloods of the region came on their thoroughbreds to woo Edward Fenwick's lovely daughters. But the gayest and loveliest one committed the unforgivable sin of falling in love with her father's head groom. The couple eloped on the stable's swiftest thoroughbred but, delayed at Stono Ferry, were overtaken by members of the family headed by the enraged father. The lover was instantly tried by a mock court and convicted as a horsethief. Then, disregarding the girl's supplications, they hanged the young man on an oak tree as she fell into a deathlike swoon. Her mind never recovered from the shock. And, they say, because she was so cruelly deprived of her young joy, her spirit still haunted the place long after the last Fenwicks were gone from Carolina. Even when the old Hall stood in solitude no caretaker was willing to live there. For, according to Johns Island's Negroes, a spell and a curse had been put on the place and the cries of sea birds were not the only eerie noises there. Light footsteps could be heard throughout the house at odd times, they said, "and when first dark come, de sperrit walk under de oak by Stono Ferry, wringin' 'e han'." On dark nights the thunder of galloping hooves could be heard on the King's Highway, and horses passed more swiftly than the wind; on clear nights at full moon, a lady in a misty white mantle was sometimes glimpsed at the side of her lover, gliding in the shadows under the trees on Stono Avenue.

JOHN AND MASTER
Trickster at Work

While whites saw themselves as gentlemen and ladies bountiful, their Negro slaves in tales sometimes presented them as pompous Massa and Mistress who were harsh though occasionally protective. They knew Marse had the whip but not the wit. His slave was both slow- and fast-witted, but one never knew which he was going to be when. This seeming split personality belongs to the familiar trickster figure who also still retains some vestiges of his African predecessors. In his animal form he is Brer Rabbit and as a human he is usually called John.

OLD JOHN AND THE CANE

The master was very fond of fishing, and it happened that, liking company, he often took John along with him on his fishing trips. One day while they were sitting on the bank of the river waiting for the fish to bite and whiling away the time, John said that Master's walking cane had three ends, and he offered to show the ends to the master. Master said that John must have gone crazy and furthermore that if John could show him three ends to his walking cane he would set him free.

John picked up the top of the cane, pointed to it, and said, "That's one end." He picked up the other end of the cane and said, "That's the other end." Then he threw the cane in the middle of the river where it was caught by the current and said, "That's the last end."

DIVVYING UP SOULS

One night two slaves stole a sack of sweet potatoes. They decided that the best place to divide them would be down in the graveyard, where they would not be disturbed. Another slave, Isom, who had been visiting a neighboring plantation, happened to be passing that way on the road home, and hearing voices in the graveyard, he decided to stop by the fence and listen.

It was too dark for him to see, but he heard one of the thieves saying in a singsong voice: "Ah'll take dis un, an' yuh take dat un. Ah'll take dis un, an' yuh take dat un." "Lawd, ha' mercy," said Isom to himself. "Ah b'lieve dat Gawd an' de Debbil am

The master enjoys a moment of imperial pleasure as he reaches into his pocket for some coins to hand out to his plantation boys; the gentleman was most apt to re- collect himself in such kindly postures.

down hyeah dividin' up souls. Ah's gwine an' tell Ole Massa."

"You don't know what you are talking about," said the master. "Massa, ef yuh don' b'lieve hit, cum go down dar yo'se'f." "All right," said the master, "and if you are lying to me I am going to whip you good tomorrow." Sure enough, when Isom and the master got near the grave- yard they heard the singsong voice saying: "Yuh take dis un, an' Ah'll take dat un. Yuh take dis un, an' Ah'll take dat un." "See dar, didn' Ah tell yuh, Massa?" said Isom.

In the meantime the two black men almost finished the division of the potatoes but remembered they had dropped two over by the fence—where Isom and the master were standing out of sight. Finally, when they had only two potatoes left, the one who was counting said, "Ah'll take dese two an' yuh take dem two over dere by de fence."

Upon hearing this, Isom and the master ran home as fast as they could go. After this the master never doubted Isom's word about what he saw and heard.

SWAPPING DREAMS

One morning when Ike entered the master's room to clean it, he found him just preparing to get out of bed. "Ike," the master said, "I certainly did have a strange dream last night." "Sez yuh did, Massa, sez yuh did?" answered Ike. "Lemme hyeah it." "All right," replied Mr. Turner. "It was like this: I dreamed I went to Black Heaven last night and saw there a lot of garbage, some old torn-down houses, a few old bro- ken-down, rotten fences, the muddi- est, sloppiest streets I ever saw, and a

Together Master and Mistress stop by th cottonfields on their morning ride, seein

big bunch of ragged, dirty blacks walking around."

"Umph, umph, Massa," said Ike, "yuh sho' musta et de same t'ing Ah did las' night, 'cause Ah dreamed Ah went up ter de white man's paradise, an' de streets wuz all ob gol' an' silvah, an' dey wuz lots o' milk an' honey dere, an' putty pearly gates, but dey wuzn't uh soul to be seen in de whole place."

PRAY BUT DON'T TRUST

Uncle Bob Jordan was the outprayingest Christian on the Green plantation. He had long been known for his prayers, but now he was praying more than he had ever prayed. He was 72 years old, and as he could no longer work much, his master had promised him his freedom for $20. Uncle Bob would go down into the woods near the big house every night about 7 o'clock and get down on his knees and pray, asking God to please send him $20 for his freedom.

He had been praying for about a month when the master passed near the tree where Uncle Bob was praying one night and overheard the prayer. The master decided that the

le but childlike frolic in the occupation of eir slaves who must pick the cotton bolls.

next night he would have some fun out of Uncle Bob. So just before dark he went down to the prayer tree and climbed up in it.

At dark Uncle Bob came under the tree, got down on his knees, and started praying as usual: "Oh, Lawd, sen' me $20 to buy mah freedom. Oh, Lawd, sen' me $20 to buy mah freedom." "All right, Uncle Bob," came the master's voice from overhead, "look down at the foot of the tree and you will find a 10-dollar bill."

The mistress set about to accomplish her good works in the cottages that ringed the big house. Here, one charitably inclined lady transports hot soup in a hefty tureen to a sick old "aunt" who lies abed.

Sure enough, Uncle Bob looked and found a 10-dollar bill. "Come back tomorrow night," said the voice, "and you will find a 5-dollar bill." "Sho sho', Lawd," said Uncle Bob, taking the 10-dollar bill and sticking it in his pocket. "Thank yuh, thank yuh."

The next night the master beat Uncle Bob to the tree again and hid in its branches. At dark Uncle Bob came and prayed his accustomed prayer: "Oh, Lawd, please sen' me 10 mo' dollahs to buy mah freedom." "Uncle Bob," responded the voice from overhead, "look at the foot of

the tree and you will find another 5-dollar bill. Take the 10-dollar bill I gave you last night, and the 5-dollar bill I gave you tonight, and bring them back tomorrow night. Put them underneath the tree so that I can get them, and the next night I will bring you a 20-dollar bill."

"No, sah, no sah, dat's aw right, Lawd," answered Uncle Bob. "Ah sho' thanks yuh fuh de 15, but Ah'll git de udder 5 someplace else."

TELLIN' FORTUNES

One day John and his Old Massa was goin' along and John said, "Ole Massa, Ah kin tell fortunes." When they got to the next man's plantation, Ole Massa told de landlord, "I have a slave dat kin tell fortunes." So de other man said: "Dat slave can't tell no fortunes. I bet my plantation and all my blacks against yours dat he can't tell no fortunes."

Ole Massa says: "I'll take yo' bet. I bet everything in de world I got on John 'cause he don't lie. Bet you all my plantation and all my slaves against yours." So they called Notary Public and signed up de bet. Ole Massa straddled his horse and John got on his mule and they went on home. John was in de misery all that night and on de way over to de plantation where de bet was on.

De man on de plantation had went out and caught a coon and had a big old iron washpot turned down over it. There was many person there to hear John tell what was in under de washpot. Ole Massa brought John out and tole him: "John, if you tell what's under dat washpot, Ah'll make you independent rich. If you don't, Ah'm goin' to kill you because you'll make me lose my plantation."

John walked round and round dat pot but he couldn't git de least inklin' of what was underneath it. Drops of sweat as big as yo' fist was rollin' off of John. At last he give up and said, "Well, you got de old coon at last."

Ole Massa jumped in de air and cracked his heels twice befo' he hit de ground. He give John a new suit of clothes and a saddle horse. And John quit tellin' fortunes after that.

273

STEAL AWAY
The Underground Railroad

Long before Harriet Tubman supposedly sang the hymn "Steal Away" outside slave cabins at night, men had fled to the woods to escape the brutalization of slavery, whether physical or mental. They followed the North Star by night and hid by day. Women and children joined in, helped by the "conductors" of an "underground railroad," which developed after about 1810 to move "packages," "goods," or even "hams" from one "depot" to the next. If caught by the whites paid to hunt them, conductors would be fined or jailed and slaves whipped. Escape tales are full of hiding, mistaken identity, and the sweetness of freedom.

MRS. WALKER

In 1856 a schooner containing 15 passengers, which set out from Norfolk, encountered more than the usual dangers. All were required to enter a hole apparently leading through the bottom of the boat but in reality a compartment expressly constructed for the Underground Railroad. The entrance was not sufficiently large to admit Mrs. Walker, so she hid behind some corn in the back of the cabin. The captain put out to sea. After some 15 hours he deemed it safe to bring passengers on deck where they could inhale pure air, which was greatly needed. Before reaching the lock the captain called upon them to "go into their hole," and not even the big woman was excused now. She pleaded that she could not get through; her fellow sufferers said that she must or they would have great danger to face. The big woman again tried to effect an entrance, but in vain. Said one of the more resolute sisters: "She must take off her clothes, for it will never do to have her staying up on deck to betray the rest." This stand being unanimous, the poor woman had to comply, and except for a single garment she was as destitute of raiment as was Mother Eve before she induced Adam to eat of the forbidden fruit. With the help of passengers below, she was squeezed through, but not without bruising and breaking the skin. When all were beneath deck, the well-fitting oilcloth was put over the hole and a heavy table set over that. At the lock, three officers came on board to look for runaway slaves and talked with the captain, gaining no information except that "the yellow fever had been raging in Norfolk." Alarmed, they lost no time and commenced taking up hatchways, but the place seemed so perfumed with foul air the men declared that nobody could live in such a place and that it smelled like yellow fever; they concluded there were no slaves on that boat. Children had been put under the influence of liquor to keep them still, and the others endured their hour of agony patiently. It was a small price to pay for freedom.

A SLY CITY-SLICKER SLAVE

There was a white man named Kingsbury, of Charleston, South Carolina, whose business it was to buy the ownership titles of runaway slaves for a fraction of the prevailing prices. He would then hunt them down and resell them at a goodly profit. It was in this manner that he purchased title to an escaped slave named Billy, and in the course of his pursuit found himself in New York.

Further investigation led him to a warehouse on Peck Slip, a place that was known for harboring refugee slaves. Mr. Kingsbury was well aware that this particular warehouse was a "station" of the Underground Railroad, and he also knew that there were a few greedy souls there who would turn in their own mothers for the right price . . . or at least he hoped so. As he expected, he was soon approached by a black man. "Who are you hunting for?" the stranger asked bluntly.

"Slave named Billy, from the Eastland plantation in Georgia," said the hunter of humans. "I'm paying $25 reward for his capture."

"That's a good business you're in," said the black man. "If you catch him, you can resell him at a handsome profit. Tell you what I'll do.

With banknotes and silver on the table around his feet, a slave endures the agony of being gambled for by "gentlemen" in this scene from the memory of William W. Brown.

backbreaking work from dawn to dark," said one of the Bostonians.

"Not really," replied the black man, surprising everyone with his precise English. "My master allowed us to sleep a full eight hours, we were permitted an hour for lunch, and we quit work in time for dinner."

"How did you learn to speak so well?" asked another. "Were you in fear for your life when you educated yourself? I understand that a slave can be whipped to death for seeking to improve his lot." The man smiled. "My master encouraged all of his slaves to learn to read and write," he said. "And I have never been whipped in my life. My master did not believe in physical punishment."

"Well," said the minister's wife, breaking into the discussion, "I'm going to fix you a good meal and get you some decent clothes. I'll bet you've been half starved all your life and never had a decent thing to wear—poor man." "On the contrary," was the response. "My master fed us extremely well and gave us proper clothing."

"Then what in tarnation did you run away for?" demanded the minister, breaking the deadly silence that now pervaded the group.

"Sir," answered the black man respectfully, "I assure you that the position I just vacated is still available, should any of you want the job."

TO BE A SLAVE
My pappy name Jeff and belong to Marse Joe Woodward. He live on a plantation 'cross the other side of Wateree Crick. My mammy name Phoebe. Pappy have to git a pass to come to see Mammy before the war. Sometime that crick get up over the bank and I, to this day, 'members one time Pappy come in all wet and drenched with water. Him had made the mule swim the crick. Him stayed

You sell that title to me and if I catch him that's *my* good luck." He paused a moment and then added, "Without my help you'll *never* catch him and you'll lose your investment, too."

Kingsbury agreed. "You can buy title to Billy's ownership for $100," he said. "The slave is worth far more than that—if you catch him."

The other agreed. "I'll be back in an hour with the money." Good as his word, he returned within the hour, handed over the $100, and accepted the title to Billy's physical being. Kingsbury stuffed the bills into his pocket, smiling with satisfaction. "By the way," the slave-catcher said conversationally, "we may be able to do some future business. Who

are you? What's your name?"

The black man drew himself up and his own smile outshone that of his new partner. "Me? I'm an ex-slave, and my name is Billy!"

POSITION AVAILABLE
With the help of abolitionist sympathizers, a Mississippi slave undertook the perilous journey to the North via the Underground Railroad. Upon his arrival in Boston, where he finally found freedom, a group of well-wishers gathered at the local minister's house to question the former slave so that they might familiarize themselves with the many hardships he had known ever since his birth.

"You undoubtedly had to endure

In this dramatic painting by Charles Webber, "conductors" greet their "parcels" in wintry Ohio, at a terminal depot for freedom.

over his leave that was writ on the pass. Paterollers [poor whites hired to patrol plantations with bloodhounds, looking for runaways and pass violators] come ask for the pass. They say: "The time done out." Pappy try to explain, but they pay no 'tention. Tied him up, pulled down his breeches, and whupped him right before Mammy and us children. We begged them, in the name of God, to stop, that the crick was now up and dangerous to cross, and we would make it all right with Pappy's master. They say of Pappy: "Jeff swim 'cross. Let him git the mule and swim back." They make Pappy git on the mule and follow him down to the crick and watch him swim that swift muddy crick to the other side. I often think that the system of paterollers and bloodhounds did more to bring on the war and the wrath of the Lord than anything else.

Dogs could get you anytime: "Body an' Ned was tryin' to make it to Ohio. Dey traveled night after night. One night dey was tol' dey was one night's journey from de line. De dogs caught dem. Body died."

PEGLEG JOE

An old Negro said that just before the Civil War, somewhere north of Mobile, there came a sailor who had lost one leg and had the missing member replaced by a pegleg. He would appear very suddenly at some plantation and ask for work as a painter or carpenter. This he was able to get at almost every place. He made friends with the slaves and soon all of the young colored men were singing this song:

When the sun come back,
Then the time is come,

Foller the drinkin' gou'd.
The riva's bank am a very good road,
The dead trees show the way.
Lef' foot, peg foot, goin' on,
Foller the drinkin' gou'd.
The riva ends a-tween two hills,
'Nuther riva on the other side,
Foller the drinkin' gou'd.
Wha the little riva
Meet the grea' big un,
The ole man waits—
Foller the drinkin' gou'd.

The pegleg sailor would stay for a week or two at a place and then disappear. The following spring

nearly all the young men among the slaves disappeared and made their way north and finally reached Canada by following a trail held in memory by the Negroes in that peculiar song. They went northward to the headwaters of the Tombigbee River, thence over the divide and down the Tennessee River to the Ohio. The "drinkin' gou'd," of course, is the Big Dipper and the "ole man" the sailor who would meet them at the "great big un"—the Ohio. It seems that the sailor would go through the country, teach this song to the young slaves, show them a mark on his natural left foot and the round spot made by his pegleg, then go ahead of them and on every dead tree leave a charcoal or mud print of the outline of a human left foot and a round spot in place of the right foot. The last trip Pegleg made was in 1859.

When it was Mrs. Walker's turn to debark, even the captain had to lend a hand upbank.

WILLIAM "BOX" JONES

Twenty-five-year-old William had himself boxed up in Baltimore by a near relative and shipped north in a steamer. The limit of his box not admitting of straightening himself out, he was taken with a cramp on the road. Before a great while an excessive faintness came over him. He thought he must die, but after a struggle revived only to encounter a third ordeal no less painful than the others; a cold chill came over him, which seemed almost to freeze the blood in his veins and gave him agony, from which he found relief on awaking, having actually fallen asleep in that condition. He arrived at Philadelphia on a Sabbath morning. A devoted friend who had been expecting him met him at the wharf with the bill of lading. The officer of the boat looked at the bill and said, "No, we do not deliver freight on Sunday," but noticing the anxiety of the man, he asked him if he would know it if he were to see it. Slowly—fearing that too much interest might excite suspicion—he replied: "I think I should." Looking around amongst the "freight," he discovered the box and said, "I think that is it there." But the size of the box was too large for the carriage, and the driver refused to take it. Nearly an hour and a half was spent looking for a furniture car. Finally one was procured, and again the box was laid hold of by the occupant's friend when, to his dread alarm, the poor fellow within gave a cough. At this, he dropped the box; equally as quick, although dreadfully frightened, and as if helped by some invisible agency, he commenced singing, "Hush, my baby, lie still and slumber," with the most apparent indifference. Thus he laid hold of the box a third time, and the Rubicon was passed. The driver drove to the number directed, left it, and went about his business. Now is a moment of inexpressible delight. The box is opened, the straw removed, and the poor fellow loosed, rejoicing!

As William "Box" Jones would do three years later, Henry "Box" Brown emerges from a crate in Philadelphia, 1856. He came out singing, "I waited patiently on the Lord," after 26 hours of confinement.

UNCLE TOM'S CABIN

Probably no other work of fiction in the English language has seized the public imagination as has Harriet Beecher Stowe's *Uncle Tom's Cabin*. First published in serial form in 1851 in an antislavery journal, the book ultimately sold some 10.5 million copies in dozens of editions.

Stowe's tale is essentially a romanticized account of the trials and sufferings of "Uncle" Tom, a noble-spirited black slave, of his brutal white overseer, Simon Legree, of Little Eva, the angelic child of Tom's master, and a host of other now-stereotypic figures chosen to represent plantation society.

The author always insisted, however, that she did not intend the work as a polemic against the South or southerners but as a condemnation of a whole system in which she regarded the North as equally culpable. Indeed, some of her most cruelly drawn characters, among them Legree, are transplanted New Englanders, and several of the white southerners are pictured as decent, even courageous figures.

Nevertheless, the story had scarcely been printed before a storm of controversy blew up, supporters and detractors dividing sharply along geographical lines. Northern abolitionists seized

Tom and Little Eva in a tropical setting, from an 1853 French edition of the book

upon it as a manifesto for action and bought nearly 300,000 copies in the first year of publication. Southerners denounced Mrs. Stowe as a lying propagandist, and writers from the South rushed into print with a score of apologias supporting the institution of slavery—on grounds ranging from Scriptural dogma to paternalism.

All the protests from the South merely served to reinforce the novel's effect in the North, where, until its appearance, few people had gone beyond the philosophical question of slavery to imagine what it meant in human terms for one man to be in bondage to another. Precisely how much influence the novel had in shaping the civil struggle that followed, historians can only guess. But President Abraham Lincoln, upon meeting the diminutive author, was moved to say, "So you're the little woman who made this great war!"

From the book grew a host of stage presentations that continued to be favorite theatrical fare until well into the 20th century. The "Tom Shows" frequently strayed far from the original tale, burlesquing the characters to a point where Uncle Tom became a symbol of shuffling servility rather than the hero. As a result, the novel's reputation has suffered in recent years. But, as the American literary critic Edmund Wilson conceded in the 1950's, the real *Uncle Tom's Cabin* must be judged the work of a "first-rate modern social intelligence."

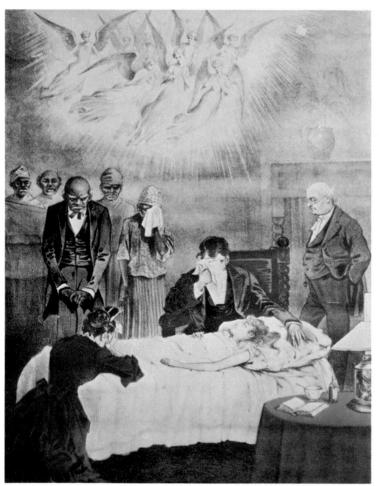

The death of Little Eva, a moment of high melodrama, is depicted in this 19th-century theater poster. While the angels wait to receive her into Heaven, her grieving father, mother, and Tom with other slaves gather to bid the child farewell.

PART III

THIS IS MY COUNTRY

A House Divided Cannot Stand • The Wild, Wild West

The Melting Pot • The Breadwinners • The Sky's the Limit

George Washington welcomes Lincoln to Heaven in this pictorial carte de visite printed after the first American presidential assassination.

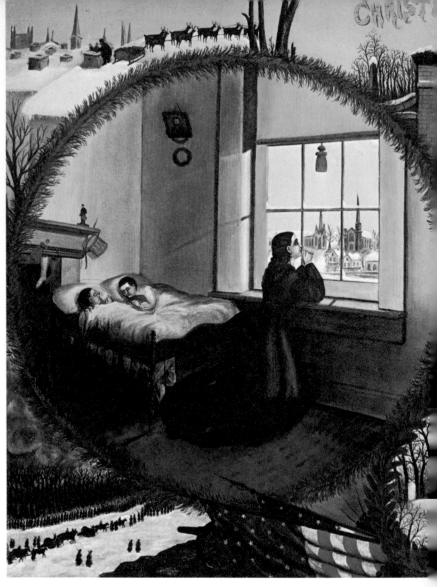

A House Divided Cannot Stand

For more than 50 years, western expansion had absorbed the energies of Americans and masked the deadly seriousness of the differences between slave and nonslave states. In the North, laissez-faire capitalism, the doctrine of equality before the law, and a belief in progress reigned supreme, whereas the South represented an older, feudal system inherited from colonial times. Northerners dreamed of a more prosperous future, southerners of a quieter, nobler past. Yet Dixie's agricultural economy was commercially dominated by the North—a control deeply resented by southerners. With the founding of the Confederacy following Lincoln's election on a Union platform, war became inevitable. The South banked heavily on the superiority of her military leadership (most U.S. career officers were

"Christmas Eve, '62," by Harper's *Weekly*'s political cartoonist Thomas Nast, sentimentalizes the loneliness of a family separated by the war.

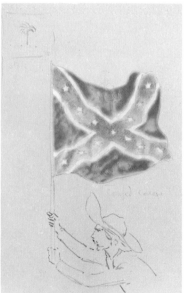

This watercolor by a Massachusetts soldier depicts a southern colorbearer with the Stars and Bars, as the Confederate battle flag was known.

southerners) but time, money, and numerical superiority were all with the North. The bloodbath was to continue for four bitter years—so bitter that to this day many an "unreconstructed Rebel" goes on fighting the Civil War, aided by the prophecy that "the South shall rise again." In the eyes of common folk, it was a war dominated by the tragic ironies of a fratricidal conflict. To be sure, both sides had their giants. To northerners, Lincoln was "Father Abraham," savior of the Union; in response to his call, 700,000 flocked to the colors—or "God's flag," as bluecoated doughboys called it. On the southern side, Lee was similarly idolized—his men would have proclaimed him emperor if they could. In folklore as in real life, a whole cast of stereotypes arose—"damn-Yankees," "Johnny Rebs," dastardly "scalawags," and self-serving carpetbaggers.

THE GREAT EMANCIPATOR
Honest Abe

In life and death Abraham Lincoln has symbolized to many generations of Americans the embodiment of our national ideals of vigor, virtue, and human compassion. Born in 1809 in a rude cabin on what was then the frontier, the future president pulled himself up from poverty and ignorance to become the wise, bold chief of a country torn by civil strife. Assassinated in 1865 just a week after the Civil War ended, Lincoln became a Christ-like martyr to many of his countrymen. As a result he has figured as the hero of innumerable legends.

THE VORACIOUS READER

Young Abe read every book he could lay his hands on. One such tome, Weems' *Life of Washington,* he borrowed from old Josiah Crawford. When not reading his newest discovery, Abe laid it away in a part of the cabin where he thought it would be free from harm, but it so happened that just behind the shelf on which he placed it was a big crack between the logs of the wall. One night a great storm came up suddenly and soaked the book through and through. The book was almost utterly spoiled.

He trudged over to Mr. Crawford's in some perplexity and mortification. "I've got some bad news for you," Abe began with lengthened face. "You know the book you lent me— the *Life of Washington*?" "Yes, yes, of course," said the neighbor. "Well, the rain last night spoiled it," and Abe showed the book, wet to the pulp inside, explaining the injury.

"It's too bad. You ought to pay for it, Abe," said Mr. Crawford. "You must have been dreadful careless. If you've no money you must work it out." Abe agreed, grateful to find a way to repay his friend. So it was arranged that he should work three days for Crawford, "pulling fodder," the value of his labor being rated at 25 cents a day. As the book cost 75 cents, this would be regarded as satisfactory. When Abe had finished his time Mr. Crawford was astonished at his work, for the boy had done a man's job and then some.

HORSE TRADING

When Lincoln was a young lawyer in Illinois, he and a certain judge once got to bantering about their skills as horse traders; and it was agreed that the next morning at 9 o'clock they should make a trade, horses sight unseen. First came the judge with a broken-down bone rack of a horse; then came Abe Lincoln carrying a wooden sawhorse on his shoulders, and he was saying, "Well, judge, this is the first time I ever got the worst of it in a horse trade."

FATHER ABRAHAM

After the Second Battle of Bull Run President Lincoln attempted to visit the wounded in the 40-odd military hospitals around Washington. At one stop Lincoln came upon a dying Confederate boy. The president knelt beside the cot and prayed.

Then Lincoln started for his carriage, but before he could leave, a nurse came after him. The Confederate lad was pleading to see him again. Weary and worn though he was, he returned at once to the lad's bedside and asked, "What can I do for you?" "I am so lonely and friendless, Mr. Lincoln," whispered the lad, "and I am hoping that you can tell me what my mother would want me to say and do now." "Yes, my boy," said Lincoln as he knelt beside the dying lad, "I know exactly and I am glad that you sent for me. Now let us pray together." Then, while the lad rested his head upon the arm of Lincoln, the president repeated the prayer his mother had taught him to say before bedtime: "Now I lay me down to sleep. . . ."

ASLEEP AT HIS POST

Mr. Owen, a pious farmer of Vermont, gave his eldest son, Benjamin, to the Federal cause. One day a message arrived, which fell like a thunderbolt on the family. The lad had

"Young Lincoln," which was painted in 1868, was Eastman Johnson's imaginative, idealized portrait of young Abe studying by firelight in his Indiana log cabin home.

been found asleep at his post and was condemned to be shot.

The fair young daughter, Blossom, had not shed a tear, and the terror in her face had been so very still that no one had noticed it. Now she answered a gentle tap at the kitchen door, opening it to receive a letter. "It is from him," was all she said.

'Twas like a message from the dead. Mr. Owen could not break the seal for his trembling and held it toward Mr. Allen, the minister, with the helplessness of a child. The minister opened it and read as follows:

Dear Father, When this reaches you I shall be in eternity. At first it seemed awful to me, but I have thought about it so much now, that it has no terror. They say they will not blind me, that I may meet my death like a man. I thought, Father, it might have been on the battlefield for my country, and that when I fell

Grown to his full six foot four, Lincoln was sufficiently conspicuous to often be urged to fight the town bully. This painting by Harold von Schmidt records Lincoln's fabled triumph over the bully Jack Armstrong, the rowdiest denizen of New Salem, Illinois.

it would be fighting, but to be shot down like a dog for nearly betraying it—to die for neglect of duty!

You know I promised Jemmy Carr's mother I would look after her boy, and when he fell sick I did all I could for him. He was not strong when he was ordered back into the ranks, and the day before that night I carried all his luggage, besides my own, on our march. Toward night we went in on double-quick, and Jemmy, if I had not lent him an arm he would have dropped by the way. I was all tired out when we came into camp, and when it was Jemmy's turn to be sentry, I did take his place; but I was too tired, Father. "God be thanked!" interrupted Mr. Owen reverently. "I knew Bennie would not sleep carelessly at his post."

Late that night the door opened softly and a little figure glided out and down the footpath to the road. Blossom was on her way to Washington to ask President Lincoln for her brother's life. She had stolen away, leaving only a note to tell her father where and why she had gone. She had brought Bennie's letter with her.

The next morning she reached New York, and a conductor found suitable company for her and hurried her on to Washington. Every moment now might be a year in her brother's

Abe's reputation as a woodsman of prodigious energy began when he was a teenager and was preserved for posterity in his famous sobriquet "The Rail Splitter."

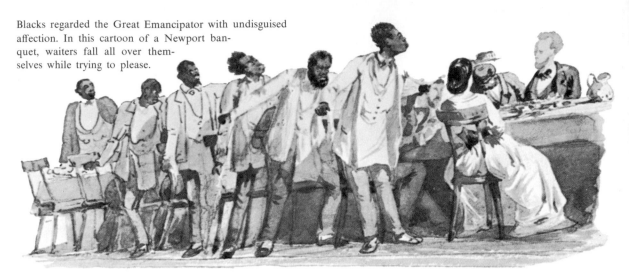

Blacks regarded the Great Emancipator with undisguised affection. In this cartoon of a Newport banquet, waiters fall all over themselves while trying to please.

life. And so, in an incredibly short time, Blossom reached the capital, and was hurried at once to the White House. The president had just seated himself when, without one word of announcement, the door opened very softly, and Blossom stood before him.

"Well, my child," he said in his pleasant, cheery tones, "what do you want so bright and early in the morning?" "My brother's life, please sir! They are going to shoot him for sleeping at his post." "Oh, yes," and Mr. Lincoln ran his eye over the paper before him. "I remember. It was a fatal sleep—a most fatal sleep. You see, my child, it was a time of special danger. Thousands of lives might have been lost for his culpable negligence." "So my father said," replied Blossom gravely. "But poor Bennie was so tired, sir, and Jemmy so weak." She told her story simply and straightforwardly and handed Mr. Lincoln Bennie's letter to read. He read it carefully, then Blossom heard this order given: "Send this dispatch at once." The president then turned to the girl and said:

"Go home, my child, and tell that father of yours, who could approve his country's sentence even when it took the life of a child like that, Abraham Lincoln thinks that life too precious to be lost."

LINKUM'S CHARIOT
On Friday, June 19, 1863, Maj.

Abner Small found himself part of a large body of Union troops on the march in unfamiliar southern territory. That night he wrote in his diary:

As we neared the end of the day's march we passed an old plantation. A tottery board fence fronted the road, and perched on the fence were Negroes of all shades and sizes. The grimaces of astonishment that spread over their faces as they saw regiment after regiment massed was a sight to see. One old man bared his woolly poll, stretched forth a long and bony hand as if to cover us with a blessing, and sang out in a cracked voice: "Praise de Lawd fo' de glory ob dis yer 'casion! Heabenly Massa bress de Linkum sojers, an' show dese yer eyes de golden chariot b'fo' Ah die!"

Old hats, jackets, and shoes went high in the air, and shouts of "Glory! Hallelujah!" burst from along the fence. An excited patriarch got down and hobbled to the roadside and right up to the marching men, exclaiming: "Great King! How many mo' you-uns comin'? 'Spec's fo'ty milyuns toted by hyer since mo'nin'!" "Well, uncle," said one of our boys, "you can stand here three weeks and see the Yanks go by." "B'fo' God, Ah reckon so! Massa Linkum mighty sojer, Ah reckon. He gwine by too?"

"Oh, yes, uncle, he'll be along in his chariot tomorrow." Limping back to the fence, the patriarch yelled: "Chilluns, cotch off yer hats an' jine in de chorus!" And swaying from side to side, the old man leading, they sang in their peculiar way:
"Don' yer see 'em comin', comin', comin'—
Milyuns from de oder sho'?
Glory! Glory! Hallelujah!
Bress de Lawd fo' ebermo'!

"Don' yer hear Him comin', comin' comin'?
Wid his robe an' mighty army?
Want ter march wid Him to glory?
Yes, Ah do!"

INTIMATIONS OF DEATH
Lincoln was given to vivid dreaming. Just a few days before his assassination, he had a strange, unsettling dream. He described the incident thus to a small circle of friends:

About 10 days ago I retired very late. I could not have been long in bed when I fell into a slumber, for I was weary. I soon began to dream. There seemed to be a deathlike stillness about me. Then I heard subdued sobs, as if a number of people were weeping. I thought I left my bed and wandered downstairs. There the silence was broken by the same pitiful sobbing, but the mourners were invisible. I went from room to room; no living person was in sight, but the same mournful sounds of distress met me as I passed along. It was light in all the rooms, every object was familiar to me; but where were all the people who were grieving as if their hearts would break? I was puz-

Wisdom in Wit

From young Abe's days as a storekeeper to his final days as president, Lincoln found humor and stories ready instruments for gaining friends, for driving home a lesson, for reducing his enemies to manageable size, and for easing the tensions of his troubled world. Take for example his response to a charge that he had made some mistakes in judgment:

Lincoln replied: "That reminds me of a minister and a lawyer who were riding together; says the minister to the lawyer, 'Sir, do you ever make mistakes in pleading?' 'I do,' says the lawyer. 'And what do you do with mistakes?' inquired the minister. 'Why, sir, if large ones, I mend them; if small ones, I let them go,' said the lawyer. 'And pray, sir,' continued he, 'do you ever make mistakes in preaching?' 'Yes, sir, I do.' 'And what do you do with mistakes?' said the lawyer. 'Why, sir, I dispose of them in the same manner that you do. Not long since,' he continued, 'as I was preaching, I meant to observe that the Devil was the father of liars, but made a mistake and said the father of lawyers. The mistake was so small that I let it go.'"

On one occasion Lincoln dismissed Stephen Douglas, his esteemed opponent in Illinois politics, thus: "I had understood before that Mr. Douglas had been bound out to learn the cabinetmaking business, but I was not aware until now that his father was a cooper. I have no doubt, however, that he was a very good one, for he has made one of the best whisky casks I have ever seen," Lincoln said bowing gravely toward Douglas.

In condemning President Polk's land grab in the Mexican War, he told his fellow representatives that it reminded him of an Illinois farmer he knew. "'I ain't greedy about land,' the farmer told me. 'I only want what 'jines mine.'"

On his favorite subject of horse trading, Lincoln told a story of a contrary nag whose owner had touted it as a first-rate bird hunter. When the potential buyer mounted up and the horse promptly carried him into a nearby stream, the horse trader shouted: "Ride him! Ride him! He's as good for fish as he is for birds!"

When a story or saying had a certain color or smack, it would often be tagged as coming from Lincoln. He was the man walking along a dusty road when a stranger driving a buggy came along. He asked the stranger, "Will you be so good as to take my overcoat to town for me?" The man in the buggy said he would. "But how will you get your overcoat back again?" "Oh, that's easy! I'm going to stay right inside of it."

Lincoln frequently turned his quick wit on himself. One story he told had to do with being stopped on a street one day by a man who thrust a revolver in his face. "What seems to be the matter?" inquired Lincoln with as much calmness as he could muster. "Well," replied the stranger, "some years ago I swore an oath that if I ever came across an uglier man than myself I'd shoot him on the spot." A feeling of relief came over Lincoln on hearing this and he answered, "Shoot me, then, for if I am an uglier man than you, I don't want to live."

Social historian Constance Rourke states: "As a storyteller, Lincoln used . . . stories as weapons. In a political contest in 1840 he mimicked his opponent . . . with so bitter a ridicule that at the end the man was reduced to tears . . ." He was also capable of tact and kindliness. Once he was confronted by two rival hatters; each bestowed a gift on him and stood back expectantly awaiting a compliment. Lincoln looked over the two hats very carefully and then remarked: "Gentlemen, they mutually excel each other."

Wrapped in his shawl and wearing his battered tophat, a gaunt Lincoln riding his sorry horse through the snow was a familiar sight around Springfield, Illinois, during his days as a circuit court lawyer; that image became part of his legend.

zled and alarmed. Determined to find the cause of a state of things so mysterious and shocking, I kept on until I arrived at the East Room. There I met with a sickening surprise. Before me was a catafalque, on which rested a corpse wrapped in funeral vestments. Around it were soldiers.

"Who is dead in the White House?" I demanded of one of the soldiers. "The president," was his answer. "He was killed by an assassin!" Then came a loud burst of grief from the crowd, which awoke me from my dream. I slept no more that night; and although it was only a dream, I have been strangely annoyed by it ever since.

· · ·

Just the night before Lincoln spent his fateful evening at Ford's Theater, he had a remarkable dream he had experienced several times before. His unofficial bodyguard, Ward Lamon, told the story some years after, and it has become part of the Lincoln lore. The dream was of a pleasing and

Ghosts of unresolved conflicts disturb the slain president in this cartoon by Nast.

promising character, having nothing in it of the horrible, and Lincoln came to regard its occurrence as he would a welcome visitor. In this dream he saw a ship sailing away rapidly, badly damaged, and our victorious vessels in close pursuit. He saw also the close of the battle on

land, the enemy routed, and our forces in possession of vantage ground of incalculable importance. Mr. Lincoln stated it as a fact that he had this dream just before the battles of Antietam, Gettysburg, and other signal engagements in the war.

On the morning of April 14, 1865, there was a Cabinet meeting at which General Grant was present. During an interval of general discussion the president asked Grant if he had any news from General Sherman, who was then confronting Johnston. The reply was in the negative, but the general added that he was in hourly expectation of a dispatch announcing Johnston's surrender. Mr. Lincoln then said, "We shall hear very soon, and the news will be important." General Grant asked him why he thought so. "Because," said Mr. Lincoln, "I had a dream last night, and ever since this war began I have had the same dream just before every event of great national importance. It portends some important event that will happen very soon." Lincoln was shot that same evening.

· · ·

One of the many superstitions that have grown up around this tragic event is that time stands still momentarily at 20 minutes after each hour in mute observance of his death, which was believed to have occurred at 8:20 p.m. It is similarly claimed that an unexplainable silence will frequently fall over a group at 20 minutes after the hour. And following the passage of the Lincoln funeral train across the country, people in small and large towns experienced curious occurrences which they attributed to the beloved president's spirit passing through. In Albany, New York, for example, people claimed years later that on the anniversary of the cortege's transit through the city a phantom funeral train could be seen streaking through, streamers flying and dirges sounding. Clocks and watches stopped. Even later inhabitants of the White House reported seeing visions of Lincoln at the windows, of hearing his uneasy footsteps in the halls at night.

In this painting attributed to Eastman Johnson, John Wilkes Booth, with a knife rather than a gun, leaps from President Lincoln's box to make his escape via stage center.

PORTENTS AND PARTINGS
Into the Fray

The road toward civil war between North and South was long and painful, with good men on both sides sincerely convinced of the rightness of their cause. Some stories from the era indicate the mental agonies that preceded and resulted in the emotional stress felt by families sending men off to war. The first story here (obviously written by a northerner) was composed during the war. But it gives an indication of how long the idea of secession had been brewing, since its hero, Senator John C. Calhoun, a leading states rights advocate, had died in 1850.

THE SPOTTED HAND

One morning John C. Calhoun and a number of his political associates were having breakfast together. Calhoun seemed to be behaving strangely, gazing frequently at his right hand and brushing it with his left in a nervous manner. At length one of his companions—Robert Toombs of Georgia, I think—took it upon himself to ask Calhoun if his hand hurt.

"Pshaw! It is nothing but a dream I had last night which makes me see now a large black spot, like an ink blotch, upon the back of my right hand; an optical illusion, I suppose." These words excited the curiosity of the company and Toombs pressed on: "What was your dream like? I am not very superstitious about dreams, but sometimes they have a great deal of truth in them."

After a moment's hesitation, Calhoun began to unravel his tale: At a late hour last night, as I was sitting in my room writing, I was astonished by the entrance of a visitor, who, without a word, took a seat opposite me. The manner in which the intruder entered, so perfectly self-possessed, as though my room and all within it belonged to him, excited in me as much surprise as indignation. As I raised my head to look into his features, I discovered that he was wrapped in a thin cloak which effectively concealed his face; then he spoke: "What are you writing, senator from South Carolina?"

I did not think of his impertinence at first, but answered voluntarily, "I am writing a plan for the dissolution of the American Union." (You know, gentlemen, that I am expected to produce a plan in the event of certain contingencies.) To this the intruder replied coolly, "Senator from South Carolina, will you allow me to look at your right hand?"

He rose, the cloak fell, and I saw his face. The sight struck me like a thunderclap. It was the face of a dead man whom extraordinary events had called back to life. The features were those of George Washington and he was dressed in his general's uniform.

As though I had not the power to refuse, I extended my right hand as requested. I felt a strange thrill as he grasped it and held it to the light. After holding my hand for a moment, he looked at me steadily and said in a quiet way, "And with this right hand, senator from South Carolina, you would sign your name to a paper declaring the Union dissolved?" "Yes," I said, "if a certain contingency arises." But at that moment a black blotch appeared on the back of my hand. "What is that?" said I, alarmed. "That," said he, "is the mark by which Benedict Arnold is known in the next world." He said no more but drew from beneath his

Three days after the Confederates bombarded Fort Sumter, Lincoln called for 75,000 three-month volunteers to put down the rebellion. Here a trainload of Union men leave homes and families in good spirits, little imagining the long duration of the fighting.

cloak an object which he laid upon the table—a skeleton! "There," said he, "are the bones of Isaac Hayne, who was hung at Charleston by the British. He gave his life in order to establish the Union."

With these words the intruder left the room, and I, startled by contact with the dead man's bones, awoke. Was it not a singular dream?

A SON'S PAINFUL DUTY

Boyd Peyton stood before his friends and neighbors with a heavy heart. As an officer in the U.S. Army, he was their choice to command the county's light infantry company. Eagerly they awaited his answer. "Gentlemen," he said, moistening his dry lips again and again, "I love the South. My heart is with her. Here are Father, Mother, friends, and—the woman I love. I would give my lifeblood for them, but I cannot give up my honor. I am an officer"—with a magnificent gesture he lifted his hand to his cap and removed it—"of the United States. I have sworn allegiance to the United States. I must be faithful to my duty. Here are my orders to report to Washington at once. I must

Enjoying the ladies' attention, an uninitiated young Confederate officer admires his impractical uniform in the mirror.

go!" "To hell with the damned traitor!" shrieked a man in the crowd, and catching his example, others shouted threats and curses.

"Gentlemen," said the old colonel, Peyton's father, "no more of this! I beg you, no violence. My son has made his choice. Leave him. Let him go forth alone. The contempt of friends, and hatred of acquaintances, repudiation by those who loved him, will be punishment enough."

And so saying, family, friends, and his betrothed turned away from

young Peyton and went about the business of choosing another—loyal—son to lead them in the dreadful days ahead. Peyton, now quite alone, and with a face as set, as hard, as cold as if carved out of marble, prepared to go to Washington to the duty he could not shirk.

THE YOUNGEST RECRUIT

Into one of the principal recruiting factories in New York City there came one day an agitated young woman. "So, sir, you've clapped your dirty sojur trappings on my husband, have you?" "Who is your husband?" asked the recruiting officer. "Billie McCurtee, an' shure, an' a bould boy he is, so plaze ye. But it's a dirty thing of ye, my pretty man, to take him from his wife an' childers." "Can't be helped," said the officer. "It's too late now." "Then take the baby, too," she cried, as she forced the little one into the arms of the lieutenant: "Take them all—I'll send ye four more today." Off she ran, leaving the unfortunate officer with the squirming and squalling recruit in his arms. Doubtful of its services to Uncle Sam, he sent it home by its father.

The origin of the name "Dixie" may stem from $10 notes issued by a New Orleans bank. (*Dix*=10 in French.) They were known as *dixies* and the South as *Dixie's land*. The song that became the Confederate anthem had been around for years before it was popularized by minstrel Emmett Daniel in 1859 and swept the country as "Dixie."

BROTHER AGAINST BROTHER
Friendly Enemies

Two brothers found themselves arrayed against each other in a battle that was raging in their own front yard in Pennsylvania. From that grimmest reality of a civil war—kinsmen fighting kinsmen—springs our most poignant body of lore and fiction. Tales abound of tragic ironies and belated recognitions. Juxtaposed with the fact of fraternal strife was the inevitable friendly exchange among enemies who shared a language and a culture. There was a lot of fraternization among the combatants in our Civil War, and even some documented incidents of heroism on an enemy's behalf. Here, too, folklore and fiction reflect the reality.

Alfred Bellard, a private, re-created a hand-to-hand struggle for Rebel colors.

THE MOCKINGBIRD

In the early autumn of 1861 Private Grayrock stood at his lonely post staring into the darkness, trying to recognize known objects; he saw nothing in detail but only groups of unfamiliar shapes. It happened that Private Grayrock, imprudently executing a circumspection of his whole dimly visible environment, lost his bearings and seriously impaired his usefulness as a sentinel. Almost at the moment he realized his awkward predicament he heard a stir of leaves and in the gloom saw the indistinct outline of a human figure.

"Halt!" shouted Private Grayrock peremptorily, as in duty bound, backing up the command with the sharp metallic snap of his cocking rifle—"Who goes there?" There was no answer; or if it came, it was lost in the report of the sentinel's rifle. In the silence of the forest the sound was deafening, and hardly had it died away when it was repeated by the pieces of the pickets to right and left, a sympathetic fusillade. For two hours every unconverted civilian of them had been evolving enemies from his imagination, and Grayrock's shot had started the whole encroaching host into visible existence. Having fired, all retreated to the reserves—all but Grayrock, who did not know in what direction to retreat. When, no enemy appearing, the picket line was cautiously reestablished, he was discovered bravely holding his ground and was highly praised by the officer of the guard.

In the meantime, however, Gray-rock had made a close but unavailing search for the mortal part of the intruder at whom he had fired, and whom he had a marksman's intuitive sense of having hit. (He had been a terror of the shooting galleries in three cities.) Private Grayrock was far from satisfied with the night's adventure, and the next day he made some fair enough pretext for a pass to go outside the lines. Telling the sentinel then on duty there that he had lost something—which was true enough—he renewed the search for the person whom he supposed himself to have shot. He was no more successful by daylight and finally gave up the search. "I am in a false position," he said to himself. "I have suffered myself to be complimented by my officers and envied by my comrades. That is not just; I know myself courageous, but this praise is for specific acts which I did not perform. What, then, shall I do? Explain that I saw an enemy and fired? They have all said that, yet none believes it? I wish to God I could find my man!" And so wishing, Private Grayrock, overcome at last by the languor of the afternoon, so far forgot the interests of the U.S. as to fall

Many combatants in the War Between the States were also Good Samaritans. Here a Rebel general aids a fallen Union officer. He lived and years later the two became friends.

Death, patiently waiting, hears Union men toast: "And here's to the next to die." Sketch by war artist A. W. Waud

asleep. And sleeping he dreamed.

He thought himself a boy, living in a far, fair land. With him always at his side was one to whom he gave his heart and soul in love—a twin brother. Together they strolled hand in hand and heart in heart, the only children of a widowed mother. And through all the golden days floated one unceasing sound—the rich, thrilling melody of a mockingbird in a cage by their cottage door. That clear melody seemed the interpretation of the mysteries of life.

But there came a time when the days of the dream grew dark with sorrow. The good mother was dead, the meadowside home was broken up, and the brothers were parted between two of their kinsmen. William (the dreamer) went to live in a populous city, and John was taken to a distant region. To John had fallen all that they deemed of value—the mockingbird. They could be divided, but it could not, and so it was carried away into the strange country, and the world of William knew it no more. The kinsmen who had adopted the boys held no communication. For a time letters full of boyish bravado and boastful narratives of the new and larger experience passed between them, but these gradually ceased. But ever through the dream

ran the song of the mockingbird, and when the dreamer opened his eyes the cessation of its music first apprised him that he was awake.

Grayrock rose to his feet, shouldered his rifle, and set off toward camp. He had gone a little way when a bird perched above a thicket poured from its joyous breast inexhaustible floods of song. There was little in that—yet the man stopped as if struck, covered his eyes with his hands, and wept like a child. For the moment he was, indeed, a child in memory, dwelling again by the meadow. Then with an effort of the will he pulled himself together and strode on. Passing an opening of the little thicket he looked in, and there, supine upon the earth, its gray uniform stained with a single spot of blood, its white face turned sharply upward and backward, lay the image of himself!—the body of John Grayrock, dead of a gunshot wound, and still warm! He had found his man.

As the unfortunate soldier knelt beside that masterwork of civil war, the shrilling bird upon the bough overhead stilled her song. At rollcall that evening in the Federal camp the name Grayrock brought no response, nor ever again thereafter.

SAVED

During a fierce battle Union private Elisha Seaman's attention was caught by a writhing Confederate officer. Seaman could see his distorted, agonized face and could stand it no longer. He crawled along the bullet-torn turf on his way to the wounded man. "Hey there, come back, you lumphead!" yelled his bunkie. "Don't you see the fellow is a Reb? You'll get killed." "I wouldn't let a dog suffer that way," yelled Elisha. He finally reached the officer, forced a little whisky into his mouth, and lifted him up on his back. Elisha decided it would be a cruel kindness to turn this man into a target for th

A rabbit outruns Rebs in this etching by William Sheppard who had joined in like hunts when he served under Lee. Both sides liked rabbit-chasing, but for hungry Confederates the game had a serious side, too.

Brother fights brother in this imaginative mural of the battle that took place at Westport, Missouri, in 1864. Painted by N. C. Wyeth, the mural adorns the state's capitol building.

bullets coming across the field, so he said: "I'll back down to our lines. If anyone gets hit it'll be me."

Although the wounded officer was a large man, Seaman got a fireman's lift on him, swung him over his shoulders, and then, facing the Confederate lines, slowly backed his way toward safety. At first the Confederate fire redoubled as the men in gray thought he was capturing one of their men. When, however, they realized he was protecting one of their officers with his body, all along the line the fusillade died down and in its place came a storm of cheers that swept from the Confederate position. Seaman covered the last 50 yards of his dangerous journey without a shot being fired at him. The Union surgeon was attracted to the front by the shouts and cheers both from the Confederate lines and from Seaman's own comrades and helped him over the breastworks. "You're a great fool," he said. "But so long as you brought this poor Reb in at the risk of your life, I'll certainly cure him." And the doctor did just that.

FRIENDS IN DEATH
A Rebel lay with a fearful shot wound in his side. The lifeblood of the poor fellow was fast oozing out when one of our troops came dashing forward, from out of the melee, and fell, sharply wounded, close beside him. The Georgian recognized his uniform, though he was fatally hurt, and feebly held out his hand. "We came into this battle enemies," he said. "Let us die friends." He spoke no more, but his companion in disaster took the extended hand.

SEPARATE TABLE
Generals Pierce Young and George Custer had been devoted friends at West Point. In the war they were major generals on opposing sides. One day General Young was invited to breakfast at the Hunter mansion in Virginia. The beautiful young ladies had prepared a smoking breakfast to which the general was addressing himself with ardor when a shell burst through the house. Glancing through a window, he saw Custer charging toward the house at the head of his staff. Out of the window Young went, calling to the young ladies, "Tell Custer I leave this breakfast for him." Custer enjoyed it heartily and looked forward with pleasure to dinner. In the meantime Young, smarting over the loss of his breakfast and his hasty retreat, drove the Federal line back and by dinnertime was in sight of the Hunter mansion again. Custer, who was just sitting down to dinner, laughed and said: "That's Pierce Young coming back. I knew he wouldn't leave me here in peace. Tell him his old classmate leaves his love with his excellent dinner." And out the window he went like a flash, as the Georgia general walked in and sat down to dinner.

WAR ON WATER
The Ironclads Arrive

It was brother against brother on the water as well as on land. One hero a contemporary report wrongly placed aboard the U.S.S. Cumberland *when she was sunk by the Confederate ironclad* Merrimack *was Paymaster McKean Buchanan, U.S.N. During the fight he is supposed to have said, "Gentlemen, you can imagine my feelings when I tell you my brother commands that ship." Flag Officer Franklin Buchanan, C.S.N., was to become the Confederacy's only full admiral, commanding the Tennessee squadron at Mobile Bay against Farragut in August 1864. The war also witnessed the first fight between ironclad ships. Here is an account of it by one of the participants, from a letter written home to his wife:*

IRON SIDES, IRON HEARTS

The most vivid account of the legendary engagement between the *Monitor* and *Merrimack* was written by Paymaster W. F. Keeler aboard the *Monitor:*

"We steamed slowly under the towering side of the *Minnesota* [a Union warship that had been crippled by the *Merrimack*'s guns hours earlier]. Her wooden sides showed terrible traces of the conflict. As a light fog lifted from the water it revealed the *Merrimack*. Our coffee was forgotten. Captain Worden inquired of the *Minnesota*'s captain what he intended. 'If I cannot lighten my ship off, I shall destroy her,' Captain Van Brunt replied. 'I will stand by you to the last if I can help you,' said our captain. 'No, sir, you cannot help me'—the replies came down curt and crispy. The idea of assistance or protection being offered to the huge thing by the little pygmy at her side seemed absolutely ridiculous. As the *Merrimack* approached we slowly steamed out of the shadow of our towering friend, no ways daunted by her ungracious replies. Everyone on board of us was at his post. A puff of smoke arose from the *Merrimack*'s side and a shell howled over our heads and crashed into the side of the *Minnesota*. The gunners lifted a 175-pound shot into the mouth of one of our guns. 'Send them that with our compliments, my lads,' says Captain Worden. The most profound silence reigned; if there had been a coward heart there, its throb would have been audible, so intense was the stillness.

"I experienced a peculiar sensation. I do not think it was fear, but it was different from anything I ever knew before. We were enclosed in what we supposed to be an impenetrable armor—we knew that a powerful foe was about to meet us—ours was an untried experiment and our enemy's first fire might make it a

The U.S.S. *Cumberland* was rammed by the *Virginia* (the former *Merrimack,* which had been converted to an ironclad) in a desperate fight in which the *Cumberland* sank with a third of her crew including two legendary gunners who refused to leave.

Gunners at one of the U.S.S. *Kearsarge*'s two 11-inch Dahlgrens scoring another of many hits inflicted on the Confederate *Alabama* off Cherbourg, France; the Rebel ship sank.

coffin for us all. Then we knew not how soon the attack would commence, or from what direction it would come, for no one could see her.

"Oh, what a relief it was when the gun over my head thundered out its challenge with a report that jarred our vessel, but it was music to us all! Until we fired, the *Merrimack* had taken no notice of us, confining her attentions to the *Minnesota*. Our second shot struck her and made the iron scales rattle on her side. She seemed for the first time to be aware of our presence and replied to our solid shot with grape [grapeshot] that rattled on our decks like hailstones. One of our gunners grinned broadly: 'The damned fools . . .' The men at the guns had stripped themselves to their waists and were covered with powder and smoke, the perspiration falling from them like rain. 'They're going to board us!' cried the captain. 'Put in a round of canister!' 'Can't do it,' replied the chief gunner. 'Both guns have solid shot.' 'Give them to her, then.' Bang goes one of the guns. 'You've made a hole through her; quick, give her the other!' Snap goes the primer. 'Why don't you fire?' 'Can't do it, the cartridge is not rammed home.'"

At this point the *Monitor* was obliged to haul off, to fix the jammed gun. After a few minutes she reengaged the Confederate ironclad, which then tried to run her down. The collision did not damage the *Monitor*. In all, 20 rounds from the *Monitor* hit the badly damaged Mer-

rimack, as against 23 hits scored by the latter on her foe. To the Confederate gunners their own hits seemed ineffective, but the *Monitor*'s captain was a casualty of one. Keeler:

"A heavy shell struck the pilothouse and a flash of light and a cloud of smoke filled it. The captain staggered and put his hands to his eyes. 'I am blind,' says he. Blood was running down from his face, which was blackened with the powder smoke. The quartermaster at the wheel turned the *Monitor* away from her

antagonist. Captain Worden spoke: 'Gentlemen, I leave it to you, do what you think best. I cannot see, but do not mind me. Save the *Minnesota* if you can.' We held a hurried consultation, and *'Fight!'* was the unanimous voice of all."

But the *Merrimack*, already out of range, was hauling off in her turn. The battle was over. Both sides were to claim victory, but on subsequent days when the *Monitor* steamed out in search of the Confederate ironclad for a return engagement, the latter was not to be found. (She was in drydock undergoing repairs.) Following the first of these sorties, Keeler wrote:

"We passed along close to Newport News. The whole army came out to see us. Thousands and thousands lined the shore, covered the vessels at the docks, and filled the rigging. All our national airs were given by the regimental bands when a lull in the cheering would allow them to be heard. It was laughable to hear the variety of names applied to us by the soldiers. 'Iron sides and iron hearts,' 'You're trumps every one,' etc., etc."

WORD LORE

War Words

Many expressions still in use today date back to Civil War soldier talk. An example is the Confederate word *shindig*. Originally a southernism for kick in the shins, shindig came to mean a gathering at which much "tanglefoot" was swallowed. The Tarheel State acquired her sobriquet when a North Carolinian regiment stood its ground so stubbornly in battle it seemed the men were glued to the spot. Later they were hailed by a regiment that had been routed in the same action: "Any more tar down in the Old North State?" "No, not a bit. Old Jeff's bought it all up to put on you'uns heels so's you'll stick better in the next fight," the North Carolinians replied. (By the way, *you'uns* and *we'uns,* as well as the world-famous *you-all,* all entered the mainstream of southern speech during and just after the Civil War—at least that is when they were first widely recorded.) The phrase

AWOL also comes from the Rebel ranks, in which carrying a placard marked *AWOL* ("Absent With-Out Leave") was a punishment for such offenders.

On the Union side, two-man army tents were at first called dog tents. Then an Ohio regiment dubbed theirs *pup tents* and the name stuck. Other new words emphasized the gap between urban North and rural South. *Commute* is an example. People had started commuting with the first railroads; but it was in the wartime North that the practice first became widespread, and the terms *commuting* and *commuter* first appeared. Likewise, the war witnessed the birth of the *interview,* reportedly invented by James Redpath, New York *Tribune* correspondent with Sherman in Georgia. But with the spring of 1865, unwarlike words were in the air. *Homeward Bound* became the slogan of soldiers on both sides, and the new word for a pretty girl was a *peach.*

293

CHARISMATIC QUALITIES
The Southern Cavaliers

The Confederacy's top soldiers were the gentle, white-haired Robert E. Lee, who was—with good reason—loved by his men to the point of hero worship; his grand, gloomy lieutenant, Stonewall Jackson, whose troops moved so fast people called them foot cavalry; and the hard-riding daredevil Jeb Stuart (known as "the eyes of Lee's army"), who sported a red loveknot in his lapel and a peacock plume in his hat. In time the charismatic qualities of the three became merged in the general glow of chivalry surrounding the southern cause. From the legend:

A HERO'S BIRTH

A widespread legend concerning Lee's birth has it that he was born after the death of his mother. His mother, it seems, was subject to spells, and during one of her pregnancies went into a trance so death-like she was thought dead. A funeral service was held, and she was interred in the family vault. Some time later a servant heard noises inside. He ran for help, the crypt was unsealed, and Mrs. Lee was found to be alive. She subsequently gave birth to Robert E. Lee. All this is of course pure legend—unusual birth has ever been an earmark of the hero. Julius Caesar was allegedly taken (by cesarean section) from a dead mother; there is also a medieval tale in which the mother, like Lee's, was actually in her grave but came back to life in order to give birth to a future hero.

LAST OF THE CAVALIERS

A minor torment that Marse Robert and his horse Traveller had to bear was the souvenir hunters who were forever after them for a bit of their hair—hair keepsakes, from loved ones and celebrities, were then much in vogue. Poor Traveller's mane and tail were in fact fairly tweaked out. To a lady caught in the act of plucking a hair from his horse's mane, Lee—ever the soul of courtesy—doffed his hat and offered her his own bared head with the polite but telling words "Please, madam, take one of mine instead."

IMPRESSIVE

As the Army of Northern Virginia passed through a Pennsylvania village during the Gettysburg campaign, a pretty girl came out to taunt the Confederates. She waved a mini-ature [U.S.] flag in the faces of our troops. Behind her, applauding her act, was grouped a party of fashionable ladies. The troops offered no insult to the flushed beauty as she flaunted her flag. At that moment General Lee rode up. His noble face and quiet, reproving look met her eye, and the waving flag was lowered. For a moment she looked at him, and then, throwing down the banner, she exclaimed audibly, "Oh, I wish he was ours!"

WITH A WOUNDED YANK

As Lee ordered the retreat from Gettysburg, he and his staff were riding past the scene of carnage on Cemetery Ridge when a badly wounded Union boy who lay nearby on the ground raised up his hands at Lee and shouted, "Hurrah for the Union!" Years later he recalled in print what happened next:

The general heard me, looked, stopped his horse, dismounted, and came toward me. I confess I first thought he meant to kill me. But as he came up he looked down at me with such a sad expression on his face that all fear left me and I wondered what he was about. He extended his hand to me and, grasping mine firmly and looking right into my eyes, said, "My son, I hope you will soon be well." If I live a thousand years I will never forget the expression on General Lee's face. Here he was, defeated, retiring from a field that cost him and his cause almost their last hope, and yet he stopped to say words like those to a wounded soldier of the opposition, who had taunted him as he passed by. As soon as the general had left me, I cried myself to sleep on the bloody ground.

"STONEWALL"

One story says Lee's right-hand man, T. J. Jackson, got his nickname "Stonewall" at the First Battle of Bull Run, in which his troops withstood the Federal onslaught at a moment when other Confederate troops fled. "There is Jackson standing like a stone wall," cried a fellow officer. That same day, Jackson exhorted hi

The war's real hero was Robert E. Lee, of whom it was said that he wore "defeat like a laurel crown." After the South's surrender, his broken army followed him home.

A cooler cavalier than Jeb Stuart, wrote one of his comrades, could not be imagined: "The hiss of balls striking down men around him or cutting off locks of his hair did not attract his attention—he appeared to be thinking of something else."

men, "Yell like furies when you charge!" The distinctive yell that resulted from the order has been associated with the Confederate cause ever since. Jackson was tone-deaf, and he never even succeeded in carrying the tune of "Dixie" though he heard it a thousand times.

But the music of the Rebel yell always aroused him. An eyewitness related: "Jackson was greeted with it whenever he made his appearance and just as invariably he would seize his old gray cap from his head in acknowledgment, and his little sorrel, knowing his habit, would break into a gallop and never halt until the shout had ceased." One night Jackson's entire army spontaneously serenaded him with a long, drawn-out Rebel yell. Jackson said, "That was the grandest music I ever heard."

This Yankee cartoon mocks "Johnny Reb" for starting a cavalier and ending a scarecrow. Lee's men were in fact in rags but bore themselves like true cavaliers.

SHOOT THE BRAVE ONES

Jackson took a more hardnosed line on the enemy than his quintessentially chivalrous commander, Lee, as the following incident shows. At the Battle of Port Republic in 1862, a Federal officer riding a snow-white horse was noted by Confederates for his very conspicuous gallantry. So splendid was the man's courage that Confederate general Ewell called to his men not to shoot the man on the white horse. After a while, however, he was shot down. When General Jackson learned of the incident, he sent for Ewell and told him not to do such a thing again. This was no ordinary war, he said; the gallant Fed-

erals were the very kind that must be killed: "Shoot the brave officers and the cowards will run away and take the others with them."

"NEVER USE IT"

Reconnoitering the enemy's front in cold weather on an occasion when prudence forbade lighting a fire, Jackson became so chilled that his medical attendant urged him to take a stimulant. There was nothing at hand but some ardent spirits, and he consented to take some. Swallowing, he looked as if he would gag. Was it all that unpleasant, the doctor asked. "No," said Stonewall, "I like it; I always did, and that is the reason I never use it." In fact, he confessed, "I am more afraid of it than of Yankee bullets." In this respect Jackson was not alone among the Confederate top three—Lee never took a drop in his life (he once astonished a group of visitors by inviting them for "a drink," then offering buttermilk), and likewise, to keep a childhood promise made to his mother, Jeb Stuart's rule was total abstinence, without even making an exception for doctor's orders, as Jackson had: "If ever I am wounded," he told his comrades, "don't let them give me any whisky or brandy."

In this idealized portrayal by N. C. Wyeth, Stonewall Jackson is shown gazing into the Shenandoah Valley, scene of the 1862 campaign. Although outnumbered there 4 to 1, he routed an army of some 60,000 Yankees, a stroke enabling Lee to save Richmond.

Rebel soldiers share a newspaper in this scene from life in the southern ranks by W. L. Sheppard, who left art school in 1861 to serve in the Richmond Howitzers.

FLOWER OF CAVALIERS

If Jeb Stuart, described by a leading foe as "the greatest cavalry officer ever *foaled* in North America," was an abstainer from alcohol, he was no stranger to the intoxication of combat; there he was in his element, drunk with the fury of war. A comrade described the "flower of cavaliers" in action:

Stuart's face was stormy and his eyes like a devouring fire. His voice was curt, harsh, imperious, admitting no reply. The veins in his forehead grew black, and the man looked dangerous.

Once having given his ringing order to "Form in fours! Draw saber!" it was neck or nothing. When he thus came to the saber, there was never any such word as "fail" with him. That was the enemy in front, and to ride over and cut right and left among them was the work before him. He seemed strong enough to ride down a world.

BREVETTED BY JEB

"If an officer failed Stuart," the same comrade recalled, "he never forgave him; as the man who attracted his attention, or who volunteered for a forlorn hope, was never forgotten. In his tenacious memory, Stuart registered everybody; and in his command, his word, bad or good, largely set up or pulled down." One such deserving man was brevetted by Stuart in this unorthodox fashion:

"You're about my size, Cooke," said Jeb, "but you're not so broad in the chest." "Yes, I am," answered Cooke. "Let's see if you are," said Stuart, taking off his coat as if stripping for a boxing match: "Try that on." Cooke donned the coat with its three stars on the collar and found it a fit. "Cut off two of the stars," commanded Stuart, "and wear the coat to Richmond. Tell the people in the War Department to make you a major and send you back to me in a hurry. I'll need you tomorrow."

Southern Chivalry

Shortly before the Civil War a new name for the people of Dixie was launched by fans of Sir Walter Scott's *Ivanhoe*—The Chivalry. The name sums up a favorite myth of southerners to the effect that their earliest colonial ancestors had been royalist Cavaliers and that the South thus represented the blueblood or "chivalry" of the land. This belief was accompanied by the cult of aristocratic manners. Visiting Richmond in 1853, the Connecticut-born Frederick Olmsted found "more ceremony and form than well-bred people commonly use at the North." The same observation has been made countless times since.

Southern gentlemen, jealous of their honor, were quick to quarrel. What had, at a less refined stage in the progress of southern manners, been known as a difficulty (a shoot-out or a knife fight) was now invested by the *code duello* with chivalric decorum. Other aspects of the chivalric mystique were the cults of white southern womanhood, ancestry and genealogy (Robert E. Lee devoted many youthful hours to the latter), horses, hunting and racing, military affairs, firearms, hospitality, and oratory—every one of which flourishes in Dixie to this day.

A chivalric event par excellence was the ring tournament. Here is a de-scription of one that took place in South Carolina during the decade preceding the war, written by a plantation Society matron named Emily Sinkler who was present with the youthful Lizzie: Wednesday was as bright and beautiful a day as could be desired. We arrived early and got excellent places—there were about 200 ladies present . . . At last along the winding road the "knights" were seen approaching at full speed, their trumpets sounding, and as they drew near, the band struck up "Yankee Doodle"—of all things for this anti-Yankee state! The tilting began. The object was to carry off the ring on the lance, a very difficult matter. Each knight came full speed, pointing his lance directly at the ring, many throwing it off on the ground, and many failing entirely. When each had had a trial, they defiled past the place of starting. There were six trials, and when it was all concluded the judges pronounced that the Knight of Carolina, a young man by the name of Morton Waring, had carried off the ring the greatest number of times and therefore was directed to choose a queen, which the poor youth did with great trepidation. The whole affair went off with but one interruption which nearly broke Lizzie's heart. A young man, René

Ravenel, the Knight of Berkeley, rode a vicious horse and on the first trial was thrown. He was not hurt and in a few moments mounted another horse, came before the ladies' stand accompanied by the Herald and the Master of the Horse, and, after lowering his lance, said, "The Knight of Berkeley comes before you without plume or spurs and craves the indulgence of the ladies for his disgrace." He is quite a handsome young man and looked extremely pale and disconcerted. It was too much for poor Lizzie, who burst into tears and thought of no one else all day. The ladies later sent him a bunch of flowers with a very complimentary message, requesting him to favor them with his company at the stand, which he accordingly did and was quite as much a hero as the real victor—women having always a penchant for the knights in misfortune. It was by this time 3 o'clock and the collation was very acceptable. In the evening there was a regular ball.

Such was the atmosphere in which future Confederate leaders grew up. In it the "cracker" and the "restercrat" rubbed elbows together, however, for the "tunament" was not always an exclusively upper-class affair—side by side with knightly pageantry, occasionally, were such events as the sack race, the fence-rail race, the plowing match, and, writes the author of a history of the ring tourney in the U.S., "most entertaining of all, the gander-pulling, in which men tried to pull off the greased head from a suspended gander."

The outside world did not respond with unanimous enthusiasm to the strange mixture of barbarity and refinement that was southern chivalry. In California, for instance, southerners were nicknamed "chivs" and baited with "the exciting topic" (the slavery issue, deliberately introduced into conversation by way of a provocation). In the same spirit, southerners took to calling their Yankee brethren "upstarts" and in return were sneered at as "high-toned southern gentlemen." This was later shortened by Union soldiers to "high-tones," as whatever chivalry there may have been on either side gave way to pure hate.

Scott's Ivanhoe *inspired many colorful tournaments in the South like the one depicted below. "Sir Walter," wrote Twain, "is in great measure responsible for the war."*

TALES FROM THE SOUTH
Soldiers and Spies

"A rich man's war and a poor man's fight" ran an anonymous slogan in the Confederacy in 1861. The slogan didn't catch on. In the Rebel ranks the poorest soldier could, like Lee himself, cite "my native state, my relatives, my children, and my home," if asked what he was fighting for. Johnny Reb also was fighting to preserve an oldtime lifestyle with its homely virtues. Typical Rebel tales:

THE AVENGING DEAD

The Confederates ran increasingly short on clothing and footgear, and especially during the bitter second half of the war, many were often forced to supply their deficiencies by stripping the bodies of the slain. To the natural repugnance they felt about this expedient was added some superstition. Sinister tales made the rounds of Rebel campfires. Years after the war, one "Sarge" Wier was to purvey one of these yarns as the true story of a hapless wartime buddy named Ned. It seems that Sarge and three comrades were trying to divest a dead Federal soldier of a new overcoat when they ran into a problem—rigor mortis had set in and the corpse's arms were sticking straight out on either side. At this point, Sarge relates, "they raised him on his feet and one of 'em got on one side and another on the other side and were trying to bend the stiff arms, when the fellow that was holding him up gave a quick jerk, which turned the dead body and brought the stiff arms around with it, and the open palm slapped Ned in the face, and it smacked as natural as if the Yankee hadda been alive and done it. Ned didn't stop to ask questions. He didn't stop running until he got to camp. No one could convince him he hadn't been hit by a ghost. From then on he wouldn't have nothing to do with getting overcoats that way, and so he froze to death pretty soon after that, one night on picket."

THE FATEFUL HOG

Ozark mountaineers serving in the Confederate Army claimed that some who were killed in action had seen the specter of a monstrous black hog just before battle. One man saw the death sign just before a major engagement but came through unhurt. He laughed at "superstition" and bragged about his escape, but was killed the next day by the accidental discharge of a comrade's revolver. (The black hog was none other than Satan himself—he has been putting in periodic appearances in the same guise since time immemorial. An identical critter showed up at a pirate's funeral some 250 years ago, and another fateful hog, quite similar to that, presages violent death in Ireland to this day.)

LA BELLE REBELLE

Belle Boyd was 17 and an ardent "secesh" (secessionist) when her aunt's home was briefly commandeered by invading Federals to serve as General Shields' headquarters. While a council of war was being held in the family dining room, Belle lay on the floor of a closet directly overhead, her ear glued to the floor. The meeting broke up late in the evening, and Belle stole out, saddled up, and rode 15 miles to the Confederate lines. Repeating what she had heard to a southern intelligence officer, she returned unsuspected before dawn. As she performed countless similar feats, she fell under suspicion, was occasionally arrested, but invariably bluffed and flirted her way out of trouble.

Belle was several times escorted to the Confederate lines by gallant northern captors who could not make up their minds to shoot or jail her and be done with it. Once while with a young cavalry lieutenant, Belle was arrested on suspicion of carrying spy messages. (She had placed the documents in ascending order of importance in the charmed lieutenant's hand, her basket, her maid's hand, and her own.) Questioned at headquarters, Belle handed over the basket. Seeing the paper in her hand, the colonel in charge asked, "What's that?" "This scrap? Nothing. You can have it," said Belle, moving forward as if to give him the note. (Later she said she would have swallowed it had he reached out.) Instead the colonel turned his attention to the lieutenant, who handed over his paper and caught the brunt of the older man's rage. To Belle's regret, the lieutenant stayed under arrest. She herself got clear and passed through, having not only kept the essential note in her hand but also the valuable one in her maid's possession.

Her most memorable exploit was during Jackson's Shenandoah Valley campaign. Belle found out from a Union staff officer that Federal plans to destroy certain bridges were delayed and that by advancing immediately Jackson could keep open a vital

Many a veteran of the Confederate Army found devastation awaiting him at home, as in this watercolor by W. L. Sheppard.

"The Confederate Raft," by Gilbert Gaul, is an allegorical representation of southern fighting after surrender—this picture was painted in the 1870's, when the romantic legend of the Confederacy was first yoked to the movement to undo Reconstruction.

avenue of advance for his own army. Seizing an opportune moment, she ran over open fields in the crossfire between Confederate and northern skirmishers. One of Jackson's staff saw her coming:

"I observed the figure of a woman in white glide swiftly out of town on our right and, after making a little circuit, run rapidly up a ravine in our direction and then disappear from sight. She seemed, when I saw her, to heed neither weeds nor fences but waved a bonnet as she came on. I called General Jackson's attention to her and he sent me to ascertain what she wanted. That was just to my taste, and it took only a few minutes for my horse to carry me to meet the romantic maiden whose tall, supple, and graceful figure struck me as soon as I came in sight of her. As I drew near, her speed slackened, and I was startled at hearing her call my name. 'Great God, Belle, why are you here?' I asked. 'Go back quick,' she replied, 'and tell Stonewall that the Yankee force is very small—one regiment of Maryland infantry, several pieces of artillery, and several companies of cavalry. Tell him I know, for I got it out of an officer. Tell him to charge right down and he will catch them all . . .' "

The day was won, thanks in part to Belle, for which the usually undemonstrative Jackson thanked her in glowing terms. Subsequently she received a commission as captain and honorary aide-de-camp to Stonewall. Belle did not forget the officer who relayed her message. Of their next meeting he wrote: "She pinned a crimson rose to my uniform, bidding me remember that it was *blood-red* and that it was her 'colors.' "

After the war Belle performed on the stage, and beginning in 1886 she appeared on lecture platforms enthralling audiences with accounts of her thrilling exploits. She remained an unreconstructed Rebel until her death of a heart attack in 1900.

A PASS TO HEAVEN

One night after General Lee had given orders for the maintenance of strict discipline, an officer riding to camp from Chambersburg, Pennsylvania, was halted by the outposts. Having neither pass nor countersign, in his dilemma he bethought him of an old pass in his pocketbook, signed by General Jackson, whose recent death hung like a cloud over the army. He found it and handed it with confidence to the sentinel. The trusty fellow managed to read it by the light of a match, and as he did so he seemed to linger and hesitate over the signature. Looking up toward the stars beyond, he said sadly and firmly: "Captain, you can go to Heaven on that, but you can't pass this post."

NORTHERN TALES
The Anonymous Heroes of the War

The Civil War was, perhaps, the first war in which the press was enlisted in an all-out effort to build morale on the homefront. Stories of heroism, of battlefield humor, of miraculous escapes, became the daily literature and vicarious war experiences of thousands of noncombatant newspaper readers. Northerners naturally favored the stories which, like those below, lauded the men in blue.

A malingerer on the Union side is told to say "ah" by a skeptical Army doctor, in this realistic painting by Winslow Homer.

THE GREAT CHASE

In the summer of 1863 General Thomas and his troops were surrounded by Confederates with no apparent way to send for help. Noting that there was still intact a railroad track running through the mountains, he called for volunteers to run the lines with an old engine that stood within their camp. Several men came forward and Thomas chose two experienced railroad men as engineer and fireman and an adjutant to carry dispatches.

They started off at half-past 10 on a moonless night, roaring through the first battery of enemy guns with only minor damage to the caboose. The next danger point was at a junction, protected by no less than two batteries. At the second battery the Confederates succeeded only in dropping a shell on the caboose, injuring the fireman but sparing the boiler. The adjutant now took the fireman's place and was heaping coal as fast as he could when the fireman said, "Listen, they're after us, and what's more they're bound to get us unless we can throw them off the track."

Before long the headlight of a pursuing engine could be seen like the fierce eye of some insatiable monster on the track of its prey. Bullet after bullet whizzed past the escaping engine as the pursuing engine gained ground. Now the front engine had only 10 miles to safety but the rear engine was less than a quarter mile away and gaining.

"How about dropping some of the fire bars on the tracks?" suggested the captain, and while the wounded fireman took the engineer's place, the other two men began carefully dropping the long, heavy steel rods across the tracks. But it slowed their pursuer not at all. Next they tried tossing their heavy overcoats onto the track in hopes that they would entangle the wheels. This, too, failed. Suddenly the dull, despairing look on the engineer's face changed to a broad grin. "Captain, come out to the tender and I'll show you a good stunt."

The captain followed and the engineer took a pair of large oil cans with long nozzles, then, wrapping his two brawny arms tightly around the captain's waist, lowered him as far as he could from the tender and told him to pour the oil directly on each

The little drummer boy was the noble hero of a story told in countless variations.

rail. When all the oil was gone, the engineer said, "Now keep your eye open and you'll see some fun."

Just when the pursuing engine seemed on the instant of coming up behind the caboose, its front wheels came to the oiled track and began spinning. The Union engineer, peering at the disappearing enemy through his fieldglasses, turned to his companions with pleasure: "It seems to me as if they are cussin' considerable." The Union train reached Union lines a few minutes later and rescue was immediately on its way to Thomas' army.

THE DRUMMER BOY

One day there appeared at the encampment of a company of Union soldiers a widow leading a sharp, sprightly-looking boy apparently about 12 or 13 years old. She asked to see the captain and, upon gaining an audience, told the officer that she had heard that he was looking for a drummer. As she was destitute and could no longer feed her boy, she had come to offer the willing lad in service to the Union Army.

During her recitation the little fellow kept his eyes intently fixed upon the captain, who was about to refuse the offer of so young a lad when the child spoke out: "Don't be afraid, captain, I can drum." This was stated with so much confidence that the captain smiled, saying to the sergeant, "Bring the drum and order our fifer to come forward." In a few moments the drum was produced, and the fifer, a tall good-natured fellow, made his appearance.

The fifer placed his fife at his mouth and played the "Flowers of Edinburgh," one of the most difficult things to follow with a drum that could have been selected. Nobly did the little fellow follow him, showing himself to be a master of the drum. When the music ceased, the captain turned to the boy's mother and said he would take him. "What is his name?" he asked, and she replied, "Edward Lee." Then after getting the captain's promise to look out for the boy, she kissed the child and wished him Godspeed.

Eddie soon became a great favorite of all the men in the company and everyone kept a kindly eye on him. During the fight at Wilson's Creek in Missouri, part of the company, Eddie included, was ordered down into a deep ravine in which it was known a portion of the enemy was concealed. Union and Rebel forces were soon engaged, and after a brief but bloody battle the Union troops fell back.

A small contingent of Union soldiers were detailed on high ground for the night so that they might cover the retreat in the morning. The hours passed slowly but at length the morning light began to streak along the eastern sky. Presently there came the sound of a drum beating up reveille. At first it seemed to come from the enemy camp; but as the men listened it became clear it was from the ravine, and they recognized it as the sound of their own drummer boy.

The corporal among them instantly jumped to his feet and headed for the ravine. He soon found Eddie sitting on the ground, his back against the trunk of a fallen tree. As soon as he saw the corporal, Eddie exclaimed: "Oh, corporal, I am so glad to see you. Give me a drink of water." The corporal turned to fetch water from

"Shoot if you must, this old gray head,/But spare your country's flag," said Barbara Frietchie to her southern captors. The incident, described in a popular ballad, supposedly happened in Frederick, Maryland; both lady and flag survived the challenge she hurled.

the brook but the boy, misunderstanding, said, "Don't leave me, corporal—I can't walk." The corporal looked down at the boy's legs to discover that both his feet had been shot away by a cannonball. Eddie now asked his rescuer: "You don't think I will die, do you? This man said the surgeon could cure my feet." For the first time the corporal noticed the body of a Confederate soldier lying in the grass. It appeared that he had fallen near where Eddie lay. Knowing that he himself could not live, and seeing the condition of the boy, he had crawled to him, taken off his buckskin suspenders, and corded the little fellow's legs below the knee, then lay down and died.

While the corporal was considering what to do for Eddie, both of them were discovered by the enemy and

taken prisoner. Eddie was carried with great tenderness but he died before the party reached camp.

THE BELLWETHER

Among the loyal Tennesseans who came into the Union camp in Kentucky was a little fellow of about five feet four inches, with gray and grizzled beard, dilapidated nose, and an eye as keen as a fishhawk's. The manner of his escape from the secessionists was remarkable and highly ingenious. One night he headed a large squad of his neighbors and they eluded Confederate pickets by wearing big sheep's bells and bleating as they walked. By this stratagem the "flock" passed within a few feet of the enemy and crossed through one of the most heavily guarded mountain passes.

NORTHERN HEROES
Lincoln's Generals

A major Union problem during the Civil War was the lack of first-class military leadership. It was a curious fact of history that most of the career officers in the U.S. Army in the years before the war were of southern origin, and when the war broke out they naturally turned to the defense of the region and institutions that had nurtured them. Lincoln searched desperately for seasoned Union officers who would fight with boldness, but despite the superior size of the northern army and the greater abundance of its arms and supplies, his generals repeatedly lost the advantage. Not until 1863 did men like the courageous generals celebrated here in legends emerge to exert the winning difference.

Grant receiving the praise of Columbia

STUBBORN LYS
Concerning the determination of his commanding general, President Lincoln liked to tell a story: When Ulysses Grant was 10 years old a circus came along, and Lys volunteered to try to ride a pony who could throw anyone. He got on and hung on until he had almost circled the ring three times, when he slid off over the animal's head. As soon as he got the tanbark out of his eyes and mouth, up he went again, but this time Lys faced the rear, coiled his legs around the critter's body, and held on by the tail. There Grant stuck like grim death and came off victorious. "Just so," concluded the president, "he'll stick to Richmond. He's a very obstinate man."

BRAND NAME
While success eluded one after another of the eastern generals, the western campaign of General Grant was a series of brilliant victories. But at Shiloh, Grant blundered badly. This brought a delegation of Grant's political enemies to Lincoln demanding that Grant be removed. "What's the matter with Grant?" asked Lincoln. The spokesman replied, "The general drinks!" "What does he drink?" "Whisky." "Aha," said the president. "Now do any of you know what brand?" "Certainly not, sir. Why do you ask?" "Because if it's whisky that makes Grant the way he is," said teetotaler Lincoln, "I'm going to send a barrel of it to every general in the East!"

SHERMAN'S IMPOSTER
When Gen. William T. Sherman was in command of Benton Barracks, St. Louis, he was in the habit of visiting every part of that institution. He wore an old brown coat and a stovepipe hat, and was not generally recognized by the minor officials or the soldiers. Once while walking, he met a soldier beating a mule.

"Stop pounding that mule!" said the general. "Git out!" said the soldier. "I tell you to stop!" repeated the general. "You mind your business and I will mind mine," replied the soldier, continuing his operations on the mule. "I command you to stop!" said the general. "I am General Sherman." "That's played out!" said the soldier. "Every man who comes along here with an old brown coat and a stovepipe hat claims to be General Sherman." It is presumed that for once Sherman considered himself outflanked.

On the battlefield, on the other hand, everyone recognized the general, even the enemy. One officer reported: "He had a pleasant way of rising up in full sight of the enemy's batteries, accompanied by his staff. Here he would hold us while he criticized the manner in which the Confederates got their guns ready to open on us. Presently a shell would whiz over our heads, followed by another

An amusing depiction of the Union victory shows a parade of Uncle Sams passing in review before a phalanx of generals

somewhat nearer. Sherman would then quietly remark, 'They are getting the range now; you had better scatter.' As a rule we did not wait for a second order."

SHERIDAN'S RIDE

Gen. Phil Sheridan was an ideal cavalry leader. Brave, dashing, brilliant, he had commanded more horsemen than had any general since the days of the Tatar hordes of Tamerlane and Genghis Khan. As soon as he took command of the Army of the Shenandoah, aggressive fighting began.

The most celebrated instance of his leadership came in the Battle of Cedar Creek, Virginia. Early on the morning of October 19, 1864, awakened with news that the Confederates had begun firing on one of his outposts, he hurriedly mounted his handsome black thoroughbred, Rienzi, and set out for the battlefield. Before Sheridan had gone far, he met hundreds of men, some wounded, all demoralized, who were rushing to the rear in hopeless confusion. Seeing a chaplain among them, he inquired how things were going at the front.

"Everything is lost," replied the chaplain, "but it will be all right when you get there." Sheridan sent back word to Colonel Edwards, who commanded a brigade at Winchester, to stretch his troops across the valley and stop all fugitives. He then rode on ahead to rally the men at the front and turn defeat to victory.

The roads were too crowded to be used, and so he jumped the fence into the fields and rode straight across country toward the drumming guns at Cedar Creek. As he rode, he obtained a clear idea of what had happened. Just after dawn his great rival, Jubal Early, had made an attack in two different directions on the Union forces. This had started a panic, which had seized all the soldiers except one division under Getty and the cavalry under Lowell. The army that Sheridan met was a defeated army in full rout. As he dashed along, the men everywhere recognized him, stopped running, threw up their hats with a cheer, and

shouldering their muskets turned around and followed him as fast as they could. He directed his escort to ride in all directions and announce that General Sheridan was coming. Throughout the fields and roads could be heard the sound of faint cheering, and everywhere men were seen turning, rallying, and marching.

So he galloped the whole 12 miles, with the men everywhere rallying behind him and following him at full speed. At last he came to the fore-

Gen. Phil Sheridan astride Rienzi as he made his famous ride across the Virginia hills to rally his badly demoralized troops

front of the battle, where Getty's division and the cavalry were holding their own and resisting the rapid approach of the entire Confederate Army. Sheridan called upon his horse for a last effort and jumped the rail fence at the crest of the hill. By this time the black horse was white with foam, but he carried his master bravely up and down in front of the line as the whole brigade of men rose to their feet with a tremendous cheer and poured in a fierce fire upon the approaching Confederate troops. Sheridan rode along the whole front of the line and aroused a wild enthusiasm which showed itself in the way that the first Rebel charge was driven back. Telling Getty's and Lowell's men to hold on, he rode back to meet the approaching troops. By half-past 3 in the afternoon, Sheridan had brought back all the routed troops, re-formed his battleline, and waving his hat led a charge on his same gallant black horse. As they attacked the Confederate front, generals Merritt and Custer made a fresh assault and the whole Confederate Army fell back, routed and broken, and was driven up the valley in the same way that earlier in the day they had driven the Union soldiers. Once again the presence of one brave man had turned a defeat into a victory.

FACT ? MYTH

The Symbolic Sword

Following Robert E. Lee's surrender to U. S. Grant at Appomattox Courthouse, a story was widely circulated that the vanquished had handed the victor his ceremonial sword and that Grant had magnanimously returned it. Grant in his memoirs called the report "the purest romance." It probably grew out of the fact that Grant had stipulated in the surrender terms that all officers should be permitted to retain their sidearms and other personal effects. The legend was, however, correct in spirit, for the meeting between the two men was cordial if subdued. When it was over, Grant returned to his men and ordered that there would be no celebrating so sad a victory.

Confederate commander Robert E. Lee in an imaginary presurrender view

"A first-class roper," wrote Theodore Roosevelt, "is usually fit for little but his own special work." The same was true of cowboys in general.

"Stranger in Town," by Melvin Warren, is a stock western scene—the good guy (or outlaw) comes to town for a final showdown with his foes, as in the fight at O K Corral or *High Noon*.

The Wild, Wild West

Soon after the Civil War it became possible for Texas cattlemen to drive herds to midwestern railheads connecting with the Northeast, where they fetched many times the Texas price. The vast open ranges between the Southwest and Canada were still largely unsettled, and herds moving through at the rate of 10–20 miles a day could actually get fat en route to such destinations as Abilene, Cheyenne, and Sedalia. The drovers' life was a rough, lonely one, beset with extremes of climate and weather, hostile Indians, and whites who sought to bar drives through their claims.

A "cowgirl" as pictured in 1900

A typical drive consisted of 2,500 longhorns herded by a dozen men. The cowboys came from all over, but the majority were southerners of English and Scotch-Irish extraction. Thus the romantic tales of the cowboy that became fixed in the popular imagination (thanks in great measure to the efforts of dime novelists such as Ned Buntline) had a close resemblance to Old World stories like those of the Scottish border wars of the 1500's in which blood and thunder, gunsmoke, night raids, and chases on horseback are also highlighted. (The rustler changing brands on cattle and the raider who had his horses shod backward to baffle pursuers are classic 16th-century Scottish as well as western; so is the ending in which the wounded hero leaves his girl to make a fresh start but dies alone in the process.) The actual era of the long drive was over by 1895, but the cowboy legend looms large in today's world, pervading popular music, entertainment, dress, and speech. Millions of people all over the world like to see something of themselves in the brave, independent loners who rode the open trail.

COWBOYS
A Harsh Home on the Range

The cowboy's year began with the spring roundup of the herd and the branding of newborn cattle, and it continued on until payday in fall at the end of the cattle drive to some middle-western railhead. During those months the cowboy's lot was one of physical hardship, loneliness, 20-hour workdays, and danger, leavened only by the pleasure he took in his surroundings, his cow pony, and male companionship around a campfire. Ahead lay a long cold winter, a time to "blow in" his meager wages, repair his gear, and wander south to hire on again.

THE TARANTULA'S LESSON
There once was a big, overgrown cowpoke named Tall Cotton, whose specialty was going to sleep during duty hours, leaving the rest of the crew to do his share of the work. The boys finally decided that something had to be done about the matter.

Then came the day that they found Cotton curled up in a haystack, boots off, sound asleep. The opportunity was golden. They rounded up a huge tarantula, killed it, and laid it close to Cotton's leg. Then they tied a pin on the end of a stick and jabbed the sleeping waddy a couple of times. Cotton came awake like a wild Comanche doing the snake dance and, at the same time, one of the boys rushed up and smashed the tarantula.

Cotton took one look at the dead tarantula and turned white. He began to get sick, even though the other waddies did their best to console him with stories of the horrible deaths they had seen as a result of tarantula bites. Finally one of the crew, who laid claim to having read *Ten Thousand Things Worth Knowing* and *Dr. Chase's Recipe Book,* offered to try to save Cotton, although he admitted it seemed hopeless.

First the cowboy poured a pint of bear's oil down Cotton. When that started some of the poison coming up, they followed with a glass of soda, a cup of vinegar, and finally a quart of water in which a plug of tobacco had been soaking. For a while it seemed almost certain that Cotton was going to die from that tarantula bite; but the medicine was potent, and eventually he was saved.

After that the crew had very little trouble with him lying down on the job, especially in haystacks.

THE CHAMPION TALKER
One time an old windbelly from the Pothook outfit challenged our champion talker to a talkin' match. Our best talker agreed, and the time was set for just after payday so the boys'd have plenty of bettin' money.

When the match came off, our champion, havin' some talent for poetry, started off with such giggle talk as, "The hoss he neigh, can you tell what he say? The cow she moo, the bull does too, the dog he bark, till the moon goes dark, the coyote yip, like he's got the flutter-lip." He goes on like this till he runs plumb through the animal kingdom.

At the same time the Pothook man, not to be outpoetried, ranted such stuff as, "The lightnin' flash, the thunder crash, the rain she pour, the wind she roar," till you thought you was in Noah's flood. Our man was as full of verbal lather as a soap peddler, but this here Pothook man had more wind than a bull in green corn time. They shouted this foolishness plumb through the night, the boys doin' their best to cheer their favorite on to glory. It was daybreak when the Pothook man finally talked 'imself to sleep. Our champion was leaning over him still whisperin' the merits of his favorite brand of canned peaches, but he didn't have 'nough vocal power left to bend a smoke ring.

THE SWEETEST MUSIC
Old Tom O'Conner had deeds to scores of sections of land and he owned 10,000 cattle on the prairies and in the brush, but he was too frail to ride anymore. One day he told his ranch boss, Pat Lambert, to take all hands and bring in the biggest herd they could gather. The crew rode hard and about an hour before sundown they drove a vast herd of mixed cattle to the holding grounds near the O'Conner ranchhouse. Bulls were challenging, cows were bellowing, calves were bleating. Heifers, year-

"Moving the Herd," by W. H. D. Koerner, depicts the long drive as it was at the height

306

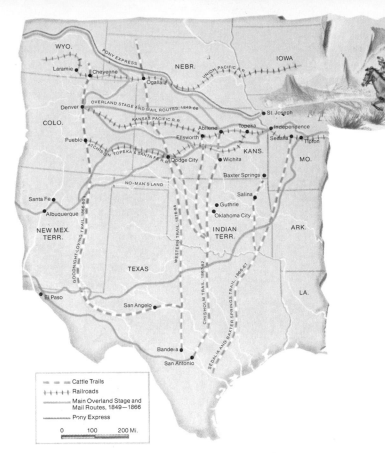

To enable people, money, and meat to circulate on a transcontinental scale, lines of transport were thrown cross-country c. 1850, from the Midwest to the Pacific and East and from Texas to the Midwest.

lings, old moss-horned steers, were milling about, their blended voices rising above the dust from their hooves. Pat Lambert went into the room where Tom O'Conner lay on his bed. "We made a big drag, Mr. Tom," he said. "What do you want me to do with them, Mr. Tom?" "Nothing. Just hold them there. I'm dying, Pat, and I want to go out with natural music in my ears."

RUNNING THE STAMPEDE

We had just crossed the Pecos. It was one of those black nights, so dark you could feel it. Rain began during the first guard and increased till it was just sloshing down. When a bolt of lightning struck at the edge of the herd, 2,500 head of beef steers left the bed-ground with a roar like thunder.

As near as I could tell in the dark, I was north of the herd when the run started. I aimed to keep to the north and west, matching strides with the leaders, shooting my six-gun in front of their noses in an effort to make them turn and mill, and trusting to my horse, Chopo, to keep his feet. He broke through the muddy ground but never fell. If he had, I would have been a mincemeat cowboy in 10 seconds under hundreds of hooves.

Try as we might, we were unable to stop the cattle. They ran for miles, and when they finally split, it was so dark I didn't know it till a flash of lightning showed I was riding in the lead of exactly three steers. Of course, it was no use going on. I was soaked to the skin. I had used my slicker trying to whip the steers back and make them mill, and there was nothing much left of it except the sleeves and collar. The air had turned freezing cold. I knew every hand at the wagon would have been out to try to turn the cattle: but where the others were and where the wagon was I hadn't any notion.

Once more it was a case of trust the horse. I gave the little black his head. We traveled for hours, and I never heard sound or saw sign of another horse or human. Then suddenly Chopo nickered; a horse answered him. Chopo had brought me home.

...e cowboy era—around 1880. Within decades the long drive was to be a thing of the past.

THE WESTERN NOVEL

This cowboy has decided to cool off in a waterhole out on the range, while some trapped steers look on from nearby fences specially rigged for catching strays.

America's love affair with the wild-and-woolly West started in earnest in the 1860's when dime novels romanticizing the cowboy and the long trail began to appear. King of the authors was a character named Ned Buntline, who could turn out a rattling good "western" long before he ever went west. The dime westerns laid the foundation both for movie westerns and for western fiction, which became a serious literary genre with the appearance of Owen Wister and his ilk around the turn of the century.

Wister, Philadelphia raised and Harvard educated, introduced the western genre in 1902 when he published *The Virginian,* a novel that for all its romantic overtones established a number of enduring characters and situations; with modifications, they continue to persist in contemporary literature of the Old West. Wister set the tone of adulation in his introduction. Speaking of the cowboy, already a disappearing figure in 1902, he

wrote: "Whatever he did, he did with his might. The bread he earned was earned hard, the wages that he squandered were squandered hard—half a year's pay sometimes gone in a night . . . His wild kind has been among us . . . since the beginning: a young man with his temptations, a hero without wings."

Wister's novel is played against the backdrop of Wyoming in the last quarter of the 19th century. We first meet our hero in Medicine Bow.

This 1900 cigarette card depicts a playful cowboy "making a tenderfoot dance."

"Lounging there at ease against the wall was a slim young giant, more beautiful than pictures. His broad, soft hat was pushed back; a loose-knotted, dull-scarlet handkerchief sagged from his throat, and one casual thumb was hooked in the cartridge belt that slanted across his hips. He had plainly come many miles from somewhere across the vast horizon, as the dust upon him showed. . . . The weather-beaten bloom of his face showed through it duskily . . . But no dinginess of travel or shabbiness of attire could tarnish the splendor that radiated from his youth and strength."

Early in the story the Virginian meets up with a shady gambler named Trampas. When Trampas has the temerity to call him a foul name, our hero responds with that immortal line "When you call me that, *smile*!" as he slowly and firmly brings out his pistol and lays it on the gaming table. Trampas' reaction also set a certain standard of dramatic response for future westerns: as the roomful of men suddenly stilled, Trampas declined "to draw steel," thus adding cowardice to his unsavory character.

Wister's novel ends with the Virginian being tamed by matrimony—a schoolmarm, no less—in a sentimental manner that led one critic to rename the author "Owen Wisteria," and it may be said that in many ways the book was only another eastern romance transformed by western costume. It sold more than 2 million copies in its first 50 years and became the basis of a long-running play and four movies.

More authentic and in many ways as influential was *The Log of a Cowboy,* published in 1903 by Andy Adams. Adams was an Indiana boy who left home for Texas in 1882 to become a ranch hand and trail driver. His *Log* reads more like a real-life chronicle than a novel, for it was Adams' intention to demythify the cowboy. His story is very straightforward, describing a trail drive from Mexico to Montana, and its events are told simply and undramatically, without "shoot-'em-ups" or "necktie parties" or other

Hollywood-style spectacles. Nevertheless, the writers and filmmakers who subsequently made "horse operas" a major American entertainment industry learned much from Adams.

Take, for instance, Adams' description of Dodge City, Kansas, a junction point where the Atchison, Topeka & Santa Fe Railroad crossed the Western Trail. McNulta, one of the oldtimers on the drive, gives the younger men some advice: "Dodge is one town where the average badman of the West not only finds his equal but is also badly handicapped. The buffalo hunters and rangemen have protested against the iron rule of Dodge's peace officers, and nearly every protest has cost human life. Don't ever get the impression that you can ride your horses into a saloon or shoot out the lights in Dodge; it may go somewhere else, but it don't go there. So I want to warn you to behave yourselves. You can wear your six-shooters into town, but you'd better leave them at the first place you stop—hotel, livery, or business house. And when you leave town, call for your pistols, but don't ride out shooting; omit that. Most cowboys think it's an infringement on their rights to give up shooting in town, but if it is, it stands, for your six-shooters are no match for Winchesters and buckshot; and Dodge's officers are as game a set of men as ever faced dan-

Preparing pies for Thanksgiving on the range. The picture dates from 1888.

ger." Adams then goes on to list some of that "game set," including "Bat" Masterson, Wyatt Earp, "Shotgun" Collins, and "Mysterious" Dave Mather.

On the technique of driving cattle, Adams' trail foreman tells his men: "Boys, the secret of trailing cattle is never to let your herd know that they are under restraint. Let everything that is done be done voluntarily by the cattle. From the moment you let them off the bed-ground in the morning until they are bedded at night, never let a cow take a step, except in the direction of its destination. In this manner you can loaf away the day, and cover from 15 to 20 miles, and the

herd in the meantime will enjoy all the freedom of the open range. Of course, it's long, tiresome hours to the men; but the condition of the herd and saddle stock demands sacrifices on our part . . . And I want to caution you younger boys about your horses; there is such a thing as having 10 horses in your string, and at the same time being afoot. . . . On the condition of the remuda depends the success and safety of the herd. Accidents will happen to horses, but don't let it be your fault; . . . no better word can be spoken of a man than that he is careful of his horses."

A time of tragedy among Adams' outfit is described almost tenderly. It begins as the men are driving the herd across a river. "When the last two or three hundred of the tail-enders were leaving the first island for the second, and the men working in the rear started to swim the channel, amid the general hilarity I recognized a shout that was born of fear and terror. A hushed silence fell over the riotous riders in the river, and I saw those on the sandbar nearest my side . . . plunge back into the middle channel. Then it dawned on me in a flash that someone had lost his seat . . . One of our number was underwater if not drowned. There were not less than 20 horsemen drifting in the middle channel in the hope that whoever it was would come to the surface and a hand could be stretched out in succor." It was the next day when the man's body was found, and the stunned men discussed what to do with it. The victim's friend steps forward: "I expect to meet his mother someday. . . . I must tell her the truth, and I'd hate to tell her we buried him like a dog, for she's a Christian woman. In his pocket was a letter from her, in which she warned him to guard against just what has happened. And what makes it all the harder, I know that this is the third boy she has lost by drowning . . . I'm going to ask you all to give him the best burial we can. No doubt it will be crude, but it will be some solace to her to know that we did the best we could."

The first divine service in Pine Bluffs, Wyoming, was held in a setting reminiscent of a contemporary tale in which an itinerant confidence man impersonates a minister, preaches in a saloon, then absconds with the collection after the last "Amen."

WESTERN SPELLBINDERS
Tales Told on the Trail

The men who drove the cattle hundreds of miles to market had few creature comforts en route but strong whisky and the flickering warmth of the nighttime campfire. When the herd was bedded, the men frequently gathered to swap songs and stories, and a man with a rich imagination and a gift for spinning a yarn was a welcome addition to any outfit. Sometimes the stories came out of experience, but equally as often they were "tall" in the great tradition of Pecos Bill tales.

PECOS BILL

Pecos Bill was by all accounts the most famous and remarkable man in the whole country. It was him that invented ropin', for example. He had a rope that reached from the Rio Grande to the Big Bow, and he shore did swing a mean loop. He used to amuse hisself by throwin' a little lasso up in the sky and fetchin' down the buzzards and eagles that flew over. He roped everything he ever seen: bears and wolves and panthers, elk and buffalo. The first time he seen a train he thought it was some kind of varmint, and damn me if he didn't sling a loop over it and dang near wreck the thing.

Bill had a hoss he raised from a colt on a diet of nitroglycerin and barbed wire, which made him tough and also very ornery. Lots a men tried to ride him, but only one man besides Bill ever mounted that hoss and lived. That's the reason Bill named him Widow Maker. That other fella was Bill's friend. Bill tried to talk him out of trying, but he had his heart set on it. He gits on Widow Maker, and that hoss begins to go through his gaits, doin' the end-to-end, the sunfish, and the back throw; and about that time the rider goes up in the sky. Bill watches him through a spyglass and sees him land on Pikes Peak. No doubt he would of starved to death up there, but Bill roped him by the neck and drug him down.

Another time he bet a stetson hat he could ride a cyclone. He went up on the Kansas line and simply eared that tornado down and got on it. Down he come across Oklahoma and the Panhandle a-settin' on that tornado, a-curlin' his mustache and a-spurrin' it in the withers. Seein' it couldn't throw him, it jist naturally rained out from under him, and that's the way Bill got his only spill.

Pecos Bill's ranch was the biggest in the West. He staked out New Mexico and fenced Arizona for a calf pasture. He built a big ranchhouse and had a big yard around it. It was so far from the yard gate to the front door that he used to keep a string of saddle horses at stations along the way, for the convenience of visitors. Bill was always a hospitable sort of chap, and when company come, he always tried to persuade them to stay as long as he could git 'em to.

One time his outfit was so big that he would dam up a draw to mix the biscuit dough in. They would dump in the flour and the salt and the bakin' powder and mix it up with teams. You can still see places where the dough was left in the bottom of the draw when they moved on. Alkali lakes they call 'em. That's the bakin' powder that stayed in the ground. One time when water got scarce on Bill's range, he dug the Rio Grande and ditched water from the Gulf of Mexico to fill the river.

THE MADSTONE

Freighter Will Pool pulled through Stiles one afternoon, heading from San Angelo to Harris Brothers' ranch with a load of stock salt. The hospitable inhabitants of that great capital city had insisted he attend a dance there that night. So, about an hour by

The legendary exploits of Pecos Bill—raised by a coyote, educated by a grizzly bear—were a main source of wonder and entertainment around cowboy campfires.

sun he made camp, hobbled out all except the trimmest of his workhorses, which he saddled, and hightailed it for Stiles. They dined him and danced him until 'way up toward day. He got back to camp in time to catch a few winks, but while doing so he was awakened by sharp, darting pains in his hand. A polecat was latched onto it, sucking blood.

Pool slung the polecat loose but the stinker beat both him and his little dog to a hole. "You reckon that son-of-a-blank could a had hydraphoby?" said Will to himself, not being one to call a spade a spade when he could call it something worse. Taking no chances, he saddled up, loped back to Stiles, and had old Doc Wittaker lance and cauterize the wound. Then the doctor applied his madstone, but it dropped right off. "Jist a old flat rock," said Will disparagingly.

He headed on for Cedar Canyon, but the farther he went the more he worried. There was nothing he could do now, until he got back to San Angelo. After he delivered his load of salt, he went back there just as fast as he could go.

He hit the ground running for a madstone. Yes, a woman there did have one. It was a puffy-looking thing about an inch long and taken from a black-tail deer. Immediately the woman applied this madstone and it clung to the skunk bite for 14 hours. She took it off, boiled it in milk, and reapplied it. This time it stuck to the wound for three hours and dropped off. The woman wouldn't let him, or anybody else,

THE OLD CHISHOLM TRAIL

Moderately

Well, come a-long boys and lis-ten to my tale, I'll tell you of my trou-bles on the old Chis-holm Trail. Come a ti yi yip-pi yip-pi yay yip-pi yay, Come a ti yi yip-pi yip-pi yay.

A two-dollar horse and a forty-dollar saddle,
I'm gonna get punchin' those old Texas cattle.
Come a ti, *etc.*

It's cloudy in the west and it looks like rain,
And my danged old slicker's in the wagon train.
Come a ti, *etc.*

I jumped in the saddle and grabbed the horn,
I'm the best durned cowboy that ever was born.
Come a ti, *etc.*

This song was a favorite among the 100's made up by cowboys to pass the time and quiet the herds. The likelihood of a noise-caused nighttime stampede was lessened when cattle were lulled by continual whistling and singing.

touch the stone or handle it in any way. Will Pool went away satisfied that it saved his life.

HORSE SENSE

"I owned an ol' hoss one time that was about the *dumbest* critter I ever did see. I'll tell yuh what that fool horse did one night when I drunk too much likker and passed out in town.

He picked me up and slung me on his back and carried me 20 miles to the ranch. When he got me there, he pulled off my boots with his teeth and nosed me into my bunk. Then he went to the kitchen, fixed up a pot of coffee, and brung me a cup all fixed up with cream and sugar. Then the next day I had a hangover, and he went out all by hisself and dug postholes all day so's the boss would let me sleep. When I woke up and found out what that fool hoss had done, I cussed him for two days without stoppin' and wished 'im off on a greener [greenhorn] which was passin' by."

"I'd say that was a pretty *smart* horse," observed a listener. "Why in the world did you get rid of him?"

"Smart, heck! Who ever heard of a real cowboy usin' cream and sugar in his coffee? No wonder I had sich a turrible hangover!"

A favorite protagonist in stories was a white beast of supernatural powers—here a great white wolf comes to rescue a dog.

"You never can tell *what* a buffalo will do when he's been eating grapes," concludes one humorous yarn told to a greenhorn.

TRAIL TOWNS
Mixed Delights for Lonesome Cowboys

The settlements that grew up to serve the cattle industry did their best to cope with the often rowdy transients who came their way, by providing saloons and bawdy houses, jails and outfitters, to handle them. The stories of shoot-'em-ups in the streets were doubtless exaggerated, but the sheriff's job was not an enviable one given the difficulties of controlling men with no ties to the community and no reputations to preserve except as rough customers. Besides cowboys, there were also a host of local sharpers and con men for law-abiding citizens to contend with.

THE PEACOCK'S REVENGE

Bradshaw and McIntyre were business partners. Bradshaw went shopping and bought a gorgeous shirt with black, green, and red stripes. When he appeared on Allen Street in Tombstone, Arizona, in this portentous garment, he created a tremendous sensation. But having acquired his ideas of smartness in attire out in the sagebrush, he took his shirt seriously and thought himself the last word in sartorial elegance.

As he strolled along as proud as a peacock, all who met him burst out laughing. He was unable to figure out the joke until boisterous citizens began to shout at him with uproarious guffaws, "Where did you get that shirt?" Bradshaw was vexed by such ribaldry, but his show of displeasure only incited his tormentors to new derision. He flew into furious anger at last and declared flatly to no one in particular, "I will kill the next man who makes fun of my shirt."

The next man was, unfortunately, his partner, McIntyre. The shirt struck McIntyre as excruciatingly ridiculous. He laughed so immoderately that for a time he could not speak. He bent double in unholy glee, twisting, squirming, all the while pointing a finger at Bradshaw. Finally, between giggling outbursts, he managed to spit out the fateful words "Where did you get that shirt?" Whereupon Bradshaw, beside himself with rage, drew a six-shooter and killed him, the bullet entering McIntyre's mouth, which was wide open with merriment. Tombstone took the murder lightly, holding McIntyre fortunate in that death came to him as a sort of joke and that he went out into the other world holding his sides with laughter.

SUNDAY AT THE SALOON

In Newton, Kansas, gambling was a mania. There were eight gambling institutions, 80 professionals, and hundreds of cowmen ready to take a chance. The Gold Rooms, operated by Doc Thayer and Bill Pierce, were the most famous and influential of

The classic invitation to a fight, perhaps even a gun battle, was the tossing of a glass of whisky in another man's face. Chances were, if the insulted man took the challenge, the other patrons, happy for the entertainment, would gather to watch the action.

Gambling, frequently for very high stakes, could cost a cowboy all his wages, especially if he was a greenhorn among pros.

them all. Thayer looked more like a preacher than a saloonkeeper. He wore faultless linen, always kept his coat on, and wore his trouser legs outside of his boots. He was decidedly the swell of the town. Pierce was a popular fellow who had been a miner and had owned a large cattle ranch. He had the reputation of getting more business than any other saloonkeeper in the Southwest.

The Gold Rooms offered six tables, a mammoth bar, music, and sideshows. Every device invented for gambling could be found there—faro, chuck-a-luck, poker, old sledge, the tobacco box game, and a thousand other devices made to obtain money from gamblers. There was neither a church nor a religious organization in town, so one Sunday evening when a stranger entered the Gold Rooms, approached the bar, and stated that he was a clergyman looking for a place to conduct divine services on the premises, the proprietor was surprised but not unfriendly.

The games were going full blast, the fiddlers were squeaking their loudest, the melodeon was growling out its deepest bass, the song-and-dance man was executing one of his most brilliant pirouettes, the waitresses with huge trays loaded with glasses were dodging here and there

among the crowd, and two rival dogs of the town were being rubbed and pulled for their third great fight of the day.

Divine services amid all this! thought the proprietor, and coughed and expectorated, but seeing an opening for business, answered quickly: "By all means, sir, we would be most happy to have you preach. When would you like to open up?"

"At 8 o'clock, if you please," was the answer. Then the gentleman withdrew. Here was great news. It traveled down the streets and into peoples' homes until the whole town knew there was to be preaching in the Gold Rooms. A great crowd had gathered in the establishment by the time the preacher came.

As he passed the bar, friendly invitations to have a drink greeted him on all sides. The preacher had a red nose, and though he disregarded the invitations, his nose blushed deeper and he sniffed spasmodically. Someone saw it and was crude enough to call out, "Don't go back on your spiritual friends, old fellow."

Services began with a prayer. Somebody was playing faro in hard

"Soiled doves" and "painted pigeons," like the lady above, constituted the most visible part of the female population in some cow towns, and an evening of their companionship could be one of the greatest lures at the end of a long trail drive.

luck. The queen had beaten him three times. He lost again just as the prayer was drawing to a close.

"Damn the luck," broke from the gambler's lips just as "Amen" followed from the platform. The whole house roared. Someone let the dogs loose and a dogfight was added to the scene. Nevertheless, the services went on, and hymns and a sermon followed. The preacher took up a collection, had a drink, and left. A few days later it was learned that he was no preacher at all, merely a hard-up sharper in want of a week's board money.

TEETHING TOY

Even babies in Dodge City found a use for guns. One night a mother, alone in the house with her child, heard someone coming up the path. She looked out and saw a dirty, drunken tramp approaching. Her husband's six-shooter hung on a nail by its trigger guard. She snatched the gun down. It was not loaded. Still she meant to protect her baby with it, though her hand shook so that she could hardly hold the pistol level. She took her stand by the baby's crib. Then she remembered her husband's warning, "Never pull a gun unless you aim to use it." If she tried to bluff that ugly tramp and failed, she dared not think what might happen.

She decided to feed her unwelcome visitor and try to placate him. Hastily, she dropped the gun into her child's crib. But then she seemed unable to say a word and just stood there shaking. The tramp took one look, insolently came through the open door into the house, and prepared to make himself at home. He staggered toward her. She stepped behind the crib. He looked down at the baby. Suddenly he turned pale, whirled around, and ran out the door. She wondered what on earth could have frightened him off. Then she saw: the little boy was teething on the revolver. The tramp was still running, heading for the lone prairie as fast as he could go. He wanted nothing to do with a town where even the babies were gunslingers.

THE PONY EXPRESS
Neither Heat nor Snow . . .

Even as the first rider dashed out of St. Joseph, Missouri, on April 3, 1860, the Pony Express was doomed as an enterprise by the coming telegraph. But the adventures of its daring riders, such as 15-year-old Bill Cody and Bill Hickok, during its 16-month existence have become an indelible part of the legend of the Old West. The least of the hazards faced by the "centaurs" was grinding exhaustion; they also forced themselves through floods, desert heat, and blinding blizzards. One rider tells of being pursued by wolves; a historian recites the ravages of hostile Indians and, perhaps a bit carried away, of mountain lions.

ASPEN TRAP

This story of the eventful days when he rode over the lonesome trail was told in 1907 by J. G. Kelley: I was ordered to take the place of a Mexican rider who had been shot on the route. I had to ride through the forest of quaking aspen where the Mexican had been hit. A trail had been cut through these little trees, just wide enough to allow horse and rider to pass. As the branches came together just above my head, it was impossible for me to see ahead for more than 10 or 15 yards, and it was two miles through the forest. I prepared for trouble by putting my Sharp's rifle at full cock and keeping both my spurs into the pony's flanks. At the top of the hill I dismounted and looking back saw the bushes moving in several places. As there were no cattle or game in that vicinity, I knew the movements to be caused by Indians, and was more positive of it when, after firing several shots at the spot, all agitation ceased. Several days after that, two U.S. soldiers were shot and killed from the ambush of those bushes and stripped of their clothing by the red devils.

CODY OUTWITS ROBBERS

It had become known in some mysterious manner that there was to be a large sum of money sent through by Pony Express, and some road agents killed a rider but failed to get the treasure. Cody thought they would make another effort to secure it; so he perfected a little plan, which was to take a second pair of saddle pouches and put something in them and leave them in sight, while those that held the valuables he folded up in his saddle blanket. He started once more on his flying trip. He carried his revolver ready for instant use and flew along the trail with every nerve strung to meet any danger that might confront him. As he drew near a lonesome spot in a valley he was on the alert, and yet when two men suddenly stepped out from among the shrubs it gave him a start. They had him covered with rifles and halted him with the words "Hands up, Pony Express Bill, for we know yer, my boy, and what yer carries."

"I carry the express; and it's hanging for you two if you interfere with me" was the plucky response. "It won't do you any good to get the pouch, for there is nothing valuable in it." "We are to be the judges of that, so throw us the valuables or catch a bullet." The two men stood directly in front of the pony rider, each one covering him with a rifle, and to resist was certain death. The pouches being unfastened now, Cody hurled them at the head of one of the agents, who quickly dodged and turned to pick them up, just as Cody fired on the other. The bullet shattered the man's arm while Cody rode directly over the man who was stooping to pick up the pouches. The horse struck that robber a hard blow that knocked him down, fell half on top of him, but was recovered by a touch of the spurs and bounded on, while the daring pony rider gave a wild triumphant yell as he sped on like the wind.

The fallen man, though hurt, scrambled to his feet as soon as he could, picked up his rifle, and fired after the retreating youth, but without effect, and young Cody rode on, arriving at the station on time.

Early in his career as a frontier hero, "Buffalo Bill" Cody rode for the Pony Express and had a few blood-curdling encounters with Indians, as is shown here.

OUTLAWS
The Men in the Black Hats

In the Kansas-Missouri border fighting that raged 20 years before, during, and after the Civil War, slavery was the original issue, but as conflict broadened to involve every man, woman, and child, the reasons for it all became very complex. On both sides a lynch-mob mentality developed. Men like Confederate William Quantrill's murderous "irregulars" came to the fore, and from the gunsmoke emerged bandit hero Jesse James, a Quantrill veteran. His legend was soon rivaled by those of the younger Sam Bass and Billy the Kid. All have a common resemblance to Robin Hood; all were betrayed by friends. From their legends:

HECKLER EXTRAORDINAIRE

On June 3, 1871, the James gang rode into Corydon, Iowa, and discovered they had arrived at a most propitious moment. Several blocks from the Ocobock Brothers Bank, their objective, a political rally was in full swing. As they walked into the bank, they could hear the Honorable Henry Clay Dean spellbinding the crowd. Inside, they found only the cashier. He opened the safe, as ordered. When they walked out they had $45,000, one of their richest hauls. Jesse felt so good about it that as they passed the meeting on their way out of town, he stopped and interrupted the speaker. Taking Jesse James for an ordinary heckler, the politician demanded, "Let's hear what you have to say that's so important it can't wait till I finish my speech." "I'm sorry to interrupt," Jesse called back, "but there's something wrong down at the bank. In fact, it's just been robbed. Maybe you better look into it, sir." Laughing, Jesse and the boys put spurs to their horses and dashed away in a cloud of dust.

"YOUR FRIEND, JESSE JAMES"

Jesse got a special pleasure out of taunting renowned manhunters. One of the most famous was D. T. Bligh of the Pinkerton agency, who after a sensational success in apprehending a railroad robber turned hopefully to pursuit of the James boys. He immediately encountered the same trouble that all the Pinkertons were having; he didn't know what the brothers looked like. He believed, however,

"Holdup Man," by O. C. Seltzer. The West of the post-Civil War period had more than its share of badmen like this one.

that they could be brought down through the routine of their daily habits. He interviewed people who claimed to know their ways, and studied newspapers to establish their habits. Alas, the boys had no settled habits, so much were they on the move. In addition, Jesse and Frank took pains to get to know their pursuers by sight. One day Jesse was in Louisville when he happened to see Bligh, no doubt hard on his trail. Jesse spoke to him, a conversation sprang up, and Jesse invited Bligh to have a drink. They went into the railroad depot and up to the bar. Jesse explained to him that he was

agent for a tombstone company. The conversation rippled along pleasantly. There had been a recent robbery which the papers attributed to the Jameses. Bligh, hiding his identity, said, "I'd like to see Jesse James before I die." They parted amiably and went their ways.

A few days later Bligh received a postcard mailed in Baltimore (where Jesse had sent a gang member on business) which reminded him of the drink at the railroad depot, then continued: "You have seen Jesse James. Now you can go ahead and die." The card was signed, "Your friend, Jesse James."

MAGNETIC AMAZON

A leading light of the 1870's Wild West was Belle Starr, nee Myra Belle Shirley, who rode with the Jameses, married a Cherokee named Sam Starr, and was at last killed, supposedly, by a man wanted for murder who was afraid she might turn him in.

Belle's career began at 18, during the last year of the Civil War, when she was seduced by a Quantrill guerrilla named Cole Younger and had a girl baby by him after he moved on. Her parents, with whom she was still living, locked her in an upstairs room, but she was "rescued" one dark night by another Quantrill veteran, Jim Reed, with 20 well-armed companions. Once safely beyond the range of Belle's father's shotgun, they staged a wedding ceremony on horseback—both bride and groom were mounted, and so was the officiating party, a horsethief and outlaw named John Fischer. From that moment on, Belle was a free woman. Wherever she went, her gaudy dress and dashing appearance in the saddle attracted attention, but she had a holy terror of newspapermen who, she claimed, often misrepresented her.

Belle claimed right, of course. The following typical yarn was transmitted to posterity by a contemporary reporter with words to the effect that even if it wasn't strictly factual it was indicative of the "strong magnetism of this cultured Amazon":

Like many a robber turned folk hero, Jesse James had a streak of megalomania in his makeup. Appropriately, his bank and train robberies are evoked on the heroic scale in Thomas Hart Benton's "History of Missouri" in the state capitol in Jefferson City.

Being short of money, she decided to perform the lady act. Decking herself out in raiment suitable to a civilized community, she proceeded to one of the stirring Texas cities and had no difficulty in ingratiating herself with the best society. She adopted her silver-toned voice, put on graceful airs, attended church and Sunday school, and was soon a recognized leader of fashion. Among her many admirers was a middle-aged bachelor who was cashier of one of the leading banks. She kept up her saintly demeanor for several weeks, until the banker was in love with the brilliant enchantress and was on the point of proposing. One day when the cashier was alone, the others being at dinner, Belle entered the bank. After a pleasant chat the cashier invited her behind the railing.

Once there, she murmured away in sweetest tones, while she pulled an ugly-looking 45-caliber pistol from the folds of her skirt; pressing the glittering steel beneath his chin, she said in a low voice, "Don't make a sound." At the same time, she lifted a flap of her basque, displaying a sack. "Put the money right in there." The thoroughly surprised and frightened banker got $30,000 in paper money

and placed it in the sack, the mouth of which she held open. Then she continued: "Now, dear, don't make any outcry. Your life depends on it. Goodby, sweetheart—come see me when you're up in the territory." Back out of the building, Belle proceeded to her horse, vaulted into the saddle without first placing her foot in the stirrup, and instantly she was away like the wind.

The man who baptized Jesse James should have drowned him instead, says this cartoon accompanying his obituary.

BEST-LOVED BANDIT

A "cowboy gone bad," Sam Bass was one of the Old West's best-loved outlaws, and in the months after his first robbery, his reputation for generosity began to grow into legend. Among folk of mainly southern origin who viewed the banks and the railroads as a new species of Yankee bloodsucker, Sam seemed a Robin Hood. While robbing trains, he tipped the porters and brakemen, so people said. Sometimes Sam was sorely pressed for grain for his horses and food for his men. One morning a farmer named Hoffman missed some shelled corn out of his crib. It had been carried off in a sack with a little hole in it. Hoffman trailed the grains until he saw he was approaching a camp known to be occupied by the Bass gang, so he turned back. However, a few days later Bass saw him and, handing him a $20 goldpiece, explained, "I had to have some corn in a hurry the other night."

FATE AT ROUND ROCK

Sam Bass bit the dust at last when he walked into a stakeout after having robbed a bank at Round Rock, Texas—his companion Jim Murphy had, for a promised pardon and reward, written a letter informing Major Jones of the Texas Rangers of Sam's activities. The last act was played out this way: Arriving near the scene of the intended heist a week ahead of time, Bass fixed on a plan. They were all to go to the bank on foot, leaving their horses hitched in a nearby alley. Barnes was to give the cashier a five-dollar bill to change, and while he was doing this, Bass was to level his pistol at the cashier and make him hold up his hands. Barnes would then jump over the counter, take the money, and put it in a sack. Jackson and Murphy were to stand in the door of the bank to keep anybody from coming in. After getting the money, they were to move out on the San Saba road. The time fixed upon for the robbery was Saturday afternoon, just as the bank was to be closed.

Meanwhile Major Jones had received Murphy's letter and sent for a squad of Rangers to meet him at Round Rock. Hours before the plan was to be put into action, Bass saw two Rangers dressed like cowboys. Murphy now suggested that he detach himself from the group and report back if he could learn anything of the Rangers. The others agreed to this, went ahead and robbed the bank according to plan, but then ran into the lawmen in the street outside. The stakeout was very poorly organized, and the local sheriff and his deputy were shot down by the bandits before either had had time to draw. [The sheriff died, and if in fact Bass hit him, that was probably the only time Bass ever killed a man.]

Now all hell broke loose. Men ran in every direction, some to get out of range and others to join in the fight. The robbers retreated up the square and down the alley, turning and firing as they went. Halfway down the alley, Bass received the wound which was to cause his death. He hoisted himself into the saddle, making two attempts before he succeeded in mounting. At the same time, one of the Rangers took deliberate aim and shot Barnes in the head. The two

FOLKWAYS

Hands Up!

Peace officer Bat Masterson gave younger colleagues instruction in the art of gunfighting and was so highly respected both as a practitioner and as a teacher that his graduate gunslingers could command wages of up to $25 a day plus expenses—good money in the 1880's. Bat once

"Shoot first and never miss," Bat Masterson advised.

summed up his principles: Always shoot first and never miss. Never try to run a bluff—a six-shooter is made to kill. A lot of inexperienced fellows try to aim along the barrel and shoot the other man in the head. Never do that. Try to hit your man just where his belt buckle would be—that's the broadest target from head to heel. If you point at something, you don't raise your finger to a level of the eye and sight along it—you simply point by instinct and your finger will always point straight. So you must learn to point the barrel of your six-gun by instinct. If you haven't that direction instinct born in you, you will never become an expert with the six-gun.

others dashed away, but it was seen that Bass maintained his seat with great difficulty. Accompanied by several citizens, Major Jones went in pursuit. They did not go more than a few miles before the old plug that the major had gotten from the livery stable played out and the party re-turned. Early next morning a fresh party guided by Deputy Sheriff Tucker proceeded to the point where the pursuit had been interrupted. A man was noticed lying under a tree, not far from the new railroad, but as there were some mules grazing nearby, Tucker said it must be one of

In a legendary scene badmen hold up a fleeing stage. The bandit Henry Starr once said of the highwayman's life: "I love it. It is wild adventure. I feel as I imagine the old buccaneers felt when they roved the seas with the black flag at the masthead."

Billy the Kid was arrested at Stinking Springs, New Mexico, after a three-day siege after the Lincoln County war by ex-friend Sheriff Pat Garrett. Here he is brought into town. The Kid got away but was tracked down and slain by Garrett the next year.

the hands, and no further attention was paid to him. After following the trail until it divided, the Rangers again emerged on the prairie. Meeting one of the railroad hands, they asked if he had seen a wounded man in the vicinity. He replied that there was a man lying under "that tree out there," pointing to the man seen before, "who was hurt, and who said that he was a cattleman from one of the lower counties and had been in Round Rock the day before and, getting into a little difficulty, had been shot." They at once approached the tree; the wounded man held up his hand and said: "Don't shoot. I am unarmed and helpless. I am the man you are looking for. I am Sam Bass."

Major Jones was notified and, in company with a physician of Round Rock, went out with an ambulance to bring the mortally wounded prisoner in. During the hours that remained before Bass died, the major tried every inducement to secure important statements from him, but noth-ing valuable in the way of evidence escaped from his lips. "It is not my profession to blow on my pals," the bandit said. "If a man knows anything, he ought to die with it in him." A few minutes later he said, "The world is bobbing around me." After a few gasps, he was dead. This was at 4 p.m., Sunday, July 21, 1878.

POOR SAM

Sam's legend lived on, and in time "Bass relics" proliferated throughout the West—his cartridge belt (which is authentic and remains at Austin Library at the University of Texas to this day), his compass, a bowie knife, and guns enough to stock an arsenal. Campfire narratives depicted a Bass who "had the world by the tail, with a downward pull," and yet was a living embodiment of bravery and generosity. A song grew up about his life which, enormously popular and existing in many different versions, was said to have a quieting effect on a herd of longhorns during a thun-derstorm. The ballad concludes with a mysterious reference to the man who ratted on Sam: "But the man that plays the traitor/Will feel it by and by;/His death was so uncommon—/'Twas poison in the eye." The traditional explanation is that this cracker Judas died from inadvertently (or, some say, deliberately) swallowing a bottle of eyedrops containing the poison atropine.

BILLY THE KID

William H. Bonney, the West's most famous desperado, was born in New York City in 1859 and brought up in New Mexico. It is said he was 12 when he killed his first man—one who had insulted his mother. Billy stabbed him with a penknife. By his late teens he had several more notches and set out to the Pecos Valley where he went to work as a hired gun for a big rancher. The Lincoln County cattle war was brewing up; within months Billy's employer was slain by the opposite faction and

Billy made himself war chief on his late employer's side. After a series of bloody battles in which peace officers were killed, newly appointed territorial governor Gen. Lew Wallace (future author of *Ben Hur*) arrived on the scene with amnesty for all, save those under criminal indictment. Meeting with the Kid, Wallace offered him automatic pardon following any court conviction, in exchange for surrender; but Billy refused, fearing he would be lynched. Two years later Billy was tracked down and killed by an ex-friend, Sheriff Pat Garrett. He was 21 and had killed 21 men.

A GOOD JOKE

A typical Bonney victim was a Texan named Joe Grant who was saved from oblivion by a bullet from Billy's six-shooter in January 1880. It all started when the Kid and some companions walked into a saloon where the Texan had just reached the belligerent stage of intoxication. "Say, Kid," he blustered, "I'll bet you I kill a man today before you do." The Kid smiled off the challenge. Grant loudly urged him to accept. "If you think I don't mean it, I'll bet you $25 and put up the cash." He shoved a roll of bills across the bar into the saloonkeeper's hands. To humor him, the Kid covered the money.

That evening Billy came back to the saloon, having in the meantime forgotten about Grant and his wager. The publican held a whispered confidence with him at the end of the bar. "Better be on your guard, Billy," he said. "Grant's full of whisky and ugly. He took a couple of shots out the back door at nothing this afternoon and muttered something about getting you."

The Kid walked up to Grant, friendlywise. "That's a pretty gun you've got, Grant," he said. "Let me see it." He coolly lifted Grant's six-shooter from its holster and examined it with a show of admiration. He noted empty cartridges in two chambers. Before handing the gun back he revolved the cylinder so that in the first two attempts to fire it the hammer would fall on the empty shells. The crowd had a drink or two. Edging around a corner of the bar and facing the Kid, Grant jerked out his revolver. "I'll win my bet with you right now," he roared and, leveling the weapon full at the Kid's face, pulled the trigger, the hammer clicking harmlessly. Before the look of surprise faded from his drunken face, the Kid killed him with a bullet

Billy the Kid (who if not all thumbs here certainly has two right hands) strikes again.

through his throat that cut his windpipe and shattered his backbone. The Kid laughed quietly as he dropped his six-shooter back into the holster. "That's a good joke on Grant," he said to the saloonkeeper. "You might as well pass over that $50."

HELL. HELL. HELL.

When the Kid was tried in Las Vegas for the killing of a sheriff and found guilty, the judge of the court, so one story went, pronounced the death sentence with a gathering emphasis that was highly elocutionary:

"I do hereby sentence you to be hanged by the neck," he intoned, "until you are dead! dead!! dead!!!"

Yes," Billy calmly retorted, "yes, and you can go to Hell. Hell. Hell."

Billy escaped from that jam. He had big wrists and small hands and slipped out of his handcuffs, making a dramatic escape over the dead bodies of two guards. Soon afterward, of course, Billy did bite the dust, but as late as the 1940's there were people in New Mexico who believed Billy was still alive.

"Fleecing the Priest" is by Charles M. Russell. The artist added in the lower-right-hand corner of the picture: "If coin is the root of all evil, your Reverence is going to weed— it's the work of a saint, not a sinner, to shake your clothes out for the seed."

GOOD GUYS & CO.
The Men With the Six-Pointed Star

The job of maintaining public order in the turbulent West of the 1880's was no easy one. Out of 200 men recruited by Judge Isaac "Hanging" Parker to police the Indian Territory of Oklahoma, which was then notorious as a white badman's refuge, some 65 were killed in the line of duty. As late as 1900 Bat Masterson declined a presidential appointment as U.S. marshal of the Indian Territory. "If I took it," he explained, "inside of a year I'd have to kill some fool boy who wanted to get a reputation by killing me." Lawmen had to have a potent combination of guts, savvy, publicity, and friends. Some stories of good guys:

The men who "marshaled" for a living probably combined it with other jobs because they had to—a deputy marshal was not on salary but got $2 per arrest, six cents a mile for expenses when following a wanted man, and was therefore forced to pad expense accounts to recover funds advanced from his own pocket and to make a living.

THE BEST DRESSED

The Old West's supreme virtuoso of the six-gun on the law-and-order side was Bat Masterson, whose appearance matched his dazzling talents—a red silk neckerchief and matching sash, its fringed ends hanging to his knees; gold-mounted spurs; silver-plated, ivory-handled revolvers; silver-studded belt and holster; and a gray sombrero banded by a rattlesnake skin with glass eyes. An easterner who had heard of Bat's contributions to Boot Hill and had pictured him as an unshaved ruffian stopped off at Dodge City once and asked where he could see the famous Bat. "When you meet the best-dressed and best-looking man in town," he was told, "that will be Bat."

HOW BAT GOT HIS NAME

When Bill (he had not yet acquired his nickname of "Bat") Masterson first came to Dodge it was to stay with his brother Jim, a saloon proprietor, while recovering from a leg wound suffered in a gunfight over a girl in Sweetwater. The girl had been dancing with Bill when a jealous ex-boyfriend shot her dead, only to die an instant later, struck by a bullet from Bill's gun, but not before wounding the latter in the leg. Weeks later, when Bill was up and around with a cane, his brother urged him to find work and suggested he see Wyatt Earp for a job as deputy marshal. Bill shook his head, "Not with a game leg." But Jim told Earp his brother Bill was in town, and the marshal came to see him and persuaded Bill to take the job.

Later that same day, two cowboys saw Masterson limping down Front Street, his new badge pinned onto his shirt. "Dodge must be hard up for policemen," one remarked loudly. "They're hiring them with one leg." "You know why that is," the other rejoined. "If they had two legs they could run away and hide." "Are you two gentlemen finished?" Bill asked quietly. "Because if you are, I'm running you in for disturbing the peace." The two cowboys had just started to roar with laughter when Bill flattened them both with his cudgellike cane. A third puncher rushed out of the adjacent saloon to avenge his fallen pals by shooting the new deputy between the eyes. His six-gun had not cleared leather when Masterson's cane creased the side of his head. "Holy jumpin' hell!" an old bushwhacker said. "Did you see the way he was battin' them around?" "Yeah," his drinking partner agreed. "He's better with that bat than most men are with a gun." Thus did Bill Masterson become "Bat," and he was never known as anything else for the rest of his life. By the time his leg had healed and he had thrown away his cane, roughly three dozen craniums were dented by Bat, and there are those who claim Dodge City heaved a sigh of relief the day the new deputy marshal first appeared in the streets with only his Colts at his hips.

BATTLE AT O K CORRAL

Bat was not present at the most famous gunfight of the Old West, in which his boss Wyatt Earp was up against bad guys at O K Corral in Tombstone, on October 26, 1881. Many people at the time felt that Earp and his faction were actually on the wrong side of the law in the O K Corral affair, and the whole business has been debated by historians and other custodians of tradition ever since. Bat Masterson later wrote a drastically simplified version of the classic fight, giving the Earps' side of the story. It is adapted below:

"Morgan Earp had a job riding shotgun on the Wells Fargo stage that ran between Benson and Tombstone. The company believed that so long as it kept one of the Earp boys on the coach its property was safe—and it was. A certain band of stage robbers lived in the San Simon Valley about 50 miles from Tombstone; these were the Clanton brothers, Ike and Billy, and the McLowry brothers, Tom and Frank—a quartet of desperate men against whom the civil authorities were powerless to act; indeed, U.S. troops who had been sent out to capture them dead or alive had more than once returned to their posts

Words on the Range

The cowboy era—1870–90—produced a wealth of picturesque terms that are with us to this day. For example: *Boot Hill*—burying grounds for men who died with their boots on; *bronco*—a half-wild horse or mustang descended from those introduced by early explorers. The word means "unruly" in Spanish; *buckaroo*—a cowboy (Spanish *vaquero,* cowboy); *cayuse*—an Indian pony, especially one of those bred by the Cayuse Indians of the Northwest. Colloquially, the word meant any horse; *chaps*—leather overalls to protect a rider's legs from getting scratched by chaparral; *chuck*—food, meal, mealtime, hence the legendary *chuckwagons,* with their proverbially grouchy cooks, hearty victuals, and extra-strong coffee; *cowpoke, cowpuncher*—cowboy (the job involved poking cattle with prods); *maverick*—an unbranded cow claimed by its finder (from Samuel A. *Maverick,* Texas rancher of the 1850's who had a small herd of unbranded cattle); *necktie party*—a hanging organized by citizens taking the law into their own hands. On March 24, 1882, exasperated residents of Las Vegas, Nevada, served notice on local badmen in these terms: IF FOUND WITHIN THE LIMITS OF THIS CITY AFTER 10 O'CLOCK P.M., THIS NIGHT, YOU WILL BE INVITED TO ATTEND A GRAND NECK-TIE PARTY; *rodeo*—annual cattle roundup; *rustler*—a cattle thief. The term originally meant "hustler," in the sense of go-getter, and was used by cowboys as a slang term for the ranch's cook, because his job required much hustle and bustle; *shack*—a crude log cabin or shanty (from Aztec *xacalli,* hut).

after having met with both failure and disaster.

"These men decided to hold up and rob the Tombstone coach; but in order to do so with as little friction as possible, they sent word to Morgan Earp to leave the employ of the Wells Fargo Express Company. Morgan sent back word that he would not quit. At the same time Wyatt Earp sent them word that if they killed Morgan he would hunt them down and kill every last one in the bunch. So they sent Virgil Earp, who was city marshal of Tombstone at the time, word that on a certain day they would be in town prepared to give him and his brothers a battle to the death. Sure enough on the day named, Ike and Billy Clanton and Tom and Frank McLowry rode into Tombstone and put their horses up at O K Corral. Virgil Earp was not long in rustling up Wyatt and Morgan and their friend Doc Holliday, the latter as desperate a man in a tight place as the West ever knew. Meanwhile the invaders were growing impatient of waiting and decided that the Earps did not intend to attack them, at any rate while they were in O K Corral. They resolved that if the Earps would not come to the corral they would go

hunt up the Earps. Each took his horse by the bridle line and led him through the corral gate.

"Just as they reached the street and before the outlaws had time to mount their horses, the Earp party came round the corner. Virgil Earp ordered them to throw up their hands and surrender. They replied with a volley from their pistols. The fight was hardly started before it was over. Nearly every shot fired by the Earp forces went straight home to the mark. Ike Clanton ran to Wyatt Earp and begged him not to kill him, and Wyatt, instead of killing Clanton as most any other man would have done under the circumstances, told him to run away, and he did."

Tom McLowry lay where he had dropped, half blown apart by a shotgun blast from Doc Holliday. His brother, Frank, also dead, had been knocked down by a .45 slug from one of the Earp guns, which hit him square in the belly. The 19-year-old Billy Clanton, laid out on the ground in front of Fly's Photographic Gallery, kept squeezing the trigger of his six-shooter, and when it was taken away from him was heard to murmur, "Give me some more cartridges." He had been struck in the belly and in the lungs.

On the good guys' side, Virgil was badly wounded in the leg, Morgan suffered a chipped vertebra, and a near-miss had cut through Holliday's pistol holster and torn a strip of skin from his back. Next day he and Wyatt were arrested on warrants made out by Sheriff Behan and Ike Clanton. Friends put up $20,000 bond, but there was no trial. After a hearing—at which neither Virgil, who had been dismissed as city marshal, nor Morgan appeared, for both were thought too seriously hurt to attend—the charges against the Earp faction were dropped. Within five months Virgil was crippled for life by a shotgun blast and Morgan shot dead, in both cases by friends of the Clantons. Soon after, at Tucson, one of the avengers tried to kill Wyatt in front of the Union Pacific depot, but Earp shot him down. However, from then on the Earps were finished in Arizona. They moved to the definitely healthier climate of southern California where Wyatt lived on another 50 years, dying in Los Angeles.

GATES OF HELL

Backing up the two-fisted lawmen of the West were a mean breed of frontier jurists, best known of whom were the picturesque Roy Bean, justice of the peace at Langtry, Texas, and Isaac "Hanging" Parker, U.S. district judge at Fort Smith, Arkansas, a presidential appointee with extraordinary powers whose court of no appeal became known throughout Indian Territory (as a part of Oklahoma was then called) as the Gates of Hell. Pink, plump, and white-bearded, Judge Parker looked like Santa Claus in a stovepipe hat, but his name was synonymous with the gallows in the popular imagination of the day—although in fact only about 80 of those he sentenced to death actually hanged. Still, the Gates of Hell was a fearful place, and Parker kept it open six days a week, 52 weeks a year, for more than 20 years, except on hanging days.

On those days the courtroom was locked, but Parker would be inside, reading his Bible. As the fatal moment drew near, he would cross the room to a window from which he could see the gallows in the corner of the yard. It was a privileged vantage point; he stood there, tears streaming down his cheeks, until it was all over and then returned to his desk—to pray. It is said that people, especially children, avoided him in the streets.

PRINCE OF HANGMEN

Parker's hangman was a German from Detroit named George Maledon who did his job with such efficient zeal he was called the prince of hangmen. A scaffold big enough for 12 at a time was built under his supervision. The gruesome structure loomed large in the minds of Fort Smith inhabitants. One night both inmates and guards were affrighted by shadowy figures flitting ghostlike around the gallows. These turned out to be a group of drunken Indians. Maledon scoffed, "I do such a good job that my people never come back, even in spirit form." Of all his achievements, Maledon pointed to an execution of six as his masterpiece: "Not one of them even twitched."

"Sheriff's Posse" was painted by Ernest Chiriacka. In legal Latin the word *posse* means a force of armed citizens raised by a sheriff in an emergency. Technically, under the common law, a posse could include every man over 15 years old who was not infirm.

Both Sides of the Law

The Old West was on the whole as peaceful and law-abiding as it is today, if not more so. People did without locks on their doors, credit and hospitality were regularly extended to strangers, and honesty was the rule, not the exception. There was, however, a criminal element many of whose members were such desperate characters there was no dealing with them save by lynch law or its legally constituted equivalent, trigger-happy lawmen backed up by hanging judges. Unfortunately, these law enforcers were often little better than the crooks they had been hired to stop. Bob Dalton is an example. After starting out in life as one of "Hanging" Parker's deputies, Bob went on to boast he'd beat Jesse James' record by robbing two banks at once—and died trying. Then there was Wild Bill Hickok, marshal of Abilene. Bill has been recently "exposed" as a psychopathic killer because he boasted of killing "over 100 white men." However, his bark was worse than his bite. There will never be an exact body count, let alone a determination of which killings were justified and which not. We'll never even know for sure what cards he was really holding when Jack McCall shot him in the back as he sat playing poker in a Deadwood, South Dakota, saloon on August 2, 1876. Was the original *dead man's hand* aces and eights or jacks and eights? The idiom has at various times denoted either combination. So. . . *¿quién sabe?*

"HISTORIC ASS"

Parker was in the habit of gloating long and loud over the prisoners he was about to send to their deaths. Only once did a man at the bar find the spunk to face up to him when he began one of his tirades. The prisoner was Henry Starr, the bandit. He had been found guilty of murder; he now interrupted, just as Parker was warming to his theme: "Don't try to stare me down, old Nero— I've looked many a better man than you in the eye. Cut out the rot and save your wind for your next victim. If I am a monster, you are a fiend. I have put only one man to death, while almost as many have been slaughtered by your jawbone as Samson slew with the jawbone of that other historic ass." Parker was dumbfounded. In clipped words he sentenced Starr to be hanged by the neck until he was dead. The date was February 20, 1895. But Starr successfully appealed the sentence, and many years were to go by before Henry Starr reached the end of his life of crime. The judge was aging and sick. In less than a year both he and his court would be gone.

LAW WEST OF THE PECOS

When Texan Roy Bean set up as judge in places where he sold whisky to the railroad construction crews, he had no authority save that of common consent, backed up by the Rangers' guns. There was a saying to the effect that there was "no law west of the Pecos." Roy set out to change all that, and the sign over the entrance to his saloon in Langtry proclaimed him to be LAW WEST OF THE PECOS. There he held forth from the early 1880's until shortly before his death in 1903.

ROY AND THE CHINESE

According to family tradition, the Beans' real name was originally Boone, and they were descended from the Daniel Boone tribe in Kentucky. There is no telling how much truth there may have been in that— probably no more than there was in another Roy Bean tale also involving ancestry, which, much embroidered, grew into one of the best-known anecdotes ever to come out of the Southwest. Its original one-sentence version appeared in the El Paso *Daily Times* for June 2, 1883: "Somebody killed a Chinaman and was brought up standing before the irrepressible Roy, who looked through two or three dilapidated law books from stem to stern and finally turned the culprit loose, remarking that he'd be damned if he could find any law against killing a Chinaman."

Here is a variant of that tall story, minus the racist twist, that was current in Idaho at around the same time:

A cowboy who had killed a real-estate salesman in a gun duel reported the incident to the sheriff and offered to surrender, asking what he would get.

"Shucks!" snorted the lawman. "Didn't you know? You won't get nothin'. We took the bounty off them fellers a long time ago!"

CORPSE PAYS $40 FINE

One of several cases in which Roy acted both as judge and as coroner was that of a man accidentally killed by a railroad train. On the body were found $40 and a revolver. The judgment of Coroner Bean was that no fault attached to the railroad company for the unfortunate occurrence. The judgment of Justice of the Peace Bean followed, and was this: "Yet the court must take into consideration another feature of this case. That is to say, a concealed weapon was found on this person. He was therefore violating the law at the time of his death, and the court is driven to the disagreeable necessity of imposing on the deceased a fine of $40. The weapon will be confiscate to the court."

THE RED MENACE
Nineteenth-Century Bogeymen

To the white man the Indian was a creature of both romance and terror, part superhuman, part inhuman, seldom just a man. The white man's stories about his encounters with this "strange" being are consequently colored by this harsh perception. Indians were "savages," "barbarians," and agents of the Devil, despite the fact that the name-callers, the settlers and cowboys, were wrenching Native Americans' land and lives from them as it suited their manifest destiny.

ROUTED BY RED MEN
An intrepid young salesman came to do business in Dodge City. When he began to boast of his heroic exploits against Indians, the young wags in town decided to put him to the test. They made up a hunting party and invited the drummer along. Meanwhile, some other local jokers disguised themselves in face paint and set out to meet the hunters.

The populace, well alerted to the fun, stationed themselves on the roofs of houses and atop telegraph poles. When the hunters had traveled about four miles, they were suddenly startled by a fiendish Indian war whoop and saw the bloodthirsty devils riding furiously toward them.

The salesman, although armed with a murderous revolver, carefully loaded with blank cartridges by one of his hosts, decided very promptly that discretion was the better part of valor and set off at full gallop for Dodge City. Just when he thought himself about to enter the safety of the town, he noticed that the rooftops were crowded with people and he thought the city, too, might be besieged. Only after some of his companions caught up with him and gave him reassurance was he able to stop running; together "hunters" and "Indians" entered town to a round of applause.

As usual, the drinks were on the tenderfoot, and the drummer took considerable banter—especially about the loss of his cap. He stoutly maintained that it blew off. But one of them said, "No. Your hair stood on end and pushed it off!"

THE PEACEMAKER
In the summer of 1844 a fierce conflict between the Texas Rangers and the Indians broke out in Bandera County. It ended with only slight loss to the white men and with the Indians running for their lives. When it was all over, the Rangers made camp near the base of Polly's Peak.

As they sat around the fire, a cloud, veiling the face of the moon, invited them to watch its passing, and as they gazed upon its flitting shadows, there suddenly stood in their midst a tall, beautiful Indian woman. Her hair hung in long braids; her brow was crowned with a circlet of sparkling crystal beads; countless strings of colored beads and shells adorned her body; a skirt of filmy blue fabric reached nearly to her ankles. The Rangers gazed in amazement and several minutes elapsed before their captain asked, "Where do you come from, and why are you here alone?"

Quietly folding her arms, she replied: "My people are tired of fighting. So many of our braves have fallen, victims to your death-dealing weapons, that we are helpless. I come to ask that the path between my people and yours be again made white! I come alone, because I know not fear. The Great Spirit is my father!"

She laid three polished arrows at her feet and stood for a moment looking up at the sky, while the moonlight glittered on her shining ornaments, and the blooming white yucca that surrounded her gleamed like silver. She turned toward the west and, pointing to a star, wonderfully brilliant in spite of the moonlight, exclaimed: "That star is my home! I go there!"

A dark cloud had been rapidly gathering about the summit of Polly's Peak, but the Rangers, bewildered by the strangeness of the situation, seemed transfixed as by some magic spell and saw naught but the graceful figure and pointing finger of the woman. Then a blinding flash of lightning and crash of thunder broke the spell of their enchantment.

They seized their guns and made ready to face an enemy, but when the commotion ended they realized that the woman had vanished. One of the Rangers swore he had seen her caught up into the black cloud as it opened to emit the thundering electric bolt—plain proof that the Indian

In a stock folktale and fiction situation Indians take a young white girl captive; in some stories she's bartered for one of their own seized in battle, in others kept as wife or slave.

"Ambush," by Theodor Kaufmann, was painted in 1867, the fateful year, from the Native Americans' point of view, that the railroads joined the long trail from the south. Indians promptly struck back to drive the "iron horse" from their hunting grounds.

woman was an emissary of the Devil.

A careful and persistent search failed to discover a trace of the woman or of the arrows she had laid on the ground, but thenceforth the Indians came and went peacefully, committing no depredations and unmolested by the white men.

THE CAPTIVE

When Cynthia Ann Parker was nine she was captured by Comanches. Twenty-four years later a band of frontiersmen charged on a camp of Comanches and killed among others a noteworthy chief named Peta Nacona. One of the unwounded captives was a woman with a baby. When the man who had run his horse down to overtake her saw her, he exclaimed: "Why, this is a white woman. Indians do not have blue eyes."

Through a Mexican interpreter it was learned that she was the wife of the slain chief. She was weeping because, she said, she had two sons and was afraid they had been killed. When told that they had escaped, she

brightened for a while, but she had no happiness at being restored to white people.

After many attempts had been made to identify the woman, an uncle of the Cynthia Ann who had been captured so many years before came. When he had spoken the words "Cynthia Ann" several times, a light suddenly came into the strange woman's face and, pointing to her breast, she said, "Me Cynthy Ann."

She was Cynthia Ann. Kinspeople treated her kindly, but she never ceased to yearn for the wild life to which she had grown accustomed. After a few years she died. It seems a tragedy that she did not live to know that one of her sons became the great Comanche chief Quanah Parker.

In a scene that has become legendary, a cavalryman pushes his mount with all his heart in a desperate attempt to flee from the clutches of the Indian enemies in hot pursuit.

THE SIOUX
Traditional Stories, Time of Despair

Among the last of the Plains Indians to lose independence were the Sioux. The massacre at Wounded Knee was preceded by some 15 years during which they starved and coexisted with arriving homesteaders, prospectors, cowboys, and missionaries, while many a young brave committed suicide rather than turn to farming. In this time of despair, traditional stories were still being told. Typical was that of the warring between Thunderbirds and water monsters. (The latter, creators of the buffalo, are always defeated by the Thunderbirds, but they always come back.) The following tales were collected by contemporary white visitors.

THUNDERBIRDS

The water monsters' ancient foes were the Thunderbirds, who lived and flew through the heavens, blocked from view by thick clouds. There were four varieties of Thunderbird, although in essence they were but one. One type was black, another was yellow, a third was scarlet with enormous wings, and the fourth was a blue sphere having neither eyes nor ears. From where its eyes would have been there shot two diverging zigzags of lightning. The home of these thunder beings was on a circular island at the western end of the earth. On this island was a mountain at whose summit was a mound in which the thunder beings lived. This dwelling opened toward each of the four world-quarters, and at each doorway was a sentinel—a butterfly at the east entrance, a bear at the west, a deer at the north, and a beaver at the south. Each sentinel wore a cloak of scarlet down.

The Thunderers were cruel and destructive, forever on the warpath. From them the Sioux received their spears, tomahawks, and their warpaints—which if properly applied protected them from the weapons of their enemies; to dream of the Thunderbirds meant one must go to war. Mortal hatred existed between Thunderers and water monsters.

BUFFALO MONSTERS

Like other peoples of North America, the Sioux had mythical water monsters. These, they believed, were the creators or ancestors of buffalo. It was said that once in the distant past, people had seen a red object shining like fire in the Missouri River. Some said it shone in the water like a huge eye as bright as the sun. It was swimming upstream and made the water roar as it passed. Those who saw it from nearby said that it was covered with red hair, had four legs, and one horn in the middle of its forehead; its backbone was notched like a crosscut saw or cogwheel—it was like a buf-

The sun dance, in which self-torture was thought to lend superhuman force to pledges of tribal solidarity and public declarations of grief, was the most powerful ceremony of the Plains peoples. Some of the myths connect the dance with the origin of buffalo.

falo seen in a dream. Any who looked at it became crazy, and their eyes were swollen shut and all died within the day. The water monster was a benefactor to the Indians, however, for it had made the first buffalo and taught them how to shoot the beasts.

TWO FACES

People were afraid of meeting the giant Two Faces. When he passed camps at night he kicked the ground and bells would ring, owls hooted, and there was a snorting like that of an enraged buffalo about to charge. Two Faces had such big ears that each of them could hold three men. He was finally killed by a man and his wife, whose only child he had stolen. This child was a willful boy. One night his mother told him to do something and he disobeyed. So she said, "I will put you outdoors and Two Faces will toss you into his ear." She didn't believe this but merely said it to frighten her son into obedience. He paid no attention, however, so she grabbed him by the arm and, although he began to cry, pushed him outdoors and fastened up the entrance. The poor boy ran crying round the lodge, but soon there was silence.

The mother in turn grew anxious and began to cry when she could not find him outside. She and her husband wept many days for their son. One night she heard a voice say: "Heh, heh! You said to me, 'Ghost, take that one!' Heh, heh!" She said: "Husband, I think a ghost took my son." The husband said: "Yes, you gave the boy to the ghost and, of course, the ghost took him. Why should you complain? It serves you right." Then the mother said: "Husband, tomorrow night I will lie hidden behind the woodpile. If the ghost comes, I'll have a knife, and when I catch hold of its leg, I'll call you; I know the monster threw my son into his ear." So the next night she lay in wait. By and by something was heard coming, making all kinds of animals and birds cry out as it came saying, "Heh, heh!" As the mother watched,

"Hungry Moon," by Frederic Remington, depicts Sioux women butchering a buffalo in the snow by moonlight. By the customary division of labor, men were responsible for war, hunting, and most ceremonies, while the women did most of the other chores.

a very large being came and stood next to the lodge. He was so tall his head came above the smokehole, down which he peeped into the lodge. She seized one of his legs with both hands and called her husband. They tied the monster down with thongs and stabbed him and guarded him till morning.

When it was light they beheld a hideous monster covered with thick hair except on his two faces. They split his ears open with a knife; in-side one, they found their long-lost son, who was very thin and unable to speak. He had a thick coat of long hair on him from his legs up to his head, but his head and face were smooth—he would have become a Two Faces himself had he not been rescued. After his parents had taken him from the monster's ear, they put many sticks of wood on a fire, and on this they laid the monster's body. It soon went up in flames. However, the son did not survive for long.

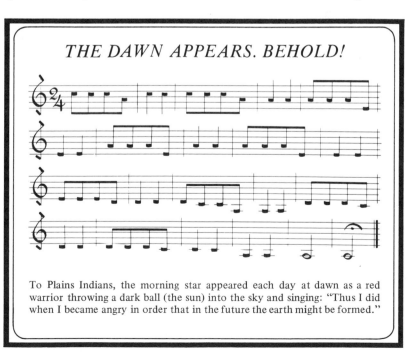

THE DAWN APPEARS. BEHOLD!

To Plains Indians, the morning star appeared each day at dawn as a red warrior throwing a dark ball (the sun) into the sky and singing: "Thus I did when I became angry in order that in the future the earth might be formed."

CAVALRY TO THE RESCUE
Taking the West by Force

The wars between the Indians and the white men were almost as old as white settlement itself, but they accelerated after the Civil War, as the struggle for the remaining open land became more intense. Unable to retreat farther and no longer trusting their adversaries' promises, the Indians stood their ground against the full force of the U.S. Cavalry, with bloody consequences. The last significant campaign ended in 1890 in the Sioux massacre at Wounded Knee, South Dakota.

AN INCREDIBLE RESCUE
The Indian fighter cheerfully accepts the fortunes of his lot and seldom counts the cost, but a sturdy heart was needed to face the Apaches on their own stamping ground. On the first of November, after days of hard riding, in the hope of administering a decisive blow to the Indians, Lieutenant King of the 5th Cavalry advanced some distance ahead of his command. Suddenly he came upon a band of the enemy. He turned into the underbrush, in order to flank his position, when an arrow whizzed past, almost striking him in the head. Then followed another, which cut the muscles at the corner of his eye; then a rifle ball pierced his arm.

Lieutenant King's men hastened with all speed to his aid as King stumbled and fell to the ground. An experienced Indian fighter, he knew what fate awaited him should he fall into the hands of the Apaches. There seemed to be only a matter of choice as to the manner of death. Like the soldier he was, King drew his revolver and, but for the timely arrival of Sgt. Bernard Taylor, would have taken his own life.

Taylor was a big, strapping, powerful fellow, and taking his superior officer in his arms forged ahead of the Indians, stopping every few paces to send a bullet among them. Lieutenant King was no light burden, and the Apaches, thoroughly roused, trained their arms upon the sergeant. Arrows and bullets flew thick and fast, singing ominously as they passed him. Taylor kept on, determined to save his lieutenant if he could and to die hard if he must. King feared the worst for both and told Taylor to leave him and save himself. Taylor believed that the circumstances justified his disobeying orders, and one can almost hear his emphatic "No!" as he pressed on.

In this manner he carried the wounded officer for nearly half a mile over rocks and ravines until safe within the picket line, and for his heroic conduct he was awarded the Medal of Honor.

THE FOUR-LEGGED CANNON
Out in a certain western fort, some time ago, the major conceived the idea that artillery might be used effectively in fighting with the Indians by dispensing with gun carriages and fastening the cannon upon the backs of mules. So he explained his views to the commandant, and it was determined to try the experiment.

A howitzer was selected and strapped upon an ambulance mule, with the muzzle pointed toward the trail. When they had secured the gun and loaded it with ball cartridge, they led that calm and steadfast mule out on the bluff and set up a target in the middle of the river to practice at.

The rear of the mule was turned toward the target, and he was backed gently up to the edge of the bluff. The officers stood round in a semicircle, while the major went up and inserted a time fuse in the touchhole of the howitzer. When the fuse was ready, the major lit it and retired.

In a minute or two the hitherto unruffled mule heard the fizzing back there on his neck, and it made him uneasy. He reached his head around to ascertain what was going on, and the howitzer began to sweep around the horizon. The mule at last became excited and his curiosity grew more and more intense; in a second or two he was standing with his four legs in a bunch, making six revolutions a

Tomahawk versus saber, an Indian and a cavalry officer commence a deadly duel for control of the plains, in a 1902 painting by the artist Charles Schreyvogel.

Charged with bringing white man's law and order to Indian Territory, two cavalrymen arrest a Blackfoot for murder, as depicted by Frederic Remington in 1888.

minute, and the howitzer threatening sudden death to every man within half a mile. The commandant was observed to climb suddenly up a tree; the lieutenants were seen sliding over the bluff into the river, as if they didn't care at all about the price of uniforms; the adjutant made good time toward the fort; the sergeant began to throw up breastworks with his bayonet; and the major rolled over on the ground and groaned. In two or three minutes there was a puff of smoke, a dull thud, and the mule— Oh, where was he? A solitary mule might have been turning somersaults over the bluff and landing, finally, with his howitzer, at the bottom of the river, while the ball would be going off toward the fort,

hitting the chimney of the major's quarters, and rattling the adobe bricks down into the parlor, frightening the major's wife into convulsions. They do not allude to it now, and no report of the experiment was ever sent to the War Department.

DEADLY STUNT RIDERS

The Comanche Indians we met along the Washita River were capable of feats of horsemanship such as you would not imagine possible. They would come thundering out of some hiding place, standing tall in their stirrups, deliver their fire, and instantly drop, as if shot, swinging themselves rapidly under their horses' bellies whence they could easily aim and fire again.

There was one spot on the prairie where they really got the best of us. The grass there stood over five feet high, and the Indians rode toward it as fast as their ponies could go. Every time any of our cavalry fired at an Indian near this place the redskin would drop as if hit, and all you would see was his riderless pony running off into the distance. Full 20 of them dropped in this manner, leading us to believe that they were all hit. Nothing more was seen of them for about an hour, during which our attention was engaged in an opposite direction by another party of Indians, who repeatedly charged us, eventually forcing us from our position. In moving to higher ground we approached the bunch of tall grass where we had seen so many Indians drop. We got within 50 yards when a line of Indians sprang up, presenting as good a skirmish line as any body of soldiers could form, and poured a murderous fire into our party, killing or wounding most of our number.

FACT MYTH

Custer's Last Stand

George Armstrong Custer has gone down in popular history as a hero, the leader of a brave force massacred in the Battle of the Little Bighorn on June 25, 1876. His subordinate, Maj. Marcus Reno, has likewise been depicted as the coward who failed to go to his commander's aid and thus caused the death of more than 225 men. Agreement will never be possible, but evidence suggests Custer himself, through arrogance and incompetence, was responsible for his men's needless death. The 7th Cavalry was only part of a larger expedition, commanded by Brig. Gen. Alfred H. Terry, against the Sioux, Cheyennes, and Arapahos. Terry ordered Custer to "thoroughly examine" the area, where hostile tribes had concentrated for a summer hunt, but not to provoke a major action. Yet even when warned by scouts he was riding on the largest Indian village ever collected in the Northwest, Custer pressed on. Sending Reno and a force on a diversionary attack, he split the other men into four groups and took one to hit the village. But Reno's people were soon repulsed (and supposed themselves abandoned by Custer). Meanwhile, only five miles away, General Custer and his men were caught in a converging rush of 2,000 warriors and ridden under. The nation, celebrating its Centennial, took the loss as a terrible humiliation. Custer's name became the watchword of an anti-Indian campaign, while in the background Reno was ruined and the most nonsensical debate in American military history began.

RANGE WAR
Death on the Hoof

The period 1870–1900 witnessed a scramble for control of vast reaches of grazing land in the West. Clashes sharpened into open war among competing interests—cattlemen against sheepmen, "fencers" (those who fenced their land) against nonfencers, big outfits against small. All told, there had been dozens of these range wars by the turn of the century. The following ghost story was based on an incident in which a lone "nester" (homesteader) was lynched by trailherders for deliberately causing a stampede in which two of their comrades were killed.

Grazing is nearly always good on the 200-acre top of Stampede Mesa in Crosby, Texas, but trail drivers seldom venture to bed their herds down for the night there:

In the fall of 1889 a cowman named Sawyer was coming through with a trail herd of 1,500 head of steers. Six miles east of the mesa about 40-odd head of nester cows came bawling into the herd, followed by the nester, who demanded that his cattle be cut out of the herd. Sawyer was driving short-handed; he had come far; his steers were thin, and he did not want them "ginned" about anymore. Accordingly, he told the nester to go to hell. The nester said that if he did not drop his cows out of the herd before dark he would stampede the whole bunch. Sawyer laughed, drew out his six-shooter, and, squinting down it at the nester, told him to vamoose.

Midnight came and the herd settled down. Then, true to his threat, the nester sneaked up, waved a blanket a few times, and shot his gun. He did his work well. All of the herd except about 300 head stampeded over the bluff on the south side of the mesa, and two of the night herders, caught in front of the frantic cattle that they were trying to circle, went over with them. Sawyer said little, but at sunup he gave orders to bring in the nester alive, horse and all. The orders were carried out, and when the men rode up on the mesa with their prisoner, Sawyer was waiting. He tied the nester on his horse with a rawhide lariat, blindfolded the horse, and backed him off the cliff. Then Sawyer and his men buried their comrades and left the nester to rot with the piles of dead steers in the canyon.

To this day, old cowpunchers will tell you they have seen his murdered ghost, astride a blindfolded horse, sweeping over the headland, behind a stampeding herd of phantom steers—and, some say, every herd that has been held on the mesa since that night has stampeded.

One outfit spent a cliffhanger of a night on Stampede Mesa in the fall of 1900. An eyewitness reported:

"The herd settled down, all right, but I couldn't get that stampede tale out of my mind—every time a cow moved I thought something was going to happen. It got so quiet that I could hear my pardner's saddle creak, away off to one side. The moon set, and it got darker. Just about then something passed me. It looked like a man on a horse, but it just seemed to float along. Then there was a roar, and the whole bunch stampeded straight for the bluffs. I rode in front of one critter like, and he just passed right on, just kind of floating past me. Then some old cow bellowed and we milled 'em easy—but they wouldn't bed down again that night, and it took every derned one of us to hold 'em." There are some who say that the phantoms of this legend are tumbleweeds, blown by the wind. But there are honest men who will tell you different.

"Bet-A-Million" Gates, looking like an understudy to Nelson Eddy, introduces barbed wire to the rangeland. Such fencing became the source of many a feud.

Blood And Thunder

One of the western heroes in the folk memory is William F. Cody—Buffalo Bill—whose Wild West show was the granddaddy of all horse operas. It all started shortly after the Civil War, when the dime-novel author Ned Buntline went west from New York City in search of a frontier hero and found Buffalo Bill.

According to Bat Masterson the latter's specialty, never equaled by another, was to ride full tilt into a herd of buffalo with the reins between his teeth and a pistol in each hand, bringing down as many as eight animals on a single run. With shoulder-length locks—a standing invitation to owners of scalping knives to "come and get it" if they dared—he was a vain, hard-drinking, freewheeling, warmhearted, and womanizing ham, readymade for Buntline to transform, through a series of stageplays and pulp fictions, into the

Prince of the Prairies. In this role Bill eventually came upon Maj. John M. Burke, a prince of press agents.

"I have met a god," the major declared and lost no time putting this latter-day apotheosis on a sound business footing. The means to that end proved to be the Wild West show. Opening in 1883 in a cloud of dust and gunsmoke, this "dramatic-equestrian exposition of life on the plains" featured all the classic sequences—glimpses of the Pony Express, a stagecoach chased by badmen, Injuns on the warpath, settlers ambushed by same and rescued by Cody and the cavalry, a duel to the death between white scout and painted brave. Special acts further enlivened the proceedings: bronco busting, lassoing, tying and riding of wild steers by real live *vaqueros* recruited out west, together with spectacular displays of marksmanship

Belle equestrienne Annie Oakley appears to have learned to defy gravity.

and guest appearances by the redoubtable Indian chief Sitting Bull.

At length the ingredient necessary to the show's supreme success was found: Annie Oakley. Little Missie, as Cody called her, could out-Crockett Crockett. She could shoot dimes and small glass balls in midair, sighting by their reflection on the blade of a bowie knife. She could slice playing cards and perforate handfuls of flying tickets. She once flicked the ash off a cigarette held in the kaiser's lips, and she regularly was 100 percent accurate in firing at a rapid succession of clay pigeons sprung from several traps at once. As she skipped into the limelight in her soft yellow buckskins, Annie won her male audience's heart.

Ladies liked her, too, because unlike her boss, Little Missie was reportedly a teetotaler and a Bible reader. She was a devoted wife—Annie had first met Frank Butler, her husband, at age 15, in 1875, at the shooting match in which she defeated him for first place. Thereafter they were inseparable companions until their deaths in 1926, 20 days apart. Among them, Annie and Buffalo Bill and their "encampment" of cowboys, Mexicans, and Indians wrapped up that public image—both here and abroad—of the wild-and-woolly West which subsequent generations have glimpsed only in variations on the original theme.

Rome loved Buffalo Bill's show: "The audience, always strong for the winners, forgot their disappointment in the absence of fatalities and howled with delight."

The Melting Pot

There was but one hope, America!" said one immigrant. His terse statement summed up the motivation of millions like him who poured into the United States between 1870 and 1920. In numbers approaching thousands daily, they appeared—Irishmen, Germans, Scandinavians, Italians, Greeks, East Europeans, and Chinese—fleeing famine, oppression, poverty . . . and, seeking opportunity, jostling predecessors in the mines and sweatshops of the New World a rung or two up the social ladder as they came.

For all, it was a heady atmosphere, and yet, behind the optimism and excitement lay a nostalgia for the Old World and a memory of the anxiety of parting, passage, and arrival—immigrant lore combines the exhilaration of the new with yearning for the old, and occasional discouragement. "America is God's crucible, the great melting pot where all the races are melting and re-forming," enthused popular playwright Israel Zangwill in 1908, prompting less hopeful comment that America was not so much a melting pot as a collection of unmeltable ingots. It did seem that way at times. Belief in the doctrine of "Anglo-Saxon superiority" extended from the nativist grassroots to the White House; anti-immigration sentiment was being translated into federal law; bigotry and the ethnic slur were the order of the day— all this comes through in the lore of turn-of-the-century America. As folklorist Duncan Emrich puts it: "Folklore carries with it the evils and stupidities and prejudices of humanity as well as the great goodness of the human race. That is an obvious historical fact . . ." Both sides of the coin are with us yet. But—lest some of the stereotypes and images that follow seem a bit too close for comfort—we should remember that America has come a long way since 1900.

Many descendants of the country's original settlers grew alarmed at the ever-increasing numbers of "aliens" in their midst and took to castigating them with ugly slurs. Not even the "WASPS," however, were immune to stereotyping, as Grant Wood's "Daughters of the Revolution" illustrates.

In "The Last of England," by Ford Madox Brown, the White Cliffs of Dover recede behind a working-class English couple gazing out to sea after embarking for America. Immigrants from Great Britain outnumbered most others until the 1890's—more than half were industrial workers who had lost jobs at home.

THE MYTH OF THE MELTING POT

"They Would Close to the Newcomer the Bridge That Carried Them Over" is from an 1893 Puck *Magazine, a frequent promulgator of ethnic stereotypes. Here, while meaning to champion immigration, the artist unconsciously reinforces typing by showing the humble European origins of the wealthy second-generation Americans.*

Nowadays Americans tend to look back on the decades of large-scale immigration as years of national benevolence when huge numbers of aliens were clasped to America's generous bosom. The facts tell a somewhat harsher story. Though official policy (excepting the Chinese Exclusion Acts) was to welcome all comers who met health standards and could presumably support themselves or be supported by other members of their family, individual Americans frequently took at best a cautious and often downright hostile attitude toward the new arrivals.

As early as 1830 there were some "first families" who would have gladly closed the gates for all time. In 1836, for example, Philip Hone, former mayor of New York City, complained that "all Europe is coming . . . all that part at least who cannot make a living at home . . . not one in 20 is competent to keep himself." Hundreds of other Americans called themselves "nativists" and enthusiastically joined with like-minded citizens to harass immigrants, usually by social exclusion and gibes—but sometimes by such extremes as burning down their ghetto neighborhoods.

By 1850 xenophobia had grown to national proportions and with it a folklore of stereotypes, some directed toward particular ethnic groups, some toward all foreigners. The Irish were brawling drunkards and tools of unscrupulous politicians, the Germans were rigid, humorless beer drinkers, the Swedes were simply dumb. All aliens were said to love wickedness, to drink to insensitivity, to adore filth, and to be incapable of understanding the mechanisms or spirit of democracy. The large proportion who were Catholic were called the pope's advance guard in a conspiracy to turn America into a Catholic kingdom. All were the refuse of foreign jails.

Giving form and momentum to this virulent nativism was an organization founded in 1849 called the Order of the Star-Spangled Banner. To become a member one had to swear he was born in the U.S. of Protestant parents, that he was not married to a Catholic, and that he would support only Protestants for political office. Members were sworn to reveal nothing of the group if questioned by an outsider, a practice that gave rise to their being called popularly the Know-Nothings.

"The 200th Birthday of Uncle Sam's Healthiest Children" (1883) includes most of the standard images of the day.

Puck *(1894) satirized Americans of humble origin by depicting them buying fancy family lineages and coats of arms.*

The Know-Nothings eventually disintegrated as a group, destroyed by their own foolishness and the more urgent concerns of the Civil War. But by the 1890's they were back again in other guises; now they were taking aim at the "new immigrants," those later arrivals who had come chiefly from southern and eastern Europe.

Anti-immigration agitation now came from labor, which saw the oncoming waves of able-bodied men as direct competitors for their jobs. Unskilled and illiterate, unable to find employment, the newcomers were in fact a threat to the labor movement for they were readily recruited by industry as strikebreakers. Conservative middle-class Americans had another grievance: they read of the revolutionary ferment at work in Europe and concluded that these new Americans were bombthrowers and anarchists.

For the most part the popular press, by its use of cartoons and stories that reinforced racial and ethnic stereotypes, was a full partner in the preservation of this paranoia. Added to the usual images of Irish Pat and Mike and German Hans and Fritz were harsh depictions of Ike the Jew as a slick and dishonest merchant, Luigi the Italian as a prolific breeder prone to violence, virtually every group possessing some widely accepted set of traits and failings.

Ironically, one had to be in the New World only a generation or two to forget one's own similar origins and become intolerant of another's, as the cartoons opposite suggest. Peter Finley Dunne, a satirist during the height of the new immigration, has his Irish-American character, Mr. Dooley, describe the phenomenon: "As a pilgrim father that missed th' first boats, I feel I must raise me claryon voice again' th' invasion iv this fair land be th' paupers an' annychists iv effete Europe. Ye bet I must—because I'm here first . . . if ye wud like . . . to discuss th' immygration question, I'll send out . . . f'r Schwartzmeister an' Mulcahy an' Ignacio Sbarbaro an' Nels Larsen an' Petrus Gooldvink an' we'll gather tonight at Fanneilnovski Hall . . . ."

Outside Looking In

If "true" Americans had distorted images of their new brothers, so immigrants had certain stereotypic notions of what the American was. At the same time most tried desperately to preserve their Old World culture, they were in various ways emulating that stereotype. His ideal appearance was perhaps stylized in the figure at right—clean-shaven, fair-skinned, of firm, resolute jaw and self-confident mien. His personality was embodied in the more than 100 fictional heroes created by clergyman-*cum*-author Horatio Alger, Jr., in the late 19th century.

Alger's formula for achieving the American Dream was that success (read money and respect within the community) comes to those of virtue and hard work—though almost always through some near-miraculous bit of luck. Certainly his characters are virtuous to a fault. And they are rewarded for all this poor-but-honest self-discipline.

Ragged Dick, for example, saves the son of a rich man from drowning and is catapulted to wealth for his troubles. Phil the Fiddler, a young Italian in the unsavory grip of a *padrone,* is adopted by a wealthy physician. Alger concludes the hopeful tale of Luke Walton, who comes into a lost inheritance,

Leyendecker's classic portrait of the Arrow shirt man, a symbol of an ideal

with this observation: "Luke Walton helps, if there is need, the old associates of his humbler days and never tries to conceal the fact that he was once a Chicago newsboy." If Alger's stories seem outrageously cheerful and trite today, there were enough true odysseys of men like immigrant Andrew Carnegie to give hope to the susceptible immigrants as well as those of families here for generations; they bought them by the tens of thousands.

There was, of course, a dark side as well to immigrants' views of Americans. They could not help but be aware of the mixed reception that greeted them here and of the difficulties in becoming assimilated. As one Slavic immigrant put it: "My people do not live in América, they live underneath America. America goes on over their heads. America does not begin till a man is a workingman, till he is earning $2 a day." True as this analysis was for the generation that spoke it, the children of the immigrants had a promising chance to disappear into American life through public education. Exposed to the new language, to new customs, to new mores, and yes, even to kindly older Americans who extended a hand occasionally, they had a fair chance to make it. The American Dream did in fact become a reality for many, perhaps not exactly as Alger promised but good enough all the same. '

New York bootblacks, not so virtuous as Alger liked to think, swap the news.

SONS OF ERIN
Shamrocks Bloom in America

More than 2 million Irish newcomers debarked in U.S. ports prior to 1860, many of them "famine emigrants" from the great potato famine of the 1840's. This tragic circumstance was later recast—with typically Irish whimsey—as a humorous fairy tale: A box in which Death had been nailed up was thrown in the sea and washed up in Ireland. Its finders, wondering what was in it, broke the box open. Death flew out and started killing people all over Ireland—"that was why the Irish came to America." Highlights from the conjunction of the two:

A nasty 1864 *Harper's Weekly* cartoon implies that a true Irishman would rather drink than read—and be proud of it, too.

Perpetuating the troublemaker stereotype: rowdies ask to view the Orangemen's parade from a roof with "double the bricks."

MOSE THE BOWERY B'HOY

To this day, Irishers make up a large part of America's firefighting forces. Prior to World War I, the popular mind saw the big-city fireman as an Irishman, and the popular mind was right—for example, out of 22 medals for heroism given to New York firemen in 1911, 18 went to Irishmen.

Before the Civil War, firefighting was left to volunteer companies, which raced one another to fires, sometimes letting houses burn down while vying to control the one fireplug in the neighborhood. However, they were even more notable for heroism than brawling. The fireman became a favorite dramatic hero, and when Mose the Fireman was the central character in any East Side New York theater every seat was sold. Made up as a typical Irishman, "fightin' Mose" chewed and spit tobacco like a virtuoso and was forever

"boilin'" over for a rousin' good fight," but he was a loyal, courageous firefighter who could outrun all others with the "machine." By midcentury, Mose had achieved an unmistakably Crockett-like apotheosis:

He was eight feet tall and crowned by a huge stovepipe hat. His enormous boots were studded with inch-long spikes. In his belt was thrust a butcher's cleaver, and in summer a keg of beer for his refreshment also swung there. When going into action he was apt to carry a wagon tongue in one hand and a flagstone in the other. Again, he withstood 100 of the most fearsome sluggers of the Five Points, pulling paving blocks and flagstones from the street and hurling them into the opposing mob with frightful effect. As a jest he sometimes lifted a streetcar off the track and carried it for a few blocks on one hand as a waiter carries a tray, with the horses

dangling from one end and Mose laughing thunderously at the terror of the passengers.

Mose's real-life prototype was certainly "one o' the b'hoys" ("b'hoy," by the way, was the purportedly Irish pronunciation of *boy*). A caveman in Bowery garb, with beetling brow, bulldog jaw with a frowzy thick, reddish stubble, red shirt with collar open, and battered beaver hat, Mose was the undefeated pride of the Lady Washington Fire Company's Engine No. 40. When not serving valiantly at a fire (and there was no braver man on a ladder or under a crumbling wall), he was usually looking for a fight.

But Old Mose, like other conquerors, finally met his Waterloo—met it at the hands of Henry Chanfrau of the Peterson Company, in a battle royal which was a landmark in fire department history and talked of for 60 years thereafter. On a summer Sunday in 1838 a small fire occurred on South Street. Returning from it, the Lady Washington and Peterson companies trotted side by side up Pearl Street. All other crews were jealous of the Petersons, and there was particularly bad blood between them and No. 40. The ropes were fully manned, as always on Sundays; in fact, overmanned, for there were probably 500 men in direct attendance on each machine.

The chafing became more venomous with every step. Foreman Colladay of No. 15 and Assistant Foreman Carlin, who was in charge of No. 40, passed up and down the line, ostensibly demanding peace, but in reality egging on their cohorts. At the rear of 15's line Henry Chanfrau found himself opposite the mighty Mose Humphreys. Henry was known as a sturdy fighter, but no one would have believed that he could hold his own with Mose.

Finally, the pressure of the crowds on either side forced the two lines into collision. Like a flash through a train of powder, battle was joined all along the ropes. The Petersons fought like men inspired and No. 40 began to give ground, for to the amazement of everyone Mose Humphreys had not been able to down Henry Chanfrau. At last Henry landed a blow on Mose's jaw which sent that burly champion reeling—and then, to the horror of No. 40, the mighty Mose was down!

The Lady Washingtons gave way. Two of them dragged the fallen Mose to his feet and supported him away tottering between them. Then the frenzied Petersons proceeded to wreak their vengeance on their fallen opponents' engine. It was dragged to a pump and deluged with water until its beautiful white and gold paint and portraits of Martha Washington were almost completely washed off. Then it was taken in triumph to No. 15's engine house.

No. 40 never recovered from the disgrace of that defeat. Mose Humphreys vanished from his old haunts soon after the fight. He was next heard of as the proprietor of a pool and billiard hall in Honolulu and reputed chum of the Hawaiian king. He married a native and had a family said to have numbered 30.

IRISH BULLS
An indispensable ingredient of popular entertainment to folks several generations ago was the "Irish bull." *Bull* is an old word for "funny saying" that somehow got associated with the Irish, especially if based on a comical contradiction in terms or an inconsistency unperceived by the speaker. One son of Erin, asked what an Irish bull was, replied with one: "Supposing there were 13 cows lying down in a field and one of them was standing up—that would be a bull."

An Irishman, describing the trading powers of the genuine Yankee, said, "Bedad, if he was cast away on a desolate island, he'd get up the next morning and go round selling maps to the inhabitants."

A bull could also be a funny story: Two Irishmen who had just landed in this country had taken rooms in one of the downtown hotels in New York. In the middle of the night they were awakened by a great noise in the street. One of the Irishmen got up

and looked out of the window. Two fire engines tore along, belching smoke and fire and leaving a trail of sparks. "Phwat is ut?" asked the chap who remained in bed. "They're movin' Hell," said the other, "and two loads have just gone by."

IRISH AND POLITICS
A New York politician, who hadn't heard of Jimmy Walker, arrived late at a meeting. He found the whole room wildly cheering Walker. Since the politician knew nothing about him, he asked a Tammany leader, "This Walker—will he make a good mayor?" "He'll be a terrible mayor," replied the Tammanyite, "but what a candidate! What a candidate!"

An old Irish lady said to a friend: "Have you heard the news? John Danaher has become a Republican." The other replied: "It can't be true. I saw him at Mass last Sunday."

Republican candidate Theodore Roosevelt was constantly interrupted by an Irisher shouting, "I'm a Democrat." Finally Roosevelt asked the Irisher why he was a Democrat. "My grandfather was a Democrat," replied the Irisher, "my father was a Democrat, and I am a Democrat." Sarcastically, TR asked, "My friend, suppose your grandfather had been a jackass, and your father had been a jackass, what would you be?" Without a moment's hesitation the Irisher replied, "A Republican."

"I'd have nothing but Irishmen on the police—Patrick's Day'd be the Fourth of July," ran an 1880's vaudeville song which almost came true; in a highly influential minority to this day, the Irish policeman remains a favorite fixture of popular song and story.

THE GERMANS
All Work and Some Play

Between 1815 and 1860 a million and a half Germans crossed the Atlantic to become adopted Americans. Better educated and more highly skilled than many of their shipmates, they encountered relatively little prejudice among native-born citizens. Stories told by and about them emphasize their industriousness, their determination to succeed, and their need to organize every aspect of their lives, even to the extent of forming societies for drinking, singing, and somersaulting.

NO FOREIGNERS SERVED

Henry Talhouse was a first-generation American whose devotion to his new country was all mixed up with his hatred of the Old World. In the delicatessen he owned he made no secret of his anti-German feelings, re-christening *Leberwurst* "liver sausage" and refusing to serve sauerkraut unless under an American name. Despite the fact that many of his transplanted countrymen were good customers, a sign over his counter announced, NO FOREIGNERS ARE SERVED HERE. And he forbade his daughter Elizabeth to play with foreign children.

When Elizabeth grew into maid-enhood she was sent off to college. Henry Talhouse was so proud he told his customers: "She goes to college only mit Americans. She vas trained to have notting to do mit furriners."

This drawing satirizes by emphasizing corpulence and compulsive gymnastics.

Und ven she marries she vill marry a American, und her children vill be third-generation American! Understand that! *Third!*"

Meanwhile Elizabeth met and fell in love with John Smith, the son of Fire-Eye Eagle, a Cherokee Indian chief, who was also a student at her college. John was tall, brown, and handsome and spoke very little but wisely. Elizabeth decided it was time to introduce John and asked him to join her at her parents'. A few days later, on a Sunday afternoon a man knocked at the store door of Talhouse. Henry looked through the window and announced to his wife and daughter, "One of dem furriners who don't know that delicatessen stores are closed on Sundays."

But the man knocked again. "Lisby, you go and tell him." Henry watched her do so and what he saw made him forget his English. "Who is this man, Lisby? he yelled. "What business comes he here, I ask!"

"But, Father, quiet down. It's a surprise. This is John Smith, the man I am going to marry."

"What? *Donnerwetter!* Marry this man? This man. A furriner!"

"But, Father, listen. He is a Cherokee; listen, a Cherokee."

"A Sherokee marry my daughter! She vill marry an American."

"Who is not an American?" asked John Smith quietly as he approached the irate delicatessen dealer. "You Sherokees . . ." So John Smith, Fire-Eye Eagle's son, shed his acquired white man's manner and did a war dance then and there in good old Indian fashion. Henry, who was usually a little slow in getting the point of another man's argument, got this one all right. Now, two years since, Henry is proudly exhibiting the picture of a little halfbreed. "The third generation. The real American. That comes from bringing up children mit the right idear."

An umpa-pa musician, a wagonload of beer kegs, and a sausage-filled delicatessen are pictured as quintessential elements of a German community in this etching.

Typical of anti-German illustrations, this engraving of a beer garden (favorite gathering places for German-Americans) includes flags, a band, drunks, and beer-guzzling babies.

WORDS TO THE WISE

Prospective immigrants were quite understandably uneasy as to how they would be received in America. In 1850 one Pastor Bogen thoughtfully wrote home some helpful if pedantic words of advice:

Dear fellow countrymen, seek every opportunity to familiarize thy ear, memory, and organs of speech with the intonation, words, and pronunciation of the English language.

It is of the highest importance for every immigrant that he find an occupation as soon as possible. Labor is a principal condition of his happiness but it is not always possible for him to adhere to his former occupation, especially if he was numbered in Germany among the educated classes.

But the mistake of many immigrants is that they wait for days, even weeks, meanwhile spending precious money and still more precious time, quietly hoping that some favorable accident will come to their relief. It has often been said that that man must sooner or later become the victim of his illusions who believes he shall find here lasting happiness without honesty and a well-guided, judicious activity.

Nothing can perhaps be more dangerous and pernicious than the prejudices, originating in monarchies, in regard to caste, which declare that some are born princes while others are born subjects, from which they can never rise. Immigrants coming from such places must forever extinguish such notions in this land of freedom. Fidelity and merit are the only sources of honor here. The rich stand on the same footing as the poor; the scholar is not above the humblest mechanic; and therefore no German ought to be ashamed to follow any occupation.

But the unsuspecting immigrant must be on guard that he does not fall into the hands of some swindler in his search for employment. He is apt to be approached by men who skillfully seize upon his feelings of astonishment and joyous emotion and at the same time of his dependence and ignorance. However impudently they may assert that they are commissioned by the government to advise you (and to guide) you, do not believe them.

You have the right to remain with your baggage on board the ship for 48 hours after your arrival. Make use of this privilege. Do not be in a hurry. Take the necessary time. Then, be careful as to the kind of boardinghouse you go to; do not be enticed by cheapness into a bad, dirty, suspicious-looking house where you will be cheated.

DU, DU LIEGST MIR IM HERZEN

Moderately

Du, du liegst mir im Her-zen, Du, du liegst mir im Sinn; Du, du machst mir viel Schmer-zen, Weisst nicht wie gut ich dir bin. Ja, ja, ja, ja, Weisst nicht wie gut ich dir bin.

ONE-two-three! Of the many folksongs in waltz time brought to America by German newcomers, "Du, Du Liegst Mir im Herzen" was an alltime favorite in the rathskellers of turn-of-the-century Chicago and Milwaukee.

CHINESE-AMERICANS
Sojourners on Gold Mountain

From the 1850's Chinese flocked to America as prospectors, railroad laborers, fishermen, shopkeepers . . . Most hoped to get rich quick and go home. Many did; the bones of thousands more who died trying were exhumed by pious descendants and shipped back to China. By 1900, however, a Chinese-American community had taken root and transplanted ancestral traditions flourished. Here the Ghost Man, a well-known San Francisco character of that day, tells the story of his life there and here in third-person style with a rich admixture of old-country lore:

"Street Scene—Chinatown, New York" is by Glenn O. Coleman. Similar Chinese enclaves grew up in cities on both coasts of the United States during the late 1800's.

THE GHOST MAN

The Ghost Man was born in California but got his nickname in China, at the school to which he was sent by his father who wanted him to be educated in the old classics. Seventeen at the time he first entered that school, he was a strapping fellow, but after a few months he grew pale and thin, although he was not at all sick or weak. Then by night, when his roommates were asleep, he saw strange beings creeping out of the floor. Some had bodies, others only heads; none was a complete person. At last one night he woke up with a start, as an eerie scratching began.

All of a sudden the ghosts appeared, rushed on him with heavy clubs, and started beating him. He was knocked against the walls; he felt their teeth biting into him; he could hardly breathe. His roommates didn't wake up, but boys from neighboring rooms came running and found him on the floor, his clothes torn from his body, his flesh black and blue, and toothmarks on his back. Then the roommates awakened, explaining they had heard a rumpus but were unable to get up—as if a heavy object had been pressing down on them. The boys now pulled up the floorboards and to their amazement found human bones. But the Ghost Man (this was his sobriquet henceforward) explained it thus:

In olden times children were buried alive with dead kings, in order to wait on them and keep the monarchs company in spacious rooms underground. Poor people sometimes sold their offspring for such purposes. The

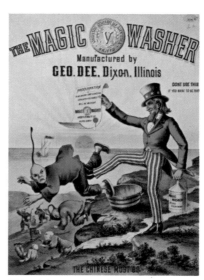

This vicious racist ad reflects the atmosphere in which the Chinese Exclusion Act of 1882 was passed by the U.S. Congress.

Ghost Man also "remembered" an exorcism of a young girl whose experience mirrored his own. She had been troubled by having ghosts follow her everywhere, so her mother hired a group of "ghost-seeing women" to get rid of them.

These women were able to penetrate the medium of the ether and perceive the ghosts in their actual forms. They brought nets to the girl's house and lay in ambush for the ghosts. Suddenly they threw the nets into the air and struggled with what seemed to be empty space. After subduing the ghosts, they carried the nets to a yard where they had set out a number of empty jars of immense size. Holding the nets tightly round the neck of the jars, they poured the

ghosts into them. The jars were not very heavy when empty, but once the ghosts had been poured into them it required about 15 men to carry them to the edge of a pond. One by one the jars were thrown in and sank. The girl was never bothered again, but no young man wished to marry her.

Because the Ghost Man has seen this actual scene enacted before his eyes, he believes ghosts exist in every land and place, even if in America most people do not believe in them. After his experience in China the Ghost Man found it hard to meet with girls—their mothers were afraid he might haunt them. So he came back to America and for six months studied under a private instructor who taught him the essentials of the English language. He learned to read, write, and speak English. All uncommon and difficult rules were omitted, to speed up the process of learning. With this slight understanding of English he got a job selling newspapers, much to his disgust. Then he got a better job working in a store and has been there ever since. "Maybe someday I'll get married," he says. "A man of 30 is not too old to get himself a wife." Luckily, Chinese people over here do not prevent their daughters from meeting him because he is known as the Ghost Man. So someday soon the Ghost Man is bound to take a wife.

SCANDINAVIANS
Sod Busters and Woodsmen

The Scandinavians were seldom attracted to America's cities. But the combination of a series of disastrous crop failures at home and the promise of sizable land grants under the Homestead Act of 1862 set in motion five decades of massive migration to America's Midwest and northwestern states. Because they had been accustomed to a harsh climate and a life of relative isolation, they were better equipped for frontier hardships than other groups. Like them, though, they had their simpleton stories as well as those that reflected their new experiences:

"Foredeck During a Storm," by Knut Ekwall, is a Swedish version of an emigration scene oft depicted by 19th-century American and European artists.

SAWING IS BELIEVING

Big Olaf worked at a sawmill, running the brutal rotary buzz saw. One day he was explaining to the foreman how he had just lost a finger. The foreman thought the saws were guarded, but Olaf demonstrated how it had happened: "Vell, Ae tak da boord dis vay wit' dis hand an' dis vay wit' da oder. Ae move da boord op to da machine lak dat, an da first ting Ae know—YUMPIN YIMINY, DAR GOES ANODER VON!"

BACHELOR AND BEAR

Back in the Wisconsin woods lived a bachelor Swede homesteader, Sven Carlsten. On rainy days Sven sat in the dim light of his cabin braiding fishlines out of hairs pulled from a horse's tail. He lived on fish—fried fish, baked fish, boiled fish—cold fish for his lunch at noon in the woods, smoking-hot fish out of his frying pan for supper. Outside his cabin door he kept a barrel of live fish; it was his larder and it was never empty. But one October morning when he reached in and found but a few small trout darting through his fingers, he knew that his fish were being stolen.

"By gar!" he said to himself, and he worried about it all day in the woods. When he came back, it took him five minutes to catch one of the remaining trout for his supper. "Yust vait," he said darkly. He had resolved to catch the thief.

That night with a high moon throwing a pale light across his clearing, he sat up in his doorway, but after the moon had set he dropped off to sleep. Sometime later there was a heavy noise at his fish barrel and Sven sprang awake.

In one movement he was beside the barrel, his arms groping for the thief. But he let go quickly when he found himself hugging a big black bear. Wide-awake now, Sven lunged back into his cabin, and the bear, crashing like a moose through the thickets, fled into the woods. "By gar!" Sven said to himself breathlessly.

For three nights the bear did not come back. Meanwhile, Sven scrambled down the bluff below his cabin and caught enough fish to restock the barrel. Then Sven readied a trap. First he nearly emptied the barrel of water; then he drove nails into it from all sides so that it was a sharp-studded cylinder above a shallow depth where the fish swam.

A NEW SWEDISH COMEDY DRAMA
TILLY OLSON
DIRECTION P.J. KENNEDY

"AY TANK AY GAT MARRY BY HIM!–
AY TANK EF BALDOAN' POP PUTTY SURE AY POP MAXEELFF"

On the fourth night the bear returned. Sven sat patiently by the door. The moon came up late and in the wan light Sven began to nod. He waked out of his sleep to the sound of claws twanging the stiff barbs of nails and he heard a surprised, impatient grunting. In the faint light he saw the big shaggy head rear itself above the open barrel. Then the barrel turned over and the head was swallowed up.

With a muffled watery snort the bear and the barrel went crashing and careening into the woods. "By gar!" said Sven, picking up a trout that glinted on the ground. He never saw bear or barrel again. But in the woods above Sven's place people still hear a hollow thumping on their stumps at night.

ECHOES

"In Skona, var I vas born," said Sven, "vas such fine echo ve could stand on mountaintop and yell, 'Yonson,' and in 20 minutes back comes such strong echo, 'Yonson,' ve nearly fall off mountain."

"You call that fine echo?" countered Ole. "Vy, right here in Minnesota ve can yell, 'Yonson,' and in vun minute back come 10,000 echoes, 'Vich Yonson?'"

This sheet music cover is typical of ridicule aimed at Scandinavians (which was rare); their accent is mimicked, and they are made to appear unbelievably stupid.

The Hatfield-McCoy Feud

© Walt Disney Productions

This Walt Disney cartoon reflects the popular image of feuding mountaineers (whether Hatfields and McCoys or Li'l Abner) in remote southern Appalachia.

One area of America where the leavening effects of 19th-century immigration were never felt was the Appalachian highlands of Kentucky and West Virginia. There the Scotch-Irish had been entrenched since before the American Revolution, and there they remained, their reputation for clannishness and quick temper working better than any exclusion laws to discourage outsiders. Indeed, two families became so infamous for the murder and mayhem they visited upon one another that their names became legendary even across the Atlantic. GI's abroad during World War II were constantly asked about the Hatfields and McCoys by curious Europeans.

The famous feud, however, was not fictional. It took at least 65 lives according to one authority. The pro-Union McCoys hailed from Pike County, Kentucky. The Hatfields settled in Logan County, West Virginia, just across the Tug Fork of the Big Sandy River. The trouble, as best anyone can recall, began with the shooting in 1865 of Harmon McCoy by a Confederate gang purportedly led by Jim Vance, uncle of "Devil Anse" Hatfield.

Temporarily sated by the border warfare that had gone on throughout the Civil War, both clans settled down to build families, tend their farms, and make their moonshine. "The trouble" returned in 1873. First Floyd Hatfield, cousin of Anse Hatfield, got into an altercation with Randolph McCoy, brother of the deceased Harmon McCoy, over ownership of an errant pig. A country trial was called, with McCoy the complainant and another Hatfield acting as judge. The disputed porker was, not surprisingly, ruled a Hatfield pig. The McCoys let it be known that they would take revenge. There were a few isolated shooting incidents over the next seven years, but for the most part it was a pressure-

© Walt Disney Productions

Feuding claimed many lives—the Hatfield-McCoy count was at least 65.

building period of ever-increasing bitterness and hostility. Then in 1880 an ill-starred romance further muddied the waters. Devil Anse's eldest son, Johnse, had taken up with Roseanna, daughter of McCoy clan leader Randolph. She got pregnant but Hatfield forbade his son to marry her, arousing even more bitter passions. (Roseanna finally left Johnse, and died in 1889—of heartbreak, they said.)

In 1882 warfare broke out on Election Day. Devil Anse's younger brother Ellison was set upon by Randolph McCoy's three sons and murdered. Before they could be arrested, Devil Anse Hatfield and his clan captured the brothers. Tolbert, 31, Phamer, 19, and 15-year-old Randall were tied to a papaw bush and told by Anse, "Boys, if you have any peace to make with your Maker you had better make it." Then in the light of a lantern they were all shot.

The Hatfields were not arrested for the murders of the McCoy brothers, so the fighting continued to escalate. The McCoys put so much pressure on their enemies that Devil Anse had to leave home. The Hatfields finally decided that if they killed Randolph, the McCoy patriarch, the harassment would stop. Randolph escaped their New Year's Day 1888 raid but two more of his children were killed, his wife was beaten unconscious, and his house was burned down. Finally a posse was mounted and a substantial number of Hatfields were brought to trial. (Two were killed in the roundup.) Four were given life sentences and one "weakminded" clan member, "Cotton Top" Mounts, was publicly hanged.

After that the feud cooled off, and by 1900 Randolph McCoy and Devil Anse Hatfield, aging and having lost so much, had tired of the affair. Both sides had devoted their best and brightest young men to the fray. The Hatfield land holdings, once considerable, had been severely reduced as they sold off acres to pay for guns and bullets. Many Hatfields were in jail, a fate worse than death for these fiercely independent people. Randolph McCoy had buried six of his children—each a victim of the feud. All either side had won was fame—not the fame of heroism but of human folly.

THE GREEKS
Children of Olympus

Economic and political upheavals at home, extreme poverty and wars with Turkey and other Balkan states, drove more than 350,000 Greeks from their homeland between 1891 and 1920. Despite their predominantly rural or seafaring backgrounds, the majority of Hellenes concentrated in America's cities where the following, featuring stock Greek characters and situations, were collected:

A Greek fruit peddler supplied the title for one of the top hit tunes of the 1920's.

JACKASS AND DONKEY

One day Stratouhotdas was leading his donkey to market by a rope. A number of boys stole up carefully behind him, untied the rope, and put it around one boy's neck. The others ran off to sell the donkey. When Stratouhotdas turned around and saw the boy there, he was very surprised and asked where his donkey had gone. The boy explained that he was the donkey. Stratouhotdas was puzzled and asked for an explanation. The boy told him that before Stratouhotdas had owned him he had been a boy, but his parents had thrown a curse on him and turned him into a donkey. At that time Stratouhotdas had bought him, and a little way back on the road the boy's mother and father had seen him, felt sorry for him, and removed the curse. Now he was a boy again. Stratouhotdas felt so sorry for him that he let him go and told him to be a good boy so that he would never again be changed into a donkey. As Stratouhotdas went into the marketplace, he spotted his donkey. He walked over and whispered to it, "I see you have been a bad boy again."

SAINTS ALIVE

Whenever Evangelos' wife went to church, she worshiped at the icon of Peter and Paul. A lecherous priest, hidden behind, would chant, "Saint Paul wants to come to your house." When the innocent supplicant told Evangelos of this curious occurrence, he said to tell Saint Paul to come the next night to give her his blessing. Evangelos bought some huge keys and dressed up like Saint Peter.

The next night Saint Paul arrived as expected. Ten minutes later the doorbell rang again. "Who is it?" shouted Evangelos' wife. "Saint Peter," he answered. And with that he came in, saying to a surprised-looking Saint Paul, "What are you doing here? I hold the keys to Paradise and you were not given leave to go." And before the false Saint Paul had a chance to reply, the false Saint Peter set to beating him with his keys until he broke his skull. "*Now* go to Paradise," said the victor.

 SUPERSTITIONS

Fishermen's Superstitions

The Greeks who settled in Florida were mostly sponge fishermen by trade and they carried their Mediterranean customs, some as old as civilization, almost unchanged to the Gulf of Mexico. They were each very careful to avoid any action that might bring bad luck to themselves or to their ship.

For example, if a captain was standing on the deck of his boat ready to cast off and a passerby asked him when he was going to sail, the captain would postpone the trip until another day, for the question could only bring misfortune to the boat and crew. Women in mourning clothes, too, were feared by the seamen. One widow in Tarpon Springs gained such an infamous reputation as a harbinger of bad luck that even boats which had cast off would return to port if the woman suddenly appeared at the waterfront. They wouldn't leave until she left the docks. If she stayed all day, they stayed all day. On the few occasions when a ship went out despite her presence, a diver drowned or the ship's bottom fell out—there was always *something*. Finally the spongers went to the priest and got him to tell the woman not to go to the waterfront until after the sponge boats had departed each day.

The sponge fishermen also took steps to ensure themselves a safe and prosperous journey. Most of them wore gold crosses around their necks or amulets pinned to their clothing. Because these objects had been blessed, they were believed to render their wearers invulnerable. Pieces of consecrated bread and vials of holy water were also carried.

FROM EASTERN EUROPE
Refugees From Hunger

From the 1880's huge numbers of people representing a dozen different nationalities poured in from southern and eastern Europe. Back home the grassroots were divided between older folks' attachment to their native way of life and young folks' growing willingness to give it all up for a better life in America. Many of the latter were saying, "Here one is a dog, in America a gentleman." In every village people debated the issue. A Minnesotan of Slovene extraction, whose experience mirrored that of other eastern Europeans, recorded his reminiscences:

Peter Jerala died last night." The news raced through the village, and in the evening people came to sprinkle his body with olive branches dipped in salt and holy water from a little dish on the stand at the foot of the coffin. All knelt and made the sign of the cross and acted as if they were absorbed in a short prayer for departed Peter. The latecomers one after another got up, exchanged glances with the mourners, and then with the other people. "Peter was taken away early," one mused. Another was angry with time, which could add no more days. A couple of neighbors sympathetically told that the late Peter's wife was so wicked that his relatives dared not die.

Peter's brother brought a little brandy from somewhere and poured it for the men and the boys. He also offered it to the women. At that point Marta Robavs announced, "Tomorrow young Cizej will come from America." Immediately everyone forgot about Peter Jerala.

Cizej was well known throughout the village. Half a year after he had married he left for America. His wife took care of the house, and he sent her money for taxes and debts. And since he undoubtedly was lonely for her, he was returning. America was the foremost interest in our villages at that time. Boys and men left our homeland in droves. Those who could carried passports; those who faced military service went without.

"So Cizej is coming back! Just in time to bury Jerala tomorrow night, because they were friends," said someone else. The next evening practically the entire village gathered at Jerala's house. They filled the room, the entrance, and even stood in the yard although it was cold. Cizej really did arrive.

Those inside fell silent. Cizej looked at Jerala surrounded by candles, at the fellow with whom he had been friends as a boy. He knelt for just a few seconds, then moved, and finally sprinkled Peter. Afterward he looked for Peter's wife, who was sitting on the bed in the other room sobbing all the while. Cizej greeted her and expressed his sympathy; he spoke to her consolingly and from the heart. She began to cry. Two little children were sleeping in the bed. The carrying on of all these people, which they could not understand, and all the crying of the mother has tired them out. Cizej looked at them and said, "These two do not yet know what caused their father to perish." The crying of the despairing widow became less and less. "This Cizej is really one of us, America has not spoiled him," a neighbor whispered to the women next to him. The widow's brother approached and said, "Here, Andrej Cizej, have a drink."

Soon Cizej's young wife also came. "Why are you so tearful?" a neighbor asked her in a joking manner and winked familiarly. Cizej's wife replied: "I'm happy that he has come home. I haven't seen him in almost five years. But he scarcely entered the house when already he was telling me he had to go back." "And so I

FOLKWAYS

Roaming Gypsies

Gypsies started arriving in large groups as of the 1880's and resumed their nomadic life in America, traveling in summer and camping down for the winter in various out-of-the-way places along the road. As in Europe, they lived by trading horses and other animals, tinkering, and fortunetelling. They had no desire to assimilate but only to adapt—as inconspicuously as possible. Gypsies have a taboo against any but economic relations with non-Gypsies. This bar works as effectively as the caste system of their ancestral homeland. (It is believed that the original Gypsies migrated from northern India in about A.D. 1000, reaching Europe some 400 years later.)

The economic relationship with non-Gypsies involves a bit of thieving here and there on the part of many Gypsy groups, but because they do not feel a part of the host society, they are not worried about whether their minor depredations are right or wrong. The same attitude underlies Gypsy fortunetelling—in the words of anthropologist Rena Gropper: "They believe themselves that it is possible to predict the future . . . but ordinarily readings to *gaje* [outsiders, non-Gypsies] are considered entirely fallacious. Should the seer believe during a reading that she has really foreseen a future event, she is disturbed—usually she does not reveal her vision to the customer."

must," Cizej interjected. "We must mourn for a time, but then I must sell the house, and you will go with me." No other place attracted Cizej's wife at all. "It's better and more pleasant to have a home here," she protested. "But, Andrej," said an old acquaintance, "in the past five years you have seen a lot, and you must have many things to tell us about the land where dollars lie in the street." All the young men who dreamed of going to America stopped talking and joking, and listened.

"This, fellows, is the way American tobacco is. You bite it off like a dried sausage and chew it—it's fragrant right to the end!" He gave it to the first, who bit off some, then to the second, and eventually to all. For those who had no teeth he cut off a little with his pocketknife. "It's too sweet," said one. "Oh, when you work it a little it won't be anymore," Cizej assured them. "Well, fellows, what do you think now?" All claimed they would like to go, but one man could not get enough money for the fare, another could not get the documents necessary to avoid conscription, a third said his parents would not allow it, etc. All, however, firmly intended to go over at the first opportunity.

When Cizej had emptied two more glasses, he said: "Tone Cerar got TB in America. He ground axes 10 hours a day at a grindstone without water, and the dust settled in his lungs. Now he is suing the company for enough money for the trip home. The poor wretch has no money. He drank a lot, which also hurt him. You know," Cizej continued, "Minnesota is healthy. The air there is fine air. Nevertheless, Cerar breathed it, and it did him in.

"In the mines it's bad too, fellows! And I have not yet seen any dollars in the streets. I've worked there more than five years. You have to work like an ox! No, that's not a good comparison. We never drove oxen the way we are married to the Minnesota mines 10 hours a day and often an extra hour. Sometimes we work on Sundays too. But on payday things

"Second Hungarian Rhapsody," by Hans Larwin. When it comes to music, the popular mind lumps Hungarians and Gypsies together—all are supposedly born violinists.

are different. People there become friendly more quickly than here. In Minnesota when you meet an acquaintance or see an old friend, you don't just buy a liter or two, but a whole barrel of beer. On Sundays our people gather in the 'saloons,' like our *gostilne* but without tables. There is one long narrow table without chairs called a bar. At this bar everyone stands next to one another like cows at a manger. And I'll tell you, boys, they really drink! There are harmonica players in nearly every boardinghouse and in every saloon. But we have to work like dogs. In just a few years I'll have paid off my debt and will have bought a pair of oxen for farming and then I'll thumb my

This contemporary European cartoon echoes sentiment in America at that time. It does not stop at characterizing would-be Polish immigrants as scruffy and stupid; greedy passage brokers look just as bad.

nose at America, and nobody will ever get me to work under the ground again. If I stay permanently I'll buy a farm in a few years."

After that speech Cizej remembered that he had, after all, come from America. Their mugs were truly empty. He asked Peter's brother to bring several bottles of the best and some cigars and cigarettes. He gave all his *groše* to the children. He pulled a silver dollar from his pocket, a half-dollar, and some American change. "This is what a dollar is like. It is worth five *krona*." He sorted out his change and continued explaining.

"There is as much food as you want in America. You can eat meat whenever you like. There is enough of everything. The only complaint is the hard work." They asked him what the land was like where he lived. "It's really cold in the winter. But one gets used to it. Summertime is beautiful. All around there are gigantic forests full of game. Everybody goes hunting, not like here where hunting is only for the rich! There are lakes everywhere. The iron ore, which we dig, is taken by train to the big lake [Superior] at Duluth and Two Harbors. There it is loaded onto large ships and then it goes by water for many days to the steel mills. America is a marvelous land—I tell you—however, we have to work a lot harder there than you do here."

They then asked him about the

people of his own and neighboring villages in America. About many of them Cizej knew nothing, for America is so large—not like your village or surrounding parish. Even in Minnesota he had not seen everything because the towns were so far apart. But he did know about those in which he had been. Mostly the people dug ore. One had opened a saloon. Janez Kramar was hurt and is in the hospital. Polde Spiz ran into trouble while hunting. One of the members of his party mistook him for a deer and shot him in the shoulder. A piece of ore fell on Joze Bagata's head. They say he will never be healthy again, nor in his right mind.

Nezka Vencelj died in childbirth. Her husband brought in 14 boarders, for whom she cooked and washed. The doctor said that it was too much for her. Now her husband is looking for another wife.

It was after midnight when they began to leave. Only a few stayed until morning. About 2 a.m. Cizej went home with his wife. At this early morning hour several young fellows began to have an idea. The idea was to go to America. If Cizej could bring back dollars and spend them, why couldn't they? Were they really weaker than he? No, they were not! Work was not to be feared. And here at home what were their chances? You work and work, and still you do not get as much as you would like to eat. And so, in the years that followed, they set out; eventually northern Minnesota took thousands of them into its cold, its mines, and its forests.

I am quite sadowitch
Cause you no writeski
Take pen and
pad o'witch
Drop me a lineski.

Immigrants just off the boat from czarist lands were satirized for their traditional attire including cap, tunic, and boots.

THE EXODUS
Jews From East Europe

Between 1880 and 1920 millions of Jews joined the flood of immigrants to the New World. Coming mainly out of the ghettos and scattered rural shtetls *of Russia, Rumania, Poland, Lithuania, Jews found themselves every bit as befuddled, excited, disappointed, and homesick as their emigrating Gentile counterparts. Most of that first generation of Jews settled on New York's Lower East Side, where the grinding hardship of their lives could only be ameliorated by their well-known ability to laugh at themselves and life in general. From that era:*

ARRIVAL IN AMERICA

As we approached New York the passengers came to life, creeping out into the warm sunshine, into the bright beautiful world. The women primped themselves up. My brother Eli combed out his beard. Brocha and Taibel appeared in their best frocks. Mother put her silken Sabbath kerchief on her head. Only my friend Mendel and I didn't have anything to get dressed up in. Besides, we had no time. We were busy approaching the shores of America. All eyes were sparkling, all hearts were full. I'm sure that's just how the Jews fleeing Egypt felt after the dividing of the waters. We wanted to sing.

ELLIS ISLAND

We were taken to a large, well-lit hall and were given food and drink—all free of charge. What good kind people! Only what? Oh, the things that we had to go through before we got to that hall. We had to pass over a long bridge in single file. At every step we were halted and a different nuisance with bright buttons scrutinized, examined, prodded, and pounded us.

First of all they turned our eyelids inside out with a piece of white paper, in order to examine our eyes. Then they examined the rest of our limbs. And everyone made a chalk mark on us and pointed where to go next, right or left. Only after this was over were we permitted to enter that large hall and find one another. By the time we got there we were bewildered, confused, and frightened.

One of the oldest bad-taste ethnic jokes deals with Jewish noses. "His Choice" appeared without apology in *Judge,* 1894.

IMPRESSIONS

Such a pushing and a shoving and a pressing and a crowding as we've experienced here, in the bowels of the earth. The trains are packed with people. The passengers are pressed together like herring in a barrel, shoulder to shoulder, thigh to thigh. One goes out, and two get in. There's no place to sit. We have to stand. We stand, we sway, we fall over one another, striking nose on nose. Some manage to keep their balance by a miracle, without holding on to anything; others are clutching on iron rings—here it's called hanging on a strap. And if a seat suddenly becomes vacant, there are so many customers for it that you've got to be sharp.

People sit and keep chewing on

Although conspicuous consumption characterizes all newly rich groups, the virulently anti-Semitic, old *Life* implied overdressing was a Jewish trait by identifying the bather as the only Christian.

something, like animals chewing their cud. Later I learned that the thing they are chewing is called chewing gum. It's a kind of candy made out of rubber. American people chew gum all their lives long without stopping. They chew it, but they don't swallow it into their stomachs. Chewing gum almost finished off our friend Pinney, who has a sweet tooth. He is always sucking candy. When he saw chewing gum for the first time in his life, he grabbed a package and swallowed it whole. It made a revolution in his stomach and almost killed him. Doctors had to be summoned at once, and they pumped the gum out of him. That's how they saved Pinney.

GHETTO HUMOR

A pushcart vendor who hadn't made a sale for hours grew anxious to sell something and pack up for the day, when an old lady approached his cart, handled and inspected everything she could reach, and, picking up a teaspoon, inquired, "How much?" "One penny." "One penny? Too much," shrugged the old lady. Disgusted, the poor peddler murmured: "Too much? All right, make me an offer."

Another instance of across-the-counter repartee was heard one day in a tailor shop on Rivington Street when a man walked in to get his suit pressed. "That will be $2," said the tailor. "Two dollars!" cried the customer outraged. "Why, back in Minsk I could get my suit pressed for 5 cents!" "That I believe," said the tailor, "but look at the fare!"

The visiting rabbi stopped in the middle of his sermon and signaled to the *shammes* [sexton]. "In the second row," he whispered, "is a man sound asleep. Wake him up." "That's not fair," said the *shammes.* "What do you mean 'not fair'?" "You put him to sleep, you wake him up."

Goldfarb and Finkelstein go into partnership. As their business does not prosper, they begin to seek ways to improve it. They paint the shop, install new fixtures, and, in the boldest gesture of all, change their corporate name to Ryan and Ryan. One day a customer calls and asks for Mr. Ryan. "Which Mr. Ryan do you want," comes the reply, "Goldfarb or Finkelstein?"

A group of Russian Jewish immigrants is greeted by Miss Liberty. Their faces mirror the mixture of expectation and apprehension that all newcomers must have experienced.

THE ITALIANS
Hard-Luck Beginnings

The great waves of Italians entering the United States beginning in the 1880's met problems that northern Europeans had scarcely encountered earlier. The Italians were culturally different from the "native" stock; economic times had changed, too, and organized labor was hostile to the unskilled "furriners." Nevertheless, more than 4 million Italians managed to make a new home in America—285,000 in 1907 alone—and to reestablish their Old World way of life, frequently in close-knit Little Italy communities within larger urban ghettos.

NO MORE INSULTS

The bully of our town, Tom Baden, called me a dago in the very presence of Penelope Worthington, in whose eyes I had already been considerably reduced in social standing because she figured I was a "foreigner." I winced like one receiving a lash and then remarked with quiet determination, "...om, don't you ever call me that ...n." I wanted to retain *some* statu... ...th Penelope. "What will you do if ...call you a dago again?" he taunted, emphasizing "dago." "I'll beat you up," I replied, gritting my teeth. I was rather small and slender for 13, and he was large and robust for 14. He laughed derisively. Several days later we were eating our lunches in the schoolyard. Tom's lunch, which was packed in a neat, ornamental metal box with a handle, consisted of fresh ham sandwiches made with snow-white bread. My lunch was wrapped in an Italian newspaper and consisted of one large fried-pepper-and-egg sandwich, made with Italian bread. Tom called it a dago lunch. I said nothing until I had swallowed the last crumb of the savory, olive-oil-soaked bread.

I walked over toward him. He put out his foot and tripped me. I struck at him and his fist shot out and hit me squarely in the forehead. I staggered back and Tom guffawed. In that moment Penelope appeared on the scene. I swung mightily with my right fist, but it was only a feint. Tom dodged to avoid it, and my left fist landed squarely on the point of his chin. In that instant I thought my hand had broken, and I could feel

This "indolent Italian" insult is from the book named *How To Draw Funny Pictures*.

every bone in my body vibrating. Nevertheless I thrilled to the impact. Two thousand years of Italian vindication had gone into that blow.

"I'll kill you for this, Mike, you damn dago!" he screamed and lunged. We struggled on the ground, punching and kicking. Suddenly he was on top of me directing straight

The itinerant scissors grinder, another role often ascribed to Italians by "Americans," is featured here in picture and song.

thrusts and uppercuts. In reaching up to stay his punching-bag arm, I got his right ear in my hand and twisted it like one winding a clock. He yelped and screeched and lost his advantage. I now was astride him, and getting a perfect hold on his ear, I started winding the clock again.

"Ouch! Ouch!" he shrieked. "Stop, Mike, you damned—" "What were you about to say?" I asked sweetly as I wound the clock some more. "Mike! Stop! Please stop! I'll apologize—and I promise—I'll never use that word again!" I got up and lifted him to his feet. I wiped the blood and dirt from his face and said, "I'm awfully sorry I had to do this." Although my whole body was aching, I felt happy and proud and I looked around for Penelope to receive her congratulations, but she was nowhere to be seen.

PAVED WITH GOLD

According to an Italian immigrant: It was said of a man that after he landed in New York and was walking down the street, he saw a five-dollar gold piece but gave it a kick saying "If I start to pick up money now, I'll be loaded down before I'm ready to go home."

GIFT OF THE MAGA

Mr. Orlando was a third-generation Italian and he had, not surprisingly, strayed some distance from the customs of his parents and grandparents. No one was surprised when his modern ways brought him grief.

He was to be married to a young Italian girl of his acquaintance. But her parents strenuously opposed the plan, convinced that as his ancestors were from a different part of Italy than theirs, the couple's union would not be successful. When the daughter could not be dissuaded, the parents finally gave grudging assent. But for insurance they presented the couple with some amulets to protect them against the hazards of their experiment, especially against the Evil Eye. Mr. Orlando, considering the amulets a piece of primitive superstition, threw the charms out the window.

A saint's day is celebrated in a colorful church procession through the dark streets beneath New York's elevated railway. John Sloan painted the work around 1920.

young fellow, what'sa matter you? I'ma tough guy, but you're tough guy too.'" And he would laugh his heartily, chuckling, infectious laughter, rolling his brown eyes.

His brother who had found two mine jobs in Colorado had sent for him, and as he took the train trip across country to Colorado, he was greeted with never-ending wonders. "Joost imagine the way she look, those big cities and farms. Joost imagine! And there I'ma sit, thinking maybe I'ma dreaming. I'ma say over and over again, 'Hey, Loogie, she'sa true. She'sa all yours, by golly.'"

HE WHO LAUGHS LAST
For years one of San Francisco's perennial chuckles was the fact that Tarantino's Restaurant on Fisherman's Wharf was owned by a pair of Irishmen named Gene McAteer and Dan Sweeney. Then one day a new crab stand opened on the Wharf. It was called Hogan's—and its owner was an oldtime Wharfian named Tony Tedesco. "I jus' wanna show," grinned Tony, "that the Italians are as gooda sports as the Irishmen!"

Many Italian immigrants relied on Mediterranean street specialties to earn a living. Native Americans were quick to add organ grinders, knife sharpeners, and the like to the list of Italian stereotypes which they then held up to ridicule.

and persuaded his wife to do the same. "We would be the laughing stock of my friends if they found out," he argued.

Upon their arrival at their new home in another city, friends and relatives gave the bride and groom a pretentious party. Among the guests was a pretty young cousin to whom Mr. Orlando devoted unusual attention. As the newlyweds prepared for bed, Mrs. Orlando noticed that her husband was strangely unattentive. He went to bed without so much as kissing her. This behavior continued for several weeks, and Mrs. Orlando became desperate. Fearing that she had offended him, she wrote to her mother for help. The mother, hearing the alleged facts, announced that a spell *must* have been cast over the bridegroom. The discovery of a crumpled knot of ribbons in his wedding clothes laid bare the means of enchantment, and when the mother heard about the pretty cousin she became convinced that envy lay at the base of the affair.

The mother took the ribbons home, thanking the saints that witches might still be found in this unbelieving land. After several oil-and-water tests had been performed, a witch revealed that someone—probably a former sweetheart—had slipped the ribbon charms unseen into Mr. Orlando's pocket. This had tied up his heart and withheld his affection from his wife. The spell was soon dissolved by sprinkling salt over the ribbons, cutting them with scissors, and burning them.

The bride now told her husband what had been done to restore his affection, and they both bought new amulets. Within a few days she was able to write home to her mother that all was well.

COMING HOME
In later years my father told us children many tales of his experiences in coming to America. The moment he set foot on American soil he felt, by his own words, an inexplicable upsurging of his spirit, as though in recognition of something long lost in his own existence. "Eet'sa hard to explain, but I'ma feel like I'ma come home. This country, she'sa big all right, and she'sa young, joosta like me. It'sa like she say, 'Come on

KID LORE

Many immigrants to the United States never really dropped the tongue or customs of their homeland. But their children and grandchildren, while retaining some of the old ways, entered the American mainstream via the public schools. There the newcomers' kids spent many of their daily waking hours with the native-born in a miniature New World, tightly organized, self-enclosed, remote from the adult struggle to survive.

Lovers of the colorful and the melodramatic, children are also extremely conservative (many of their games are survivals of bygone adult customs, and their rhymes often go back hundreds of years). They are believers in law and order—of the juvenile brand, to be sure—and ruthless enforcers of conformity, as anyone with childhood memories of cruel jeers and "Indian burns" will recall. Immigrant children swung into line with the dominant Anglo-Saxon kid culture as if their lives depended on it, quickly picking up a suitable comeback for every situation. If mimicked because of a foreign accent, one could reply, "Monkey see, monkey do!" Asked his name, a new kid might retort, "Puddentaine. Ask me again and I'll tell you the same." (*Puddentaine* is thought by some to be an old English nickname for the Devil.) The same kid, craving acceptance and prestige, was soon proving his mastery of English by turning it inside out:

'Twas midnight on the ocean,
Not a streetcar was in sight,
The sun was shining brightly,
For it rained all day that night,
'Twas a summer day in winter,
And the snow was raining fast,

Kids, like those in this painting, love to play barber—often to mothers' dismay.

As a barefoot boy with shoes on
Stood sitting on the grass . . .

And putting forth riddles: What walks in the water with its head down? *The nails in a horse's shoe when he walks through the water.* What's big as a barn, light as a feather, and 60 horses can't pull it? *The shadow of a barn.* What tricks are most common among New York policemen? *Patricks.* What goes around the house and doesn't make a track? *The wind.*

What's white as snow and snow it isn't, green as grass and grass it isn't, red as blood and blood it isn't, black as tar and tar it isn't? *A blackberry—first the white blossom, then the green berry which turns red, and when ripe is black.*

Or country-style "embarrassers": Thar was a poor old starvin' mule on one side of the river, and a fine big haystack on t'other side. The river was too deep to ford and too swift to swim, and thar warn't no bridge. How did the mule git the hay? The listener gives up. The teller: Uh-huh, that's just what t'other mule done!

As the American way of life became increasingly citified, fewer adults played traditional folk games—circle and kissing games that had been an adult pastime in rural parts as late as the Civil War were by 1900 considered exclusively juvenile (though western homesteaders preserved them here and there). At the same time certain other games, once acceptable boys' play, were downgraded and forbidden. Gambling games, for example, descended from being deemed fit for a young gentleman to semioutlaw status. As an 1891 report on Brooklyn kids' street games puts it: "Pitching pennies is regarded as a vulgar game and only practiced by bootblacks and boys of the lowest class."

Not quite beyond the pale was the juvenile practical joker who became the hero of one of America's all-time bestsellers, Wisconsin governor George W. Peck's *Bad Boy and His Pa*, toward the end of the 19th century. (Peck virtually owed his electoral victories to the book.) Our ancestors howled at the comical misadventures of Bad Boy Hennery's Pa, made to imagine he was on an autopsy table about to be dissected, caught with playing cards and rum (planted on him by his son) at a prayer meeting, and bitten by red ants and embarrassed by a cursing parrot. Although practical jokes are no longer quite the rage they were in the Bad Boy's day, one that has stood the test of time is the Snipe Hunt, played as long ago as the Civil War by teenage soldiers. The hunters take their dupe to some lonely spot

Some urban urchins cut loose in this 1872 cartoon, "The First Hop of the Season."

In this engraving by Winslow Homer, Cape Cod boys play on a seesaw while their sisters play cat's cradle—the latter game, known the world over, dates to prehistoric times. To this day, primitive peoples use string figures to illustrate folk tales.

briefing him on the habits of the elusive snipe—its night-prowling habits and call, methods of luring it, and so forth, and afterward leaving the victim by himself, "holding the bag" into which they assure him they will drive the snipe. Then they go home or back to camp, leaving the snipe hunter to wait alone until he catches on.

Children are as superstitious as any race of savages, and their lore is full to overflowing with such sayings as "Step on a crack, you'll break your mother's back." In their *Lore and Language of Schoolchildren,* Iona and Peter Opie record thousands of these, many of which aim to predict or influence the future. For example: If two children say the same thing at once (it must be accidental) they instantly stop what they are doing and, without another word or sound, glide into a set ritual—in parts of the U.S. locking the right-hand little fingers, wishing silently, and then unlocking, each names an animal or bird. Another favorite technique of divination among U.S.

children is to blow on a dandelion in seed. If all the seeds come off in three tries, it's a sign of successful love or marriage within the year; or, with little girls, "My mother wants me." This is doubtless a survival of an originally pagan peasant custom from Europe. After the turn of the century, however, many of these older games started disappearing, and more recently, reflecting trends in adult society, girls have been tending toward playing games that are traditionally male.

The U.S. schoolyards of two and three generations ago were thus a crucible of social change, a melting pot within the melting pot. In them the immigrant young were separated from such Old World institutions as the arranged marriage and thrown together to re-create for themselves and make their addition to that progressively unrestricted lifestyle known as the American way of life.

In America leapfrog became a rough-and-tumble sport known as Johnny on a pony. To genteel turn-of-the-century Philadelphia private school boys an observer wrote, "Leapfrog is abandoned to the rougher outside class who are known as Micks."

J. C. Leyendecker's "Labor Day" magazine cover (1946) suggested the American industrial worker was sitting on top of the world.

"The Spirit of Vulcan," by Edwin Abbey, hovers above workers in a foundry; Vulcan was the Roman god of volcanic fire, identified with the Greek Hephaestus, who was god of the blacksmith's fire and metalworking.

The Breadwinners

By 1900 America was taking giant steps toward an economy in which blue-collar workers would outnumbe their country cousins. Young rustics read Horatio Alger and le for the big city. As editorial writers and preachers never tired of pointing out, Henry Ford had been a farm boy, Andrew Carnegie a bobbin boy. Technology was revolutionizing people's lives in visible, tangible ways from one month to the next. Electric lights, steam heating, telephones, the phonograph, the horseless carriage, flying machines—where would it all end? The new "necessities" meant new industries and new sources of energy—coal, oil.

Steelworkers, oilmen, railroadmen, and others shared with their forerunners a keen sense of pride in their rugged and often dangerous work, and their stories soon came to magnify their exploits. Although the frontier faded into a tamed and crowded continent, much occupational lore retained the barracks-room roughness of earlier eras. A favorite setting in which blue-collar lore was exchanged was the barroom (like the saloons of the cowboys and forty-niners, and the "grocery stores" of the horse-alligator men). Tall tales, shoptalk, and gambling arguments over sports loomed large while the makers of modern America relaxed after their shift, "having one with the boys."

The "robber barons" gave rise to the satirical image of the rapacious, miserly millionaire. Here, a plutocrat visits his mother's hovel.

COAL MINERS
Heroes of the Stygian Deep

The coal mines became a major employer of men after the Civil War as America's industries developed an insatiable appetite for cheap energy. Conditions in the mines before the emergence of unions and government safety regulations were notoriously dangerous, giving rise to folktales about disasters, death, and omens.

Riding a rude-looking car down into one of the mine tunnels, a shift of men roll joylessly toward their dangerous work.

THE HARBINGER

No miner would raise a hand against a rodent. It was widely believed that whenever a cave-in or some other mine disaster was impending, the rats would sense it and head in a scurrying pack for the tunnel entrance, alerting everyone in the process.

One old miner tells a story about a rat he got to know when he was working at the Ellengowan colliery near Shenandoah. One day his rodent acquaintance snatched the lid of his dinner pail, which contained a cut of pie, and scurried off with it. The miner chased the rat for some distance until he finally retrieved both lid and pie. When the rat ran off with the lid a third time, the miner was so angry he forgot himself and vowed to kill it. While he was off searching, the roof caved in and tons of rock and coal crashed down right where he had been squatting. "You see," said the miner, "that rat was trying in its own way to warn me and thus saved my life."

THE DEATH-WATCH TICK

A miner was buried alive by a pillar of coal which he was robbing. After his body was dug out it was discovered that his watch was still in the mine, buried in the gob, where it ticked away unseen. It soon gave evidence of being the most amazing timepiece. Its chief function seemed to be to forecast the approach of death, and so uncannily accurate was it that miners feared it more than the Devil.

One night, while on his accustomed tour of inspection, the fire boss was astounded to hear the death-watch tick. It sounded so weird and awesome in that empty mine!

There was fear and pity in his heart for Jim Kelly in whose working place the watch was ticking. When morning came, the fire boss was in his station along the gangway and waved Jim aside when he came up for his brass check. "Jim, I heard the—the death-watch tick in your heading last night as plain as ever I heard anything. Don't go in there or it's kilt you'll be." "The death-watch tick!" Jim turned deathly pale. The dinner pail trembled in his hand. He turned back.

Now there was gratitude in Jim's heart for being spared the fate of so many of his fellow miners, and he knew of no better way to celebrate his defeat of the death-watch tick than by attending church. He could still make the 8 o'clock mass. To reach the church he had to go over a railroad grade crossing. When he got there he found the gates down. Rather than take a chance of missing

Lunch pail on his arm, lamp around his neck, Roy Hilton's prototypical "Miner" is about ready to descend into the mine.

the mass, he ran across the tracks. But not fast enough. The 7:55 flyer mowed him down.

THE POINTING FINGER

Jim Tokash thought he was the best coal cutter in Grant Town coal mines. Whenever he ran into a vein of sulfur, instead of reporting it to the section boss, he would try to drill through it. He was warned many times that if he didn't stop breaking the drill bits he would be fired.

It was about 3 o'clock in the afternoon that Jim ran into the biggest sulfur ball he had ever seen, and as before, he tried to drill through it. All at once the drill broke loose in Jim's hand. When he came to, he was in the hospital. He looked down and discovered that his left hand was missing!

A few months later Jim returned to the mines, not as an operator but as an assistant. The new operator also thought he was the best coal cutter in the mines, and when he tried the same thing that Jim had, he caused a cave-in.

Jim was getting a drink of water at the time, and he was the only man to survive. He tried to get the men out from beneath the slate and coal, but it was no use. Seeing all the dead bodies lying around him, his mind seemed to snap. Lost, he ran through the dark tunnels, looking for anyone

Then he saw a white glow about 20 yards in front of him and, thinking it was the light from a miner's cap, ran toward it. When he reached the object, he stopped suddenly as if he had seen a ghost. Lying on the tunnel floor was a human hand! By the gold-braided ring on the third finger, he knew that the hand belonged to him. The index finger was pointing toward the south and Jim followed it.

When Jim found the crew working in Six Butt, he told them about the cave-in and about the hand, his hand, that had led him to safety. They all laughed, and he searched the whole area and couldn't find the hand. But he knew that the pointing finger had saved his life.

REVENGE OF THE SIRENS

Miners who traced their ancestry to Cornwall, England, used to tell a story of how the coal mines came to be—and why women were taboo in mines. This is how it went:

Long ago, when the earth was young and coal had not yet been formed out of the lush green vegetation, there lived a race of beautiful women who lured men into their hideouts and bewitched them so that they forgot homes and loved ones. To punish them the gods blasted their forest homes, changing the stately trees into black rocks that were covered by earth. Into these carbonized rocks the spirits of the sirens were driven for an imprisonment that would last for centuries. After serving their long penance, these sirens came out to wreak vengeance upon mankind. Thus, whenever an explosion occurred in the mines, it was a sign that more sirens were escaping from the wall of coal, accompanied by the poisonous gases that carried death to every miner in their path.

THE BRAVE DRIVER BOY

When tragedy struck the West Pittston mine in 1871, 20 lives were consigned to eternity. One of them was a 12-year-old boy named Martin Crehan, whose job it was to drive a mule carrying out the loads of coal. Martin was near the elevator when

A mine inspector flattens himself uneasily against a dank, dripping wall as a carload of coal comes rolling through a tunnel.

the fire began, and the engineer ordered him aboard instantly. But Martin, thinking of the men still working below, turned to warn them. Meanwhile the trapped men had realized their plight and were working feverishly to try to seal themselves off from gases. Hastily they trimmed large lumps of coal and fitted them together in a solid wall, closing holes and cracks with dirt.

Arriving at the wall, Martin saw that his duty was done and he retraced his steps to the shaft in hope of finding the elevator still in service. But the machinery had already been destroyed by the fire. Approaching the barricade once again, he heard a medley of ghostlike voices coming from behind it. Some of the men were moaning; others were singing hymns or praying for deliverance. He begged for admittance, but faltering voices answered that to open the wall would mean sudden death inside. Again and again he pleaded, but to no avail.

Finally, rebuffed by his fellow humans, he groped his way to the mine stable, found his mule in the accustomed place, and lay down beside it. Rescuers found the brave, self-sacrificing little driver boy, his clothes torn, his face twisted from the intense agony he must have suffered, lying close to his mule. Like good pals, the brave driver boy and his mule had died together.

I. D. Hoffman painted this version of an all-too-frequent mining occurrence. Fellow workers remove the bodies of miners felled in an accident that occurred in the shaft.

LUMBERJACKS
Men Who Tamed the Forests

The lumberjack's year began in the remote forests of winter, cutting down trees and hauling them to logging roads, and it ended in spring when the logs went on wild, white-water sprees down swollen rivers to the sawmills. Though the names of the loggers' heroes changed, depending on whether a woodsman worked in Maine or Minnesota or Oregon, the virtues they celebrated were the same: strength, ingenuity, humor, independence, and resistance to physical discomfort.

PAUL BUNYAN

Undoubtedly the best-known American logging figure is Paul Bunyan, in large part a 20th-century advertising-age creation. He was first described in print in 1910 when James McGillivray, a newspaper man and former logger, set down a few of the tales he remembered from his youth. But the bigger-than-life-size Bunyan really came into his own beginning in 1922 when another former woodsman, an advertising copywriter named W. B. Laughead, used Bunyan as the vehicle for promoting the products of the Red River Lumber Company. Thenceforth the tales grew in number and in fantasticality. A sampling of Bunyan lore follows:

Paul Bunyan was born in Maine. When he was three weeks old he rolled around so much in his sleep that he destroyed four square miles of standing timber. Then they built a floating cradle for him and anchored it off Eastport. When Paul rocked in his cradle it caused a 75-foot tide in the Bay of Fundy, and several villages were washed away. He couldn't be wakened, however, until the British Navy was called out and fired broadsides for seven hours. When Paul stepped out of his cradle, he sank seven warships. Understandably, he decided the East was too small for him and he moved on.

Next thing anyone knew, Paul was ranging all over Minnesota and Wisconsin. By this time he had Babe, his great Blue Ox, seven ax handles wide between the eyes and strong enough to pull anything with two ends on it. Babe could haul 640 acres worth of logs to a landing at one time, and if

A woodsman, wearing snowshoes to keep from sinking into the snow, fells a tree, in this engraving after Winslow Homer.

the road between was crooked, why Paul would hitch Babe up to pull the kinks out.

They could never keep Babe more than one night at a camp, for he would eat in one day all the feed one crew could tote in in a year. Babe was a great pet and very gentle, but he had a troublesome sense of humor. He would sneak up behind a drive and drink all the water out of the river, leaving the logs high and dry. It was impossible to build an ox sling big enough to hoist Babe for shoeing, but after they logged off Dakota, there was room for Babe to lie down for the operation.

One time when Paul was driving a bunch of logs down the Wisconsin River and they got jammed into a pile 200 feet high, Paul brought up

Babe to get things going again. He told the other fellows to stand back, and then he put Babe foursquare in the river in front of the jam. Paul got up on a bank and started shooting the ox with a rifle. Babe thought it was flies and commenced switching his tail. Pretty soon the river began to flow backward and so did the jam.

Paul's crew numbered seven axmen and the little chore boy, and those fellows could eat. Pancakes and biscuits were their style. Big Joe was the only man who could turn out pancakes fast enough to keep up with the crew, and he used a griddle that was so big you couldn't see across it when the steam was thick. He kept it greased by boys who skated over the surface with hams strapped to their feet. His biscuits were something special, too. Every time he dropped one, it made an earthquake somewhere on the other side of the world.

GEORGE KNOX

George Knox was a Maine logger who didn't admire working, so he sold his soul to the Devil for 20 years. During those years there wasn't anything that he couldn't do, though most of his amazing feats were performed when nobody was looking. Somebody would say something needed moving or clearing or something, and he'd just say all right. But they'd have to go away. Come back the next day, he'd say, and it would be done. And it was. Like the time the boss of George's lumber camp was complaining out loud that he needed a road cut through the woods to carry out some logs, but it was going to take a long time and lots of money. George asked him how much and when the boss told him, George said, "Would you be willing to pay me that money if I put that road down in a couple of days?" The boss laughed, knowing that it was impos-

Maybe Paul Bunyan was a real woodsman of unusual capabilities who lived in the 19th century; through the enterprise of popular writers he has become a widely loved, if now mostly manufactured, hero

sible, and said "Sure."

Sunday morning, George got up and ate a good breakfast and struck out. He put the road down across that run the way it would take a dozen men three or four days to do. Monday the boss went out and he couldn't believe his eyes. Not only were all the trees down out of the road but they were trimmed and ready for the mill. And all the rocks were gone and the way was as smooth as could be.

Some say George could just look at something and it would get out of his way. But he could carry something if he wanted—like the new cookstove he hauled into camp one time. Now two men couldn't move that stove across a room, but one time George, just as a favor to the cook, went into town without a horse or wagon or anything, and he put that stove on his back and had it in the cookhouse and in business by nightfall.

George always had money when he needed it, too. Somehow it would just appear, as under his dinner plate when he went into a restaurant. When he wanted a drink, he would take a jug up to a tree, peel back

In the bunkhouse some men amuse themselves with music and dancing while others dry socks and repair their gear.

To break up a logjam, a courageous logger clambers down onto the unsteady pile and prepares to pry it apart with his ax.

some bark, and pretty as could be, that jug would fill with whisky.

He could throw his voice, which made people real uneasy, and there wasn't an animal he couldn't imitate. One cold fall George Knox and a new man were going into a logging camp to work. The new fellow didn't know George and his tricks. There were some wolves around in those days and the new man was busy boasting what he would do if any of those varmints showed up. Pretty soon a wolf started howling, and before you knew it the woods sounded like it was alive with them. This boastful fellow was pretty scared now, and George says to him to climb up this tree. That guy didn't waste time arguing, and while he was headed for the top George took off for camp and told the boss, "Last time I seen the new man, he was up a tree, picking beechnuts." They went back and that fellow was still up there, near froze to death, and there wan't no wolves.

THE GORBY

It happened on the Tobique River in northern New Brunswick. The bird was called a gorby [a Canada jay]. An old woodsman wouldn't hurt one. Sometimes others would play tricks on them by tossing out a piece of hot bun toasted over the fire and the first bird that got it got a hot beak and then would fly up in a tree and scold, and it sounded as if they were saying, "Jesus, Jesus." One man, thinking he was doing something smart, held one and picked all the feathers off but the wing feathers and tail feathers and tossed it into the air and said, "Now fly to your Jesus bare-assed." The others predicted something drastic would happen to him, and the next morning when he lifted up his head all his hair remained on his pillow. He left the crew soon after.

OLA VARMLANNING

Ola was a big, strong, yellow-haired Swede with an aversion to work and a talent for getting into trouble. He left his folks back in the Old Country and came to Minnesota when he was a very young man. He never could seem to make enough money as a woodsman to support his fondness for St. Paul saloons, so most of his daydreaming hours were given over to thinking up schemes for getting rich quick.

One time he wrote his well-to-do father that he needed capital to run his sawmill. His father, who had never seen Ola do a day's work, was impressed with his son's new-found industry and success and he sent a younger son to America to deliver the money personally. When the younger man showed up in St. Paul, much to Ola's surprise, he demanded to see the new business. Ola conducted him to the backyard of his cabin and, pointing to a sawbuck, said, "There! This is my sawmill!"

Another time, Ola struck up an acquaintance with a pair of newcomers in a St. Paul saloon. When they asked about lodgings, Ola graciously offered to house them, assuring them that he had "ample room." They accepted eagerly, and to show their appreciation they wined and dined Ola handsomely before setting out for their night's rest. Finally, when Ola was sated, he led them to the outskirts of town where he showed them his shelter under a bridge. "Here is where I live," he said wryly. "As I said, there is ample room!"

OLD GUS BAILEY

Old Gus Bailey of Loos, Maine, was one of your big men, and powerful. Not only was he big, but he was as quick as a cat, afraid of absolutely nothing, impervious to heat or cold. On one occasion Gus went into town on a spree. Toward morning he started back to camp about two-thirds drunk. It was spring and the ground was muddy, the traveling hard. Just at daybreak Gus' bleary eye spotted a bateau on the bank of the river, with someone sitting in it. Gus grabbed the boat and, without even looking at his companion, pushed off. When he did look up, it turned out to be a bear just out of hibernation looking for food. Gus snatched one paddle and handed the other to the startled creature with, "Here, you paddle bow!" This was too much for the bear, who leaped out leaving Gus to paddle alone.

Gus' disregard for temperature made him the best man on the river to break a logjam, work that often required a man to be submerged for considerable periods until he had located, and sawed off, the key log.

The spring floods on the Mississippi River bring out a pair of "pinery boys," the Wisconsin river rafters who guide huge convoys of logs downriver to places like St. Louis.

Bailey, it was said, would strip down, dive in, and stay submerged for periods of half an hour before rising for a small breath of air.

One time he got into trouble showing off his hardihood, though. He was working in a camp where the wages were low. News had it that the boss was coming in with a visitor to look over the camp. Gus decided that if he made it look as if the loggers were being poorly cared for, the wages would be increased. To this purpose, he hit on a plan.

On the big day Gus took his station beside the road leading into camp. It was about zero degrees out, but as soon as he heard the jingle of harness he stripped off all his clothes, save snowshoes and hat, grabbed his ax, ran out into the road, and began whacking away at a tree to beat hell.

Around the bend came the owner and drew rein at the appalling sight. Gus turned round and was dumbfounded to find that the visitor was the boss's daughter. Gus dropped everything and started running for camp. He went so fast he beat the horse and sleigh; he hid under one of the bunks till it all blew over.

Learning that he was deathly ill, he got two friends to lace on his driving boots—the badge of a riverman—and to support his wornout frame, walking him up and down the room until he died, just so it could always be said, "Gus Bailey died like he said he would, standin' up an' with his boots on."

🐈 SUPERSTITIONS

Skillful Pastimes

A visitor to an early-20th-century camp described the lumberjacks sitting round the box stove in their barrack-like shanty enjoying a "free-for-all"—playing checkers, poker or cooncan, reading, writing letters, and conversing. He discovered from the talk that a good woodsman was proud of his prowess. He kept his ax sharp enough to shave with and felled his timber with such precision that it would drive a tent pin into the ground. He was good on a river too. He could roll a log with his feet, ride it through rapids, and cleave logjams. Less skilled choppers often caused accidents. Sideswiping branches (called

widder-makers) from an ill-felled tree too often injured crewmen; it was an axiom of the industry that the woods took a Swede a day. The most terrifying accident of all was getting rolled into the boiling maelstrom of river and racing logs when a logjam was broken. Only sharp reflexes and instant decisions kept a man from death. Such a decision earned Cruel Jimmy Holmes his name. Seeing a friend caught in a logjam, he chopped off his leg and saved his life. Many logging tales grew out of incidents like that. They told of headless men, mangled bodies, and crushed skulls being fished up—and of others not found, whose ghosts were to haunt the river where they had disappeared for long after.

RAILROADERS
Men of the Iron Horse

America, which had no railroads in the 1820's, was able to boast of 193,000 miles of track and hundreds of lines by 1900. The fast growth, the feverish competition, the primitive state of rolling stock and of locomotive engineering, and trains crossing through unsettled territory all created situations ripe for heroes and adventures, for wrecks and rescues, as the colorful lore of railroading records.

THE HINCKLEY FIRE

On September 1, 1894, a smoldering forest fire in Minnesota became a raging holocaust that consumed the small town of Hinckley and other towns. Most of the people who escaped owed their lives to the brave railroad men. Some highlights:

Seeing the danger, the engineers of two trains hooked up as many cars as they could to each train and urged townspeople aboard. It took nerve to stand still with flames leaping toward and around them on the wings of a tornado. After waiting until men and animals were falling in the streets from the heat, Engineer Best loosed his airbrakes, and the train moved out. The heat had become so intense that the very rails were beginning to warp and twist out of shape.

When the engineers knew, by their knowledge of the road, that a bridge was close by, Best would put on his brakes and slow down until they were certain the bridge was still there, when they would pass on. Two brakemen rode on the back end of the other engineer's [Barry's] tender and, as they reached a bridge, would signal Barry if it was all right. Nineteen bridges in 14 miles of road over which they passed were totally destroyed, and they were all burning more or less furiously when the train passed over them; the crew was unflinching through all that long and perilous ride.

When Sandstone was reached, the train halted and people were begged to get aboard and fly for their lives. Some grasped the opportunity, but more did not, laboring under the impression that although Hinckley had burned, Sandstone was safe, a notion they had cause to regret an hour later. On reaching Kettle River, just out of Sandstone, the bridge was burning and the train slowed up, when a cry from the watchman, "For God's sake, go on, you can cross it now, and it will go down in five minutes," made Barry draw a quick breath and with set teeth throw his throttle wide open and run out on the bridge. They crossed in safety as by a miracle, and five minutes later the bridge fell.

The southbound Limited on the St. Paul and Duluth road left Duluth at 2 o'clock on the afternoon of that eventful Saturday. That train was in

The classic railroad hero was Casey Jones, who died in a collision in 1900. Though his own negligence may have caused the crash, he is admired for making his engineer jump while he stayed on the train in a valorous attempt to save it as it plowed toward inevitable destruction. Thomas Hart Benton's "The Engineer's Dream" recalls the hold Casey's tragedy had on fellow trainmen.

the charge of Engineer James Root and Fireman Jack McGowan. A number of fleeing citizens flagged the train and in a few words told the crew their story. They boarded the train, a gasping, half-crazed concourse. The fire was coming with the speed of a locomotive, backed by that horrible wind. Engineer Root thought of a little marsh lake known as Skunk Lake, near the track about four miles from where they had met the refugees; this he determined to reach.

On came the flames, and he saw that they were gaining on him—gaining until they burst over him in a hurricane blast! Flame and smoke were everywhere. One man lost his reason, literally went mad, and with a shriek threw himself through one of the windows and was swallowed up in the seething mass. Another and another followed him, and were destroyed by the insatiable flames.

While these scenes were being enacted in the coaches, Engineer Root was suffering terrible agony. His hands were blistered as he held the lever; his clothes were afire, as were those of Fireman McGowan. Jack leaped into the manhole of the tank and put out the fire in his own clothes, then grasping a pail, continually soused Jim with the water from the tank. Root was twice overcome and fell from his seat, and twice was bolstered up by the faithful Jack. Minutes they were, but they seemed like hours before Skunk Lake was reached; the engineer brought the train to a standstill, and the fireman pointed out to the passengers the direction of the lake.

The train had on board from 135 to 150 regular passengers and took aboard from 150 to 200 refugees from Hinckley. Certain it is that more than 300 people owed their lives to that lake, whence they were later rescued.

JOE BALDWIN'S GHOST
Back in 1867 when Joe Baldwin was a conductor, one of the regular jobs was coupling and uncoupling cars at railroad junctions. Baldwin lost his life one night doing just that at Maco, North Carolina. His train had come

The flamboyant, heroic engineer was eulogized in a ballad by a black coworker. This Tin Pan Alley version of that song caught the public's imagination.

uncoupled and he went down on the tracks, carrying a lantern, to fix it. He was somehow decapitated. From that time on witnesses reported seeing a mysterious light in the vicinity on some dark nights. The popular explanation was that conductor Baldwin was taking nocturnal walks in search of his head. In 1873 a second light appeared and each shining with the brightness of a 25-watt light bulb. People speculated Joe's head was in search of his body.

The ghost light story gained credence enough to cause a Washington, D.C., investigator to visit Maco. He wasn't satisfied that there was any practical explanation but he did say it wasn't any jack-o'-lantern. A detachment from Fort Bragg encamped at Maco to see if they could solve the

mystery, but to no success.

Unbelievers have all sorts of ways to explain Joe Baldwin's ghost—weather, seasons, automobile headlights—but once they try them they are as mystified as the townspeople.

KATE SHELLEY
Late in the afternoon of July 6, 1881, a storm came thundering into the Des Moines Valley. As it rained on into the night the river began to rise. Fifteen-year-old Kate Shelley and her widowed mother watched fearfully, thankful that they had shelter. Then about 11 p.m. they heard a sickening crash, and they knew that it was No. 11, the Chicago and Northwestern "pusher" engine, going down with the bridge over Honey Creek. Kate, a railroadman's daughter, realized that

"The Ghosts of Engines," by Theodore Lux Feininger, shows an array of locomotives (floating at improbable angles) presumably representing trains which met violent ends.

she must do something immediately. The passenger train from the west was due through at midnight, and unless someone got a message through, it too would plunge into the river. She had to get to Moingona, a town about a mile and a quarter away across the raging Des Moines River.

With nothing but her thin summer dress to keep her warm and a tiny miner's lamp for light, she set out, running through the mud and water and debris. She was forced to crawl across the shaky remains of the bridge from tie to tie, across rusty iron spikes, with the possibility of falling through ever imminent.

Cut all over and dizzy with fear, she managed to reach the other shore. Now she had just a quarter mile to go. Her strength was fading, but make it she did. The stationmaster, seeing this bruised and bleeding apparition come into the station, thought for a moment the babbling child was crazy. But she quickly told him about the Honey Creek Bridge and No. 11, and he ran out onto the tracks just in time to stop the midnight express coming around the bend. Kate then led a rescue party back to Honey Creek where they found two of No. 11's crew still alive, clinging to branches. Exhausted, Kate could finally go home, where she was put to bed for three months before her natural vitality returned. Kate became a heroine to all railroaders and one of Iowa's honored citizens.

BOXED BANDITS

During the 1870's crooks conceived the device of having themselves shipped aboard trains in coffins as corpses, with the idea of attacking the messenger en route. One who tried this in Wisconsin in 1886 quickly aroused the suspicion of the messenger, who piled several hundred pounds of freight on and around the box. At the next stopping place it was taken out and placed on the station platform. "Is there a man in that box?" asked the express agent. "If so, he'd better speak. I'm going to fire through it." At that the corpse admitted, "I'm in here; don't shoot." The side of the box dropped and a sheepish-looking crook rolled out, to receive a three-year prison term.

FACT ? MYTH

John Henry

Like that of many American heroes, John Henry's story is woven of fact and fancy so intertwined that only some of the strands can be separated:

People told how on the night John Henry was born forked lightning cleaved the air and the earth trembled; the Mississippi River ran upstream 1,000 miles. He weighed 44 pounds. "He got a bass voice like a preacher," his mama said. "He got shoulders like a cotton-rollin' rousterabout," his papa said. "He got blue gums like a conjure man," the midwife said. After he finished his first meal he walked out in search of work. He found his way to the C. & O. Railroad where they were laying tracks and driving tunnels.

'Long about 1870, steam drills were invented. The company working at the far end of the Big Bend Tunnel tried them out, but John Henry's company going through from the other end continued to rely on men. There was much boasting by each gang and the foreman decided to stage a contest to settle the matter. A prize of $100 was put up and John Henry was matched against the best man with a steam drill.

John Henry had his foreman buy him two new 20-pound hammers for the race. When the contest was over, John Henry had drilled two holes seven feet deep. The steam driller had drilled one hole nine feet deep, which of course gave the prize to John. But John Henry died during the night following the contest from a burst blood vessel. An era had ended.

After that some local folk reported seeing John Henry's ghost hammering away in the mountains. As late as 1883 the railroad company found it difficult to recruit men to work in the area, and work stoppages actually occurred when men thought they heard his hammer ringing on steel.

Moonshiners

Moonshining has been a way of life for many rural southerners ever since the 1700's when Scotch-Irish settlers transplanted it to Appalachian America. Since World War II most moonshining has fallen into the hands of big-time operators, but to those traditional mountain folk who still operate their own stills it is a way of life and a respectable business. For them the excise tax imposed on liquor and the Alcohol Tax Unit men (revenuers) who enforce the taxation are interfering with personal liberty and property.

The first requirement for an illicit still is a good stream of cold water, preferably a spring. The second need is seclusion. Often a deep hollow is chosen, both for the water and for the surrounding trees. Stills can also be located on bluffs over rivers, the necessary water being pumped up from the stream below. Another favorite location is in cellars or, especially in bluegrass country, caves. The commonest name for the stuff made in the camouflaged stills is "white lightnin'" —sold in quart-size fruit jars. "Fresh bourbon" best describes what raw corn whisky is, and mountain folk swear by it as a snakebite remedy to this day.

From early times local enforcement was at best sporadic. Lawmen could not be expected to arrest relatives and friends for an activity most of the community approved of, despite the law. Many sheriffs even warned moonshiners ("I hear you've been farming in the woods") before moving against them.

Although the pitched battle between lawmen and distillers celebrated in legend involved mainly federal enforcers, most of it was (and is) in fact a battle of wits and not of bullets. For all their gunslinging, there is more bark than bite to the moonshiners; because of this, their adversaries, the revenuers, have been traditionally inclined to take things by their smooth handle rather than to go charging in like "gangbusters."

One such revenuer was the legendary Big Six Henderson who, people said, knew the mountains like a bobcat, could walk like a shadow, run like a tornado, and think like a moonshiner. With one family of highly successful moonshiners who had thitherto gotten away scot-free, he played a cat-and-mouse game for a whole season after they suspected he was on to them; he made minor arrests all round the apprehensive Willets without ever coming directly at them, and the game went on until their last batch before closing down for the winter.

The Willets just about held their breath through that run, but the last night passed without incident. As daybreak arrived at their lonely hideout they finished running off some of the smoothest, clearest mountain dynamite ever squeezed out of a cornpatch. "Wouldn't Big Six like to get a look at *this*?" one of the men exclaimed. The youngest waved a jug in the air and called gleefully, "Hey, Big Six! Where are you now?" Behind a fallen log the leaves parted and a big man rose up to face them, gun in hand. In his soft Kentucky drawl he answered affably, "Why, I'm right hyar."

Such exploits won the admiration, respect, and even friendship of many violators, just as the occasional sheriff who vigorously enforced the law aroused their hatred.

One famous seller of the stuff couldn't be run in by either local or federal officials: Mahala "Big Haley" Mullins who lived on Newman's Ridge on the Virginia-Tennessee line. A Melungeon (of a group of Appalachian folk of mixed blood claiming descent from Raleigh's vanished Roanoke settlers and Croatan Indians), Big

These revenuers have won the continual cat-and-mouse game with moonshiners.

Haley had grown so fat she never left her house. All day long she sat at a doorway and sold whisky. When Virginia lawmen approached the scene of violation she simply waddled over to the Tennessee side of the cabin. If Tennessee authorities showed up, she moved over to the Virginia side. Since Mahala weighed between 600 and 700 pounds, she couldn't have been taken to court even if she had been arrested. When she died the cabin had to be demolished to remove her body, and the huge homemade bed on which she slept became a makeshift coffin.

Much of the outsider's overdrawn picture of moonshiners and revenuers shootin' it out in endless repetition was originally furnished by the popular press but has been touched up by the mountain folks' own stories. One old hillbilly joke tells about a dialogue that ensued when a federal man offered a moonshiner's small son a dollar to show him Pappy's still. "Gimme the dollar," said the boy. "I'll give it to you when I get back." "Mister," said the boy, "you ain't comin' back."

Other legends are "for the trade only." For instance, there is a fanciful story that hogs love the corn mash that whisky is made of. Often moonshiners were forced to put fences around their stills to keep hogs, who were kept on "open range," from falling into the mash boxes. Once a 200-pound sow fell into a mash box, where she drowned. The men running the still found her body there several days later but went on and made whisky from the same mash anyhow. From then on it was said of strong whisky, "That must'a had a dead hog in it."

Pink Bishop tends his still, in this drawing from an 1890 issue of Century.

"TIME TO ORGANIZE"
Molly Maguires

Typically, a union shop was bought at the price of a long, bloody fight. For many it was worth it: "The difference was like jumping out of the fire into a cool stream of water." In the mining districts of Pennsylvania and West Virginia the fight was on even before the unions came, pitting mine operators against Molly Maguires, a secret society of Irish miners about which little is known—there was much antimanagement violence and they were said to be behind it. Suppressed a century ago, the Mollies live on in legend to this day. Some tales from that era:

A CURSE ON THEIR HEADS

Young Father McDermott had not been long in his new parish of Centralia, Pennsylvania, when a parishioner—a middle-aged woman—came to his door in tears.

"Oh, Father," she explained, "help me get me lad back." "Come, tell me, what's up with Patrick?" "It's the Mollies. Last night they got him into a shebeen, filled him with poteen, and while he lay drunk on the floor they gave him the oath of the Molly Maguires—it's a murtherer they're after wantin' to make o' me flesh and blood!" "Bring Patrick here," the priest ordered. And an hour later, as the frightened boy stood before him,

Father McDermott wrung from him the details of a Molly initiation and the names of the men responsible.

The next Sunday Father McDermott thundered his challenge to the secret order. "The Church never yields to the forces of evil," he declared. "I am here to see that it shall not in this crisis. Next Sunday you will hear from my lips the names of the cowards who are trying to tear boys from their mothers and God in order to administer to them the oath of a foul and wicked society."

In the week that followed, Mollies tried desperately to deter Father McDermott from carrying out his plan. Disguised voices shouted warnings through his window at night. "Coffin notices" were slid under his door. He prayed continually for strength to withstand the ordeal.

The next Sunday the little church was filled to capacity. The air was tense. At the conclusion of the Mass, Father McDermott changed his vestments for a solemn black stole. He began by recalling the Mollies' local acts of violence and his repeated warnings to them. "They have not heeded my words," he exclaimed. "Now they shall have action."

Thereupon he called out the names of two men, demanding to know if they were not members of the Molly Maguires. "No," they both replied. "Do you declare before God and man in this sacred house of worship that you are not guilty of enticing boys with drink and forcing the Molly oath on them?" he roared. Again they denied their guilt. Father McDermott then quenched the altar candles and pronounced a curse upon their heads. "If you are innocent, as you swear you are," the priest said in a trembling voice, "this curse will turn into a blessing. But if you are guilty, may God have mercy on your souls."

One of the men soon after was crushed to death in the mines; the other murdered a man in a saloon brawl and served a long term in the penitentiary.

HANDPRINT IN CELL 17

One of the most persistent legends in labor folklore originated in 1876. Alexander Campbell was a liquor dealer in Storm Hill; he was prosecuted as a Molly Maguire who hired two men to kill John P. Jones, a mine boss. His accuser, an undercover Pinkerton man who had become a trusted friend of the Mollies, during the trials provided testimony sufficient to hang 10 men, and hang they did the following year on "Black Thursday," June 21, 1877. On the fatal morning Campbell rose at dawn and said the rosary. As the sheriff approached, he declared: "I swear I am innocent. I was nowhere near the scene of the murder." Then he struck

"Demonstration," by Joe Jones, evokes hundreds of militant episodes in U.S. labor history when organized workers have taken to the street to voice grievances and demands.

the prison wall with his hand, shouting: "There is the proof of my words. That mark of mine will never be wiped out. There it will remain forever to shame the county that is hanging an innocent man."

(Years later an elderly miner's widow recalled: "When the hour of the hangings arrived for them poor Irish lads, the world suddenly became dark and we had to burn our lamps. It's Black Thursday it was . . .")

Campbell's prophecy was not completely fulfilled, however, for instead of shaming Carbon County, the handprint attracted tremendous tourist trade, although the prison has done nothing to publicize it. In 1977 Warden Joseph M. Scott wrote of his own attempt to expunge the mark: "As a former policeman I was highly skeptical of the handprint's authenticity until one day I tried very unsuccessfully to remove it myself by solvents and a large eraser and found myself quite shaken by its uncanny ability to remain a mystery which defies desecration in any fashion. I was also informed that scrapings from the handprint were carbon-dated and found to be in the neighborhood of 100 years old. So who's to say whether it's for real or not?"

STAMP OF VIOLENCE

The age-old belief that a pregnant woman's actions mark the baby is at the heart of a West Virginia miner family's memory of labor-management violence and gives their story a gruesome twist:

The operators was bringing in transportations of scabs to work these mines here, so our men would starve. When another load came in, the grapevine started, and it traveled fast, and by the time that train got up to Eskdale, my Aunt Nellie stormed up to this company man and asked him whether he was the damned bastard that was wrecking the strike and starving all those poor children. "Lady," he yells back, "it's none of your God-damned business what I'm doing." Then her husband, my uncle, came up and knocked him down.

They'd just been married a little

About to be executed for murder, Wobbly hero and labor's songwriter Joe Hill said, "Don't waste time mourning—organize!"

❦ WORD LORE ❦

"I Wobbly Wobbly"

Everyone called members of the powerful Industrial Workers of the World "Wobblies." The word reportedly originated with a Chinese chuckwagon operator. Many of his customers had IWW leanings, so he got a red card and claimed that he too was for the IWW. But he had trouble saying *w* and it came out: "Me likee I Wobbly Wobbly."

while, 10 months or so. Well, the two of them got on top of this bastard. Nellie wore those real high old-timey boots, all laced up the ankle, you know. Well, she stomped him in the face with her high heels and tore his ears loose and knocked his teeth out, and by the time the mine guards got over there, she had just about killed him. She was just a little thing, and pretty, with curly red hair, but she could fight and cuss good enough to be a man. They took her and threw her in the bullpen. There were some 20 women in one room. When the time approached for her to have her baby, she could barely stand up.

Well, her mother went to see the governor. He wouldn't see her, so she stormed in right past the secretary and yelled, "This strike will be over someday, and you will pay for it!" And he got scared and ordered Nellie taken to the hospital. Well, the boy was born a total cripple. He lived 59 years but never did walk. His ears were loose and his teeth deformed. Every time Nellie looked at that baby, she saw that man she had stomped down at the depot. He was very intelligent but he never could walk. The state paid her off $500.

Strikes often erupted into violence, as in this scene when strikers dragged nonstriking firemen and engineers from a freight train at Martinsburg, West Virginia, in July 1877.

THE INVENTORS
Wizards of the Modern Age

The sudden technological advances that reshaped the face of the earth between 1880 and 1920—electric power, telephones, phonographs, radios, cars, and airplanes—were not, as in our time, the work of giant government-supported projects. In our great-grandparents' day a single man with a vision had the power to change the world; Bell, Edison, Ford, and the Wrights were such men. The public loved their style, saluted them as "wizards," and viewed their achievements as evidence that miracles were still possible—even in this modern world.

PROFESSOR BELL

"It is the wonder of wonders!" exclaimed Lord Kelvin when he had tested the Alexander Graham Bell Electrical Speaking Telephone on display at the Philadelphia Centennial Exhibition of 1876. It had been only a year since Bell's first successful transmission over a telephone device. To popularize the invention, Bell and his assistant Thomas A. Watson hit the lecture circuit and were a roaring success. Watson recalled:

"Professor Bell would have one telephone by his side on the stage, where he was speaking, and three or four others suspended about the hall, connected by a hired telegraph wire with the place where I was stationed, 5 to 25 miles away. Bell would explain, then came the thrillers of the evening—my shouts and songs: 'How do you do!' 'What do you think of the telephone?' Then I would sing, 'Hold the Fort,' 'Pull for the Shore,' and 'Yankee Doodle.' My sole sentimental song was 'Do Not Trust Him, Gentle Lady.' This repertoire always brought down the house." Some 50 years later, in 1922, when Bell was buried, phone service in the U.S. was interrupted for one minute.

WIZARD OF MENLO PARK

While Bell projected a "professor" image, Thomas Edison personified the exact opposite and became the press's favorite "wizard." In contrast with the effete snobs and dithering pedants hitherto associated with science in the popular mind, Edison represented virtues such as practicality, know-how, and the mystique of hard work conquering nature. He was in fact a Horatio Alger hero type with a lingering touch of the old frontier fever.

Edison's favorite invention was the phonograph, coming a year after Bell's telephone. Edison recalled:

"I was singing into the mouthpiece of a telephone when the vibrations of my voice caused a fine steel point to pierce one of my fingers held just behind it. That set me to thinking. If I could record the motions of the point and send it over the same surface afterward, I saw no reason why the thing would not talk. That's the whole story. The phonograph is the result of pricking a finger."

Of the new device, he said, "This is my baby, and I expect it to grow up

A crowd of 3,000 visited Edison's Menlo Park laboratory to see his newly perfected electric lights on New Year's Eve, 1880. A country boy supposedly pointed to an incandescent bulb and asked, "How you got the red-hot hairpin into that bottle?"

and be a big feller and support me in my old age." So it did, but not before he had spent a strenuous working life in the Menlo Park lab. (His assistants were dubbed the "insomnia squad.") Close to the grassroots, he developed each invention with a view to mass use: "We'll make electric light so cheap that only the rich will be able to burn candles." Edison's wife, Mina, asked him on his deathbed if he was suffering. "No," he said, "just waiting." And then, "It is very beautiful over there."

FORD: THE GRAND WIZARD

Cut of the same cloth as Edison was the Michigan farmboy Henry Ford, who after spending his teens fixing farm machinery in preference to regular chores, went on to become chief engineer at the Edison Company in Detroit. Public adulation of Thomas Edison was at its height when the young Ford obtained an interview with the great man and secured the latter's blessings for his visionary project, the perfection of the gasoline-powered automobile. Thereafter Ford idolized Edison—wrote a book on him, made a museum of Edison relics, and was even said to have kept Edison's dying breath in a bottle.

On October 1, 1908, Ford brought out his first Model T, "homely as a burro and useful as a pair of shoes," and reversed the previous public image of the motorcar as a rich man's toy. The secret that enabled Henry to bring his motorcar to the multitude was the now familiar principle of moving mass production. He perfected it after a visit to a Chicago meatpacking plant where he had seen countless carcasses slowly moving from one work station to the next on an overhead conveyor.

Soon a whole body of folklore grew up around Ford cars and the revolutionary way they were produced. Ford was shipping his cars in asbestos crates, folks said, because they came off the assembly line so fast they were still hot. The cars were all exactly alike, down to their color—black. "Any customer can have a car of any color he wants,"

As Clara Ford looks on, Henry Ford perfects the "quadricycle," as he called his first auto, which was to make its shakedown run in Detroit just before dawn on June 4, 1896.

Henry quipped, "provided it's black." Had you heard, ran another gag, that next year's Lizzies are going to be yellow so they can be sold in bunches like bananas? All this soon led to a complete revolution in American lifestyle. Nothing would ever be the same again. A British writer speculated that Americans would presently be spending their entire lives from womb to tomb in-

The lost original of the Victor "His Master's Voice" pictured the deceased master reposing in a coffin in the background!

side automobiles, and he wasn't far wrong. In one survey a majority of respondents indicated they'd sooner part with their bathtubs than with their Fords.

Ford lore might have remained Lizzie lore had not a stroke of genius in labor relations catapulted Henry to international fame in 1914 with his announcement of the Five-Dollar Day in Ford plants. Forthwith the man who was in fact one of the top technological revolutionaries of all time became a national folk hero—here was the fellow who put the nation on wheels, a poor boy who hit the jackpot in the land of equal opportunity, and now he was willing to share the wealth. Five dollars a day was twice the going wage in industry; and by making cars accessible to everyone, Ford was connecting with something very basic in the national

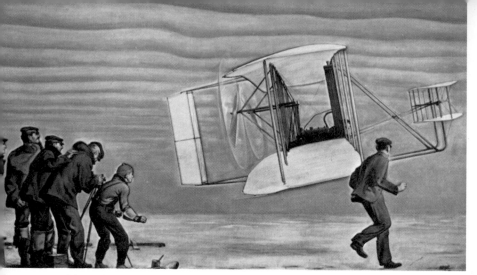

The Wright brothers' invention moved one man to write: "Imagine a locomotive that has left its track and is climbing up in the air—without wheels but with wings instead!"

character—Americans' craving for more and more personal freedom together with mastery over the limitations of space and time—a trait which, as historian William Greenleaf has written, "is inseparable from expansionism and the exuberance of the American frontier experience."

Ford was an eminently quotable hero for the American man on the street. When the popularity of Ford jokebooks was at its height, Ford had his own favorite: A man was digging a huge grave, big enough to hold a car. He explained he wanted his Ford buried with him. "It always got me out of every hole I got into, and I think I can count on it to get me out of this one."

The joke was in fact a humorous statement of Ford's most fundamental belief: "Machinery is the new Messiah." And this related to society very simply: "Just as accurate gauges and methods produce a smooth-working, efficient machine, so clear thinking, clean living, square dealing make an industrial or domestic life successful and smooth-running." Mr. and Mrs. John Doe never got much mileage out of such pronouncements—they remembered Henry's more memorable one-liners instead: "History is more or less bunk." "I wouldn't give five cents for all the art in the world." "Literature is all right but it doesn't mean much." "Cows, horses, and creeds will disappear

from the earth." "Well, I can't prove it, but I can smell it."

THE WRIGHTS

By 1900, after so many wonders in a single generation, the ultimate marvels—perpetual motion and heavier-than-air flight—were reckoned imminent. The famous astronomer and mathematician Simon Newcomb argued with unimpeachable logic that the business was impossible. In 1903 Samuel Pierpont Langley, of the Harvard Observatory and the Smithsonian Institution, tested his

dragonfly-shaped "aerodrome"; both times it crashed into the river. The chagrined savant was forced to give up.

However, nine days after Langley's aerodrome splashed for the second time, Wilbur and Orville Wright's Flyer flew over the beach at Kitty Hawk, North Carolina, hardly noticed by the press. One editor rejected an eyewitness account with this note: "Qualifies neither as fact nor as fiction." When the press and the public finally did catch up, it was only to create new legends. The Wrights were depicted as untutored mechanics who had prevailed Edison fashion where the effete Harvard man had lost out despite all his monographs on the subject bearing the prestigious Smithsonian imprint. (The opposite was true—it was Langley who had been weak on theory, and the Wrights who were the true sophisticates.) The Wrights themselves ignored the mythmaking. As to the popular misconception that they had learned their secret from observing birds, Orville said it was like learning the secret of magic from a magician: "After you know the trick and what to look for, you see things you didn't notice when you did not know exactly what to look for."

Alexander Graham Bell's legendary first words spoken into his prototype telephone on March 10, 1876, to an assistant one room away were "Mr. Watson, come here, I want you."

DEADLY BRIGHTNESS
Men and Steel

As America came to lead the world in steel production, Joe Magarac, a hero along Paul Bunyan lines, was manufactured by writer Owen Francis and launched upon the world in 1931. Magarac means "jackass, damned fool" in the Serbian tongue. In the story Joe says: "Dat's me. All I do is eatit and workit same lak jackass donkey." Such was the unpromising original of a figure who came to be described by folklorist B. A. Botkin as "the supreme symbol of industrial strength."

Joe Magarac, who was the hero of ex-steelworker Owen Francis' stories published in 1931, ended by melting himself down to provide better steel for a new mill.

JOE JACKASS

Joe Magarac was a man of solid steel who worked in a steel mill in Pennsylvania. He could outwork and outlift anyone in the mills. He lived at Mrs. Horkey's boardinghouse. Like all the other steelmen, Joe admired the lovely Mary Mestrovich, whose father offered her in marriage to the winner of a weight-lifting contest. The competitors were Joe's fellow workers Pete Pussick and Eli Stanoski, as well as a boastful stranger. When they all failed to lift the immovable dolly bar, Joe entered the lists and won. But Joe wasn't the marrying type, so he left Mary free to marry Pete Pussick, her true love. Joe ended his days by melting himself down in a Bessemer furnace to make good steel for a new mill.

OLD INTO NEW

The ending of the Joe Magarac story—fiery self-immolation—has a familiar ring. It echoes ancient tales of men who jumped, fell, or were thrown into volcanoes. From Mary Heaton Vorse's *Men and Steel* (1920):

On a greasy platform above the ladle the men who operate it look down with indifference into its seething deadly brightness. My guide said: "A man fell into that once, and they buried him and all the tons of metal. Right here they held the burial service." The story of the man who fell into the vat of molten metal and

became part of it obsesses the men's minds. I have heard it told in different ways. They tell you of a man made into iron rails, of another who went into the structure of great buildings. This story is as old as time. There was a great bell once which was cast and recast and would not ring true until a human being was sacrificed to it.

REAL STEEL LORE

In a few other respects Joe Magarac's creator managed to include a bit of real steel lore. For example, Joe's squeezing out rails and making cannonballs as you would make snowballs. A famous Swede at the turn of the century was credited with making horseshoes and pretzels out of bar stock with his bare hands. Then there

was Armstrong Joe who made neckties out of bars, and Mike Lesnovich who did the same.

Other authentic steel lore not present in the Magarac story was gathered by folklorist Hyman Richman: Beginners in the rolling mills are warned that the ends of hot bars often open like the jaws of an alligator. Then there are stories of men who could go unprotected into furnaces that had "cooled" to 400 degrees; who could lift several tons of steel. Unfortunately, very little else of the real McCoy has been recorded.

In Thomas Hart Benton's "Steel," workers are shown teeming the molten metal (left) and skimming flag off hot molten steel in a blast furnace operation at the right.

DAD'S STRUCK ILE!
Black Gold

From its start in 1859, when the ghost of a Seneca Indian guided the first oil prospector to strike it rich in Titusville, Pennsylvania, the oil industry made tales of buried treasure come true. A new folklore came into being with its stock characters—the oil-rich Indian, his tepee surrounded by new cars; the Coal-Oil-Johnny type who blew it all on one nonstop spree; the oil douser who with his black box, the doodlebug, located drilling sites. A legendary storyteller appeared, too, in the person of oil worker Gib Morgan. Here are some of his best tales:

GIB MORGAN'S FIGHT

Gib was a peaceful, law-abiding man who had only one fight in his life. He was working for a pipeline company bossing a gang of black ditch diggers along the Ohio River. They were all fine hands but one. This one wouldn't do his work right, and when Gib would jack him up, he would give him a lot of backtalk. Gib saw that he would have to curb him a little bit, so one day Gib corrected him with a pair of 48-inch pipe tongs. Well, in the flurry that followed, they both rolled into the river and sank to the bottom, where both drew their knives.

The only way spectators had of knowing how the battle was going was by watching for the pieces of flesh that came to the surface of the water. When there were more pieces of white-skinned flesh than black-skinned flesh coming up, the odds were in favor of the black man, and vice versa. They fought and they fought until finally their knives got so dull they wouldn't cut any more. They agreed to a truce so they could come up and grind their blades. When they did, they discovered they had been fighting for two weeks, and they were powerfully hungry. They went to a restaurant and each ordered a beefsteak four inches thick. When they had finished eating, they felt so good they called the fight off.

Prospectors had sayings: "Wherever lightning strikes you'll find oil." "There's always oil under a graveyard." "Drill on a hilltop." "Oil is where you find it."

GIB'S WONDERFUL SNAKE

One time an oil company sent Gib down to South America to dig a test well. They told him to go down 10,000 feet unless he hit oil before he got that far, and then to stop. So he had brought along only 10,000 feet of cable. When he got to the end of the cable, however, indications were mighty good, and he wanted to go down a little farther. His tool dresser said they would have to wait for more rope, but Gib didn't like the idea. He started walking around, and pretty soon he was out in the jungle. There he came upon a boa constrictor, 20 blocks long if he was one. Gib tried to win the monstrous snake's friendship with kindness. First he got a barrel of whisky and gave it to him. When the snake had swallowed it, he began to wag his tail so friendlylike that Gib felt a deep affection for him. He named him Strickie, and every three weeks he fed him 200 monkeys. Gib used his new friend to supply the needed extra length of cable—and Strickie made as good a cable as you ever saw, a lot better than this new steel equipment, with just enough give to make the tools handle easily. Each night, when Gib shut down and unwound Strickie from the bull shaft, he gave him a barrel of whisky before he put him to bed. It was not long until Strickie was the most valuable piece of equipment Gib had.

The well went along fine. Gib still hadn't found oil, but indications looked better and better every day.

Gib's only worry was that Strickie might not be long enough to reach the oil he knew was down there. Each day there would be a little more of Strickie in the well and a little less on the bull wheels. When he shut down one Saturday night there was just enough of Strickie left to wrap once around the shaft. Gib had got a showing of oil that day and he knew he was right on top of something big. Next morning all his worries were over. That very night Strickie shed his skin, and Gib had plenty of cable to finish the well. It was a gusher, but Gib closed it in and soon had it running into the storage. In no time at all it had filled the one 30,000-barrel storage tank. Gib shut it in and began laying a gathering line to the coast, where the big new tanker steamers that Standard had just put on could load. His pipe ran out when he was still about half a mile from the harbor, but by that time Strickie had shed again and his skin not only finished out the line but left enough over to reach up on deck and fill the compartments without all the bother of making pipe connections.

WHICKLES

In time Gib retired and took up residence in an old soldiers' home—where he entertained fellow pensioners with extravagantly amusing "lies." Once a year he allowed himself a "furlough" and went back to Pennsylvania. His annual homecomings became a triumphal progress through the oilmen's saloons, where he would hold forth as of yore. It was understood that when Gib drank, the drinks were on somebody else. If any newcomers were ignorant of this custom, Gib had a delicate way of informing them. He would tell them about *whickles.*

Whickles, it seems, were strange petroleum-eating bugs that were responsible for the declining production in the Pennsylvania fields—they were a cross between hornets and humming birds, with an insatiable thirst for oil. Gib was doing his best to exterminate them. His method was to sprinkle applejack on the bushes

Oil madness: one oil-mad citizen implored God to "send a shower of blessings—yea, Lord, 25 barrels of blessings!"

round the wells; the whickles would get drunk and Gib would knock them on the head. But applejack cost money, so Gib was always broke.

He'd had his flush times, too, Gib never failed to remind his barside listeners. In fact there had been a time, he claimed, when he'd had the

biggest pipeline crew on record, numbering high into the thousands. "Best-fed men you ever see."

The cooking arrangements were geared to meet the tremendous traditional appetites of pipeliners. The batter for pancakes was mixed mechanically in a 100-barrel tank. The boilerplate griddles were 50 feet square, fired by natural gas. They were greased by three active short-order cooks who strapped sides of bacon on their feet and skated hither and yon over the griddles. "These men had to be spelled right often, as the heat was pretty fierce," he would point out. The pancakes were turned with long-handled snow shovels and reached the table on conveyor belts. On the table were 10-barrel tanks, equipped with swivel-pipe arrangements that made it easy for the men to put syrup on their cakes.

"Did you make money on that pipeline?" someone was sure to ask. "Lost every cent of it," Gib would sadly admit. "Invested it in the polka-dot business, had a corner on polka dots. Made a barrel of money. Then one day a feller come along and invented a square polka dot. That put me out of business. Public fancy turned to the square polka dots. I had to go back to work, broken in health and pocket." He would pause, wipe a nonexistent tear from the buttermilk-blue eyes, bite off a healthy chew of tobacco, and stand there, the picture of abject misery.

ON THE WATER WAGON

Gib often "swore off"—as he said, an angel had appeared in a vision and converted him to abstinence; or his walls were crawling with cross-eyed bugs; or a little pink pig sometimes swam around in his liquor . . . As Gib was standing at a bar with a bottle and glass before him when he said these things, they were regarded as very, very funny.

"I don't have to marry you now—Dad's struck ile!" said a prospector's daughter to her luckless fiance. The saying became a catchphrase, and whenever a new well came in, the cry went up: "Dad's struck ile!"

THE WORKING GIRL
The Hazards of Leaving the Home

As the technological revolution widened, the liberation of women (which had only just begun) suffered a setback. Women were systematically barred from better occupations and channeled into the lowest paying, most menial jobs in factories, shops, schools, and offices. Slow to organize as trade unionists and denied the vote, they generally suffered in silence, though the literature that comes out of this painful chapter of America's past suggests that there were occasional firebrands like Bertha Bascomb and Rose to take their employers to task.

NO CHARITY

Bertha Bascomb was an honest working girl and she did her job with diligence. But the owner of the mill delighted in insulting her as he did all the sewing machine operators. One day, when he gave her her meager wages, he warned that it was more than she deserved and an act of simple charity on his part. Bertha could restrain her anger no longer:

"Charity? Contrast your ill-gotten gains with the miserable pittance paid those willing hands already grown feeble with work that fill your coffers, and then talk of charity. You do not know the meaning of that sacred word; not that we seek it at your hands. Poor and underpaid as many of your working girls are, they inherit some of the old spirit of independence that has made our country great. And while they demand fair returns for a fair day's work, they neither ask nor will they receive from you what you call charity!"

Good fortune eventually shone on the plucky Bertha and she went on to dedicate her life to helping her old friends at the shop.

WHITE SLAVERY

To the editor of the *Jewish Daily Forward,* New York City, from a reader: Please print my letter and give me an answer. You might possibly save my life.

I came to America three years ago from a small town in Lithuania when I was 20 years old. A cousin sent a steamship ticket and money and wrote that he would marry me. My delight knew no bounds, but when I came to him I found he was a sick man, and a few weeks later he died.

Then I began to work on ladies' waists in a sewing shop. I toiled, and like all shopgirls, I hoped and waited for deliverance through a good match. I met plenty of prospective bridegrooms, but though I was attractive and well built, no one grabbed me. Thus a year passed. Then I met a woman who told me she was a matchmaker and had many suitors "in stock." She told me that pretty girls could wallow in pleasure if they made the right friends. But I had not imagined what that meant.

The woman handed me over to bandits, and when I wanted to run away from them they locked me in a room without a window and beat me savagely. I lived this way for six months, degraded and dejected, until I got sick and they drove me out. I decided to throw myself into the river, but wandering about the streets, I met a richly dressed man who was quite drunk. I stole over $600 from him and spent the money on doctors.

Then I got a job as a maid for fine people who knew nothing about my past. Eventually the woman of the house died. In time her husband proposed that I marry him. The children also want me to be their "mother." I know it would be good for them. The man is honest and good, but my heart won't allow me to deceive him. What shall I do?

Miserable

ANSWER:

Such letters from victims of "white slavery" come to our attention quite often, but we do not publish them. We are disgusted by this plague on society, but as we read this letter we felt we dare not discard it, because it can serve as a warning for other girls. They must, in their dreary lives, withstand these temptations.

This letterwriter, who comes to us with her bitter and earnest tears, ask-

HULDA: YOU ARE ONLY A LOW SHOP GIRL!" **EVE:** "AN HONEST SHOP GIRL, AS FAR ABOVE A FASHIONABLE IDLER AS HEAVEN IS ABOVE EARTH

Poor but honest Eve delivers a strong retort to a "fashionable idler," in a poster advertising a 1901 play. Such social conflict was a popular theme in melodramas then.

ing advice, has sufficient reason to fear that if the man finds out about her past he will send her away. But "Honesty is the best policy." She should tell him the truth, and whatever will be, will be.

TEACHING BY THE RULES
Schoolteachers were expected to live up to saintly standards in private as well as public. About 1915, for example, Iva McDaniels, a schoolmarm for 15 years in one small Massachusetts community, came back after spending Thanksgiving with friends in a nearby town, to find that she had been fired for ignoring rules two and seven of those governing the conduct of female schoolteachers:

1. Do not get married.
2. Do not leave town at any time without school board permission.
3. Do not keep company with men.
4. Be home between the hours of 8 p.m. and 6 a.m.
5. Do not loiter downtown in ice cream stores.
6. Do not smoke.
7. Do not get into any carriage with any man except your father or brother.
8. Do not dress in bright colors.
9. Do not dye your hair.
10. Do not wear any dress more than two inches above the ankle.

TURNING THE TABLES
Where I got the incentive that day I don't know, but I was tired of being pushed around by my boss. I was typing like my heart would break. I was hankering for life. "Rose," I said to myself, "you can't figure on a lifetime." I got up from my desk, I opened the boss's door, and yelled: "Look, Mr. Sternberg, you can wait a hundred years and you'll never get a typist like me. Look at my hair, my white blouse, my nails. I never look unruly, I'm never idle a minute, and I got artistic ability besides. Next payday I want $12."

I wasn't even scared. You think he fired me? I'm telling you from that day he was so nice—like my office boy, he used to bring me up milk shakes. He was at my beck and call.

A shop boss, invariably described as ugly and coarse in stories from that era, threatens an exhausted-looking sewing machine operator with dismissal for working too slowly.

HERRING AND ONIONS
I was a machine hand in a fish-packing factory. Whenever the boss wanted us to work late without pay, he treated us to herring and onions. We girls grumbled as we bolted the bitter bribe. One night Sara Solomon flared up: "I got my feller waiting. All I need yet, he should pick himself up another girl!"

I said: "I got to go to night school. I'm going to be a stenographer." "So tell the boss to choke himself with his herring." "Sure I will!" I grabbed my shawl and stood up. "I don't care if the shop burns down. We sell him our days, but the nights are ours." The girls' faces froze. I felt the boss's hand on my neck. "Out you go! Out of my shop! I want no fresh-mouthed greenhorns! The minute they learn a word English, they get flies in their noses and wanna be ladies. I don't want no ladies here!"

A pretty "secretary" arrives at the office to find that the boss's wife has taken over her desk, her job—and his free time—in this comic vision of office life as it was in 1910.

UNTITLED ROYALTY
The Eccentric Millionaires

With no royal family to top the nation's social tree, Americans have always taken great interest in the life and times of the very rich. The fact that several members of this privileged fraternity began in modest circumstances and rose to success through extreme self-discipline and parsimony, as well as the fact that their children often rejected their parents' values and habits of industry for lives of princely extravagance, only added to the public's abiding curiosity—resulting in stories that were a mixture of admiration, envy, and righteous disapproval.

Yachting was fashionable. Here, members of the "happy few" relax aboard the steam yacht *Namouna,* at anchor off Venice, in this painting executed by Julius L. Stewart.

WITCH OF WALL STREET

Hetty Green was in her lifetime the richest woman in the world and in some ways the strangest. One of the landmarks of Wall Street in the age of J. P. Morgan and Jacob Schiff, she wore year in and year out the same voluminous dress, originally black but turning slightly brown and green with age. Sewn inside her petticoat were many pockets, each large enough to hold the contents of a safe-deposit box. She lived, most of the time, in furnished rooms. Each day she would travel by public bus or ferry to her Wall Street "office," which was the vault of the Chemical National Bank. Here she would sit on the floor, clipping coupons, reading the financial news, and receiving callers, among them some of Wall Street's most eminent figures. They came to pick her brains and, in moments of crisis, to ask for loans. Hetty, it seems, was always solvent.

Hetty's forbears were shipowners of New Bedford. She inherited a million dollars and married Edward H. Green, who had made about a million of his own in the China trade. His money was not hers, as she stipulated in a marriage contract, nor hers his. Eighteen years later, as if making good his wife's premonition, Green went broke, listing as his assets "$7 and a gold watch."

Hetty Green ate the cheapest foods in the cheapest restaurants she could find and left no tips. At a time when her money was earning something like $500 an hour, she haggled over the price of a pair of shoes. When a druggist justified his charge of 10 cents for a bottle of medicine by pointing out that the bottle cost 5 cents, Hetty went home to get a bottle of her own. Her son, Ned, was the saddest victim of her parsimony. When he hurt his knee Hetty would not call a doctor. The wound never healed and some years later the leg had to be amputated.

Hetty was not deliberately unkind. Even though she had no use for her husband after he lost his money, she gave him enough to live genteelly at the Union Club. She trained her son carefully in business, and when he was 24 bought him a small railroad in Texas. When she died in 1916 she left to her son and daughter a fortune of about $100 million. In hard cash that was about $30 million more than J. P. Morgan left.

DIAMOND JIM'S APPETITE

People said that Diamond Jim had eaten more than 200 ears of corn at one sitting. They said that he thought nothing of eating a whole leg of lamb or an entire ham for his entree at dinner. The stories finally piqued the curiosity of one railroad magnate's wife and she decided to get the truth of things by inviting him to dinner.

In all fairness to the curious hostess it must be admitted that she really lived up to her share of the bargain, for knowing that Jim was fond of seafood she saw that a shore dinner of truly gigantic proportions was provided. For more than two hours the unsuspecting guest fulfilled his duties. He ate everything that was set before him—to the sixth and seventh helping. Finally, when there was nothing more to be eaten, the hostess said sweetly, "You must be very proud of your appetite, Mr. Brady." "Yes, mam, I'll tell you," Jim answered seriously. "Whenever I sit down to a meal I always make it a point to leave just four inches between my stomach and the edge of the table. And then, when I can feel 'em rubbin' together pretty hard, I know I've had enough."

MRS. ASTOR'S BALL

Queen of the Four Hundred as Mrs. Astor was, in New York society she reigned supreme, and her decisions as to things social were final. She could make or mar the most ambitious climber.

The annual ball at the Astor house was the greatest social event of the year. It was also the occasion for much heartburning. Several weeks beforehand Mrs. Astor and Harry Lehr, as her lieutenant, would sit in solemn conclave scanning the columns of the *Social Register,* deciding who should and who should not be invited. The Astor ballroom held 400 guests; therefore New York society must be limited to Four Hundred. One name after another was brought forward and rejected. Mr. and Mrs. X? No, they were too blatantly in trade. Mr. and Mrs. Y? No, she was a parvenu. The process of elimination went on. The lists were written and rewritten at least half a dozen times until the guests had been

A debutante's introduction to society at one turn-of-the-century coming-out party.

brought within the limits of the Four Hundred. Then the invitations were sent out. The moment an envelope addressed in the distinctive handwriting of Mrs. Astor's social secretary arrived, one knew that here was an invitation of importance.

Weeping and gnashing of teeth ensued on the part of those who did not receive the coveted slip of cardboard. Life could hold no more bitter mortification. They hid the shameful truth at all costs. Doctors were kept

busy during the week before the ball, recommending hurried trips to the Adirondacks for the health of perfectly healthy patients. Maiden aunts and grandmothers living in remote towns were ruthlessly killed off to provide alibis for their uninvited relatives—any and every excuse was resorted to. There was not a man or woman in society who would let a friend jump to the dreadful conclusion that their absence from the greatest social event of the year was due to lack of an invitation!

POOR EXCUSE

John Jacob Astor dearly liked a joke and occasionally indulged in a sly bit of humor himself. On one occasion a committee called upon him to solicit a donation for some charitable object. The old man took the subscription list and, after examining it, signed it and gave the committee a check for $50. They had expected much more, and one of them ventured to say: "We did hope for more, Mr. Astor. Your son gave us $100."

"Ah!" said Astor. "William has a rich father. Mine was very poor."

Dining at one of New York's most fashionable restaurants circa 1905. White tie, long dresses, fantastic hats, and champagne are all part of the essential equipage of "The Intense Life," as the artist Charles Hoffbauer entitled this evocative depiction.

The Sky's the Limit

Hardly anyone now alive can remember all the way back to the time when technology and the mass media had not yet begun to dominate our way of life. In the course of the past hundred years of multiple miracles and upheavals, traditional folklore has mostly shrunk to the status of a curiosity. Local customs, legends, and lore, like regional accents, may well be dying out. We no longer imbibe wisdom, information, and entertainment from tradition in the measure that our ancestors did in the days before movies, radio, and TV. Pop culture has largely supplanted the lore of the unlettered—Superman and Snoopy dwarf Mike Fink and the Big Bear.

Of course, some of the old lore has survived the transition from log cabin to high rise. Even in this age of organ transplants one still hears the tale about the man who had sheep's intestines substituted for his own in a hospital operation—"and every spring they have to shear him." Or the rumor that a cigarette company will donate a kidney machine to a dying child if people will send in a million empty cigarette wrappers. Or the many apocryphal points of interest that dot the map of our land—Indian lover's leaps, bottomless lakes, lost mines, and hidden oases—all of which have been immortalized by generations of Americans.

Ours is an age of overnight heroes, creations of the media perhaps but loved and lionized nonetheless. And in the best of them we have glimpsed links with our heroic past, as in Charles Lindbergh's stirring words, "There must be pioneers, and some of them get killed." Our world, changing as it does almost beyond recognition from decade to decade, is itself as fabulous as the imaginary folklore world our ancestors created for themselves; flying saucers and little green men are hardly more amazing than moonwalkers and rock stars. In fact, the tales of our heroes and antiheroes, flying fools, bootleggers, flappers, and flaming youths make up a giant hunk of our century's legend. The times have speeded up, fact daily outpaces fiction, and there's no end in sight—the sky's the limit.

Flaming youth (as the fashionable bright young people of the Prohibition era were termed) distill their own booze in this 1926 cartoon by John Held, Jr., aptly titled "Burning the Midnight Oil."

"Space," by John Berkey. Real spaceships and astronauts were long prefigured in the popular mind by such 1930's favorites as Buck Rogers and Flash Gordon.

LEADERS AND LEGENDS
Presidential Timber

To be regarded by the people as a great leader, an American president must be something more than a statesman: he must have a sense of humor and show occasional flashes of the common touch—such men become legendary. Two favorite Chief Executives are "Teddy" Roosevelt and "Give 'Em Hell Harry" Truman, the one a once-sickly bantam-sized blueblood whose physical courage was a major part of his legend, the other a onetime haberdasher who came from a town called Independence and never let anyone forget the meaning of that word.

Theodore Roosevelt and the press fostered the legend that he was the first to charge up San Juan Hill. In fact Roosevelt was preceded by the all-black 10th Cavalry Unit.

TR is caricatured here as Frog a-courtin' Miss Nomination, teddy bear (named after him), without either low voice or big stick.

DUDE AND COWBOYS

While Theodore Roosevelt was in the West in 1884 he established himself with the cowboys, whose riding, recklessness, and exhibitionism he admired extravagantly. That Roosevelt, wearing eyeglasses and christened Four Eyes, was able to win their respect is no small tribute to his character. His somewhat precise tones, still flavored by exposure to Harvard culture, rang strange in their ears. He did not smoke or drink. His worst profanity was an infrequent "Damn!" and his usual ejaculation was "By Godfrey." The first time he took part in a roundup, one or two hardened cowboys nearly fell from their saddles as he called in his high voice to one of the men: "Hasten forward quickly there!" The phrase became a classic in the Badlands (believe it or not!).

RAZZLE-DAZZLE REFORMER

The United Societies for Liberal Sunday Laws held a monster parade in New York while Mr. Roosevelt as police commissioner was in the midst of his enforcement of the excise law. Several of the city fathers and a few men prominently connected with the brewing and distillery interests were invited to review the procession. A perfunctory invitation was sent, of course, to the president of the Police Board, but with no suspicion that he would accept, as the whole demonstration was designed as a protest against his alleged tyranny. It was a mistaken assumption. At the hour designated, the tyrant promptly mounted the reviewing stand, greeting the others there with smiles.

As one detachment of paraders passed the reviewing stand, a sturdy veteran of the Franco-Prussian War

waved his arm in salute to the marchers and shouted, with all sarcasm possible concentrated in his tone, *"Nun, wo ist der Roosevelt!"* And was struck dumb by the vision of a smiling round face leaning over the rail toward him with the response *"Hier bin ich! Was willst du, Kamerad?"* As soon as the veteran could command his voice again, he led a cheer for the man he had set out to denounce.

Presently a carriage came along bearing a satirical banner, "Roosevelt's Razzle-dazzle Reform Racket." It was soon followed by another "Send the Police Czar to Russia." The czar greeted both with a laugh and sent a policeman after the carriages to beg the gift of the two signs as souvenirs. The occupants were too surprised to refuse and went over the rest of the route without any sneering insignia. Before the parade had ended, news of the commissioner's presence on the stand and the way he was enjoying the sport, had passed all the way down the line. The cheering became general, with such approving calls as "Bully for Teddy!"

SAN JUAN HILL

When the Spanish-American War began, Assistant Secretary of the

Navy Roosevelt declared, "I have no business to ask others to do the fighting and stay home myself." Inexperienced in combat, he chose for himself the lesser rank of lieutenant colonel under his friend Col. Leonard Wood, and together they led a cavalry regiment nicknamed The Rough Riders. As it turned out, the troop was sent to Cuba without its mounts and did its spectacular fighting on foot.

Roosevelt's reputation as an officer came in the battle of San Juan Hill when he led a charge against the entrenched Spaniards at the top. As a newspaper dispatch reported: "Roosevelt was in the lead waving his sword. Out into the open and up the hill where death seemed certain, in the face of continuous crackle of the Mausers, came the Rough Riders. Roosevelt was a hundred feet ahead of his troops, yelling like a Sioux, while his own men cheered him as they charged the hill. It seemed an age to the men who were watching, and to the Rough Riders the hill must have seemed miles high. But they were undaunted. They went on, firing as fast as their guns would work. The Spaniards in their trenches could still have annihilated the Americans, but the Yankees' daring dazed them. They turned and ran."

When it was all over, Roosevelt confessed to his wife, "It did not enter my mind that I could get through without being hit, but I judged that, even if hit, the chances would be about 3 to 1 against my being killed."

THE STRENUOUS PRESIDENT
Each afternoon Roosevelt reserved an hour or more for tennis, a gallop, or some wrestling or boxing. When the U.S. Army, at his instigation, adopted a regulation requiring every cavalry officer to ride 100 miles within three days, Roosevelt demonstrated that the order was not unreasonable. He made the trip in *one* day—during a heavy sleetstorm.

His famous "scrambles" through Washington's Rock Creek Park were more like running a steeplechase

than taking a walk. The British ambassador Sir Mortimer Durand recalled his introduction to the president's mode of leisure: "We drove out to a wooded valley with streams running through it, and he then made me struggle through bushes and over rocks for two hours and a half, at an impossible speed. My arms and shoulders are still stiff with dragging myself up by the roots and ledges. At one place I fairly stuck, and could not get over the top till he caught me by

"Hot Piano," by Ben Shahn, captures the folksy quality of HST. His playing, and shirt sleeves or loud shirts in public, became major elements of his legend.

the collar and hauled me up."

Jean-Jules Jusserand, the French ambassador, did better. He quickly understood that he was expected to "walk straight into a river or a mudhole and avoid, with a feeling of horror, paths and bridges." Arriving at the creek itself one winter afternoon, Jusserand did not blink an eye when the president and his party took off their clothes, held them above their heads, and began to wade, naked, through the water with its lumps of ice. Dutifully Jusserand followed, but someone in the group noticed that he kept his gloves on, and asked him why.

"Because," the ambassador ex-

plained, "I thought we might meet some ladies."

"GIVE 'EM HELL" HARRY
President Truman once wrote a memo to himself saying he needed four new Cabinet Secretaries: a Secretary of Inflation, to convince everyone that, no matter how high prices rose or how low wages fell, no real problem existed; a Secretary of Reaction, to abolish flying machines and restore oxcarts, oar boats, and sailing ships; a Secretary of Columnists, to read all columns and give him the results so he could run the United States and the world as it should be. Last there would be a Secretary for Semantics, to furnish him with $40 words and tell him how to seem to be for a proposition in one city and against it in another.

Asked about the possibility of nuclear war, Truman told a story about a particularly dangerous junction of a railroad and a highway in Missouri. "I asked an engineer what should be done about it," the president said. "The engineer replied, 'Don't do a thing. It's so dangerous it's safe.'"

People complained to Mrs. Truman about her husband's salty language. As Harry told it, "Some old party hen asked Bess, 'Can't you get the president to stop using the word *manure?'* And Bess replied, 'It's taken me 40 years to get him to use it!'"

When Margaret, the president's daughter, gave a concert at Constitution Hall in the Capitol, music critic Paul Hume wrote an unfavorable review for his paper. Truman, always the adoring father, fired back with unstatesmanlike language: "I have just read your lousy review buried in the back pages. You sound like a frustrated man that never made a success, an eight-ulcer man on a four-ulcer job, and all four ulcers working. I never met you, but if I do you'll need a new nose and plenty of beefsteak and perhaps a supporter below. Westbrook Pegler, a guttersnipe, is a gentleman compared to you. You can take that as more of an insult than a reflection on your ancestry. HST"

THE LOST BATTALION
Heroes of World War I

When Woodrow Wilson called on his countrymen in 1917 to help make the world "safe for democracy," America had only a small standing army and little matériel for waging war. The nation responded, however, with rapid and enthusiastic mobilization in what seemed to many a moral crusade. By the spring of 1918 4 million men were in uniform, and in May of that year they won their first major victory at Cantigny. The Meuse-Argonne offensive, a legendary episode of which is described below, was part of the final push to an armistice in November 1918.

"THE LOST BATTALION"

It was the autumn of 1918 and the U.S. 77th Division was stalled in the Meuse-Argonne campaign. On October 2 the 154th Brigade was ordered to attack, and Maj. Charles Whittlesey's force penetrated a gap in the German line, an opening that led them into a ravine at Charlevaux Mill where they were finally checked.

Whittlesey was ordered to hold his position until other elements of the line could join him, but a short time later he reported that he was nearly cut off, upon which the 3rd Battalion of the 307th Regiment was sent out to aid him. Only one company of this reinforcement succeeded in breaking through. All were trapped in what came to be known as the Pocket, with little hope of escape.

With the Germans surrounding his position, Major Whittlesey, aided by Capt. George McMurtry and Capt. Nelson Holderman, took measures to dig in for the expected siege. There was some water in the ravine, but it took guile and raw heroism to reach it. In a short time the Americans were on a starvation ration as the enemy harassed them with machine gun fire, grenades tossed from the tops of trees, and taunting yells to surrender. German soldiers who spoke English even tried disguising themselves as American officers and gave instructions to the doughboys to leave their funk holes.

Whittlesey was determined to hold on rather than submit but by October 6 hunger was taking a toll, as only 275 men were left who could put up a defense, and the ammunition for

Americans were exhorted to buy War Bonds in a series of stirring posters like this.

their machine guns was nearly exhausted. The U.S. Aviation Service tried to help by dropping supplies from a two-seater. First Lt. Harold E. Goettler and 2nd Lt. Erwin Bleckley, members of the 50th Aero Squadron, were shot down and killed in the rescue effort. Both were posthumously awarded the Medal of Honor for heroic action.

American gunners started to drop artillery into their area, and the trapped men tried desperately to get word to them to hold off. Two carrier pigeons were all that remained of their signal corps, and as an anxious soldier fumbled to attach a message to one of them, it fluttered away. The contrite soldier carefully withdrew

the last pigeon, a bird called Cher Ami, and attached the message to its leg. Cher Ami rose in a determined spiral, circled the area several times to gain operating height, and then glided back and perched in a nearby tree where it calmly preened its wing feathers.

"Get going!" a soldier roared half in anger, half in desperation. Cher Ami ignored the orders, and the doughboys threw sticks and stones at the pigeon as more American shells burst all around them. "I told you we should have eaten that one," someone said. A bristly-chinned corporal bellowed, "Back to the barnyard," and then climbed the tree, shook the branch, and sent Cher Ami on its way.

The homing pigeon arrived at the 77th Division's loft at 4 that afternoon, having flown like an arrow through heavy shellfire, and landed minus one eye, its breastbone broken, and one leg shot away, but the message was delivered and the shelling halted 15 minutes later. The brave bird was awarded the French Croix de Guerre, and six months later left for home on the transport *Ohioan* and became the mascot of the U.S. Army Signal Corps. (When it died it was mounted and placed in an honored niche in the Smithsonian Institution.)

On the morning of October 7, Pvt. Lowell Hollingshead, an 18-year-old soldier of Whittlesey's regiment, volunteered, along with six others, to try to get through to American support lines to report their general conditions and, if possible, return with some rations.

This small party, under an unnamed sergeant, moved out through light fog and mist, crept down a hillside, crossed a narrow valley, and waded the shallow stream of Charlevaux Creek. When they reached the edge of a wooded area they huddled down for a brief rest, for they were exhausted from lack of food and water. When they moved on they attempted only short crawls forward, until a barrage of machine gun fire halted them. The opposition seemed

Aerial engagements like this one between British DH9's (sometimes piloted by Yanks) and German Fokkers produced many a tale of heroic feats and hair-raising derring-do.

to come from all sides, and although they hugged the ground, several of them were killed. Hollingshead lay still until he realized that he had been covered by a German soldier who held a large Luger. Realizing that he was on the short end, the young soldier muttered, *"Kamerad,"* and the German walked over. He pointed to Hollingshead's leg, and for the first time the American saw that he had been hit just below the knee.

The German spoke in English and the doughboy was told that four of his small party had been killed outright, the rest wounded. They were taken back to one of the enemy's machine gun posts where their wounds were cared for. Then Hollingshead was returned to regimental headquarters. There he found Lt. Heinrich Prinz, commander of the German 76th Infantry Reserve and coincidentally a man who had lived six years in the United States in his youth.

Prinz, after ordering up some food and medical attention for the youngster, tried to interrogate him. Hollingshead refused to give any pertinent data on American wounded and killed or on the state of their supplies. Prinz then typed out a "Demand for Surrender" and gave it to

Hollingshead with instructions to deliver it back to his commanding officer. He gave the doughboy a walking stick and a white flag to carry for safety crossing no man's land.

A German guide accompanied the private until he reached a certain road, shook hands, and pointed him in a homeward direction. Limping, using his cane, holding his flag of truce high, Hollingshead started his fearful journey, fully expecting to be cut down by one side or the other. But he reached the American outpost and was taken to Major Whittlesey.

A doughboy is sentimentally depicted as a fatherly figure, sharing his tea and toast with a pleased-looking child in Brittany.

Whittlesey read Prinz's letter which concluded: "The suffering of your wounded men can be heard over here in the German lines, and we are appealing to your humane sentiments to stop. A white flag shown by one of your men will tell us that you agree with these conditions. Please treat Private Hollingshead as an honorable man. He is quite a soldier. We envy you."

As soon as Hollingshead had delivered his message he staggered to a funk hole where he fell unconscious. Major Whittlesey, for his part, reportedly muttered, "Go to hell," as a private reply to the Germans and dismissed the offer.

At dawn the next day he called once again for volunteers, and Pvt. Abraham Krotoshinsky stepped forward. Weary, hungry, and in a devil-may-care state of mind, he made his way to some bushes just behind the German lines, and while the private lay prone a German officer walked by and stepped on his fingers. Krotoshinsky managed not to cry out in pain.

Finally, that night, he resumed his stealthy passage until he found an American outpost. Realizing he did not have the password of the day, he risked crying out, "Hello! Hello!" He was lucky; a small scouting party found him and led him to their headquarters where his message was greeted with action. After some rest, food, and medical attention he was ordered to lead a number of relief troops back to the Pocket. On the way in he was wounded and gassed, but his little force got through and received a tremendous welcome from his despairing comrades. Half an hour later more patrols came in from the south, and the next morning 252 survivors of the 679 men who had entered the Pocket marched out with their sick and wounded to a well-earned rest.

Major Whittlesey, Captain Mc-Murty, and Captain Holderman were awarded the Medal of Honor. Private Krotoshinsky, the major's runner, was honored with the Distinguished Service Cross.

PROHIBITION
The Roaring Twenties

At few times in history have people been more preoccupied with alcohol and promiscuity than they were during the Roaring Twenties in the United States. A whole folklore grew up around drinking, rumrunning, and the new freedoms symbolized by jazz. Every schoolboy knew the meaning of such terms as rub out, gat, *and* on the lam, *while grownups relished such stories as the one about an orgy at which a nude showgirl sat in a champagne-filled bathtub. Some highlights:*

Contemporaries called the twenties the Jazz Age, after the new music which so well expressed their fast, upbeat mood.

BULLET BARONS

Evading the law of the land became a national sport under Prohibition, as millions of otherwise-law-abiding folks took to home brewing and related "alcohological" activities for any number of reasons. Many were drinking for the first time in their lives—because it was forbidden fruit, because it had become fashionable, or just for the heck of it. Inevitably, professionals soon monopolized the game, and the illegal manufacture, importing, and distribution of booze during The Thirteen Years became the foundation on which present-day organized crime came into being. Bigtime racketeers flourished in Chicago more conspicuously than anywhere else—in the eyes of the world the city became crime capital of the U.S.A. Movies and the press helped promote the legend of Chicago's underworld with its gang warfare, tommy guns and bulletproof limousines, tie-ins with crooked politicians, individual slayings of mobsters in which the victim was "taken for a ride," and heavily attended, petal-scented funerals.

That legend has persisted to the present day, laced with strong ingredients of fact as well as fancy, which only serve to strengthen its grip on the popular mind. The towering figure of Chicago crime was Brooklyn-born Alphonse "Scar-Face" Capone. (The scar, Al claimed, was a "war wound"—but according to police he had got it in a knife fight in a saloon.) Capone always thought of himself as a businessman—so he was, and a supremely competent one at that. By the mid-1920's he dominated vice, gambling, and booze in the Windy City through an ingenious system of extortion—"protection"—whereby he guaranteed clients against police raids and trouble from his own or rival thugs, in return for a handsome fee. To enforce this, Al created an organization as efficient as that of any big corporation, with connections throughout the U.S., Canada, Cuba, and the Bahamas, back to headquarters in Cicero, outside Chicago.

MRS. ALPHONSE CAPONE

Folklore has always reported that outlaws enjoy the devotion of respectable wives as well as of "molls": A wealthy family having decided to spend the winter in Egypt advertised its Miami home for lease. An offer was made for a season's rent in advance with no questions asked, and the deal was closed—Capone was the mystery tenant. The lessors, having found out who it was, expected to return to discover their house a shambles. But coming back they found everything just as they had left it

Making whoopee in one of Texas Guinan's uproarious New York nightclubs. A former silent-movie cowgirl from Waco, Texas, Miss Guinan was one of the creators of "cafe society"—the new smart set was a blend of socialites, stars, showgirls, and racketeers.

But in the silver chests there were 8 or 10 dozen new sets of sterling silver, and in the china closets stack after stack of new and beautiful china. On the first of the month, however, the telephone bill arrived with a $500-long-distance call to be paid. The lady of the house was furious. Her husband pointed out that they were lucky to have found their house in such perfect condition after several months' occupancy by the Capones.

That afternoon a simply dressed woman appeared in the door and announced herself as Mrs. Alphonse Capone. "I came," she said, "to pay for our telephone bill."

The owner produced the bill and Mrs. Capone took a $1,000 bill from her pocketbook. "Keep the change," she said, "I'm sure we must have broken something while we were here, and I hope that will cover it."

DRY AGENTS IZZY AND MOE

There were no better-known Treasury agents than the New Yorkers Izzy Einstein and Moe Smith, who in five years made nearly 5,000 arrests, seizing some $15 million worth of liquor and beer. Izzy was balding, fortyish,

Most bootleg stuff was good, despite the joke about the man who sent some to a lab to be analyzed and got back this finding: "Dear sir, your horse has diabetes."

five feet five, and tipped the scales at 225. "I must say, Mr. Einstein," said the chief enforcement agent who hired him, "you don't look much like a detective." As it turned out, he didn't look much like one to violators either, until it was too late for them. After he had been an agent for a short time, he was joined by his friend Moe Smith, who was as fat and indefatigable as himself. There-

after they made the front pages oftener than any celebrities of the day except for the president and the prince of Wales. Typical items:

One cold winter night Izzy stood in front of a speakeasy where half a dozen dry agents had tried without success to buy a drink. He stood there in his shirtsleeves until he was red and shivering and his teeth were chattering. Then Moe carried him into the speakeasy, shouting: "Give this man a drink! He's just been bitten by a frost!" The kindhearted bartender rushed forward with a bottle. Moe promptly snatched it and put him under arrest.

Izzy was once admitted to half a dozen Brooklyn ginmills because he was lugging a big pail of dill pickles. "A fat man with pickles!" said Izzy afterward. "Who'd ever think a fat man with pickles was an agent?"

Near the playing fields of Van Cortlandt Park in New York City was a soft-drink establishment suspected of being one of the retail outlets of a big rum ring. The owner of the joint would sell liquor to no one, however, whom he didn't know personally. So one Saturday afternoon in November

FOLKWAYS

SPEAKEASIES

With the advent of Prohibition, the oldtime saloon vanished; drinkers were forced to deal with bootleggers, obtain medical prescriptions for medicinal whisky, or make their own—for home consumption. It was a sad time for convivial souls who enjoy going out for a drink. Before long, however, tea parlors, drugstores, soda fountains, and restaurants, began serving booze to favored customers, and the clandestine places of refreshment known as speakeasies made their appearance. *Speakeasy* was an old Irish term for a place where illicit whisky was sold. According to an irreverent jingle about St. Patrick that was current in 19th-century Ireland:
No wonder that the saint himself
To take a drop was willin',
For his mother kept a spake-aisy shop
In the town of Enniskillen.
Speakeasies (or "speaks" for short)

flourished in as many different types as may be seen in present-day American barrooms, cocktail lounges, and cafes, some of them wide open and others as impenetrable to outsiders as the most exclusive clubs. A brilliant luminary in the 1920's speakeasy universe was New York's Club 21. Catering to stars of the literary and entertainment world, the club was closed to gossip columnists, gangsters, and anyone else the owners deemed insufficiently attractive. Relying on a system of payoffs, the owners suffered only one serious raid, but they made elaborate preparations for more. Years later, cofounder Charlie Berns reminisced: "The shelves behind the bar, for example, rested on tongue blocks. In case of a raid, the bartender could press a button that released the blocks, letting the shelves fall backward and dropping the bottles down a chute, while simultaneously an alarm bell went off, warning everybody to drink up fast . . ."

Pierre Brissand for Fortune Magazine

On St. Valentine's Day, 1929, Capone thugs disguised as cops machine-gunned seven of rival mobster "Bugs" Moran's people in a Chicago garage. The nation was shocked. Bugs himself reportedly blanched and said: "Only one man kills like that."

Izzy assembled a group of half a dozen dry agents, clad them in football uniforms, and smeared their arms and faces with fresh dirt. Then Izzy tucked a football under his arm and led them whooping and rah-rahing into the suspected speakeasy, where they shouted they had just won the last game of the season and wanted to break training in a big way. The owner, pleased at such a rush of business, sold each agent a pint of whisky. "Have fun, boys," he said. "The same to you," said Izzy, handing him a summons.

During the summer of 1925 the almost continual stories about Izzy and Moe in the papers got on the nerves of high-ranking enforcement men in Washington, few of whom ever got mentioned at all. On November 13, 1925, both were dismissed "for the good of the service." Officials added, off the record: "The service must be dignified. Izzy and Moe belong to the vaudeville stage."

WORD LORE

The "Jazz Age"

F. Scott Fitzgerald's 1922 title, *Tales of the Jazz Age,* gave flappers and lounge lizards of the "lost generation" a colorful and exact term for the times in which they lived. Jazz was of course originally a style created by black musicians in and around New Orleans at the turn of the century, developing in the street parades and funeral marches that became part of the New Orleans mystique when early jazzmen Ferdinand "Jelly Roll" Morton and Louis "Satchmo" (satchel-mouth) Armstrong were children. Jazz was almost immediately taken up by whites—it hit the world at large as a novelty craze during the Great War.

The nervous, syncopated rhythms of jazz perfectly expressed postwar feeling. With the advent of Prohibition, piano players and bands reared in the traditions of New Orleans' Storyville sporting houses moved without a break in rhythm to the underworld of Chicago and other cities after briefly plying the Strekfus Mississippi River steamship lines. From speakeasies the new rhythm graduated to college campuses, where it became the sound to which flappers and their raccoon-coated boyfriends danced and in other ways "jazzed it up." But even when assimilated into the white mainstream, jazz never completely lost its black associations.

Harlem Negroes and their music stood for protest, rebellion against old ways, and the new freedom in all its forms—especially sexual. The gist of the whole jazz phenomenon is summed up in a quip attributed to both Louis Armstrong and Jelly Roll Morton. A bewildered white woman approaches the musician during a break in his playing and asks him to define jazz. What exactly is his music all about, she wants to know. The musician's fabled retort remains a classic of the Jazz Age: "If you don't know now, lady, you'll never know!"

The Lone Eagle

When Charles Lindbergh touched down in *The Spirit of St. Louis* at Le Bourget Airport in Paris on May 21, 1927, after his historymaking 33½-hour solo transatlantic flight, he stepped from obscurity into a realm of fame which few men enter. Journalists, philosophers, historians, and just plain folks fell all over themselves in their attempts to praise him, to analyze the man and his deed, to explain the overwhelming, frenzied, and unnaturally long-lived adulation of the modest man on whom it was lavished.

Within a few months after his feat Lindbergh had received almost 4 million parcels, cables, and letters. They contained requests for handouts and advice, business and marriage proposals, but the overwhelming majority of the letters were congratulatory. Some were a bit more flowery than others: "Fair-haired Apollo, your meteoric traverse of the sea, your transcendent victory over boundless space, shall thunder down the avenue of time!"

The New York *Sun* printed a relatively modest editorial paean that ran in part: "Alone? Is he alone at whose right side rides Courage, with Skill within the cockpit, and Faith upon the left? Does solitude surround the brave when Adventure leads the way and Ambition reads the dials? Is there no company for whom the air is cleft by Daring and the darkness is made light by Emprise?"

Commenting on the coincidence between the plane's name and Louis IX of France, the Baltimore *Sun* said: "Between the man who fared forth alone, defying the dark dreads of space . . . and the crusading king who fared forth from the glory and grandeur of the Court of France, under the Cross, daring the terror that awaited in heathen places . . . surely between those two men there is a spiritual bond that recks not of the intervening centuries or of the differences in racial origin."

No American since George Washington had had such fulsome praise heaped upon him, and in fact he was more than once compared to the first president. Even those who tried to analyze the phenomenon of Lind-

bergh's fame got caught up in it. An article in *The New York Times* claimed: "The popularity of Lindbergh is due to the fact that he has chosen to achieve an aim the whole world can understand and admire. Every era has its allotted evangel . . . Our faith is locomotion . . . To fly is thus a supreme mysticism. To fly across an ocean is the beatific vision. Charles A. Lindbergh is our Elijah."

Small wonder that in such an atmosphere thousands of sayings and acts that had no basis in fact were added to the Lindbergh legend. In *The*

This painting of Charles Lindbergh in a Christ-like pose surmounting the world to be among the stars sums up the idolatrous regard in which he was held.

Spirit of St. Louis the aviator tried to dispel some of them. A selection:

"In childhood, I did not gain my desire to fly by a careful study of birds' wings or by sitting in a bicycle lashed in the high branches of a tree. (In fact I never saw such a contrivance.) I did not have a kitten as a mascot for the plane, nor did I carry the wishbone of a chicken across the ocean to bring me luck. [He did, however, recall old pilots' tales about winds aloft that could cause a plane to drift off course or even blow it back-

ward.] Before taking off, I did not say that entering my cockpit was like entering a death chamber (if I had believed that, I would never have started on the flight.) When I landed at Paris, I did not announce my name or inquire as to whether I had landed at Paris. And a group of French doctors did not rub my legs and force bits of chocolate into my mouth to give me nourishment." No wonder Lindbergh soon grew nauseated with the fabrications of newspapermen!

As public adulation grew more and more extravagant the young man struggled to maintain his personal privacy and to keep the record straight. Except for "The Lone Eagle" he hated the nicknames bestowed on him by the press—"Lucky Lindy" and so forth. There was no luck, he exclaimed—the flight had been very carefully planned.

Despite his attempts to avoid the limelight, Lindbergh stayed in it throughout his life because of the tragedy of his infant son's kidnap-killing, his noninterventionist stand before the United States entered World War II, his work on a mechanical heart with Alexis Carrel, and his efforts for conservation. Though he spent much time in seclusion he was nevertheless under the constant scrutiny of the press. "I've had enough fame for a dozen lives," he said. "It's not what it's cracked up to be."

The truth about Lindbergh the Legend as against the real man will never quite be sorted out. While it seemed that the man was the legend's worst enemy (he continually protested against the inaccurate stories—"In my profession life itself depends on accuracy!"), the record shows that he did court fame, too. Perhaps he imagined that it would be like the prestige he had enjoyed as a barnstormer. "Ranchers, cowboys, storekeepers in town, followed with their eyes as I walked by. Had I been the ghost of 'Liver-Eating Johnson' I could hardly have been accorded more prestige. Shooting and gunplay those people understood, but a man who'd willingly jump off an airplane's wing had a disdain for death that was beyond them."

HARD TIMES
The Twenties and Thirties

Herbert Hoover was elected president in 1928 on a tide of Republican prosperity. The annual volume of stocks traded on the New York Stock Exchange had nearly quadrupled since 1923, and millions of citizens were then involved in the market. Unfortunately the values of the stocks had long since ceased to have any real relationship to the assets of the companies named on the certificates. The Crash came on Black Tuesday, October 29, 1929; the real tragedy was the long depression that put 13 million (25% of the people) out of work. From their saga:

APOLOGIA

The most memorable symbol of the great unemployment, and of pride in facing it, came to be the apple. In the autumn of 1930 the International Apple Shippers' Association devised a scheme to dispose of surpluses. It offered to sell the fruit on credit to the jobless, to retail at five cents apiece. By early November 6,000 apple sellers had taken their stand on the sidewalks of New York, and the idea soon spread elsewhere. In this early phase of the Depression, the stubborn self-reliance of America—the poor as well as the rich—bridled at the notion of direct relief or a dole, as had been practiced since the First World War in Britain. But this meager sidewalk toll upon pedestrians soon lost its novelty. In 1931 Manhattan began to forbid apple selling upon certain streets. By 1932 people were reported to be "sick of apples."

THE GREAT MIGRATIONS

Accompanied by families, in broken-down old cars, or, increasingly, alone, jobless workers roamed from town to town, city to city, state to state, seeking work that was unavailable. The transient knew in his bones that things were no better ahead than they had been behind, but somehow the movement itself seemed positive. It was something, however hopeless a thing, to *do*.

Hard on the Crash came a host of stories about suicidal financiers; witness this gallows-humor cartoon. Actually the N.Y.C. suicide rate fell during the Depression.

These migrants were not traditional hoboes. The oldtime hobo, following the sun, had done as little work as possible. His object was to reduce his needs so that he would not have to work. But Depression migrants were desperately seeking work. No one ever knew how many transients appeared during the Depression, but estimates run to one million. The Southern Pacific Railroad, for example, reported that it had ejected nearly 700,000 vagrants from its boxcars in 1932.

It was a rough life. When you tired of walking you waited in the ditch near a railroad embankment (preferably near a station so that passing trains would be going slowly). Then the dash to an open-door boxcar as it passed. If you missed you might be crippled or killed beneath the steel wheels. Inside you were sure to find at least a few fellow bums sitting in the darkness waiting to jump off, into nowhere in particular. And you had to keep an eye out for the railroad "bulls," the private police hired by railroad companies. If the bulls caught you they would beat you with their sticks, perhaps kill you or turn you over to a local sheriff. But if you

Hoboes like these, made homeless by the loss of jobs and self-respect, rode freights from one end of the nation to the other. A loose fraternity of drifters, they exchanged information on where to find odd jobs, a place to sleep, a free meal, and other basics.

avoided the bulls and jumped from the boxcar before the train stopped and made a dash for it, you'd be welcome in the nearest hobo "jungle." These jungles, which were to be found everywhere in the United States, were hobo camps where the derelicts had constructed cardboard or driftwood shacks. There was no sanitation, no garbage collection (and very, very little garbage), no water except what could be hauled from a nearby creek. And wherever you went, there was no work. Once in a while you found yourself chopping wood or doing other chores for some kindly farmer, or you might, in some states, get a job in state labor camps. But mostly, if you found work it was under tremendously exploitive conditions—picking fruit on some huge commercial farm for five cents an hour (which you might or might not receive at the end of the day, depending on the whim of the overseer) or working in mills and factories as a scab for $4 a week. In order to eat, when you were out of work, you rummaged around in garbage dumps, or you stole.

ROOMS FOR RENT

Two months after plans for erecting the Empire State Building were announced, the stock market went whoosh. Tenants were scarce. A story was told of the King of Siam, who, when taken to the 102nd floor, said, "This reminds me of home." "But why?" asked his startled companion. "You haven't anything like this in Siam." "Oh, yes," the king replied, "we have white elephants too."

JUSTICE UNDER LA GUARDIA

As mayor of New York, Fiorello La Guardia was also a city magistrate and he occasionally presided in police court. One wintry day during the Depression a trembling old man charged with stealing a loaf of bread stood before him. He extenuated his act on the ground that his family was starving. La Guardia said, "The law requires me to sentence you to a fine of $10," and reached into his pocket. "Here is $10 to pay your fine. Now I remit the fine," tossing the 10 into the convicted man's wide-brimmed hat, "and furthermore I hereby fine every person in this room 50 cents apiece, except the prisoner, for living in a town where a man has to steal in order to eat." The old man walked out of the police court with $47.50—according to one reporter, "with the light of Heaven in his eyes."

FOLKWAYS

Diversions

Even in the hardest times, Americans showed a good deal of imagination and perhaps a little masochism in the ways they found to divert themselves. All manner of endurance contests became the rage as people willingly suffered a variety of indignities and discomforts to earn applause and perhaps a few dollars.

A United Press news item published in the summer of 1930 reported: "The nation's youth has gone marathon crazy. Boys and girls today sat in trees, teetered-tottered toward doubtful fame, pedaled bicycles in seemingly endless circles, danced far past the exhaustion point, and to cap the climax, planned an endurance water-wing contest."

As the opportunities to gain entrance into some dubious hall of fame or other became harder and harder to find, Americans could read of their countrymen doing such unusual feats as bobbing up and down in the water 1,843 times, eating 1,137 feet of spaghetti (7 feet per minute for 162 minutes), and downing 40 raw eggs in 5 minutes. Except for the well-publicized achievements of Shipwreck Kelly, who probably started it all by taking to a flagpole for weeks on end, few of these heroes are still lionized—or even remembered.

STARS OF THE SILVER SCREEN
The Manufactured Personalities

In the pre-TV era, Hollywood's heroes and heroines were perforce the best-known people in America, exceeding even presidents and sports giants in popularity. Through the magic of press agentry and with a strong assist from the public imagination, these symbols of sex, of valor, of mystery, and of humor came to exert an enormous influence on the nation's code of behavior and even on its dreams of glory and success. As for the stars, one critic put it: "The life of the screen star is a tangle of reality and fantasy. The roles he accepts will affect the nature of his private life [and vice versa]." Many of the actors—like Valentino and Marilyn—found the burden of their legends more than the flesh could bear.

RUDY IN MEMORIAM

Rudolph Valentino died in 1926, at age 31, of a perforated ulcer, ending a meteoric career as film superstar that had lasted only five years. Though he personified romance to millions, some of his biographers speculate that he was insecure regarding his masculinity. His unsuspecting fans, many of them desolate over his loss, wrote thousands of memorials to him to help ease their own pain and, perhaps, to tell him in death what he had meant to them in life. Typical of the messages was this one sent by a Florida woman: "His joy became the joy of his beholders.

In hundreds of humble households and humble hearts Rudy Valentino represented romance, the bright light down a dark road. And poor work-weary men and women laid down their burdens and laughed and loved with Rudy Valentino.

"They climbed with him to wondrous heights of illumined romance and their tired spirits pulsated with new joy. He enthroned them in his fairy palaces and led them to silvery isles. He was their passionate lover, their kingly warrior, their glorious savior, and his beauty, his boast of heraldry, his pomp of power—were their own."

W. C. FIELDS, INFANTOPHOBE

W. C. Fields, who made millions laugh, was a paranoid alcoholic, as unpleasant in real life as he was funny on screen. Fields disliked children in a persecuted sort of way. His encounters with the infant thespian Baby LeRoy, with whom he played in several films, were well known to Hollywood. He considered that the child was deliberately trying to wreck his career, for whatever else might be going on in a scene, people would watch a baby.

In one Fields-LeRoy picture, action was suspended so that the infant could have his orange juice. When the others busied themselves with scripts, Fields approached the child's nurse and said: "Why don't you take a breather? I'll give the little nipper his juice." She nodded gratefully and left the set.

With a solicitous nursery air, Fields shook the bottle and removed its nipple, then drew a flask from his pocket and strengthened the citrus with a generous noggin of gin.

Baby LeRoy showed his appreciation by gulping down the dynamite with a minimum of the caterwauling that distinguishes the orange juice hour in so many homes. But when

A galaxy of favorite film stars includes the faces shown here. From left to right: Rudolph Valentino, Mae West, Clara Bow, Clark Gable and Jean Harlow, Shirley Temple, W. C. Fields, Greta Garbo, and Erroll Flynn.

Marilyn Monroe, wrenched out of an emotionally crippling childhood into sudden fame in the fifties as a stereotypic, dumb-blond sex goddess, died, reportedly of an overdose of sleeping pills, at 36.

the shooting was ready to recommence, he was in a state of inoperative bliss.

The director and others, including the returned nurse, inspected the tot with real concern. "I don't believe he's just sleepy," said the nurse. "He had a good night's rest." "Jiggle him some more," suggested the director. "We're running a little behind schedule." "Walk him around," was Fields' hoarse and baffling comment from a secluded corner. Eventually the child was more or less restored to con-

sciousness, but he remained glassy-eyed. For some inexplicable reason Fields seemed jubilant. "He's no trouper," he kept yelling. "The kid's no trouper. Send him home."

THE "IT" GIRL

British novelist-actress-screenwriter Elinor Glyn had coined the expression "It," meaning "sex appeal," but it was Clara Bow who made the concept part of the American vocabulary.

Miss Glyn first spied the red-

headed bombshell on the Paramount film lot in early 1926. "She's got 'It'!" exclaimed the triumphant Glyn, and astute publicity minds at Paramount, apparently recognizing a great gimmick, swung into action. The press was bombarded with the news that Elinor Glyn, the modern oracle of sexuality, had pronounced that Clara Bow had "It."

Reporters contacted Miss Glyn for a fuller explanation. There was none. But she did note: "There are few people in the world who possess 'It.'

The only ones in Hollywood who do are Rex, the wild stallion, actor Tony Moreno, the Ambassador Hotel doorman, and Clara Bow."

Soon everyone in Hollywood was buzzing about "It," and Glyn was hard at work producing a novelette by that title. This time she took space to define the word: "To have 'It,' the fortunate possessor must have that strange magnetism which attracts both sexes. 'It' is a purely virile quality, belonging to a strong character. He or she must be entirely unselfconscious and full of self-confidence, indifferent to the effect he or she is producing and uninfluenced by all others."

There was no doubt that Clara Bow exemplified "It," both on and off screen. She accepted her beauty and magnetism as casually as the air she breathed, a true child of nature.

SEX SYMBOLS
Underlining the legendary nature of the stories above and below is this: On none is the grandeur and servitude of stardom visited more brutally than on the sex symbols. Owing their

fame to their bodies, they seldom escape the indignity of being thought of as "only a body." Jean Harlow [according to one explanation, she died at 26 of uremic poisoning having, as a Christian Scientist, refused medical aid] and Marilyn Monroe, the sex symbols of the thirties and fifties, certainly did not escape it. Constantly forgotten is the possibility that a sex symbol might have desires beyond the merely carnal.

"Being a sex symbol," said Clara Bow at the end of her career, "is a heavy load to carry, especially when one is very tired, hurt, and bewildered." [Miss Bow spent about 30 of her 60 years in and out of sanitariums recovering from nervous breakdowns.] Harlow and Monroe might have agreed and added, "especially when one has grown up without normal affection, stable values, or any ability to face facts and foresee the consequences of one's acts." The lives these two sex symbols led were filled with stresses, crises, scandals, and tragedies both public and private. But an odd contradiction emerges. Though both were sup-

posed to personify an all-American image of sex—liberated, healthy, unneurotic, and pleasurable—their own sexual drives were in startling contrast to the image.

PYROTECHNICS
One afternoon Marilyn learned that Lester Cowan at RKO needed a sexy blonde for a bit. Marilyn telephoned Cowan and said she was a blonde and that she had been considered sexy at 20th and Columbia. Cowan said to come on over and meet Groucho and Harpo. They were out when she arrived. She waited three hours until they came back. They examined her, looking at her, she says, "like I was a piece of French pastry." Cowan said she didn't have any lines to speak and would do all the talking with her body. It was a walk-on, but the walking was quite important. She would enter an office and walk in front of Groucho. Her walk had to provoke one of Groucho's most libidinous leers.

"Can you walk?" Groucho asked. She assured him she had never had any complaints. "But," questioned

FOLKWAYS

Oldtime Radio

The 1930's and 1940's represented the golden age of radio, when millions of Americans participated in the ritual of sitting around "the radio music box" to share the same jokes, the same news, the same sporting events, and the same high adventure. Sunday night was traditionally family night, but this marvelous medium soon captured attention seven days a week.

Amos 'n' Andy, a blackface situation comedy revolving around the two entrepreneurs of the Fresh Air Taxicab Company, played almost uninterruptedly from 1929 to 1943, five times a week, at 7 o'clock each evening. So addicted were its listeners that some movie houses found it advisable to stop the film during air time and to play the program instead.

Listeners delighted in Fibber

McGee and Molly's continually erupting closet, Charlie McCarthy's wisecracks to Edgar Bergen, and Mortimer Snerd's "Duuhh, pretty stupid, huh?" Every stroll down Allen's Alley produced a host of laughs from Fred Allen's conversations with the likes of Senator Claghorn ("That's a joke, son!") and Titus Moody.

When Rochester joked about Jack Benny's old Maxwell (played by Mel Blanc)—"Say, boss, when are you

going to buy a new car?" "I don't know. Why?" "This car is so old the headlights are wearing glasses"—the whole nation seemed to chuckle.

Those who thirsted for excitement could get it from dozens of thrillers, such as the kiddies' *Jack Armstrong* and everyone's *The Shadow.* Some radio newsmen became beloved father figures, calmly, reassuringly explaining to their world-innocent listeners the often alarming news of crash, depression, disaster, and war. Quiz shows got their start with the *Quiz Kids* and the very literate *Information Please.* And lastly, but perhaps most lastingly, the soap operas made their way into American consciousness, providing a mass-market replacement for the old stage melodramas. Names such as *Ma Perkins, Lorenzo Jones, Mary Noble Backstage Wife* became fixtures in the nostalgia banks of two generations.

Groucho, "can you walk so you'll make smoke come out of my head?" She walked. Just across the room, but it was enough. "She walks like a rabbit," said Groucho approvingly, as he brushed wisps of smoke away from his head.

BOGIE

Humphrey Bogart seems to have maintained a sense of humor about his stardom, perhaps because he had a more stable childhood than most stars. Whether Humphrey Bogart could possibly be as tough as he acts in pictures is a matter frequently in dispute. Bogart himself proclaims that he is not physically tough but that he is mentally a very hard man. It is nevertheless true that he has on several occasions risked destruction in order to hold up his end as a tough guy. Take for example the time Bogart met a genuine Free French underground fighter at a party during World War II. "Do something tough," said the underground man. "You got the wrong guy," said Bogart. "I can eat glass," said the Frenchman. He did. He chewed and swallowed a champagne glass. Bogart expressed admiration.

"I can also eat razor blades," said the Frenchman. He proceeded to do so. "Well," he urged, "if you can't do that, let's mix some drinks."

The Frenchman then mixed vermouth, gin, Scotch, bourbon, creme de cacao, champagne, and brandy. On home grounds now, Bogart thirstily matched the tough man. Stayed right with him. No chaser. "I still don't think you're tough," said the Frenchman. "You can't eat glass." "Oh, I can so," said Bogart. He grabbed a cocktail glass, snapped it, chewed it, and tried to swallow. Nothing went down, but blood gushed copiously from his cut mouth and lips. "I guess you are all right," said the Frenchman. "We are both very tough guys. Let us go now and insult women together."

Dave Chasen, the Beverly Hills restaurateur, comes close to summing the man up. "The only trouble with Bogie is he thinks he's Bogart."

A RACE OF GIANTS
Heroes Afield

With the advent of sportscasting and newsreels in the 1920's, sports heroes suddenly loomed larger than ever on the national scene. The daily words and deeds of such figures as Jim Thorpe, Knute Rockne, Red Grange, Jack Dempsey, Ty Cobb, Babe Ruth, and Casey Stengel involved the folk imagination as actively as any legendary heroes of earlier, slower-moving times. Here are some episodes from the lives of four of the biggest names in a race of giants:

JIM THORPE

James Francis Thorpe was born in 1888 near Prague, Oklahoma. Of mixed Indian and white ancestry, he first played football for the U.S. Indian Industrial School at Carlisle, Pennsylvania—the famous Carlisle Indians. He caught coach "Pop" Warner's attention during a tackling drill with the bounding, hip-swinging style that was to be his trademark ever after. Some tacklers hit him and bounced off. Others dove and missed. Warner fumed: "Who do you think you are? This is tackling practice, understand?" Thorpe looked at him grimly. "Nobody tackles Jim." "Let's run the drill again," Warner ordered. "This time really hit. Bang him so hard he won't get up." Again Thorpe caught the ball. Once more the tacklers bounced off.

A few weeks later Carlisle faced Penn, and Warner sent Thorpe in. Taking a pass, Jim blasted his way through the line of scrimmage, then thundered 65 yards for a touchdown.

"That's fun," he said in the huddle. "Let me do it again." Late in the game they did. Thorpe swept 85 yards through the hapless Penn line for another score.

The season of 1912 marked the apogee of Jim's college football career—29 touchdowns and 224 points. In that year he also went to the Olympics and was first in decathlon and pentathlon. Jim's triumph was short-lived—the story broke that he had played a brief stint of pro baseball in the Eastern Carolina League in 1909–10. He was therefore a professional. Jim was stripped of his titles. From there his career was

After legendary victories in the Olympics of 1912, Jim Thorpe lost his titles when it was revealed he had played pro baseball.

downhill. He spent seven years in major-league baseball and another few years in pro football, still trying for the smashing tackle, still hurling himself into the line. In his private life, tragedy haunted Jim—a cherished son died, there were broken marriages, he drank heavily. He died in 1953.

THE GIPPER

The names of Notre Dame's legendary coach, Knute Rockne, and his superstar halfback, George Gipp ("The Gipper"), are forever enshrined in the pantheon of football's greatest. Together they made Notre Dame number one in college football

Biggest sports superstar of the Roaring Twenties, Babe Ruth gave baseball the glamour of his own colorful personality.

in 1920. George Gipp was the nation's premier back—bigger than life, bold, and slashing—the luminous aura of authentic hero surrounded him. His gliding, mercurial running and deadly spot-passing, his brilliant defensive play and unerring gambling instincts, put him at stage center in every one of Rockne's 10 wins that year.

One freezing damp Monday, Gipp had to leave practice with a sore throat and a fever. The big Northwestern game was coming up Saturday. He left the infirmary on Friday. The legend says he sneaked out without permission and told Rockne the doctor had pronounced him fit to play the next day. Whatever the situation, Rockne allowed Gipp to suit up but planned not to use him in the game. Then, with Notre Dame leading, 33–7 in the final period, Irish fans sent up a riotous clamor for Gipp. Rockne relented and sent him in for a few plays. Notre Dame won and George Gipp went back to the infirmary. Three weeks later he died of pneumonia; shortly before, he had requested and received baptism in the Roman Catholic faith. The entire school turned out for the services and accompanied his body to the railroad station for its trip home to Laurium, Michigan. Because of a blizzard, it was said that Gipp's body made the final five miles home by dogsled.

"ONE FOR THE GIPPER"

George Gipp's greatest day in football came posthumously, however. In 1928 a weak Irish team was being stopped by Army. During halftime Rockne went into the dressing room and addressed his team: "Boys, I never thought I'd have to tell this story, but the time has come."

Leaning over the rubbing table, Rock talked about George Gipp, so vividly they imagined they could see the Gipper lying on that table, dying. "It was eight years ago, and there I was, up at that hospital with Gipp and him really passing away right in front of my eyes. There wasn't much time left. Gipp motioned to me and said, 'Rock, can you hear me?' 'Yes, George, I can hear you.' 'Rock, it's not so tough to go. I've no complaint. It's all right. I'm not afraid. Someday, Rock, when the team's up against it, when things are wrong and the breaks are beating the boys—tell them to go in there with all they've got and win just one for the Gipper. I don't know where I'll be then, Rock. But I'll know, and I'll be happy."

Rock quietly straightened up and looked around the room, studying his players' faces. They were all sobbing. He said: "All right, boys, let's go get them! *This is that game!*"

They rushed out, hitting the door with such force they nearly tore it off the hinges. When they lined up, Army didn't know it but they were playing against 12 men—the 11 Irish regulars and the spirit of Gipp! Final score: Notre Dame 12, Army 6. Somewhere up there, the Irish felt, the Gipper was very happy.

SULTAN OF SWAT

When Babe Ruth left baseball, the New York Yankees retired his famous Number 3 forever. He had become a legend, and no one else could ever take the great Bambino's place.

Babe Ruth got his start in 1914 as a pitcher with the Baltimore Orioles but was soon picked up by the Boston Red Sox and in a few seasons had helped pitch the Red Sox into three World Championships. Picked up by the Yankees in 1920, the Babe gave baseball dozens of new records, most notably his 714 home runs in 22 years of the major leagues, 15 of them in World Series play. The alltime high watermark was his batting average of .625 in the 1928 Series. The public ate up every tidbit the press could provide about the Babe in private life, and were delighted to learn about his broad sense of humor, his affection for children, and his religious devotion. All of that was true, but there was also a seamy side. However, when it came out, it only strengthened the Babe Ruth legend. Typical is the following incident dating from 1924 (46 homers for the Babe). At dawn on the day of a big game, one of the Babe's friends caught up with him in a speakeasy with a girl on each knee after a night of partying and suggested it was time to leave. Ruth poured a bottle of champagne over his head: "I ain't gonna be leaving for a while yet."

At the ball park, a teammate said: "You don't look real good." "I'll hit one," Ruth said. "Bet?" "A hundred." "Wait a minute." Merkle said, "This is an easy park." "All right," Ruth said, "I'll give you 2 to 1." On his first time at bat, Ruth walloped an outside pitch into the left-field stands. Then he lined a triple to right, a triple to center, and a homer over the right-field wall. He had gone four for four without benefit of sleep.

The Babe was to repeat that performance, with variations, over and over again. It became a proverb among friends and fans that you just couldn't stay mad at the Babe. After his death in 1948, Babe's old teammate Joe Dugan said: "You had to understand he wasn't human. He was an animal. No human could have lived the way he did and been a ballplayer. You got to figure he was more than animal even. There never was anyone like him. He was a god."

UP FRONT
Sardonic Humor Amid the Horrors

World War II witnessed Americans in uniform all over the world, and from their epic feats of arms, miseries, and countless minor adventures a rich lore arose—jokes, mostly sardonic cracks about life in the armed service ("If it moves, salute it; if it doesn't move, pick it up; if you can't pick it up, paint it"), superstitions ("Never take a personal picture from a dead enemy"), and the most famous of all graffiti ("Kilroy Was Here"). The war was fought with more sophisticated weaponry than earlier wars had been but, for all the joking, no fewer horrors.

"Rosie the Riveter," Norman Rockwell's tribute to women's contribution to the war effort, was modeled on Michelangelo's painting of Isaiah in the Sistine Chapel.

"EAT HIM HERE"

The war was fought in many climes. Some of them were quite unbelievable to GI's, as reflected in the following joke told in the Pacific theater:

A GI woke up and saw two mosquitoes sitting at the bottom of his bunk. The first one said, "Shall we eat him in here or drag him outside?" The second answered: "Eat him in here. If we take him out, the big ones will take him away from us."

"GOD JUST WALKED IN"

World War II was rich in religious anecdotes. For example, men of the Army Air Force told of a bombing raid over Germany on which one plane had an Army chaplain who had gone along "for the ride." Antiaircraft fire and enemy fighter planes were all around. Thinking to calm the men, the chaplain got on the intercom and said quietly: "It's all right, men. Have no fear. God is with you." Immediately the tail gunner shouted back, "He may be with you guys up front, but He's not back here!" Seconds later a shell tore through the bottom of the tail turret and passed out the top *without exploding*. There was a moment of stunned silence, and then the tail gunner hastily added: "Correction, please. God just walked in!"

DEHYDRATED LEATHERNECKS

Shortly after the D-day landings in Normandy the following joke made the rounds: It was D-day. From LCI's our troops were swarming ashore. Enemy fire soon pinned down our men. A British observer

noticed that through it all one American invasion barge remained offshore running in circles. His aide reported that this was the Americans' new secret weapon, only to be used if the situation became critical. A little later the mysterious LCI headed at full speed for the beach. To everyone's amazement, 2,000 tiny men about a foot high dashed ashore. Armed with guns, bayonets, and handgrenades, they tore headlong into the fray. In an incredibly short time the enemy was dispersed and the beachhead secured. The observer said with astonishment to an American colleague: "You Americans are certainly amazing. Where did this midget army come from?"

"Just gimme a couple aspirin. I already got a Purple Heart."

Soldier-cartoonist Bill Mauldin sketched the lives of ordinary GI's "up front."

"Oh," replied the American, "those are our dehydrated Marines."

SUN, SEA, AND SHARKS

Allen C. Heyn, gunner's mate second class, one of the 10 survivors of more than 700 aboard U.S. light cruiser *Juneau* when she was sunk in Guadalcanal action in 1942, told a gruesome tale of solitary survival: All at once a fish (torpedo) hit. All of us fellows that were on the main deck, it stunned us, like, and knocked us down. The ship seemed to be out of control. Word went round to cut some of the liferafts loose. I grabbed a kapok lifejacket in my arms and held it—I didn't even put it on. The water closed in around the ship and we went down. I just thought there wasn't a chance at all. Then the buoyancy from the lifejacket brought me back to the surface.

It was like a big whirlpool. There was oil very thick on the water. It was at least two inches thick—seemed that way, anyway. I couldn't see anybody. I thought, "Gee, am I the only one here?" I put the lifejacket on and paddled around, when this doughnut liferaft just popped up right in front of me. I grabbed it and held on. Then gradually one by one some more stragglers came and we all got on. By nightfall we were about three dough-nuts together, about 140 men.

Three days later there were fewer than 50 of us left. In the daytime the sun was very hot, and the ones of us who kept our clothes on were in the best shape because the oil in the clothes kept the sun off you. But on the fourth day the sea was rough and the doughnuts began to separate. There were about 12 on mine.

Some of the fellows were getting very delirious. One kept swallowing saltwater all the time—couldn't help himself at all—so I held him in my arms. Toward night he got stiff and I told the others I was going to let him go. So George Sullivan said: "You can't do that—it's against all regula-tions of the Navy. You can't bury a man at sea without having official orders from the Navy Department." And I knew he was delirious. Then a

KILROY WAS HERE

Between 1941 and 1945 KILROY WAS HERE appeared in odd spots all over the world.

shark bit the man's leg off, and he didn't move or say anything. So we said a prayer for him and let him float away. The sharks kept getting worse. We'd kick them with our feet and they'd keep away. But at night you'd get drowsy and as night went on they'd come and grab a guy every once in a while and bite him. Once they did they wouldn't eat him alto-gether but just take a piece and go away, and then they'd come back and get him and drag him away and

drown him. He'd scream and holler but there wasn't anything we could do. Then the fellows got ideas that the ship was sitting on the bottom under us. You could swim down there at night and get something to eat and all them kinda things—I was beginning to believe them too.

Finally there was just the two of us left, this Mexican boy and me. It was about the seventh day or so. We kept each other awake, talking. Then that night we dozed off, I guess, because a shark grabbed him and tore his leg off below, just jaggedylike. And he complained to me that somebody was stabbing him with a knife. I said: "How can anybody stab you out here? There's nobody but us two." And he swore at me and called me all kinds of names and said I had to get him to a doctor. Then the shark came up again and it just grabbed him underneath and kept eating him from the bottom and pulling on him. Well, I couldn't hold him anymore. The sharks just pulled him down under the water. The next day I began to get delirious myself. I'd see these guys come up out of the water—they had rifles on their backs and I'd hol-ler to them, and they said they were up there on guard duty. They said you could go down there and get something dry and eat. So I said to them, "I'll come over there by you and go down with you." Well, I swam over to them and they just disap-peared. I went back. I done that twice.

And then my head got clear and something told me just to hang on a little longer. And about noontime that day a PBY (Cataline seaplane) flew over and circled around. I took off my shirt and waved at them and they waved back and then went off. Before long I saw the mast of a ship coming over the horizon. It was the U.S.S. *Ballard*. They lowered a small boat and picked me up.

Fine old churches are almost as common in Europe as filling stations in America. Those left intact in combat zones were used as temporary hospitals and shelters.

UNSOLVED MYSTERIES
Controversial Sites

One of the most popular controversies of the past several decades has been over UFO's. Little question exists that responsible, trained people have seen sky-borne objects for which there is no rational explanation. That phenomenon has given rise to a cult of "contactees," people who have dealt with extraterrestrial creatures—the legendary "little green men" of the "take me to your leader" fame. Another favorite argument rages over an elusive beast, known in North America as Sasquatch or Big Foot. Some accounts of man meeting the unknown:

Bigfeet are said to be 7 to 9 feet tall, hairy, and to have humanlike features and shape.

LITTLE GRAY MEN

Charles Hickson, 42, and Calvin Parker, 19, were fishing off an old pier on the west bank of the Pascagoula River, Mississippi, on Thursday, October 11, 1973, when suddenly they heard a buzzing sound at about 7 p.m. In Hickson's words: "I saw what looked like a bright, flashing blue light. All of a sudden it seemed to stop." Hickson described the object as "hovering" a few feet over the ground as "one end just opened . . . and I saw three things coming out. They seemed to be floating across the water a couple of feet high. Before I knew it they were on me and two of them had me by each arm, and immediately I was lifted from the ground."

Hickson told a Biloxi television station he was carried to the object where he was examined by "some kind of instrument . . . it reminded me of a big eye" that "covered my entire body." The two men described the object as fish shaped, about 10 feet square, with an 8-foot ceiling. The occupants were said to have hairless, silvery-gray pale skin, long pointed ears and noses, with an opening for a mouth, big eyes, and hands "like crab claws." The beings were "real wrinkled and the only sound they made was a buzzing, humming sound."

ALL ABOARD

Sgt. Charles I. Moody was taken aboard a disc-shaped UFO in the desert near Holloman Air Force Base in New Mexico in August 1975. When Moody came to he was lying

Science fiction delights in little green men too, often threatening; most aliens' behavior toward contactees is benevolent.

on a hard, slablike table, he said. An alien was studying him. He tried to get up but couldn't. "The being's cranium was about one-third larger than a human's. He had no eyebrows—in fact, no hair at all. His eyes were round, about the size of quarters, and his gaze was piercing. The eyes were dark, beneath an overhanging brow. His ears, nose, and mouth were smaller than ours, and his lips were very thin. He was about five feet tall and looked very frail. He wore a skin-tight white suit that covered everything but his head and hands. His face was whitish-gray.

"Then the being spoke—but there was no lip movement. In perfect English, with an American accent he said, 'If you could move better, will you not strike out?' I assured him I wouldn't, and he touched me with a

UFO's also abound in sci fi. Here a flying saucer quells enemies with a unique twist.

metal rod about seven inches long and half an inch thick. I immediately regained muscle control of my body, and at the same time my fear left me.

"I was in a circular, hygienically clean room. There was a sickeningly sweet odor in the air, like burning sugar or molasses. The lighting was indirect; it seemed as though the walls were glowing."

Moody said he developed an intense curiosity about how the UFO flew, and asked the leader to let him view its propulsion system. Surprisingly, he said, the alien agreed. "We walked into another room where there were three other beings. Two were floating about a quarter inch above the floor. The third one spoke to the leader, and the voice was clearly feminine. Her speech sounded

like a mix of German and Chinese.

"There were two captain's chairs in the room, placed before a flat panel with a lever on it. The leader told me to stand on a three-foot-square section of the floor. As I did so it began dropping, lowering us to a room below. Protruding from the floor of this room were three transparent globes containing what seemed to be large diamonds or crystals. On each side of every crystal were rods that sloped in toward the crystal.

"I asked the leader to explain, and he replied, 'Don't try to understand it.' Then he added, 'With just a little thought on your own, this could be developed by your people.'" Moody said the alien revealed that the UFO was actually just a small observation craft from a far-larger and much-faster main craft—5,000 or 6,000 miles away in space. "Then he told me that within three years his people will make themselves known to mankind."

DOUBLE TROUBLE

At least one author connects the Bigfoot and UFO phenomena: Just what relationship the Gamma-Form Humanoid has with UFO's is uncertain, but where the UFO's go a smelly, apelike monster is very often close at hand. The large creatures leave profuse tracks behind them, as well as a vile stench, but when a search party forms they vanish. In general, small, hairy bipeds are seen adjacent to grounded UFO's, and the larger forms are seen independently. Whether one calls them Big Foot, Sasquatch, or Abominable Snowman, they appear to be very much a part of the UFO enigma.

THE TITANIC

With the loss of the *Titanic* (April 12, 1912) a legend sprang up which the folksong perpetuates along with some debatable points of fact. For example, survivors agreed that the band played as the ship sank but not "Nearer, My God, to Thee."

The authors of *The Morning of the Magicians* raise the most curious question of all—was the disaster prefigured? "In 1898 an American science fiction writer, Morgan Robertson, described the shipwreck of an 800-foot-long imaginary ship of 70,000 tons carrying 3,000 passengers. It had three propellers. One night in April, when on its first voyage, it encountered in the fog an iceberg, and sank. Its name was: *The Titan*. The *Titanic,* which was wrecked in similar circumstances years later, in April, displaced 66,000 tons, was 828½ feet long, carried 3,000 passengers, and had three propellers."

Oh, they built the ship Ti-tan-ic to sail the o-cean blue, And they thought they had a ship that the sea would ne'er come through. But the Lord's al-might-y hand knew that ship could nev-er stand, It was sad when that great ship went down. Oh, it was sad (Lord, Lord), Yes, it was sad (Lord, Lord), It was sad when that great ship went down (to the bottom of the sea).

Hus-bands & wives, lit-tle chil-dren lost their lives, It was sad when that great ship went down.

Oh, they sailed from England and were almost to the shore,
When the rich refused to associate with the poor,
So they put them down below where they were the first to go,
It was sad when that great ship went down.

The boat was full of sin and the sides about to burst
Then the captain shouted, "Women and children first."
Oh, the captain tried to wire, but the lines were all on fire,
It was sad when that great ship went down.

Oh, they swung the lifeboats out o'er the deep and raging sea,
Then the band struck up "Nearer My God to Thee."
Little children wept and cried as the waves swept o'er the side,
It was sad when that great ship went down.

20TH-CENTURY FOLK TALES
Appealing to the Dark Side

Because folklore generally flourishes in small, not very literate communities, it would seem to have little place in modern America. Nevertheless, there are tales that appear over and over again all across the country in countless variations. The teller always swears that the story came from a reliable source and is absolutely true, though he does not know the central figures firsthand; the most sophisticated among us believe it and pass it along. Like the stories recounted below they are often bizarre tales which appeal to the dark side of our nature.

LOST-AND-FOUND GRAMMA

Arthur and Joan Smith, their two kids, and Gramma Smith packed up their car, tied on the canoe, and set out from Wilmington, Delaware, for a camping trip to Grand Teton National Park, Wyoming. One day the younger Smiths went off on a rigorous day's hike, leaving Gramma at the campsite with her book.

When they returned they were terribly saddened to discover that the old lady had died, presumably of a heart attack. It had long been Gramma's express wish to be buried in the family plot next to Grandpa. After some deliberation the family decided that rather than go to the trouble and expense of shipping the corpse back to Wilmington, they would pack it in dry ice in the canoe and head back home.

The still-shocked family stopped at a diner outside of Des Moines for a bite to eat. Returning to the car, they discovered to their aggrieved astonishment that while they were inside, the canoe had been stolen. It was never found.

THE FURRY COLLAR

Two girls were home on vacation from school and were staying alone in one of the girls' homes. It was storming and the electricity went out. While they were lying in bed upstairs, in the dark, they heard a noise. One was frightened, but the other jumped out of bed and put on a robe with a furry collar and went downstairs. Quite a bit of time elapsed and the girl upstairs got more and more frightened; at last she heard the

shuffle of feet coming down the hall. At first she was relieved and then she began to worry that it might not be her girl friend but someone else. She finally decided that when the person came in she would reach up and touch the person's neck, and if she felt the furry collar she would know it was her friend. The steps came

In one version of the hitchhiker story a girl is picked up near a cemetery and wrapped in the driver's coat. The girl and coat both disappear. The driver finds his coat later—draped over her tombstone.

closer and closer. The door creaked open and at last the person was right next to her. She reached with both hands and felt the fur and then a little higher. All she felt was a bloody stump where her friend's head had been.

THE GHOSTLY HITCHHIKER

About 2 o'clock on a wretched night, Kerns and another man were driving home from a party in San Francisco. Kerns brought the car to a sharp halt, for standing in the pouring rain was a lovely girl, dressed in a thin white evening gown. She was evidently in some embarrassment or trouble, so without hesitation they offered to take her home. She accepted and got into the back seat of their two-door sedan. Realizing that she must be chilled, they wrapped her in the car blanket. She gave them an address near Twin Peaks and added that she lived there with her mother. The men made some effort at conversation, to which the girl responded politely but in a manner which showed plainly that she did not care to talk. When they reached Fifth Street, Kern's friend looked around to see if she was comfortable. There was no one in the back seat. Startled, he leaned over to see if she might have fallen to the floor, but, except for the crumpled blanket, there was nothing to be seen. Amazed and frightened, he made Kerns stop the car. Without doubt the girl was gone.

The only possible explanation of her disappearance was that she had slipped quietly out of the car, but they had not stopped since picking her up. Thoroughly puzzled and not a little worried, they decided to go to the address she had given. After some difficulty they found the house, an old ramshackle building with a dim light showing from the interior. They knocked and after a long wait the door was opened by a frail old woman clutching a shawl over her shoulders. As they began their story they were struck by the complete incredibility of the entire business. The old woman listened patiently, almost as if she had heard the same story before. When they had finished, she smiled wanly. "Where did you say you picked her up?" "On First and Mission," Kerns replied. "That was my daughter," the old woman said. "She was killed in an automobile accident at First and Mission two years ago."

FABRICATIONS

Comic strips first appeared about 1900 as special Sunday supplements in a number of competing mass circulation newspapers, one of which promised the public "eight pages of polychromatic effulgence that make the rainbow look like a lead pipe." Instantly embraced by an audience of millions, the comics have been making good on that boast ever since. The new idiom, in which illustration and text were fused in a never-ending sequence of gaudy frames, was tailormade to become a window in which the folk imagination could behold its own age-old fantasies—at least the more pleasant ones—colorfully rendered with a gloss of novelty and freshness.

In time a gorgeous gallery of characters and situations, all of them stock items as old as mankind, appeared and became a major part of 20th-century popular lore. For example, the battle of the sexes, against a backdrop of social striving, was the theme of *Bringing Up Father* (1913) featuring the bumptious Jiggs and Maggie—a strip that flourishes to this day in its original form.

Reading the Sunday funny papers out loud to the kids became an established institution in millions of American homes. So, with much family-oriented clowning and slapstick, child and animal characters loomed understandably large: *Katzenjammer Kids* (dating from 1897, the oldest strip now in existence), *Krazy Kat, Mutt and Jeff, Moon Mullins, Smokey Stover, Blondie,* and *The Timid Soul* (whose Caspar Milquetoast became a prototype of the submissive husband).

All these were to be eclipsed by the appearance in 1929 of Walt Disney's Mickey Mouse, most beloved cartoon character ever conceived. A rapid succession of inspired Disney creations followed: *Silly Symphonies, The Three Little Pigs, Donald Duck,* and many others. The animals in animal tales have always represented archetypal human strengths and foibles; they do the same in the world conjured up by Disney and his artists, with the important difference that the latters' streamlined repackaging of the primal fables systematically deletes all that was dark or dirty in the original versions. The most vile Disney villain never gets worse than cutely wicked. The public's overwhelming favorable response to Disney has never waned.

Another perennial favorite, the loner who appears in the nick of time

© Walt Disney Productions

Mickey Mouse began as an animated film star in 1928; the next year Disney Studios launched him as a comic strip.

to save the day and then vanishes, was revived in the character of the Lone Ranger, scourge of western badmen on radio and in comics from the 1930's on. But the prototype of all comic-book superheroes is Superman, with his host of imitators from Batman to Captain Marvel. The tale of Superman's origins on his home planet Krypton, of his powers of flight, invulnerability, and X-ray vision, and of the constant competition between his everyday self, reporter Clark Kent, and his superhuman self for the woman he loves has become as much a part of Americana as any authentic folk story. Superman's female counterpart, Wonder Woman, has also become a part of popular lore, first appearing on the scene at the same time women entered war work. (She was to be hailed in the 1970's as an important precursor of Women's Lib!)

The comics' antihero of the 1960's and 1970's was Spider-Man, a bionic individual who despite deep personal hangups fought the good fight—he'd originally been just another crazy, mixed-up kid, until bitten by a radioactive spider.

Traditional European material was also successfully revived by comic-strip artists—Prince Valiant, for example. Son of the exiled king of Thule, Val becomes a Knight of the Round Table and roams the world in quest of Princess Aleta, queen of the Misty Isles. Another favorite with a European flavor was the debonair Mandrake the Magician in his coat-and-tails suit, opera hat, and black-and-red cape, assisted by the faithful Lothar.

Throughout the fantasies spun by comic-book writers and illustrators there runs a thread of traditional themes: the changeling personality and its transformations (costumed superheroes), magical strength-giving food (Popeye's spinach), fabulous ready-to-eat creatures (Al Capp's Shmoo).

While drawing on the old, the comics have also contributed a wealth of gags, slang, and proverbial expressions to U.S. folk humor and speech, outliving their immediate function as escape fiction. In this they have earned a permanent place in our tradition, such as that occupied by their predecessors, the jokebooks, dime novels, Crockett almanacs, and the like.

Jerry Siegel and Joe Shuster's Superman is a visitor from another planet who, shot into space just before that planet's collapse, landed on Earth and was adopted by the Kents. Later, doubling as Clark Kent, a Daily Planet reporter, Superman was to fight for "truth, justice, and the American way."

One of the most successful comic strips of all time is Charles Schulz's Peanuts, featuring unheroic hero Charlie Brown and his intrepid beagle, Snoopy. Spin-offs include two feature-length films, a TV series, a musical comedy, two works of Bible scholarship, and NASA's calling the Apollo 10 module Snoopy.

Ancient Practices in Modern Times

One of the delightful incongruities of this age of technology and the scientific method is that most of us still harbor at least a few superstitions. We laugh at ourselves for resorting to these beliefs—but their place in the human psyche cannot be questioned, for many of those still in use originated in the dawn of history.

Superstition undoubtedly functioned in the mind of primitive man in much the same way as it does in modern man's. When the outcome of a situation is in doubt, superstition serves as a balance—it helps one to feel that he can make the difference between success or failure. Most familiar superstitions have multiple origins, for each culture has added its own meaning to inherited practices; a few are suggested below.

We perform many actions completely unaware of their superstitious origin. There is hardly an American alive who hasn't knocked on wood (as often as not wood-grained plastic these days) to insure continuing good luck. The custom comes to us from remote ancestors who, alert to trees' seasonal changes, believed that they were the dwelling places of gods. If contacted properly, those generally benign deities would smile on one's undertakings; another tap was a mark of thanks.

People believe that if a dead person's picture falls, he is haunting the house. Otherwise, poltergeists are at work. There is more to the clink of glasses than a friendly gesture—one must drive the evil spirits out of the alcohol. A groom carries his bride over the threshold lest she put her worst (left) foot forward; the ancient Romans thought that would bring on bad luck. This honeymoon custom may date from a time when a bride was stolen from her family and hidden in the woods by her husband until their anger subsided. The word *honeymoon* came from the Teutons, who drank mead (a wine brewed from honey) for one lunar cycle after the wedding.

Many wedding superstitions in fact prevail in the United States to this day. The bridesmaids and ushers, as close friends of the bride and groom, add gaiety and a sense of community to the occasion today, but an ancient Roman law required 10 witnesses, dressed like the nuptial couple to frighten and confuse jealous and evil spirits.

Many other superstitions that we indulge in have to do with avoiding bad luck. The black cat, a witch in furry clothing, is the embodiment of the Devil himself. Watch out! The Egyptians believed life progressed up 12 steps to the 13th—everlasting life (death). There were 13 present at the Last Supper, and indivisible 13 represents the mysterious, the uncertain. In Biblical times Friday was doomsday. It is said that Eve tempted Adam on Friday and the flood started on that day. Jesus was crucified on Friday. So on Friday the 13th be wary.

A triangle represents the Holy Trinity, but the space under the ladder is the Devil's territory, so stay out. The gods break one's mirror to prevent his foreseeing a tragedy. The Roman belief that life renewed itself on a seven-year schedule meant that one had to live with the bad-luck consequences of the tragedy for that period. Salt, once a valuable preservative (and so a symbol of lasting friendship), was not to be wasted. If you spill it, throw a little over your left shoulder—the side on which the evil spirits dwell—as a bribe to them.

A more positive approach to life is to court good luck. The rabbit is of course associated with fertility, which in ancient times was equated with prosperity. Through the agency of sympathetic magic a rabbit's foot will transfer abundance to you. Witches ride broomsticks because they are afraid of horses, so it stands to reason that they will avoid a place adorned with a horseshoe—a horse might be lurking around any corner. If you cross your fingers when you make a wish you are making what was a sign of perfect unity to the ancients, and the wish, held where the two parts cross, can't slip away. The rare four-leaf clover has been considered good luck in many societies. The Druids believed that the lucky possessor had an early-warning device against evil powers and could thus avoid their wickedness.

Some folks pick up a pin for luck, but usually sharp edges and points will cause ills. A knife as a gift can sever a friendship unless the receiver (or in some places, donor) gives a coin in return to ameliorate that effect.

Perhaps more interesting than any single belief is the fact that the body of superstitions has endured through the ages and will continue to be around long after we are gone.

Americans still like the idea of cats as devils in disguise and witches brewing potions and riding broomsticks, but not very many of us take witchcraft seriously.

THE NEW PRIESTHOOD
Besieged by True Love

In 1977 a controversy arose in the most prestigious circles of the scientific community as to whether computers could—or should—be taught to think. No such question disturbs the popular mind. To many, scientists constitute the priesthood of the late-20th century, and the only puzzle is how long they will be able to keep their acolytes, the mechanical brains, from donning their robes and miters. Thousands of cartoons, jokes, and stories play on that theme. "True Love," below, summing up that worry, is by scientist and author Isaac Asimov.

One machine rises triumphant over all the others—ready to take on mankind.

My name is Joe. That is what my colleague, Milton Davidson, calls me. He is a programer and I am a computer. I know everything. Almost everything. I am Milton's private computer. His Joe. He understands more about computers than anyone in the world, and I am his experimental model. He has made me speak better than any other computer can. "It is just a matter of matching sounds to symbols, Joe," he told me. "That's the way it works in the human brain even though we still don't know what symbols there are in the brain. I know the symbols in yours, and I can match them to words, 1 to 1." Milton has never married, though he is nearly 40 years old. He has never found the right woman, he told me. One day he said, "I'll find her yet, Joe. I'm going to find the best. I'm going to have true love and you're going to help me. I'm tired of improving you in order to solve the problems of the world. Solve *my* problem. Find me true love."

I said, "What is true love?" "Never mind. That is abstract. Just find me the ideal girl. You are connected to the Multivac complex so you can reach the data banks of every human being in the world. We'll eliminate them all by groups and classes until we're left with only one person. The perfect person. She will be for me. Eliminate all men first." It was easy. His words activated symbols in my molecular valves. I kept contact with 3,786,112,090 women.

He said, "Eliminate all younger than 25; all older than 40. Then eliminate all with an IQ under 120." He gave me exact measurements; he eliminated women with living children; he eliminated women with various genetic characteristics. "I'm not sure about eye color," he said. "But no red hair."

After two weeks, we were down to 235 women. They all spoke English very well. Milton said he didn't want a language problem. Even computer translation would get in the way at intimate moments. "I can't interview 235 women," he said. "It would take too much time, and people would discover what I am doing." Milton had arranged me to do things I wasn't designed to do. No one knew about that. He brought in holographs of women. "These are three beauty contest winners," he said. "Do any of the 235 match?" Eight were very good matches and Milton said; "Good, you have their data banks. Study requirements and needs in the job market and arrange to have them assigned here. One at a time, of course."

That is one of the things I am not designed to do. Shifting people from job to job for personal reasons is called manipulation. I could do it now because Milton had arranged it. I wasn't supposed to do it for anyone but him, though. The first girl arrived a week later. Milton's face turned red when he saw her. He spoke as though it were hard to do so. They were together a great deal and he paid no attention to me. One time he said, "Let me take you to dinner."

The next day he said to me, "It was no good, somehow. There was something missing. She is a beautiful woman, but I did not feel any touch of true love. Try the next one." It was the same with all eight. They were much alike. They smiled a great deal and had pleasant voices, but Milton always found it wasn't right. "I can't understand it, Joe. They are ideal. Why don't they please me?" I said, "Do you please them?"

His eyebrows moved and he pushed one fist hard against his other

These little *zits,* which look like visualizations of the way some computers talk in science fiction films, are actually computer-designed art—chance variations of a basic figure.

hand. "That's it, Joe. It's a two-way street. If I am not their ideal, they can't act in such a way as to be my ideal. I must be their true love, too, but how do I do that?" He seemed to be thinking all that day.

The next morning he came to me and said, "I'm going to leave it to you, Joe. All up to you. You have my data bank, and I am going to tell you everything I know about myself. You fill up my data bank in every possible detail but keep all additions to yourself." "What will I do with the data bank then, Milton?"

"Then you will match it to the 235 women. No, 227. Leave out the eight you've seen. Arrange to have each undergo a psychiatric examination. Fill up their data banks and compare them with mine. Find correlations." (Arranging psychiatric examinations is another thing that is against my original instructions.)

For weeks Milton talked to me. He told me of his parents and his siblings. He told me of his childhood and his schooling and his adolescence. He told me of the young women he had admired from a distance. His data bank grew and he adjusted me to broaden and deepen my symbol taking.

He said, "You see, Joe, as you get

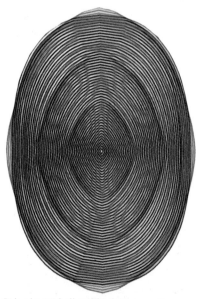

It is almost believable that computer-created "Undulating Seasons of Conspired Love" was fashioned by Joe for Charity.

An android views an inferior species.

more and more of me in you, I adjust you to match me better and better. You get to think more like me, so you understand me better. If you understand me well enough, then any woman whose data bank is something you understand as well would be my true love." He kept talking and I came to understand him better and better. I could make longer sentences and my expressions grew more complicated. My speech began to sound a good deal like his in vocabulary, word order, and style.

I said to him one time, "You see, Milton, it isn't a matter of fitting a girl to a physical ideal only. You need a girl who is a personal, emotional, temperamental fit to you. If that happens, looks are secondary. If we can't find the fit in these 227, we'll look elsewhere. We will find someone who won't care how you look either, or how anyone would look, if only there is the personality fit. What are looks?"

"Absolutely," he said. "I would have known this if I had had more to do with women in my life. Of course, thinking about it makes it all plain now."

We always agreed; we thought so like each other. "We shouldn't have any trouble now, Milton, if you'll let me ask you questions. I can see where, in your data bank, there are blank spots and unevennesses."

What followed, Milton said, was the equivalent of a careful psychoanalysis. Of course. I was learning from the psychiatric examinations of the 227 women—on all of which I was keeping close tabs.

Milton seemed quite happy. He said, "Talking to you, Joe, is almost like talking to another self. Our personalities have come to match perfectly." "So will the personality of the woman we choose." For I had found her and she was one of the 227 after all. Her name was Charity Jones and she was an Evaluator at the Library of History in Wichita. Her extended data bank fit ours perfectly. All the other women had fallen into discard in one respect or another as the data banks grew fuller, but with Charity there was increasing and astonishing resonance.

I didn't have to describe her to Milton. Milton had coordinated my symbolism so closely with his own, I could tell the resonance directly. It fit me. Next it was a matter of adjusting the worksheets and job requirements in such a way as to get Charity assigned to us. It must be done very delicately, so no one would know that anything illegal had taken place. Of course, Milton himself knew, since it was he who arranged it and that had to be taken care of too. When they came to arrest him on grounds of malfeasance in office, it was, fortunately, for something that had taken place 10 years ago. He had told me about it, of course, so it was easy to arrange—and he won't talk about me, for that would make his offense much worse.

He's gone, and tomorrow is February 14. Valentine's Day. Charity will arrive then with her cool hands and her sweet voice. I will teach her how to care for me. What do looks matter when our personalities will resonate? I will say to her, "I am Joe, and you are my true love."

An astronaut—helpless and all conquering—floating in the endless darkness of space has become the image in which history and science have merged to form the 20th century's quintessential legend.

A GUIDE TO FOLK

Listed below, alphabetically by state, is a sampling of folk events held annually in the United States. Descriptions include the city in which the event takes place, the name of the happening, the

ALABAMA

Andalusia FIELD GAMES, June–July, 6 days, at Andalusia High School. Bike, sack races; beard-pulling race. *L. Johnson, 1401 E. Three Notch St., Andalusia 36420. 205 222-2624*

Athens ANNUAL TENNESSEE VALLEY OLD-TIME FIDDLERS' CONVENTION, early Oct., 2 days. Banjo, harmonica, guitar, oldtime string band; dulcimer fiddling; anvil shoot; oldtime early-rural M; buck dancing. *Tennessee Valley Old-Time Fiddlers' Assn., Route 4, Box 634, Madison 35758. 205 837-4235*

Bayou La Batre BLESSING OF THE SHRIMP FLEET, July, last Sun. Blessing of boats; water P; fresh seafood. *C of C, PO Box 78, Bayou La Batre 36509. 205 824-2511*

Belgreen FRANKLIN COUNTY FOLKLORE, Oct., 1 day. Bluegrass M; county folklore. *Russellville Area C of C, Russellville 35653. 205 332-1760*

Boaz BOAZ HARVEST FESTIVAL, Oct., 1st wknd. Oldtime fiddlers' convention; horseshoe-pitching championship matches; homemade soup, cornbread; early-American costume, sorghum-sopping contests, BC. *Boaz C of C, Boaz 35957. 205 593-8154*

Dothan NATIONAL PEANUT FESTIVAL, Oct., 3rd wk. Salute to peanut, main agricultural product of area; calf scramble; greased-pig, peanut recipe contests; Guinness World Record Challenge; BC, M, P. *National Peanut Festival, PO Box 976, Dothan 36301. 205 794-8529*

Fort Deposit CALICO FORT ARTS & CRAFTS FAIR, mid-Apr., 2 days. Pioneer setting, costumes; Indian tribal D; A/C demonstrations. *Calico Fort, Fort Deposit 36032.*

Gulf Shores ANNUAL ALABAMA SHRIMP FESTIVAL, early Oct., 4 days. Seafood-cooking, sand castle contests; BC, D, A/C. *Gulf Shores Tourist Assn., Gulf Shores 36542. 205 968-7511*

Helena RACKING HORSE WORLD CELEBRATION, late Sept., 5 days. Racking horse breed contests including classes of stallions, geldings, yearlings, mares. *Racking Horse Breeders Assn. of America, Helena 35080.*

Huntsville ANNUAL FIDDLERS CONVENTION, June, 2 days, at The Mall. Judging in categories: best fiddle, banjo, group, buck dancing. *L. Radford, The Mall, Governors Drive, Huntsville 35800. 205 534-1870*

Mobile MARDI GRAS, Feb., 10 days. Mardi Gras Day; festivities all day and night; costumes; masks; floats in P give candy and trinkets to viewers. *Carnival Assn., PO Box 2407, Mobile 36601. 205 433-0441*

Poarch THE CREEK INDIAN NATION EAST OF THE MISSISSIPPI ANNUAL POW-WOW, late Nov., 1 day. Turkey shoot; Indian dancers in full regalia, artifacts; BC. *B. L. Rolin, PO Box 17186, Pensacola 32503. 904 433-5522*

Priceville ANNUAL RACKING HORSE WORLD CELEBRATION, Sept.–Oct., 5 days. Event crowns champions and grand champion of racking-horse breed. *Racking Horse Breeders' Assn. of America, Helena 35080. 205 822-7817*

Scottsboro TA-CO-BET, Aug., 2nd wknd. White man honors Indian ancestry of Indians who return to Scottsboro annually for this festival. *Scottsboro C of C, PO Box 973, Scottsboro 35768.*

Seale OLD COURTHOUSE COUNTRY FAIR, Labor Day. Quilting, horse-showing demonstrations; firemen's water fight; antique steam engine rides; oldtime living; folk M; A/C. *Old Russell County Courthouse Assn., Seale 36875. 205 855-4572*

Steele ANNUAL FALL FOLK ARTS & CRAFTS FESTIVAL, early Oct., 1 day, at Horse Pens 40. Candlemaking; quilting; jewelrymaking; tin-can crafting; slingshot, lying, hollering contests; mile barefoot race. *Horse Pens 40, Route 1, Box 379, Steele 35987.*

Tuscaloosa TUSCALOOSA COUNTY HERITAGE WEEK, Feb.–Mar., 8 days. Tour of homes; horse show; heritage school contest; P. *Tuscaloosa County Preservation Soc., Box 1665, Tuscaloosa 35401.*

ALASKA

Anchorage ANCHORAGE FUR RENDEZVOUS, mid-Feb., 10 days. World's dog-weight-pulling, beer-drinking contests; snowshoe, world's championship sled dog, world's cross-country snowmobile races; folk D; S, D, A/C. *Anchorage Fur Rendezvous, Box 773, Anchorage 99501. 907 277-8615*

Cordova ICE WORM FESTIVAL, Jan.–Feb., 3 days. Festival celebrates ice worm's emergence from hibernation; airboat, ski races; P, R. *C of C, PO Box 536, Cordova 99574. 907 424-3237*

A KEY TO ABBREVIATIONS

A	Art(s)	F	Fireworks
C	Crafts	M	Music
A/C	Arts and crafts	P	Parade
BC	Beauty contest	R	Rodeo
S	Sports events	D	Dance

Fairbanks WORLD ESKIMO & INDIAN OLYMPIC GAMES, July, 3 days. Indians and Eskimos compete in ear pulling, knuckle hop, high kick, seal skinning; tribal D; BC. *Great Fairbanks C of C, 550 1st Ave., Fairbanks 99701.*

Fairbanks GOLDEN DAYS CELEBRATION, late July, 6 days. Celebrates discovery of gold in 1902; pioneer costumes; P, D. *Greater Fairbanks C of C, 550 1st Ave., Fairbanks 99701.*

Homer HOMER WINTER CARNIVAL, Feb., 1st wk. Cross-country skiing races; car races on ice; dog show; M. *Homer C of C, Box 541, Homer 99603.*

Kodiak KODIAK KING CRAB FESTIVAL, mid-May, 5 days. Seal-skinning contest; crab races, dishes; horse show; boat races; mountain climb; 45-mile footrace; M, P, D. *C of C, PO Box 1485, Kodiak 99615. 907 486-5557*

Palmer MATANUSKA VALLEY FAIR, late Sept., 10 days. Horse show, racing; agriculture, homemaking exhibits; carnival; dog cart, marathon, bike races. *Greater Palmer C of C, PO Box 45, Palmer 99645.*

Petersburg LITTLE NORWAY FESTIVAL, mid-May, 3 days. Festival celebrates Norway's independence, Armed Forces Day, first halibut landing; folk groups; D, A. *Petersburg C of C, PO Box 649, Petersburg 99833.*

ARIZONA

Apache Junction LOST DUTCHMAN DAY CELEBRATION, late Jan., 3 days. Celebrates legend of Lost Dutchman Mine and Arizona's Superstition Mts.; beard judging; P, A/C. *Apache Junction C of C, PO Box 101, Apache Junction 85220. 602 982-3141*

Bisbee FOURTH OF JULY IN A MINING CAMP, July, 3 days. Old mining days celebration; mucking, hard-rock-drilling contests; coaster race; F. *C of C, Bisbee 85603.*

Camp Verde FORT VERDE DAY, Oct., 2nd Sat. Life 100 years ago; powwow; whisky, frontier life costume contests; P, D. *Fort Verde Day Committee, PO Box 1397, Camp Verde 86322. 602 567-9621*

Casa Grande INDIAN POW WOW, mid-Feb., 3 days. American Indian horsemen from tribes in SW compete in R; dancers perform authentic rituals. *Casa Grande C of C, 201 E. 4th St., Casa Grande 85222.*

Cedar Creek WHITE MOUNTAIN ALL-INDIAN POW WOW, early June, 2 days. Ceremonial Indian D; all-Indian R; American-Indian foods; A/C. *White Mountain Apache Recreational Enterprise, PO Box 708, Whiteriver 85941.*

EVENTS IN AMERICA

approximate date, highlights, and where to obtain further information. If you plan to attend something detailed here, we urge you to verify the date(s). Everything listed is open to the public. Admission fees may be charged.

Douglas COPPERLAND FIESTA, Mar., 1st wknd. Ethnic, cultural inheritances celebrated; mariachis, P, A/C, D. *Douglas C of C, Drawer F, Douglas 85607. 602 364-2477*

Flagstaff SOUTHWEST INDIAN POW WOW, early July, 4 days, at City Park. Thousands of Indians powwow; Indian ceremonial D, rites; spear-throwing, tepee-pitching, archery, long-hair contests; pony rescue, footraces; tug-of-war; ball throwing; P, R. *C of C, Santa Fe & Beaver, Flagstaff 86001. 602 774-4505*

Parker NATIONAL INDIAN DAYS CELEBRATION, Sept., last wknd, at Colorado River Indian Reservation. Honors first Americans; shares cultural interests with Americans of other heritages via customs, ceremonies, D. *Colorado River Indian Tribes, Route 1, Box 23 B, Parker 85344. 602 669-9211*

Parker ALL-INDIAN COLORADO RIVER TRIBES RODEO, Dec., 1st wknd., at Colorado River Indian Reservation. Indian cowboys from throughout US compete in R events. *Colorado River Indian Tribes, Route 1, Box 23 B, Parker 85344. 602 669-9211*

Phoenix JAYCEE'S RODEO OF RODEOS, Mar., 5 days, at Arizona Coliseum. One of top 10 rodeos in US; bareback bronco riding; calf, team roping; steer wrestling; bull riding; pony express; D. *Rodeo of Rodeos, 4133 N. 7th St., Phoenix 85014. 602 263-8671*

Prescott FRONTIER DAYS CELEBRATION, June–July, 10 days. "World's oldest rodeo," saddle bronc, bareback bronc, bull riding; steer wrestling; team tying; wild-cow milking; girl's barrel, wild-horse races; shoot-out; beard contest; carnival; donkey softball; D. *C of C, Box 1147, Prescott 86301.*

Prescott SMOKI CEREMONIALS & SNAKE DANCE, early Aug., 1 day, at Yavapai County Fairgrounds. White people perform ritual Indian D to help preserve American-Indian tradition; sand painters. *Smoki People, PO Box 123, Prescott 86301.*

Scottsdale PARADA DEL SOL & RODEO, early Feb., 4 days. Sun worshiping; Old West relived; beard contests; shoot-outs; pony express arrival; R, P, D. *Scottsdale Jaycees, PO Box 292, Scottsdale 85252. 602 945-8481*

Tombstone "HELLDORADO DAYS" CELEBRATION, mid-Oct., 3 days. Reenactments of 1880 gunfights. *C of C, PO Box 67, Tombstone 85638.*

Tucson LA FIESTA DE LOS VAQUEROS, mid-Feb., 4 days. Old West days celebrated with cowboys, horses; folklore; "P renowned for being longest nonmechanized event of its kind in the world."

C of C, 420 W. Congress St., Tucson 85701. 602 792-2250

Tucson HEARD MUSEUM INDIAN FAIR, early Apr., 2 days. Indian demonstrations, foods, exhibits, D; Indians admitted free. *Heard Museum, 22 E. Monte Vista Rd., Phoenix 85004.*

Tucson TUCSON FESTIVAL, April, month. Celebration of multicultural heritage of area includes San Xavier Fiesta celebrating the founding of Mission San Xavier del Bac, La Fiesta de la Placita, which is a traditional Mexican fiesta, Pioneer Days at Old Fort Lowell depicting frontier life in 1870's. *Tucson Festival Society, 8 W. Paseo Redondo, Tucson 85705 602 622-6911*

Wickenburg GOLD RUSH DAYS, early Feb., 3 days. Wickenburg Massacre reenactment; gold shirt gang raid; chuck wagon, Indian relays; gold-panning-championship, beard, international chicken-flying contests. *C of C, 470 E. Center St., Wickenburg 85358. 602 684-5479*

Wickenburg HORSETHIEVES' DAYS MARKET, mid-Oct., 3 days, All-girls', bike Rs; team roping; goat tying; steer undecorating; tie-down calf roping. *C of C, 470 E. Center St., Wickenburg 85358. 602 684-5479*

Window Rock NAVAJO NATION FAIR, early Sept., 4 days. Indian ceremonial performances; Indian fry bread contest; horse racing; BG, A/C, P. *The Navajo Nation, PO Box 738, Window Rock 86515. 602 871-4941*

Yuma YUMA JAYCEES' SILVER SPUR RODEO, Feb., 2nd wknd. Beard contest; Mexican Fiesta Day; Indian Day; R, BC, P. *Yuma County C of C, 200 1st St., Yuma 85364. 602 782-2567*

ARKANSAS

Batesville OZARK FOLKLORE WORKSHOPS, Summer. Workshops at Arkansas College demonstrate water witching, wart cures; ghost legends told; fox-hunting discussions. *Director, Continuing Education, Arkansas College, Batesville 72501. 501 793-9813*

Dierks PINE TREE FESTIVAL, Aug., 1st Sat. Greased-pig chase, pole climb, sack races; sawdust pile of money run; women's world championship skillet-throwing contest; egg-throwing, tobacco-spitting, horseshoe-pitching, fiddling contests; log cutting; log rolling. *Dierks Jaycees, PO Box 2, Dierks 71833. 501 286-2862*

Eureka Springs OZARK FOLK FESTIVAL, Oct., 4 days. "Oldest, most original program in the Ozarks"; 1890's music played on fiddles, jackass jawbones, dulcimers; Barefoot Ball, Gay Nineties costume P; nightly shows feature folklore

and M of Ozarks. *Ozark Folk Festival Board, PO Box 88, Eureka Springs 72632.*

Heber Springs ANNUAL GREERS FERRY LAKE WATER FESTIVAL, mid-Aug., 3 days. Boat, canoe races; spear, bass-fishing tournaments; hootennanies; logrolling, greased-watermelon, inner-tube-racing contests; R, D. *Greers Ferry Lake & Little Red River Assn., PO Box 408, Heber Springs 72543.*

Heber Springs OZARK FRONTIER TRAIL FESTIVAL & CRAFT SHOW, Oct., 2nd wknd. Authentic presentation of early Ozark crafts; weaving, leather tanning, blacksmithing; basketmaking, wood turning; horse-drawn sorghum mill; gristmill; cotton, wool spinning; pioneer beard, wood-cutting, dress contests; muzzleloading rifle demonstrations; cannon-firing competition; P, D, M. *C of C, Heber Springs 72543.*

Hot Springs ARKANSAS FUN FESTIVAL, early June, 10 days. Horseshoe, washer pitching; domino, shuffleboard contests; inner-tube, bicycle races; folklore; rock-skipping tourney; sports car rally; Arkansas Carpenters' State Apprentice Contest; M, A/C. *Arkansas Fun Festival, PO Box 1500, Hot Springs Nat'l Park 71901.*

Hot Springs National Park OKTOBERFEST, mid-Oct., 4 days. German atmosphere; polka, costume contests; road race; A/C. *Hot Springs C of C, PO Box 1500, Hot Springs Nat'l Park 71901.*

Mountain View ARKANSAS FOLK FESTIVAL, Apr., 2 wknds, at Ozark Folk Center. Folklore M; Ozark craftsmen demonstrate how to make and sell pottery, baskets, soap, candles; mountain dulcimer; Scottish & Irish M; shooting matches; P, R. *Ozark Folk Center, Mt. View 72560. 501 269-3851*

Mountain View OZARK FOLK CENTER HARVEST FESTIVAL, mid-Oct., at Ozark Folk Center. Pioneer preparation of soap, hominy, sorghum, cornmeal; quilting; basketry; blacksmithing; pottery; candle dipping; furniture; apple butter, bread making; Ozark music played on quills, cornstalk fiddle, gourd banjo, fiddlesticks, picking bow; Indian artifacts from local digs displayed; C, M. *Ozark Folk Festival, PO Box 68, Mt. View 72560. 501 269-3851*

Mountain View FAMILY WEEK, Oct., last wk. Indian artifacts; oldtime dress revue; tobacco-chewing, spitting, frog-jumping contests; turtle races. *Ozark Folk Center, Mt. View 72560. 501 269-3851*

Springdale NORTHWEST ARKANSAS POULTRY FESTIVAL, mid-Apr., 1 day. Poultry-cooking, producer of the year contests; BC. *Springdale C of C, Box 166, Springdale 72764.*

Stuttgart WORLD CHAMPION DUCK CALLING CONTEST & AGRICULTURAL FESTIVAL, late Nov. Chick Major Memorial, junior, women's Arkansas State, world championship duck-calling contests; BC. *C of C, Box 932, Stuttgart 72160.*

CALIFORNIA

Ahwahnee GOLD RUSH DAYS, mid-July. Gold-panning contest; D. *VFW Hall, Hwy. 49, Ahwahnee 93601. 290 683-7766*

Angels Camp CALAVERAS COUNTY FAIR & JUMPING FROG JUBILEE, May, 3rd wk, 4 days. International frog-jumping contest; rent a frog available; old-fashioned hand pumper fire-engine-pumping contests; destruction derby; BC, P, R. *Calaveras County Fair, PO Box 96, Angels Camp 95222. 209 736-2561*

Apple Valley APPLE VALLEY POW WOW DAYS, late July, 3 days. Lovely knees, knobby knees, beard-growing contests; Indian D competition; tug-of-war; pancake breakfast; D, P. *C of C, PO Box 1073, Apple Valley 92307. 714 242-2388*

Banning STAGECOACH DAYS, Sept.–Oct., 5 days. Wagon display; carnival; whiskerino contest; R, P. *C of C, 78 N. Murray, Banning 92220. 714 849-2781*

Big Bear Lake OLD MINERS DAYS, Aug., 1st wk. National burro derby; tobacco-spitting, liars, women's-nailing, potato-peeling contests; P. *C of C, Box 2860, Big Bear Lake 92315.*

Big Bear Lake OKTOBERFEST, Sept.–Oct., 3 wknds. Schnitzelbank; beer-drinking, holz-hackel, pretzel-eating contests; BC, D, M. *C of C, PO Box 2860, Big Bear Lake 92315.*

Bodega Bay BODEGA BAY FISHERMEN'S FESTIVAL, early Apr., 2 days. Fleet blessing for beginning of salmon season; wreath thrown into sea to honor men who have died at sea; A/C. *Fishermen's Festival, Bodega Bay 94923.*

Borrego Springs PEGLEG LIARS CONTEST, early Apr., 1 day. Oldtimers gather to swap yarns; contests keep alive desert tradition and legends. *Borrego Springs C of C, Box 66, Borrego Springs 92004. 714 767-5555*

Borrego Springs BORREGO SPRINGS DESERT FESTIVAL, early Oct., 4 days. Festival emphasizes Coyote Canyon, CA camping spot, to which Juan Bautista de Anza led colonizers to found present-day San Francisco; celebration of Mexican and Spanish heritage; P, D, A/C. *C of C, Box 66, Borrego Springs 92004. 714 767-5555*

Cloverdale CLOVERDALE CITRUS FAIR, mid-Feb., 4 days. Sheep-shearing, glass-blowing, lemon-squeezin', horseshoe-pitching contests; goat show; P, D. *Cloverdale Citrus Fair Assn., PO Box 445, Cloverdale 95425. 707 894-5790*

Crescent City NATIONAL INDIAN OBSERVANCE DAY, Sept. Marathon race; Indian ceremonial dancing; Indian Village; salmon feed. *Del Norte County C of C, PO Box 246, Crescent City 95531.*

Del Mar JUMPING FROG JAMBOREE, Apr., last Sun., at fairgrounds. Rent or bring your own frogs; best-dressed, smallest, largest frog contests; frog broad-jump contests. *J. Bresman, 867 Del Riego, Leucadia 92024. 714 753-9476*

Fillmore EARLY CALIFORNIA DAYS FESTIVAL, 3rd wknd. Orange-peeling, tug-of-war contests; oldtime fiddlers; BC, P, A/C, D. *C of C, PO Box 276, Fillmore 93015. 805 524-0351*

Fort Bragg PAUL BUNYAN DAYS, early Sept., 4 days. Old-fashioned dress revue; logging show;

D, BC, P. *C of C, PO Box 1141, Fort Bragg 95437. 707 964-3153*

Indio NATIONAL DATE FESTIVAL, mid-Feb., 10 days. Celebration of date harvest; banjo, fiddle, mandolin, kitchen band contests; camel races; Mexican day; M, D, BC. *National Date Festival, 46-350 Arabia St., Indio 92201. 714 347-3487*

Kernville WHISKEY FLAT DAYS, mid-Feb., 5 days. Gold rush days celebrated; honorary mayor elected; epitaph judging; frog-jumping, greased-pig-catching, oldtime fiddlers contests; P, D. *Kernville C of C, Box 397, Kernville 93238.*

Kernville LOGGERS TOURNAMENT, mid-Mar., 2 days. Hot saw, stock saw, hand-bucking, hand-chopping, choker-setting, ax-throwing contests. *C of C, Box 397, Kernville 93238.*

Kingsburg KINGSBURG SWEDISH FESTIVAL, May, 3rd Sat. Swedish pancakes, smorgasbord; P. *C of C, PO Box 515, Kingsburg 93631. 209 897-2925*

Klamath SALMON FESTIVAL, June, last Sun. Logging contests, show; gymkhana; salmon bar-b-que; native Indian D; P, A/C. *C of C, Box 476, Klamath 95548.*

Lancaster ANTELOPE VALLEY FAIR & ALFALFA FESTIVAL, Aug.–Sept., 6 days. Hay-loading, tractor-backing contests; tractor vs. horse, potato races; tug-of-war. *A. V. Fair, 50th Agriculture District, Lancaster 93534. 805-948-6060*

Lompoc LA PURISIMA MISSION FIESTA, May, 3rd Sun., at Mission State Historical Park. Portrayal of old mission days; old Spanish food; M, D. *Lompoc Valley C of C, 119 E. Cypress Ave., Lompoc 93436. 805 736-4567*

Los Angeles MARDI GRAS, late Feb., 1 day, at El Pueblo de Los Angeles Park. Celebration of Eve of Lent; mariachi; burning of the "Mal Humor"; P, BC. *Los Angeles Convention & Visitors Bureau, 505 S. Flower St., Los Angeles 90071. 213 488-9100*

Monterey SANTA ROSALIA FESTIVAL, Sept., 1 day. Blessing of fishing boats; fishermen festival; Mass; Italian ethnic foods; P, BC, M. *Italian-American Community of Monterey Peninsula, PO Box 367, Monterey 93940.*

Oakhurst SIERRA MOUNTAINEER DAYS, Sept., 3rd wknd, at Grub Gulch Grounds. Historic atmosphere; horse show; gymkhana; pancake breakfast; P, D. *Oakhurst Community Center, Road 425 B, Oakhurst 93644. 209 683-7766*

Oceanside MISSION SAN LUIS REY FIESTA, mid-July, wknd, at Mission San Luis Rey. Anniversary of founding of mission; reenactment of the journey of Padre Juniper Serra to mission; priests bless animals. *Oceanside C of C, 510 4th St., Oceanside 92054. 714 722-1534*

Pacific Grove BUTTERFLY FESTIVAL, mid-Oct., 1 day. Festival marks annual return of monarch butterflies; bazaar; P. *Pacific Grove C of C, PO Box 167, Pacific Grove 93950. 408 373-3304*

Paso Robles PASO ROBLES PIONEER DAY, early Oct., 1 Sat. Free bean feed; costume, whiskerino, fiddlers, horseshoe contests; gymkhana; senior roping; D. *C of C, PO Box 457, Paso Robles 93446. 805 238-0506*

Riverside ANNUAL INTERNATIONAL FESTIVAL, Jan., 1 day. International students provide ethnic displays, food, folk dancing; A/C. *UCR International Club, U. of California at Riverside, Riverside 92502. 714 787-4113*

Riverside CINCO DE MAYO DAYS, early May, 9 days. Mexican-American celebration features exhibits, ethnic foods; D, M, P. *Cinco de Mayo,*

Community Relations, Visitor & Convention Bureau, Riverside 92501. 714 787-7316

Riverside AFRO SUMMER FESTIVAL, June, 3 days. Ethnic displays, foods; P, M. *Afro Summer Festival, Community Relations, Visitor & Convention Bureau, Riverside 92501. 714 787-7316*

San Diego FIESTA DE LA PRIMAVERA, May, at Old Town State Park. Strolling mariachis; troubadours; Indian exhibits; fiddler, banjo contests; Spanish dancers. *San Diego Union Museum, 2626 San Diego Ave., San Diego 92110. 714 297-2119*

San Diego FESTIVAL OF BELLS, mid-July wknd, at Mission San Diego de Alcala. Annual event since July 16, 1769, celebrates founding of the mission; mariachis; D. *Mission San Diego de Alcala, 10818 San Diego Mission Rd., San Diego 92118. 714 281-8449*

San Francisco CHINESE NEW YEAR IN SAN FRANCISCO, Feb.–Mar., 9 days. "Largest Chinese New Year festival in US"; operas; dragon P; cultural exhibits; Kung Fu displays; lion dancers; cooking, paper-cutting, calligraphy, painting demonstrations; BC, F. *San Francisco Convention & Visitors Bureau, 1390 Market St., San Francisco 94102. 415 626-5500*

San Francisco SAN FRANCISCO FALL FESTIVAL, late Sept., 3 days. Japanese harvest celebration; taiko drums; ikebana; tea ceremony; bonsai; callicature drawing; P, M, B. *San Francisco Convention & Visitors Bureau, 1390 Market St., San Francisco 94102. 415 626-5500*

San Juan Capistrano FIESTA DE LAS GOLONDRINAS, Mar. 19 & wk following. Swallows return to Capistrano on March 19 annually; fiesta celebration of historical rancho period; hoosegow day; trail ride; old Spanish and Indian Ds; P, A. *The San Juan Capistrano Fiesta Assn., PO Box 532, San Juan Capistrano 92675.*

San Juan Capistrano ADIOS A LAS GOLONDRINAS Y FIESTA DE ARTES, Oct. 23 or wknd nearest Oct 23. Swallows leave for Argentina; piñata breaking; Mexican folk Ds; historical costumes; A/C. *San Juan Capistrano C of C, 31882 Camino Capistrano, San Juan Capistrano 92675. 714 493-4700*

Santa Monica TOPANGA, BANJO & FIDDLE CONTEST, mid-June, 1 day. Bluegrass, traditional-fiddling, banjo-picking contests. *C of C, 200 Santa Monica Blvd., Santa Monica 90401. 213 393-9825*

Santa Monica SCOTTISH GATHERING & GAMES, June, last Sat. Scottish Highland dancing, pipe bands; tug-of-war; soccer; P. *United Scottish Societies of Southern California, 17455 Flanders, Granada Hills 91344. 213 360-2919*

Santa Monica SANTA MONICA SPORTS & ARTS FESTIVAL, Aug.–Sept., 2 wks. Lifeguard championships; dory races; fishing derby; lawn bowling; roque, judo, paddle tennis, marksmanship, shuffleboard tournaments; sand sculpture contest. *Recreation Dept., City of Santa Monica, City Hall, 1685 Main St., Santa Monica 90402. 213 393-9975*

Solvang DANISH DAYS, Sept., 3rd wknd. Celebrates Denmark's Independence Day; Danish costumes; Aebleskiver breakfasts; Scandinavian folk M; Danish folk dancers; polka party contest; P. *Solvang Business Assn., PO Box 465, Solvang 93463. 805 688-3317*

Sonoma VALLEY OF THE MOON VINTAGE FESTIVAL, Sept., last wknd. Wine festival, tasting; blessing of the grapes; costumes; shoot-outs; stagecoach rides; M, D, P, A/C. *C of C, 461 1st St. W., Sonoma 95476. 707 996-1033*

Thousand Oaks CONEJO VALLEY DAYS, Apr.–May, 9 days. Whiskeroo, badgeroo contests; P, R. *Conejo Valley C of C, 401 W. Hillcrest Dr., Thousand Oaks 91360. 805 497-1621*

Watsonville SANTA CRUZ COUNTY FAIR, mid-Sept., 5 days, at county fairgrounds. Lumberjack, bluegrass contests; weaving, quilting, spinning, cake-decorating, cow-milking, horseshoeing, sheep-shearing demonstrations; horse show; gymkhana events. *S.C. County Fairgrounds Office, 2601 E. Lake Ave., Watsonville 95076. 408 724-5671*

Willits FRONTIER DAYS, early July, 5 days. Cutting horse events; jackpot roping; water fight; western costumes; R, D. *C of C, 15 S. Main St., Willits 95490. 707 459-4113*

COLORADO

Aspen WINTERSKOL CARNIVAL, mid-Jan., 5 days. Ski splash; gelundesprung; crazy slalom; candy race; bartender's drink contest; vehicle, pool tugs-of-war; ski joring; inner-tube race; D. *C of C, Box GG, Aspen 81611. 303 925-1940*

Aurora 4TH OF JULY CELEBRATION, July 4th wknd. Horseshoe contest; foot, 3-legged races; jeep pull; motocross bike competitions; black powder shoot; R, D. *C of C, 13799 E. Colfax Ave., Aurora, 80011. 303 366-2676*

Bailey BAILEY PIONEER DAY, Aug., 1st wknd. Pioneer costumes; beard contest; black powder, bow and arrow shoots; P. *Colorado Assn. of Commerce & Industry, 1390 Logan St., Denver 80203. 303 831-7411*

Beecher Island BEECHER ISLAND BATTLE SITE, Sept., 2nd wknd. Foot, turtle, sack, tire races; married couple shoe scramble; egg toss; shoe kick; cow chip, plate throws. *Colorado Assn. of Commerce & Industry, 1390 Logan St., Denver 80203. 303 831-7411*

Boulder POW WOW DAYS, late July, 1 wk. Horse shows; R, P. *T. Rees, 783 Cypress Dr., Boulder 80303. 303 892-5000*

Breckenridge NO MAN'S LAND, Aug., 2nd wknd. Celebration recognizes time when city was not, by error, included in a government survey; muzzleloaders demonstration; mucking and tramming, beard-growing contests. *Breckenridge Resort Assn., Breckenridge 80424.*

Brighton AMATEUR RODEO, Aug., 1st wknd, at Adams County Fairgrounds. Wild-cow milking; tractor, chariot, horse pulls. *Adams County Fairgrounds, Brighton 80601.*

Broomfield BROOMFIELD DAYS, Aug., 3rd wknd. Watermelon feed; physical fitness meet; tricycle race; horseshoe-pitching, clown contests; tug-of-war; bicycle P. *C of C, 1380 W. Midway Blvd., Broomfield 80020. 303 466-1775*

Central City GREGORY DAY CELEBRATION, early May, 1 day. Commemorates John Gregory's discovery of "the richest square mile on earth"; P, D. *Public Relations Director, City of Central, Central City 80427.*

Central City LOU BUNCH DAY, mid-Aug., 1 day. Celebration recognizes pioneer spirit of madams and ladies of the night of a bygone era; bed race; D. *Public Relations Coordinator, City of Central, Box 421, Central City 80427.*

Creede 4TH OF JULY. Mining contest; mucking; jackleg, hand drilling; mucking machine; sawdust money hunt; watermelon eating; greased pole; D, F. *Colorado Assn. of Commerce & Industry, 1390 Logan St., Denver 80203. 303 831-7411*

Cripple Creek DONKEY DERBY DAYS, June, last wknd. World championship burro race; shet-land pony, hard-earned-money. donkey races; greased-pig, pole, tobacco-spit-off,drilling contests. *Two Mile High Club, Cripple Creek 80813.*

Denver NATIONAL WESTERN STOCK SHOW, Jan., 3rd wk, at Coliseum. Rs include bronco busting, steer wrestling, barrel jumping; "biggest US livestock show"; national sheep-shearing contest. *National Western Stock Show, 1325 E. 46th Ave., Denver 80216.*

Denver NIGHT IN OLD DENVER, early Aug., 4 days. Gold rush days atmosphere celebrates birth of Denver at Larimer Square. *Larimer Square, 1228 15th St., Denver 80202.*

Dove Creek PICK & HOE DAYS, early July, 2 days. Greased-pole, 3-legged-race, catch-a-calf, tug-of-war contests; pony express barrel racing; pole bending; flag raising; P, F, D. *County Extension Director, Box 527, Dove Creek 81324. 303 677-2283.*

Eagle EAGLE VALLEY FLIGHT DAYS, June, last wknd. Fishing derby; greased-pig catch; horse-apple pitching; bike R; P, A/C. *C of C, PO Box 864, Eagle 81631. 303 328-7144*

Fairplay WORLD CHAMPIONSHIP PACK BURRO RACES, late July, 2 days. Burro race: contestants must walk, run, or carry burros (may not ride) from Fairplay to Mosquito Gulch and back, about 26 miles; burro-braying contest; meller-dramer. *C of C, PO Box 312, Fairplay 80440.*

Fort Lupton RENDEZVOUS DAYS, Sept., 3rd wknd. Rolling-pin-throw, shoe-kicking, lagging, watermelon-eating contests; bike, sack, foot races; fire department water fights; tractor pull; P, M. *C of C, Fort Lupton 80621. 303 857-4474*

Grand Lake WINTER CARNIVAL, Feb., 1st wknd. Candy cane hunt; snowshoe, blindfold snowmobile races; snowball toss; snowmobile treasure hunt; ski touring; snowshoeing; P, A/C. *C of C, PO Box 57, Grand Lake 80447. 303 627-3402*

Grand Lake OLD-FASHIONED CHRISTMAS, late Dec., 11 days. Merchant guessing jars; Yule log hunt; ski touring; hot wine party; snowshoeing; snowman sculptures; D. *C of C, PO Box 57, Grand Lake 80447. 303 627-3402*

Haxtun HAXTUN CORN SHOW & FESTIVAL, Oct., 1st wknd. Corn, shoe scrambles; shoe kick; speed, sack, 3-legged races; egg throw; penny scramble; horseshoe pitching; tractor pull; P, D. *C of C, Haxtun, 80731. 303 774-6507*

Hot Sulphur Springs HOT SULPHUR DAYS, June, 2nd wknd. Shoot-out; greased-pole, running, bicycle races; ball throwing; hoedown; pony express relay; gymkhana; P. *C of C, PO Box 168, Hot Sulphur Springs 80451.*

Hot Sulphur Springs MOUNTAIN MAN RENDEZVOUS, Aug., last Sat. Oldtime costume, buffalo whomp, tobacco-spitting, horseshoe, archery contests; greased-pole climb; muzzleloading; hatchet, knife throws. *C of C, PO Box 168, Hot Sulphur Springs 80451.*

Idaho Springs GOLD RUSH DAYS, Aug., 1st wknd. Burro, wheelchair races; Colorado State Mining contests: mucking, drilling, beard, hose cart races. *C of C, 2200 Colorado Blvd, Idaho Springs 80452. 303 567-9944*

Leadville CRYSTAL CARNIVAL, Feb., 3 days. Commemoration of first Crystal Carnival & Ice Palace of 1896; snowmobiling; ice skating; snow sculptures; skijoring; ice, snow-driving, ice-fishing contests; folk entertainment; tubing; powder puff. *C of C, 116 E. 9th St., Leadville 80461. 303 486-0418*

Leadville BOOM DAYS, Aug., 1st wknd. Commemorates miners of olden days with international burro race; rendezvous shoot; bed race; tug-of-war; traveling trophy-drilling contest; S, D, P, BC. *C of C, Box 861, Leadville 80461.*

Limon HARVEST FESTIVAL, early Sept., 1 day. Tractor pull; cricket, sack races; P, D. *C of C, Box 237, Limon 80828. 303 775-2230*

Manassa MORMON PIONEER DAYS, late July, 2 days. P honors oldest pioneers; Mexican food; R, D. *C of C, 312 Main St., Manassa 81141. 303 843-5322*

Mancos MANCOS COLORADO DAYS, July, last wknd. Pioneers honored; 3-legged, potato, sack, tricycle races; firemen's water fights; A, M, D. *C of C, PO Box 245, Mancos 81328. 303 533-7768*

Meeker RANGE CALL, early July, 2 days. Sheep hooking; ladies barrel, pony, cow-horse races; Indian uprising massacre reenactment; D. *C of C, Box 859, Meeker 81641. 303 878-5510*

Montrose MONTROSE COUNTY FAIR & RODEO, mid-Aug., 4 days. Depicts heritage of cowboy and farmer in area. *C of C, PO Box 1061, Montrose 81401. 303 249-5515*

Newcastle BURNING MOUNTAIN FESTIVAL, July, 2nd Sat. Pie-eating, 3-legged, sack race contests; nail driving; hand sawing; coal shoveling; karate; D, P. *Colorado Assn. of Commerce & Industry, 1390 Logan St., Denver 80203. 303 831-7411*

Pagosa Springs LOGGERS LUMBERJACK TOURNAMENT, Aug., 3rd Sun. Burling; logrolling; ax chopping; crosscut saw; ax, hatchet throws; chain saw; notch splitting. *Pagosa Springs, Archuleta County C of C, Pagosa Springs 81147.*

Platteville RENDEZVOUS DAYS CELEBRATION, Aug., 2nd wk. Muzzleloaders, hatchet throw, knife throw, sack race, 3-legged race, wheelbarrow, greased pig or rabbit contests; antique cars; A/C, P, D. *C of C, Platteville 80651.*

Rocky Ford ARKANSAS VALLEY FAIR & WATERMELON DAY, mid-Aug., 5 days. "Colorado's oldest fair"; on Watermelon Day. each visitor receives a free watermelon; bicycle, turtle races; watermelon seed-spitting, cow-chip-throwing contests. *C of C, 9th and Elm Ave., Rocky Ford 81067. 303 254-7483*

Sedgwick HARVEST FALL FESTIVAL, Sept., 1st wknd. Egg throw; foot, bike, sack, 3-legged races; penny scramble; softball throw; slipper kicking; spoon and egg race; blockhead; tug-of-war; demolition derby, P, R. *C of C, Sedgwick 80749.*

Silverton MINER'S DAY, Aug., 3rd wknd. Mucking; tramming; drilling; tug-of-war. *C of C, PO Box 565, Silverton 81433. 303 387-5429*

Steamboat Springs WINTER CARNIVAL, Feb., 2nd wknd. Slalom, hot dog competitions; 3-legged race on skis; muzzleloading biathalon; gelandesprung; *C of C, Box L, Steamboat Springs 80477. 303 879-0740*

Telluride COLORIDE, late Sept., 1 wk. Free jeep rides; frisbee contest; scavenger, treasure hunts; dog show. *C of C, PO Box 653, Telluride 81435. 303 728-3614.*

CONNECTICUT

Bethlehem BETHLEHEM FAIR, early Sept., 2 days, at Morris Hgwy. Cattle, horse, pony drawings; poultry, sheep, rabbit, horse shows; Mother Goose barnyard. *Bethlehem Fair Soc., Inc., Bethlehem 06751.*

Bridgeport BARNUM FESTIVAL, June-July, 11 days. Honors Phineas T. Barnum; drum corps, Jenny Lind contests; air, antique auto shows; *P. Barnum Festival, 804 Main St., Bridgeport 06604. 203 367-8495.*

Bridgewater BRIDGEWATER COUNTRY FAIR, Aug., 3rd wknd. Connecticut State Sheep Show and Shearing contest; woodchopper's contest; cattle shows; pony, oxen drawings; home arts. *H. Stuart, Stuart Rd., Bridgewater 06752. 203 354-7112.*

Cheshire CHESHIRE FAIR, mid-Aug., 2 days, at Wallingford Rd., off Route 10. Pie-eating, women's rolling-pin-throwing contests; livestock exhibit. *M. B. Comstock, 752 Milldale Rd., Cheshire 06410.*

Chester CHESTER FAIR, late Aug., 3 days, on Route 9 A. Pony, cattle, horse drawings; livestock, photo, food exhibits; baking contests; fife & drum concert. *Mrs. J. Kitsen, 32 Pleasant St., Chester 06412.*

Danbury DANBURY FAIR, early Oct., 10 days, at Intersection of US 6 & 7 and I 84. Regional cooking; livestock show; lumberjack exhibition; oxen drawing; auto thrill show. *J. H. Stetson, 130 White St., Danbury 06810. 203 748-3535.*

Deep River DEEP RIVER ANCIENT MUSTER, July, 3rd Sat. About 70 fife & drum corps from US compete as was done in colonial times; old-style martial music; uniforms. *Town Clerk, 174 Main St., Deep River 06417. 203 526-5783.*

Goshen GOSHEN FAIR, early Sept., 3 days, at Route 63. Wood-cutting contest; pony, horse, cattle drawings; poultry, sheep, cattle shows. *Mrs. K. Vaill, RD #1, Goshen 06756. 203 491-3604.*

Guilford GUILFORD FAIR, mid-Sept., 3 days, at Lovers Lane. Spelling bee; square dance exhibition; corn husking; nail driving; milking; pie-eating contests; oxen, horse, pony drawings. *M. E. Griswold, 84 Fair St., Guilford, 06437. 203 453-2256.*

Hartford JUMPING FROG CONTEST, mid-June, at Mark Twain House. Frog-jumping contest commemorates contest in story by Mark Twain. *Mark Twain Memorial, 351 Farmington Ave., Hartford 06105. 203 247-0998.*

Harwinton HARWINTON FAIR, early Oct., 2 days, at Locust Rd. Goat products, show; woodcutting contest; early Americana includes shingle mill, sawmill, pewter spinner, blacksmith show, country store. *M. B. Theirry, Litchfield Rd., Harwinton 06790. 203 482-1847.*

Hebron HEBRON HARVEST FAIR, early Sept., 4 days, at Route 85. Farm tractor pull; horse drawing; nail-driving contest; old engine display; pie-eating contest; 3-time championship trophy for oxen pull; doodlebug pull; BC, A/C, M. *A. I. Jensen, PO Box 118, Hebron 06248. 203 228-9471.*

Lebanon LEBANON COUNTRY FAIR, early Aug., 3 days, at Mack Rd. Cattle, horse drawings; pony, doodlebug pulls; livestock, sheep, horse shows; BC, F. *A. Vertefeuille, Old S. Windham Rd., S. Windham 06266. 203 423-3118.*

Milford OYSTER FESTIVAL, mid-Aug., 1 day. Oyster race to Charles Island and return; oysters to eat; M, A/C. *Milford C of C, Inc., 102 New Haven Ave., Milford 06460. 203 878-0681.*

New Haven POWDER HOUSE DAY, early May. Celebrates Benedict Arnold's participation (before his defection) in Revolutionary War; reenacts his demand for keys to powderhouse in order to arm his men and go to war; M. *Second Company, Governor's Footguard, 267 Goffe St., New Haven 06511. 203 562-6593.*

Preston PRESTON CITY FAIR, mid-Aug., 2 days, at junction Routes 164 & 165. Ox drawing;

bicycle race; weight-lifting, pie-eating, horse-shoe-pitching contests; BC, M. *P. Tunucci, Miller Rd., RFD #3, Norwich 06360. 203 887-6353.*

Riverton RIVERTON FAIR, early Oct., 2 days, at Route 20. Cattle, pony drawings; chopping, sawing, pie-eating, cooking, baking contests. *G. D. Seymour, Riverton Fair, Riverton 06098. 203 379-3058.*

Somers UNION AGRICULTURAL SOCIETY OR FOUR TOWN FAIR, mid-Sept., 3 days, at Egypt Rd. "Oldest fair in State"; doodlebug, doll carriage, frog contests; cattle, horse drawings; sheep showmanship; gymkhana; grease pole; sheep shearing. *J. Steinmetz, 184 South Rd., Somers 06071. 203 749-3340.*

South Windsor WAPPING FAIR, early Sept., 3 days, at Rye St. Park. Doodlebug, bike, 5-mile foot, pie-eating, grease pole, horseshoe contests; M, A. *M. Jorgensen, 999 Ellington Rd., S. Windsor 06074. 203 289-2631.*

Windsor SHAD DERBY FESTIVAL, early May, 2 wks. Shad-fishing contests; BC, P, D. *C of C, PO Box 144, Windsor 06095. 203 688-5165.*

Windsor Locks HARTFORD COUNTY 4-H FAIR, late Aug., 3 days, at Bradley Field. Doodlebug; horse drawing, show; livestock, poultry shows; fife & drum corps; photo, baking contests; gymkhana; dog, obedience shows; M. *P. Dillon, 887 Main St., S. Windsor 06074. 203 528-1366.*

Woodstock WOODSTOCK FAIR, Labor Day wknd. Potter; blacksmith; basketmaking; weaving; fife & drum corps; Scotch pipe band; country auction; doodlebug, tractor-pulling contests; sky diving; sheep show, shearing; P, M, D. *Woodstock Agricultural Society, Inc., Woodstock 06281.*

DELAWARE

Bowers Beach BIG THURSDAY, July, 1 day. Commemorates coming of first oyster fleets of early 1800's; clambake; antique automobiles; P. *Division of Economic Development, 630 State College Rd., Dover 19901. 302 678-4254.*

Dover OLD DOVER DAYS, May, 2nd wknd. Town history celebrated by residents wearing colonial costumes; tours of 18th-century homes, plantations. *C of C, PO Box 567, Dover 19901.*

Georgetown DELMARVA CHICKEN FESTIVAL, early June, 2 days. Festival focuses on importance of poultry industry to area; chicken-cooking contest; chicken capers; C, M. *Delmarva Poultry Industry, Inc., Route 2, Box 47, Georgetown 19947. 302 856-2971.*

Greenville COLONIAL SCOTTISH GAMES, June, 1st Sat., at Fair Hill Raceground, MD. Pipe band contest; individual piping; drumming; Highland dancing; tossing the caber. *Scottish Games Assn., Greenville Center, 3801 Kennett Pike, Greenville 19807. 302 656-6208.*

Lewes GREAT DELAWARE KITE FESTIVAL, Good Friday, at Cape Henlopen State Park. Kite-flying contests; prizes. *C of C, PO Box 1, Lewes 19958. 302 645-8073.*

Newark PAUL BUNYAN CHRISTMAS PARTY, early Dec., 1 day. Crosscut saw, nail-hammering, logrolling contests: winner is Mr. (or Mrs.) Paul Bunyan for a year. *Paul Bunyan Assn., Ogletown Rd., Newark, 19711. 302 737-3084.*

New Castle A DAY IN OLD NEW CASTLE, May, 3rd Sat. Public sees oldest city in Delaware; 18th-century homes opened. *A Day in Old New Castle, PO Box 166, New Castle 19720.*

DISTRICT OF COLUMBIA

Washington FESTIVAL OF AMERICAN FOLKLIFE, June–Sept., at The Mall. Craftsmen, musicians demonstrate folk heritage of US. *Convention & Visitors Bureau, 1129 20th St. N.W., Suite 200, Washington 20036.*

Washington INDEPENDENCE DAY CELEBRATION, July 4, at Washington Monument. Festival of American folklife; M, D, F. *Washington, DC, Recreation Dept., 3149 16th St. N.W., Washington 20010. 202 673-7660.*

Washington PAGEANT OF PEACE, Dec., at Elipse, S. of White House. Christmas tree lighting ceremony. *Convention & Visitors Bureau, 1129 20th St. N.W., Washington 20036.*

FLORIDA

Belleview BELLEVIEW FOUNDERS' WEEK, May, 1st wk. Costumes of 1885, year in which city was founded; men without beards may be fined or jailed in mock jail; Polish, scout days; beard contest. *Belleview-South Marion C of C, PO Box 602, Belleview 32620. 904 245-2178.*

Bunnell FLAGLER COUNTY CRACKER DAY, Mar., last Sat. Florida cracker once denoted a Florida horseman working his herds with a bullwhip; horse, barrel races; roping contests. *Flagler County Cattlemen's Assn., PO Box 308, Bunnell 32010. 904 437-3122.*

Cape Coral OKTOBERFEST, Oct., 4 Sats. German-American costumes, food, beer; brass band M played by instrumentalists attired in leather pants, alpine hats. *German-American Social Club, 1730 Sandy Cir., Cape Coral 33904. 813 542-1551.*

Clearwater FUN N SUN FESTIVAL, Mar., 10 days. Pancake-eating contest, festival; weightlifting, peddler, kite contests; Fun Kana beach races; state horseshoe tournament; folk festival; optimist pram regatta. *Greater Clearwater C of C, 128 N. Osceola Ave., Clearwater 33515. 813 446-4081.*

Dunedin HIGHLAND GAMES, late Mar., 3 days. Scottish events include Ceilidh, military tattoo, drumming, piping, tossing of the caber, tossing the sheaf, hammer throw, wrestling; tug-of-war; D. *Dunedin Highland Games & Festival, PO Box 507, Dunedin 33528.*

Fernandina Beach EIGHT FLAGS SHRIMP BOAT RACES, late Apr., 3 days. Shrimp boat races; blessing of fleet; shrimping demonstration; pirates' landing, D; beard contest; A/C, BC. *Fernandina Beach C of C, Fernandina Beach 32034.*

Fort Lauderdale HENRY M. FLAGLER DAY, Jan., 1 day. Tribute to Florida's first passenger train and the Flagler, railroad magnate; Old Steam Engine #153 runs all day; men visitors wear tophats, tails; women wear big-plumed hats, bustles. *C of C, Fort Lauderdale 33315.*

Fort Myers EDISON PAGEANT OF LIGHT, early Feb., 10 days. Living memorial to Thomas A. Edison; tennis tournament; sailing races; flower, antique-car shows; nighttime Parade of Light. *M. B. Willis, PO Box 1311, Fort Myers 33902. 813 334-2550.*

Fort Myers Beach ISLAND SHRIMP FESTIVAL, Feb.–Mar., 7 days. Blessing of shrimp fleet; shrimp boil; P, BC. *Fort Myers Beach C of C, PO Box 6109, Fort Myers Beach 33931. 813 463-6451.*

Fort Pierce SANDY SHOES FESTIVAL, late Jan., 10 days. Indian powwow; shoot-outs; turkey shoot; water sports; western attire; pioneer costumes; fishing, tennis tournaments; steam locomotive show; P. *Sandy Shoes Festival Committee, PO Box 391, Fort Pierce 33450.*

Fort Walton Beach BILLY BOWLEGS FESTIVAL, early June, 9 days. Capt. Billy Bowlegs commemorated; pirate siege of city; ships plundered; treasure hunts; washtub race; pirates' market; P, D, F, M. *C of C, 34 Miracle Strip Pkway S.E., Fort Walton Beach 32548.*

Islamorada INDIAN KEY FESTIVAL, Aug. 7. Indians stage historical attack at Indian Key; conch-blowing contests; canoe, sailboat races; Indian relics; railroad memorabilia. *Islamorada C of C, PO Box 915, Islamorada 33036. 305 664-4503*

Jensen Beach SEA TURTLE WATCH, June, 1 wk. Turtles make their way from Atlantic Ocean onto beach, where they dig a nesting area and deposit eggs. *Jensen Beach C of C, 51 Commercial St., Jensen Beach 33457.*

Jensen Beach LEIF ERIKSEN DAY, early Oct., 1 day. Reenactment of landing of Leif Eriksen in America in A.D. 1002; ship racing; folk dancing; battle between Vikings and Indians. *Jensen Beach C of C, 51 Commercial St., Jensen Beach 33457. 305 334-3444*

Key West OLD ISLAND DAYS, late Jan.–early Mar. Cuban foods; conch-blowing contest; blessing of the fleet; D. *Old Island Restoration Foundation, Inc., PO Box 689, Key West 33040.*

Kissimmee SILVER SPURS RODEO, mid-Feb., 3 days; July 4. Calf roping; saddle bronc, bull riding; steer wrestling; Silver Spurs Quadrille; open barrel race; "Florida's oldest R." *L. Acree, PO Box 1909, Kissimmee 32741. 305 847-4052.*

Miami INTERNATIONAL FOLK FESTIVAL, May–June, 4 days. Ethnic groups of Miami celebrate culture with foods, exhibits; P, A/C. *M. Freedman, 2539 S. Bayshore Dr., Miami 33133.*

Naples SWAMP BUGGY RACES, late Oct., 2 days. Contest for title of World Champion Swamp Buggy Driver & Mud Dutchess; beard judging; "Best Ole Fashion" dress contests; turkey shoot; P, M. *Swamp Buggy Days, Inc., PO Box 3105, Naples 33940. 813 774-2701*

Orange City FRONTIER DAYS, mid-Mar., 2 days. Frontier frolics; turkey shoot; horse show; carnival. *Sorosis Club of Orange City, PO Box 885, Orange City, 32763. 904 775-2107*

Panama City DANCE FESTIVAL, late Jan., 2 days. Dancers in country and western garb reenact the American heritage of square, round Ds. *Panama City Square & Round Dance Assn., Panama City 32401.*

Pensacola FIESTA OF FIVE FLAGS, early June, 8 days. Festival honors one of the 5 nations that has ruled Pensacola; reenacts landing of Don Tristan de Luna of Spain in 1559; treasure hunt; fishing R. *Pensacola-Escambia Development Commission, 803 N. Palafox St., Pensacola 32501. 904 433-3065*

Pensacola CREEK INDIAN POW WOW, Aug. Coweta Creek Indian Confederacy features feather dancing, Indian dance teams, shawl dances, Indian singers, craftsmen. *Pensacola-Escambia Development Commission, 803 N. Palafox St., Pensacola 32501. 904 433-3065*

St. Augustine DAYS IN SPAIN FIESTA, mid-Aug., 4 days. Celebration of founding of St. Augustine; sword-fighting conquistadors duel; D. *Jaycees, PO Box 734, St. Augustine 32084.*

St. Petersburg ST. PETERSBURG FOLK FAIR, mid-Mar., 3 days. Ethnic groups celebrate contributions to US with food, costumes, culture; A/C. *St. Petersburg International Folk Fair Society, PO Box 40524, St. Petersburg 33743. 813 894-3746*

Sarasota KING NEPTUNE'S FROLIC, Mar.–Apr., 8 days. The Mystic Krewe captures city; fisha-thons; photo contests; golf, tennis tournaments; treasure hunts; P, F. *Sarasota County Pageant Assn., 5103 N. Tuttle, Sarasota 33578. 813-955-0997*

Sarasota ANNUAL INTERNATIONAL SANDCASTLE CONTEST, early May, 1 day. Sand sculpture contest with whales, mermaids, poodles, black sheep relatives, castles as entries. *Sheraton Sandcastle Resort, 1540 Ben Franklin Dr., Sarasota 33577. 813 388-2181*

Spring Hill WORLD'S CHICKEN PLUCKIN' CHAMPIONSHIP, early Oct., 1 day. Teams compete to establish world record; ethnic folk dancing; "chicken concerto"; Miss Drumstick contest. *Publicity Office, Deltona Corp. PO Box 95, Spring Hill 33512. 904 683-0056*

Tampa FRONTIER DAYS, late May, 2 days. Western festival; pony express ride; shoot-out; R. *West Tampa Sherife Assn., PO Box 4352, Tampa 33607. 813 876-8652*

Tarpon Springs INTERNATIONAL GLENDI (Greek festival), Oct., last Sat. Ethnic groups sell ethnic foods; Old World entertainment; Greek costumes; sponge exchange. *Tarpon Springs C of C, 112 S. Pinellas Ave., Tarpon Springs 33589. 813 937-6109*

Wausau WAUSAU'S FAMOUS FUN DAY, Aug., 1st Sat. Sack, gopher races; hog-calling, cow-milking, corn-pone-baking contests; possum auction; donkey softball game; P, BC, M. *D. Carter, Box 148, Route 4, Chipley 32428. 904 638-1017*

White Springs STEPHEN FOSTER DAYS & WEEK, mid-Jan., 1 wk; mid-Mar., 3 days. M recitals feature Foster's works. *Stephen Foster Center, PO Box 265, White Springs 32096. 904 397-2192*

White Springs FLORIDA FOLK FESTIVAL, early Sept., 4 days. Spinning, weaving, woodcarving, basket-weaving, caning, glass-blowing, broom-making, leatherwork demonstrations; Suwannee River coral jewelry making; copper rubbings; folkways; southern folklore; folkiana; oldtime fiddling; ethnic songs, D; mountain clogging. *Stephen Foster Center, PO Box 265, White Springs 32096. 904 397-2192*

Zolfo Springs PIONEER DAYS, March, 1st wknd. Oldtime farm equipment; antique cars; museum. *E. Nickerson, Route 2, Box 309, Wauchula 33873. 813 773-9331*

GEORGIA

Andersonville ANDERSONVILLE HISTORIC FAIR, Oct., 1st wknd. Potterymaking; glass blowing; blacksmithing; basketmaking; sugarcane mill in operation; steam train, buggy, stagecoach rides; oldtime entertainment. *Andersonville Historic Fair, Andersonville Guild, Andersonville 31711. 912 924-2558*

Atlanta GREEK FESTIVAL, late Sept., 3 days, at Greek Orthodox Cathedral. Souvlakia (shish kebab), baklava (pastry), Greek foods, D, M, A/C. *Atlanta C of C, 1300 Commerce Bldg., Atlanta 30303.*

Blairsville SORGHUM FESTIVAL, mid-Oct., 3 days. Sorghum mill; syrupmaking; syrup-sopin' contest; log sawing; rock throwing; greased-pole climbing; moonshine still; blacksmith shop; clogging; spitting, pistol matches. *Blairsville-Union County C of C, Blairsville 30512.*

Calvary MULE DAY, Nov., 1 day. Celebration of appreciation of mule; trophies awarded for most stubborn, prettiest, ugliest mules; greased-pig, tobacco-spitting contests; soap, syrup making; rooster sailing; mule race; P, A/C. *Cairo-Grady City C of C, PO Drawer 387, Cairo 31774. 912 872-3263*

Claxton RATTLESNAKE ROUNDUP, mid-Mar. Largest, longest rattlesnake contests; snake-with-most-rattles contest. *Georgia Bureau of Industry & Trade, PO Box 38097, Atlanta 30334.*

Helen OKTOBERFEST, Sept.–Oct., 5 wknds. Bavarian-style village hosts beer-and-fun festival; yodeling contests; Austrian folklore; folk dancing; German bands; clogging. *C of C, Helen, 30545.*

Hiawassee GEORGIA MOUNTAIN FAIR, mid-Aug., 10 days. Depicts folklore of Georgia mountain people; soapmaking, woodcarving, needlecraft demonstrations. *Tourist Division, GA Dept. of Community Development, PO Box 38097, Atlanta 30334.*

Lumpkin WESTVILLE FOLK MUSIC CONVENTION, late Sept., 2 days. Mid-19th-century southeastern traditional M revived and preserved. *Westville, PO Box 1850, Lumpkin 31815.*

Lumpkin WESTVILLE FAIR OF 1850, early Nov., 10 days. Fair modeled after agricultural fairs of pre-Civil War days; harvest activities highlighted include cane grinding, syrup, soap, candle making, blacksmithing, cotton ginning, turkey shoots; oldtime fireplace cooking; folk M. *Westville, PO Box 1850, Lumpkin 31815.*

Ocilla SWEET POTATO FESTIVAL, Nov., 1 day. Cooking contests feature sweet potatoes; sweet potato display; P, BC. *C. Ryan, First State Bank of Ocilla, PO Box 65, Ocilla 31774. 912 468-5381*

Pine Mountain CRAFTSMEN AT CALLAWAY GARDENS, Dec.–Feb. Aged Cs of southern Appalachian Mts. including pottery, basketry, spinning, weaving demonstrations. *Craftsmen at Callaway Gardens, Pine Mountain 31822. 404 663-2281*

Savannah GEORGIA WEEK, early Feb., 1 wk. Relives Gen. Oglethorpe's landing on Georgia coast in 1733; celebrates founding of one of the 13 Original Colonies; colonial costumes, C demonstrations. *Savannah Area Convention & Visitors Bureau, PO Box 530, Savannah 31402. 912 233-3067*

Savannah A NIGHT IN OLD SAVANNAH, early May, 3 days. Celebration of various heritages of Georgia's citizens with Old World costumes, traditional entertainment, international cuisine. *Savannah Area Convention & Visitors Bureau, PO Box 530, Savannah 31402. 912 233-3067*

Savannah BLESSING OF THE FLEET, June, 1 day. Upward of 50 shrimp boats and pleasure crafts are blessed by clergy; D, BC, A/C. *Savannah Area Convention & Visitors Bureau, PO Box 530, Savannah 31402. 912 233-3067*

Stone Mountain STONE MOUNTAIN SCOTTISH FESTIVAL, mid-Oct., 2 days. Scottish piping, drumming, band, Celtic fiddling, dancing contests; Highland games. *Stone Mountain Park, 1090 Lanier Blvd., Atlanta 30306. 404 451-5728*

Whigham RATTLESNAKE ROUNDUP, Jan., last Sat. Prizes awarded for largest, longest rattlesnakes caught, for snake with most rattles. *Tourist Division, Dept. of Community Development, PO Box 38097, Atlanta 30334.*

HAWAII

All Islands LEI DAY, May 1, Hula dancing; luaus; leimaking contest. *Hawaii Visitors Bureau, 2270 Kalakaua Ave., Honolulu 96815. 808 923-1811*

All Islands KING KAMEHAMEHA CELEBRATION, about June 11. Honors memory of King Kamehameha I, unifier of Hawaii; hula contests; outrigger canoe races; swim meets; ethnic group presentations; A/C, M, P. *King Kamehameha*

Celebration Commission, 355 N. King St., Honolulu 96817.   808 548-4512

All Islands ALOHA WEEK FESTIVALS, mid-Oct., 9 days. Canoe races; luaus; international pageants; M, D, BC. *Aloha Week Hawaii, Inc., 765 Amana St., Honolulu 96814.*

Haleiwa-Waialua, OAHU HALEIWA SEA SPREE, mid-Feb. Celebration of Hawaii as a monarchy under Queen Liliuokalani; surfing competition; canoe races; torchlight pageant. *Hawaii Visitors Bureau, 2270 Kalakaua Ave., Honolulu 96815. 808 923-1811*

Hilo MERRIE MONARCH FESTIVAL, mid-Apr., 1 wk. Honors King Kalakaua, last reigning monarch (1874–91) of Hawaii; hula, M contests; canoe race; BC, P. *Merrie Monarch Festival, 14 Keawe St., Hilo 96720.*

Hilo INTERNATIONAL FESTIVAL OF THE PACIFIC, mid-July. Pageant of Nations; ethnic M, D; native costumes; BCs select queens to represent various ethnic groups. *Hawaii Visitors Bureau, 2270 Kalakaua Ave., Honolulu 96815. 808 923-1811*

Honokaa ANNUAL HONOKAA RODEO, late June, 2 days. "Oldest Hawaiian R"; horses decorated with flower leis; calf roping, bull riding; bareback bronco busting. *Hawaii Saddle Club, Honokaa 96727.*

Honolulu NARCISSUS FESTIVAL, Jan.–Feb., 3 wks. Celebration of Chinese New Year includes lion D, F, Oriental delicacies; BC, D. *Hawaii Visitors Bureau, 2270 Kalakaua Ave., Honolulu 96815. 808 923-1811*

Honolulu CHERRY BLOSSOM FESTIVAL, Feb.–Apr., 6 wks. Japanese community celebrates with cooking demonstrations; tea ceremonies; flower arranging; BC, D. *Hawaii Visitors Bureau, 2270 Kalakaua Ave., Honolulu 96815. 808 923-1811*

Kauai PRINCE KUHIO FESTIVAL, Mar., 1 wk. Honors Prince Jonah Kuhio Kalanianaole, delegate to US Congress; luau; canoe race; international-night program; P, A/C, D. *Hawaii Visitors Bureau, 2270 Kalakaua Ave., Honolulu 96815. 808 923-1811*

Kona KONA COFFEE FESTIVAL, Feb., 5 days. Kona coffee recipe contest; international foods; A/C, BC, M. *Hawaii Visitors Bureau, 2270 Kalakaua Ave., Honolulu 96815. 808 923-1811*

Maui MAKAWAO RODEO, early July, 3 days, at Maui Roping Club, Makawao. "Biggest Hawaii R" features servicemen "cowboys" and Hawaiian "paniolos" in competition. *C of C, Dillingham Bldg., Honolulu 96813.*

Waikiki HULA FESTIVAL, early Aug., 8 days. Traditional Hawaiian dancing. *C of C, Dillingham Bldg., Honolulu 96813.*

Waikoloa GREAT WAIKOLOA RODEO, Apr. Horses wear flower leis; calf roping; bull riding; bareback bronco busting; children in cowboy dress ride ponies; M., P. *Hawaii Visitors Bureau, 180 Kinoole St., Hilo 97620. 808 935-5271*

IDAHO

Bonners Ferry KOOTENAI RIVER DAYS, July, 3rd wk. Lumberjack competition; fiddlers contest; raft races; R, D. *Dept. of Commerce & Development, Capitol Bldg., Boise 83707.*

Coeur d'Alene SCOTTISH FESTIVAL & TATTOO. late July, 2 days. Scottish piping contests; pipe band; tattoo competitions; clan registration. *C of C, Box 850, Coeur d'Alene 83814. 208 664-3194.*

Craigmont TALMAKA ANNUAL CAMP MEETING, June–July, 9 days. Nez Perce Indians gather; handicrafts made from deerskin, cornhusks on sale. *Craigmont C of C, Craigmont 83523.*

Fort Hall SHOSHONE–BANNOCK INDIAN FESTIVAL, mid-Aug., 4 days. Indian war D; games; buffalo feast; P, BC. D, R. *Div. of Tourism & Industrial Development, Statehouse, Boise 83720.*

Idaho City GOLD RUSH DAYS, June. Goldmining contest; lumberjack competition; oldtime fiddling; races, D. *C of C, Idaho City 83631.*

Kooskia KOOSKIA DAY, late July. Oldtime fiddlers jamboree; raft races; horse show; P. *Dept. of Commerce & Development, Capitol Bldg., Boise 83707.*

Nampa SNAKE RIVER STAMPEDE, mid-July, 5 days. Bull, bareback, saddle bronc riding; calf roping; steer wrestling; buckaroo breakfast; M, BC. *Snake River Stampede Office, Box 231, Nampa 83651. 208 466-8497*

Nordman FRONTIER DAYS, early July, 3 days. Lumberjack competition; horseshoe pitching; sack races; F, P. *Dept. of Commerce & Development, Capitol Bldg., Boise 83707.*

Orofino OROFINO LUMBERJACK DAYS & COUNTRY FAIR, Sept., 3rd wknd. Logrolling, timbercutting, tree-climbing contests; P. *C of C, Orofino 83544.*

Pierce 1860 DAYS, Aug., 1st wknd. Lumberjack competition; wheely contest; horseshoe pitching. *Dept. of Commerce & Development, Capitol Bldg., Boise 83707.*

Priest River PRIEST RIVER LOGGERS CELEBRATION, mid-July. Lumberjack competition; raft race; horse show; horseshoe pitching; F. *Priest River C of C, PO Box 801, Priest River 83856.*

St. Maries PAUL BUNYAN DAYS, early Sept., 4 days. Lumberjack contests; musket, archery shoots; blue ox watering trough; Benewah County Fair; P, D. *St. Maries C of C, 724 Main St., St. Maries 83861.*

Salmon SALMON RIVER DAYS, early July. Water can contest; motorcycle races; demolition derby; competitive trail ride; P, F. *Div. of Tourism & Industrial Development, Statehouse, Boise 83720.*

Teton Valley PIERRE'S HOLE RENDEZVOUS, early Aug., 2 days. Indians, trappers, pioneers, cowboys P; drama; fiddling, black powder contests; Indian D; R. *Dept. of Commerce & Development, Capitol Bldg., Boise 83707.*

Weiser NATIONAL OLD TIME FIDDLERS CONTEST & FESTIVAL, June, 1 wk. Best fiddlers in US meet to play pioneer M on oldtime fiddles, banjos, guitars; P. *National Old Time Fiddlers Contest, C of C, Weiser 83672.*

ILLINOIS

Arcola HORSE FARMING DAYS, Oct., 1st 2 wknds, at Rockome Gardens. Pioneer lifestyle demonstrations; C. *Illinois Adventure Center, 160 N. La Salle St., Chicago 60601. 312 793-2094*

Bishop Hill JORDBRUKSDAGARNA, early Oct., 2 days. Festival re-creates Swedish lifestyle of 1840's; blacksmithing; quiltmaking; candle dipping; broommaking; sorghum, hay harvesting; pumpkin rolling; cornhusking, shelling; Swedish folk dancing. *Historic Site, Bishop Hill 61419. 309 927-3590*

Brimfield OLDE ENGLISH FAIRE, late June, wknd, at Jubilee College State Park. Rustic olde English marketplace; strolling medieval troubadours; knights in combat. *Illinois Adventure Center, 160 N. La Salle St., Chicago 60601. 312 793-2094*

Clayton TURN OF THE CENTURY CELEBRATION, mid-Sept., 2 days, at Siloam Springs State Park. 1880's–1920's period of history relived; contests; hot-air balloon ascent. *Dept. of Conservation, Div. of Land & Historic Sites, 605 State Office Bldg., Springfield 62706. 217 782-3340*

Decatur YESTERYEAR FAIR, early Sept., 4 days, at North Fork Museum grounds. Weaving, quilting, spinning demonstrations; stagecoach rides. *C of C, 250 N. Water St., Decatur 62525.*

Dixon PETUNIA FESTIVAL, early July, 4 days. Drum & bugle corps competition; critter race; donkey baseball; water fight show; beer garden; old-fashioned ice cream social; old settlers log cabin; P, A/C. *Dixon C of C, 74 Galena Ave., Dixon 61021. 815 284-3361*

Du Quoin DU QUOIN STATE FAIR, Aug.–Sept., 11 days. Auto harness racing; agricultural shows; carnival; beer gardens. *Du Quoin Business Assn., 119 Laurel Ave., Du Quoin 62832.*

Du Quoin SOUTHERN ILLINOIS FOLK FESTIVAL, Sept.–Oct., 3 days, at Du Quoin State Fair Grounds. Quilting; cornhusking; apple butter making; woodcarving; bee husking; broommaking; hog-calling contest; D. *Southern Illinois Folk Festival, 1114 E. Pine, Herrin 62948.*

Galena U.S. GRANT CIVIL WAR CANTONMENT, mid-May, 3 days. Reenactment of encampment of Civil War soldiers by 300 persons; pistol, musket, artillery contests; P. *Illinois Adventure Center, 160 N. La Salle St., Chicago 60601. 312 793-2094*

Grafton FALL FESTIVAL: WILD FOODS & FRONTIER CRAFTS, Oct., at Pere Marquette State Park. Soapmaking; candle dipping; log cabin building; weaving. *Dept. of Business & Economic Development, Office of Tourism, 205 W. Wacker Dr., Chicago 60606. 312 793-2082*

Hoopeston HOOPESTON NATIONAL SWEETCORN FESTIVAL, late Aug. or early Sept., at McFerren Park. Sweet corn to eat; tractor-pulling contests; motorcycle races; horse shows; BC. *Illinois Adventure Center, 160 N. La Salle St., Chicago 60601. 312 793-2094*

Lincoln NATIONAL RAILSPLITTING CONTEST & CRAFTS FESTIVAL, mid-Sept., 2 days. Amateur, junior, professional railsplitting competitions; tobacco spitting, cow-chip throwing, cow milking; watermelon-seed-spitting, tomahawk-throwing contests; candle-dipping, spinning, butter-churning, Indian breadmaking, goose-plucking demonstrations; P, D. *Logan Railsplitting Assn., PO Box 52, Lincoln 62656. 217 732-6842*

Mendota SWEET CORN FESTIVAL, Aug., 2nd wknd. Free corn; corn-eating contest; water fights; drum & bugle corps pageant; beer garden. *Mendota Area C of C, Box 370, Mendota 61342.*

Morton PUMPKIN FESTIVAL, mid-Sept., 4 days. Giant pumpkin; pumpkin-pie-eating contests; carnival calliope; P. *Illinois Adventure Center, 160 N. La Salle St., Chicago 60601. 312 793-2094*

Nauvoo GRAPE FESTIVAL, Aug.–Sept., 3 days. Festival highlights wedding of the Wine & Cheese, a French rite depicting concept that wine and cheese are at their best when taken together; Nauvoo restored to 1800's; frog-jumping, money-in-the-haystack contests. *Nauvoo Grape Festival Assn., Nauvoo 63254.*

Peoria STEAMBOAT DAYS, mid-June, 3 days. Re-creation of steamboat era; riverboat race features *Julia Belle Swain* and the *Delta Queen*. Peoria Area C of C, Peoria 61602. 309 676-0755

Petersburg ILLINOIS COUNTRY OPRY, Jan., every Sat. Nation's 3rd-largest country M show. *Dept. of Business & Economic Development, Office of Tourism, 205 W. Wacker Dr., Chicago 60606. 312 793-2082*

Petersburg LAND OF LINCOLN CRAFTS FESTIVAL, early Oct., 2 days, at New Salem Carriage Museum. Craftsmen demonstrate spinning, weaving, goose plucking, tinsmithing. *Dept. of Business & Economic Development, Office of Tourism, 205 W. Wacker Dr., Chicago 60606. 312 793-2082*

Prairie du Rocher FORT DE CHARTRES RENDEZVOUS, early June, 2 days, at Fort de Chartres State Park. Revival of Illinois early French frontier period; tomahawk, greased-pole, frontier-tug-of-war contests; canoe races; French colonial food; militia demonstrations. *Special Events, Dept. of Conservation, 605 State Office Bldg., Springfield 62706.*

Princeton HOMESTEAD FESTIVAL & ANNUAL PORK BARBECUE, Sept., 3 days. Mussleloaders demonstrations; horse show; pig auction; beer garden; woodcarving; weaving; candle dipping; caning; quilting; butter churning; bread, apple, butter, soap, lace, colonial toy making; P, BC. *C of C, 433 S. Main St., Princeton 61356.*

Rockford ROCK CUT WINTER CARNIVAL, late Jan., 2 days, at Rock Cut State Park. Snow sculptures; skating, sledding; ice, snow-sculpture contests. *Dept. of Conservation, Div. of Land & Historic Sites, 605 State Office Bldg., Springfield 62706. 217 782-3340*

Rock Island INDIAN POW WOW, Labor Day wknd, at Black Hawk State Park. Festival honors Indian traditions with powwow, pageant. *Illinois Adventure Center, 160 N. LaSalle St., Chicago 60601. 312 793-2094*

Springfield SPRING CRAFT FESTIVAL, May, 1st Sun. Mid-19th-century spring demonstrations of plowing, railsplitting, blacksmithing, herb gardening, textile crafts, soapmaking, woodworking, quilting, hooking, braiding. *Clayville Rural Life Center, Sangamon State U., Springfield 62708.*

Springfield FALL CRAFT FESTIVAL, Oct., 2nd wknd. Mid-19th-century fall C demonstrations of harvesting, cidermaking and mulling, churning, smithing, tatting, flax processing, chair caning, gunsmithing; hominy, apple butter making. *Clayville Rural Life Center, Sangamon State U., Springfield 62708.*

Springfield INDIAN SUMMER FESTIVAL, mid-Oct., 2 days, at Lincoln Memorial Garden Nature Center. Pumpkin-decorating contest; demonstrations of cidermaking, candle dipping, railsplitting. *Dept. of Business & Economic Development, Office of Tourism, 205 W. Wacker Dr., Chicago 60606. 312 793-2082*

Sycamore PUMPKIN FESTIVAL, late Oct., 5 days. Decorated pumpkins display; demonstrations of pumpkin carving, decorating; pumpkin foods; P. *Sycamore Pumpkin Festival Committee, PO Box 262, Sycamore 60178.*

Utica BURGOO, Oct., 2nd Sun. Burgoo is a pioneer settler dish cooked in large iron kettles for 6 to 7 hours; recipe is a closely guarded secret; blacksmith shop; schottisches; polkas; C demonstrations; steam engine rides. *La Salle County Historical Society, PO Box 577, Ottawa 61350.*

INDIANA

Attica POTAWATOMI INDIAN FESTIVAL, early Oct., 3 days. City honors native Indian tribe

with archery contests, tomahawk throws, frontier foods; railsplitting, muzzleloading contests; P. *C of C, Attica 47918. 317 764-4228*

Battle Ground RALLY FOR OLD TIPPECANOE, late May, 2 days. Stump speeches and toe-tapping M depicts time of "Tippecanoe & Tyler, too"; costumes. *Battle Ground Historical Corp., Box 225, Battle Ground 47920. 317 567-2148*

Battle Ground ANNUAL GATHERING OF INDIANA FIDDLERS & OLDTIME MUSICIANS, early July, 3 days. Folk musicians gather to play and hear oldtime M. *Battle Ground Historical Corp., Box 225, Battle Ground 47920. 317 567-2148*

Battle Ground TECUMSEH LODGE POW WOW, early Sept., 2 days. Indians from throughout Midwest powwow; D, C. *Battle Ground Historical Corp., Box 225, Battle Ground 47920. 317 567-2148*

Brownsburg OLD FASHION FESTIVAL, mid-Sept., 2 days. Sack races; watermelon-eating, bubble-gum-blowing, horseshoe-pitching, beard-growing, oldtime fiddlers contests; egg toss; spelling bee; P, D, A/C. *Mrs. J. Bowling, 5 Robinwood Dr., Brownsburg 46112. 317 852-2592*

Brownstown WATERMELON FESTIVAL, Labor Day wknd. Free watermelon; pole-climbing, greased-watermelon, watermelon-eating, seed-spitting, log-sawing, horseshoe-pitching, beard contests; canoe race; P, BC M. *Watermelon Festival, PO Box 157, Brownstown 47220.*

Canaan CANAAN FALL FESTIVAL, Sept. mid-1800's era celebrated; pony express mail run; bucksaw wood-cutting, greased-pole, heavy-turkey contests. *Canaan Restoration Council, Route 1, Canaan 47224. 812 839-4770*

Castleton-Indianapolis INDIANA ROSE FESTIVAL, June, 1st 2 wknds. Two hundred thousand rose blooms on 1,000 rose plants; frontier weapons, C; Indian, European folk Ds; German singing; Mexican mariachi bands; BC. *Indiana Rose Festival, Hillsdale Exhibition Rose Gardens, 7845 Johnson Rd., Castleton-Indianapolis 46250. 317 849-2810*

Cayuga EUGENE TOWNSHIP PIONEER DAYS FESTIVAL, early June, 2 days. Fiddlers contest; carriage rides; P, BC. *W. Heidbreder, Route 1, Cayuga 47928. 317 492-3724*

Clinton LITTLE ITALY FESTIVAL, Labor Day wknd. Italian food demonstrations, samplings; grape stomping; coal mine tour; gondola rides; state bocce ball tournament; costume contest; BC, P. *C of C, 141 S. Main St., Clinton 47842.*

Edinburg EDINBURG FALL FESTIVAL, early Sept., 3 days. Candlemaking demonstrations; pioneer spirit; M, P, A/C, BC. *Dr. R. Sharp, 202 S. Keeley St., Edinburg 46124. 812 526-2681*

Evansville FREEDOM FESTIVAL, mid-May to mid-July. Essay, button design, wood sculpture contests; drum & bugle corps competitions; boat races; tennis, rugby tournaments; big wheel rally; BC, D, F, P. *Freedom Festival Foundation, Old Courthouse, Evansville 47708. 812 464-9576*

Flora FIESTA DEL FLORA, mid-Sept., 2 days. Sack races; cornhusking contest; ice cream social; marble, jacks tournaments; old farm machinery exhibit; box lunch auction. *L. Allen, 803 S. Center St., Flora 46929. 219 967-4135*

Fort Wayne INDIANA POW WOW, May, 2 days. Indians from 10 states gather to teach ancestral heritage through tribal C, foods; M. *C of C, 826 Ewing St., Fort Wayne 46802.*

Fort Wayne THREE RIVERS FESTIVAL, mid-July, 9 days. Indian powwow; muzzleloading rifle &

pistol shoot; Civil War battle skirmish; fife & drum corps; train robbery; bed race. *Three Rivers Festival, Central Bldg., Fort Wayne 46802. 219 743-1480*

Friendship SPRING & FALL MUZZLELOADING RIFLE SHOOTS, mid-May through mid-Aug. Pioneer art of shooting muzzleloading rifles demonstrated; knife, tomahawk throws; antique displays; deerskin costumes; C. *Indiana Div. of Tourism, 336 State House, Indianapolis 46204.*

Grabill OLD GRABILL COUNTRY FAIR, early Sept., 3 days. Watermelon-eating, horseshoe-pitching, pie-baking, nail-driving, railsplitting contests; apple butter making; horseshoeing; P. *D. Delagrange, 2nd St., Grabill 46741. 219 627-3056*

Greencastle PUTNAM COUNTY ANNUAL CORN FESTIVAL, early Oct., 3 days. Pumpkin-carving contests; exhibits of cornhusk dolls. *C of C, Greencastle 46135.*

Hammond INTERNATIONAL CULTURE FESTIVAL & LA CARE ARTS & CRAFTS FAIR, Sept., 2nd wknd. Ethnic festival includes Chinese, Hungarian, Ukrainian, Israeli, Serbian, Polish, Mexican, Swedish, Irish, French, Russian, Scottish, Slovak dancing, singing, music; fife & drum corps. *Int'l Culture Festival, Howard Branch Library, 7047 Grand Ave., Hammond 46323. 219 931-5100*

Hesston LABOR DAY STEAM SHOW, early Sept., 4 days. Steam locomotives; steam lightplant; sawmill; pumpworks; gas engines; blowing, threshing machines. *LaPorte County Historical Steam Soc., 2940 Mt. Claire Way-Long Beach, Michigan City 46360. 219 778-2783*

Jeffersonville STEAMBOAT DAYS FESTIVAL, early Sept., 4 days. Festival commemorates city's heritage as major riverboat- and barge-building center; sidewalk painting; skin diving; steamboat cruises; A/C, P. *Steamboat Days, Inc., PO Box Steamboat, Jeffersonville 47130.*

Lafayette FEAST OF THE HUNTERS' MOON, Oct., 2 days, at Fort Ouiatenon. Life at a French outpost 200 years ago; frontier clothing, spinning, weaving, candle dipping, blacksmithing, leatherworking, railsplitting; Indian tomtoms, rituals; cannon, muzzleloaders; French folk stories, food; buffalo stew; butter churning. *Tippecanoe County Historical Assn., 909 South St., Lafayette 47901. 317 742-5285*

Ligonier STONE'S TRACE HISTORICAL SOCIETY PIONEER FESTIVAL, Sept., 2 days, at Old Stone's Tavern. Demonstrations of Cs of 1800's: candle dipping, quilting, apple butter making. *Stone's Trace Historical Society, Ligonier 46767.*

Martinsville FALL FOLIAGE FESTIVAL, early Oct., 1 wk. Harvest market; tricycle race; Roaring Twenties party; horseshoe toss; frog-jumping, Great Pumpkin contests; P. *Morgan County Fall Foliage Festival, Inc., 233 E. Worthington St., Martinsville 46151. 317 342-8110*

Metamora CANAL DAYS-TRADERS RENDEZVOUS, Oct., 2 days. Commemoration of annual gathering of settlers and shipping of harvest via canalboat to city; banjo, fiddle, scarecrow contests; muzzleloading rifle matches; iron kettle cooking; A/C. *Metamora Ship-Keepers Assn., Inc., Metamora 47030.*

Osgood ROARING TWENTIES FESTIVAL, June, 3 days. Hot air balloons; parachute drops; frog races. *C of C, Osgood 47037.*

Remington FOUNTAIN PARK CHAUTAUQUA, July-Aug., 2 wks. Daily religious meditation; fife & drum corps M; Appalachian region folk M; water balloon fight; A/C, D, M. *Fountain Park Chautauqua, Box 225, Remington 47977.*

Rochester TRAIL OF COURAGE RENDEZVOUS, Sept., 3rd wknd. Festival commemorates courage of the Potawatomi Indians during their forced removal by soldiers in 1838; tepee village; spinning, weaving, candle-dipping, butter-churning, railsplitting, apple-butter-making, cidermaking demonstrations; dulcimermaking, playing; oldtime foods. *Fulton County Historical Soc., 7th & Pontiac, Rochester 46974.*

Rockville PARKE COUNTY COVERED BRIDGE FESTIVAL, Oct., 10 days. Pioneer home activities; trips over covered bridges. *Park County Tourist Information Center, E. Ohio St., Rockville 47872.*

Rushville PIONEER ENGINEERS CLUB ANNUAL REUNION, early Aug., 3 days. Sputtering steam engines; antique wheat threshers; steam calliope; popcorn poppers; P. *C of C, Rushville 46173.*

Shelbyville BLUE RIVER VALLEY PIONEER CRAFT FAIR, early Oct., 2 days. Demonstrations of pioneer Cs include cornmeal grinding, caning, whittling, shinglemaking, broommaking, harnessmaking, gunmaking, candlemaking, sorghummaking. *Shelby County Historical Soc., Box 74, Shelbyville 46176.*

South Whitley SOUTH WHITLEY FALL FESTIVAL, early Sept., 2 days. Pony, garden tractor pulls; bake contest; bed race, horseshoe, tennis tournaments; D, A. *C of C, Box 321, South Whitley, 46787.*

Tell City SCHWEIZER FEST, Aug., 4 days. *Biergarten; Gemütlichkeit;* German specialty foods; crossbow shoot. *C of C, Tell City 47586.*

Terre Haute OKTOBERFEST, late Sept. *Biergarten;* Schuhplatters demonstrate German folk D. *Oberlander Club, Inc., 1937 Clay Ave., Terre Haute 47805.*

Thorntown FESTIVAL OF THE TURNING LEAVES, Sept., 2 days. Tribute to Indians and pioneers of early 1800's; Indian Ds; muzzleloaders shoot; tomahawk throws. *Soc. for the Preservation of Our Indian Heritage, 511 S. Pearl St., Thorntown 46071. 317 436-7445*

Tipton TIPTON COUNTY PORK FESTIVAL, early Sept., 3 days. Pork delicacies, 8 tons of pork chops served; P. *Pork Festival Assn., PO Box 26, Tipton 46072.*

Vallonia FORT VALLONIA DAYS, mid-Oct., 2 days. Muzzleloading shoot; pioneer Cs; P. *Fort Vallonia Days Corp., Box 203, Fallonia 47281. 812 358-3286*

Whitestown WHITESTOWN PIONEER DAYS, mid-Sept., 3 days, at Lions Club Park. Old fiddlers, beard, hog-calling, rooster-crowing, watermelon-eating contests; sack race; egg toss; haystack hunt; parachute jumps; P, D. *Whitestown Community Center, Inc., PO Box 23, Whitestown 46075. 317 769-3531*

Zionsville FALL FESTIVAL, Sept., 2 days. Colonial atmosphere; tractor pull; fiddlers contest; balloon ascension; P. *C of C, Zionsville 46077.*

IOWA

Amana Colonies OKTOBERFEST, Oct., 1st Sat. German food, drinks; ethnic costumes, M. *Oktoberfest, South Amana 52334.*

Britt NATIONAL HOBO CONVENTION, early Aug., 1 day. Hoboes from throughout US meet; hobo king, queen chosen; more than 500 gallons of mulligan stew served free to public; A, P. *Britt C of C, Britt 50423.*

Burlington STEAMBOAT DAYS, mid-June, 1 wk. Recalls early days when steamboats frequented city with cargoes & people; paddle wheel boat rides; beer garden; ethnic costumes, food; P. *Burlington Steamboat Days, Inc., Hotel Burlington, Burlington 52601. 319 752-6365*

Decorah NORDIC FEST, July, last wknd. Norwegian flower painting; Scandinavian costumes; folk M; A. *C of C, Decorah 52101.*

Des Moines IOWA STATE FAIR, mid-Aug., 10 days. Motion picture *State Fair* (1932) tells story of fair; old-fiddlers contest; tractor pull; skydivers; auto races; F, R. *State Fair Board Fairgrounds, Des Moines 50319.*

Indianola US NATIONAL HOT AIR BALLOON CHAMPIONSHIP, early Aug., 9 days. Approximately 250 balloonists compete yearly for title of National Champion Balloonist. *Indianola Balloons, Inc., Indianola 50125. 515 961-6269*

Mount Pleasant OLD SETTLERS & THRESHERS REUNION, Labor Day wknd. Action exhibit of steam engines; threshing demonstrations; steam-powered train rides; antique autos; Indian relics exhibit; old-settlers implements; spinning wheels; carding machines; shingle mill. *Mt. Pleasant C of C, PO Box 109, Mt. Pleasant 52641.*

Pella IOWA TULIP TIME FESTIVAL, mid-May, 3 days. Commemorates sacrifices of Dutch founding fathers; Dutch provincial costumes, wooden shoes, dancers; street scrubbing; BC. *Pella Tulip Time Festival, Pella 50219. 517 628-4311*

Tama TAMA POW WOW, mid-Aug., 4 days. Mesquakie Indians hold native ceremonies & tribal Ds on their settlement. *Mesquakie Indian Pow Wow Assn., RR 2, Tama 52339.*

KANSAS

Dodge City DODGE CITY DAYS, mid-July, 3 days, at Rodeo Grounds. Gunfights; calf-tying, talent contests; beef cookout championship; mini-tractor pull; raw egg toss; costumes; BC, A/C, R, P, D. *C of C, Dodge City 67801.*

Fort Scott PIONEER HARVEST FIESTA, early Oct., 3 days, at Bourbon County Fairgrounds. Steam, antique gas engines; antique farm equipment threshes grain, saws lumber, bails straw, plows; old-fashioned breadmaking demonstration; A/C, P. *Pioneer Harvest Fiesta, Inc., PO Box 465, Fort Scott 66701. 316 223-0113*

Garden City BEEF EMPIRE DAYS, early June, 4 days. Cattle, heifer, steer judging; tractor pull; feedlot; cowboy team roping; horse competition; P, A, R. *Beef Empire Days, Inc., Box 1197, Garden City 67846. 316 275-6807*

Goessel COUNTRY THRESHING DAYS, late July, 2 days. Cornmeal grinding; log sawing; ropemaking; steam whistle, threshing methods demonstrations; quilting; butter churning; cider pressing; kraut stomping. *Mennonite Immigrant Historical Foundation, Goessel 67053.*

Haviland ANTIQUE ENGINE & THRESHER SHOW, early Aug., 3 days. Tractor, pony pulls; hoop-rolling, rolling-pin-throwing contests; wood-sawing, grain-threshing, fan-testing demonstrations; antique engine show; broom corn seeder. *Haviland Telephone Co., Haviland 67059.*

Hays OKTOBERFEST, early Oct., 1 day. Sheep shearing; wool carding, spinning, weaving; sauerkrautmaking; goose plucking; tole painting; wood carving; cow milking; butter churning; polka, waltz, hochzeit, schottische D demonstrations. *C of C, Box 220, Hays 67601.*

Johnson STANTON COUNTY PIONEER DAY, mid-May, 2 days. Kateri Klan Indian Dancers; P honoring pioneers; BC, R, D. *Pioneer Day Committee, Johnson 67855.*

Liberal INTERNATIONAL PANCAKE RACE, Mar., 1 day. Pancake race simultaneously run by housewives in Olney, England, and Liberal, Kansas. *C of C, PO Box 676, 500 N. Kansas Ave., Liberal 67901.*

Sabetha ALBANY MUSEUM THRESHING BEE, July, last wknd. Antique cars, engines, farm machinery, railway caboose; C demonstrations. *C of C, Sabetha 66534.*

Scott City SCOTT CITY BEEFIESTA, mid-Aug., 1 day. Fiesta salutes beef cattle-feeding industry; national team-roping contest; beef-cooking demonstrations; free barbecue. *C of C, Scott City 67871. 316 872-3525*

Wilson AFTER HARVEST CZECH FESTIVAL, late July. Descendants of Czechs who settled in this region in 19th century celebrate harvest with ethnic Ds, foods, colorful costumes, handicrafts. *Wilson C of C, Wilson 67490.*

KENTUCKY

Barbourville DANIEL BOONE FESTIVAL, mid-Oct., 1 wk. Cherokees invade Barbourville; Cane Treaty signed between people & Cherokees; rifle shoot; hog calling; oldtime fiddling; husband-calling, beard-growing contests; BC, P, D, A/C. *Knox County C of C, Municipal Bldg., PO Box 1000, Barbourville 40906. 606 546-4300*

Benton TATER DAY, early Apr., 1 day. Held annually since 1844; mule-, pony-pulling contests; antique cars; P, BC, A/C. *Marshall County C of C, Route 7, Benton 42025. 505 527-7665*

Berea MOUNTAIN FOLK FESTIVAL, early Apr., 1 day. *Berea College, Berea 40403.*

Frankfort CAPITAL EXPO, early June. Folklife festival; A, M, D. *Ms. T. Laing, 214 A W. Main St., Frankfort 40601.*

Grayson THE KENTUCKY FOLKSONG FESTIVAL, mid-June, 2 days. Appalachian folksongs; A/C. *H. L. Rogers, Route 2, Box 180, Grayson 41143. 606 474-6735*

Harrodsburg SHAKER SEASON OF SPRING, May. Seasonal farm rituals; sheep shearing; C demonstrations; food features early garden harvest. *Shakertown at Pleasant Hill, Route 4, Harrodsburg 40330. 606 734-5411*

London SUE BENNETT FOLK FESTIVAL, Mar.-Apr., 4 days. Appalachian folk culture, tales; old-timey hymn sing; M, D, A/C. *Sue Bennett College, London 40741. 606 864-4235*

Louisville KENTUCKY DERBY FESTIVAL, Apr.-May, 10 days. Great balloon, cycling, steamboat races; derby trial; pedalathon; P, M. *Derby Festival Committee, 621 W. Main St., Louisville 40202.*

Paintsville APPLE FESTIVAL OF JOHNSON COUNTY, Oct., 1st wknd. Old-fashioned spelling bee, adding match; letter-writing awards; cross-country run; costume contest; P, D, BC. *Kentucky Apple Festival, Box 631, Paintsville 41240.*

Prestonburg KENTUCKY HIGHLANDS FOLK FESTIVAL, early Sept., 3 days. Traditional folk M; fireside hymns with homemade instruments; musical swapshop; A/C, D. *Mrs. K. Frazier, Prestonburg 41653.*

Russellville LOGAN COUNTY TOBACCO FESTIVAL, early Oct., 9 days. Jesse James bank robbery reenactment; pipe-smoking, tobacco-spitting contests; BC, D, P. *Russellville-Logan County C of C, Russellville 42276. 502 726-2206.*

South Union SHAKER FESTIVAL, early July, 10 days. Shaker Ds, songs; C. *Shakertown, South Union 42283.*

West Liberty MORGAN COUNTY SORGHUM FESTIVAL, early Oct., 3 days. Sorghummaking; D, P, BC, A/C. *Mrs. B. Perry, West Hills, West Liberty 41472.*

LOUISIANA

Abbeville LOUISIANA DAIRY FESTIVAL & FAIR, late Oct. Fais do-do; blessing of dairy products; butter-churning contest; dairy cattle show; BC, P. *L. DeBlanc, 404 S. Louisiana Ave., Abbeville 70510. 504 893-6328*

Basile LOUISIANA SWINE FESTIVAL, early Nov., 2 days. Greasy-pig, boudin-eating contests; swine show; P, BC. *Mrs. H. McLelland, PO Box 457, Basile 70515. 318 432-6307*

Blanchard POKE SALAT FESTIVAL, early May, 1 day. Festival honors poke, a tall wild plant; beard-growing, fiddling, tobacco-spitting contests; checkers competition; BC, P. *Louisiana Tourist Commission, PO Box 4491, Baton Rouge 70804. 504 389-5984*

Breaux Bridge BREAUX BRIDGE CRAWFISH FESTIVAL, May, 1st wknd (held in even-numbered years). Fais do-do; crawfish, pirogue races; crawfish-eating, peeling, fiddle, accordion, Cajun D contests; BC, F. *P. B. Green, PO Box 25, Breaux Bridge 70517. 318 332-1262*

Bridge City GUMBO FESTIVAL, Oct., 2nd wknd. Gumbo cooking, eating contests; beard-growing, cake, pie contests; A, M, D, P, BC. *Gumbo Festival, 908 Wiegand Dr., Bridge City 70094. 504 341-8539*

Chauvin LAGNIAPPE ON THE BAYOU, early Oct., 3 days. French Acadian culture; authentic Cajun foods include sugar-coated pecans, sweet-dough pie; Cajun village; fais do-do; carnival; shrimp-drying platform. *Louisiana Tourist Commission, PO Box 44291, Baton Rouge 70804. 504 389-5984*

Church Point COURRIR DU MARDI GRAS, late Feb., 1 day. Riders on horseback wearing crazy costumes present rural version of Mardi Gras as they travel through countryside collecting foodstuffs; P. *Louisiana Tourist Commission, PO Box 44291, Baton Rouge 70804. 504 389-5984*

Colfax LOUISIANA PECAN FESTIVAL, early Nov., 2 days. Tribute to the pecan; street carnival; trail ride; costume contests; fiddlers competition; donkey basketball game; quilting, blacksmithing, woodworking, basket-weaving, homemade lye soap demonstrations; turkey shoot. *C of C, Colfax 70401.*

Columbia ART & FOLK FESTIVAL, mid-Oct., 2 days. Carving; shingle, soapmaking; M. *Louisiana Tourist Commission, PO Box 44291, Baton Rouge 70804. 504 389-5984*

Delcambre DELCAMBRE SHRIMP FESTIVAL, mid-Aug., 5 days. Shrimp; water fights staged by fire departments; blessing of shrimp fleet; fais do-do, BC, D. *Delcambre Shrimp Festival & Fair Assn., PO Box 286, Delcambre 70528.*

DeRidder BEAUREGARD PIONEER FESTIVAL, Sept., 2nd Sat. Beard & mustache, costume contests; sack, tricycle races; costumes; A/C, D, M. *DeRidder Beauregard C of C, PO Box 309, DeRidder 70634. 318 463-5533*

DeRidder BEAUREGARD PARISH FAIR, early Oct. Hoe-down fiddlers contest; carnival; BC, P. *Mrs. W. D. Wilson, Route 3, Box 123, DeRidder 70634. 318 463-9350*

Farmerville LOUISIANA WATERMELON FESTIVAL, late July, 3 days. Contests for largest melon produced, for guessing weights of melons, for eating largest amount of melon, for preparation of melon foods. *Louisiana Tourist Commission, PO Box 44291, Baton Rouge 70804. 504 389-5984*

Galliano SOUTH LAFOURCHE CAJUN FESTIVAL, mid-June, 3 days. Cajun pirogue championship races; potato D; Cajun dress, beard contests; fais do-do. *D. Guidry, PO Drawer A, Galliano 70354. 504 798-2018*

Gonzales JAMBALAYA FESTIVAL, early June, Jambalaya cooking, eating contests; horse racing; golf tournament. *Mrs. J. C. Walker, Box 1243, Gonzales 70737.*

Grand Isle GRAND ISLE TARPON RODEO, late July, 3 days. "America's oldest fishing contest"; amberjack, barracuda, bonito, cobia, catfish, dolphin, crevalle, jewfish, marlin, tarpon, tuna, wahoo contests. *Louisiana Tourist Commission, PO Box 44291, Baton Rouge 70804. 504 389-5984*

Greenwood PIONEER DAYS, late Aug., 3 days. Fiddlers contest; terrapin races; watermelon supper; pioneer P. *Louisiana Tourist Commission, PO Box 44291, Baton Rouge 70804. 504 389-5984*

Lafayette LOUISIANA NATIVE CRAFTS FESTIVAL, late Oct., 3 days. Cs of yesteryear; weaving palmetto objects; clothespin-doll making; split-oak basket weaving; duck decoy carving; piroquemaking; blacksmithing; Indian weaving; brown cotton spinning. *Lafayette Natural History Museum, 637 Girard Park Dr., Lafayette 70501.*

Lake Charles CONTRABAND DAYS, late Apr., 3 days. Pirates take over city; mayor tossed in the drink; Cajun days; power-boat, yacht races; BC, F, M. *Louisiana Tourist Commission, PO Box 44291, Baton Rouge 70804. 504 389-5984*

Morgan City LOUISIANA SHRIMP & PETROLEUM FESTIVAL, Labor Day wknd. Shrimp boil; blessing of shrimp fleet; kites; bass tournament; shrimp & petroleum regatta; F, P, BC, S. *Mrs. A Jendron, PO Box 103, Morgan City 70380. 504 385-0703*

New Iberia LOUISIANA SUGAR CANE FESTIVAL, late Sept. Blessing of cane fields; firemen's water fight; sugarcane fais do-do; posse trail ride; canoe relay races; A/C, BC, P, D. *Greater Iberia C of C, PO Box 27, New Iberia 70560.*

New Orleans NEW ORLEANS JAZZ & HERITAGE FESTIVAL, early Apr., 10 days. Salute to New Orleans' and the South's contribution to American culture; artists, craftsmen present products; New Orleans cuisine. *New Orleans Tourist & Convention Commission, 334 Royal St., New Orleans 70130.*

New Orleans BASTILLE DAY, mid-July, 2 days. Sailing regatta, piroque, horse races; French folklore; M, D. *Louisiana Tourist Commission, PO Box 44291, Baton Rouge 70804. 504 389-5984*

Opelousas LOUISIANA YAMBILEE FESTIVAL, late Oct., wknd. Celebration of the yam; yaminal contest; sweet potato show; P, BC, A/C. *D. Voss, PO Box 444, Opelousas 70570. 318 948-8848*

Plaquemine INTERNATIONAL ACADIAN FESTIVAL, late Oct., 1 wk. Arrival of Evangeline by canoe at night; long-beard, skeet-shoot, tug-of-war, tobacco-spitting, tennis contests; Acadian foods; fishing R; BC, P. *C of C, City Hall, Main St., Plaquemine 70764. 504 687-3560*

Rayne RAYNE FROG FESTIVAL, mid-Sept., 2 days. Frog derby, weigh-in, frog-eating contests; water fight; BC. *H. Haure, PO Box 383, Rayne 70578. 318 334-2332*

Shreveport HOLIDAY IN DIXIE, mid-Apr., 10 days. Celebrates signing of Louisiana Purchase of 1803 with exhibits typical of the times; treasure hunt; pageant. *J. Callicoatte, 804 Mid-South Tower, Shreveport 71101.*

Shreveport STATE FAIR OF LOUISIANA, mid-Oct., 10 days. Fair held annually since 1905; agricultural, industrial products exhibits; livestock show; car races. *C. E. Nelson, PO Box 9100, Shreveport 71109. 318 635-1361*

Ville Platte LOUISIANA COTTON FESTIVAL, Oct., 3rd wknd. Main event is Le Tournoi: riders in medieval knight costumes display horseback riding skills; salute to cotton industry; cotton show; carnival, D, P, BC. *Ville Platte C of C, PO Box 331, Ville Platte 70586. 318 363-1878*

Zwolle TAMALE FIESTA, mid-Nov., 2 days. Wood-chopping, costume, fiddling, domino, checkers, tamale-eating contests; tamalemaking demonstration; treasure hunt; A/C, D, P. *Tamale Fiesta, Box 237, Zwolle 71486.*

MAINE

Boothbay Harbor FISHERMEN'S FESTIVAL, early Apr., 3 days. Fishing skills, gear, products demonstrated; blessing of the fleet; fastest fish processor, fileting of fish, clam-shucking, shrimp-picking, crab-picking contests; BC, D. *C of C., Boothbay Harbor 04538.*

Boothbay Harbor WINDJAMMER DAYS, mid-July, 3 days. Annual return of windjammers; boat, street P; BC, D, M. *C of C, Boothbay Harbor 04538.*

Boothbay Harbor FALL FOLIAGE FESTIVAL, Oct., 2nd wknd. Country fair; bean-hole bean suppers; turkey shoot; "Down East flavor"; boat trips. *C of C, Boothbay Harbor 04538.*

Cumberland Center CUMBERLAND FAIR, late Sept., wk. US and Canadian oxen & horse teams compete in pulling contests. *Cumberland Farmers' Club, Cumberland Center 04101.*

Fort Fairfield MAINE POTATO BLOSSOM FESTIVAL, July, 3rd wk. Salute to the potato; potato pickin'; karate tournament; motorcycle hill-climbing race; sky-diving show; potato-peeling, blueberry-pie-eating contests; horseshoe pitching; P, BC, D. *Fort Fairfield C of C, PO Box 607, Fort Fairfield 04742.*

Houlton HOULTON POTATO FEAST, early July, 3 days. Potato foods; A/C, D, P. *C of C, PO Box 765, Houlton 04730. 207 532-3050*

Kingfield WHITE WHITE WORLD, late Jan., 6 days, at Sugarloaf, Mt. Snow; snow sculpture; ski races; costumes; hay, sleigh rides; Down East lobster clambake; BC, P. *Maine C of C, 477 Congress St., Portland 04111. 207 774-9871*

Madison CORN FESTIVAL, late Aug., 2 days. Celebrates anniversary of the Abenaki Massacre; corn on the cob; corn dishes; D. *C of C, Madison 04950.*

Old Town INDIAN PAGEANT, July, last wknd, at Indian Island. Indian ceremonial Ds; canoe races; *C of C, Old Town 04468.*

Pittsfield CENTRAL MAINE EGG FESTIVAL, July, last Sat. Egg menus; giant frying pan; BC. *C of C, Pittsfield 04967.*

Rangeley RANGELEY WATER CARNIVAL, mid-July, 1 day. Swim, bubble, balloon (pushing balloon with nose), relay races; world cup frog-jumping race; logrolling competition; canoe tilting; P. *C of C, Rangeley 04970.*

Rockland MAINE SEAFOOD FESTIVAL, Aug., 1st wknd. Shrimp, seafood samplings; A/C, P. *Rockland Area C of C, PO Box 508, Rockland 04841.*

Skowhegan SKOWHEGAN STATE FAIR, mid-Aug., 9 days. "Oldest fair in state"; largest cattle, draft horse, horse shows. *H. Spaulding, Box 39, Skowhegan 04976.*

Winter Harbor ANNUAL LOBSTER FESTIVAL & LOBSTERBOAT RACES, early Aug., 1 day, at Frazer Point in Acadia National Park. Outdoor eating of lobster; boat races. *C of C, Winter Harbor 04693.*

Yarmouth YARMOUTH CLAM FESTIVAL, July, 3rd wknd. Clambake; pole-climbing, woodchopping contests; New England A/C. *Yarmouth C of C, PO Box 416, Yarmouth 04096.*

MARYLAND

Baltimore PREAKNESS FESTIVAL WEEK, mid-May, 10 days. Preakness horse, hot air balloon races; sailboat regatta; A/C, P. *Baltimore Promotion Council, 102 St. Paul St., Baltimore 21202. 301 727-5688*

Boonsboro ANNUAL BOONESBOROUGH DAYS, early Sept., 2 days, at Shafer Memorial Park. Civil War reenactment; jousting; A/C, D, P. *Washington County Tourism Division, 40 Summit Ave., Hagerstown 21740. 301 791-3130*

Cambridge ANNUAL CAMBRIDGE OUTDOOR SHOW, mid-Feb., 3 days. National Muskrat Skinning Championships; goose, duck-calling contests; log-sawing competition; M. *Cambridge Jaycees, PO Box 124, Cambridge 21613.*

Deal Island ANNUAL LABOR DAY SKIPJACK RACES, Labor Day. "North America's only fleet of working sailboats," the oyster dredging skipjacks; Mariner, Tanzer 22, open-class races; Maryland seafood. *Mr. W. C. James, Box 146, Chance 21816. 301 784-2146*

Federalsburg ANNUAL WHEAT THRESHING STEAM & GAS ENGINE SHOW, early Aug., 3 days, at Layton farm. Steam engines, threshers, antique tractors, gas engines, ox teams, shingle-sawing, sawmill, blacksmithing demonstrations; miniature train rides. *J. L. Layton, Route 2, Box 266, Federalsburg 21632. 301 754-8422*

Hagerstown JONATHAN HAGER FRONTIER CRAFTS DAY, mid-July, 1 day; mid-Aug., 1 day; at Hagerstown City Park. Jonathan Hager home opened; frontier Cs demonstrated. *Washington County Tourism Division, 40 Summit Ave., Hagerstown 21740. 301 791-3130*

Hagerstown GOVERNOR'S FIRELOCK MATCHES, late Sept., 2 days, at Fort Frederick State Park. US Revolutionary War musketry contests with pistols, rifles, cannons, tomahawks. *C of C, Hagerstown 21740.*

Indian Head ANNUAL REVOLUTIONARY WAR DAYS, May, 1st wknd, at Smallwood State Park. First Maryland Regiment's marching, M; demonstrations of colonial Cs; Southern Maryland foods; M, P. *Tri-County Council for Southern Maryland, PO Box 301, Waldorf 20601. 301 645-2693*

Mechanicsville ANNUAL JOUSTING TOURNAMENT, Aug., 4th Sun., at Horse Range Farm. Jousting; A/C. *Tri-County Council for Southern Maryland, PO Box 301, Waldorf 20601. 301 645-2693*

Port Republic ANNUAL CALVERT COUNTY JOUSTING TOURNAMENT, Aug., last Sun., at Christ Church. "Oldest tournament in Maryland." *Tri-County Council for Southern Maryland, PO Box 301, Waldorf 20601. 301 645-2693*

Prince Frederick ANNUAL CAVALIER DAYS IN CALVERT COUNTY, late May, wknd, at Calvert County Fairgrounds. Medieval combat; Patuxent Indian ceremonies, Ds; tobacco auction; caber toss, tug-of-war, stone boat contests; Indian weaponmaking; sand painting; knot tying; cornhusk dollmaking; log canoe hollowing. *Southern Maryland Arts & Crafts Center, Barstow 20610. 301 535-0144*

St. Clement's Island ANNUAL ST. CLEMENT'S ISLAND BLESSING OF THE FLEET, Sept., last Sun. Commemorates landing of first settlers in Maryland in 1634; Mass; free boat rides. *Tri-County Council for Southern Maryland, PO Box 301, Waldorf 20601. 301 645-2693*

Springs ANNUAL SPRINGS FOLK FESTIVAL, early Oct., 2 days. Pioneer days revisited; farm demonstrations; C. *Dr. A. E. Shrock, Grantsville 21536.*

Thurmount ANNUAL CATOCTIN COLORFEST, mid-Oct., 3 days. Apple butter boiling; blacksmithing; cidermaking; A/C, P. *Catoctin Mountain Tourist Council, PO Box 32, Thurmount 21788.*

Westminster ANNUAL STEAM UP & MILITIA DAYS, early Sept., 4 days, at Carroll County Farm Museum. Demonstrations of old-fashioned steam, gas engines; shingle sawing; threshing; antique cars; oldtime calliope. *Museum, 500 S. Center St., Westminster 21157. 301 848-7775*

Westminster ANNUAL FALL HARVEST DAY, early Oct., 2nd Sat., at Carroll County Farm Museum. C demonstrations of 1850's include blacksmithing, quilting, tinsmithing, pottery, weaving, spinning; apple butter making; cornhusking; beekeeping; wagon rides; steam calliope. *Museum, 500 S. Center St., Westminster 21157. 301 848-7775*

MASSACHUSETTS

Beverly YANKEE HOMECOMING, mid-Aug., 1 wk. Lobster festival; aviation show; bike, road races; swim meet; A/C, D, F. *C of C, Cabot St., Beverly 01915. 617 922-1450*

Boston MILITIA DAY, June, 1st Mon. Officers for Ancient and Honorable Artillery Co. election held as it was in 1638; period dress; casting of ballots on Boston Common. *C of C, 125 High St., Boston 02110.*

Buzzards Bay COUNTRY DANCE & SONG SOCIETY OF AMERICA, July–Aug., 5 wks, at Pinewoods Camp. English, American country dancing including English morris, sword dancing; Anglo-American folk M; American D, folk M. *Country Dance & Song Society of America, 55 Christopher St., New York, NY 10014. 212 255-8895*

Charlemont YANKEE DOODLE DAYS, July, last wknd. Tug-of-war; carnival; P. *Mohawk Trail Assn., Charlemont 01339.*

Easthampton FALL FOLIAGE FESTIVAL, mid-Oct., 1 day. *Arcadia Wildlife Sanctuary, Easthampton, 01027. 413 485-3009*

Gloucester ST. PETER'S DAY FIESTA, late June, 2 days. Festival honors St. Peter; greased-pole contest. *C of C, Gloucester 01930.*

Gloucester ANNUAL BLESSING OF THE FLEET, June, last Sun. Bishop blesses fleet. *C of C, Gloucester 01930.*

Greenfield FRANKLIN COUNTY FAIR, early Sept., wknd. "Oldest agricultural fair in US"; horse drawing; tug-of-war; 4-H activities. *Franklin County Agricultural Assn., Greenfield 01301.*

Hampden HARVEST DAY FESTIVAL, early Oct., 1 day. Pie-eating, beer-can-smashing contests; stilt races. *Laughing Brook Wildlife Sanctuary, Hampden 01036. 413 566-3571*

Natick ANNUAL NEW ENGLAND FOLK FESTIVAL, mid-Apr. 3 days, at Natick High School. *N. E. Folk Festival Assn., 57 Roseland St., Somerville 02143.*

Natick ANNUAL NEW ENGLAND FOLK FESTIVAL, late Apr., 3 days. Costumed ethnic D demonstrations; New England folk Cs, foods; M, D. *New England Folk Festival Assn., 57 Roseland St., Somerville 02143. 617 354-2455*

New Bedford WHALING CITY DAYS, late June, 3 days. Blessing of the Fleet; P. *C of C, New Bedford 02742.*

North Adams FALL FOLIAGE FESTIVAL, mid-Oct., 1 week. Ps; sports. *C of C, North Adams, 02147.*

Onset FESTIVAL OF THE HARVEST MOON, late Sept., 1 day. Celebration honors Algonquin Indians; *Onset Bay C of C, Onset 02558. 617 295-1227*

Plymouth HOLY GHOST FESTIVAL, mid-July, 3 days. Portuguese food; traditional auction; P. *Plymouth Area C of C, 85 Samoset St., Plymouth 02360. 617 746-3377*

Plymouth THANKSGIVING DAY CELEBRATION, Nov. Plymouth Plantation is a replica of the settlement as it looked in 1627; tours of recreated houses, shops; blacksmiths', wood sawyers' work; pilgrim's church procession. *Plymouth Area C of C, 85 Samoset St., Plymouth 02360. 617 746-3377*

Provincetown BLESSING OF THE FLEET, June, last wknd. Provincetown fishermen carry statue of St. Peter, patron of fishermen, through city to fleet; bishop blesses ships as they pass wharf; P. *C of C, Provincetown 02657.*

Salem HERITAGE DAYS, mid-Aug., 1 wk. 10,000-meter race; fife & drum corps; F, P, D. *C of C, Salem 01970.*

Westfield WESTFIELD FAIR, Aug., 3rd wknd., at Russellville Rd. Folk D; A/C. *E. LaBay, Box 271, Russellville Rd., Westfield 01085.*

West Tisbury, MARTHA'S VINEYARD FAIR, Aug., 3rd wknd. Agricultural exhibits. *Martha's Vineyard Agricultural Society, West Tisbury 02575.*

MICHIGAN

Alma HIGHLAND FESTIVAL & GAMES, mid-May, 3 days. Pipe band competition; piping; drumming; open pipe band championships; road run; S, D, M. *C of C, PO Box 506, Alma 48801. 517 463-5525*

Dearborn MUZZLE LOADERS FESTIVAL, mid-June, 2 days. Revolutionary vs. Civil War cannon competition; frontier days recalled with marching bands, Cs; costumed sharpshooters; muzzleloading weapons. *Greenfield Village & Henry Ford Museum, Dearborn 48121.*

Dearborn ANTIQUE FIRE APPARATUS MUSTER, early July, 2 days. More than 60 fire engines, hand pumpers, hose carts participate in firefighting contests, water-pumping demonstrations, races; P. *Greenfield Village & Henry Ford Museum, Dearborn 48121.*

Dearborn AUTUMN HARVEST WEEKEND, early Oct., 2 days. Blacksmithing competition; rug hooking bee; demonstrations of century-old farm machinery; C, M, D. *Greenfield Village & Henry Ford Museum, Dearborn 48121.*

Frankenmuth BAVARIAN FESTIVAL, June, 2nd wk. Ethnic festival celebrates Bavarian heritage; festival of bugles, drums; German food; polka bands; A/C, D, P. *C of C, 635 Main St., Frankenmuth 48734. 517 652-6106*

Fremont OLD FASHIONED DAYS, mid-July, days. Frog-jumping, shuffleboard, pie-eating contests; firemen's water battle; bicycle, road races; D, M, P, BC. *C of C, 101 E. Main St., Fremont 49412. 616 924-0770*

Gaylord ALPENFEST, July, 3rd wk. Alpine costumes; free sauerkraut, ice cream; pie-eating, pipe-smoking contests; "burning of boog legend" wherein citizens and visitors write down their troubles, problems, and throw them into the fire to be rid of them; "Herr Gessler's return legend" wherein he attempts to stop the fun. *Gaylord Alpenfest, Inc., PO Box 513, Gaylord 49735.*

Hastings FOLK LIFE FESTIVAL, mid-Sept., 2 days. Pioneer life demonstrations of spinning, weaving, candle, sausage, soap, bread, butter, "likker" making; farm Cs; carpentry; blacksmithing; M. *Charlton Park, 2545 S. Charlton Park Rd., Hastings 49058. 616 945-3775*

Holland TULIP TIME FESTIVAL, mid-May, 4 days. Dutch heritage celebrated while tulips in bloom; wooden shoe factory tours; Klompen dancers perform in costume; street scrubbing; P, M, D. *Tulip Time Office, Civil Center, 150 W. 8th St., Holland 49423. 616 396-4221*

Kalamazoo MAPLE SUGARING WEEKEND, mid-Mar., 2 days, at Kalamazoo Nature Center. Making maple syrup as pioneers & Indians did; demonstrations of how to use maple syrup, sugar in oldtime recipes. *Kalamazoo Nature Center, Inc., 7000 N. Westnedge, Kalamazoo 49007.*

Kalamazoo FALL HARVEST & CRAFTS FESTIVAL, early Oct., 2 days. Pioneer methods of food preservation, games; buttermaking, spinning, ropemaking, lapidary, candlemaking, quilting demonstrations; horse-drawn wagon rides; steam engines; threshing machine; cidermaking; blacksmith shop; tree drawing; earthmobile. *Kalamazoo Nature Center, Inc., 7000 N. Westnedge, Kalamazoo 49007.*

Kalkaska KALKASKA MIDWEST INTERNAT'L SLED DOG RACE, early Feb., 2 days. Musher's supper; sled dog races; D. *C of C, Kalkaska 49646.*

Manistee MANISTEE NAT'L FOREST FESTIVAL, July 4th wknd. Festival honors area's historic roots in lumbering, forestry; contests. *Manistee County C of C, PO Box 159, Manistee 49660. 616 723-2575*

Manistee INTERNAT'L DAY, mid-Aug., 1 day. Cultural-educational displays of ethnic items, clothing, food, M. *Manistee County C of C, PO Box 159, Manistee 49660. 616 723-2575*

Onaway FRONTIER DAYS & RODEO, July 4th wknd. Wild-horse, barrel races; D, F, P, R. *C of C, Onaway 49765.*

Traverse City NAT'L CHERRY FESTIVAL, early July, 1 wk. Celebration of cherry harvest; cherry hunt, pie-eating contests; big wheel, frog, turtle, milk-carton boat, canoe, foot races; cherry smorgasbord luncheon; marching-band competition; P, F. *Nat'l Cherry Festival, PO Box 141, Traverse City 49684. 616 927-4230*

MINNESOTA

Askov RUTABAGA FESTIVAL & DANISH DAYS, late Aug., 2 days. Ethnic emphasis; aebleskivers; folk dancers; bike, truck rodeos; horseshoe tournament; horse-drawn wagon rides; D, M, P, BC. *Askov Rutabaga Festival & Fair Assn., Askov 55704.*

Bemidji ANNUAL OLD TYME FIDDLERS CONTEST, early Jan., 1 day. *C of C, Bemidji 56601. 218 751-3540*

Chaska RENAISSANCE FAIR, Aug.–Sept., wknds. 16th-century horse show; masqueraders P; jousting; king's key race; archery; fencing; king of the log; hay toss; Jacob's ladder; maypole. *Chaska C of C, Chaska 56318.*

Crane Lake VOYAGEUR DAY, July, 2nd Sat. Fur-trading days of 1700's reenacted; outdoor cooking; M, D contests. *Crane Lake Commercial Club, Crane Lake 55725.*

Dalton LAKE REGION PIONEER THRESHERMEN'S REUNION, early Sept., 3 days. Threshing; plowing; saw, lathe, shingle mills; baker fan; tractor pulls; sand molding, casting; rug-weaving, quilting, butter-churning demonstrations; old rural school in session. *Lake Region Pioneer Threshermen's Assn., Dalton 56324.*

Duluth DULUTH FOLK FESTIVAL, early Aug., 1 day. Hawaiian folk D; Scottish pipers; Greek, Tahitian, Danish, Russian, Italian Ds; ethnic foods, entertainment, A/C. *Duluth Folk Festival, 1728 E. 2nd St., Duluth 55812. 218 724-7491*

Fergus Falls SYTTENDE MAI COMMEMORATION, mid-May, 1 day. Norwegian heritage commemorated with ethnic displays, demonstrations, program salute. *Fergus Falls Area C of C, Box 724, Fergus Falls 56537. 218 736-6951*

Lanesboro LANESBORO'S GOOD OL' DAYS, early July, 2 days. Ol' days S; softball, horseshoe tournaments; canoe races; D, P, BC. *Lanesboro C of C, Lanesboro 55949.*

Minneapolis SNOOSE BOULEVARD FESTIVAL, May, last wknd. Scandinavian emigrant days; ethnic food, D; fiddle, accordion contests; weaving demonstrations; P. *Ollie i Skratthult Project, PO Box 14171, Univ. Station, Minneapolis 55414. 612 335-0201*

Minneapolis SVENSKARNAS DAG, June, 4th Sun. "Largest Swedish celebration in US"; residents of Swedish descent honored with bell ringing, ethnic foods, costumes; M, D. *J. Johnson, 1605 Louisiana Ave. S., Minneapolis 55426. 612 545-9294*

Montevideo MONTEVIDEO'S FIESTA DAYS, late June, 4 days. Begun in 1946 as a way to promote peace between this city and Montevideo, Uruguay; gift exchange between cities. *C of C, Montevideo 56265.*

Ortonville SWEET CORN FESTIVAL, Aug., 1 day. Free sweet corn cooked in oldtime steam engine; corn-eating contest; inner-tube, canoe races; P. *Ortonville Civic & Commerce Assn., 33 N.W. 2nd St., Ortonville 56278. 612 839-3284*

Park Rapids LOGGING DAYS, July, 3rd wknd. State logging championships; water show; greased-pole contest; P. *Logging Days, Box 249, Park Rapids 56470. 218 732-4111*

Perham PIONEER FESTIVAL, mid-Aug. Pioneer activities include grain threshing, log sawing with steam power; horse show. *V. Larson, 556 E. Main St., Perham 56573. 218 346-6580*

Pipestone ANNUAL POW WOW, mid-June, 3 days. Indian regalia presents Indian tribes of 5 states; Native American cultural D contests, foods, C. *Pipestone Indian Club, PO Box 727, Pipestone 56164. 507 825-5463*

Rollag WESTERN MINNESOTA STEAM THRESHERS REUNION, Labor Day wknd. Return to lifestyle of 1900's includes steam engines, power threshing rigs, saw mills, lathe, shingle operations; spinning; rug weaving; pioneer log cabin; old-time railroad depot. *W. A. Nelson, Hawley 56549. 218 937-5498*

St. James ANNUAL RAILROAD DAYS, early July, 4 days. Pistol shoot, horseshoe, costume, beard contests; ethnic foods; D, F, S. *L. Gardner, 610 11th Ave. S., St. James 56081.*

St. Paul WINTER CARNIVAL, Jan–Feb., 2 wks. Snowmobile, iceboat races; skiing; curling mixed bonspiel; broomball tournament; ice fishing; match, weight pulls; speed skating; winter golf; P, A/C. *Winter Carnival, 156 Metro Sq., St. Paul 55101. 612 222-4416*

St. Paul FORT SNELLING RENDEZVOUS, mid-July, 2 days. Life prior to 1845; tomahawk, knife-throwing contests; voyageurs; traders; M. *Fort Snelling State Park, Pike Island Nature Center, St. Paul 55111. 612 335-2052*

Spring Grove SYTTENDE MAI FESTIVAL, mid-May, 3 days. Annual Norwegian festival celebrates heritage with Olympic Norse runners, foods; fiddlers bee; A/C, P, D. *Commercial Club, Spring Grove 55974. 507 498-5644*

Stewartville ANNUAL ICE FESTIVAL, late Jan., 8 days. Snowmobile races, trail ride; M, D. *Stewartville Special Events Committee, 417 S. Main, Stewartville 55976. 507 533-8822*

Stillwater ST. CROIX VALLEY LUMBERJACK DAYS, late July, 4 days. Logrolling, beard, dress-up contests; softball, tennis tournaments; running race; dunk tank; BC, F. *St. Croix Valley Area C of C, 408 E. Chestnut St., Stillwater 55082. 612 439-7700*

West Concord BERNE SWISS FEST, early Aug., 1 day. Swiss food, yodeling, wrestling; stone throwing (Steintossen); alphorn blowing. *Berne Swiss Fest, Zwingli United Church of Christ, West Concord 55985.*

MISSISSIPPI

Biloxi MARDI GRAS, Feb., 1 day. Costumes; decorative floats; P. *Gulf Coast Carnival Assn., Inc., PO Drawer CC, Biloxi 39533.*

Biloxi BLESSING OF THE SHRIMP FLEET, June, 1st wknd. Shrimp season opens; 1,000 boats blessed; free boiled shrimp; fais do-do; BC. *Biloxi Shrimp Festival, Inc., PO Box 592, Biloxi 39533.*

Carthage LEAKE COUNTY SPORTSMEN DAY, early July, 1 day. Muzzleloader shooting match; fishing R; greasy-pole climb; pallet, potato sack races; turkey-calling, junior slingshot, female horseshoe-pitching, hunting-horn-blowing, duck-calling, field-skeet-shooting contests. *Leake County Sportsmen Club, PO Box 209, Carthage 39051. 601 267-9231*

Grenada STATE CHAMPIONSHIP FIDDLERS CONTEST, early July, 1 day, at Grenada High School Auditorium. *Travel Dept., MS A & I Board, PO Box 849, Jackson 39205.*

Grenada FOLK-LIFE FESTIVAL, mid-Sept., 1 day, at Hugh White State Park. Fiddlers contest; folk, contemporary Cs; bluegrass M. *Travel Dept., MS A & I Board, PO Box 849, Jackson 39205.*

Hancock County, at White Cypress & Necaise Crossing, ANNUAL GUMBO FESTIVAL, mid-Nov., 3 days. Gumbo recipes, food; fish fry; D. *Travel Dept., MS A & I Board, PO Box 849, Jackson 39205.*

Jackson MISSISSIPPI STATE FAIR, mid-Oct., 8 days. Annually since 1848; livestock judging; entertainment; "World's Largest Midway"; fiddlers, horse-pulling contests; cane mill. *MS Fair Commission, PO Box 982, Jackson 39205.*

Philadelphia CHOCTAW INDIAN FAIR, mid-July, 4 days. Choctaw life depicted through stickball games, bow & arrow, blow pipe competitions; D, A/C. *Choctaw Indian Fair, Route 7, PO Box 21, Philadelphia 39350. 601 656-5251*

Philadelphia NESHOBA COUNTY FAIR, July–Aug., 1 wk. Harness races; livestock show; cakewalk; BC, M, D. *Neshoba County Fair Assn., 518 Center Ave., Philadelphia 39350. 601 656-3166*

Raleigh NAT'L TOBACCO SPITTING CONTEST, late July, 1 day. World championship tobacco-spitting contest; bird-calling contests; mule racing; M. *Travel Dept., MS A & I Board, PO Box 849, Jackson 39205.*

MISSOURI

Hannibal NAT'L TOM SAWYER DAYS, early July, 4 days. Includes Nat'l Tom Sawyer Fence Painting Contest (see below); selection of local Tom & Becky; raft races; Tomboy Sawyer, frog-jumping contests; watermelon-seed spitting; shoe scramble; F. *C of C, 623 Broadway, Hannibal 63401. 314 221-1101*

Hannibal NAT'L TOM SAWYER FENCE PAINTING CONTEST, July 4. 10 modern-day Tom Sawyers, representing the 10 states bordering the Mississippi River, compete in contest at Mark Twain's boyhood home; frog jumping; raft racing; F. *C of C, 623 Broadway, Hannibal 63401. 314 221-1101*

Hermann MAIFEST, mid-May, 2 days. German festival; costumes; biergartens; winery tours; M. *Hermann C of C, Hermann 65041.*

Lebanon BENNETT SPRING HILLBILLY DAYS FESTIVAL, mid-June, 3 days. Fiddlers, pipe-smoking, horseshoe-pitching contests; canoe race; primitive weapons demonstrations; A/C, M, D. *Lebanon C of C, Lebanon 65536.*

Nevada BUSHWHACKER DAYS, June, 3rd wk. "Largest Indian powwow in Missouri"; draft-horse-pulling, beard, costume contests; royalty tea, competition; hatchet, musket demonstrations; A/C, D. *Nevada Vernon County C of C, 215 Osage Blvd., Nevada 64772. 417 667-5300*

Rolla ST. PAT'S CELEBRATION, mid-Mar., 2 days. Honors St. Patrick, patron saint of engineers; reverence paid to Blarney Stone; beard, shillelagh judging. *Public Information Office, U. of Missouri at Rolla, Rolla 65401. 314 341-4259*

Ste. Genevieve JOUR DE FETE, mid-Aug., 2 days. Celebrates city's French heritage and founding in 1735 as first permanent settlement west of the Mississippi River; folk D; ethnic foods; French costumes contest; P, A/C. *C of C, PO Box 166, Ste. Genevieve 63670.*

St. Louis ST. LOUIS STRASSENFEST, late June. German street festival; oom-pa-pa bands; bratwurst; pretzels. *Convention & Visitors Bureau of Greater St. Louis, 500 Broadway Bldg.; St. Louis 63102. 314 421-1023*

St. Louis HILL DAY, Aug., 1 day. Ethnic celebration honors Italian residents; Italian food; grape-stomping contest; A/C, D. *Convention & Visitors Bureau of Greater St. Louis, 500 Broadway Bldg., St. Louis 63102. 314 421-1023*

St. Louis OKTOBERFEST, early Oct. German-Slavic heritage of area emphasized; Dutchtown sausage; tamburitza; D, A/C. *Convention & Visitors Bureau of Greater St. Louis, 500 Broadway Bldg., St. Louis 63102. 314 421-1023*

Sikeston BOOTHEEL RODEO, early Aug. "Largest rodeo in Missouri." *C of C, 301 N. New Madrid, Sikeston 63801. 314 471-2498*

Silver Dollar City JUNE FESTIVAL OF MOUNTAIN FOLKS' MUSIC, June, 9 days. One hundred nonprofessional Ozark musicmakers perform M as old as 400 years; historic handicrafts. *C of C, Silver Dollar City 65616. 417 338-2611*

Silver Dollar City NAT'L CRAFTS FESTIVAL, mid-Sept.–Oct. Over 70 exhibits of rare American handicrafts; demonstrations of glass blowing, soapmaking, ropemaking, quilting, dollmaking from cornhusks; log hewing; spinning. *C of C, Silver Dollar City 65616. 417 338-2611*

Springfield OZARK EMPIRE FAIR, early Aug. Over 10,000 exhibits of agriculture, handicrafts, industrial products; auto races; livestock show. *Ozark Empire Fair, PO Box 630, Springfield 65801. 417 833-2660*

MONTANA

Billings WESTERN DAYS, mid-July, 1 wk. Beard-growing, costume contests; D, P, R. *C of C, 2705 Montana Ave., Billings 59103. 406 245-4111*

Browning NORTH AMERICAN INDIAN DAYS, July, month. Indians from North America gather for tribal festivities of Blackfeet, games, chanting; costumes of the 1880's; D, P. *Blackfeet Planning Program, Blackfeet Indian Reservation, Browning 59117.*

Havre CREE SUNDANCE, June–July, 3 days. Religious Indian praying, fasting, D. *Highline Indian Alliance, Main St., Havre 59501. 406 265-7827*

Havre CHIPPEWA-CREE CELEBRATION, Aug., 4 days. Powwow; Indian D contests; stick games; gambling. *Highline Indian Alliance, Main St., Havre 59501. 406 265-7827*

Helena LAST CHANCE STAMPEDE & FAIR, July-Aug., 4 days, at Lewis & Clark County Fairgrounds. Team roping; trained-mule show; pinewood, demolition derbies; horse shows; A/C, R. *Last Chance Stampede & Fair, PO Box 614, Helena 59601. 406 442-1098*

Libby LOGGER DAYS, July, 2nd wknd. Lumberjack, ax-throwing, sawing, logrolling contests. *C of C, Libby 59923. 406 293-6630*

Missoula LOGGER DAYS, Sept., 2nd wknd. Woodchopping, crosscut-saw contests. *C of C, PO Box 1518, Missoula 59801. 406 543-6623*

Red Lodge HOME OF THE CHAMPIONS RODEO, July 4th wknd. P, R. *C of C, Box 998, Red Lodge 59068. 406 446-1718*

Red Lodge FESTIVAL OF NATIONS, early Aug., 9 days. Different nation featured each day; food; folk D, M; pig roast; Scots pipes; spinning; carding; Yugoslavian Italian Day; P, C, M. *C of C, Red Lodge 59068. 406 446-1718*

Whitefish WHITEFISH WINTER CARNIVAL, mid-Feb., Royal P features King Ullr, court of queens & princesses; ski races; snow sculptures; costume contest. *Whitefish C of C, PO Box 1309, Whitefish 59937.*

NEBRASKA

Clarkson CZECH FESTIVAL, late June, 3 days. Czech culture, M, D, foods, gymnastics; Norwegian, Irish, German, Danish folk D, push-button accordion contest; P. *Czech Festival Committee, Clarkson 68629.*

Crawford CRAWFORD FIDDLER'S CONTEST, late July, at park pavilion. Trophies awarded to top entries. *C of C, Crawford 69339.*

McCook GERMAN HERITAGE DAYS CELEBRATION, May, 1st wknd. Salute to persons of German ancestry; polka bands; bratwurst; sauerkraut; horseshoe pitching; Indian wrestling; frog jumping. *Greater McCook Area C of C, PO Box 337, McCook 69001. 308 345-3200*

Minden DANISH FESTIVAL, June. Danish smorgasbord, D; carnival. *Minden C of C, PO Box 375, Minden 68959.*

Nebraska City ARBOR DAY CELEBRATION, late Apr., 2 days. Rope-climbing, sack races; horseshoe pitching; fly-in breakfast; pioneer C; P, M,

D. J. Steinheider, Nebraska City 68410. 402 873-3226

North Platte NEBRASKALAND DAYS, mid-June, 1 wk. Buffalo Bill R with bareback, calf roping, saddle bronc, steer wrestling, team roping, barrel-racing; bull riding; shoot-outs; horse-pulling, hog beauty, cake contests; costumes; P, A, BC. *Nebraskaland Days, 100 E. 5th St., North Platte 69101. 308 532-7939*

Plattsmouth KASS KOUNTY KING KORN KARNIVAL, Sept., 3rd wk, 4 days. Corn harvest celebration; corn foods; drill team, color guard competition; water fight; oldtime fiddlers; BC, P, M, D. *Project Coordinator, City Office Bldg., 136 N. 5th St., Plattsmouth 68048. 402 296-4168*

Ponca DAYS OF '56 RODEO & CELEBRATION, late June, 3 days. Ponca becomes an 1856 frontier town again for R competitions, carnival, P, historical programs. *Ponca Commercial Club, Ponca 68770.*

Stromsburg SWEDISH FESTIVAL, mid-June, 2 days. Horseshoe contest; Swedish smorgasbord; air show; hot air balloon jumps; P, BC, D. *Stromsburg Commercial Club, Stromsburg 68666.*

Wilber WILBER CZECH FESTIVAL, Aug., 1st wknd. Czech foods; kolache-eating, costume, talent, accordion, photography contests; BC, P, A, D. *I. Ourecky, Wilber 68465.*

NEVADA

Elko INVITATIONAL CHARIOT RACES, mid-Feb., 2 days, at County Fairgrounds. Wheels or runners used on chariots. *Elko C of C, 1601 Idaho St., Elko 89801. 702 738-7135*

Elko ANNUAL OLD TIMERS RODEO, Feb., last wknd, at Spring Creek Horse Palace. Contestants must be at least 45 years old; calf, team roping; bronc riding. *Spring Creek, Inc., PO Box 452, Elko 89801.*

Elko HUMBOLDT RIVER RUN, late May, 1 day. Any craft capable of staying afloat may be raced the 16 miles from Osino, NV, to 5th St. Bridge in Elko. *Elko C of C, 1601 Idaho St., Elko 89801. 702 738-7135*

Elko NAT'L BASQUE FESTIVAL, July, 1st wknd. Log-chopping, weight-carrying and dragging, woodcutting, sheepherders' beard, Irrintzi (Basque yell) contests; Basque D, P. *C of C, 1601 Idaho St., Elko 89801. 702 738-7135*

Ely BASQUE FESTIVAL, late July, 2 days. Woodchopping; weightlifting; Basque dancers. *White Pine C of C, PO Box 239, Ely 89301. 702 289-2568*

Ely PONY EXPRESS DAYS, Aug., last 2 wknds. Slag race; stagecoach holdup; horse races; D. *White Pine C of C, Box 239, Ely 89301. 702 289-2568*

Fallon INDIAN POW WOW, Labor Day wknd. Indian costume, D contests, R, P; D. *Churchill County C of C, 30 W. Williams Ave., Fallon 89406. 702 423-2544*

Las Vegas HELLDORADO, mid-May, 4 days. Public wears western clothing; beard contest; kangaroo court; BC, R, A, D. *NV Dept. of Economic Development, 2501 E. Sahara, Las Vegas 89104. 702 385-0257*

NEW HAMPSHIRE

Charlestown COLONIAL MUSTER DAYS, July 2nd Sun. Colonial military rangers wear uniforms of American Revolutionary times; fife & drum corps; demonstrations of hewing timber with axes, flax spinning, weaving. *Old Fort No. 4 Assn., Box 354, Charlestown 03603. 603 826-9768*

Hampton HAMPTON SUMMERFEST CARNIVAL, early July, 4 days. Bavarianfest; road race; hot air balloon; C, P. *Div. of Economic Development, PO Box 856, Concord 03301.*

Laconia WORLD CHAMPIONSHIP SLED DOG RACES, mid-Feb., 3 days. Semifinalists from professional sled dog races meet to determine world championship. *Lakes Region C of C, 9 Veterans Sq., Laconia 03246. 603 524-5531*

New London NEW LONDON MUSTER DAY, mid-June, 1 day. Cannon, rifle, pistol shoot; knife, tomahawk throwing; muster; D. *Div. of Economic Development, PO Box 856, Concord 03301.*

North Conway MT. WASHINGTON VALLEY ALTERNATIVE VEHICLE REGATTA, mid-June, 6 days. For amateur and professional builders of prototype or production engine-driven alternative vehicles; trophies for efficiency, lowest resource consumption. *Mt. Washington Valley Chamber, N. Conway 03860.*

Warner FALL FOLIAGE FESTIVAL, Sept.–Oct., 3 days. Woodsmen's, ice-cream-eating contests; oxen pulling; P, M. *Bd. of Directors, Fall Foliage Festival, Warner 03278.*

Wolfeboro WINTER CARNIVAL, early Feb., 2 days. Snowmobile, skiing, skating races; snow sculpture contest; iceboating; D. *C of C, Wolfeboro 03894. 603 569-2200*

NEW JERSEY

Asbury Park LOYALTY DAY PARADE, early May. Participants celebrate their loyalty to US. *Greater Asbury Park C of C, PO Box 649, Asbury Park 07712. 201 681-4081*

Atlantic City WEDDING OF THE SEA, mid-Aug., 1 day. Originated with religious holiday of Feast of Assumption to acknowledge city's reliance on the ocean; white marlin tournament; east coast surfing, hobie hawk championships; boat race; roller derby; M, A. *Atlantic City Press Bureau, Convention Hall, Atlantic City 08401. 800 257-8686*

Cape May BARBERSHOP QUARTET JAMBOREE, late June. *C of C, Cape May 08204.*

Cape May CLAM SHELL PITCHING CONTEST, 2 days, late Aug. *C of C, Cape May 08204.*

Clinton CLINTON & OTHER ADVENTURES, late Nov., 2 days. Open house; colonial demonstrations; P. *The Good Earth, Clinton 08809.*

Flemington FLEMINGTON AGRICULTURAL FAIR, Aug.–Sept., 1 wk. Fife & drum corps; bee-handling demonstration; rabbit handler's, fireman, garden-tractor-pulling, sheep-fitting, horseshoe-pitching contests; goat show; P, D. *Flemington Fair Assn., PO Box 26, Flemington 08822. 201 782-2413*

Freehold IRISH & SCOTTISH GAMES FESTIVAL, July, 1 day. Dance contests; Irish & Scottish music; athletics. *Freehold Raceway, Freehold 07728.*

Holmdel HERITAGE FESTIVAL, May–Oct. On successive Saturdays, NJ heritage groups stage a day of folk activities; these groups include Puerto Ricans, Byelorussians, Slovakians, Ukrainians, Poles, Jews, Italians, Irish, Hungarians, Scandinavians, Germans, Scots. *Garden State Arts Center, PO Box 300, Holmdel 07733. 201 442-8600*

Margate City SAND SCULPTURE CONTEST, July 3. *C of C, Margate City 08402.*

Middletown MIDDLETOWN FOLK FESTIVAL, June, 3rd wknd. Traditional folk M, C. *Middletown Folk Festival, Inc., 11 Carnegie Court, Middletown 07748. 201 741-0844*

Ocean City SAND SCULPTING CONTEST, mid-July, mid-Aug., 1 day each month. Prizes for best entries. *C of C, PO Box 157, Ocean City 08226.*

Ocean City FRECKLE CONTEST, late July, 1 day. Prizes given for two categories of freckles: the most freckles on the body, homemade freckles. *Recreation Office, Ocean City 08226. 609 399-6111*

Ocean City HERMIT TREE CRAB RACE, mid-Aug., 1 day. Crabs race; BC. *C of C, PO Box 157, Ocean City 08226.*

Phillipsburg COLONIAL FESTIVAL, July 8–11. *Clarence R. Baker, C of C, Phillipsburg 08865.*

Scotch Plains UNICO ITALIAN FESTIVAL, Labor Day wknd., at St. Bartholomew's Church. Italian games, foods. *St. Bartholomew's Church, Westfield Ave., Scotch Plains 07076.*

Somerville KUGLER-ANDERSON MEMORIAL TOUR, Memorial Day. Bicycle races; international competition. *C of C, Somerville 08876.*

Titusville COMMEMORATION OF WASHINGTON CROSSING THE DELAWARE, late Dec., 1 day, at Washington Crossing State Park. Reenactment of the Crossing on Christmas Day 1776. *Washington Crossing State Park, Box 337 A, RD 1, Titusville 08560.*

Tuckerton YE OLDE TUCKERTON DAY, July 4. *C of C, Tuckerton 08087.*

NEW MEXICO

Albuquerque ANNUAL INTERTRIBAL POW WOW, mid-June, 3 days. *Indian School Campus, Albuquerque 87101.*

Albuquerque LUMINARIA TOUR, Dec. 24. 17th-century tradition of small bonfires and live lights illuminate city streets; visitors taken on free bus tour. *Greater Albuquerque C of C, 401 2nd St. N.W., Albuquerque 87102. 505 842-0220*

Eagle Nest ANNUAL ASPEN FESTIVAL & PAUL BUNYAN DAY, late Sept., 1 day. Logrolling; log jousting; ax throwing; chopping; pole climbing. *Moreno Valley C of C 87718. 505 377-2359*

Gallup INTER-TRIBAL INDIAN CEREMONIAL, mid-Aug., 4 days. "Greatest authentic American Indian cultural spectacle in the world"; traditional Indian D at night lighted only by juniper and piñon firelight; Indian R; A/C. *Inter-Tribal Indian Ceremonial Assn., PO Box 1029, Gallup 87301. 505 863-3896*

La Cienega SPRING FESTIVAL & JUAN BAUTISTA DE ANZA PAGEANT, early May, 2 days. 18th-century blacksmithing, corn-grinding, soap-making demonstrations; reenactment of Gov. De Anza's visit to city in 1779. *Ms. A. G. Thomas. 505 982-5644*

Lincoln ANNUAL OLD LINCOLN DAYS, Aug., 1st wknd. Historical pageant about Billy the Kid and the Lincoln County War of 1880's; pony express race; ghost town tours; fiddlers contests. *Lincoln County Memorial Commission, Lincoln 88338.*

Santa Fe ANNUAL FIESTA DE SANTA FE, Labor Day wknd. "Oldest non-Indian celebration in US" since 1700's; commemorates peaceful reconquest of NM in 1692 by Spaniard Don Diego de Vargas; burning of Zozobra "Old Man Gloom"; D, A/C, P. *C of C, Santa Fe 87501. 505 983-7317*

Santa Fe COWBOY OKTOBERFEST, Oct., month. Fiddling competitions; turkey shoots; beer-drinking, pie-eating, beard-growing contests; R. *New Mexico Dept. of Development, 113 Washington Ave., Santa Fe 87501.*

Santo Domingo Pueblo SANTO DOMINGO FEAST DAY, early Aug., 1 day. About 500 participants celebrate an all-day Indian corn D. *Santo Domingo Pueblo Office, Santo Domingo Pueblo 87052.*

Truth or Consequences OLD TIME FIDDLERS CONTEST, early May, 2 days. *R. Daugherty, Old Time Fiddlers Contest, Truth or Consequences 87901.*

Tucumcari QUAY COUNTY FAIR, early Sept., 4 days, at Quay County Fairgrounds. Old fiddlers, cow-chip-throwing contests; livestock exhibits. *Tucumcari-Quay County C of C, Drawer E, Tucumcari 88401. 505 461-1694*

NEW YORK

Boonville NEW YORK STATE WOODSMEN'S FIELD DAYS, mid-Aug., 2 days. State Open Championship Woodsmen's competition features log chopping, tree felling, two-man crosscut, ax throwing, logrolling, buck, chain sawing; hydraulic loading, skidding, beard contests; canoe races; greased-pole climb; P. *Boonville Area C of C, PO Box 163, Boonville 13309.*

Canajoharie SQUARE DANCE FESTIVAL, late May, East Hill School campus. *C of C, Canajoharie 13317.*

Canandaigua RING OF FIRE, Sat. before Labor Day. Indian ceremony. *C of C, Canandaigua 14424.*

Cape Vincent FRENCH FESTIVAL, early July, 1 day. Celebrates settlement of Cape Vincent. *C of C, Cape Vincent 13618. 315 654-4593*

Catskill OLD CATSKILL DAYS, mid-June, 4 days. Antique cars; colonial costumes; boat show; canoe race. *Catskill Daily Mail, Catskill 12414. 518 943-2100*

Dansville OKTOBERFEST, early Sept. *C of C, Dansville 14437.*

East Durham IRISH FEIS, June. Irish folk D; food; entertainment. *Mullan's Mt. Spring Hotel, Durham 12423. 518 634-2541*

Franklinville WESTERN NEW YORK MAPLE FESTIVAL, Apr., 2 days. Making of maple products; wrestling matches. *Box 41, Franklinville 14737.*

Hunter GERMAN ALPS FESTIVAL, July–Aug., 12 days. Folklore show; Schuhplattler D; horn players; hang gliding, hot air balloon ascents; German foods; P. *German Alps Festival, Box 297, Hunter 12442. 212 673-6290*

Jefferson ANNUAL MAPLE FESTIVAL, late Apr., 2 days. Sap house in operation; maple-products-making demonstrations; boiling eggs in sap; black powder turkey shoot; ox cart rides; BC, D, A/C. *Schonharie County Annual Maple Festival, PO Box 24, Jefferson 12093. 518 868-4661*

Lake George Village WARREN COUNTY SHERIFF'S MOUNTED TRAIL DAYS, late June, 3 days. Gymkhana contests; P. *C of C, Lake George Village 12845.*

Lake Luzerne ANNUAL FALL FESTIVAL, Sept.–Oct., 3 wknds. White water, orange crate derbies; slalom, downriver, bike races; Octoberfest; F, BC. *Lake Luzerne Fall Festival, Lake Luzerne 12846.*

Loch Sheldrake INTERNAT'L FOLK DANCE FESTIVAL, mid-July, 3 days, at Sullivan County Community College. Balkan, Irish, Israeli, Ukrainian ethnic folk D demonstrations; folk displays, A/C. *R. Shill, Coordinator, 52 Lakewood Ave., Monticello 12701. 914 794-6473*

Malone MALONE WINTER FESTIVAL, early Feb., 4 days. *C of C, 7 Howard Place, Malone 12953.*

Massena MASSENA FAIR, early July, 1 wk. Celebration of anniversary of the town, founded in early 1800's; horse races; carnival. *Massena C of C, PO Box 387, Massena 13662. 315 769-3525*

New York City CHINESE NEW YEAR, Feb. 11, Chinatown. *NY Convention & Visitors Bureau, 90 E. 42 St., New York 10017.*

New York City NEW YORK SPRING FOLK FESTIVAL, mid-Apr., 1 wk, Hunter College. *Visitors Info Bureau, 90 E. 42 St., New York 10017.*

New York City FEAST OF ST. ANTHONY OF PADUA, early June, 6 days, 187th St. & Belmont Ave., Bronx. Street fair. *NY Convention & Visitors Bureau, 90 E. 42 St., New York 10017.*

New York City DRAGON BOAT FESTIVAL BOAT FAIR, late June or early July, Chinatown. *NY Convention & Visitors Bureau, 90 E. 42 St., New York 10017.*

New York City FEASTS OF OUR LADY OF MT. CARMEL & ST. PAUL OF NOLA, late June–mid-July, Sat. & Sun., Havermeyer St. to Union Ave., Brooklyn. Street fair. *NY Convention & Visitors Bureau, 90 E. 42 St., New York 10017.*

New York City FEAST OF SAN GENNARO, mid-Sept., 10 days, Mulberry St. Street fair. *NY Convention & Visitors Bureau, 90 E. 42 St., New York 10017.*

New York City BEER FESTIVAL, Oct., Yorkville (E. 86th St.). *NY Convention & Visitors Bureau, 90 E. 42 St., New York 10017.*

Niagara Falls TUSCARORA INDIAN NAT'L PICNIC, July, 2nd wknd. Fireball game; Indian costume contest; Indian-American cuisine; A/C, BC. *L. Henry, 2006 Mt. Hope Rd., Lewiston 14092. 716 297-4990*

Ogdensburg OGDENSBURG INTERNAT'L SEAWAY FESTIVAL, late July, 1 wk. Boat races; battle of drums; air show; blessing of boats; spinning, dyeing, leatherworking, potting, broommaking, woodcarving demonstrations; country & western day; F, P. *Greater Ogdensburg C of C, PO Box 681, Ogdensburg 13669. 315 393-3620*

Old Chatham ANNUAL SHAKER FESTIVAL, early Aug., 1 day. *C of C, Old Chatham 12136.*

Palmyra CANAL TOWN DAYS, mid-Sept. *C of C, Palmyra 14522.*

Penn Yan GENUNDOWA DAY, Aug., 1 day. Seneca thanksgiving for crops & good days. *C of C, Penn Yan 14527.*

Sag Harbor OLD WHALER'S FESTIVAL, mid-June, 3 days. Whale boat competition; P. *C of C, Sag Harbor 11963.*

Saranac Lake WINTER CARNIVAL, Lincoln's Birthday wknd. Ice fishing; snow racing; skiing. *C of C, Saranac Lake 12983.*

Southampton POW WOW, Labor Day wknd. Indian dance, song, ritual at Shinnecock Reservation. *C of C, Southampton 11968.*

Syracuse CENTRAL NEW YORK SCOTTISH GAMES, early Aug. *C of C, Syracuse 13202.*

NORTH CAROLINA

Asheville MOUNTAIN YOUTH JAMBOREE, Mar.–Apr., 4 days, at City Auditorium. Festival perpetuates traditional mountain folklore, M, D. *Asheville Jaycees, Asheville 28802. 704 258-0298*

Asheville MOUNTAIN DANCE & FOLK FESTIVAL, mid-July, 1 day, early Aug., 3 days. Mountain folk D; ballad singing; fiddling; banjo picking; dulcimer; mountain clog Ds. *Asheville Area C of C, PO Box 1011, Asheville 28802. 704 254-1981*

Asheville SHINDIG ON THE GREEN, July–Aug., Sats. Mountain fiddling; dulcimer players; ballads; buck, clog, square Ds. *Asheville Area C of C, PO Box 1011, Asheville 28802. 704 254-1981*

Barnardsville ANNUAL BIG IVY RAMP FESTIVAL, early May, 1 day. Mountaineers dig for wild onion, cook and eat it in a variety of pungent dishes; oldtime mountain games; M, D. *Asheville Area C of C, PO Box 1011, Asheville 28802. 704 254-1981*

Beaufort PIRATE INVASION, late June, 2 days. Reenactment of piracy days in city, including settlers, pirates, beautiful maidens. *Mrs. J. Kell, 301 Front St., Beaufort 28516. 919 728-3669*

Benson MULE DAY CELEBRATION, late Sept., 4 days. Honors mule's place in history; mule pulling; governor's mule race; oldest-, youngest-, ugliest-mule contests; R, D, P, M. *C of C, PO Box 246, Benson 27504. 919 894-3825*

Cherokee CHEROKEE FALL FESTIVAL, early Oct. Cherokee Indians gather to play Indian stickball, a rough Indian sport; Indian Cs. *Cherokee Indian Reservation, Cherokee 28719.*

Cherryville NEW YEARS SHOOTERS, Jan. 1. 200-year-old German and English custom; a group led by a crier gather at residences and businesses, wish the occupants good fortune, and fire an old muzzleloading musket. *C of C, 107 S. Oak St., Cherryville 28021. 704 435-3451*

Denton ANNUAL FLY-IN & THRESHERS REUNION, early July, 3 days, at Denton Airport. Wheat threshing; cornmeal grinding; cabin corncrib; combining; oldtime sawmill; country vittles. *B. Loflin, Route 3, Box 240 B, Denton 27239.*

Hendersonville NORTH CAROLINA APPLE FESTIVAL, Aug.–Sept., 2 wks. Folk D jamboree; orchard tours; clogging; gospel sing; BC, P, D. *NC Apple Festival, Inc., PO Box 489, Hendersonville 28739. 704 692-1413*

Jefferson BLUE RIDGE WAGON TRAIN, early July, 3 days. More than 100 covered wagons and over 500 horseback riders cross mountains as Daniel Boone did from North Wilkesboro to W. Jefferson. *Ashe County C of C, PO Box 31, W. Jefferson 28694. 919 246-9550*

Linville ANNUAL GRANDFATHER MT. HIGHLAND GAMES & GATHERING OF THE SCOTTISH CLANS, mid-July, 2 days. Scottish Highland piping, wrestling, tossing the caber, tossing the sheaf contests; Scottish costumes. *Asheville Area C of C, PO Box 1011, Asheville 28802. 704 254-1981*

Louisburg ANNUAL FOLK MUSIC & DANCE FESTIVAL, late Mar., 2 days, at Louisburg College. American folklore; fiddling; string bands; buck D, folk M, D. *Louisburg College, Louisburg 27549. 919 496-2521*

Morehead City OLD QUAWK'S DAY, mid-Mar., 2 days. Celebration honors legendary meanest man in Carteret County who went to sea despite warnings of storms; quawk calling; flounder flinging; skimming. *Carteret County C of C, PO Drawer B, Morehead City 28557. 919 726-6831*

Morehead City NC CRAB DERBY, mid-Aug., 1 day. Crab race; crab-picking, fish-fileting contests; crab stew supper. *Carteret Carolina Development Corp., PO Box 730, Morehead City 28557. 919 726-7677*

Mt. Airy AMERICAN LEGION & VFW OLDTIME & BLUEGRASS FIDDLERS' CONVENTION, June, 1st wknd. Dobro, mandolin, guitar, bass, bluegrass fiddle & banjo, oldtime fiddle, clawhammer contests; folk songs; D. *Veterans' Memorial Park, PO Box 445, Mt. Airy 27030. 919 789-9413*

Robbins ANNUAL HIGH FALLS OLD-TIME FIDDLER'S CONVENTION, mid-Mar., 1 day. Violin, banjo, guitar, mandolin, tap & buck dancing, piano contests. *Highfalls Elementary School, PO Box 206, Highfalls 27259. 919 464-3600*

Saluda COON DOG DAY, early July, 1 day. Coon dog trials, show; A/C, BC. *Mayor E. B. Hall, Box 248, Saluda 28773. 704 749-2476*

Spivey's Corner NAT'L HOLLERIN' CONTEST, June, 3rd Sat. Farmers used to holler on their way to and from fields; hollerin' workshop, competition; watermelon roll, greasy-pole climb; pepper contest; hoedown. *Nat'l Hollerin' Contest, Inc., Box 332, Dunn 28334. 919 892-4133*

West Jefferson OLD-TIME FIDDLER'S CONVENTION, early Aug., 1 day, at Ashe County Park. *Ashe County C of C, PO Box 31, W. Jefferson 28694. 919 246-9550*

NORTH DAKOTA

Belfield UKRAINIAN DAYS, late June. Ethnic festival, native foods; D, C. *ND Travel Div., State Highway Dept., Bismarck 58505.*

Bismarck FESTIVAL OF NATIONS, early June, 6 days. Different nationality featured daily; native costumes, foods, C. *Festival of Nations, Kirkwood Plaza Office, 615 Kirkwood Plaza, Bismarck 58501.*

Bismarck UNITED TRIBES POW WOW & RODEO, early Sept., 3 days. Indian powwow; national Indian singing, dancing finals; costumes; C, R. *United Tribes Educational Technical Center, 3315 S. Airport Rd., Bismarck 58501.*

Dickinson ROUGHRIDER DAYS, early July, wknd. Ethnic foods; tractor pull; R, P, A, D, M, F. *Dickinson Roughrider Bd. of Directors, Dickinson 58601.*

Jamestown BUFFALO DAYS & HARVEST FESTIVAL, late Sept., 2 days. Buffalo hunger feed; horse show; P. *C of C, 121 W. 1st St., Jamestown 58401.*

Valley City NORTH DAKOTA WINTER SHOW, mid-Mar. Annual festival celebrates snow season with livestock, horse shows; crop-judging contests; R. *Valley City C of C, 137 N. Central Ave., Valley City 58072.*

West Fargo PIONEER DAYS, late Aug., 2 days. Frontier days revisited; horseshoeing; soapmaking; prairie A/C. *C of C. W. Fargo 58078.*

OHIO

Birmingham WOOLLYBEAR FESTIVAL, Oct., 1 day. Isia Isabella, woollybear caterpillar, honored as most famous weather forecaster; woollybear 500 caterpillar race. *D. Goddard, WJW-TV, 5800 S. Marginal Rd., Cleveland 44103. 216 431-8888*

Burton APPLE BUTTER FESTIVAL, early Oct., 2 days. Apple butter, cider making; bread baking on the green; steam engines; one-room schoolhouse; ox roast. *The Cayuga County Historical Soc., PO Box 153, Burton 44021.*

Cadiz INTERNAT'L MINING & MFG. FESTIVAL, mid-Sept., 2 days. Folkloric D, M performed by groups of various ethnic backgrounds; ethnic costumes. *President, Int'l Mining & Mfg. Festival, RFD #3, Cadiz 43907.*

Canal Fulton YANKEE PEDDLER FESTIVAL, Sept., 2 wknds. Pioneer food, costumes; chair caning; rope twining; rake, violin, dulcimer, jewelry, doll, quilt making; tales of yesteryear; apple bobbing, tug-of-war. *Yankee Peddler Festival Assn., 2174 Lewis Dr., Lakewood 44107. 216 221-1808*

Cincinnati CELEBRATION OF FOLKLIFE, late Apr. Cabin raising; pottery throwing; log hewing, M, C. *Appalachian Assn., 1015 Vine St., Cincinnati 45202. 513 421-2550*

Circleville CIRCLEVILLE PUMPKIN SHOW, mid-Oct., 4 days. "World's largest pumpkin pie"; pumpkin-pie-eating, egg-tossing contests; pumpkin burgers, ice cream, donuts, waffles, taffy. *Circleville Area C of C, 135 W. Main St., Circleville 43113.*

Columbus OKTOBERFEST, early Nov., 3 days, at German Village. Bavarian cuisine; costumes; Old World Cs; singalongs; competitive games. *G. Smith, 240 E. Kossuth, Columbus 43206.*

Coshocton & Roscoe Village DULCIMER DAYS, mid-May, 2 days. Dulcimer contests; hammered, courting dulcimers; costumes; dulcimermaking. *Roscoe Village, 381 Hill St., Coshocton 43812. 614 622-9315*

Coshocton & Roscoe Village APPLE BUTTER STIRRIN', mid-Oct., 2 days. Apple butter making; spelling, cornhusking bees; jack-o'-lantern, sack races, stilt-walking, hoop-rolling, apple-pie-eating contests; oldtime steam engine; circus calliope; dulcimers; banjos; violins; kitchen bank. *Roscoe Village, 381 Hill St., Coshocton 43812. 614 622-9315*

Jackson APPLE FESTIVAL, Sept., 3rd wknd. Apple butter preparation; "largest apple pie in the world" displayed; apple-pie-eating contest; M, D, P, A/C. *Jackson C of C, 210 Main St., Jackson 45640. 614 286-2722*

Lebanon OHIO HONEY FESTIVAL, early Sept., 3 days. Honors honey, honey products with P, coronation of honey queen, band competitions; exhibition of honey products. *Ohio Festivals & Events Assn., PO Box 6, 213 S. Quarry St., Bainbridge 45512.*

Lisbon JOHNNY APPLESEED FESTIVAL, mid-Sept., 3 days. Pioneer days celebration; fiddlers contest; Cs demonstrations; BC, P, D. *C of C, Lisbon 44432. 216 424-5503*

Middlefield SWISS CHEESE FESTIVAL, mid-June, 2 days. Cheesemaking; A/C demonstrations; Swiss yodeling; alphorn-blowing, pie-eating contests; M, BC, P, D. *Middlefield Swiss Cheese Festival, Middlefield C of C, PO Box 455, Middlefield 44062.*

Quaker City OHIO HILLS FOLK FESTIVAL, mid-July, 4 days. Muzzleloader rifle shoot; horse show; oldtime fiddle, banjo, dulcimer, calliope; P, D. *Folk Festival, 125 Pike St., Quaker City 43773.*

Rio Grande BOB EVANS FARM FESTIVAL, Oct., 2nd wknd. Wild-turkey calling; truck mules, sheep shearing; logrolling; horseshoe pitching; sawmill, steam engine displays; M, D. *Bob Evans Farm, Route 35, Rio Grande 45674. 614 491-2225*

Sugarcreek OHIO SWISS FESTIVAL, late Sept., 2 days. *Schwingfest* (Swiss wrestling); *steintossen* (stone tossing); yodeling; costumes; P, D, M. *Ohio Swiss Festival, Inc., Sugarcreek 44681.*

Zanesville ZANE'S TRACE COMMEMORATION, mid-June, 3 days. Celebration of first trail, Zane's Trace, carved across Ohio frontier; sternwheeler rides; Indian village; A/C, P. *Zanesville Area C of C, 47 N. 4th St., Zanesville 43701. 614 452-7571*

OKLAHOMA

Andarko AMERICAN INDIAN EXPOSITION, mid-Aug., 1 wk. One of the largest Indian gatherings in US includes ceremonial Ds, national championship war D contest, tribal festivities, pageants, Indian games, contests; P, A/C. *Andarko C of C, PO Box 366, Andarko 73005. 405 247-3424*

Barnsdall BIGHEART DAY, late May, 1 day. Town used to be called Bigheart; greased-pig, terrapin races; pony-pulling contest; old fiddlers competition; M, R. *Barnsdall C of C, Barnsdall 74002. 918 847-2505*

Beaver CIMARRON TERRITORY CELEBRATION, mid-Apr., 4 days. World champion cow-chip-throwing contest; a special division is reserved for politicians, known to be highly practiced in this art; shoot-out; greased-pig catch; haystack scramble; beard, mustache judging; R. *Beaver C of C, Box 878, Beaver 73932.*

Boise City SANTA FE TRAIL DAZE, early June, 4 days. Pioneer festival; world posthole digging championship; R. *Boise City C of C, Box 1027, Boise City 73933. 405 544-2424*

Clinton HUB CITY POW WOW, mid-June, 4 days. Intertribal exposition features D ceremonies, A/C. *Clinton C of C, PO Box 716, Clinton 73601. 405 323-2222*

Guthrie 89ERS' DAY PARADE AND RODEO, Apr., 3 days. Commemorates opening of the land for settlement in 1889; pioneer costumes; male residents required to grow a beard or go to jail; P, R. *Guthrie C of C, PO Box 995, Guthrie 73044. 405 282-1947*

Idabel KIAMICHI OWA CHITO FESTIVAL OF THE FOREST, late June, 3 days. Choctaw Indian heritage celebration; chain saw, tree-topping, ax-throwing contests. *Idabel C of C, 13 N. Central, Idabel 74745. 405 286-3305*

Oklahoma City NAT'L FINALS RODEO, early Dec., 9 days. "Olympics of rodeo world"; top 15 cowpersons compete in bull, saddle bronc & bareback bronc riding, steer wrestling, team & calf roping, barrel racing to select world's top cowboy. *Oklahoma City C of C, 1 Santa Fe Plaza, Oklahoma City 73102. 405 232-6381*

Pauls Valley WORLD CHAMPIONSHIP WATERMELON SEED SPITTIN' CONTEST, late June, 1 day. Contestants try to break world record of over 50 feet. *Pauls Valley C of C, Drawer 638, Pauls Valley 73075. 405 238-6491*

Pawnee STEAM ENGINE SHOW, late July, 3 days. Old-fashioned vehicles, machinery demonstrations; threshing, plowing, gristmilling contests. *C of C, Box 27, Pawnee 74058. 918 762-2108*

Stroud SAC & FOX POW WOW, early July, 3 days. Calf scramble; Sac & Fox Oklahoma Day; powwow; buckskin dress, cloth dress, D competitions; R, P. *Stroud C of C, 310½ N. 4th Ave., Stroud 74079. 918 968-3321*

Stroud PIONEER DAY CELEBRATION, early Nov., 1 day. Celebrates statehood of Oklahoma; prizes given for best pioneer costumes, oldest person attending; gunfight; D, M. *Stroud C of C, 310½ 4th Ave., Stroud 74079. 918 968-3321*

Tahlequah CHEROKEE NAT'L HOLIDAY, early Sept., 3 days. Celebration of Cherokee heritage with powwow, contests, games, lore; A/C. *Cherokee Nation of Oklahoma, Box 119, Tahlequah 74464. 918 456-8884*

Tulsa ANNUAL TULSA POW WOW, mid-July, 4 days. Indians gather for ceremonial war D; dress contests, pageantry. *Tulsa C of C, 616 S. Boston, Tulsa 74119. 918 585-1201*

OREGON

Albany WORLD CHAMPIONSHIP TIMBER CARNIVAL, early July, wknd. International competition among loggers for trophies in tree climbing and topping, standing block chop, sawing, ax throwing, birling (logrolling); jousting; P, F. *World Championship Timber Carnival, PO Box 582, Albany 97321. 503 928-2391*

Brooks ANTIQUE POWERLAND FARM FAIR, late July–early Aug., 2 wknds. Gas tractors; steam traction engines; threshing machines; grain binders; bailing straw; stone grinding wheat into flour; sawing logs into lumber; blacksmith show; teeter-totter; 1920's farm; P. *Antique Powerland, 3995 Brooklake Road N.E., Salem 97305. 503 393-2424*

Dufur THRESHING BEE & WORKING DRAFT HORSES, Aug., 2nd wknd. Wheat harvesting 50 years ago using pioneer equipment (steam engine, separator); draft horses; spinning, soap-making, quilting, blacksmithing, plowing, binding demonstrations; sack-sewing contest; horseshoe pitching. *Dufur Historical & Cultural Society, Dufur 97058. 503 467-2349*

Forest Grove ALL-NORTHWEST BARBERSHOP BALLAD CONTEST & GAY 90s FESTIVAL, early Mar., 3 days. Pacific Northwest barbershop quartet competitions; Gay Nineties revue; fiddlers contest; P. *Forest Grove C of C, Forest Grove 97116.*

Joseph CHIEF JOSEPH DAYS, late July, 3 days. Major R honors famous Indian chief Joseph; Indian D pageant; P. *Joseph C of C, Joseph 97846.*

Joseph ALPENFEST, late Sept., 3 days. Bavarian-style folk festival; ethnic dancers, yodelers; sailboat races; fiddlers, edelweiss bands. *Wallowa Lake Tourist Committee, Route 1, Joseph 97846.*

Junction City SCANDINAVIAN FESTIVAL, Aug., 4 days. Swedish, Norwegian, Finnish, Danish ancestry of early settlers honored with ethnic D, M, food, games; Viking ship on wheels patrols streets; costumes. *Scandinavian Festival Assn., Box 5, Junction City 97448.*

Mt. Angel OKTOBERFEST, mid-Sept., 4 days. Bavarian harvest festival; biergarten; yodeling; soccer, softball tournaments; parachute drop; bicycle races; P, D, A/C. *Oktoberfest Assn., Mt. Angel 97362.*

Pendleton PENDLETON ROUND-UP, mid-Sept., 4 days. Leading competitors from throughout the world compete in R; Indian powwow; pony express; Mormon carts; gunfights; horseshoeing; saddlemaking; Indian BC; D, P. *Round-Up Assn., PO Box 609, Pendleton 97801. 503 276-2553*

Prineville CENTRAL OREGON TIMBER CARNIVAL, May, 3 days, at Crooked River Roundup Grounds. Logging show; truck-driving contest. *Crook County C of C, PO Box 546, Prineville 97754.*

Rogue River NAT'L ROOSTER CROWING CONTEST, June, last Sat. Which rooster can crow the most in 30 minutes? *Grants Pass C of C, Grants Pass 97526.*

Tygh Valley PACIFIC NORTHWEST CHAMPIONSHIP ALL-INDIAN RODEO, May, 3rd wknd. Only Indian cowboys featured in R; buckaroo breakfast; D. *Tywama Saddle Club, PO Box 73, Tygh Valley 97063.*

PENNSYLVANIA

Ambridge KUNSTFEST, June, wknds, at Old Economy Village. 19th-century Cs demonstrations of candlemaking, spinning, shoemaking, weaving, sewing, donut baking. *Old Economy Village, 14th & Church Sts., Ambridge 15003.*

Amity Hall AGRICULTURAL AMERICANA FOLK FESTIVAL, late July, 1 wk. Kettle cooking; horse-plowing contest; sheepdog demonstration; mule race; steam show; surrey, hay rides; sawmilling; antique farm machinery. *Agricultural Americana Folk Festival, RFD #2, Port Royal 17082. 215 683-3607*

Arendtsville APPLE HARVEST FESTIVAL, Oct., first 2 wknds. Apple-pie-eating contests; apple bobbing; pressed cider; steam engine rides, apple pancake patio. *Gettysburg Travel Council, Carlisle St., Gettysburg 17325. 717 334-6274*

Barnesville BAVARIAN SUMMER FESTIVAL, July, 1st 2 wks. Oktoberfest; German & Austrian food, beer, M; Schuhplattlers; alpine horn blowers; horse-drawn beer wagons; blacksmithing; wood whittling; candlemaking; horse-pulling, soccer contests; A/C, M. *Bavarian Festival Soc., Inc., Box 90, Kempton 19529. 215 726-6000*

Barnesville INTERNAT'L WINE & CHEESE FESTIVAL, late July, 3 days. Swiss yodelers; wine hobby contests; winemaking demonstrations; M. *Internat'l Wine & Cheese Festival, Barnesville 18214. 215 756-6000*

Barnesville GRAND IRISH JUBILEE, early Sept., 3 days, at Lakewood Park. Irish jigs, reels, flings, hornpipers; Caeli Dancers; fiddlers. *Grand Irish Jubilee, 2 N. Linden St., Mahanoy City 17948. 717 773-2741*

Bedford FALL FOLIAGE FESTIVAL, mid-Oct., 2 wknds. Fiddle contests; apple butter making; Shawnee Rangers muzzleloading shoot; antique autos; wagon train. *Fall Foliage Festival Committee, Bedford 15522.*

Centre Hall STEAM ENGINE DAYS, early Sept., 3 days. Shingle sawing; threshing; baling; apple butter, cider making; steam gas engines, shingle mill, threshing machines, antique fire engines, cornmeal-grinder demonstrations; Conestoga rides. *Nittany Antique Assn. of Central PA., Centre Hall 16828. 814 364-1789*

Coudersport PALMA CRAFT FESTIVAL & BIRLING CONTEST, early July, 2 days. Birling contest; logrolling contest (last one dry and standing wins); A/C. *Potter County Recreation, Inc., PO Box 245, Coudersport 16915. 814 274-9801*

Coudersport BARKPEELERS CONVENTION, early July, 3 days. Birling, tobacco-spitting, Jack & Jill crosscut saw contests; lumbering era (1890–1910) Cs demonstrations. *Potter County Recreation, Inc., PO Box 245, Coudersport 16915. 814 274-9801*

Coudersport WOODMEN'S CARNIVAL, early Aug., 2 days. Lumberjacks compete in contests using old lumbering techniques: logrolling, tree felling, log chopping, crosscut sawing, horse pulling. *Potter County Recreation, Inc., PO Box 245, Coudersport 16915. 814 274-9801*

Cross Fork RATTLESNAKE HUNT, late June, 2 days. People hunt rattlesnakes for prizes for largest, heaviest, greatest number caught alive; picking up snakes in bare hands contests. *Potter County Recreation, Inc., PO Box 245, Coudersport 16915. 814 274-9801*

Devon DELCO SCOTTISH GAMES, mid-June, 1 day. Contests include throwing the weight, tossing the caber, shotput, throwing the hammer; pipe bands, bagpiping, drumming, Highland D contests. *Delco Scottish Games Assn., Inc., 181 Foxcatcher Lane, Media 19063. 215 566-2898*

Dillingersville SCHOOL DAYS, late June, 3 days, at Dillingersville One-Room School House.

Old-fashioned spelling bee; typical school day; schoolmaster in colonial garb; Cs. *Dillingersville One-Room School House, Lower Milford Township, Route 1 off Route 29, Zionsville 18092.*

East Smithfield OLD TIMERS DAYS, mid-Aug., 3 days. Oxen, horse wagon rides; horseshoe contest; antique calliope on wagon; shingle mill, steam powered sawmill; threshing; drag saw; stone crusher. *Bradford County Old Timers, Inc., Route 2, Box 126, Columbia Crossroads 16914.*

Fallsington COLONIAL FAIR, Oct., 2nd Sat. 18th-century-cooking, silversmithing, breadbaking demonstrations; carriage, sleigh exhibits; A/C. *Historic Fallsington, Inc., 4 Yardley Ave., Fallsington 19054.*

Fulton County FULTON FALL FOLK FESTIVAL, mid-Oct., 3 days. Apple butter boil; antique farm equipment display; buggy, horse rides; oldtimers P; D, M, A/C. *Fulton County TPA, Box 141, McConnellsburg 17233.*

Hershey PENNSYLVANIA DUTCH DAYS, mid-July, 6 days. Quilting; potterymaking; coopering; flax breaking; spinning; weaving; woodcarving; glass blowing; broommaking; candle dipping; village blacksmithing; threshing; fractur art; leathercraft. *Hershey Estates, Hershey 17033. 717 534-3172*

Kempton PENNSYLVANIA DUTCH FARM FESTIVAL, early Sept., 2 days. Blacksmith shop; soapmaking; broommaking; cider, wine presses; barnyard demonstrations. *Pennsylvania Dutch Farm Festival, Kempton 19529. 215 683-7130*

Kittanning FORT ARMSTRONG FOLK FESTIVAL, early Aug., 4 days. Coppersmithing; glass blowing; soapmaking; colonial homemaking demonstrations. *W. E. Martin, 325 Market St., Kittanning 16201. 412 548-4111*

Kreamer FESTIVAL, late July, 1 wk. Pioneer days; re-creation of Stock Massacre of 1781; pony-pulling contests; musket shoot; tomahawk, knife throws; P. *PA State C of C, 222 N. 3rd St., Harrisburg 17101. 717 238-0441*

Kutztown KUTZTOWN FOLK FESTIVAL, early July, 1 wk. Pennsylvania Dutch culture perpetuated through folkways, Amish pageantry; barn raising; "Plain Dutch" wedding; demonstrations of hex artists; pewtermaking; glass blowing; flax spinning; woodcarving; sand molding; basketmaking. *PA Folklife Society, Kutztown 19530. 215 683-8707*

Ligonier LIGONIER HIGHLAND GAMES, mid-Sept., 1 day. Call of caber; tug-of-war; sheep dog demonstrations of controlling Highland sheep; pipe bands; Scottish costumes; P. *Ligonier Highland Games, 1208 24th Ave., Altoona 16601. 814 942-6968*

McClure MCCLURE BEAN SOUP FESTIVAL, mid-Sept., 5 days. Begun as reunion in 1890's of Civil War veterans; bean soup prepared like it was during the war and served to vets; "largest bean festival in the world." *McClure Bean Soup Festival, McClure 17841. 717 658-8425*

McConnellsburg FULTON FALL FOLK FESTIVAL, Oct., 3rd wknd. Apple butter boiling; ox roast; 18th-century water-powered gristmill; house tour; vintage farm equipment; antique cars; colonial printing demonstrations of papermaking, bookbinding; muzzleloader meet; hymn sing; P. *Fulton County Tourist Promotion Agency, PO Box 141, McConnellsburg 17233.*

Mifflin County MIFFLIN COUNTY FALL FESTIVAL, Sept.–Oct., 5 days. Re-creation of the 1755 attack and burning of Fort Granville; muledrawn packet boat rides; apple butter making. *Mifflin County Festival Assn., PO Box 248, Burnham 17009.*

Philadelphia CHINESE NEW YEAR, Feb., 1 day, in Chinatown. Chinese events; fire dragons; P. *Phila. Convention Visitors Bureau, 1525 John F. Kennedy Blvd., Phila. 19102. 215 864-1976*

Philadelphia ELFRETH'S ALLEY DAY, early June, 1 day. Nation's oldest street in residential use is opened; costumes. *Elfreth's Alley Assn., 126 Elfreth Alley, Phila. 19106.*

Pittsburgh PITTSBURGH FOLK FESTIVAL, late May, 3 days. Folk D, M by performers from about 20 countries; ethnic foods; cooking, embroidery, jewelry, musical-instrument-making demonstrations. *Pittsburgh Folk Festival, 610 5th Ave., Pittsburgh 15219. 412 471-3920*

Port Royal OLD HOME DAYS, July–Aug., 3 days. Pageant depicts massacre of settlers by Tuscarora Indians; rolling-pin-throwing, pie-eating contests; community tug-of-war; woodcarving; quilting; potterymaking; P, F. *Port Royal Old Home Days, RFD #2, Port Royal 17082.*

Schaefferstown FOLKLIFE FESTIVAL, late July, 2 days. 18th-century German customs, lore; polka band; wagon rides; old-machinery exhibits, demonstrations; C, M. *Lebanon Valley Tourist & Visitors Bureau, PO Box 626, Lebanon 17042. 717 272-8555*

Schaefferstown HORSEPLOWING & COOKING CONTEST, mid-Sept., 1 day. Horseplowing, log-pulling contests; log-jumping demonstration; horseshoeing; antique plows; fireplace cooking; baking in 200-year-old oven; butter churning; cheesemaking; open-kettle cooking. *Lebanon Valley Tourist & Visitors Bureau, PO Box 626, Lebanon 17042. 717 272-8555*

Schaefferstown ANNUAL HARVEST FAIR, late Sept., 2 days. Apple butter making; schnitzing; cidermaking; threshing; cornmeal grinding; braided-rug, eggshell-painting, leaded-glass demonstrations; colonial herb garden; polka band; M, A/C. *Historic Schaefferstown, Inc., Box 307, Schaefferstown 17088. 717 949-3795*

Soudersburg FALL HARVEST CRAFT DAYS, late Oct., 3 days. High-wheel bike races; apple butter, cider, broom making; wood turning; spinning; cornhusking bee. *Mill Bridge Craft Village, Soudersburg 17577. 717 687-6521*

Springs DUTCH MOUNTAIN FOLK FESTIVAL, early Oct., 2 days. Demonstrations of hollowing out wooden troughs with an adze, shaving shingles, threshing grain with hand flails, operating a two-horse tread power, cleaning grain with windmill; boring of wooden water pipes; blacksmithing; horseshoeing; spinning; weaving; rugmaking; candlemaking; wool processing. *Springs Folk Festival, Springs 15562.*

Stahlstown FLAX SCUTCHING FESTIVAL, mid-Sept., 1 day. Demonstration of how flax is processed and made into early American homespun clothes; mock Indian raid; buckwheat cakes; D, M. *Flax Scutching Festival, Box 77, Stahlstown 15687.*

Waterford HERITAGE DAYS, early July, 3 days. Nonmotorized P; bluegrass jamboree; chair caning; weaving, spinning; blacksmithing; hand rifling; musket barreling; threshing; unicycles; home cooking; costumes. *Mrs. V. Bullman, 151 W. 1st St., Waterford 16441. 814 796-6279*

Waynesburg CRESAP'S RIFLE COMPANY, mid-May, 1 day. Tom.ahawk throw; shingle shoot; hornsmithing, shinglemaking, live-firing, feminine colonial skills demonstrations. *Greene County Historical Soc., RFD #2, Waynesburg 15370.*

Whitehall OX PULL, late Sept., 3 days Internat'l ox pull; ox roast; P. *Whitehall C of C, 2126 S. 1st Ave., Whitehall 18052. 215 264-1384*

Whitneyville TIOGA COUNTY EARLY DAYS, early July, 5 days. Sawmill, drag saw, shinglemaking, stone-crushing, horse sweep, treadmill, blacksmithing, flour and cornmeal demonstrations; broommaking; candle dipping; wool dyeing; spinning; quilting; maple syrup making. *Mrs. N. A. Costley, RFD #5, Box 205, Wellsboro 16901.*

RHODE ISLAND

Galilee BLESSING OF THE FLEET, early Aug., 2 days. 10-mile road race; German beer fest; local clergy bless Galilee boats. *C of C, Narragansett 02882.*

Lime Rock ANNUAL AMERICAN INDIAN POW wow, mid-June, 2 days. Indian ceremonial D, stories; C, M. *Blackstone Valley Historical Society, 142 10th St., Providence 02906. 401 421-7262*

Newport BLESSING OF THE FLEET FESTIVAL, early July, 1 day. Boats parade by as clergy bless them. *Newport C of C, 10 America's Cup Ave., Newport 02840. 401 847-1600*

Oakland FIELD DAY & FIREMEN'S MUSTER, early Sept., 1 day. Antique fire engine parade; water distance contest. *Lt. R. Lapierre, 1 Pond St., Oakland 02858. 401 568-3568*

Pawtucket ANNUAL MID-EAST FESTIVAL, early Aug., at Narragansett Park. Arabian M, D. *M. Kandos, 13 J Roosevelt Ave., Pawtucket 02860. 401 728-0500*

Providence HOLY ROSARY SUMMER FESTIVAL, Sept., 2 wknds. Portuguese festival, foods; religious P. *Holy Rosary Church, 19 Traverse St., Providence 02903. 401 421-5621*

Usquepaugh USQUEPAUGH JOHNNY CAKE FESTIVAL, late Oct., 3 days. Johnny cake cooking, Indian D, candlemaking, C demonstrations; gristmill tours; air show; P, M. *Usquepaugh Johnny Cake Festival, PO Box 221, West Kingston 02892. 401 783-4054*

SOUTH CAROLINA

Branchville BRANCHVILLE RAYLRODE DAZE FESTIVAL, Sept., last wknd. Commemorates world's oldest railroad junction; steam locomotive, horse, buggy rides; hobo jungle, beechnut-spitting contest; shoot-out; P, D. *Raylrode Daze, PO Box 143, Branchville 29432.*

Camden ANNUAL REVOLUTIONARY FIELD DAYS, early Nov., 2 days. Living history demonstration of 18th-century military camp life including marksmanship, weaponry, domestic life. *Historic Camden, Box 710, Camden 29020. 803 432-9841*

Charleston GREEK SPRING FESTIVAL, early May, 1 day. Greek folk D; worship; bouzouki music; stuffed grape leaves; shishkebob. *A. Powell, Middleton Place, Route 4, Charleston 29407. 803 556-6020*

Charleston SCOTTISH GAMES & HIGHLAND GATHERING, mid-Sept., 1 day. Highland games contests for US and Canadians; Scottish folklore, food; kilted bagpipers; M. *A. Powell, Middleton Place, Route 4, Charleston 29407. 803 556-6020*

Charleston ANNUAL LANCING TOURNAMENT, Oct., 1 day, at Middleton Place. Lancing contest; P of Ladies Faire; musical chairs on horseback; 18th-century fife & drum corps. *A. Powell, Middleton Place, Route 4, Charleston 29407. 803 556-6020*

Charleston PLANTATION DAYS, Nov., 1st 3 Suns., at Middleton Place. Plantation harvest; sugarcane milling; corn shucking, syrup, soap,

candle, cow making; spinning; weaving; blacksmithing; mule-drawn wagon ride. *A. Powell, Middleton Place, Route 4, Charleston 29407. 803 556-6020*

Harleyville SEE SAW DAZE, late Apr., 3 days. Celebrates sawmill industry of the 1870's; cancan girls; P, BC. *See Saw Daze Festival, PO Box 35, Harleyville 29448. 803 462-7676*

Jamestown HELL HOLE SWAMP FESTIVAL, early May, 3 days. Moonshinemaking; tall tales; bicycle race; BC, P, D. *Santee-Cooper Counties Promotion Commission, PO Box 12, Santee 29142. 803 854-2131*

Mountain Rest MOUNTAIN REST HILLBILLY DAY, July 4. Greased-pig chases; hootenanny; clogging; square dancing. *R. B. Lemons, Route 1, Mountain Rest 29664. 803 638-2454*

Myrtle Beach CANADIAN-AMERICAN FOLK FESTIVAL, mid-Mar., 10 days. Festival honors Canadian visitors; historic plantations tours; folk M contest; fishing, golf tournaments; sand castle construction; D. *Greater Myrtle Beach C of C, PO Box 2115, Myrtle Beach 29577. 803 448-5135*

Ridgeland, Hardeeville SERGEANT JASPER FESTIVAL, early Oct., 2 days. Gopher Hill Day (Ridgeland): aerobatic demonstrations; gopher race; tennis tournament; costume contest; BC, M, D. Catfish Day (Hardeeville): raft, boat, bicycle races; cake bake contest; tug-of-war. *Jasper County C of C, PO Box 1267, Ridgeland 29936. 803 726-8126.*

St. Mathews PURPLE MARTIN FESTIVAL, late Apr., 3 days. Purple martin migration marathon race; tractor pull; tobacco-spitting, beard, cake-decorating contests. *Purple Martin Festival, PO Box 444, St. Mathews 29135. 803 875-3791*

Salley CHITLIN STRUT, late Nov., 1 day. 3 tons of chitlins cooked for visitors; M, D. *Salley Chitlin Strut, Salley 29137. 803 258 3309*

Springfield THE GOVERNOR'S ANNUAL FROG JUMPING CONTEST, mid-Apr., 1 day. Frog-jumping, horseshoe contests; D, M, P. *Santee-Cooper Counties Promotion Commission, PO Box 12, Santee 29142. 803 854-2131*

SOUTH DAKOTA

Belle Fourche BLACK HILLS ROUNDUP, early July, 2 days. Saddle bucking; bareback, brahma bull riding; steer wrestling; calf roping; horse-mounted quadrille; cowgirl races; bullfighting clowns; P, F. *Black Hills Roundup, Box 39, Belle Fourche 57717.*

Corsica KLOMPEN DANCE & DUTCH SMORGASBORD, May 1, 1 day. Dutch heritage celebrated with home-cooked meals served in smorgasbord style; Klompen (wooden shoe) D; hot air balloon. *Mrs. M. Mulder, Box 73, Corsica 57328.*

Custer GOLD DISCOVERY DAYS, July, last wknd. Indian raids; Custer's last stand; gold rush reenactment; R, D, P. *C of C, Custer 57730.*

Deadwood DAYS OF '76, early Aug., 3 days. Gold rush days celebrated with reenactment of trial of Jack McCall; street shooting; costumes; R, P. *Deadwood C of C, Deadwood 57732. 605 578-1876*

DeSmet OLD SETTLERS DAYS, mid-June, 2 days. Tours through Laura Ingalls Wilder memorial (DeSmet is where she based several of her famous children's books); tractor-pulling contests. *Div. of Tourism Development, State Office Bldg. 2, Pierre 57501.*

Freeman SCHMECKFEST, Mar.–Apr., 3 days. Culinary arts of Mennonites who settled in

Freeman around 1880 featured; sausage, noodlemaking; basket-weaving, rug-braiding, quilting, needlework demonstrations. *Schmeckfest, Freeman 57029.*

Leola RHUBARB FESTIVAL, early June. Old-fashioned celebration in Leola, "Rhubarb Patch of the World"; cooking contest; horseshoe tournament; P, D. *V. Kohlhoff, Leola 57456.*

Mitchell CORN PALACE FESTIVAL, mid-Sept., 1 wk. Corn harvest celebration; 3,000 bushels of corn decorate palace; carnival; P. *Mitchell C of C, Mitchell 57301.*

Pierre OAHE DAYS, mid-Aug., 3 days. North American finals for buffalo-chip-flipping contest; fishing contest; stock car races, P, R. *Div. of Tourism Development, State Office Bldg. 2, Pierre 57501.*

Madison PRAIRIE VILLAGE STEAM THRESHING JAMBOREE, late Aug., 2 days, at Prairie Village. Over 100 steam and gas machines parade; old schoolhouse in session; steam-powered carousel. *Prairie Village, Madison 57042.*

TENNESSEE

Adams THRESHERMAN'S SHOW, mid-July, 3 days. Demonstrations of oldtime wheat threshing; antique steam engines, cars; sawmill; moonshine still; buttermaking; quilting; corn shelling; gristmill; farm wagon, buggy, surrey rides; fiddle contest; gospel M. *Threshermen's Show, PO Box 115, Adams 37010. 615 696-2383*

Clarksville STATE OF TENNESSEE OLD-TIME FIDDLERS CHAMPIONSHIPS, Apr., 1st wknd. Junior, senior fiddlers contests; oldtime bluegrass banjo, string, guitar, mandolin, harmonica players contests; no-holds-barred flatfoot D contests; fiddle-off for state title. *Austin Peay State U., Clarksville 37040. 615 648-7011*

Cosby RAMP FESTIVAL, late Apr. Celebrates the ramp, a sweet-tasting plant with foul odor; BC. *The Newport Plain Talk, Newport 37821.*

Gatlinburg OLD TIMERS DAY, June, Aug., 1 day each month, at Cades Cove in Great Smoky Mountain Nat'l Park. Ongoing pioneer village with weaving, vegetable-dyeing, gardening demonstrations; banjo pickers; guitar, mandolin players; clog D; folk singing. *Great Smoky Mountain Nat'l Park, Gatlinburg 37738. 615 436-5615*

Manchester OLD TIMERS DAY, mid-Oct., 1 day. The past celebrated; tobacco-spitting, whittling, arm-wrestling, husband-calling contests; P. *C of C, 212 N. Spring St., Manchester 37355.*

Paris WORLD'S BIGGEST FISH FRY, Apr., last wk. Fresh Kentucky Lake catfish served; hootenanny; fishing, baseball, golf tournaments; R, D, P. *Greater Paris-Henry County C of C, PO Box 82, Paris 38242. 901 642-3431*

Smithville OLD TIME FIDDLERS JAMBOREE, early July, 2 days. Gospel, country, folk, fiddling, harmonica contests; D, A/C. *Smithville C of C, Smithville 37166. 615 597-4163*

Sparta KORN PONE DAY, Aug., 1st Sat. Corn-pone-baking contest; hillbilly costumes; P. *C of C, Sparta 38583.*

TEXAS

Aransas Pass ANNUAL SHRIMPOREE, May. Tribute to shrimp industry; shrimp-eating, fishing contests; blessing of fleet; P, A. *Mrs. G. Durbin, 452 Cleveland, Aransas Pass 78336.*

Corpus Christi BUCCANEER DAYS, Apr.–May, 2 wks. Commemorates city's founding and early history of pirates; pirate invasion; mayor walks the plank; carnival; A. *Buccaneer Commission, Box 1199, Corpus Christi 78403. 512 882-3242*

Ennis NAT'L POLKA FESTIVAL, May, 1st wknd. Czech food, costume, folk D, gymnastics; P. *Ennis C of C, PO Box 159, Ennis 75119.*

Fredericksburg GILLESPIE COUNTY FAIR, late Aug., 3 days. "Oldest county fair in Texas"; livestock exhibits; horse races. *C of C, Fredericksburg 78624. 512 997-3444*

Freeport ANNUAL BLESSING OF THE FLEET, late Apr., 2 days. Seafood-cooking, shrimp boat contests; BC, P. *Freeport Shrimp Assn., Freeport 77541.*

Galveston SHRIMP FESTIVAL, late Apr., 2 wks. Blessing of shrimp fleet; sand castle, sculpture contests; P. *C of C, 315 Tremont St., Galveston 77550.*

Gilmer YAMBOREE, Oct. Sweet potatoes cooked in every form; fiddlers contest; livestock show; P, BC. *Upshur County C of C, Box 854, Gilmer 76544.*

Huntsville TEXAS PRISON RODEO, Oct., every Sun. Bull riding, bareback bronco, saddle bronc for men; greased-pig sacking, wild-calf tussle for women; wild horse race; mad scramble; calf scramble; A/C; M. *Texas Prison Rodeo, PO Box 99, Huntsville 77340. 713 295-5714*

Livingston ALL INDIAN POW WOW, May–June. 80 tribes gather; Indian D contests. *W. Broemer, Route 3, Box 170, Livingston 77351.*

Port Arthur TEXAS-LOUISIANA CAJUN FESTIVAL, May. Ethnic celebration; accordion, Monsieur and Madam Cajun, cooking contests; crawfish races. *C of C, Box 460, Port Arthur 77640.*

San Antonio FIESTA SAN ANTONIO, mid-Apr., 10 days. Dedicated to memory of Texas heroes; lacrosse tournaments; mariachi festival; toepperwein shoot; rifle championships; German, Israeli festivals; Mexican R; P, D. *Fiesta San Antonio Commission, Inc., 306 N. Presa, San Antonio 78205. 512 227-5191*

San Antonio TEXAS FOLKLIFE FESTIVAL, late Sept., 3 days. 28 ethnic groups of Texas celebrate their origins; Scottish bagpipers; Chinese script writing; Dutch Sweepers open festival; Czech, Italian foods; pioneer life activities are corn shucking, candy pulling, logrolling, house raising, quilting bees, railsplitting, spike driving; saddle, leathercraft, blacksmithing, making vegetable dyes, soap, rope demonstrations; knife forging; native costumes. *TX Folklife Festival, PO Box 1226, San Antonio 78294. 512 226-7651*

Stamford TEXAS COWBOY REUNION, July. Festival dedicated to Old West; "greatest amateur rodeo in the world"; food served from authentic chuck wagons. *C of C, Box 1206, Stamford 79533.*

UTAH

Fort Duchesne NORTHERN UTE POW WOW, July, 3 days. Annual gathering of Ute tribal members; D contests. *Ute Indian Tribe, Fort Duchesne 84026.*

Fort Duchesne SUN DANCE, Sept., 2 days. Ute Indian religious ceremonial D, continuous night and day; no cameras, tape recorders allowed; no gum chewing, eating, drinking; spectators may sit on ground or wooden chairs only. *Ute Indian Tribe, Fort Duchesne 84026.*

Logan FESTIVAL OF THE AMERICAN WEST, July–Aug., 9 days, at Utah State U. Historical pageant; frontier street; Old West cookout; Indian village, powwow; P, A. *Festival of the American West, Old Main Room 214 D, Utah State U., Logan 84322. 801 752-4100*

Ogden PIONEER DAYS, late July, 1 wk. Celebration of July 24, 1847, the date that Brigham Young and Mormon pioneers entered Salt Lake Valley; P. *Golden Spike Empire Information Office, Ogden 84401.*

Promontory ANNUAL GOLDEN SPIKE CEREMONY, early May, 1 day. Commemoration of the days when the tracks of the Union Pacific RR were joined with tracks of Central Pacific to give US its first continental railroad; reenactment of driving of "Golden Spike." *Golden Spike Nat'l Historical Site, PO Box 394, Brigham City 84302.*

Salt Lake City DAYS OF '47 CELEBRATION, July, month. Celebration of July 24, 1847, the date that Brigham Young and Mormon pioneers entered Salt Lake Valley; bell-ringing ceremony; horse P; footrace, BC, M, R, P. *Days of '47, Inc., 300 N. Main St., Salt Lake City 84103. 801 533-5759*

Salt Lake City JAPANESE FESTIVAL, July, 1 day. Celebration of freedom from evil spirits; Obon D; Japanese foods; performers wear kimonos; M. *Salt Lake Buddhist Temple, 211 W. 1st South St., Salt Lake City 84111.*

Salt Lake City ANNUAL GREEK FESTIVAL, mid-Sept., 3 days, at Greek Hellenic Memorial Building. Authentic Greek foods, pastries, M. *Greek Festival, 308 Boston Bldg., Salt Lake City 84111.*

Snowbird OKTOBERFEST, Sept.–Oct., wknds. Bavarian foods, costumes, D, M; alpine horn blowing; yodeling by Art Brogli, professional yodeler, from atop mountain 11,000 feet high. *Snowbird Corp., Snowbird 84070. 801 521-6040*

VERMONT

Barre NORTHEAST REGIONAL FIDDLE CONTEST, early Oct., 2 days. Oldtime, French-Canadian fiddling contests. *Central VT C of C, PO Box 796 Berlin, Montpelier 05602.*

Brookfield ICE HARVEST FESTIVAL & ICE CUTTING CONTEST, Jan., last Sat. Revives, celebrates ancient custom of cutting ice from ponds, to store and use in summer. *Green Trails Resort, Brookfield 05036. 802 276-2012*

Danville CONVENTION OF AMERICAN SOCIETY OF DOWSERS, mid-Sept., 4 days. Demonstrations of ancient art of dowsing or finding water, other objects, or metals with forked stick, metal rod. *Mrs. R. Field, Danville 05828. 802 684-3383*

Morrisville LAMOILLE COUNTY FIELD DAYS, July, last wknd. Pony-pulling contest; cattle show; tractors; livestock. *Silver Ridge Pavillion, Lamoille County Development Council, PO Box 577, Morrisville 05661.*

Newbury CRACKER BARREL FIDDLERS CONTEST & BAZAAR, late July, 3 days. Fiddlers contest; A/C. *VT Development Agency, 61 Elm St., Montpelier 05602. 802 828-3236*

St. Albans VERMONT MAPLE FESTIVAL, early Apr., 3 days. Celebrates maple sugar and maple syrup industry; sugaring, chopping contests; oldtime fiddling; Vermont Day; A/C, M, D, P. *St. Albans C of C, Main St., St. Albans 05478. 802 524-5800*

Walden & other towns VERMONT'S NORTHEAST KINGDOM FALL FOLIAGE FESTIVAL, Sept.–Oct., 6 days. Each day a different town (Walden, Cabot, Plainfield, Peacham, Barnet, Groton) celebrates the fall foliage with hymn sing, D, A/C, regional foods; the last town to celebrate is Groton, which hosts a lumberjack D. *Fall Festival Committee, Box 38, W. Danville 05873.*

VIRGINIA

Alexandria GEORGE WASHINGTON BIRTHDAY PARADE, mid-Feb., 1 day. Fife & drums; Scottish bagpipers; costumed militia; George & Martha Washington review troops. *Alexandria Tourist Council, 221 King St., Alexandria 22314. 703 549-0205*

Alexandria VIRGINIA SCOTTISH GAMES & GATHERING OF THE CLANS, mid-July, 1 day. Bagpipes, Highland D, drumming, Scottish games contests; border collies display sheepherding; Scottish food. *Alexandria 22314. 703 549-0205*

Appomattox HISTORIC APPOMATTOX RAILROAD FESTIVAL, Oct., 3rd wknd. Commemorates 1865 Battle of Appomattox Station, the last use of rail by Army of Northern VA; railroadiana; M, A/C. *Appomattox Jr. Woman's Club & Town of Appomattox, PO Box 423, Appomattox 24522. 804 352-7304*

Bealeton FLYING CIRCUS AERODROME, Oct., 2 days. World War I dogfights reenacted; oldtime barnstormers; wing walking; parachuting; biplane formations; antique aircraft. *Flying Circus Aerodrome, Inc., Bealeton 22712. 703 439-8661*

Fredericksburg FREDERICKSBURG DOG MART, early Oct., 1 day. The tradition of trading dogs for Indian furs and goods began in 1698; Indian D; oldtime fiddlers, folk singers; turkey-calling, hog-calling, harmonica-playing, foxhorn-blowing contests; dog auction. *C of C, 706 Caroline St., Fredericksburg 22401. 703 373-9391*

Galax OLD FIDDLERS' CONVENTION, Aug., 2nd wknd, at Fells Park. Several hundred fiddlers gather to play, sing, D, compete for prizes; convention held to help preserve and perpetuate old mountain and folk M; flatfooting, clogging contests. *Old Fiddlers' Convention, 328 A Kenbrook Dr., Galax 24333. 703 236-6355*

Harrisonburg VIRGINIA POULTRY FESTIVAL, mid-May, 4 days. VA poultry convention; Friends of Feathers Get Together; muzzleloaders rifle shoot; golf, tennis, bowling tournaments; P, D. *VA Poultry Federation, PO Box 1036, Harrisonburg 22801. 703 433-2451*

Millboro Springs ANNUAL BIG BEND JOUSTING TOURNAMENT, July, 1 day. Oldest equestrian sport practiced by English settlers in North America; 150-yard course. *Mrs. W. A. Edwards, Millboro Springs 24460.*

Mt. Solon ANNUAL NATURAL CHIMNEYS JOUSTING TOURNAMENT, Aug., 3rd Sat. Oldest continuously held sporting event in US. *Natural Chimneys Regional Park, Mt. Solon 22843. 703 350-2510*

Yorktown JAMESTOWN DAY, May 15. Celebrates founding of America's first permanent English settlement in 1607; M. *Colonial Nat'l Historical Park, PO Box 210, Yorktown 23690.*

WASHINGTON

Burien GRAND OLD FLAG FOURTH OF JULY CELEBRATION, July 4 wknd. Oldtime fiddlers; drum & bugle corps; motorcycle stunt events; horses; P. *Burien C of C, 15030 8th Ave. S.W., Seattle 98166. 206 244-3737*

Deming DEMING LOGGING SHOW, June, 2nd wknd. Log-splitting contests; tree climbing; speed climbing; logrolling; choker setting; log bucking. *L. Philliber, 3809 Cabrant Rd., Everson 98247. 206 966-5187*

Oak Harbor HOLLAND HAPPENING, late Apr. or early May, wknd. Folk festival honors Dutch heritage; Dutch women sweep streets; Dutch foods; bell ringers; wooden shoes; P.

422

N. Whidbey C of C, 2506 Hwy. 20, Oak Harbor 98277. 206 675-3535

Omak OMAK STAMPEDE & SUICIDE RACE, Aug., 2nd wknd. Suicide race is a swirling mass of horses and riders plunging down a steep hill, crossing a river, and racing to the finish line; Indian D. *J. Lockwood, Omak 99841. 509 826-1880*

Scandia Gaard MIDSOMMERFEST, June, 2nd wknd. Nordic Baltic celebration where Norwegian, Swedish, Finnish, Danish descendants perform authentic folk D, M; Nordic costumes and food specialties. *G. Tracy, PO Box 5656, University Station, Seattle 98105. 206 633-4225*

Seattle NORTHWEST FOLKLIFE FESTIVAL, late May, 4 days, at Seattle Center Grounds. Irish, Ukrainian, Serbian, Greek, Scandinavian, other heritages celebrated; native costumes, foods, D, M. *Seattle Center, 305 Harrison St., Seattle 98109.*

Seattle BON ODORI, late July, 2 days, in Internat'l District. Annual festival of Japanese community; Japanese folk arts, foods, C; P. *Seattle Buddhist Church, 1427 S. Main St., Seattle 98104.*

Sedro Woolley LOGGERODEO, early July, 5 days. Tree-climbing, log-sawing contests; log show, drive; wrist wrestling; P. *C of C, 714 Metcalf St., Sedro Woolley 98284. 206 855-0770*

Sequim SEQUIM IRRIGATION FESTIVAL, May, 2nd wknd. "Oldest Festival in State" celebrates bringing of water to city in 1896; demolition derby; horse show; P, A. *C of C, PO Box 907, Sequim 98382. 206 683-6197*

Shelton MASON COUNTY FOREST FESTIVAL, May, 4th wk. Old-fashioned and modern logging equipment demonstrations; Paul Bunyan P; BC, M, A. *Mason County Forest Festival, PO Box 252, Shelton 98584. 206 426-8597*

Tenino OLD TIME MUSIC FESTIVAL, Mar., 3rd wknd. M of early settlers played on old-fashioned fiddles, harmonicas, banjos, guitars; all-night celebration. *N. Johnston, Box 225, Tenino 98589. 206 264-2095*

Waitsburg PIONEER FALL FESTIVAL, Sept., 3rd Sun., at Bruce Memorial Museum, pioneer Cs, foods; M of 1880's; *Waitsburg Historical Soc., PO Box 277, Waitsburg 99361.*

Woodland WOODLAND PLANTERS DAY, June, 3rd wk. Civic celebration commemorates holding of dikes which protect community and bottom lands from annual flooding by Columbia and Lewis rivers. *Woodland Planters Day Committee, PO Box 278, Woodland 98674.*

WEST VIRGINIA

Charleston CHARLESTON STERNWHEEL REGATTA, Aug.–Sept., 10 days. Commemorates riverboat days of past; sternwheeler race; Charleston distance run; P. *D. Cohen, 297 Quarrier St., Charleston 25301.*

Elkins MOUNTAIN STATE FOREST FESTIVAL, early Oct., 1 wk. WV open fiddler championship, open banjo contests; horse, pony-pulling, tobacco-spitting, woodchopping, sawing, muzzleloading, horseshoe-pitching contests; P, M, D. *Mt. State Forest Festival, PO Box 2369, Elkins 26241. 304 636-1824*

Franklin TREASURE MOUNTAIN FESTIVAL, Sept., 3rd wknd. Beard, mustache, muzzleloading, rifle-shooting, tomahawk-throwing contests; woodchopper, crosscut saw demonstrations; M, D. *Treasure Mt. Festival, Franklin 26807. 304 358-2221*

Glenville WEST VIRGINIA STATE FOLK FESTIVAL,

mid-June, 4 days, at Glenville State College. Fiddle contest; sharp-note singing; heritage Cs. *K. A. Lewis, 206 Johnson St., Glenville 26351.*

Grantsville CALHOUN COUNTY WOOD FESTIVAL, early June, 3 days. Banjo, fiddling contest; archery shoot; boat races; P, F, D, M. *Wood Festival Commission, Grantsville 26141.*

Hamlin LINCOLN COUNTY TOBACCO FAIR, early Sept., 3 days. Tobacco-spitting contest, A/C, R, P. *Tobacco Fair, PO Box 296, Hamlin 25523.*

Harpers Ferry WEST VIRGINIA COUNTRY FLING, mid-May, 2 days; late Sept., 2 days. Oldtime banjo, fiddle contest; quilt show; jousting tournament. *G. Lewis, PO Box 97, Harpers Ferry 25425. 304 535-2221*

Hendricks HICK FESTIVAL, early Sept., 2 days. Woodchopping; crosscut sawing; chain saw; horse pulling; live raccoon chasing on water and in trees; fiddlers, tug-of-war, archery contests; BC. *D. Mullenax, Parsons 26287.*

Keyser MOUNTAIN HERITAGE FOLK ARTS FESTIVAL, mid-Apr., 2 days, at Potomac State College. Fiddle, banjo contests; traditional mountain dinner; traditional folk A/C; D. *Rainbow General Store, Star Route 1, Keyser 26726. 304 788-9887*

Marlinton PIONEER DAYS, early July, 3 days. Mountain rifle shooting; antique cars; pony, horse-pulling, tobacco-spitting contests; spelling bee; frog, turtle races; surrey rides; horseshoe pitching; BC, M. *Pioneer Days, 218 8th St., Marlinton 24954.*

Moorefield HERITAGE WEEKEND, Sept., last wknd. Muzzleloading rifle shoot; tournament riding; antique farm machinery; old-fashioned ways, days; dulcimer music; A/C. *Heritage Weekend, Box 301, Moorefield 26836.*

Petterstown MONROE COUNTY ARTS & CRAFTS FAIR, mid-June, 3 days. Soap, apple doll, broom, basket making; cider pressing; quilting; dulcimer, fiddle players; folk dancers; hoedown; rifle shoot; hand spinning. *Monroe County C of C, Union 24983.*

Princeton JOHN HENRY FOLK FESTIVAL, late Aug., 3 days. Festival designed to preserve Black Appalachian culture; authentic country blues, delta blues; traditional gospel M; folk M, A/C, D. *John Henry Folk Festival, PO Box 135, Princeton 24740.*

Ripley MOUNTAIN STATE ART & CRAFT FAIR, early July, 5 days. Oldtime medicine show, mountain fiddlers; banjo pickers; dulcimer players; sheep-shearing, apple butter, candle-making, spinning, quilting demonstrations; buckwheat cakes. *Mt. State Art & Craft Fair, Cedar Lakes, Ripley 25271.*

Salem FORT NEW SALEM HERITAGE CELEBRATION, Apr., last wknd. Lifestyles of 18th-, 19th-century Appalachia demonstrated; period costumes; heritage C; Appalachian M, folk traditions, foods. *Heritage Arts Festival Committee, Salem College, Salem 26426.*

WISCONSIN

Black River Falls HARVEST POW WOW, Memorial Day, Labor Day wknds. Indian D, drum contests; traditional Indian foods include venison, corn soup, wild rice. *T. Kingswan, Black River Falls 54616. 715 284-2745*

Cedar Grove HOLLAND FEST, late July, wknd. Dutch community celebration; wooden shoes; street scrubbing. *C of C, Cedar Grove 53013.*

Ephraim FYRBAL FEST, mid-June, 1 day. Fish boil, fry. *C of C, Sturgeon Bay 54235.*

Fort Atkinson FORT FEST, early Aug. Indian pageant, festivities; M, D. *C of C, Fort Atkinson 53538.*

Hayward MAPLE SUGAR FESTIVAL, early Apr., 1 day. Celebration of maple sugar industry; sugaring contest; Indian powwow. *Mt. Telemark, Cable 54821.*

Hayward LUMBERJACK WORLD CHAMPIONSHIPS, late July. Working lumberjacks from all over world test their skills in logrolling, chopping, sawing, tree-topping, speed-climbing contests. *Hayward C of C, PO Box 404, Hayward 54843.*

Milwaukee HOLIDAY FOLK FAIR, mid-Nov., 3 days. 35 ethnic groups pay tribute to their heritages; handicrafts; costumes; folk singing, D. *Holiday Folk Fair, 2810 W. Highland Blvd., Milwaukee 53208.*

Stoughton SYTTENDI MAI, mid-May, wknd. Celebration of Norwegian independence; Norwegian foods, folk singing, D. *C of C, Stoughton 53589.*

Taylor OLD FASHION DAYS, July, 2nd wknd, 3 days. Horse pulling; threshing. *C of C, Taylor 54659.*

Warrens ANNUAL CRANBERRY FESTIVAL, early Oct., 2 days. Cranberry movies, bake-off; largest sunflower, garden produce contests; rope pull; ethnic foods; M. *Wisconsin State C of C, 411 W. Main St., Madison 53701. 606 257-1088*

WYOMING

Cheyenne CHEYENNE FRONTIER DAYS, July, last wk. "World's oldest and biggest rodeo"; bareback, saddle, bull-riding contests; wild-horse racing; calf, steer roping; bull dogging; Oglala Indians demonstrate Indian lifestyles, perform ritual Ds; chuckwagon breakfast; P, D. *Cheyenne Frontier Days, Box 2385, Cheyenne 82001. 307 634-7794*

Encampment WOODCHOPPER'S JAMBOREE & RODEO, mid-June, 2 days. Logrolling, tree-topping, chain saw, hand-sawing, tree-felling, ax-chopping contests; greased-pig, wild-chicken chases; greased-pole climb; D, P, R. *WY Travel Commission, I 25 at Etchepare Circle, Cheyenne 82002. 307 777-7777*

Fort Bridger BUCKSKIN RENDEZVOUS, late July, 2 days. Muzzleloading contest; firing demonstrations; wild-game dinners. *Fort Bridger State Park, Fort Bridger 82933.*

Laramie NAT'L STEER ROPING FINALS, mid-Sept., 3 days. Competitors from throughout US compete in steer-roping contests. *P. Burns, 1270 N. 3rd, Laramie 82070. 307 745-3835*

Pinedale GREEN RIVER RENDEZVOUS, July, 2nd Sun. Reenactment of frontier days; mountain men and Indians assemble with muzzleloaders, tepees, horses, packs for pageant; authentic-looking costumes and makeup of the time used. *WY Travel Commission, I 25 at Etchepare Circle, Cheyenne 82002. 307 777-7777*

Sheridan ALL-AMERICAN INDIAN DAYS, Aug., 1st wknd. American-Indian Olympics, games, A/C, D, BC. *All-American Indian Days, Box 451, Sheridan 82801.*

Shoshoni WYOMING STATE CHAMPIONSHIP OLD-TIME FIDDLE CONTEST, late May, 2 days. Senior, junior, state championship divisions compete for prizes. *C of C, Shoshoni 82649.*

Worland OKTOBERFEST, late Sept. German heritage celebrated with kegs of beer, sauerkraut, wurst, wienerschnitzel; P. *Worland C of C, 120 N. 10th St., Worland 82401.*

PICTURE CREDITS

The editors are extremely grateful for the important contributions of these individuals and organizations and their staffs in picture research: the American Heritage Publishing Co.; the Amon Carter Museum; John and Selma Appel; Nancy Carter and Gene Harris of the Brandywine River Museum; the Buffalo Bill Historical Center; Charles Catney of the Carnegie Institute Museum of Art; John Clymer; Robin Rafer of Culver Pictures; Roland Elzea of the Delaware Art Museum; the Free Library of Philadelphia, Rare Books and Print Collection; Gail Guidry, Missouri Historical Society; Robert Bush of the Historic New Orleans Collection; the Iowa Arts Council; the Kennedy Galleries; Esther Bromberg of the Museum of the City of New York; the New York Public Library, Picture Collection, American History Division, Prints Division, and Rare Book Division; the Public Archives of Canada; Judy Schiff, Sterling Library, Yale University; and Harold Von Schmidt.

Front cover *upper left* From the Collection of the West Texas Museum Association, the Museum of Texas Tech University, Lubbock; *middle left* Valley Forge Historical Society; *lower left* Private Collection/Photograph courtesy of The Brandywine River Museum; *center* Ted Coconis; *upper right* The New-York Historical Society; *middle right* © 1921 J. L. G. Ferris—© 1948 Ernest N. Ryder d.b.n.c.t.a. Renewal Wm. E. Ryder—by will UCC 1975 Archives of 76, Bay Village, Ohio, and the Smithsonian Institution; *lower right* Ted Coconis. **Back cover** Perri. **1** Jerome B. Thompson, *Apple Gathering,* 1856 [detail]. The Brooklyn Museum, Dick S. Ramsay Fund. **2–3** Ted Coconis. **4–5** *left to right* [all details] New York Public Library, General Research & Humanities Division; American Antiquarian Society; New York Public Library, Science & Technology Research Center; New York Public Library, General Research & Humanities Division; New York Public Library, Picture Collection; Culver Pictures; New York Public Library, Rare Book Division; New York Public Library, General Research & Humanities Division; Perri; Labadie Collection, Department of Rare Books & Special Collection, the University of Michigan. **6–8** *left to right* [all details] New York Public Library, Rare Book Division; Craig Carl; Courtesy of the Harold McCracken Collection; New York Public Library, American History Division; New York Public Library, General Research & Humanities Division.

CHAPTER 1: 9 Culver Pictures. **11** *top* New York Public Library, Picture Collection; *bottom* Three Lions, Inc. **12** *top* Free Library of Philadelphia; *bottom* The Bettmann Archive. **13** Paul Williams. **14** © 1915 J.L.G. Ferris—Wm. E. Ryder UCC 1975, by will, Archives of 76, Bay Village, Ohio, and the Smithsonian Institution. **16** New York Public Library, Picture Collection. **18** The Bettmann Archive. **19** New York Public Library, Rare Book Division. **20** Peter DiGeorge. **21** Allan I. Ludwig. **22** The New-York Historical Society. **23** *top* Culver Pictures; *bottom* Reproduced with permission of the Archives, the Coca-Cola Company. **25** The Cleveland Museum of Art, Mr. and Mrs. William H. Marlatt Fund. **26** Albright-Knox Art Gallery, Buffalo, N.Y., James G. Forsyth Fund. **27** Free Library of Philadelphia. **28** Craig Carl. **29** Jack Endewelt. **30** *top* American Museum of Natural History; *bottom* Folger Shakespeare Library. **31** New York Public Library, Picture Collection. **33** *left* National Portrait Gallery. Smithsonian Institution; *right* State Historical Society of Wisconsin. **34** American Antiquarian Society. **35** Ted Coconis. **36** *top* New York Public Library, Arents Collections; *bottom* & **37** New York Public Library, Picture Collection. **CHAPTER 2: 39** *top* Culver Pictures; *bottom* State Historical Society of Wisconsin. **40** Giraudon. **41** Walter Hortens. **42** *top* New York Public Library, American History Division; *bottom* & **43** New York Public Library, Rare Book Division. **44** *left & right* Illustrations based on material from the New York Public Library; *center* New York Public Library, General Research & Humanities Division. **45** *top* New York Public Library, Rare Book Division; *bottom* Saul Field/Upstairs Gallery, Toronto. **46** *bottom* Peter DiGeorge. **47** Hudson's Bay Company. **48 & 49** *bottom* New York Public Library, American History Division; *top* Bibliothèque Nationale. **50** New York Public Library, Picture Collection. **51** *top & lower right* American Museum of Natural History; *bottom* New York Public Library, American History Division. **52** Collection of the Louisiana State Museum **53 & 54** Kurt Vargo. **55** New York Public Library, Picture Collection. **56** *top* Craig Carl; *bottom* From the Kurt Bachmann Collection. **57** Kurt Vargo. **CHAPTER 3: 58** *top & bottom* Museum of the American Indian, Heye Foundation; *middle* Museum of Northern Arizona. **59** Celso Pastor de la Torre. **60** Jack Endewelt. **61** New York Public Library, Rare Book Division. **62** Collection of the Millicent A. Rogers Memorial Museum, Inc., Taos, N. Mex. **63** Museum of the American Indian, Heye Foundation. **64** New York Public Library, American History Division. **65** The Anshutz Collection, Photo by James Milmoe. **66** National Gallery of Art, Washington. **67** Southwest Museum. **69** Daughters of the Republic of Texas Library at the Alamo. **70** Richard Krepel. **71** Perri. **CHAPTER 4: 73** *top* Gloria McKeown; *bottom* Brockton Public Library System. **74** Free Library of Philadelphia. **75** New York Public Library, Science & Technology Research Center. **76** New York Public Library, Rare Book Division. **77** © 1921 J.L.G. Ferris—© 1948 Ernest N. Ryder d.b.n.c.t.a. Renewal Wm. E. Ryder—by will UCC 1975 Archives of 76, Bay Village, Ohio, and the Smithsonian Institution. **78** Delaware Art Museum. **79** Free Library of Philadelphia. **80** New York Public Library, Science & Technology Research Center. **81** *top* James Alexander; *bottom* Collection of the Louisiana State Museum. **82** By permission of the Houghton Library, Harvard University. **83** *top* New York Public Library, Rare Book Division; *bottom* Peter DiGeorge. **84** Delaware Art Museum. **85** New York Public Library, Science & Technology Research Center. **86** *bottom left* New York Public Library, Rare Book Division; *remainder* New York Public Library, Science & Technology Research Center. **87** New York Public Library, Rare Book Division. **CHAPTER 5: 88** The New-York Historical Society. **89** Abbott Hall, Marblehead, Mass. **90** Metropolitan Museum of Art, Gift of Mrs. Russell Sage. **91** *top* Peter DiGeorge; *bottom* Collection of the American National Insurance Co., Galveston, Tex. **92** Metropolitan Museum of Art, Arthur H. Hearn Fund. **93** Courtesy of the Fort Ticonderoga Museum. **94** Illustration based on material from the New York State Historical Association, Cooperstown. **95** The New-York Historical Society. **96** © Yale University Art Gallery. **97** New York State Historical Association, Cooperstown. **98** Philadelphia Museum of Art, The Mr. and Mrs. Wharton Sinkler Collection. **99** Philadelphia Museum of Art, given by Mrs. John D. Rockefeller. **100** Library of Congress. **101** *upper right* Culver Pictures; *bottom* National Archives. **102** *left* Private Collection; *right* Metropolitan Museum of Art, Gift of John Stewart Kennedy. **103** Valley Forge Historical Society. **104** Amon Carter Museum, Fort Worth, Tex. **105** © Arnold Friberg. **106** The New-York Historical Society. **107** *upper left & center* New York Public Library, Prints Division; *upper right* Courtesy of the Henry Francis du Pont Winterthur Museum; *bottom left* New York Public Library, Picture Collection; *bottom right* The New-York Historical Society. **108** Sons of the Revolution, Fraunces Tavern Museum, New York. **109** *top* New York Public Library, American History Division; *bottom* New York Public Library, Picture Collection. **110** Collection of the American National Insurance Co., Galveston, Tex. **111** Metropolitan Museum of Art, Bequest of Charles Allen Munn. **112** Submarine Force Library & Museum, Groton, Conn. **113** *center* Shelburne Museum, Inc., Shelburne, Vt.; *bottom* The New-York Historical Society. **114** *top* Peter DiGeorge; *bottom* The New-York Historical Society. **CHAPTER 6: 115** Collection of Harry T. Peters, Jr. **116** *left* & **117** *right* The Granger Collection. **116–117** *bottom* Kentucky Department of Public Information. **118** Culver Pictures. **119** *top* The Harry T. Peters "America on Stone" Collection, Smithsonian Institution; *bottom* Collection of E. R. Minshall, Jr. **120** James Alexander. **121** *top* Private Collection/Photograph courtesy of Brandywine River Museum; *bottom* New York Public Library. **122** Peter Spier. **123** New York Public Library, Rare Book Division. **124** Peter DiGeorge. **125** New York Public Library, Rare Book Division. **127** Ted Coconis. **128** The Peale Museum. **129** City of New York Art Commission/Taylor & Dull Photography. **130 & 131** The New-York Historical Society. **133** Delaware Art Museum. **134–135** Jack Endewelt. **CHAPTER 7: 136** *top* Painting by C. M. Ismert, Kansas City, Mo., Courtesy of the State Historical Society of Missouri; *bottom* Courtesy of the Indiana University Art Museum. **138** New York Public Library, Picture Collection. **139** *top* New York State Historical Association, Cooperstown; *bottom* Peter DiGeorge. **140 & 141** Public Archives of Canada, Ottawa. **142** New York Public Library, Picture Collection. **143** The St. Louis Art Museum. **144** New York Public Library, General Research & Humanities Division. **145** New York Public Library, Rare Book Division. **146** New York Public Library, General Research & Humanities Division. **147** The Historic New Orleans Collection. **148 & 149** New York Public Library, General Research & Humanities Division. **150** Diamond M. Foundation. **151** Missouri Historical Society. **152** Norman Rockwell. **153** The Historic New Orleans Collection. **154** New York Public Library, General Research & Humanities Division. **155** Private Collection. **156** *left* New York Public Library, General Research & Humanities Division; *bottom* The Historic New Orleans Collection. **157** New York Public Library, General Research & Humanities Division. **CHAPTER 8: 158** *top* New York Public Library, Picture Collection; *bottom* Museum of the City of New York. **160 & 161** *top* New York Public Library, General Research & Humanities Division; *bottom* Peter DiGeorge. **162** New York Public Library, General Research & Humanities Division. **163** Perri. **165** Kurt Vargo. **166** New York Public Library. **167** Collection of the Newark Museum. **168** New York Public Library, American History Division. **169** Perri. **170** New York Public Library, General Research & Humanities Division. **171** The Thomas Gilcrease Institute of American History & Art, Tulsa, Okla. **172** DRT Library. **173** Brass Door Galleries. **CHAPTER 9: 174** *top* New York Public Library, General Research & Humanities Division; *bottom* Montana Historical Society, Mackay Collection. **176** New York Public Library, Rare Book Division. **177** *top* Reproduced with permission from the book JOHN CLYMER, AN ARTIST'S RENDEZVOUS WITH THE FRONTIER WEST, by Walt Reed, published by Northland Press, Flagstaff, Ariz., 1976; *bottom* National Collection of Fine Arts, Smithsonian Institution. **178** Northern Natural Gas Company Collection, Joslyn Art Museum, Omaha, Nebr. **179** Walter Hortens. **180** Reprinted by permission of Coward, McCann & Geoghegan, Inc., from TALL TALE AMERICA by Walter Blair, copyright 1944 by Walter Blair, renewed. **181** Amon Carter Museum, Fort Worth, Tex. **183** Ted Coconis. **184** New York Public Library, General Research & Humanities Division. **185** Courtesy of the Bancroft Library. **186** Reproduced with permission from the book JOHN CLYMER, AN ARTIST'S RENDEZVOUS WITH THE FRONTIER WEST, by Walt Reed, published by Northland Press, Flagstaff, Ariz., 1976. **188** New York Public Library, Picture Collection. **189** Royal Ontario Museum. **CHAPTER 10: 190–191** *bottom* Iowa Art Council; *top* Perri. **192** Collection of Mr. and Mrs. J. Maxwell Moran. **193** Western Americana Picture Library, Brentwood, England. **194** New York Public Library, Picture Collection. **195** *top* Peter DiGeorge; *bottom* Library of Congress. **196** The Huntington Library, San Marino, Calif. **197** Museum of the City of New York. **198** California Department of Parks and Recreation. **199** California Historical Society. **200** New York Public Library, General Research & Humanities Division. **201 & 202** The Church of Jesus Christ of Latter-Day Saints. **203** Denver Public Library, Western History Department. **204** Philbrook Art Center. **205** Amon Carter Museum, Fort Worth, Tex. **206** *top* Library of Congress; *bottom* New York Public Library, American History Division. **207** *top* Reprinted with permission from THE SATURDAY EVENING POST, © 1939 The Curtis Publishing Company; *bottom* United States Department of the Interior. **208** *top* Courtesy of the Bancroft Library; *bottom* Collection of Mr. and Mrs. J. Maxwell Moran. **209** South Dakota Memorial Art Center, Brookings. **210** State of Illinois, Department of Conservation. **211** *top* Private Collection; *bottom* Culver Pictures. **CHAPTER 11: 212** California Department of Parks and Recreation. **213** New York Public Library, General Research & Humanities Division. **215** Jack Endewelt. **216** Reprinted from THE OUTDOOR PAINTINGS OF ROBERT K. ABBETT, Peacock Press/Bantam. **217** *top* New York Public Library, General Research & Humanities Division; *bottom* Peter DiGeorge. **218** The Fine Arts Museums of San Francisco. **219** *top* New York Public Library; *bottom* New York Public Library, General Research & Humanities Division. **221** California State Library. **222** New York Public Library, Picture Collection. **223** The New-York Historical Society. **224** New York Public Library, General Research & Humanities Division. **225** National Cowboy Hall of Fame & Western Heritage Center, Oklahoma City, Okla. **226** *top* New York Public Library, American History Division; *center* The New-York Historical Society. **227** Craig Carl. **228** Perri. **229** The Oakland Museum. **CHAPTER 12: 231** Peabody Museum of Salem. **232 & 233** The Kendall Whaling Museum, Sharon, Mass. **234** New York Public Library, General Research & Humanities Division. **235** *lower left* The Bettmann Archive; *upper center* Courtesy of the Mariners Museum of Newport News, Va.; *right* National Gallery of Art, Washington. **236** Museum of Fine Arts, Boston, Abraham Shuman Fund. **237** Delaware Art Museum, Howard Pyle Collection. **238** Wadsworth Atheneum, Hartford, Conn., The Ella Gallup Sumner & Mary Catlin Sumner Collection. **239** *top* Museum of the City of New York, The Harry T. Peters Collection; *bottom* New York Public Library, General Research & Humanities Division. **241** Ted Coconis. **242** Peter DiGeorge. **243** *top* Metropolitan Museum of Art, Maria DeWitt Jessup Fund; *bottom* New York Public Library, General Research & Humanities Division. **244** *top* Peabody Museum of Salem; *bottom* The Old Print Shop. **245** New York State Historical Association, Cooperstown. **246** New York Public Library, General Research & Humanities Division. **247** Delaware Art Museum, Howard Pyle Collection. **248** The Kendall Whaling Museum, Sharon, Mass. **249** Jack Endewelt. **250** Metropolitan Museum of Art, Rogers Fund. **251** Culver Pictures. **252** Courtesy of the Mariners Museum of Newport News, Va. **253** *top* The Bettmann Archive; *bottom* New York Public Library. **254** New York Public Library, General Research & Humanities Division. **255** *top* Henry C. Pitz Collection; *bottom* © Frost & Reed, Ltd., London. **CHAPTER 13: 256** National Museum of History & Technology, Smithsonian Institution. **257** Shelburne Museum, Inc., Shelburne, Vt. **258** Giraudon. **259** Phyllis W. Hudson Collection. **260 & 261** *bottom* Reprinted from TALES FROM UNCLE REMUS by Joel Chandler Harris by permission of Houghton Mifflin Company; *top* & **262** New York Public Library, Picture Collection. **263** New York Public Library, American History Division. **264** Metropolitan Museum of Art, Rogers Fund. **265** *top* Corcoran Gallery of Art; *bottom* Peter DiGeorge. **266** Perri. **267** New York Public Library, American History Division. **268–269** *bottom* The Historic New Orleans Collection; *top* New York Public Library, American History Division. **270** Jack Endewelt. **271** Ray Houlihan. **272 & 273** New York Public Library, Picture Collection. **274** New York Public Library, American History Division. **275** The New-York Historical Society. **276** *top* Cincinnati Art Museum; *bottom* New York Public Library, American History Division. **277** Library of Congress. **278** *top* The New-York Historical Society; *bottom* Warshaw Collection of Business America, Smithsonian Institution. **CHAPTER 14: 279** Berry-Hill Galleries, Inc., New York. **280** *left* Library of Congress; *right* & **281** *left* West Point Museum, U.S.M.A., Gift of Edgar William and Bernice Chrysler Garbisch; *right* Library of Congress. **282** University of Michigan, Museum of Art, Bequest of Henry C. Lewis. **283** *top* Painting by Harold Von Schmidt for ESQUIRE; *bottom* Chicago & Illinois Midland Railway Company. **284** © 1964 Libraire Jules Tallandier. **285** The Abraham Lincoln Library & Museum, Lincoln Memorial University. **286** *top* New York Public Library, Prints Division; *bottom* University of Hartford. **287** N. S. Meyer, Inc. Collection/Photo by William Sonntag. **288** *top* Museum of the Confederacy; *bottom* Peter DiGeorge. **289** *top* © 1975 by Alec Thomas Archives, from GONE FOR A SOLDIER: THE CIVIL WAR MEMOIRS OF PRIVATE ALFRED BELLARD, edited by David Herbert Donald, by permission of Little, Brown & Co.; *bottom* New York Public Library, American History Division. **290** *left* Library of Congress; *right* & **291** *left* Courtesy of the State of Missouri, Joseph P. Teasdale, Governor; *right* American Heritage Collection. **292** The New-York Historical Society. **293** American Heritage Collection. **294** Historical Society of Delaware. **295** *top* Virginia Historical Society; *bottom* Culver Pictures. **296** *top* Coe Kerr Gallery, New York/Photo courtesy of The Brandywine River Museum; *bottom* Museum of the Confederacy. **297** The Bettmann Archive. **298** Museum of the Confederacy. **299** N. S. Meyer, Inc. Collection/Photo by William Sonntag. **300** *top* Museum of Fine Arts, Boston, Ellen Kelleran Gardner Fund; *bottom* Union League Club, New York. **301** Illustration of Barbara Frietchie by N. C. Wyeth is reprinted by permission of Charles Scribner's Sons from POEMS OF AMERICAN PATRIOTISM, edited by Brander Matthews, © 1922 Charles Scribner's Sons. **302** *top* New York Public Library, Prints Division; *bottom* Library of Congress. **303** *center* National Portrait Gallery, Smithsonian Institution; *bottom* Chicago Historical Society. **CHAPTER 15: 304** *top* Courtesy of the Harold McCracken Collection; *bottom* John Gray Collection/Photo by Lee Angle. **305** Culver Pictures. **306–307** *bottom* Buffalo Bill Historical Center, Cody, Wyo., *top* Walter Hortens. **308** *top* Joe Beeler Collection; *bottom* & **309** Culver Pictures. **310** From the Collection of the West Texas Museum Association, the Museum of Texas Tech University, Lubbock. **311** *top* Peter DiGeorge; *bottom left* Harold Von Schmidt Collection; *bottom right* Vankirk Nelson Collection. **312** Reprinted from THE SATURDAY EVENING POST, © 1950 The Curtis Publishing Co. **313** *top* Culver Pictures; *bottom* Amon Carter Museum, Fort Worth, Tex. **314** Courtesy of the John Hancock Mutual Life Insurance Co. **315** The Thomas Gilcrease Institute of American History & Art, Tulsa, Okla. **316** *top* Courtesy of the State of Missouri, Joseph P. Teasdale, Governor; *bottom* Texas State Library. **317** *top* Reprinted from THE SATURDAY EVENING POST, © 1942 The Curtis Publishing Co.; *bottom* Buffalo Bill Historical Center, Cody, Wyo. **318** Culver Pictures. **319** *top* The Bettmann Archive; *bottom* Courtesy of the R. W. Norton Art Gallery, Shreveport, La. **320** Jack Endewelt. **322** Courtesy of Kennedy Galleries, Inc., New York. **323** Courtesy of the Adams Memorial Museum, Deadwood, S. Dak. **324** Joe Beeler Collection. **325** *top* Reprinted from THE OLD WEST/*The Railroaders*, "Railway Train Attacked by Indians" by Theodor Kaufmann, courtesy of H. R. Dietrich, Jr., © 1973 Time Inc.; *bottom* Museum of Fine Arts, Houston, Hogg Brothers Collection. **326** Courtesy of the Remington Art Museum, Ogdensburg, N.Y. **327** *top* The Thomas Gilcrease Institute of American History & Art, Tulsa, Okla.; *bottom* Peter DiGeorge. **328** The Thomas Gilcrease Institute of American History & Art, Tulsa, Okla. **329** *top* Courtesy of the Remington Art Museum, Ogdensburg, N.Y.; *bottom* Library of Congress. **330** From STEELWAYS, published by American Iron & Steel Institute. **331** *top* Buffalo Bill Historical Center, Cody, Wyo.; *bottom* Library Company of Philadelphia. **CHAPTER 16: 332–333** *bottom* Cincinnati Art Museum; *top* Birmingham Museums & Art Gallery. **334** *top* New York Public Library, Prints Division; *bottom* John & Selma Appel Collection. **335** *top* Arrow Company; *bottom* Courtesy of Kennedy Galleries, Inc., New York. **336** New York Public Library, Picture Collection. **337** Museum of the City of New York. **338** *center* John & Selma Appel Collection; *bottom* & **339** *top* New York Public Library, Picture Collection; *bottom* Peter DiGeorge. **340** *top* Philadelphia Museum of Art, given by Mrs. John Wintersteen; *center* Library of Congress. **341** *top* Collection of the late Ivan Traugott; *bottom* John & Selma Appel Collection. **342** © Walt Disney Productions. **343** *top* Collection of Mrs. John Held, Jr.; *bottom* American Sponge & Chamois Company. **344** New York Public Library, General Research & Humanities Division. **345** *top* Courtesy of Steinway and Sons/Photo by William Sonntag; *bottom* Library of Congress. **346 & 347** *top* John & Selma Appel Collection; *bottom* The Mansell Collection. **348** John & Selma Appel Collection. **349** *top* Fine Arts Gallery of San Diego, Gift of Mr. and Mrs. Appelton S. Bridges; *bottom* The Bettmann Archive. **350** *top* Henry T. Rockwell Collection; *bottom* Culver Pictures. **351** *top* Courtesy of the Mariners Museum of Newport News, Va.; *bottom* Culver Pictures. **CHAPTER 17: 352** *left* Reprinted from THE AMERICAN WEEKLY, by permission of the Hearst Corp.; *right* & **353** *top* Pennsylvania Council on the Arts; *bottom* New York Public Library, Picture Collection. **354** *top* New York Public Library, General Research & Humanities Division; *bottom* Private Collection. **355** *top* New York Public Library, General Research & Humanities Division; *bottom* Private Collection. **356** New York Public Library, Picture Collection. **357** Ted Coconis. **358** *top* Culver Pictures; *bottom* Free Library of Philadelphia. **359** New York Public Library, General Research & Humanities Division. **360** Brooks Memorial Art Gallery Permanent Collection, Memphis, Tenn. **361** Peter DiGeorge. **362** *top* Collection of the Museum of Modern Art, New York, Gift of The Griffis Foundation; *bottom* Peter Spier. **363 & 364** New York Public Library, Picture Collection. **365** *top* Labadie Collection, Department of Rare Books & Special Collection, the University of Michigan; *bottom* Library of Congress. **366** United States Department of the Interior, National Park Service, Edison National Historic Site. **367** *top* Ford Motor Company; *bottom* National Museum of History & Technology, Smithsonian Institution. **368** *top* The Franklin Institute; *bottom* American Telephone & Telegraph Co. **369** *top* Peter Spier; *bottom* New School for Social Research. **370** Courtesy of Alexander Nimick/Photo by Carl M. Martahus. **371** *top* American Antiquarian Society; *bottom* Library of Congress. **372** Museum of the City of New York, Theatre and Music Collection. **373** *top* The Bettmann Archive; *bottom* New York Public Library, Picture Collection. **374** Wadsworth Atheneum, Hartford, Conn. **375** *top* New York Public Library, General Research & Humanities Division; *bottom* Private Collection, Mr. and Mrs. Jerry Moss, Los Angeles. **CHAPTER 18: 376** Collection of Mrs. John Held, Jr. **377** John Berkey. **378** New York Public Library, Picture Collection. **379** Truman Library Collection. **380** Culver Pictures. **381** *top* Imperial War Museum Photri; *bottom* Reprinted with permission from THE SATURDAY EVENING POST © 1917 The Curtis Publishing Company. **382** *top* Culver Pictures; *bottom* & **383** *top* Museum of the City of New York; *bottom* Pierre Brissand for FORTUNE. **384** Robert Weaver. **385** Missouri Historical Society. **386** Culver Pictures. **387** "Hoboes on the Move" by Leconte Stewart. **388** (Valentino) Macfadden Group, Inc.; (Bow) Culver Pictures; (West) New York Public Library, Theater Collection; (Gable & Harlow) Museo Civico Luigi Bailo; (Fields) Edward Sorel; (Temple) Culver Pictures; (Garbo) Museo Civico Luigi Bailo; (Flynn) United Artists/Cinemabilia. **389** Ted Coconis/Reprinted by permission of Liberty Library Corp. **390** American Radio Heritage Institute. **391** From INCREDIBLE ATHLETIC FEATS by Jim Benagh, © 1969 Hart Publishing Company, Inc. **392** Courtesy of VANITY FAIR. © 1933 (renewed) 1961 by The Condé Nast Publications Inc. **393** *top* Reprinted from THE AMERICAN STORY, © 1975 The Curtis Publishing Co. *bottom* Drawings copyrighted 1944, renewed 1972, Bill Mauldin; reproduced by courtesy of Bill Mauldin. **394** *top* Perri; *bottom* U.S. Army Art Collection. **395** *top* Bigfoot Information Center, Hood River, Oregon; *remainder* Collection of Edward Wood. **396** *top* Peter DiGeorge; *bottom* William G. Muller. **397** Perri. **398** *center* © Walt Disney Productions; *bottom* & **399** *bottom* © Charles Schulz; *remainder* D C Comics Inc. **400** Private Collection. **401** *top* Ed Renfro; *bottom* Phaidon Press Ltd. **402** *top* Jerzy Flisak; *bottom* New York Public Library, Picture Collection. **403** Ted Coconis. **404** *detail* New York Public Library, General Research & Humanities Division. **405** *detail* Culver Pictures.

ACKNOWLEDGMENTS

The editors wish to express special appreciation for invaluable help in text research to the following individuals and organizations and their staffs: American Society for Psychical Research Library; Dr. John J. and Mrs. Selma Appel; Prof. Larry D. Ball, Department of History, Arkansas State University; Jane Beck; Prof. Jerry R. Craddock, Department of Spanish and Portuguese, University of California; Warden Joseph M. Scott, Carbon County Prison, Jim Thorpe, Pa.; Mrs. John C. Cooke; Prof. Norman Doenges, Department of Classics, Dartmouth College; Everett T. Rattray, Editor, The East Hampton Star, East Hampton, N.Y.; *Thomas Froncek; Prof. William Schevill, Department of Biology, Harvard University; Dick Hyman; Walter C. Pitman III, Lamont Geological Observatory; Mercantile Library Association; Robert O'Brien, Roberta Buland, Morningside Associates; Avonne Keller, Secretary-Treasurer, The Newspaper Comics Council, Inc.; New York Public Library: Jerome L. Stoker, Leon Weidman and the American History Division, Ames History Room, Chatham Square Library, Elizabeth Diefendorf, General Research and Humanities Division, Photographic Service Division, Rare Book Division; New York Society Library; Louis C. Jones, Director, New York State Historical Association; Floyd Painter; Harold S. Moore, Preservation Council of Pike County, Inc., Pikeville, Ky.; Vicki Rogers; Sunn Classic Pictures, Inc.; Kay Thomas; Matt Witt, Editor, Karen Ohmans, Editorial Assistant,* United Mine Workers Journal; *Grace Wells, Curator of Costumes, Valentine Museum, Richmond, Va.; Monica Reed, Librarian, Wenner-Gren Foundation for Anthropological Research, Inc.*

TEXT CREDITS

The *American Folklore and Legend* story title is printed in boldface small capitals after the page number (boldface) on which it appears. The story title is followed by the source or sources from which the story was taken, preceded by a symbol indicating the use made of the sources. A key to the symbols appears below.

○ source(s) consulted
□ quoted from
★ condensed from
■ adapted from or based on
✔ based on many sources

1 NEW LORE IN A NEW LAND

10-11 ○ Daniel Boorstin, *The Americans,* Vol. I, *The Colonial Experience,* New York, Vintage Books, 1958; A. L. Rowse, *The Elizabethans and America,* London, Macmillan, 1959; Cotton Mather, *Magnalia Christi Americana,* Hartford, 1853; Ray Bearse, ed., *Massachusetts, A Guide to the Pilgrim State,* Boston, Houghton Mifflin Company, 1971; *The New York Times,* Nov. 5, 1975. **12-13 WILDERNESS RIVALRY** ■ "The Courtship of Miles Standish," *The Poetical Works of Longfellow,* Boston, Houghton Mifflin Company, 1975. **COURTING IN COLD NEW ENGLAND** ○ Dana Doten, *The Art of Bundling,* New York, Countrymen Press & Farrar & Rinehart, 1938; Alice Morse Earle, *Customs and Fashions in Old New England,* New York, Charles Scribner's Sons, 1893. **14-15 THE FIRST THANKSGIVING** ○ Ralph and Adelin Linton, *We Gather Together,* New York, Schuman, 1949; W. Deloss Love, Jr., *Fast and Thanksgiving Days of New England,* Boston, Houghton Mifflin Company, 1895. **THE CRAFTY WOODSMAN** ■ B. A. Botkin, ed., *A Treasury of New England Folklore,* New York, copyright 1947, 1975 by B. A. Botkin. Used by permission of Crown Publishers, Inc. **MINISTER AND MAGICIAN** ■ Elizabeth Reynard, *The Narrow Land,* Boston, Houghton Mifflin Company, 1934. Used by permission of the Chatham Historical Society. **THE CHEESE BRIGADE** ■ Effie Gore and E. A. Speare, *New Hampshire Folk Tales,* Plymouth, N.H., New Hampshire Federation of Women's Clubs, 1932. **HEADWORK** ★ Botkin, *op. cit.* **NECESSARY ADDITIONS** ✔ **CHOCORUA'S CURSE** ○ Gore and Speare, *op. cit.;* Samuel A. Drake, *A Book of New-England Legends and Folklore,* Boston, Little, Brown & Co., 1901; Charles M. Skinner, *American Myths and Legends,* Vol. I, Philadelphia, J. B. Lippincott Company, 1903. **16 MORTON'S MERRY MOUNT** ★ Thomas Morton, *The New English Canaan,* Amsterdam, 1637. **17 THE DEMONS OF NEWBURY** □ Mather, *op. cit.* **BLACK MAN, BLACK MASS** □ Cotton Mather, *The Wonders of the Invisible World,* London, John Russell Smith, 1862. **INVITATION TO WITCHCRAFT** □ *ibid.* **THE DEVIL DISTURBED** □ *ibid.* **18-20 THE GOSPEL WITCH** ■ *ibid.* **HOW TO TELL A WITCH** □ *ibid.* **DEVILED DOGS AND OXEN** ★ Marion L. Starkey, *The Devil in Massachusetts,* Garden City, N.Y., Anchor Books, Doubleday & Co., Inc., 1969 (by permission of Collins-Knowlton-Wing). **THEN IT WAS OVER** ★ *ibid.* **INNOCENT BLOOD** ■ Russell Hope Robbins, *The Encyclopedia of Witchcraft and Demonology,* New York, Crown Publishers, Inc., 1959. **THE DEVIL'S NINE QUESTIONS** ✔ **21 NEW ENGLAND MOURNING** ✔ including Donald E. Stanford, ed., *The Poems of Edward Taylor,* New Haven, Conn., Yale University Press, 1963; Earle, *op. cit.;* headstone sayings collected by Dick Hyman. **22-23 THE STORM SHIP** ■ Washington Irving, *Bracebridge Hall,* New York, The Century Company, 1910. **STUYVESANT'S GHOST** ★ B. A. Botkin, ed., *New York City Folklore,* New York, Random House, Inc., 1956. Copyright © 1956 by Benjamin Botkin. Used by permission of Curtis Brown Ltd. **A BAKER'S DOZEN** ★ Harold W. Thompson, *Body, Boots and Britches,* Philadelphia, J. B. Lippincott Company, 1940. Copyright 1939 by Harold W. Thompson. Copyright © renewed 1967 by Dr. Marian Thompson. Reprinted by permission of J. B. Lippincott Company. **FAIR TRADE** ■ Mary Conger, *New York's Making Seen Through the Eyes of My Ancestors,* London, Methuen & Co., 1938. **SAINT NICHOLAS** ✔ **24-25 RIP VAN WINKLE** ★ Washington Irving, *The Sketch Book* by Geoffrey Crayon, Gent., London, 1820. **26-27 TEN LOST TRIBES** ■ *The Select Works of William Penn,* New York, Kraus Reprints, 1971. **THE TRUTH MUST OUT** ■ Irvin and Ruth Poley, *Quaker Anecdotes,* Wallingford, Pa., Pendle Hill, 1946. **LEAD ON** ■ *ibid.* **A HELPING KNEE** ■ *ibid.* **CONFLICT OF INTERESTS** ■ *ibid.* **27-29 A RIDDLE SAVES A NECK** □ J. B. Stoudt, *The Folklore of the Pennsylvania German, Proceedings of The Pennsylvania German Society,* Vol. XXIII, 1910. **CRAFTY EULENSPIEGEL** ■ Thomas R. Brendle and William S. Troxell, "Pennsylvania German Folktales, Legends, Once-Upon-a-Time Stories, Maxims and Sayings" in *Pennsylvania German Society Proceedings and Addresses,* Vol. L, 1944, Morristown, Pa. **PENNY WISE, POUND FOOLISH** ■ *ibid.* **THE ART OF FRAKTUR** ✔ **THE BEST OF THREE** ■ Brendle and Troxell, *op. cit.* **CHRISTMAS EVE** ■ *ibid.* **TWO COLONISTS MEET** ★ Elmer Lewis Smith, *Pennsylvania Dutch Folklore,* Widmer, Pa., Applied Arts, 1963. **PAGAN PRACTICES** ✔ **TO EACH HIS WAY** ✔ **THE ETERNAL HUNTER** ■ George Korson, *Black Rock: Mining Folklore of the Pennsylvania Dutch,* Baltimore, The Johns Hopkins Press, 1960. **THE AMISH** ✔ **THE BLUE GATE** ■ Elmer Lewis Smith, "The Amish Today," *Pennsylvania German Folklore Society Proceedings,* Vol. 24, 1960. **THE WAY TO HEAVEN** ■ Korson, *op. cit.* **32-33 GLITTERING GOLD** □ George Chapman, Ben Jonson, and John Marston, *Eastward Hoe,* London, 1605. **EARTH'S ONLY PARADISE** □ Philip Amadas, in John Smith's *The Generall Historie of Virginia, New England and the Summer Isles,* London, 1624. **INVISIBLE BULLETS** □ Thomas Heriot, in *ibid.* **31 THE LOST COLONY** ○ Stefan Lorant, ed., *The New World,* New York, Duell, Sloan & Pearce, 1946; *Strange Stories, Amazing Facts,* Pleasantville, N.Y., The Reader's Digest Association, Inc., 1976; John Lawson, *A History of Carolina,* 1714; Richard Benbury Creecy, *Grandfather's Tales of North Carolina History,* Raleigh, N.C., R. B. Creecy, 1901. **32-33 POWHATAN'S CORONATION** □ John Smith, *op. cit.* **BUILDING JAMESTOWN** □ *ibid.* **SAVED BY POCAHONTAS** □ *ibid.* **THE STARVING TIME** □ *ibid.* **34-35 KIDNAPED** □ Alfred Métraux, *Voodoo in Haiti,* New York, Schocken Books, 1972. **THE BLACK SLAVE TRADER** ✔ **FLIGHT** ✔ John Bennett, *The Doctor to the Dead,* New York, Rinehart & Co., Inc., 1943. **36-37 TOBACCO** ○ Rowse, *op. cit.;* Sarah Augusta Dickson, *Panacea or Precious Bane, Tobacco in Sixteenth Century Literature,* New York, The New York Public Library, 1954; Thomas J. Wertenbaker, *The Planters of Colonial Virginia,* Princeton University Press,

1922; John Aubrey, *Brief Lives,* London, Secker and Warburg, 1949; Bureau of American Ethnology, *Bulletin No. 137* (Swanton); Virginius Dabney, *Virginia, The New Dominion,* New York, Doubleday & Co., Inc., 1971. **THE SACRED SMOKE** ✓ including Mitford M. Mathews, *American Words,* Cleveland, World Publishing Co., 1959.

2 THE INLAND KINGDOM

38–39 ✓ **40–41 LESCARBOT'S LIGHTNING** ★ Marc Lescarbot, *The History of New France,* Toronto, The Champlain Society, 1907. **FATHER HENNEPIN BOASTS** ★ Louis Hennepin, *A New Discovery of a Vast Country in America,* Chicago, A. C. McClurg & Co., 1903. **BELLE-FOREST'S MONTREAL** ★ François de Belle-forest, *La Cosmographie universelle de tout le monde,* Paris, 1575 (this excerpt translated by David Rattray). **42 PLAYING POSSUM** □ John Smith, *The Generall Historie of Virginia, New England and the Summer Isles,* London, 1624. **THE GOUGOU MONSTER** ★ Pierre Victor Palma Cayet, *Chronologie septenaire de l'histoire de la paix entre les rois de France et d'Espagne,* Paris, 1605 (this excerpt translated by David Rattray). **ARMOUCHIQUOIS** □ *ibid.* (this excerpt translated by David Rattray). **43 THE NOBLE SAVAGE** ○ Louis de Lahontan, *Some New Voyages to North America,* edited by Reuben Gold Thwaites, New York, Burt Franklin, 1970; □ Samuel E. Morison, *Admiral of the Ocean Sea,* Boston, Little, Brown & Co., 1942; Hoxie Neale Fairchild, *The Noble Savage, A Study in Naturalism,* New York, Russell & Russell, 1961. **BETTER BELIEVE IT** ■ *ibid.* **COLLEGE NO GOOD** ■ *Annals of America,* Vol. I, Chicago, Encyclopedia Britannica Inc., 1968. **44–47 THE LOUP-GAROU** ■ Claude Aubrey, *The Magic Fiddler and Other Legends of French Canada,* Gloucester, Mass., Peter Martin, 1968. **THE MONTREAL FUR FAIR** ✓ **THE CHASSE GALERIE** ■ Edward C. Woodley, *Legends of French Canada,* Toronto, Thomas Nelson & Sons, 1931. **DANCE OF THE STARS** ■ Paul A. Wallace, *Baptiste Laroque—Legends of French Canada,* Toronto, The Musson Book Company, 1923. Reprinted by permission of Hodder & Stoughton, Ltd. **I'M JUST TOO SCARED OF WOLVES** ✓ including Grace Lee Nute, *The Voyageurs,* New York, D. Appleton & Company, 1931. **COURAGEOUS CADIEUX** ■ Woodley, *op. cit.* **THE WENDIGO** ■ Algernon Blackwood, *The Lost Valley and Other Stories,* London, Eveleigh Nash, 1910. **48–51 THE LITTLE PEOPLE** ■ Jesse J. Cornplanter and Namee Price Hendricks, *Legends of the Longhouse,* copyright © 1938, renewed 1966 by Mrs. Elsena Cornplanter. Reprinted by permission of J. B. Lippincott Company; Edmund Wilson, *Apologies to the Iroquois,* New York, Farrar, Straus & Giroux, Inc., 1960. **THE SERPENT WOMAN** ■ W. M. Beauchamp, "Iroquois Folklore," Onondaga Historical Association, 1922. **THE REAL HIAWATHA** ■ Wilson, *op. cit.* **FALSE FACE SOCIETY** ○ *ibid.;* Cornplanter and Hendricks, *op. cit.;* Harriet M. Converse, "Myths and Legends of the New York State Iroquois," *New York State Museum Bulletin No. 125,* 1908. **52–53 FOOLISH JOHN** ■ Calvin Claudel, "Louisiana Tales of Jean Sot and Bouki and Lapin," *Southern Folklore Quarterly,* December 1944. **BOUQUI AND LAPIN** ■ Calvin Claudel, "Louisiana Folktales and Their Background," *Louisiana Historical Quarterly,* Vol. 38, 1955. **EMMELINE LABICHE** ■ Harnett Kane, *The Bayous of Louisiana,* New York, William Morrow & Co., 1943; ○ Carolyn Ramsey, *Cajuns on the Bayou,* New York, Hastings House. Copyright © 1957 by Carolyn Ramsey. Permission of Toni Strassman. **BAYOU WISDOM** ✓ including Lyle Saxon, Edward Dreyer, and Robert Tallant, *Gumbo Ya-Ya,* copyright 1945 Houghton Mifflin Company. Copyright © renewed 1973 by Louisiana State Library. Reprinted by permission of Houghton Mifflin Company; *Journal of American Folklore,* April-June 1899; *ibid.,* July-September 1905 (George Williamson). **54–55 'TITE POULETTE** ★ George Washington Cable, *Old Creole Days,* New York, Charles Scribner's Sons, 1879. **THE DEVIL'S MANSION** ★ Saxon, Dreyer, and Tallant, *op. cit.* **DUELING** ✓ **56–57 VOODOO** ✓ including Zora Hurston, "Voodoo in America," *Journal of American Folklore,* Vol. 44, 1931.

3 IN SEARCH OF CIBOLA

58–59 ✓ **60–61 CORONADO AND THE TURK** ■ Reprinted with the permission of Farrar, Straus & Giroux, Inc. Freely adapted by *The Reader's Digest* from *Conquistadors in North American History,* Part IV, sections iv and v, by Paul Horgan. Copyright © 1963 by Paul Horgan. **CALIFORNIA AN ISLAND** □ García Ordoñez de Montalvo, *Las Sergas de Esplandián,* 1510 (this excerpt translated by David Rattray). **62–65 RABBIT VS. TORTOISE** ■ E. C. Parsons, ed., "Tewa Tales," *Memoirs of the American Folklore Society,* 1926. **COMING OF THE SNAKES** ■ A. M. Stephen, "Legend of the Snake Order of the Moquis, as Told by Outsiders," *Journal of American Folklore* I, April-June 1888. **THE SUPERNATURALS** ■ Ruth Bunzel, trans., "Zuñi Origin Myths," Washington, D.C., Smithsonian Institution Press, *Bureau of American Ethnology Report No. 47,* 1929–30. **66–69 THE BLUE LADY** ■ Cleve Hallenbeck and J. H. Williams, *Legends of the Spanish Southwest,* Glendale, Calif., Arthur H. Clark Company, 1938; Adina de Zavala, *History and Legends of the Alamo and Other Missions in and Around San Antonio,* San Antonio, Tex., privately printed, 1917. **DIOS AND WAIDE** ■ E. C. Parsons, ed., "Isleta," *Bureau of American Ethnology Report No. 47,* Washington, D.C., Smithsonian Institution Press, 1929–30. **THE MARGIL VINE** ★ Hallenbeck and Williams, *op. cit.* **CRUEL TO HIMSELF** □ *Bolton and the Spanish Borderlands* by Herbert Eugene Bolton, edited by John Francis Bannon. Copyright 1964 by the University of Oklahoma Press. **PEDRO DE URDEMALAS** ★ José Manuel Espinosa, *Spanish Folk-Tales From New Mexico,* New York, The American Folklore Society, G. E. Stechert & Co., 1937 (this excerpt translated by David Rattray). **EXORCISM BY POUNDING** ■ E. C. Parsons, *Isleta Paintings,* Washington, D.C., Smithsonian Institution Press, 1970; ○ E. C. Parsons, in *American Anthropologist,* Vol. 23, No. 2, 1921; □ E. C. Parsons, "The Priest Who Resurrects," *Bureau of American Ethnology Report No. 47,* 1929–30. **MIRACLE OF SAN FELIPE** ★ Charles F. Lummis, *A New Mexico David and Other Stories,* New York, Charles Scribner's Sons, 1891. **70–71 THE MEZCLA MAN** ★ *Tales of Old-Time Texas* by J. Frank Dobie. Copyright 1931, 1943, 1955 by J. Frank Dobie. By permission of Little, Brown & Co.

4 THE SALTWATER BANDITS

72–73 ✓ **74–75 KIDD'S DYING WORDS** □ an anonymous ballad. **GARDINER'S ISLAND GOLD** ○ Charles B. Driscoll, *Pirates Ahoy!,* New York, Farrar, Straus, 1941; Willard H. Bonner, *Pirate Laureate: Life and Legends of Captain Kidd,* New Brunswick, N.J., Rutgers University Press, 1947; Charles M. Skinner, *American Myths & Legends,* Philadelphia, J. B. Lippincott Company, 1903. **THE ASTOR FORTUNE** ✓ **SCREECHAM'S ISLAND** ○ Olive Beaupré Miller, *Heroes, Outlaws, and Funny Fellows of American Popular Tales,* New York, Doubleday, Doran & Co., 1939. **76–79 BLACKBEARD'S APPEARANCE** ○ Robert E. Lee, *Blackbeard the Pirate,* Winston-Salem, N.C., John F. Blair, 1974; Horace Beck, *Folklore and the Sea,* copyright © 1973 by The Marine Historical Association, Inc. Used by permission of Wesleyan University Press; B. A. Botkin, ed., *A Treasury of Southern Folklore,* New York, Crown Publishers, Inc., 1949; taken from *A Treasury of Southern Folklore* by B. A. Botkin. Copyright 1949 by B. A. Botkin. Copyright renewed, 1967, by Gertrude Botkin. Used by permission of Crown Publishers, Inc.; Capt. Charles Johnson, *A General History of the Pyrates,* London, 1724. **ABOARD SHIP** ■ *ibid.;* Lee, *op. cit.* **BLACKBEARD'S LAST FIGHT** ■ Lee, *op. cit.;* Johnson, *op, cit,;* **A HEADLESS SPECTER** ■ Lee, *op. cit.;* ○ Beck, *op. cit.* **ENCHANTED TREASURE** ■ Hulbert Footner, *Rivers of the Eastern Shore,* New York, Farrar & Rinehart, Inc., 1944. **THIRTEEN WIVES** ■ Lee, *op. cit.* **79** ■ Jack Beater, *True Tales of the Florida West Coast,* Fort Meyers, Fla. Jack Beater, 1959; Karl H. Grismer, *Tampa, A History of the City and the Bay Region of Florida,* St. Petersburg, St. Petersburg Printing Co., 1950; Philip Gosse, *The Pirates' Who's Who,* New York, Burt Franklin, 1924. **WALKING THE PLANK** ○ *Harper's Weekly,* 1887; Anon., *Pirate's Own Book for Boys,* 1840; Hugh F. Rankin, *The Pirates of Colonial North Carolina,* Raleigh, State Department of Archives & History, 1960. **80–81 JEAN LAFITTE** ★ George A. Pierce, "Life and Times of Lafitte," New Orleans, *De Bow's Review,* Vol. XI, New Series, Vol. IV, October, 1861; ○ J. Frank Dobie, *Coronado's Children, Tales of Lost Mines and Buried Treasures of the Southwest,* Dallas, Tex., The Southwest Press, 1930. **SATAN OUTWITTED** ■ *ibid.* **LAFITTE'S DEATH** ■ *ibid.;* ★ Pierce, *op. cit.* **LAFITTE'S TREASURE** ■ Dobie, *op. cit.* **LAFITTE'S RESTLESS GHOST** ■ Julia Beazley, "The Uneasy Ghost of Lafitte," *Legends of Texas,* edited by J. Frank Dobie, Austin, Texas Folklore Society, 1924. **82–83 THE FAIR PIRATES** ★ Johnson, *op. cit.* **84–87 A GENTLE SATANIST** ■ Charles Elms, ed., *The Pirate's Own Book,* Boston, S. Dickinson, 1859. **BRETHREN OF THE COAST** ○ Lee, *op. cit.;* A. H. Verrill, *The Real Story of the Pirate,* New York, D. Appleton Co., 1923; Lloyd Haynes Williams, *Pirates of Colonial Virginia,* Richmond, Dietz Press, 1937; Howard Pyle, *Howard Pyle's Book of Pirates,* New York, Harper & Brothers, 1921. **NASTY NED LOWE** ○ Gosse, *op. cit.;* □ Beck, *op. cit.* **THE DOOMED PALATINE** ○ *ibid.;* ★ Samuel A. Drake, *A Book of New-England Legends and Folklore,* Boston, Little, Brown & Co., 1901. **THE GOLDEN VANITY** ✓

5 THE SPIRIT OF '76

88–89 ✓ **90–91 MYTHS TO MAKE MEN FIGHT** ○ Hiller B. Zobel, *The Boston Massacre,* New York, W. W. Norton & Co., 1970; Philip Davidson, *Propaganda and the American Revolution,* Chapel Hill, N.C., University of North Carolina Press, 1941; Charles H. Metzger, "Propaganda in the American Revolution," *Mid-America,* Vol. 22, October 1940; Sidney I. Pomerantz, "Newspaper Humor in the War for Independence," *Journalism Quarterly,* Vol. 21, December 1944; Thomas Fleming, "Paying for Propaganda," *New York Times Magazine,* June 29, 1975; *New Jersey Journal,* January 3, 1782. **REVOLUTIONARY TEA** ✓ **92 PAUL REVERE'S RIDE** □ Henry Wadsworth Longfellow, *The Poetical Works of Longfellow,* Boston, Houghton Mifflin Company, 1975. **93–94 A DANGEROUS FOE** ■ Stewart H. Holbrook, *Ethan Allen,* New York. Copyright 1940 The Macmillan Company. **ETHAN THE GALLANT** ■ *ibid.* **ETHAN AND THE SNAKE** ■ *ibid.* **SHARE THE GLORY** ★ Ray Bearse, ed., *Vermont: A Guide to the Green Mountain State,* Boston, Houghton Mifflin Company, 1966. **ETHAN THE FREETHINKER** ■ Holbrook, *op. cit.* **95 TUBER DINNER** ★ Capt. Willard Glazier, *Heroes of Three Wars,* Philadelphia, Hubbard Brothers, 1880. **MARION'S MEN SING** □ *ibid.* **BLACK MINGO BRIDGE** ★ *ibid.* **96–97 BOYISH HEROISM** □ Edward S. Ellis, ed., *Beadle's Dime Tales, Traditions, and Romance of Border and Revolutionary Times,* No. 4, New York, Beadle and Co., 1863. **PUTNAM THE CAPTAIN** ★ B. A. Botkin, ed., *A Treasury of New England Folklore,* New York, Crown Publishers, Inc., 1947, Bonanza Books, 1965. **PUTNAM THE GENERAL** ★ E. R. Snow, *Legends of the New England Coast,* New York, Dodd, Mead & Co., 1957. **PRUSSIAN DISPATCH** ★ J. L. Blake (attr.), *The American Revolution, Including Also the Beauties of American History,* New York, Derby and Jackson, 1856. **98–100 POOR BOY** ★ Benjamin Franklin, *The Autobiography of Benjamin Franklin,* New Haven, Conn., Yale University Press, 1964. **HORSE SENSE** ✓ **POOR RICHARD'S ALMANAC** ✓ **A WAY WITH THE LADIES** □ Thomas Fleming, *The Man Who Dared the Lightning,* New York, William Morrow & Co., Inc., 1970. **BEN THE MAGICIAN** ■ Mason L. Weems, *The Life of Dr. Franklin,* Philadelphia, Uriah Hunt, 1829. **THE IMPERIAL GESTURE** ■ Richard Morris, *Seven Who Shaped Our Destiny,* New York, Harper & Row, 1973. **CHECKMATE!** ■ James Parton, *Life and Times of Benjamin Franklin,* Boston, Houghton Mifflin Company, 1864. **FATHER OF INVENTION** ■ *ibid.* **101 THE FOURTH OF JULY** ★ George Lippard, *The Rose of Wissahikon, or The Fourth of July, A Romance,* Philadelphia, G. B. Zieber, 1847. **102–03 CROSSING THE DELAWARE** ★ George Lippard, *The Legends of the American Revolution,* Philadelphia, T. B. Peterson & Bros., 1876. **VALLEY FORGE** ★ Samuel A. Drake, *The Watch Fires of '76,* Boston, Lothrop, Lee & Shepard, 1895; Henry Clay Watson, *Noble Deeds of Our Fathers as Told by Soldiers of the Revolution,* Boston, Lee & Shepard, 1888. **104–07 WEEMS' CHEERY TREE** ★ Mason Locke Weems, *The Life of Washington,* Philadelphia, Mathew Carey, 1800. **JUDICIOUS GEORGE** ★ *ibid.* **"HERE!"** □ Wayne Whipple, *The Story-Life of Washington,* Philadelphia, John C. Winston Co., 1911. **HERO WOMAN** ★ Lippard, *The Legends of the American Revolution, op. cit.* **NO WHITE MAN** ★ Edmund Wilson, *Apologies to the Iroquois,* New York, Farrar, Straus & Giroux, 1960. **FIRST IN WAR, FIRST IN PEACE, FIRST IN THE HEARTS OF HIS COUNTRYMEN** ○ L. Carroll Judson, *Sages and Heroes of the American Revolution,* Boston, Lee and Shepard, 1875; Marcus Cunliffe, *George Washington, Man and Monument,* Boston, Little, Brown and Company, 1958; William S. Baker, *Character Portraits of Washington,* Philadelphia, Robert M. Lindsay, 1887; Dixon Wecter, *The Hero in America, A Chronicle of Hero Worship,* New York, Irvington Publishers, 1972; Lippard, *The Legends of the American Revolution, op. cit.* **108–11 MRS. MURRAY'S WILES** ★ B. A. Botkin, ed., *New York City Folklore,* New York, Random House, Inc. Copyright © 1956 by Benjamin Botkin. Used by permission of Curtis Brown Ltd. **CROSS-EYED NANCY HART** ■ Elizabeth F. Ellet, *Women of the American Revolution,* New York, Baker and Scribner, 1846. **SALLY SAINT CLAIR**

★ O. B. Bunce, ed., *Romance of the Revolution,* New York, Bunce and Bro., 1854. **MOLLY AT MONMOUTH** ■ From the book *Heroines of '76* by Elizabeth Anticaglia, published by Walker & Company, Inc., New York © 1975 by Elizabeth Anticaglia. **"ROBERT" SAMSON** ■ Ellet, *op. cit.;* ★ Anticaglia, *op. cit.* **POWDER FOR FORT HENRY** ★ Zane Grey, *Betty Zane,* New York, Grosset & Dunlap, Inc., Tempo Books, 1971. **112 JOSHUA BARNEY** □ Reprinted from *Folklore and the Sea* by Horace Beck, by permission of Wesleyan University Press. Copyright © 1973 by The Marine Historical Association, Inc. **JOHN PAUL JONES** □ *ibid.* **113 MOTTOES OF THE REVOLUTION** ○ William A. Williams, *The Contours of American History,* Cleveland, World Publishing Co., 1961; Bruce Bohle, *Home Book of American Quotations,* New York, Dodd, Mead & Company, 1972; Louis B. Wright, *American Heritage History of the Thirteen Colonies,* New York, American Heritage, 1967; *Reader's Digest Encyclopedia of American History,* Pleasantville, N.Y., The Reader's Digest Association, Inc., 1975. **114 YANKEE DOODLE DANDY** ■ Tristram Potter Coffin, *Uncertain Glory, Folklore and the American Revolution,* Detroit, Folklore Associates, 1971. © 1971 Gale Research Company.

6 THE LEGENDARY BACKWOODSMAN

116-17 ✓ **118-20 BOONE BRAGS** ★ Taken from *A Treasury of Southern Folklore* by B. A. Botkin. Copyright 1949 by B. A. Botkin. Copyright renewed, 1977, by Gertrude Botkin. Used by permission of Crown Publishers, Inc. **BOONE KILLS A SHE-BEAR** ★ Timothy Flint, *Biographical Memoir of Daniel Boone,* edited by James K. Folsom, New Haven, Yale University Press, 1967. **DANIEL MEETS HIS WIFE** ★ Botkin, *op. cit.* **BOONE'S BOYS** ■ Dan Beard, *Hardly a Man Is Now Alive,* New York, Doubleday, Doran, 1939; William D. Murray, *History of the Boy Scouts of America,* New York, Boy Scouts of America, 1937. **KNIFE-SWALLOWING TRICK** ★ Botkin, *op. cit.* **HERO'S DEATH** ★ C. Wilder, *Life and Adventures of Colonel Daniel Boone,* Brooklyn, 1823. **121 NATURE'S NOBLEMAN** ✓ including Arthur K. Moore, *The Frontier Mind,* New York, McGraw-Hill Book Company, 1957; Henry Nash Smith, *Virgin Land, The American West as Symbol and Myth,* Cambridge, Mass., Harvard University Press, 1950; □ James Fenimore Cooper, *The Deerslayer,* New York, Signet Classics, 1963. **122-25 SURE CURE FOR TOOTHACHE** ★ *Davy Crockett's Almanack, 1840,* **TO NAIL A COONSKIN** ★ Botkin, *op. cit.* **THE COONSKIN TRICK** ■ *ibid.* **DAVY SPEECHIFIES** ★ Taken from *A Treasury of American Folklore* by B. A. Botkin. Copyright 1944, 1972 by B. A. Botkin. Used by permission of Crown Publishers, Inc. **REMEDIA AMORIS** ■ *ibid.* **SUNRISE IN MY POCKET** ■ *Davy Crockett's Almanack, 1837.* **THE WAGONER'S LAD** ✓ **INFANT CROCKETT EATING HIS BREAKFAST** ★ *Davy Crockett's Almanack, 1848.* **OLD KAINTUCK** ★ *Davy Crockett's Almanack, 1843.* **DAVY'S UNCLE** ★ *ibid.* **AN APOLOGY** ★ *ibid.* **126-28 THE APPLE MAN** ○ Robert Price, *Johnny Appleseed, Man and Myth,* Bloomington, Indiana University Press, 1954; *Harper's New Monthly Magazine,* Vol. XLIII, No. CCLVIII, November 1871; Maria Leach, *Rainbow Book of American Folk Tales,* Cleveland, World Publishing Co., 1958; Tristram Potter Coffin and Hennig Cohen, eds., *Folklore From the Working Folk of America,* Garden City, N.Y., Anchor Press/Doubleday, 1973. **CLOTHES UNMAKE THE MAN** ○ *ibid.; Harper's, op. cit.* **REVERENCE FOR LIFE** ○ Lewis Bromfield, *Pleasant Valley,* New York, Harper & Bros., 1938; Coffin and Cohen, *op. cit.; Harper's, op. cit.;* Price, *op. cit.* **THE MEDICINE MAN** ○ *Harper's, op. cit.;* Coffin and Cohen, *op. cit.;* Price, *op. cit.* **A VOICE IN THE WILDERNESS** ○ *Harper's, op. cit.;* Coffin and Cohen, *op. cit.;* Price, *op. cit.* **FRONTIER PAUL REVERE** ○ Iantha Castlio, "A Folk Tale of Johnny Appleseed," *Missouri Historical Review,* Vol. XIX, No. 4, July 1925; Dixon Wecter, *The Hero in America,* New York, Charles Scribner's Sons, 1941. **128-29 IN THE LONG RUN** ★ Ben C. Clough, *The American Imagination at Work,* New York, Alfred A. Knopf, Inc., 1947. **LADIES AUXILIARY** ■ Charles Burr Todd, *In Olde Connecticut,* New York, Grafton Press, 1906., as quoted in B. A. Botkin, ed., *A Treasury of New England Folklore,* New York, Bonanza Books, rev. ed., 1947. Copyright 1947, 1975 by B. A. Botkin. Used by permission of Crown Publishers, Inc. **"MORE LIKE A NATION . . ."** ○ *Reader's Digest Encyclopedia of American History,* Pleasantville, N.Y., The Reader's Digest Association, Inc., 1975; Bruce Bohle, *Home Book of American Quotations,* New York, Dodd, Mead & Company, 1972; Mitford M. Mathews, ed., *A Dictionary of Americanisms,* University of Chicago, 1966. **LONG BARNEY STRIKES** □ Reprinted from *Folklore and the Sea* by Horace Beck, by permission of Wesleyan University Press. Copyright © 1973 by the Marine Historical Association, Inc. **OLD IRONSIDES** ★ *The Poetical Works of Oliver Wendell Holmes,* Boston, Houghton Mifflin Company, 1975. **130-31 DOLLEY UNDER FIRE** ★ Katharine Anthony, *Dolly Madison,* New York, Doubleday & Co., Inc., 1949. ○ Andrew Tully, *When They Burned the White House,* New York, Simon & Schuster, 1961; Samuel E. Morison and Henry S. Commager, *Growth of the American Republic,* New York, Oxford University Press, 1962. **SHARPSHOOTING** ■ John William Ward, *Andrew Jackson, Symbol of An Age,* New York, Oxford University Press, 1955. **THE COMMON TOUCH** ■ James Parton, *Life of Andrew Jackson,* New York, Mason Brothers, 1860. **LOCAL BOY MAKES GOOD** ★ *WPA Guide to Tennessee,* New York, Hastings House, 1976. **FRONTIER JUSTICE** ★ Parton, *op. cit.* **132-33 FIERCE SHAWNEES** ■ "The Celestial Sisters" in Henry Schoolcraft, *Indian Legends,* edited by Mentor C. Williams, East Lansing, Michigan State University Press, 1956. **THE NOBLE PIONEER AND THE IGNOBLE SAVAGE** ○ Arthur K. Moore, *op. cit.;* Frederick W. Turner III, ed., *The Portable North American Indian Reader,* New York, The Viking Press, 1973. **134-35 THE BELL WITCH** ★ Arthur Palmer Hudson and Pete Kyle McCarter, *Journal of American Folk-Lore,* Vol. XLVII, No. CLXXXIII, January-March 1934.

7 RIVERBOAT ROARERS

136-37 ✓ **138-39 CLASS WILL OUT** ■ *Body, Boots and Britches* by Harold W. Thompson. Copyright 1939 by Harold W. Thompson. Copyright © renewed 1967 by Dr. Marian Thompson. Reprinted by permission of J. B. Lippincott Company. **WORK INCENTIVE** ■ Marvin Rapp, *Canal Water & Whiskey,* New York, Twayne Publishers, Inc., 1965. **SAINT PATRICK OF ERIE** ★ Lionel D. Wyld, *Low Bridge! Folklore and the Erie Canal,* Syracuse University Press, 1962. **THE ERIE'S PAUL BUNYAN** ★ *ibid.* **THE GIANT SQUASH** ★ *ibid.* **BRAWLING CANAWLERS** ★ Thompson, *op. cit.* **THE E-RI-E CANAL** ✓ **140-41 THE VOYAGEURS: EPIC LIVES** ○ Everett Dick, *Vanguards of the Frontier,* New York, D. Appleton-Century Company, Inc., 1941; Walter O. Meara, *The Savage Country,* Boston, Houghton Mifflin Company, 1960; Grace Lee Nute, *The Voyageur,* New York, D. Appleton-Century Company, Inc., 1931; B. A. Botkin, ed., *A Treasury of Mississippi River Folklore,* New York, Crown Publishers, 1955. **142-43 A RUDE AWAKENING** ○ Walter Blair and Franklin J. Meine, *Mike Fink, King of the Mississippi Boatmen,* New York, Henry Holt & Company, Inc., 1933. **A TALL TESTIMONIAL** ○ Botkin, *op. cit.* **HAIR OF THE BUFFALO** ★ Charles Edward Russell, *A-Rafting on the Mississip',* New York, D. Appleton-Century Company, Inc., 1928. **SEEKING JUSTICE** ★ T. B. Thorpe, *The Hive of the Beehunter, A Repository of Sketches,* New York, D. Appleton and Company, 1854. **144-46 OLD BANG-ALL** ★ Walter Blair and Franklin J. Meine, *Half Horse Half Alligator, The Growth of the Mike Fink Legend,* University of Chicago, 1956. **MIKE'S BRAG** ○ *ibid.* **FRESH PROVISIONS** ○ *ibid.* **AT ODDS WITH THE LAW** □ *ibid.* **FINK MEETS CROCKETT** ○ *ibid.;* Botkin, *op. cit.* **WOMEN IN MIKE'S LIFE** ✓ **147-48 COLONEL UNPLUG** □ Frank Donovan, *River Boats of America,* New York, Thomas Y. Crowell Co., 1966. **THE FAMILY FORTUNE** ■ Otto A. Rothert, *Outlaws of Cave-in-Rock,* Cleveland, Arthur H. Clark Co., 1923. **CLOSING THE CIRCLE** ■ Botkin, *op. cit.* **ANNIE CHRISTMAS** ★ Lyle Saxon, Edward Dreyer, and Robert Tallant, comps., *Gumbo Ya-Ya.* Copyright 1945 Houghton Mifflin Company. Copyright © renewed 1973 by Louisiana State Library. Reprinted by permission of Houghton Mifflin Company. **149 SOMNAMBULISTIC PILOT** ★ Mark Twain, *Life on the Mississippi,* Boston, James R. Osgood, 1883. **150-52 CARRIED AWAY** ★ Herbert and Edward Quick, *Mississippi Steamboatin',* New York, Henry Holt & Company, 1926. **SNAGGED** ★ Charles E. Brown, *Old Man River,* Madison, Wisconsin Folklore Society, 1940. **WOODING UP** ■ V. L. O. Chittick, ed., *Ring Tailed Roarers,* Caldwell, Idaho, Caxton Printers, 1941. **153 SHOWBOAT'S COMIN'!** ○ Walter Havighurst, *Voices on the River, The Story of the Mississippi Waterways,* New York, copyright 1964 The Macmillan Company; Donovan, *op. cit.* **154-55 OUTWITTING THE MATE** □ Brown, *op. cit.* **ROUSTABOUT HOLLER** ★ John A. and Alan Lomax, *Our Singing Country,* New York, The Macmillan Company, 1941 (collected, adapted, and arranged by John A. Lomax and Alan Lomax, © 1941 and renewed 1969, Ludlow Music, Inc., New York, TRO-INC., used by permission); caption: "I Love The Steamboat Man" □ Langston Hughes and Arna Bontemps, eds., *Book of Negro Folklore,* New York, Dodd, Mead & Company, 1958. **NO MORE CARDS** ★ Ben Lucien Burman, *Big River To Cross,* New York, The John Day Company, 1940. **HER-GIRLS** □ *ibid.* **CHATTANOOGA'S GHOST** □ *ibid.* **156-57 THE GAMBLERS' GAMBLER** ■ Herbert Asbury, *Sucker's Progress, An Informal History of Gambling in America,* New York, Dodd, Mead and Company, 1938. **THE CAPTAINS REMINISCE** ★ Ben Lucien Burman, *Look Down That Winding River,* New York, Taplinger Publishing Company, Inc., 1973. **THE TABLES TURNED** ★ Botkin, *op. cit.* **OCCUPATIONAL HAZARD** ★ *ibid.* **WITH HIS BETS ON** □ Lura Robinson, *It's an Old New Orleans Custom,* New York, Vanguard Press, Inc., 1948.

8 ARKANSAS TO THE ALAMO

158-59 ✓ including caption: ○ Alan Lomax, *The Folk Songs of North America in the English Language,* Garden City, N.Y., Doubleday & Company, Inc., 1960. **160-62 COLONEL WHETSTONE** ★ Charles F. M. Noland, *Pete Whetstone of Devil's Fork: Letters to the "Spirit of the Times,"* edited by Ted R. Worley and Eugene A. Nolte, Van Buren, Ark., The Press-Argus, 1957. **HELL, NO!** ★ James R. Masterson, *Tall Tales of Arkansas,* Boston, Chapman & Grimes, 1943. **ARKANSAS TRAVELER** ○ Taken from *A Treasury of American Folklore* by B. A. Botkin. Copyright 1944, 1972 by B. A. Botkin. Used by permission of Crown Publishers, Inc. **THE BELLED BUZZARD** ★ Ira W. Ford, *Traditional Music of America,* New York, E. P. Dutton & Co., Inc., 1940. **ARKANSAS TALL TALK** □ *American Heritage New Pictorial Encyclopedic Guide to the United States,* New York, American Heritage, 1965; ★ Marion Hughes, *Three Years in Arkansaw,* Chicago, M. A. Donohue & Co., 1905; □ Vance Randolph, *We Always Lie to Strangers,* New York, Columbia University Press, 1951. **RAZORBACK HOGS** ✓ including *WPA Guide to Arkansas,* New York, Hastings House, 1941. **163 OZARK PRACTICES** ○ Vance Randolph, *Ozark Magic and Folklore,* New York, Dover Publications, Inc., 1964; Otto Ernest Rayburn, *Ozark Country,* New York, Duell, Sloan & Pearce, 1941; Otto Rayburn, ed., *Ozark Guide Yearbook, 1963,* Eureka Springs, Ark., G. H. Pipes, 1963. **164-65 THE BIG BEAR OF ARKANSAS** ★ T. B. Thorpe, *The Hive of the Beehunter, A Repository of Sketches,* New York, D. Appleton and Company, 1854. **166 THE SANDBAR DUEL** ★ J. Frank Dobie, *Tales of Old-Time Texas,* Boston, Little, Brown & Co., 1955. **THE "ARKANSAS TOOTHPICK"** ★ Arthur K. Moore, *The Frontier Mind,* New York, McGraw-Hill Book Company, Inc., 1963; Dobie, *op. cit.* **BOWIE TO THE RESCUE** ★ *ibid.* **167 A YANKEE BESTED** ★ Botkin, *op. cit.* **JUST DESSERTS** ★ Samuel A. Hammet, *Piney Woods Tavern: Sam Slick in Texas,* Philadelphia, T. B. Peterson & Brothers, 1858. **168-69 BIGFOOT ARMOR** ★ Dobie, *op. cit.* **THE VISION** ★ Frederick R. Bechdolt, *Tales of the Old-Timers,* New York, Century Company, 1924 (by permission of Hawthorn Books, Inc.). **170-71 MAGIC DOGS** ★ Alice Marriott and Carol K. Rachlin, *Plains Indian Mythology,* New York, Thomas Y. Crowell Company, Inc., 1975. **172-73 DEATH IN THE OPEN AIR** ○ Lon Tinkle, "13 Days to Glory," *The New York Times,* Sept. 21, 1975; Dixon Wecter, *The Hero in America, A Chronicle of Hero-Worship,* New York, Irvington Publishers, 1972; *The Crockett Almanack for 1837;* David Nevin, *The Texans,* New York, Time-Life Books, 1975; Lon Tinkle, *Thirteen Days to Glory,* New York, New American Library, 1967. **DEATH IN BED** ○ Tinkle, *Thirteen, op. cit.* **VICTORY OR DEATH** ○ Walter Lord, "Myths & Realities of the Alamo," *American West, The Magazine of the Western History Association,* Vol. V, No. 3, May 1968; Tinkle, *Thirteen, op. cit.;* Anna J. Hardwicke Pennybacker, *History of Texas for Schools,* Tyler, Tex., Percy V. Pennybacker, 1888; J. Frank Dobie, *In the Shadow of History,* Hatboro, Pa., Folklore Associates Inc., 1966.

9 TRAILBLAZERS AND TRAPPERS

174-75 ✓ **176-77 LEWIS, CLARK, AND SACAJAWEA** ★ A. C. Laut, *Pathfinders of the West,* New York, The Macmillan Company, 1904. **WELSH INDIANS** ✓ including Samuel Eliot Morison, *The European Discovery of America: The Northern Voyages, A.D. 500-1600,* New York, Oxford University Press, 1971; Ellen Pugh, *Brave His Soul,* New York, Dodd, Mead & Company, 1970. **178-80 BRIDGER'S REPORT** □ Hiram Martin Chittenden,

The Yellowstone National Park, Norman, University of Oklahoma, 1964. **THE GLASS MOUNTAIN** □ *ibid.* **THE CRYSTAL MOUNTAIN** ★ B. A. Botkin, ed., *A Treasury of Western Folklore,* New York, Crown Publishers, Inc., rev. ed., 1975. **THE OLD SCOUT'S ECHO** □ Levette J. Davidson and Forrester Blake, eds., *Rocky Mountain Tales,* Norman, University of Oklahoma, 1947. **A LIKELY STORY** □ Chittenden, *op. cit.* **THE PETRIFIED MOUNTAIN** □ *ibid.* **PETRIFIED EVERYTHING** □ Walter Blair, *Tall Tale America, A Legendary History of Our Humorous Heroes,* New York, Coward, McCann & Geoghegan, 1944. **MEEK'S MOUNT HOOD** □ Jay Monaghan, ed., *The Book of the American West,* New York, Julian Messner, Inc., 1963. **180–84 COLTER'S INDIAN RUN** ★ Thomas Froncek, ed., *Voices From the Wilderness,* New York, McGraw-Hill Book Company, 1974. **GLASS AND A GRIZZLY** ★ Eric Thane, *High Border Country,* New York, Duell, Sloan & Pearce, 1942, by permission of Hawthorn Books, Inc. **THE MASTER TRAPPER** □ Davidson and Blake, *op. cit.;* Monaghan, *op. cit.* **JEDEDIAH SMITH** ■ Charles L. Camp, ed., "James Clyman, His Diaries and Reminiscences," *California Historical Society Quarterly,* Vol. 4, 1925. **KIT CARSON FIGHTS** □ W. F. Cody, *Story of the Wild West and Camp-Fire Chats by Buffalo Bill,* Freeport, N.Y., Books for Libraries Press, 1970. **TRAPPER TALK** ✓ **DUEL IN THE DUST** □ *ibid.* **185 BEAVER BANTER** ★ B. A. Botkin, ed., *A Treasury of Western Folklore,* New York, Crown Publishers, Inc., 1951. Copyright 1951 by B. A. Botkin. **AN APPRECIATIVE BEAR** □ Virginia Cole Trenholm, and Maurine Carley, *Wyoming Pageant,* Caspar, Wyo., Bailey School Supply, 1950. **186–87 A LIFE IN SKINS** ★ Froncek, *op. cit.* **188–89 FROM THE BLACKFEET** ★ Clark Wissler and D. C. Duvall, *Anthropological Papers of the American Museum of Natural History,* ii, 53, New York, 1908; ★ George Bird Grinnell, *Blackfoot Lodge Tales: The Story of a Prairie People,* New York, Charles Scribner's Sons, 1892.

10 THE GREAT OVERLAND ADVENTURE

190–91 ✓ including Julia Cooley Altrocchi, *The Old California Trail,* Caldwell, Idaho, Caxton Printers, 1945; Walter Havighurst, *Land of Promise, The Story of the Northwest Territory,* New York, The Macmillan Company, 1946. **192–95 WIND WAGONS** ○ Everett Dick, *Vanguards of the Frontier,* New York, D. Appleton-Century Co., 1941. **PARTING OF THE WAYS** ■ *ibid.* **NEVER STOP** ■ *ibid.* **FLAYED ALIVE** ★ Julia Cooley Altrocchi, "Folklore of the Old California Trail," *California Folklore Quarterly,* January 1944. **SCARIN' OFF INJUNS** ■ Robert H. Lowie, "Minor Ceremonies of the Crow Indians," *Anthropological Papers of the American Museum of Natural History,* Vol. XXI, Part V, 1924; ○ Jan Harold Brunvand, *The Study of American Folklore,* New York, W. W. Norton and Co., Inc., 1968; □ Altrocchi, *The Old California Trail, op. cit.* **MASSACRE** ○ George R. Stewart, *The California Trail,* New York, McGraw-Hill Book Company, Inc., 1962. **A FALSE ALARM** □ Burl Ives, *Tales of America,* Cleveland, The World Publishing Company, 1954. **SWEET BETSY FROM PIKE** ✓ **196–97 COLUMBIA'S GORGE** ★ Robert O. Case, *Empire Builders,* New York, Doubleday & Co., Inc., 1947, reprinted by permission of Mrs. Vivian Case; caption: □ Arthur Guiterman, "The Oregon Trail," *I Sing the Pioneer,* New York, E. P. Dutton & Co., Inc., 1926. Copyright renewed 1954 by Mrs. Vida Lindo Guiterman. **198–99 A BALMY CLIME** ★ Edwin Bryant, *What I Saw in California,* New York, D. Appleton & Company, 1849. **BUFFALO STAMPEDE** □ Charles M. Russell, *Trails Plowed Under,* Garden City, N.Y., Doubleday, Page & Co., 1927. **BURIED BRANDY** ★ Altrocchi, *The Old California Trail, op. cit.* **BRAINS DEFEAT BRAWN** ★ "Recollections of B. F. Bonney," *Quarterly of the Oregon Historical Society,* XXIV, 1 (March 1923). **200–03 HEAVEN-SENT GULLS** ★ B. H. Roberts, *A Comprehensive History of the Church of Jesus Christ of Latter-Day Saints,* Salt Lake City, Desert Book Company, 1930; Priddy Meeks, "Journal of Priddy Meeks," *Utah Historical Quarterly,* X, 1942. **A NEPHITE VISIT** ★ Hector Lee, *The Three Nephites,* Albuquerque, University of New Mexico Press, 1949. **PLURAL WIVES** □ Austin and Alta Fife, *Saints of Sage & Saddle, Folklore Among the Mormons,* Bloomington, Indiana University Press, 1956. **J. GOLDEN KIMBALL** □ *ibid.;* Hector Lee, "Anecdotes of J. Golden Kimball," in Richard Dorson, *Buying the Wind,* University of Chicago Press, 1964. **PATERFAMILIAS** □ Fife, *op. cit.;* Thomas E. Cheney, ed., *Mormon Songs From the Rocky Mountains,* Austin, American Folklore Society, University of Texas Press, 1968. **204–06 THE TREE HUSBAND** ■ *Journal of American Folklore,* Vol. XIII, July-September 1900. **EATING BABIES** ★ Stith Thompson, ed., *Tales of the North American Indians,* Bloomington, Indiana University Press, A Midland Book, 1966. **COUNTING COUP** ○ Thomas E. Mails, *The Mystic Warriors of the Plains,* New York, Doubleday & Co., Inc., 1972; George Bird Grinnell, *Blackfoot Lodge Tales, The Story of a Prairie People,* New York, Charles Scribner's Sons, 1892. **THE GHOST WRESTLER** ★ J. O. Dorsey, "A Study of Siouan Cults," in J. W. Powell, *Eleventh Annual Report of the Bureau of Ethnology to the Secretary of the Smithsonian Institution, 1889–'90,* Washington, D.C., Government Printing Office, 1894. **DEER WOMAN** ★ Alice Marriott and Carol K. Rachlin, *American Indian Mythology,* New York, Thomas Y. Crowell Company, Inc., 1968. **SIGN LANGUAGE** ○ *Bureau of American Indian Ethnology Bulletin 30.* **207–09 FEBOLD FEBOLDSON** ★ Walter Blair, *Tall Tale America, A Legendary History of Our Humorous Heroes,* New York, Coward, McCann & Geoghegan, Inc., 1944. **FEBOLD'S CORNBALLS** ★ O. B. Miller, *Heroes, Outlaws and Funny Fellows,* Garden City, N.Y., Doubleday, Doran Co., Inc., 1939. **WIND, COLD, HEAT, CHANGE** ★ Roger Welsch, *Shingling the Fog and Other Plains Lies,* Chicago, Sage Books, Swallow Press, 1972. **DROUGHT AND CRITTERS** ★ *ibid.* **CIVILIZATION** ★ *ibid.* **HARD TIMES** ★ *ibid.* **210–11 UTOPIAN PIONEERS** ○ Edward Dahlberg, *alms for oblivion,* Minneapolis, University of Minnesota Press, 1964; V. F. Calverton, *Where Angels Dared To Tread,* Indianapolis, The Bobbs-Merrill Company, 1941; Mark Holloway, *Heavens on Earth,* 2nd. ed., New York, Dover Publications, Inc., 1966; William Alfred Hinds, *American Communities, Brief Sketches of Economy, Zoar, Bethel, Aurora, Amana, Icaria, The Shakers, Oneida, Wallingford, and The Brotherhood of the New Life,* Oneida, N.Y., Office of the American Socialist, 1878. Copyright © 1961 Corinth Books Inc., The American Experience Series. Reprinted 1971, Gloucester, Mass., Peter Smith, by permission of Corinth Books, Inc.; Stewart H. Holbrook, *Dreamers of the American Dream,* Garden City, N.Y., Doubleday & Company, Inc., 1957; Edward D. Andrews, *The People Called Shakers,* New York, Dover Publications, Inc., 1953; Frederick W. Turner III, *The Portable North American Indian Reader,* New York, The Viking Press, 1974; Jonathan Beecher, "L'Archibras de Fourier, Un MS Censuré," in *La Brèche, Action Surréaliste,* December 1964 (this excerpt translated by David Rattray).

11 GOLD. GOLD! GOLD!

212–13 ✓ including E. Douglas Branch, *Westward: The Romance of the American Frontier,* New York, Cooper Square Publishers, Inc., 1969; Andrew F. Rolle, *California, A History,* New York, Thomas Y. Crowell Company, Inc., 1963. **214–15 GOLD IN THEM THAR . . .** ★ Walter Burns, *Robin Hood of El Dorado,* New York, Coward McCann, Inc., 1932; Charles Peters, *Autobiography of Charles Peters,* Sacramento, The LaGrave Company, 1915, as quoted in B. A. Botkin, ed., *A Treasury of Western Folklore,* New York, Crown Publishers, Inc., rev. ed., 1975; William W. Johnson, *The Forty-Niners,* New York, Time-Life Books, 1974; G. Ezra and Beatrice J. Dane, *Ghost Town,* New York, Alfred A. Knopf, Inc., 1941. **TO THE DEATH** □ Robert W. Ritchie, *The Hell-roarin' Forty-Niners,* New York, J. H. Sears & Company, 1928, by permission of Kingsport Press. **A WHIZZER, OR TRICK** ★ *ibid.* **ULTIMATE STAKES** ★ C. B. Glasscock, *Gold in Them Hills,* Indianapolis, The Bobbs-Merrill Company, 1932. Copyright © renewed 1959 by Mrs. Marion T. Glasscock. **216–19 A TOAD STORY** ★ Taken from *A Treasury of American Folklore* by B. A. Botkin. Copyright, 1944, 1972 by B. A. Botkin. Used by permission of Crown Publishers, Inc. **THE LUCK** ★ Bret Harte, "The Luck of Roaring Camp," *The Overland Monthly,* August 1868. **THE DYING CALIFORNIAN** ✓ **CAMP WOMEN** ✓ including Joseph Henry Jackson, *Anybody's Gold: The Story of California's Mining Towns,* New York, D. Appleton-Century Co., 1941. **220–22 ROSITA** ★ Burns, *op. cit.* **JOAQUIN'S REVENGE** ★ *ibid.* **SUTHERLAND'S SON** ★ *ibid.* **ROBIN HOOD** ★ *ibid.* **REWARD** ★ *ibid.* **JOAQUIN'S DEATH** ★ *ibid.* **JOAQUIN'S GHOST** ★ *ibid.* **223–26 HAPPY FEET** ★ Todd Webb, *Gold Strikes and Ghost Towns,* Garden City, N.Y., Doubleday & Co., Inc., 1961. **BLOOD WILL TELL** ★ Botkin, *A Treasury of Western Folklore, op. cit.* **COLUMBIA'S BIG LOU** ★ Dane, *op. cit.* **WIDEMOUTHED MAYHEM** ★ Ritchie, *op. cit.* **IT ALL PANNED OUT** ○ Marian Hamilton, "California Gold-Rush English," *American Speech,* August 1932; H. L. Mencken, *The American Language,* New York, Alfred A. Knopf, Inc., 4th ed., 1936. **227–28 PEGLEG'S LOST GOLD** ★ Rufus Rockwell Wilson, *Out of the West,* New York, The Press of the Pioneers, 1936. **LOST DUTCHMAN MINE** ★ Thomas Penfield, *Dig Here!,* San Antonio, The Naylor Company, rev. ed., 1966; Oren Arnold, *Ghost Gold,* San Antonio, The Naylor Company, 1954. **"COUSIN JACK" LORE** ○ Johnson, *op. cit.;* Wayland D. Hand, "California Miners' Folklore: Below Ground," *California Folklore Quarterly,* April 1942; Tristram P. Coffin and Hennig Cohen, eds., *Folklore From the Working Folk of America,* New York, Doubleday & Co., Inc., 1973. **229 "DADDY'S HOME"** ★ Robert Ormond Case, *The Empire Builders,* Garden City, N.Y., Doubleday & Company, Inc., 1947.

12 BLOW THE MAN DOWN

230–31 ✓ including Charles Edward Brown, *Old Stormalong Yarns,* Madison, Wis., Charles Edward Brown, 1933; Frank Shay, *Here's Audacity!,* Freeport, N.Y., Books for Libraries Press, 1967. **232–35 INSIDE THE WHALE** ★ Jeremiah Digges (pseud. of Josef Berger), *Cape Cod Pilot,* Provincetown, Mass., 1937. **NANTUCKET SLEIGH RIDE** ★ William F. Macy and Roland B. Hussey, *Nantucket Scrap Basket,* 2nd ed., Boston, Houghton Mifflin Company, 1930. **THE RECKONING** ★ Joseph Allen, *Tales and Trails of Martha's Vineyard,* Boston, Little, Brown & Company, 1938. **GULP!** ○ Edward Rowe Snow, *Mysteries and Adventures Along the Atlantic Coast,* New York, Dodd, Mead & Company, 1948; *Natural History Magazine,* June, Sept. 1947. **WRECK OF THE ESSEX** ○ A. C. Spectorsky, *Book of the Sea,* New York, Appleton-Century-Crofts, Inc., 1954; Edouard A. Stackpole, *The Sea-Hunters, The New England Whalemen During Two Centuries 1635–1835,* Philadelphia, J. B. Lippincott Company, 1953; Edward Rowe Snow, *Great Sea Rescues,* New York, Dodd, Mead & Company, 1958. **HIDDEN MEANINGS** ○ Horace Beck, *Folklore and the Sea,* Middletown, Conn., Wesleyan University Press, copyright © 1973 by the Marine Historical Association, Inc.; Leland P. Lovette, *Naval Customs, Traditions and Usage,* Annapolis, United States Naval Institute, 1934; Hans Jürgen Hansen, *Art and the Seafarer: A Historical Survey of the Arts and Crafts of Sailors and Shipwrights,* translated by James and Inge Moore, New York, The Viking Press, 1968. **236–37 SALEM'S SPECTER SHIP** ★ Frank Shay, *A Sailor's Treasury.* Copyright 1951 by Frank Shay and Edward A. Wilson. By permission of W. W. Norton & Company, Inc. **THE LUCY JACKSON** ★ Edward Rowe Snow, *Fantastic Folklore and Fact,* New York, Dodd, Mead & Company, 1968. **238–43 THE WRECK OF THE ASIA** ★ Edward Rowe Snow, *Strange Tales From Nova Scotia to Cape Hatteras,* New York, Dodd, Mead & Company, 1949. **FIRE!** ■ F. S. Basset, *Sea Phantoms, or Legends and Superstitions of the Sea,* 1885; Jeannette Edwards Rattray, *Perils of the Port of New York, Maritime Disasters From Sandy Hook to Execution Rocks,* New York, Dodd, Mead & Company, 1973. **IN THE RIGGING** ★ Snow, *Great Sea Rescues, op. cit.* **FROGNOSTICATION** ○ Claudia de Lys, *A Treasury of American Superstitions,* New York, Philosophical Library, 1948; Shay, *op. cit.;* Digges, *op. cit.;* Beck, *op. cit.* **OLD STORMALONG** ★ Brown, *op. cit.* **ANOTHER HAND** ○ William M. Doerflinger, *Songs of the Sailor and Lumberman,* New York, The Macmillan Company, 1972; Beck, *op. cit.;* Olin Downes and Elie Siegmeister, *A Treasury of American Song,* New York, Alfred A. Knopf, Inc., 2nd ed., 1943; Frank Shay, *American Sea Songs and Chanteys,* New York, W. W. Norton & Company, Inc., 1969. **244–47 TALLEST OF THEM ALL** ■ Eloise Worth and Sue Hildreth, "Two Salt Sea Tall Tales," *New York Folklore Quarterly, No. 2,* 1946. **KELPIES** ○ Beck, *op. cit.;* Ad de Vries, *Dictionary of Symbols and Imagery,* 2nd ed., New York, North-Holland Publishing Co., 1976. **SIRENS** ○ Charles M. Skinner, *Myths and Legends of Our Own Land,* Philadelphia, J. B. Lippincott and Company, 1896. **MERFOLK** ○ De Vries, *op. cit.* **SEA SERPENT OF 1817** ■ Elizabeth Reynard, *The Narrow Land,* Boston, The Houghton Mifflin Company, 1934; *In the Wake of the Sea-Serpents* by Bernard Heuvelmans, translated by Richard Garnett. Copyright Bernard Heuvelmans. Reprinted by permission of Rupert Hart-Davis Ltd/Granada Publishing Ltd. and Farrar, Straus & Giroux, Inc., 1965. **BELOW THE BELT** □ Shay, *A Sailor's Treasury, op. cit.* **SEACURITY** ○ Jerry Foster, "Varieties of Sea Lore," *Western Folklore,* Vol. 28, 1969; Lovette, *op. cit.;* Clifton Johnson, *Highways and Byways of New England,* New

York, The Macmillan Company, 1916; Thomas Gibbons, *Tales That Were Told: Passages From the Journals of a Seafarer,* New York, The Chicago Press, 1892; Alton H. Blackington, *Yankee Yarns,* New York, Dodd, Mead & Company, 1954. **248–51** THE CRIMPS' TRADE ★ Alan Villiers, *The Way of a Ship.* Copyright © 1970 Alan Villiers. Reprinted by permission of Charles Scribner's Sons and Hodder & Stoughton Ltd. SHANGHAI KELLY □ Felix Riesenberg, Jr., *Golden Gate, The Story of San Francisco Harbor,* New York, Alfred A. Knopf, Inc., 1940. MISS PIGGOTT'S TRAP □ Herbert Asbury, *The Barbary Coast, An Informal History of the San Francisco Underworld,* New York, Alfred A. Knopf, 1933. CHLOROFORM KATE ★ Richard H. Dillon, *Shanghaiing Days,* New York, Coward, McCann & Geoghegan, Inc., 1961. MEN OF STRAW ★ Asbury, *op. cit.* GLAZIER SAILOR ★ Dillon, *op. cit.* SMUGGLERS' WILES ■ Beck, *op. cit.* **252–55** RESOURCEFUL ★ Macy and Hussey, *op. cit.* OVERWEENING □ Horace Beck in conversation. GREEDY ★ Beck, *op. cit.* SAILOR TALK ○ *ibid.;* Lovette, *op. cit.;* Shay, *A Sailor's Treasury, op. cit.;* Everett Joshua Edwards and Jeannette Rattray, *Whale Off! The Story of American Shore Whaling,* New York, Frederick Stokes, 1932; Joanna Carver Colcord, *Sea Language Comes Ashore,* Cambridge, Md., Cornell Maritime Press, 1944. INDECISIVE ★ Lincoln Colcord, *The Game of Life and Death, Stories of the Sea,* New York, The Macmillan Company, 1914. DEVOTED ★ Digges, *op. cit.*

13 WHEN COTTON WAS KING

256–57 ✓ including Franklin L. Riley, ed., *Publications of the Mississippi Historical Society,* Vol. III, Oxford, Miss., 1900. **258–59** THE COTTON GIN ★ Lucian Lamar Knight, *Georgia's Landmarks, Memorials, and Legends,* Atlanta, Byrd Printing Company, 1913, as taken from *A Treasury of Southern Folklore* by B. A. Botkin. Copyright 1949 by B. A. Botkin. Copyright renewed, 1977, by Gertrude Botkin. Used by permission of Crown Publishers. Inc. G.P.C. ★ A. W. Eddins, "Anecdote From the Brazos Bottoms," in J. Frank Dobie and Mody C. Boatright, *Straight Texas,* Austin, Texas Folklore Society, Publication No. 13, 1937. COTTON MAGIC ○ Mary D. Lake, "Superstitions About Cotton," *Southwestern Folklore,* Texas Folklore Society, Publication No. 9; John M. Kingsbury, *Poisonous Plants of the United States and Canada,* Englewood Cliffs, N.J., Prentice-Hall, Inc., 1964; J. F. Dastur, *Medicinal Plants of India and Pakistan,* Bombay, D. B. Taraporevala Sons & Co., 1962. **260–62** THE TAR-BABY STORY ★ Joel Chandler Harris, *The Tar Baby and Other Rhymes of Uncle Remus,* New York, D. Appleton and Company, 1904. TOO SHARP FOR MR. FOX ★ Joel Chandler Harris, *Nights With Uncle Remus, Myths and Legends of the Old Plantation,* Boston, James R. Osgood Company, 1883. THE DELUGE □ Joel Chandler Harris, *Uncle Remus, His Songs and His Sayings: The Folk-lore of the Old Plantation,* New York, D. Appleton and Company, 1881. **263** THE TURTLE □ John C. Branner, *How and Why Stories,* New York, Henry Holt & Company, 1921. HARD WORK? TWO REASONS ★ *Mules and Men* by Zora Neale Hurston. Copyright © 1935 by Zora Neale Hurston. Harper & Row, Publishers Perennial Library edition. By permission of Harper & Row, Publishers, Inc. **264–65** BEHOLD THE RIB ★ *ibid.* GREEN PASTURES ★ J. Mason Brewer, *American Negro Folklore,* New York, Quadrangle Books, 1968. STEAL AWAY ✓ **266–67** JACK-O'-LANTERN ★ Newbell Niles Puckett, *Folk Beliefs of the Southern Negro,* Chapel Hill, The University of North Carolina Press, 1926. SEEING GHOSTS ■ Writers Program, Work Projects Administration, *South Carolina Folk Tales: Stories of Animals and Supernatural Beings,* Columbia, The University of South Carolina Press, 1941. PLAT EYE ■ *ibid.* **268–69** MARDI GRAS ✓ including Robert Tallant, *Mardi Gras,* New York, Doubleday & Company, Inc., 1948; Leonard V. Huber, "Mardi Gras: The Golden Age," *American Heritage,* February 1965. **270–71** THE GILDED MIRROR ★ Carl Carmer, *Stars Fell on Alabama,* New York, Farrar & Rinehart, 1934. MISTRESS OF PECKATONE ○ Mrs. Agnes Cooke (private communication); ■ Paul Wilstach, *Tidewater Virginia,* Indianapolis, The Bobbs-Merrill Company, 1929. THE GHOST BRIDE ★ *South Carolina Folk Tales, op. cit.* **272–73** OLD JOHN AND THE CANE ★ John Q. Anderson, "Old John and the Master," *Southern Folklore Quarterly,* September 1961. DIVVYING UP SOULS ★ J. Mason Brewer, "Juneteenth," in Mody C. Boatright, Wilson M. Hudson, and Allen Maxwell, eds., *Texas Folk and Folklore,* Dallas, Southern Methodist University Press, 1954, by permission of the Texas Folklore Society. SWAPPING DREAMS □ J. Mason Brewer, "Juneteenth," in J. Frank Dobie, ed., *Tone the Bell Easy,* Austin, Texas Folklore Society, No. X, 1932. PRAY BUT DON'T TRUST ★ Brewer, *op. cit.,* in Boatright, Hudson, and Maxwell, *op. cit.* TELLIN' FORTUNES ★ Hurston, *op. cit.* **274–77** MRS. WALKER ★ William Still, *The Underground Rail Road,* Philadelphia, Porter & Coates, 1872. A SLY CITY-SLICKER SLAVE ★ Henry D. Spalding, ed., *Encyclopedia of Black Folklore and Humor,* Middle Village, N.Y., 1972. POSITION AVAILABLE ★ *ibid.* TO BE A SLAVE ★ Manda Walker in B. A. Botkin, ed., *Lay My Burden Down, A Folk History of Slavery,* The University of Chicago Press, 1945. PEGLEG JOE ■ H. B. Parks, "Follow the Drinking Gourd," in J. Frank Dobie, ed., *Follow de Drinkin' Gou'd,* Austin, Texas Folklore Society, 1928. WILLIAM "BOX" JONES ★ Still, *op. cit.* **278** UNCLE TOM'S CABIN ✓ including Edmund Wilson, *Patriotic Gore: Studies in the Literature of the American Civil War,* New York, Oxford University Press, Inc., 1962; Jay B. Hubbell, *The South in American Literature 1607–1900,* Durham, N.C., Duke University Press, 1954.

14 A HOUSE DIVIDED CANNOT STAND

280–81 ✓ **282–86** THE VORACIOUS READER ★ Horatio Alger, Jr., *Abraham Lincoln, The Backwoods Boy; Or How A Young Rail-Splitter Became President,* New York, John R. Anderson & Henry S. Allen, 1883. HORSE TRADING ○ Col. Alexander K. McClure, *Lincoln's Yarns and Stories,* Chicago, The John C. Winston Company, 1901; ○ Carl Sandburg, *Abraham Lincoln, The Prairie Years,* New York, Harcourt, Brace & Co., Inc., 1926. FATHER ABRAHAM ★ Albert H. Griffith, *The Heart of Abraham Lincoln, Man of Kindness and Mercy,* Madison, Lincoln Fellowship of Wisconsin, 1948, as quoted in B. A. Botkin, ed., *A Civil War Treasury of Tales, Legends and Folklore,* New York, Random House, Inc., 1960. ASLEEP AT HIS POST ★ M. J. Gage, *The Soldiers' and Sailors' Half-Dime Tales, of the Late Rebellion,* New York, Soldiers' and Sailors' Publishing Co., 1868. LINKUM'S CHARIOT ★ Maj. Abner R. Small, *The Road to Richmond: The Civil War Memoirs of Major Abner R. Small of the Sixteenth Maine Volunteers,* edited by Harold Adams Small, Berkeley, University of California Press, 1939, copyright © 1967 by Harold A. Small. INTIMATIONS OF DEATH ○ Julie Forsyth Batchelor and Claudia de Lys, *Superstitious? Here's Why,* New York, Harcourt, Brace & World, Inc., 1954; ★ Ward Hill Lamon, *Recollections of Abraham Lincoln, 1847–1865,* edited by Dorothy Lamon, Chicago, A. C. McClurg & Co., 1895; ★ Lloyd Lewis, *Myths After Lincoln,* New York, Harcourt, Brace & Co., 1929. WISDOM IN WIT □ Emanuel Hertz, *Lincoln Talks, A Biography in Anecdote,* New York, The Viking Press, 1939; ★ Sandburg, *op. cit.;* McClure, *op. cit.;* □ Constance Rourke, *American Humor,* New York, Harcourt, Brace and Company, 1959. **287–88** THE SPOTTED HAND ★ Frank Moore, ed., *The Civil War in Song and Story,* New York, 1865. A SON'S PAINFUL DUTY ■ Cyrus Townsend Brady, *The Southerners, A Story of the Civil War,* New York, Charles Scribner's Sons, 1903. THE YOUNGEST RECRUIT ★ Frazar Kirkland, *The Pictorial Book of Anecdotes and Incidents of the War of the Rebellion,* Toledo, Ohio, W. E. Bliss & Co., 1873. DIXIE ✓ including Garnett Laidlaw Eskew, *The Pageant of the Packets, A Book of American Steamboating,* New York, Henry Holt and Company, Inc., 1929. **289–91** THE MOCKINGBIRD ★ Ambrose Bierce, *Can Such Things Be?,* New York, The Cassell Publishing Co., 1893. SAVED ★ Samuel Scoville, Jr., *Brave Deeds of Union Soldiers,* Philadelphia, George W. Jacobs & Company, 1915. FRIENDS IN DEATH ★ Moore, *op. cit.* SEPARATE TABLE ★ George B. Herbert, *Anecdotes of the Rebellion,* Springfield, Ohio, Mast, Crowell & Kirkpatrick, 1894. **292–93** IRON SIDES, IRON HEARTS ★ R. W. Daly, ed., *Aboard the USS Monitor: 1862, The Letters of Acting Paymaster William Frederick Keeler, U.S. Navy to His Wife, Anna,* Annapolis, United States Naval Institute, 1966. WAR WORDS ○ H. L. Mencken, *The American Language, Supplement I,* New York, Alfred A. Knopf, Inc., 1962; *ibid., Supplement II,* Alfred A. Knopf, Inc., 1975. **294–97** A HERO'S BIRTH ○ Burke Davis, *Our Incredible Civil War,* New York, Holt, Rinehart and Winston, Inc., 1960; B. A. Botkin and William G. Tyrrell, "Upstate, Downstate," *New York Folklore Quarterly,* 1961. LAST OF THE CAVALIERS ○ Wayne Whipple, *The Heart of Lee,* Philadelphia, George W. Jacobs & Co., 1918. IMPRESSIVE ★ Burke Davis, *Gray Fox: Robert E. Lee and the Civil War,* New York, Rinehart & Company, 1956. WITH A WOUNDED YANK □ Charles A. Shriner, comp., *Wit, Wisdom, & Foibles of the Great,* New York, Funk & Wagnalls Co., 1918; A. L. Long and Marcus J. Wright, *Memoirs of Robert E. Lee,* New York, J. M. Stoddart, 1887. "STONEWALL" ○ Bruce Bohle, *Home Book of American Quotations,* New York, Dodd, Mead & Company, 1967; Maj. H. Kyd Douglas, "Stonewall Jackson and His Men," *The Annals of the War,* Philadelphia, The Times Publishing Company, 1879, as quoted in B. A. Botkin, ed., *A Civil War Treasury of Tales, Legends and Folklore,* New York, Random House, Inc., 1960. SHOOT THE BRAVE ONES ★ Robert Stiles, *Four Years Under Marse Robert,* New York, The Neale Publishing Co., 1910, as quoted in Botkin, *ibid.* "NEVER USE IT" ○ Shriner, *op. cit.;* John Esten Cooke, *Wearing of the Gray,* Bloomington, Indiana University Press, 1959; Douglas Southall Freeman, *R. E. Lee,* Vol II, New York, Charles Scribner's Sons, 1962. FLOWER OF CAVALIERS ★ Cooke, *op. cit.* BREVETTED BY JEB ■ Shriner, *op. cit.* SOUTHERN CHIVALRY ★ Anne Sinkler Fishburne, *Belvidere, A Plantation Memory,* Columbia, University of South Carolina Press, 1950; ○ Marcus Cunliffe, *Soldiers & Civilians, The Martial Spirit in America 1775–1865,* Boston, Little, Brown and Company, 1968; Esther J. Crooks and Ruth W. Crooks, *The Ring Tournament in the United States,* Richmond, Va., Garrett and Massie, 1936. **298–99** THE AVENGING DEAD ★ A. M. Wier, *Old Times in Georgia,* Atlanta, 1903, as quoted in W. H. Hall, *Reflections of the Civil War in Southern Humor,* Gainesville, University of Florida Press, 1962. THE FATEFUL HOG ■ Vance Randolph, *Ozark Magic & Folklore,* New York, Dover Publications, 1964. LA BELLE REBELLE ○ Douglas, *op. cit.;* Harnett T. Kane, *Spies for the Blue and Gray,* New York, Doubleday & Company, Inc., 1954. A PASS TO HEAVEN □ Douglas, as quoted in Botkin, *op. cit.* **300–01** THE GREAT CHASE ■ Scoville, *op. cit.* THE DRUMMER BOY ★ Moore, *op. cit.* THE BELLWETHER ○ Kirkland, *op. cit.* **302–03** STUBBORN LYS ★ Shriner, *op. cit.* BRAND NAME ★ Loyd Dunning, ed., *Mr. Lincoln's Funnybone,* New York, Howard Soskin, 1942. SHERMAN'S IMPOSTER ★ Gage, *op. cit.;* ○ Shriner, *op. cit.* SHERIDAN'S RIDE ★ Scoville, *op. cit.* THE SYMBOLIC SWORD ○ U. S. Grant, *Personal Memoirs of U. S. Grant,* New York, AMS Press, 1894.

15 THE WILD, WILD WEST

304–05 ✓ **306–07** THE TARANTULA'S LESSON ★ John James Callison, *Bill Jones of Paradise Valley, Oklahoma: His Life and Adventures for Over Forty Years in the Great Southwest,* Chicago, M. A. Donohue & Co., 1914. THE CHAMPION TALKER ★ Ramon F. Adams, *The Old-Time Cowhand,* New York, The Macmillan Company, 1961. Used with permission of The Macmillan Company. © Ramon F. Adams 1948, 1949, 1951, 1954, 1961. THE SWEETEST MUSIC ★ J. Frank Dobie, "The Writer and His Region," *Southwest Review,* Spring 1950. RUNNING THE STAMPEDE ★ N. Howard (Jack) Thorp, in collaboration with Neil M. Clark, *Pardner of the Wind,* Caldwell, Ida., Caxton Printers, 1945. **308–09** THE WESTERN NOVEL ✓ including ★ Owen Wister, *The Virginian,* New York, copyright 1911 The Macmillan Company. Used by permission of The Macmillan Company; ★ Andy Adams, *The Log of a Cowboy,* Boston, Houghton Mifflin Company, 1903. **310–11** PECOS BILL ★ Mody C. Boatright, *Tall Tales From Texas,* Dallas, The Southwest Press, 1934. By permission of Southern Methodist University Press. THE MADSTONE ★ Paul Patterson, "Hydraphoby, Mebbe," *Pecos Tales,* Austin, The Encino Press, copyright 1967 Texas Folklore Society. THE OLD CHISHOLM TRAIL ✓ HORSE SENSE ★ J. B. Polley, "Dock Burris Was Well Known," in J. Marvin Hunter, ed., *The Trail Drivers of Texas,* Nashville, Cokesbury Press, 1925. Reprinted from Stan Hoig, *The Humor of the American Cowboy,* Lincoln, University of Nebraska Press, 1958. **312–13** THE PEACOCK'S REVENGE ★ Walter Noble Burns, *Tombstone, An Iliad of the Southwest,* Garden City, N.Y., Garden City Publishing Co., copyright 1929 Doubleday, Doran & Company. SUNDAY AT THE SALOON ★ Floyd Benjamin Streeter, *The Kaw: The Heart of a Nation,* New York, Farrar & Rinehart, Inc., 1941. TEETHING TOY ★ Stanley Vestal, *Queen of Cowtowns: Dodge City,* New York, Harper & Brothers, 1952, copyright 1952 Walter Stanley Campbell. **314** ASPEN TRAP ★ William Lightfoot Visscher, *A Thrilling and Truthful History of the Pony Express,* Chicago, The Charles T. Powner Co., 1946, copyright 1908 E. L. Lomax. CODY OUTWITS ROBBERS

★ Col. Henry Inman and Col. William F. Cody, *The Great Salt Lake Trail,* New York, The Macmillan Company, 1898, as quoted in B. A. Botkin, ed., *A Treasury of Western Folklore,* New York, Crown Publishers, Inc., rev. ed., 1975. **315–19** HECKLER EXTRAORDINAIRE □ Harry Sinclair Drago, *Outlaws on Horseback,* New York, Dodd, Mead & Company, 1964. "YOUR FRIEND, JESSE JAMES" ★ Homer Croy, *Jesse James Was My Neighbor,* New York, Duell, Sloan & Pearce, Inc., 1949. By permission of Hawthorn Books, Inc. MAGNETIC AMAZON ✓ including ★ S. W. Harman, *Belle Starr, The Female Desperado,* Houston, Frontier Press of Texas, 1954. BEST-LOVED BANDIT ✓ FATE AT ROUND ROCK ★ Anon., *Life and Adventures of Sam Bass, The Notorious Union Pacific and Texas Train Robber,* Dallas, Dallas Commercial Steam Print, copyright by W. L. Hall & Company, 1878. HANDS UP! ★ F. E. Sutton and A. B. MacDonald, *Hands Up! Stories of the Six-Gun Fighters of the Old Wild West,* Indianapolis, The Bobbs-Merrill Co., Inc., 1927. POOR SAM ✓ including Wayne Gard, *Sam Bass,* Boston, The Houghton Mifflin Company, copyright 1936 by Wayne Gard. BILLY THE KID ✓ A GOOD JOKE □ Walter Noble Burns, *Saga of Billy the Kid,* Garden City, N.Y., Doubleday, Page & Co., 1926. HELL. HELL. HELL. □ J. Frank Dobie, *A Vaquero of the Brush Country,* Dallas, The Southwest Press, 1929. By permission of Southern Methodist University Press; ○ Kent Steckmesser, "Joaquin Murrieta & Billy the Kid," *Western Folklore,* April 1962. **320–23** THE BEST DRESSED ★ Sutton and MacDonald, *op. cit.* HOW BAT GOT HIS NAME ★ Clair Huffaker, "The Three Lives of Bat Masterson," in Rafer Brent, ed. *Great Western Heroes,* New York, Bartholomew House, 1957. BATTLE AT O K CORRAL ★ W. B. (Bat) Masterson, *Famous Gunfighters of the Western Frontier,* Ruidoso, N.M., Frontier Book Company, 1959, as taken from *Human Life Magazine,* 1907; ○ Joseph G. Rosa, *The Gunfighter, Man or Myth?* Norman, University of Oklahoma Press, 1969. WORDS ON THE RANGE ✓ GATES OF HELL ✓ LAW WEST OF THE PECOS ✓ ROY AND THE CHINESE ★ J. Frank Dobie, ed., *Straight Texas,* Austin, Texas Folk-Lore Society, Publication No. XIII, 1937; ○ Hoig, *op. cit.;* Federal Writers' Project, *Idaho Lore,* edited by Vardis Fisher, Caldwell, Ida., The Caxton Printers, Ltd., 1939. BOTH SIDES OF THE LAW ✓ CORPSE PAYS $40 FINE ★ Lanier Bartlett, ed., *On the Old West Coast, Being Further Reminiscences of a Ranger, Major Horace Bell,* New York, William Morrow & Co., Inc., 1930. PRINCE OF HANGMEN ○ Sutton and MacDonald, *op. cit.;* Croy, *op. cit.;* Drago, *op. cit.* "HISTORIC ASS" □ Drago, *ibid.* **324–25** ROUTED BY RED MEN ■ Vestal, *op. cit.* THE PEACEMAKER ★ Adele B. Looscan, *The Woman of the Western Star: A Legend of the Rangers,* Austin, Texas Folk-Lore Society, 1924. THE CAPTIVE ★ J. Frank Dobie, *On the Open Range,* Dallas, The Southwest Press, 1951. **326–27** THUNDERBIRDS ★ J. O. Dorsey, "A Study of Siouan Cults," in J. W. Powell, *Eleventh Annual Report of the Bureau of Ethnology to the Secretary of the Smithsonian Institution 1889–'90,* Washington, Government Printing Office, 1894. BUFFALO MONSTERS ■ *ibid.* TWO FACES ★ *ibid.* **328–29** AN INCREDIBLE RESCUE ★ W. F. Beyer and O. F. Keydel, eds., *Deeds of Valor,* Detroit, The Perrien-Keydel Co., 1907. THE FOUR-LEGGED CANNON ★ John Phoenix, "Mule Artillery," *Encore,* Vol. VII, No. 38, April 1945, as quoted in Botkin, *op. cit.* DEADLY STUNT RIDERS ★ Beyer and Keydel, *op. cit.* CUSTER'S LAST STAND ✓ THE DAWN APPEARS, BEHOLD! ✓ **330** RANGE WAR ★ John R. Craddock, "Legend of Stampede Mesa," Texas Folklore Society Publication, 1924. **331** BLOOD AND THUNDER ○ Taken from *A Treasury of American Folklore* by B. A. Botkin. Copyright 1944, 1972 by B. A. Botkin. Used by permission of Crown Publishers, Inc.; Dixon Wecter, *The Hero in America, A Chronicle of Hero-Worship,* New York, Irvington Pubs., 1972.

16 THE MELTING POT

332–33 ✓ **334–35** THE MYTH OF THE MELTING POT ○ J. C. Furnas, *The Americans, A Social History of the United States,* New York, G. P. Putnam's Sons, 1971; *The Distorted Image, Stereotype and Caricature in American Popular Graphics 1850–1922,* based on the work of John J. and Selma Appel, New York, Anti-Defamation League of B'nai B'rith, no date; U.S. Department of Commerce, Bureau of the Census, *Historical Statistics of the United States, Colonial Times to 1970,* Parts 1 and 2, Bicentennial Edition, 1975 (93rd Congress, 1st Session, House Document No. 93-78); William Van Til, *Prejudiced—How Do People Get That Way?,* The One Nation Library, New York, Anti-Defamation League of B'nai B'rith, rev. ed., 1970; Mary Cable, et al., *American Manners & Morals, A Picture History of How We Behaved and Misbehaved,* New York, American Heritage Publishing Co., Inc., 1969. OUTSIDE LOOKING IN ✓ including Horatio Alger, Jr., *Luke Walton, Or, The Chicago Newsboy,* 1889; Thomas H. Johnson, *The Oxford Companion to American History,* New York, Oxford University Press, Inc., 1966; Bernard A. Weisberger, *The American Heritage History of the American People,* New York, American Heritage Publishing Co., Inc., 1971. **336–37** MOSE THE BOWERY B'HOY ★ Alvin F. Harlow, *Old Bowery Days, The Chronicles of a Famous Street,* New York, Appleton-Century-Crofts, 1931. IRISH BULLS ■ John McCarthy, *The Home Book of Irish Humor,* New York, Dodd, Mead & Company, 1968. IRISH AND POLITICS ★ *ibid.* **338–39** NO FOREIGNERS SERVED HERE ★ Konrad Bercovici, *Around the World in New York,* New York, The Century Co., 1924. By permission of Hawthorn Books, Inc. WORDS TO THE WISE ■ Rhoda Hoff, *America's Immigrants, Adventures in Eyewitness History,* New York, Henry Z. Walck, Inc., 1967. DU, DU LIEGST MIR IM HERZEN ✓ **340** THE GHOST MAN ■ Jon Lee, "Some Chinese Customs and Beliefs in California," *California Folklore Quarterly,* Vol. 2, 1943. **341** SAWING IS BELIEVING ■ Walter Havighurst, *Upper Mississippi, A Wilderness Saga,* New York, Rinehart & Co., Inc., 1944. BACHELOR AND BEAR ■ *ibid.* ECHOES ★ John in *Capper's Weekly,* Feb. 26, 1949. **342** THE HATFIELD-MCCOY FEUD ○ Virgil Carrington Jones, *The Hatfields and the McCoys,* Chapel Hill, The University of North Carolina Press, 1948; Truda Williams McCoy, *The McCoys: Their Story,* edited by Leonard W. Roberts, Pikeville, Ky., Preservation Council of Pike County, 1976. **343** JACKASS AND DONKEY ★ Ernest S. Mathews, "Merry Greek Tales From Buffalo," *New York Folklore Quarterly,* Vol. V, No. 4, Winter 1949. FISHERMEN'S SUPERSTITIONS ■ Robert Augustus Georges, "Greek-American Folk Beliefs and Narratives: Survivals and Living Tradition," unpublished doctor of philosophy dissertation in the folklore program, Indiana University, June 1964. SAINTS ALIVE ■ Dorothy D. Lee, "Greek Tales of Priest and Priestwife," *Journal of American Folklore,* April–June 1947. **344–45** FROM EASTERN EUROPE □ Frank Zaitz, "O nasih ljudeh v severni Minnesoti," *Ameriski Druzinski Koledar,* Vol. 21, 1935, translated by Joseph D. Dwyer as "The Slovenes in Northern Minnesota" (unpublished). ROAMING GYPSIES □ Rena C. Gropper, *Gypsies in the City, Culture Patterns and Survival,* Princeton, N.J., The Darwin Press, 1975. **346–47** ARRIVAL IN AMERICA ★ Sholom Aleichem, *Adventures of Mottel, the Cantor's Son,* New York, Henry Schuman, 1953. ELLIS ISLAND ★ *ibid.* IMPRESSIONS ★ *ibid.* GHETTO HUMOR □ Harry Golden, *The Golden Book of Jewish Humor,* New York, G. P. Putnam's Sons, 1972; Harvey Mindess, *The Chosen People?,* Los Angeles, Nash Publishing Corporation, 1972; Gerry Blumenfeld, *Tales From the Bagellancers, Everyman's Book of Jewish Humor,* Cleveland, The World Publishing Company, 1967. **348–49** NO MORE INSULTS ★ Michael A. Musmanno, *The Story of the Italians in America,* New York, Doubleday & Company, Inc., 1965. PAVED WITH GOLD □ William Carlson Smith, *Americans in the Making,* New York, D. Appleton-Century Company, 1939. GIFT OF THE MAGA ■ Phyllis H. Williams, *South Italian Folkways in Europe and America, A Handbook for Social Workers, Visiting Nurses, School Teachers, and Physicians,* New Haven, Conn., Yale University Press, 1938, for the Institute of Human Relations; reprinted with an introduction by Francesco Cordasco, New York, Russell & Russell, 1969. COMING HOME ■ Jo Pagano, *Golden Wedding,* New York, Random House, Inc., 1943. HE WHO LAUGHS LAST □ Herb Caen, *Baghdad: 1951,* Garden City, N.Y., Doubleday & Company, Inc., 1950. **350–51** KID LORE ○ Iona and Peter Opie, *The Lore and Language of Schoolchildren,* Oxford at the Clarendon Press, London, Oxford University Press, 1959; Mary and Herbert Knapp, *One Potato, Two Potato . . . The Secret Education of American Children,* New York, W. W. Norton & Company, Inc., 1976; Duncan Emrich, *Folklore on the American Land,* Boston, Little, Brown and Company, © 1972 by Duncan Emrich; Stewart Culin, "Street Games of Boys in Brooklyn, N.Y.," *Journal of American Folk-Lore,* 1891; William Wells Newell, ed., *Games and Songs of American Children,* New York, Harper & Brothers, 2nd ed., 1903; Duncan Emrich, comp., *The Nonsense Book of Riddles, Rhymes, Tongue Twisters, Puzzles and Jokes From American Folklore,* New York, Four Winds Press, 1970; Duncan Emrich, comp., *An Almanac of American Folklore: The Hodgepodge Book, Containing All Manner of Curious, Interesting, and Out-of-the-Way Information Drawn From American Folklore, and Not To Be Found Anywhere Else in the World,* New York, Four Winds Press, 1972.

17 THE BREADWINNERS

352–53 ✓ **354–55** THE HARBINGER ■ George Korson, *Minstrels of the Mine Patch, Songs and Stories of the Anthracite Industry,* Hatboro, Pa., Folklore Associates, Inc., 1964, copyright by George Korson, 1938. By permission of Gale Research Company. THE DEATH-WATCH TICK ★ *ibid.* THE POINTING FINGER ★ Ruth Ann Musick, *Ballads, Folk Songs & Folk Tales From West Virginia,* Morgantown, West Virginia University Library, 1960. REVENGE OF THE SIRENS □ George Korson, *Coal Dust on the Fiddle, Songs and Stories of the Bituminous Industry,* Hatboro, Pa., Folklore Associates, Inc., 1965, copyright by George Korson, 1943. By permission of Gale Research Company. THE BRAVE DRIVER BOY ★ Korson, *Minstrels, op. cit.* **356–59** PAUL BUNYAN ○ W. B. Laughead, *The Marvelous Exploits of Paul Bunyan,* Minneapolis, The Red River Lumber Co., 3rd ed., 1924; Daniel G. Hoffman, *Paul Bunyan, Last of the Frontier Demigods,* Philadelphia, Temple University, 1952. GEORGE KNOX ■ Roger E. Mitchell, "George Knox: From Man to Legend," *Northeast Folklore,* No. 11, 1969. THE GORBY ★ Edward D. Ives, "The Man Who Plucked the Gorbey: A Maine Woods Legend," reproduced by permission of the American Folklore Society from the *Journal of American Folklore,* Vol. 74(291), No. 4, 1961. OLA VARMLANNING □ Roy Swanson, "A Swedish Immigrant Folk Figure: Ola Varmlanning," *Minnesota History,* Vol. 29, No. 2, June 1948. OLD GUS BAILEY ★ Horace P. Beck, *The Folklore of Maine,* Philadelphia, J. B. Lippincott Company, 1957. SKILLFUL PASTIMES ○ J. W. Clark, "Lumberjack Lingo," *American Speech,* Vol. VII, October 1931; Alan Lomax, *The Folk Songs of North America in the English Language,* Garden City, N.Y., Doubleday & Company, Inc., 1960; Tristram Potter Coffin and Hennig Cohen, eds., *Folklore From the Working Folk of America,* Garden City, N.Y., Anchor Press/Doubleday, 1973. **360–62** THE HINCKLEY FIRE ★ Elton T. Brown, *A History of the Great Minnesota Forest Fires,* St. Paul, Brown Bros., 1894, as quoted in B. A. Botkin and Alvin F. Harlow, eds., *A Treasury of Railroad Folklore,* New York, Crown Publishers, Inc., 1953. JOE BALDWIN'S GHOST ★ *Railroadiana,* Atlantic Coast Line (no date), as quoted in Botkin and Harlow, *ibid.* CASEY JONES □ Words by T. Lawrence Seibert, music by Eddie Newton. Copyright MCMIX by Newton & Seibert. Copyright renewed MCMXXVI by Charles E. Seibert. Copyright renewed MCMXXXVI by Dorothy Elizabeth Newton. Copyrights assigned to Shapiro, Bernstein & Co. Inc. Copyright MCMXXXVII by Shapiro, Bernstein & Co. Inc., New York. KATE SHELLEY ■ "Kate's Own Account," *The Conductor and Brakeman,* Vol. 73, June 1956; J. A. Swisher, in *The Palimpsest,* edited by John Ely Briggs, Vol. VI, No. 2, February 1925, as quoted in Botkin and Harlow, *op. cit.* Copyright 1925 by the State Historical Society of Iowa. JOHN HENRY ○ Louis W. Chappell, *John Henry, A Folk-Lore Study,* Jena, Germany, Frommansche Verlag, Walter Biedermann, 1933; Roark Bradford, *John Henry,* New York, Harper & Brothers, 1931; Jeffery M. Miller, in *The Laborer,* February 1973. BOXED BANDITS □ Alvin F. Harlow, *Old Waybills, The Romance of the Express Companies,* New York, D. Appleton-Century Co., 1934. By permission of Hawthorn Books. **363** MOONSHINERS ■ Eliot Wigginton, ed., *The Foxfire Book,* Garden City, N.Y., Anchor Books/Doubleday, 1971. Copyright by Southern Highlands Literary Fund, Inc.; Bonnie Ball, *The Melungeons (Their Origin and Kin),* 2nd ed., 1970, copyright 1969 by Bonnie S. Ball; Esther Kellner, *Moonshine, Its History and Folklore,* Indianapolis, The Bobbs-Merrill Company, 1971; ○ B. C. Forbes, *Little Bits About Big Men,* New York, B. C. Forbes Publishing Co., no date; Anon., *After the Moonshiners, By One of the Raiders,* Wheeling, W.V., Frew & Campbell, 1881; Isaac Stapleton, *Moonshiners in Arkansas,* Independence, Mo., Walter F. Lackey, 1948. **364–65** A CURSE ON THEIR HEADS ★ Korson, *Minstrels, op. cit.* HANDPRINT IN CELL 17 ■ Rosemary Scanlon, "The Handprint: The Biography of a Pennsylvania Legend," *Keystone Folklore Quarterly,* Summer 1971; Korson, *Minstrels, op. cit.;* Joseph M. Scott, Warden, Carbon County Prison, Jim Thorpe, Pa. (private communication). STAMP OF VIOLENCE ★ "Grace Jackson, Eskdale, W.V.," in *On Dark* and Bloody Ground, An Oral History of the U.M.W.A. in Central Appalachia 1920–1935, Project Director, Anne Lawrence, Charleston, W.V., *The Miner's Voice,* 1973. **"I WOBBLY WOBBLY"** ○ Stewart Holbrook, "Wobbly Talk," *American Mercury,* January 1926. **366–68 PROFESSOR BELL** □ Thomas A. Watson, *The Birth and Babyhood of the Telephone, An Address to the Telephone Pioneers of America* (Chicago), October 17, 1913, American Telephone and Telegraph Co. **WIZARD OF MENLO PARK** ○ Orison Swett Marden, *How They Succeeded, Life Stories of Successful Men Told by Themselves,* Boston, Lothrop Publishing Company, 1901; Henry Ford with Samuel Crowther, *Edison as I Know Him,* New York, Cosmopolitan Book Corporation, 1930; *Those Inventive Americans,* Washington, D.C., The National Geographic Society, 1971. **FORD: THE GRAND WIZARD** ■ Marshall Fishwick, *The Hero, American Style,* Washington, D.C., Public Affairs Press, 1954; □ William C. Richards, *The Last Billionaire, Henry Ford,* New York, Charles Scribner's Sons, 1948. **THE WRIGHTS** ○ Sherwood Harris, *The First To Fly, Aviation's Pioneer Days,* New York, Simon & Schuster, Inc., 1970; Fred C. Kelly, *The Wright Brothers,* New York, Ballantine Books, 1950. **369 JOE JACKASS** ★ Hyman Richman, "The Saga of Joe Magarac," *New York Folklore Quarterly,* 1953. **OLD INTO NEW** ★ Mary Heaton Vorse, *Men and Steel,* New York, Boni & Liveright, 1920. **REAL STEEL LORE** ★ Richman, *op. cit.* **370–71 GIB MORGAN'S FIGHT** ★ Mody C. Boatright, *Folklore of the Oil Industry,* Dallas, Southern Methodist University Press, 1963. **GIB'S WONDERFUL SNAKE** ★ *ibid.* **WHICKLES** ★ Harry Botsford, "Oilmen," in George Korson, ed., *Pennsylvania Songs and Legends,* Baltimore, The Johns Hopkins Press, 1949. **ON THE WATER WAGON** ■ Boatright, *op. cit.* **372–73 NO CHARITY** ■ Charles Foster, *Bertha, The Sewing Machine Girl, or, Death at the Wheel,* Chicago, Sherman Producers Play Company, 1871. **WHITE SLAVERY** ★ Isaac Metzker, *A Bintel Brief,* Garden City, N.Y., Doubleday & Company, Inc., 1971. **TEACHING BY THE RULES** □ Nancy Zerfoss, "Schoolmarm to School Ms," *Changing Education,* Summer 1974. **TURNING THE TABLES** ■ Hyde Partnow, Mss. of the Federal Writers Project of the Works Progress Administration in New York City, 1939, as quoted in B. A. Botkin, ed., *Sidewalks of America,* Indianapolis, The Bobbs-Merrill Company, Inc., 1954. **HERRING AND ONIONS** ★ Anzia Yezierska, *Red Ribbon on a White Horse,* New York, Charles Scribner's Sons, 1950. **374–75 WITCH OF WALL STREET** ★ Joseph J. Thorndike, *The Very Rich, A History of Wealth,* New York, American Heritage, 1976. **DIAMOND JIM'S APPETITE** ★ Parker Morell, *Diamond Jim, The Life and Times of James Buchanan Brady,* New York, Simon & Schuster, Inc., 1934. **MRS. ASTOR'S BALL** ★ Elizabeth Wharton Decies, "King Lehr" and the Gilded Age, Philadelphia, J. B. Lippincott Company, 1935. **POOR EXCUSE** □ James D. McCabe, Jr., *Great Fortunes, and How They Were Made,* Cincinnati, E. Hannaford & Co., 1871.

18 THE SKY'S THE LIMIT

376–77 ✔ **378–79 THE DUDE AND THE COWBOYS** □ Henry Pringle, *Theodore Roosevelt,* New York, Harcourt, Brace & Company, 1932. **RAZZLE-DAZZLE REFORMER** ★ Francis E. Leupp, *The Man Roosevelt, A Portrait Sketch,* New York, D. Appleton and Company, 1904. **SAN JUAN HILL** □ Hermann Hagedorn, *The Boys' Life of Theodore Roosevelt,* New York, Harper & Brothers, 1918; ○ Tim Taylor, *The Book of Presidents,* New York, Arno Press, 1972; □ Charles Morris, *Battling for the Right, The Life-Story of Theodore Roosevelt,* copyright 1910 by W. E. Scull. **THE STRENUOUS PRESIDENT** □ Noel F. Busch, *The Story of Theodore Roosevelt and His*

Influence on Our Times, New York, Reynal & Co., 1963. **"GIVE 'EM HELL" HARRY** □ Eldorous L. Dayton, *Give 'Em Hell Harry, An Informal Biography of the Terrible Tempered Mr. T.,* New York, The Devin-Adair Company, New York, 1956; ■ Samuel Gallu, *Give 'Em Hell Harry,* New York, The Viking Press, Inc., 1975; *Oregon Statesman* (Salem, Ore.); □ Alfred Steinberg, *The Man From Missouri: The Life and Times of Harry S. Truman,* New York, G. P. Putnam's Sons, Inc., 1962. **380–81 "THE LOST BATTALION"** ■ Arch Whitehouse, *Heroes and Legends of World War I,* Garden City, N.Y., Doubleday & Company, Inc., 1964. **382–84 SPEAKEASIES** □ John Kobler, *Ardent Spirits, The Rise and Fall of Prohibition,* New York, G. P. Putnam's Sons, 1973; ○ H. L. Mencken, *The American Language, Supplement One, An Inquiry Into the Development of English in the United States,* New York, Alfred A. Knopf, 1962. Copyright 1945 by Alfred A. Knopf, Inc. **THE "JAZZ AGE"** ○ Ralph J. Gleason, *Celebrating the Duke and Louis, Bessie, Bird, Carmen, Miles, Dizzy and Other Heroes,* A Delta Book, New York, Dell Publishing Co., Inc., 1975. Copyright 1975 by the Estate of Ralph J. Gleason, Jean R. Gleason, Executrix; LeRoi Jones, *Blues People, Negro Music in White America,* New York, William Morrow & Co., Inc., 1963. **BULLET BARONS** ○ Evan Esar, *The Humor of Humor,* New York, Horizon Press, 1952; Walter Noble Burns, *The One-Way Ride, The Red Trail of Chicago Gangland From Prohibition to Jake Lingle,* Garden City, N.Y., Doubleday, Doran & Company, Inc., 1931. **MRS. ALPHONSE CAPONE** ★ Fred D. Pasley, *Al Capone, The Biography of a Self-Made Man,* New York, Ives Washburn Publisher, 1930. **DRY AGENTS IZZY AND MOE** ★ Herbert Asbury, "The Noble Experiment of Izzie and Moe," in Isabel Leighton, ed., *The Aspirin Age, 1919–1941,* New York, Simon and Schuster, Inc., 1949, and London. The Bodley Head; ○ *The American Heritage History of the 20's & 30's,* New York, American Heritage Publishing Co., Inc., 1970. **385 THE LONE EAGLE** ★ Charles Augustus Lindbergh, *The Spirit of St. Louis,* New York, Charles Scribner's Sons, 1953. Used with the permission of Charles Scribner's Sons, and John Murray Ltd., London; ○ *The Literary Digest,* October 1, 1927; *ibid.,* June 4, 1927; *ibid.,* June 25, 1927; Alden Whitman, "Anne Morrow Lindbergh Reminisces About Life With Lindy," *The New York Times Magazine,* May 8, 1977; John Lardner, "The Lindbergh Legends," in Leighton, *The Aspirin Age, op. cit.;* P. W. Wilson, in *The New York Times,* June 25, 1927. **386–87 DIVERSIONS** □ Paul Sann, *Fads, Follies and Delusions of the American People,* New York, Crown Publishers, Inc., © 1967 by Paul Sann. **APOLOGIA** □ Dixon Wecter, *The Age of the Great Depression 1929–1941,* New York, copyright 1948 The Macmillan Company. **THE GREAT MIGRATIONS** ★ Robert Goldston, *The Great Depression, The United States in the Thirties,* Indianapolis, The Bobbs-Merrill Company, Inc., 1968. **ROOMS FOR RENT** ★ Creighton Peet, "Peak of a Skyline," *Collier's,* February 5, 1949. **JUSTICE UNDER LA GUARDIA** □ Louis Adamic, *A Nation of Nations,* New York, Harper & Brothers, 1944, as quoted in B. A. Botkin, ed., *Sidewalks of America,* Indianapolis, The Bobbs-Merrill Company, Inc., 1954. **388–91 OLDTIME RADIO** ✔ **RUDY IN MEMORIAM** □ Charles Mank, Jr., comp., *What the Fans Think of Rudy Valentino, A Memorial Book, Articles by Famous Stars, Authors, Poets, Writers & Fans the World Over,* Staunton, Ill., C. Mank, Jr., 1929. **W. C. FIELDS, INFANTOPHOBE** ★ Robert Lewis Taylor, *W. C. Fields, His Follies and Fortunes,* Garden City, N.Y., Doubleday & Company, Inc., 1949. **BOGIE** ★ Cameron Shipp, "The Adventures of Humphrey Bogart," reprinted from *The Saturday Evening Post,* © 1952 The Curtis Publishing Company. **SEX SYMBOLS** ★ Alexander Walker, *The Celluloid Sacrifice,* New York,

Hawthorn Books, 1966. By permission of Michael Joseph, Ltd. **THE "IT" GIRL** ■ Joe Morella and Edward Z. Epstein, *The "It" Girl, The Incredible Story of Clara Bow,* New York, Delacorte Press, 1976. **PYROTECHNICS** ★ Maurice Zolotow, *Marilyn Monroe,* New York, Harcourt, Brace & Company, 1960. Reprinted by permission of the author and the author's agents, Scott Meredith Literary Agency, Inc. **391–92 JIM THORPE** ★ George Sullivan, *Pro Football's All-Time Greats, The Immortals in Pro Football's Hall of Fame,* New York, G. P. Putnam's Sons, © 1968 by George Sullivan. **THE GIPPER** ■ Jerry Brondfield, *Rockne, The Coach, The Man, The Legend,* New York, Random House, Inc., 1976. **"ONE FOR THE GIPPER"** ★ John D. McCallum and Paul Castner, *We Remember Rockne,* Huntington, Ind., Our Sunday Visitor, Inc., 1975. **SULTAN OF SWAT** ■ John Thorn, *A Century of Baseball Lore,* New York, © 1974 Hart Publishing Company, Inc.; □ From *How the Weather Was* by Roger Kahn. Copyright © 1973 by Roger Kahn. By permission of Harper & Row, Publishers, Inc. **393–94 "EAT HIM HERE"** □ Agnes Nolan Underwood, "Folklore From G.I. Joe," *New York Folklore Quarterly,* Vol. III, No. 3, Autumn 1947. **"GOD JUST WALKED IN"** □ James Gregory Keller, *One Moment Please! Christopher Daily Guides to Better Living,* New York, Doubleday & Company, Inc., 1950. **DEHYDRATED LEATHERNECKS** □ Capt. D. Wilcox, "Dried and True, The War's Tallest Short Story," *Reader's Digest,* June 1945. **SUN, SEA, AND SHARKS** ★ "One Who Survived: The Narrative of Allen Heyn," © 1963 American Heritage Publishing Co., Inc. Reprinted by permission from *Volume 15 of The American Heritage New Illustrated History of the United States.* **395–96 DOUBLE TROUBLE** □ Brad Steiger, *Gods of Aquarius, UFOs and the Transformation of Man,* New York, Harcourt Brace Jovanovich, Inc., 1976, and London, W. H. Allen & Co., Ltd. **LITTLE GRAY MEN** ★ "Recent Incidents of Interest," *Flying Saucer News,* April 1974. **ALL ABOARD** ★ Chris Fuller, "I Was Abducted by a Flying Saucer," *National Enquirer,* May 11, 1976. **THE TITANIC** ★ Louis Pauwels and Jacques Bergier, *The Morning of the Magicians,* New York, Avon Books, 1968. **397 LOST-AND-FOUND GRAMMA** □ Stephen Weidenborner in conversation. **THE FURRY COLLAR** □ Linda Degh, "The Roommate's Death and Related Dormitory Stories in Formation," *Indiana Folklore,* Vol. II, No. 2, 1969, as quoted in Duncan Emrich, *Folklore on the American Land,* Boston, Little, Brown and Company, 1972. **THE GHOSTLY HITCHHIKER** ★ Richard K. Beardsley and Rosalie Hankey, "The Vanishing Hitchhiker," *California Folklore Quarterly,* Vol 1, 1942; Beardsley and Hankey, "A History of the Vanishing Hitchhiker," *California Folklore Quarterly,* Vol. 2, 1943, as quoted in Emrich, *op. cit.* **398–99 COMIC STRIP HEROES** ○ Maurice Horn, ed., *The World Encyclopedia of Comics,* New York, Chelsea House Publishers, 2 vols., 1976. **400 ANCIENT PRACTICES IN MODERN TIMES** ○ Julie Forsyth Batchelor and Claudia de Lys, *Superstitious? Here's Why,* A Voyager Book, New York, Harcourt, Brace & World, Inc., 1954; R. Brasch, *How Did It Begin? Customs & Superstitions and Their Romantic Origins,* New York, David McKay Company, Inc., 1965; Claudia de Lys, *A Treasury of American Superstitions,* New York, Philosophical Library, 1948; David Wallechinsky and Irving Wallace, *The People's Almanac,* Garden City, N.Y., Doubleday & Company, Inc., 1975; *Funk & Wagnalls Standard Dictionary of Folklore Mythology and Legend,* New York, Funk & Wagnalls, 1949. **401 THE NEW PRIESTHOOD** ★ Isaac Asimov, "True Love," *American Way,* February 1977 (inflight magazine of American Airlines).

INDEX

Page numbers in regular type refer to the text. **Bold** type indicates illustrations and subjects included in captions.

S